Scotland's
Highlands & Islands

KT-416-264

**Northern Highlands
& Islands**
p166

**Inverness & the
Central Highlands**
p109

**Southern
Highlands &
Islands**
p42

EAST SUS
W
21

Contents

CRAIG EASTON / LONELY PLANET ©

RED DEER, KNOYDART
PENINSULA P159

PETE SEAWARD / LONELY PLANET ©

KINLOCH CASTLE P161

Contents

Welcome to
Scotland's Highlands & Islands

The hills and glens and wild coastline of Scotland's Highlands and islands offer the ultimate escape – one of the last corners of Europe where you can discover genuine solitude.

Lonely Landscapes

Since the 19th century – when the first tourists began to arrive, inspired by the Romantic movement – the Scottish Highlands have been famed for their wild nature and majestic scenery. Today, the region's biggest draw remains its magnificent landscape. At almost every turn is a vista that will stop you in your tracks, from the bluebell woods, gentle hills and warm autumn colours of Loch Lomond and the Trossachs to the primeval grandeur of Coigach and Assynt, where pillared peaks rear above gnarled and ancient gneiss. Keep your camera close.

Outdoor Adventures

Scotland's mountains, lochs and seaways offer some of the most rewarding outdoor adventures in Europe. As well as classic challenges such as the West Highland Way and the ascent of Ben Nevis, there are wilderness walks through the roadless wilds of Knoydart and Sutherland, and spectacular summits such as An Teallach, Stac Pollaidh and Suilven. Mountain bikers can enjoy a multitude of off-road routes, from easy trails through pine forests to strenuous coast-to-coast rides, while the turbulent tidal waters around the Outer Hebrides, Orkney and Shetland provide the ultimate test of paddling mettle for sea-kayakers.

Legend & Tradition

Legend and tradition run deep in the Highlands. Crumbling forts and monastic cells were once home to Gaelic chieftains and Irish saints; lonely beaches and mountain passes once echoed to the clash of clan battles; and empty glens are still haunted by the ghosts of the Clearances. History is everywhere – in the abandoned crofts preserved on a hillside like fossil fragments; in the proud profile of broch and castle silhouetted against a Highland sunset; in the Gaelic lilt of Hebridean speech and the Nordic twang of Shetland dialect.

A Taste of Scotland

An increasing number of visitors have discovered that Scotland's restaurants have shaken off their reputation for deep-fried food and unsmiling service and can now compete with the best in Europe. A newfound respect for top-quality local produce means that you can feast on fresh seafood mere hours after it was caught, beef and venison that was raised just a few miles away from your table, and vegetables that were grown in your hotel's own organic garden. And top it all off with a dram of single malt whisky – rich, evocative and complex, the true taste of Scotland.

Why I Love Scotland's Highlands & Islands

by Neil Wilson, Author

It's the weather. Yes, seriously. We get four proper seasons here (sometimes all of them in one day) and that means that you get to enjoy the same landscapes over and over again in a range of different garbs – August hills clad in purple heather, native woodlands gilded with autumn colours, snowpatched winter mountains, and Hebridean machair sprinkled with a confetti of spring wildflowers. And the unpredictability of the weather means that even the wettest day can be suddenly transformed by parting clouds and slanting shafts of golden light. Sheer magic.

For more about our authors, see page 304

Above: Hiker on the summit of Ben A'an, overlooking Loch Katrine (p52)

Scotland's Highlands & Islands

Shetland Islands Hermaness

- Ulsta
- Toft
- Hillswick
- Lerwick ▲

Shetland Birdlife
British birdwatching's most impressive experience (p239)

Atlantic Ocean

North Sea

To Shetland Islands (see Inset)

Orkney Islands
- Kirkwall
- Stromness

Old Man of Hoy
Tallest sea stack in Britain (p234)

ELEVATION

| 1000m |
| 700m |
| 500m |
| 300m |
| 200m |
| 100m |
| 0 |

- Fraserburgh
Rattray Bay
- Peterhead
- Banff
- Huntly
- Dufftown
- Elgin
- Nairn
- Grantown-on-Spey

- John O'Groats
- Dunnet Head Mey
- Dunnet
- Wick
- Scrabster Thurso
- Strathy Point Melvich
- Lybster
- Helmsdale
- Brora
- Golspie
- Portmahomack
Moray Firth
- Tain
- Invergordon
- Black Isle
- Dingwall Inverness
- Strathpeffel

- Bettyhill
- Tongue
- Cape Wrath
- Durness
- Kinlochbervie
Enard Bay
- Lochinver
- Ullapool
- Gairloch
- Lairg
- Bonar Bridge
- Dornoch
Loch Shin

Ben Hope (927m) ▲
Ben More Assynt (998m) ▲
Beinn Dearg (1084m) ▲
An Teallach (1062m) ▲
Loch Maree

ATLANTIC OCEAN

- Butt of Lewis
- Stornoway
The Minch
- Tarbert
- North Harris
- Lochmaddy
- Uig
- Trotternish
- Portree
- Dunvegan
- Isle of
The Little Minch

Callanish Standing Stones
Mysterious prehistoric stone circle (p212)

Beaches of South Harris
Spectacular white-sand beaches (p214)

North Sea

58°N

60°N

59°N

2°W

3°W

4°W

5°W

6°W

7°W

8°W

1°W

ROAD DISTANCES (mi)
Note: Distances are approximate

	Fort William	Inverness	Kyle of Lochalsh	Mallaig	Oban	Scrabster	Ullapool
Inverness	66						
Kyle of Lochalsh	76	82					
Mallaig	44	106	34				
Oban	45	110	120	85			
Scrabster	185	119	214	238	230		
Ullapool	90	135	88	166	161	125	

Scale: 100 km / 50 miles
40 km / 20 miles

Cairngorms
Playground for outdoor enthusiasts (p126)

Ben Nevis
Climb the highest Munro of them all (p153)

The West Highland Way
The best Highland hiking (p99)

Cuillin Hills
Craggy peaks and inaccessible pinnacles (p201)

Picturesque Iona
Scotland's most sacred island (p93)

The Road to the Isles
Stunning scenery and Jacobite history (p156)

Glen Coe
Dramatic scenery meets deep history (p146)

Scotland's Highlands & Islands'

Top 19

Whisky

1 Scotland's national drink – from the Gaelic *uisge bagh,* meaning 'water of life' – has been distilled here for more than 500 years. More than 100 distilleries are still in operation, producing hundreds of varieties of single malt, and learning to distinguish the smoky, peaty whiskies of Islay, say, from the flowery, sherried malts of Speyside has become a hugely popular pastime. Many distilleries offer guided tours, rounded off with a tasting session, and ticking off the local varieties is a great way to explore the whisky-making regions.

Walking the West Highland Way

2 The best way to appreciate the scale and grandeur of Scotland's landscapes is to walk them. Despite the wind and midges and drizzle, walking here is a pleasure, with numerous short- and long-distance trails, coastal paths and mountains begging to be trekked. Top of the wish list for many hikers is the 95-mile West Highland Way (p99) from Milngavie (near Glasgow) to Fort William, a challenging, week-long walk through some of the country's finest scenery, finishing in the shadow of its highest peak, Ben Nevis.
Hikers approach Beinn Dòrain near Bridge of Orchy (p105)

MONTY RAKUSEN / GETTY IMAGES ©

DEREK DAMMANN / GETTY IMAGES ©

2

Cuillin Hills

3 In a country famous for its stunning scenery, the Cuillin Hills (p201) take top prize. This range of craggy peaks is near-alpine in character, with knife-edge ridges, jagged pinnacles, scree-filled gullies and acres of naked rock. While they're a paradise for experienced mountaineers, the higher reaches of the Cuillin are off limits to the majority of walkers. Not to worry – there are easy trails through the glens and into the corries, where walkers can soak up the views and share the landscape with red deer and golden eagles. Loch Slapin and the peak of Bla Bheinn (p200)

Seafood

4 One of the great pleasures of a visit to Scotland is the opportunity to indulge in the rich harvest of the sea. The cold, clear waters around the Scottish coast provide some of the most sought-after seafood in Europe, with much of it being whisked straight from the quayside to waiting restaurant tables from London to Lisbon. Fortunately there are plenty of places to sample this bounty right here, with Oban (p84) topping the list of towns with more than their fair share of seafood restaurants.

Castles

5 Whether you're looking for grim, desolate stone fortresses looming in the mist, picture-postcard castles such as Eilean Donan (p193), or luxurious palaces built in expansive grounds by lairds more concerned with status and show than with military might, the Highlands sport the full range of castles, reflecting the region's turbulent history. Most castles have a story or 10 to tell of plots, intrigues, imprisonments and treachery, and a worryingly high percentage have a phantom rumoured to stalk their parapets. Eilean Donan (p193)

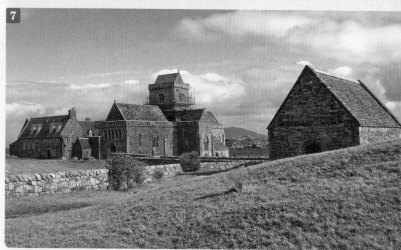

Marine Wildlife

6 Scotland is one of the best places in Europe for seeing marine wildlife. In high season (July and August) many cruise operators on the west coast, notably on the Isle of Mull (p86), can almost guarantee sightings of Minke whales and porpoises, and the Moray Firth is famous for its population of bottlenose dolphins. Basking sharks – at up to 12m, the biggest fish to be found in British waters – are also commonly seen. And it's not just the wildlife that makes a boat trip a must – don't miss the chance to visit the Corryvreckan whirlpool. Bottlenose dolpins, Chanonry Point (p120)

Picturesque Iona

7 Legend has it that when St Columba left Ireland in 563 to found a missionary outpost on Scotland's west coast, he kept sailing until he found a spot where he could no longer see his homeland on the southern horizon. That place was the little jewel of Iona (p93) – Scotland's most sacred island, and one of its most beautiful, with lush green pastures bordered by pink granite rocks, white shell-sand beaches and shallow, turquoise waters. The abbey stands on the site of Columba's first chapel. Iona Abbey (p93)

Ceilidhs

8 A *ceilidh* (pronounced kay-li) is a traditional evening of Scottish dancing with music provided by fiddles, *bodhrans* (handheld drums) and other instruments, has evolved into something of a tourist spectacle, but there are still plenty of places including Inverness, where *ceilidhs* are staged for the locals – and visitors are always welcome. Don't worry if you don't know the steps; there's usually a 'caller' to lead the dancers through their paces, and no one cares if you get it wrong as long as you're enjoying yourself!

Glen Coe

9 Scotland's most famous glen (p146) combines those two essential qualities of the Highland landscape – dramatic scenery and deep history. The peacefulness and beauty of this valley today belie the fact that it was the scene of a ruthless 17th-century massacre that saw the local MacDonalds murdered by soldiers of the Campbell clan. Some of the glen's finest walks – to the Lost Valley, for example – follow the routes used by clansmen and women trying to flee their attackers, where many perished in the snow. Buachaille Etive Mor (p146)

Island Hopping

10 Much of the unique character of western and northern Scotland is down to the expansive vistas of sea and islands – there are more than 700 islands off Scotland's coast, of which almost 100 are inhabited. A network of ferry services links these islands to the mainland and each other, and buying an Island Rover ticket (unlimited ferry travel for 15 days) provides a fascinating way to explore. It's possible to hop all the way from Arran or Bute to the Outer Hebrides, touching the mainland only at Kintyre and Oban.

Oban (p80)

Standing Stones of Callanish

11 Few sights conjure up the mystery and romance of the Highlands and islands like the prehistoric monuments that punctuate the landscape from Orkney to the Western Isles. The 5000-year-old Callanish Stones (p212) on the Isle of Lewis – contemporaries of the pyramids of Egypt – are the archetypal stone circle, with beautifully weathered slabs of banded gneiss arranged as if in worship around a central monolith. To experience the stones at dawn, before the crowds arrive, is to step back in time, and sense something deep and truly ancient.

Road to the Isles

12 Immortalised in song and story, the 'Road to the Isles' (p156) is the route from Fort William to Mallaig – jumping-off point for the Isle of Skye, the Small Isles and beyond to the Outer Hebrides. Steeped in Jacobite history – Bonnie Prince Charlie passed this way several times around 1745 – the route (followed by both road and railway) passes through some of Scotland's finest scenery, with views over dazzling white-sand beaches and emerald waters to a horizon pricked by the sharp peaks of Eigg, Rum and Skye. Glenfinnan, on the Road to the Isles (p156)

TOM MARTIN / GETTY IMAGES ©

Climbing Ben Nevis

13 The allure of Britain's highest peak is strong – around 100,000 people a year set off up the summit trail (p153), though not all will make it to the top. Nevertheless, the highest Munro of them all is within the ability of anyone who's reasonably fit – treat Ben Nevis with respect and your reward (weather permitting) will be a truly magnificent view and a great sense of achievement. Real walking enthusiasts can warm up by hiking the 95-mile West Highland Way first.

Old Man of Hoy

14 From the Mull of Kintyre to Duncansby Head, the patient craftsmanship of the sea has whittled the Scottish coastline into a profusion of sea stacks, chasms and natural arches. Many stacks are nicknamed 'old man', but none compare to the grandest old man of them all. At 137m tall (a third taller than London's Big Ben), the Old Man of Hoy (p234) is the tallest sea stack in Britain. Hike from Rackwick Bay for a spectacular view of the stack and, if you're lucky, rock climbers in action.

Sea Kayaking

15 The convoluted coastline and countless islands of Scotland's western seaboard are widely recognised as one of the finest sea-kayaking areas in the world (p35). Paddling your own canoe allows you to explore remote islands, inlets, creeks and beaches that are inaccessible on foot, and also provides an opportunity to get close to wildlife such as seals, otters, dolphins and seabirds. There are dozens of outfits offering guided kayaking tours for beginners, from a half day to a week, either camping on wild beaches or staying in comfortable B&Bs.
Loch Duich (p193)

Shetland Birdlife

16 Sparsely populated, and with large areas of wild land, Scotland is an important sanctuary for all sorts of wildlife. Amazing birdwatching is on offer throughout the country, but the seabird cities of the Shetland Islands (p239) take first prize for spectacle. From their first arrival on the sea cliffs in late spring to the raucous feeding frenzies of high summer, the vast colonies of gannets, guillemots, puffins and kittiwakes at Hermaness, Noss and Sumburgh Head provide one of British birdwatching's most impressive experiences. Atlantic puffin

SANDRA LEIDHOLDT / GETTY IMAGES ©

Cairngorms

17 In the bare, boulder-strewn, 1200m-high plateau of the Cairngorms (p126), Scotland harbours its own little haven of subarctic tundra. The haunt of ptarmigan and snow bunting, red deer and reindeer, these austerely beautiful granite mountains provide a year-round playground for outdoors enthusiasts, from summer hiking and mountain biking along winding trails through the ancient Caledonian pine forest to skiing, snowboarding and full-on mountaineering on the snowy summits in the midst of winter. Ben Avon

Northwest Highlands

18 The Highlands abound in breathtaking views, but the far northwest is truly awe-inspiring. The coastal road between Durness and Kyle of Lochalsh (p182) offers jaw-dropping landscapes at every turn: mountain and sea are entwined in a gloriously scenic embrace, from the vertiginous sea cliffs of remote Cape Wrath to the distinctive pillared peaks and lonely lochs of Assynt, and the haunting, desolate beauty of Torridon. These and the warm Scottish welcome found in classic Highland inns make this an unforgettable corner of the country. Plockton (p191) and the Torridon Hills

Beaches of South Harris

19 Scotland's Highlands and islands are never going to be famous for bucket-and-spade seaside holidays, but when it comes to scenically spectacular beaches, the region is up there with the best. And the vast stretches of blinding white shell-sand that line the west coast of South Harris (p214) in the Outer Hebrides are among the most beautiful in Europe – grass-covered dunes sprinkled with pink and yellow wildflowers, clear sparkling waters that range from turquoise to emerald, and sunset views that take your breath away. Luskentyre (p214)

Need to Know

For more information, see Survival Guide (p279)

Currency
Pound Sterling (£)

Language
English
Gaelic and Lallans

Visas
Generally not needed for stays of up to six months. Not a member of the Schengen Zone.

Money
ATMs widely available. Credit cards widely accepted.

Mobile Phones
Uses the GSM 900/1800 network. Local SIM cards can be used in European and Australian phones. Patchy coverage in remote areas.

Time
UTC/GMT plus one hour during summer daylight saving time, UTC/GMT the rest of the year.

When to Go

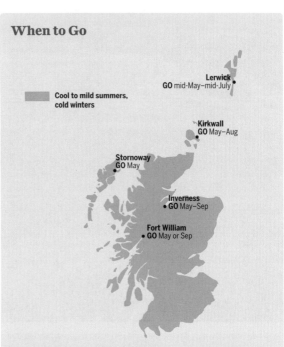

Cool to mild summers, cold winters

Lerwick
GO mid-May–mid-July

Kirkwall
GO May–Aug

Stornoway
GO May

Inverness
• GO May–Sep

Fort William
• GO May or Sep

High Season
(Jul & Aug)

➡ Accommodation prices 10% to 20% higher (book in advance if possible).

➡ Warmest time of year, but often wet, too.

➡ Midges at their worst.

Shoulder Season
(May, Jun & Sep)

➡ Wildflowers and rhododendrons bloom in May and June.

➡ Best chance for dry weather; fewer midges.

➡ June evenings have daylight till 11pm.

Low Season
(Oct–Apr)

➡ Rural attractions and accommodation often closed.

➡ Snow on hills November to March.

➡ In December it gets dark at 4pm.

➡ Can be very cold and wet November to March.

Useful Websites

Lonely Planet (www.lonely planet.com/scotland) Destination information, forums, hotel bookings, shop.

VisitScotland (www.visitscot land.com) Official tourism site; booking services.

Internet Guide to Scotland (www.scotland-info.co.uk) Best online tourist guide to Scotland.

Traveline (www.travelinescot land.com) Public transport timetables.

WalkHighlands (www.walkhigh lands.co.uk) Detailed walking guide with maps.

Important Numbers

Country code	☏ +44
International access code	☏ 00
Ambulance	☏ 112 or ☏ 999
Fire	☏ 112 or ☏ 999
Mountain rescue	☏ 112 or ☏ 999
Police	☏ 112 or ☏ 999

Exchange Rates

Australia	A$1	£0.55
Canada	C$1	£0.56
Euro zone	€1	£0.79
Japan	¥100	£0.57
New Zealand	NZ$1	£0.49
USA	US$1	£0.62

For current exchange rates, see www.xe.com.

Daily Costs

Budget:
Less than £35

➡ Dorm beds: £12–22
➡ Wild camping: free
➡ Food from supermarket: £5–10

Midrange:
£40–120

➡ Double room at midrange B&B: £50–100
➡ Bar lunch: £10; dinner at midrange restaurant: £25
➡ Car hire: £35
➡ Petrol costs: around 15p per mile

Top End:
Over £120

➡ Double room at high-end hotel: £130–250
➡ Dinner at high-end restaurant: £40–60
➡ Flights to islands: £65–130 each way

Opening Hours

Opening hours may vary throughout the year, especially in rural areas where many places have shorter hours, or close completely, from October or November to March or April.

Banks 9.30am to 4pm or 5pm Monday to Friday; some are open 9.30am to 1pm Saturday

Pubs & Bars 11am to 11pm Monday to Thursday, 11am to 1am Friday and Saturday, 12.30pm to 11pm Sunday

Shops 9am to 5.30pm (or 6pm in larger towns) Monday to Saturday, and often 11am to 5pm Sunday

Restaurants Lunch noon to 2.30pm, dinner 6pm to 9pm or 10pm

Arriving in Scotland

Edinburgh Airport (p279) Trams to Edinburgh city centre every eight to 10 minutes from 6.15am to 10.45pm (£5); buses every 10 to 15 minutes from 4.30am to midnight (£4); night buses every 30 minutes from 12.30am to 4am (£3.50); taxis cost £16 to £22 (about 20 minutes to the city centre)

Glasgow Airport (p287) Buses to Glasgow city centre every 10 to 15 minutes from 6am to 11pm (£6); night buses hourly 11pm to 4am, half-hourly 4am to 6pm (£6); taxis cost £22 to £26 (about 30 minutes to city centre)

Getting Around

Transport in Scotland can be expensive compared to the rest of Europe; bus and rail services are sparse in the more remote parts of the country. For timetables, check out Traveline Scotland (www.travelinescotland.com).

Car Useful for travelling at your own pace, or for visiting regions with minimal public transport. Cars can be hired in every town or city. Drive on the left.

Train Relatively expensive, with extensive coverage and frequent departures in central Scotland, but only a few lines in the northern Highlands and southern Scotland.

Bus Cheaper and slower than trains, but useful for more remote regions that aren't serviced by trains.

Boat A network of car ferries link the mainland to the islands of western and northern Scotland.

For much more on **getting around**, see p287

If You Like...

Outdoor Adventures

Fort William The self-styled 'Outdoor Capital of the UK'; a centre for hiking, climbing, mountain biking and winter sports. (p149)

Shetland One of Scotland's top coastlines for sea kayaking, with an abundance of bird and sea life to observe from close quarters. (p239)

Laggan Wolftrax Mountain biking for all abilities, from easy forest trails to black-diamond down-hilling. (p132)

Cairngorms Winter skiing and summer walking amid the epic beauty of this high, subarctic plateau. (p126)

Thurso An unlikely surfing mecca, but once you've got the drysuit on the waves are world-class. (p178)

Scapa Flow The scuttling of the German High Seas Fleet at the end of WWI has made this one of Europe's top diving sites. (p230)

Prehistoric Sites

Skara Brae Most famous of all is Orkney's neolithic village, where circular houses uncovered by eroding sand dunes preserve Stone Age furniture and fittings. (p231)

Maes Howe This enormous passage tomb, with a corbelled roof skillfully constructed from stone slabs, has the added intrigue of Viking graffiti. (p230)

Ring of Brodgar One of Scotland's most evocative prehistoric sites, this vast circle of weathered sandstone slabs impresses with sheer scale. (p231)

Callanish Standing Stones Gnarled fingers of gneiss shaggy with lichen, the stones of Callanish are contemporary with the pyramids of Egypt. (p212)

Kilmartin Glen With hill forts, chambered cairns, standing stones and rock carvings, this is Scotland's biggest concentration of prehistoric sites. (p64)

Old Scatness This Shetland site is still being investigated, offering the chance to see archaeologists at work. (p245)

Rural Museums

Arnol Blackhouse Preserved in peat smoke since its last inhabitant left in the 1960s, a genuine slice of 'living history'. (p211)

Highland Folk Museum Fascinating outdoor museum populated with real historic buildings reassembled here on site. (p131)

Scottish Crannog Centre Head back to the Bronze Age in this excellent archaeological reconstruction of a fortified loch house. (p145)

Tain Through Time Very entertaining local museum with comprehensive display on Scottish history and Tain's silversmithing tradition. (p170)

Stromness Museum Delightful small-town museum with exhibits on the Orkney fishing industry, the World Wars, and local marine wildlife. (p232)

Coastal Scenery

Ardnamurchan The most westerly point on the British mainland is also one of the most scenic, with superb sunset views north and south to the islands of Skye and Mull. (p154)

Achiltibuie This remote village enjoys a gorgeous coastal setting, looking out across the jewel-like Summer Isles to the distant mountains of Wester Ross. (p185)

Applecross Majestic views of the hills of Skye and magical sunset moments at this isolated village. (p191)

Tongue Wild sea lochs penetrate the rocky coast like steely blades on this lonely stretch of the north coast. (p180)

Top: Ring of Brodgar (p231), Orkney
Bottom: Fingal's Cave (p95), Isle of Staffa

Arisaig & Morar Long strands of silver sands and stunning panoramas to the isles of Eigg and Rum. (p157)

Unst The most northerly point of the British Isles boasts seabird cities ranged on ragged cliffs, and the lighthouse-topped stack of Muckle Flugga. (p248)

Classic Hikes

West Highland Way The grand-daddy of Scottish long-distance walks, the one everyone wants to do. (p99)

Glen Affric to Shiel Bridge A classic two-day cross-country hike, with a night in a remote hostel. (p118)

Great Glen Way The easiest of Scotland's long-distance paths, linking Fort William to Inverness – can be done as an extension of the West Highland Way. (p120)

Speyside Way Follow the mighty River Spey through the heart of whisky country to the mountain resort of Aviemore. (p35)

Cape Wrath Trail From Fort William to Scotland's north-west corner through some of the country's most remote landscapes. (p184)

Machair Way A peaceful and leisurely path along the beaches and wildflower-strewn dunes of the Uists. (p216)

Remote Islands

Iona Beautiful, peaceful (once the day trippers have left) and of huge historic and cultural importance, Iona is the jewel of the Hebrides. (p93)

Eigg The most intriguing of the Small Isles, with its miniature mountain, massacre cave and singing sands. (p161)

Jura Wild and untamed, with more deer than people, and a dangerous whirlpool at its northern end. (p77)

Handa Huge cliffs, raucous sea-bird colonies, and a view of the Great Stack of Handa are your reward for a hike to the western edge of this small but beautiful island. (p183)

Westray & Papa Westray These magical islands at Orkney's northern end have great accommodation and eating options, coastal scenery, birdwatching, and historic sights. (p237)

St Kilda Remote, spectacular and difficult to get to, the soaring stacks of St Kilda are the ultimate tick for island collectors. (p213)

Natural Wonders

Old Man of Hoy While most of the Orkneys is fairly flat, Hoy is rugged and rocky; its spectacular west coast includes Britain's tallest sea stack. (p234)

Corryvreckan Whirlpool One of the world's three most powerful tidal whirlpools, squeezed between Jura and Scarba. (p79)

Falls of Measach A trembling suspension bridge provides a scary viewpoint for one of Scotland's most impressive waterfalls. (p188)

Quiraing Skye has many impressive rock formations, but the weird world of the Quiraing takes first place for strangeness. (p205)

Fingal's Cave Accessible only by boat, this columnar sea cave inspired Mendelssohn's *Hebrides Overture*. (p95)

Falls of Lora The surge of the sea through the narrow mouth of Loch Etive creates the country's most impressive tidal whitewater rapids. (p97)

Historic Castles

Dunvegan Castle The ancient seat of Clan Macleod is home to fascinating relics, including the legendary Fairy Flag. (p204)

Duart Castle Commanding the entrance to the Sound of Mull, this Maclean stronghold is one of the oldest inhabited castles in Scotland. (p88)

Dunrobin Castle The largest country house in the Highlands offers a peek at the opulent lifestyle enjoyed by the Duke of Sutherland. (p173)

Kisimul Castle Seat of Clan MacNeil, this archetypal Highland castle is perched on a Hebridean islet, accessible only by boat. (p218)

Eilean Donan Castle Perfect lochside location conveniently located by the main road to Skye makes this the Highlands' most photographed fortress. (p149)

Wild Beaches

Sandwood Bay A sea stack, a ghost story, and 2 miles of windblown sand – who could ask for more? (p183)

Kiloran Bay A perfect curve of deep golden sand, the ideal vantage point for stunning sunsets. (p79)

Bosta A beautiful and remote cove filled with white sand beside an Iron Age house. (p212)

Durness A series of pristine sandy coves and duney headlands surround this northwestern village. (p181)

Scousburgh Sands Shetland's finest beach is a top spot for birdwatching, as well as for a bracing walk. (p245)

Sanday This aptly named member of Orkney's North Isles is one giant sand dune, with many spectacular stretches of white-sand beach. (p236)

Month by Month

January

The nation shakes off its Hogmanay hangover and gets back to work, but only until Burns Night comes along. It's still cold and dark, but if there's snow on the hills the skiing can be good.

🍴 Burns Night

Suppers all over Scotland (and the world, for that matter) are held on 25 January to celebrate the anniversary of national poet Robert Burns, with much haggis, drinking of whisky and reciting of poetry.

✨ Up Helly Aa

Half of Shetland dresses up with horned helmets and battleaxes in this spectacular re-enactment of a Viking fire festival, with a torchlit procession leading the burning of a full-size replica of a Viking longship.

Held in Lerwick on the last Tuesday in January.

February

The coldest month of the year is usually the best for winter hillwalking, ice-climbing and skiing. The days are getting noticeably longer now, and snowdrops begin to bloom.

🏃 Fort William Mountain Festival

The UK's 'Outdoor Capital' celebrates the winter season with skiing and snowboarding workshops, talks by famous climbers, kids' events and a festival of mountaineering films.

April

The bluebell woods on the shores of Loch Lomond come into flower and ospreys arrive at their Loch Garten nest. Weather is improving, though heavy showers are still common.

☆ Shetland Folk Festival

The end of April sees this engagingly eccentric music festival, with traditional music from around the world staged everywhere

from Lerwick pubs to remote island village halls.

May

Wildflowers bloom on the Hebridean machair and puffins arrive at their Orkney and Shetland nesting colonies – May is when the Scottish weather is often at its best.

🍷 Spirit of Speyside

Based in Dufftown, this festival of whisky, food and music involves five days of distillery tours, cooking, art and outdoor activities – and plenty of knocking back the 'water of life'. Held late April to early May in Moray and Speyside.

🏃 Scottish Series Yacht Races

The scenic harbour at the West Highland fishing village of Tarbert fills with hundreds of visiting yachts for five days of racing, drinking and partying.

✨ Feis Ile

B&Bs in Islay are booked out for this week-long celebration of traditional Scottish music and whisky. Events include *ceilidhs*, pipe-band performances, distillery tours and whisky tastings.

June

Argyllshire is ablaze with pink rhododendron blooms. The long summer evenings (known in Orkney and Shetland as the simmer dim) stretch on till 11pm.

RockNess

The 'world's most beautiful rock festival' gathers on the shores of Loch Ness for three days of live music, chilling out and monster-watching.

UCI Mountain Bike World Cup

Around 20,000 mountain-biking fans gather at Nevis Range near Fort William for the spectacular World Cup downhill and 4X finals.

St Magnus Festival

It barely gets dark at all at midsummer, making a magical setting for this celebration of music, poetry, literature and the visual arts. Held late June in Orkney.

July

School holidays begin at the start of July; the busiest time of year for campsites and B&Bs begins. It's high season for Shetland birdwatchers, with sea cliffs loud with nesting guillemots, razorbills and puffins.

Mendelssohn on Mull

A week-long festival of free classical music concerts

at various venues in Mull, Iona and Oban.

Hebridean Celtic Festival

The gardens of Lews Castle in Stornoway provide the scenic setting for this four-day extravaganza of folk, rock and Celtic music.

August

Highland games are taking place all over the region, but the midges are at their worst. On the west coast, this is the peak month for sighting minke whales and basking sharks.

Plockton Regatta

Plockton Bay fills with sails as a fortnight of yacht and small-boat racing culminates in Regatta Weekend with a street party, concert and *ceilidh*.

Argyllshire Gathering

Oban is the setting for one of the most important events on the Scottish Highland Games calendar, which includes a prestigious pipe-band competition.

September

School holidays are over, midges are dying off, wild brambles are ripe for picking in the hedgerows, and the weather is often dry and mild – an excellent time of year for outdoor pursuits.

Braemar Gathering

The biggest and most famous Highland Games in the Scottish calendar,

traditionally attended by members of the Royal Family, featuring Highland dancing, caber-tossing and bagpipe-playing. Held early September in Braemar, Royal Deeside.

October

Autumn brings a blaze of colour to the forests of Highland Perthshire and the Trossachs, as the tourist season winds down and thoughts turn to log fires and malt whiskies in country house hotels.

Cowalfest

Dunoon and the lovely Cowal peninsula play host to this 10-day walking festival. As well as a huge range of guided walks, there are mountain-bike rides, horse rides, orienteering, exhibitions, art, theatre and concerts.

Enchanted Forest

Crowds gather in the Explorers Garden at Pitlochry to experience this spectacular sound-and-light show. Three weeks of events occasionally spill into November.

December

Darkness falls mid-afternoon as the shortest day approaches. The often cold and wet weather is relieved by Christmas and New Year festivities, and the chance of seeing the Northern Lights in Orkney and Shetland.

Itineraries

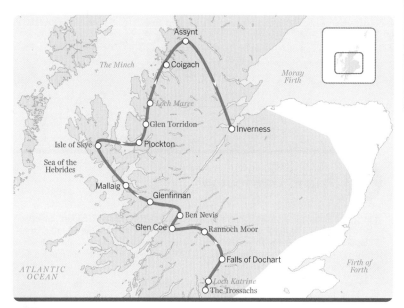

 **A Highland Fling**

Begin this tour with a visit to the **Trossachs** for your first taste of Highland scenery; take a cruise on **Loch Katrine** and spend the night in Callander. Continue north via the Falls of Dochart at Killin and the fringes of Rannoch Moor.

The mountain scenery becomes more impressive, culminating in the grandeur of **Glen Coe**. Keen hill walkers will pause for a day at Fort William to climb **Ben Nevis** (plus another day to recover!) before taking the Road to the Isles past glorious Glenfinnan and the Silver Sands of Morar to **Mallaig**. Overnight here and dine at one of its seafood restaurants.

Take the ferry to the **Isle of Skye**, spending a day or two exploring Scotland's most famous island, before crossing the Skye Bridge back to the mainland, then head north via the pretty village of Plockton to the magnificent mountain scenery of **Glen Torridon**. Spend a day or two hiking here, then follow the A832 alongside lovely Loch Maree and continue north into the big-sky wilderness of **Coigach** and **Assynt**, before making your way back south with an overnight in **Inverness**.

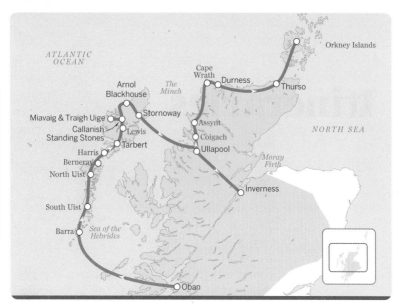

 Island Hopscotch

This route is usually done by car, but the Oban–Barra–Stornoway–Ullapool–Inverness loop also makes a brilliant cycle tour (around 270 miles, including the 60 miles from Ullapool ferry terminal to Inverness train station, making both start and finish accessible by rail). CalMac's Island Hopscotch ticket No 8 includes all the ferries needed for the Outer Hebrides part of this route.

From Oban it's a five-hour ferry crossing to **Barra**; you'll arrive in the evening so plan to spend the night there (book ahead). In the morning, after a visit to romantic Kisimul Castle and a tour around the island, take the ferry to **South Uist**. Walk along the wild beaches of the west coast, sample the local seafood and, if you've brought your fishing rod, look forward to a bit of sport on the island's many trout lochs. There are good places to stay at Polochar, Lochboisdale and Lochmaddy (two nights should be enough).

Keep your binoculars handy as you follow the road north through Benbecula and North Uist, as this is prime birdwatching country. If you're camping or hostelling, a night at **Berneray** is a must before taking the ferry to **Harris**. Pray for sun, as the road along Harris' west coast has some of the most spectacular beaches in Scotland. The main road continues north from Tarbert (good hotels) through the rugged Harris hills to Lewis.

Don't go directly to Stornoway, but take a turn west to the **Callanish Standing Stones** and **Arnol Blackhouse** museum – the highlights of the Western Isles. If you have time (two days is ideal), detour west to the beautiful beaches around **Miavaig** and **Traigh Uige**; there's plenty of wild and semiwild camping.

Spend your final night in the Hebrides in **Stornoway** (eat at Digby Chick), then take the ferry to **Ullapool**, where you have the choice of heading straight to Inverness, or continuing north around the mainland coast through the jaw-dropping wilderness of **Coigach** and **Assynt**, and on via Cape Wrath and Durness to Thurso, where the ferry to the **Orkney Islands** awaits.

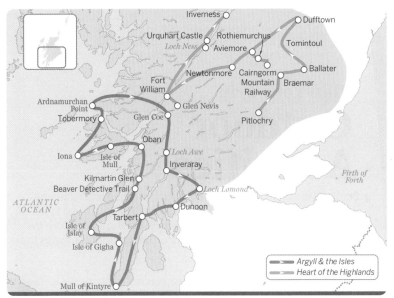

Argyll & the Isles
Heart of the Highlands

 10 DAYS Argyll & the Isles

 **1 WEEK Heart of the Highlands**

Argyll & the Isles

Begin with a scenic drive across the Cowal peninsula from Dunoon to Portavadie, via Benmore Botanic Garden and Tighnabruaich, then take the ferry to the pretty fishing village of **Tarbert**. Devote a day to exploring the Kintyre peninsula, taking in Campbeltown, the Mull of Kintyre and a trip to the Isle of Gigha. Then allow at least two days for touring **Islay** and its famous distilleries.

Back on the mainland, head north through Knapdale – visit the **Beaver Detective Trail** – to the prehistoric sites of **Kilmartin Glen** and then on to the bustling ferry port of **Oban**. Take the ferry to Craignure for a tour of the **Isle of Mull**, making sure to visit Duart Castle and Iona, before spending a night at **Tobermory**. Then take another ferry to Kilchoan, allowing a trip to **Ardnamurchan Point**, the most westerly point of the British mainland, before the scenic drive along the shores of Loch Sunart to Corran Ferry.

Head back south via the splendour of Glen Coe and the minor road through Glen Orchy to reach **Loch Awe**. From here you can return to your starting point by way of Inveraray and Loch Lomond.

Heart of the Highlands

Beginning in **Pitlochry**, abandon the main A9 road to the north and enjoy a day's scenic drive east across the hills on the A924, and then north on the A93 through the ski area of Glenshee to the remote **Braemar**. Spend a night here, then either hike in the Cairngorm hills nearby or visit Balmoral Castle before spending your second night at **Ballater.**

From here the rollercoaster A939 takes you north to Tomintoul; then it's back roads via Glenlivet to **Dufftown**, the capital of Speyside whisky. Next day, take your time visiting distilleries along the Spey valley to Aviemore, in the heart of Cairngorm National Park. Take least two nights here to explore the ancient pine forests of **Rothiemurchus** and to take a trip on the **Cairngorm Mountain Railway**.

Then head west, stopping to discover the Highland Folk Museum at **Newtonmore** before continuing to **Fort William**. Overnight here, then spend a morning exploring **Glen Nevis** and head north along the Great Glen to see **Urquhart Castle** and **Loch Ness** – leave time for a monster-spotting cruise – and finish up in **Inverness**.

Plan Your Trip
Outdoor Activities

Scotland is a brilliant place for outdoor recreation and has something to offer everyone, from those who enjoy a short stroll to full-on adrenaline junkies. Although hiking, biking, fishing and golf are the most popular activities, there is an astonishing variety of things to do.

Need to Know

Best Time to Go

May, June and September are the best months for hiking and biking – best chance of dry weather and less chance of midges

Best Outdoor Experiences

Hike the West Highland Way, climb Ben Nevis, cycle-tour the Outer Hebrides, mountain bike a black trail at Laggan Wolftrax, sea kayak in Shetland

Essential Hill Walking Gear

Good waterproofs, spare warm clothing, map and compass, mobile phone (but don't rely on it), first-aid kit, head torch, whistle (for emergencies), spare food and drink

Safety Checklist

Check the weather forecast first, let someone know your plans, set pace and objective to suit slowest member of party, don't be afraid to turn back if it's too difficult

Walking

Scotland's wild, dramatic scenery and varied landscape has made walking a hugely popular pastime for locals and tourists alike. There really is something for everyone, from after-breakfast strolls to the popular sport of Munro bagging.

The best time of year for hill walking is usually May to September, although snow can fall on the highest summits even in midsummer. Winter walking on the higher hills of Scotland is for experienced mountaineers only, requiring the use of an ice axe and crampons.

What to Bring

Highland hikers should be properly equipped and cautious, as the weather can become vicious at any time of year. After rain, peaty soil can become boggy, so always wear stout shoes or boots and carry extra food and drink – many unsuspecting walkers have had to survive an unplanned night in the open. Don't depend on mobile phones (although carrying one with you is a good idea, and can be a life saver if you can get a signal). If necessary, leave a note with your route and expected time of return in the windscreen of your car.

Maps

Britain's national mapping agency, the Ordnance Survey (OS), caters to walkers with a wide range of maps at different scales. The Landranger series at 1:50,000 (1.25 inches to 1 mile; £5.99 per sheet) is the standard hiker's map. If you want more detail, the Explorer series at 1:25,000 (2.5 inches to 1 mile; £7.99 per sheet) shows features such as field boundaries and fences. Both series are also available as 'Active' versions (£12.99 and £13.99), which are completely waterproof. Tourist offices and bookshops usually stock a selection, or you can buy them online.

Alternatively, look out for the excellent, weatherproof walkers' maps published by Harveys at scales of 1:40,000 and 1:25,000. These are tailored to particular walking and climbing areas such as Ben Nevis or the Cairngorms, and there are also maps dedicated to long-distance footpaths.

Further Information

Every tourist office has leaflets (free or for a nominal charge) of suggested walks that take in local points of interest. Lonely Planet's *Walking in Scotland* is a comprehensive resource, covering short walks and long-distance paths; its *Walking in Britain* guide covers Scottish walks, too. For general advice, VisitScotland produces a **Walking Scotland** (http://walking. visitscotland.com) website that describes numerous routes in various parts of the country, and also offers safety tips and other useful information.

Other useful sources:

➡ **Mountaineering Council of Scotland** (www. mcofs.org.uk)

➡ **Ordnance Survey** (www.ordnancesurvey. co.uk)

➡ **Ramblers' Association Scotland** (www. ramblers.org.uk/scotland)

➡ **Scottish Mountaineering Club** (www.smc. org.uk)

Mountain Biking

A combination of challenging, rugged terrain, a network of old drove roads, military roads and stalkers' paths, and legislation that enshrines free access to the countryside has earned Scotland a reputation as one of the world's top mountain-biking destinations. Fort William has hosted the UCI Mountain Bike World Championships every year since 2007.

THE RIGHT TO ROAM

There is a tradition of relatively free access to open country in Scotland, a tradition that was enshrined in law in the 2003 Land Reform (Scotland) Bill, popularly known as 'the right to roam'. The **Scottish Outdoor Access Code** (www.outdooraccess-scotland.com) states that everyone has the right to be on most land and inland waters, providing they act responsibly. You should avoid areas where you might disrupt or disturb wildlife, lambing (generally mid-April to the end of May), grouse shooting (from 12 August to the third week in October) or deer stalking (1 July to 15 February, but the peak period is August to October). You can get up-to-date information on deer stalking in various areas through the **Heading for the Scottish Hills service** (www.outdooraccess-scotland.com/hftsh).

You are also free to pitch a tent almost anywhere that doesn't cause inconvenience to others or damage to property, as long as you stay no longer than two or three nights in any one spot, take all litter away with you, and keep well away from houses and roads. (Note that this right does not extend to the use of motorised vehicles.)

Local authorities aren't required to list and map rights of way, so they're not shown on Ordnance Survey (OS) maps of Scotland, as they are in England and Wales. However, the **Scottish Rights of Way & Access Society** (www.scotways. com) keeps records of these routes, provides and maintains signposting, and publicises them in its guidebook, *Scottish Hill Tracks*.

The Highlands and islands offer everything from custom-built forest trails with berms, jumps and skinnies to world-class downhill courses such as those at Laggan Wolftrax and Nevis Range. But perhaps the region's greatest appeal is its almost unlimited potential for adventurous, off-road riding. Areas such as the Angus Glens, the Cairngorms, Lochaber, Skye and most of the Northwest Highlands have large roadless regions where you can explore to your heart's content.

Top trails include Glen Feshie, Glenlivet and Rothiemurchus Forest in the Cairngorms, Spean Bridge to Kinlochleven via the Lairig Leacach and Loch Eilde Mor, and the stretch of the West Highland Way between Bridge of Orchy and Kinlochleven. The 37-mile loop from Sligachan on Skye (south through Glen Sligachan to Camasunary, over to Kilmarie, and back north via Strath Mor) was voted by *Mountain Bike Rider* magazine as the best off-road trail in the whole of Britain.

But the ultimate off-road experience is a coast-to-coast ride. There is no set route and no waymarking, so it's as much a planning and navigational challenge as a physical one. A coast-to-coast can be as short as the 36 miles from Ullapool to Bonar Bridge via Glen Achall and Glen Einig, or as long as the 250 miles from Aberdeen to Ardnamurchan (90% off-road).

The most popular route, though, is from Fort William to Montrose (starting and finishing at a railway station) via Fort Augustus, Aviemore, Tomintoul, Ballater and Edzell, taking in the Corrieyairack Pass, the Ryvoan Pass, Glen Builg, Glen Tanar and Glen Esk (195 miles). You can camp wild along the way or book accommodation at B&Bs and hostels. Alternatively join a guided expedition with an organisation such as **Wilderness Scotland** (☑01479-42 0020; www.wildernessscotland.com) or **Scottish Mountain Bike Guides** (☑0800 689 0188; www.scottishmountainbikeguides.com).

Mountain-Biking Centres

Nevis Range (☑01397-705825; www.nevisrange.co.uk; gondola return trip per adult/child £11.50/6.75; ☺10am-5pm summer, 9.30am-dusk winter, closed mid-Nov–mid-Dec) Ski resort offering summer sport in the form of a world-championship downhill course, and a 3.7-mile red-grade cross-country trail from the top station of the gondola.

Witch's Trails (☑01397-702184; scotland.forestry.gov.uk/visit/witchs-trails) Has 22 miles of forest road and single-track in the shadow of Ben Nevis. Hosts the annual cross-country world championships and the annual 10 Under The Ben endurance event.

Laggan Wolftrax (p132) Forest centre near Newtonmore with everything from novice trails and a bike park to hard cross-country and a challenging black route with drop-offs, boulder fields and rock slabs.

Highland Wildcat (www.highlandwildcat.com; ☺dawn-dusk) FREE The hills above Golspie harbour have the biggest single-track descent in the country (390m drop over 4 miles, from the top of Ben Bhraggie almost to sea level). Plenty for beginners and families, too.

Learnie Red Rocks (☑01463 791575; scotland.forestry.gov.uk/visit/learnie-red-rocks) Just north of Rosemarkie; 10 miles of forest trails plus fun park, for all levels of skill and experience.

Kyle of Sutherland Trails (☑01408-634063; scotland.forestry.gov.uk/visit/carbisdale) Rocks and boardwalks add some technical challenges to 10.5 miles of blue-, red- and black-graded forest trails with great views.

OFFICIAL LONG-DISTANCE FOOTPATHS

WALK	DISTANCE	FEATURES	DURATION	DIFFICULTY
Great Glen Way	73 miles	Loch Ness, canal paths, forest tracks	4 days	easy
Speyside Way	66 miles	follows river, whisky distilleries	3-4 days	easy-medium
West Highland Way	96 miles	spectacular scenery, mountains & lochs	6-8 days	medium

Cycling

Cycling is an excellent way to explore Scotland's Highlands and islands. There are hundreds of miles of forest trails and quiet minor roads, and dedicated cycle routes along canal towpaths and disused railway tracks. Depending on your energy and enthusiasm, you can take a leisurely trip through idyllic glens, stopping at pubs along the way, or head off on a long and arduous road tour.

The network of signposted cycle routes maintained by **Sustrans** (www.sustrans.org. uk) makes a good introduction. Much of the network is on minor roads or cycle lanes, but there are long stretches of surfaced, traffic-free trails between Callander and Killin, between Oban and Ballachulish, and on Royal Deeside.

But it's the minor roads of the Northwest Highlands, the Outer Hebrides, Orkney and Shetland that are the real attraction for cycle tourers, offering hundreds of miles of peaceful pedalling through breathtaking landscapes. The classic Scottish cycle tour is a trip around the islands of the west coast, from Islay and Jura north via Mull, Coll and Tiree to Skye and the Outer Hebrides (bikes travel for free on Calmac car ferries).

Further Information

VisitScotland publishes a useful free brochure, *Active Scotland,* and has a website with more information (http://active. visitscotland.com). Many regional tourist offices have information on local cycling routes and places to hire bikes. They also stock cycling guides and books.

For up-to-date, detailed information on Scotland's cycle-route network contact Sustrans. The **Cyclists' Touring Club** (www. ctc.org.uk) is a membership organisation offering comprehensive information about cycling in Britain.

Birdwatching

Scotland is the best place in the British Isles (and in some cases, the only place) to spot bird species such as the golden eagle, white-tailed eagle, osprey, corncrake, capercaillie, crested tit, Scottish crossbill and

ptarmigan, and the country's coast and islands are some of Europe's most important seabird nesting grounds.

There are more than 80 ornithologically important nature reserves managed by **Scottish Natural Heritage** (www.snh.gov. uk), the **Royal Society for the Protection of Birds** (www.rspb.org.uk) and the **Scottish Wildlife Trust** (www.swt.org.uk).

Further information can be obtained from the **Scottish Ornithologists Club** (www.the-soc.org.uk).

Whale Watching

In contrast to Iceland and Norway, Scotland has cashed in on the abundance of minke whales off its coast by embracing whale watching rather than whaling. There are now dozens of operators around the coast offering whale-watching boat trips lasting from a couple of hours to all day; some have whale-sighting success rates of 95% in summer.

The best places to base yourself for whale watching include Oban, the Isle of Mull, Skye and the Outer Hebrides. Orkney and Shetland offer the best chance of spotting orcas (killer whales) while the Moray Firth has a resident population of bottle-nosed dolphins. While seals, porpoises and dolphins can be seen year-round, minke whales are most commonly spotted from

BEATING THE MIDGES

Forget Nessie. The Highlands have a real monster in their midst: a voracious, blood-sucking female fully 2mm long, known as *Culicoides impunctatus* – the Highland midge. (The male midge is an innocent vegetarian.) The bane of campers and as much a symbol of Scotland as the kilt or the thistle, they can drive sane folk to distraction as they descend in swarms of biting misery. Though mostly vegetarian too, the female midge needs a dose of blood in order to lay her eggs. And like it or not, if you're in the Highlands in summer, you've just volunteered as a donor.

The midge season lasts from late May to early September, with June to August being the worst months. Climate change has seen warmer, damper springs and summers that seem to suit the midges just fine – in recent years they've increased both in numbers and in range. They're at their worst in the morning and evening, especially in calm, overcast weather; strong winds and strong sunshine help keep them away.

You can get an idea of how bad they are going to be in your area by checking the midge forecast (www.midgeforecast.co.uk).

Be Prepared

Cover up by wearing long trousers and long-sleeved shirts, and (if they're really bad) a head net (available in most outdoor shops for £4 to £5) worn over a brimmed hat. Also be sure to use a repellent.

Many kinds of repellents have been formulated over the decades, some based on natural ingredients such citronella and bog myrtle, but until recently there was only one that worked reliably – DEET, which is a nasty, industrial chemical that smells bad, stings your eyes and seems to be capable of melting plastic. A new repellent called Saltidin claims to be both effective and pleasant to use (marketed under the brand name Smidge).

However, there's another substance that has shot to prominence since 2005 despite not being marketed as an insect repellent. Avon's 'Skin So Soft' moisturiser spray is so effective that it is regularly used as a midge repellent by professionals including the Royal Marines, forestry workers and water engineers, as well as thousands of outdoor enthusiasts. You can find it in most outdoor stores in the west of Scotland. Not only does it keep the midges away, but it leaves your skin feeling 'velvety soft'.

June to August, with August being the peak month for sightings.

The website of the **Hebridean Whale & Dolphin Trust** (www.whaledolphintrust.co.uk) has lots of information on the species you are likely to see, and how to identify them. A booklet titled *Is It a Whale?* is available from tourist offices and bookshops, and provides tips on identifying the various species of marine mammal that you're likely to see.

Outfits operating whale-watching cruises include:

Aquaxplore (☎0800 731 3089; www.aquaxplore.co.uk; ⊗Apr-Oct)

Gairloch Marine Cruises (☎01445-712636; www.porpoise-gairloch.co.uk)

MV Volante (☎01681-700362; www.volanteiona.com; ⊗Jun-Oct)

Sea Life Surveys (☎01688-302916; www.sealifesurveys.com; Ledaig)

Sea.fari Adventures (☎01852-300003; www.seafari.co.uk; Ellenabeich; ⊗Apr-Oct)

Golf

Scotland is the home of golf. The game has been played in Scotland for centuries and there are more courses per head of population here than in any other country. Most clubs are open to visitors; details can be found at www.scotlands-golf-courses.com.

St Andrews is the headquarters of the game's governing body, the Royal and Ancient Golf Club, and the location of the world's most famous golf course, the Old Course. Although the major championship courses, including those at Carnoustie, Royal Troon and Turnberry, are in the south of the country, there are some superb courses in the Highlands, such as Royal Dornoch, Tain and Nairn. Many visiting golfers enjoy the challenge of the wild and some eccentric golf courses can be found dotted among the islands, such as Machrie on Islay, Askernish on South Uist and Whalsay in Shetland.

VisitScotland publishes *Golf in Scotland* (http://golf.visitscotland.com), a free annual brochure listing course details, costs and clubs, as well as information on where to stay.

Fishing

Fishing – coarse, sea and game – is enormously popular in Scotland; the lochs and rivers of the Highlands and islands are filled with salmon, sea trout, brown trout and Arctic char. Fly-fishing in particular is a joy – it's a tricky but rewarding form of angling, closer to an art form than a sport.

Fishing rights to most inland waters are privately owned and you must obtain a permit to fish in them – these are usually readily available from the local fishing tackle shop or hotel, which are also great sources of advice and local knowledge. Permits cost from around £5 to £20 per day but salmon fishing on some rivers –

notably the Dee, Tay and Spey – can be much more expensive (up to £150 a day).

For wild brown trout the close season is early October to mid-March. The close season for salmon and sea trout varies between districts; it's generally from mid-October to mid-January.

FishPal (www.fishpal.com/scotland) provides a good introduction, with links for booking fishing on various rivers and lochs.

Kayaking & Canoeing

The islands, sea lochs and indented coastline of Scotland's Highlands and islands provide some of the finest sea kayaking in the world. There are sheltered lochs and inlets ideal for beginners, long and exciting coastal and island tours, and gnarly tidal passages that will challenge even the most expert paddler, all amid spectacular scenery and wildlife – encounters with seals, dolphins and even whales are relatively common.

The inland lochs and rivers offer excellent Canadian and white-water canoeing. Lochs Lomond, Awe and Maree all have uninhabited islands where canoeists can set up camp, while a study of the map will suggest plenty of cross-country expeditions involving only minor portages. Classic routes include Fort William to Inverness along the Great Glen; Glen Affric; Loch Shiel; and Loch Veyatie–Fionn Loch–Loch Sionascaig in Assynt.

THE SPEYSIDE WAY

This long-distance footpath follows the course of the River Spey, one of Scotland's most famous salmon-fishing rivers. It starts at Buckie and first follows the coast to Spey Bay, east of Elgin, then runs inland along the river to Aviemore in the Cairngorms (with branches to Tomintoul and Dufftown). At only 66 miles, the main walk can be done in three or four days, although including the branch trails to Dufftown and Tomintoul will push the total walking distance to 102 miles (allow seven days).

This route has also been dubbed the **Whisky Trail** as it passes near a number of distilleries, including Glenlivet and Glenfiddich, which are open to the public. If you stop at them all, the walk may take considerably longer than the usual three or four days!

The *Speyside Way* guidebook by Jacquetta Megarry and Jim Strachan describes the route in detail. Or check out the route at www.speysideway.org.

There are dozens of companies offering sea kayaking and canoeing courses and guided holidays, including the following:

Arran Adventure Company (☏01770-303479; www.arranadventure.com)

NorWest Sea Kayaking (☏01571-844281; www.norwestseakayaking.com)

Rockhopper Sea Kayaking (www.rockhopperscotland.co.uk)

Sea Kayak Shetland (☏01595-840272; www.seakayakshetland.co.uk)

Skyak Adventures (☏01471-820002; www.skyakadventures.com; Breakish)

Wilderness Scotland (☏01479-420020; www.wildernessscotland.com)

Further Information

➡ **Scottish Canoe Association** (www.canoescotland.org) Publishes coastal navigation sheets and organises tours, including introductory ones for beginners.

➡ *The Northern Isles* (by Tom Smith & Chris Jex) A detailed guide to sea kayaking the waters around Orkney and Shetland.

➡ *The Outer Hebrides* (by Mike Sullivan, Robert Emmott and Tim Pickering) A detailed guide to sea kayaking around the Western Isles.

➡ *Scottish Sea Kayak Trail* (www.scottishseakayaktrail.com; by Simon Willis) Covers the Scottish west coast from the Isle of Gigha to the Summer Isles.

Winter Sports

There are five ski centres in Scotland, offering downhill skiing and snowboarding.

Cairngorm Mountain (www.cairngorm-mountain.org; 1-day ski pass per adult/child £33.50/20) Has almost 30 runs spread over an extensive area (1097m).

Glencoe Mountain Resort (p146) Has only five tows and two chairlifts (1108m).

Glenshee Ski Resort (☏01339-741320; www.ski-glenshee.co.uk; 1-day lift pass £29) Situated on the A93 road between Perth and Braemar; offers the largest network of lifts and the widest range of runs in all of Scotland (920m).

Lecht 2090 (www.lecht.co.uk) The smallest and most remote centre, on the A939 between Ballater and Grantown-on-Spey (793m).

Nevis Range (p32) Near Fort William; offers the highest ski runs, the grandest setting and some of the best off-piste potential in Scotland (1221m).

The high season is from January to April but it's sometimes possible to ski from as early as November to as late as May. It's easy to turn up at the slopes, hire some equipment, buy a day pass and head right off.

VisitScotland's *Ski Scotland* brochure is useful and includes a list of accommodation options. General information, and weather and snow reports, can be obtained from **Ski Scotland** (www.ski-scotland.com) and **WinterHighland** (www.winterhighland.info).

THE ANCIENT ART OF MUNRO BAGGING

At the end of the 19th century an eager hill walker, Sir Hugh Munro, published a list of Scottish mountains with summits of more than 3000ft (914m) above sea level. He couldn't have realised that in time his name would be used to describe any Scottish mountain over 3000ft. Many keen hill walkers now set themselves the target of reaching the summit of (or bagging) all of Scotland's 282 Munros.

To the uninitiated it may seem odd that Munro baggers see venturing into mist, cloud and driving rain as time well spent. However, for those who can add one or more ticks to their list, the vagaries of the weather are part of the enjoyment, at least in retrospect. Munro bagging is, of course, more than merely ticking off a list – it takes you to some of the wildest and most beautiful corners of Scotland.

Once you've bagged all the Munros you can move on to the Corbetts – hills over 2500ft (700m), with a drop of at least 500ft (150m) on all sides – and the Donalds, lowland hills over 2000ft (610m). And for connoisseurs of the diminutive, there are the McPhies: 'eminences in excess of 300ft (90m)' on the Isle of Colonsay.

Top: Mountain biking on a forest trail

Bottom: Surfer at Brimms Ness, Thurso (p178)

Horse Riding

There are hundreds of miles of beautiful woodland, riverside and coastal trails to be ridden in the Highlands, and seeing the country from the saddle is a wonderful experience even if you're not an experienced rider.

VisitScotland publishes the *Riding in Scotland* brochure (http://riding.visit scotland.com), which lists riding centres around Scotland.

The **Trekking & Riding Society of Scotland** (www.ridinginscotland.com) can provide information on horse-riding courses and approved riding centres.

Scuba Diving

It may lack coral reefs and warm waters but Scotland offers some of the most spectacular and challenging scuba diving in Europe. There are spectacular drop-offs, challenging drift dives (the Falls of Lora is a classic) and fascinating wildlife ranging from colourful jewel anemones and soft corals to giant conger eels, monkfish and inquisitive seals. There are also hundreds of fascinating shipwrecks.

Dive sites such as Scapa Flow in the Orkney Islands, where the seven remaining hulks of the WWI German High Seas Fleet, scuttled in 1919, lie on the sea bed, and the oceanic arches, tunnels and caves of St Kilda rank among the best in the world.

For more information on the country's diving options contact the **Scottish Sub Aqua Club** (www.scotsac.com).

Surfing

Even with a wetsuit on you definitely have to be hardy to enjoy surfing in Scottish waters. That said, the country does have some of the best surfing breaks in Europe.

The tidal range is large, which means there is often a completely different set of breaks at low and high tides. It's the north and west coasts, particularly around Thurso and in the Outer Hebrides, which have outstanding, world-class surf. Indeed, Lewis has the best and most consistent surf in Britain, with around 120 recorded breaks and waves up to 5m.

For more information contact **Hebridean Surf** (www.hebrideansurf.co.uk).

Regions at a Glance

Which parts of the Highlands and islands you choose to visit will naturally depend on how much time you have, and whether you've been here before. First-time visitors will want to squeeze in as many highlights as possible, so could try following the well-trodden route through the Trossachs, Pitlochry, Inverness, Loch Ness and Skye.

It takes considerably more time to explore the further-flung corners of the country, but the jaw-dropping scenery of the northwest Highlands and the gorgeous white-sand beaches of the Outer Hebrides are less crowded and ultimately more rewarding. The long journey to Orkney or Shetland means that you'll want to devote more than just a day or two to these regions.

Southern Highlands & Islands

Wildlife
Islands
Food

Whales & Eagles

This region is home to some of Scotland's most spectacular wildlife, from magnificent white-tailed sea eagles in Mull, to majestic minke whales and basking sharks cruising the west coast. It's also where the beaver – extinct here for centuries – has been re-introduced into the wild.

Island-hopping

Island-hopping is one of the best ways to explore the western seaboard, and the cluster of islands here – Islay with its whisky distilleries, wild and mountainous Jura, scenic Mull and the little jewel of Iona, and the gorgeous beaches of Colonsay, Coll and Tiree – provide a brilliant introduction.

Seafood

Whether you dine at a top restaurant in Oban or Tobermory, or eat with your fingers on the harbourside, the rich harvest of the sea is one of the region's biggest drawcards.

p42

Inverness & the Central Highlands

Activities
Royalty
Legends

Hiking & Skiing

The Cairngorm towns of Aviemore and Fort William offer outdoor adventures galore. Be it climbing Ben Nevis, walking the West Highland Way, biking the trails around Loch Morlich or skiing the slopes of Cairngorm, there's something for everyone.

Royal Deeside

The valley of the River Dee (often called Royal Deeside) between Ballater and Braemar has been associated with the royal family since Queen Victoria acquired her holiday home, Balmoral Castle.

Loch Ness Monster

Scotland's most iconic legend, the Loch Ness monster, lurks in the heart of this region. You might not spot Nessie, but the magnificent scenery of the Great Glen makes a visit worthwhile, as does Culloden battlefield, the undoing of another Scottish legend, Bonnie Prince Charlie.

p109

Northern Highlands & Islands

Scenery
Activities
History

Mountains & Lochs

From the peaks of Assynt and Torridon, to the jagged rock pinnacles of the Cuillin Hills, to the dazzling beaches of the Outer Hebrides, the big skies and lonely landscapes of the northern Highlands and islands are the very essence of Scotland, a wilderness of sea and mountains that remains one of Europe's most unspoilt regions.

Climbing & Kayaking

The northwest's vast spaces are one huge adventure playground for hikers, bikers, climbers and kayakers, providing the chance to see some of the UK's most spectacular wildlife.

The Clearances

The abandoned rural communities of the north teach much about the Clearances, especially Arnol Blackhouse and Skye Museum of Island Life. The region is also rich in prehistoric remains, including the famous standing stones of Callanish.

p166

Orkney & Shetland

History
Wildlife
Music

Skara Brae

These treeless, cliff-bound islands have a fascinating Viking heritage and unique prehistoric villages, tombs and stone circles. Predating the pyramids of Egypt, Skara Brae is northern Europe's best-preserved prehistoric village; Maes Howe is one of Britain's finest Neolithic tombs.

Birdwatching

Shetland is a birdwatcher's paradise, its cliffs teeming in summer with gannets, fulmars, kittiwakes, razorbills and puffins, and Europe's largest colony of Arctic terns. Several nature reserves include Hermaness on Unst, Scotland's northernmost inhabited island.

Folk Tradition

The pubs of Kirkwall, Stromness and Lerwick are fertile ground for exploring the traditional-music scene, with impromptu sessions of fiddle and guitar music. Both Orkney and Shetland host annual festivals of folk music.

p220

On the Road

Orkney & Shetland
p220

Northern Highlands & Islands
p166

Inverness & the Central Highlands
p109

Southern Highlands & Islands
p42

Southern Highlands & Islands

Why Go?

The impossibly complex coastline of Scotland's southwest harbours some of its most inspiring corners. Here, sea travel is as important as road and rail – dozens of ferries allow you to island-hop from the scenic splendour of Arran to majestic Mull or Tiree's lonely sands, via the whisky distilleries of Islay, the wild mountains of Jura, the scenic delights of diminutive Colonsay and Oban's sustainable-seafood scene.

On fresh water too, passenger ferries, vintage steamboats, canoes and kayaks ply the lochs of Loch Lomond and the Trossachs National Park, a memorable concentration of scenic splendour that's very accessible from Glasgow or Edinburgh but possessed of a wild beauty.

Wildlife experiences are a highlight here; from the rasping spout of a minke whale to the 'krek-krek' of a corncrake. You can spot otters tumbling in the kelp, watch sea eagles snatch fish from a lonely loch and thrill to the sight of dolphins riding the bow-wave of your boat.

Best Places to Eat

➡ Callander Meadows (p57)

➡ Starfish (p66)

➡ Café Fish (p90)

➡ Seafood Temple (p84)

➡ Brodick Bar (p71)

Best Places to Stay

➡ Monachyle Mhor (p57)

➡ Lake of Menteith Hotel (p51)

➡ Calgary Farmhouse (p91)

➡ Iona Hostel (p94)

➡ Argyll Hotel (p94)

When to Go
Oban

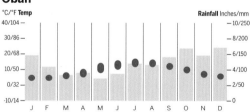

May Fèis Ìle (Islay Festival) celebrates traditional Scottish music and whisky.

Jun Roadsides and gardens become a blaze of colour with deep-pink rhododendron blooms.

Aug The best month of the year for whale-watching off the west coast.

Southern Highlands & Islands Highlights

1 Exploring the lovely lochscapes and accessible walking and cycling routes of the **Trossachs** (p50)

2 Visiting the smoky heavyweights of the whisky world on their peaty home turf of **Islay** (p76)

3 Blowing away the cobwebs on scenic, activity-packed **Isle of Arran** (p68)

4 Visiting the white waters of the **Corryvreckan whirlpool** (p79) of the north end of lonely Jura

5 Journeying through wildlife-rich **Mull** (p86) to reach the holy emerald isle of **Iona** (p93)

6 Hiking the **West Highland Way** (p44) along the eastern shore of Loch Lomond

7 Tucking into a platter of fresh local langoustines at the seafood restaurants in **Oban** (p80)

8 Teeing off on the great-value old and new courses at **Machrihanish** (p67) down the Kintyre peninsula

LOCH LOMOND & AROUND

The 'bonnie banks' and 'bonnie braes' of Loch Lomond have long been Glasgow's rural retreat – a scenic region of hills, lochs and healthy fresh air within easy reach of Scotland's largest city. Today the loch's popularity shows no sign of decreasing.

Loch Lomond

Loch Lomond is mainland Britain's largest lake and, after Loch Ness, the most famous of Scotland's lochs. Its proximity to Glasgow (20 miles away) means that the tourist honeypots of Balloch, Loch Lomond Shores and Luss get pretty crowded in summer. The eastern shore, which is followed by the West Highland Way long-distance footpath, is quieter and offers a better chance to appreciate the loch away from the busy main road.

Loch Lomond straddles the Highland border. The southern part is broad and island-studded, fringed by woods and Lowland meadows. However, north of Luss the loch narrows, occupying a deep trench gouged out by glaciers during the Ice Age, with 900m mountains crowding either side. The length of Loch Lomond means that access between the western part of the national park and the Trossachs is either in the far north of the region via Crianlarich or the far south via Drymen.

🏃 Activities

Walking

The **West Highland Way** (www.west-highland-way.co.uk) runs along the loch's eastern shore, while the **Rob Roy Way** (www.robroyway.com) heads from Drymen to Pitlochry via the Trossachs. The **Three Lochs Way** (www.threelochsway.co.uk) loops west from Balloch through Helensburgh and Arrochar before returning to Loch Lomond at Inveruglas. There are numerous shorter walks around: get further information from information centres.

Rowardennan is the starting point for ascents of **Ben Lomond** (974m), a popular and relatively straighforward (if strenuous) 7.5-mile round trip (five to six hours). The route starts at the car park just past the Rowardennan Hotel.

Other Activities

The mostly traffic-free **Clyde and Loch Lomond Cycle Way** links Glasgow to Balloch (20 miles), where it links with the **West Loch Lomond Cycle Path**, which continues along the loch shore to Tarbet (10 miles). The park website details some other local routes.

CanYou Experience   CANOEING, CYCLING
(📞 01389-756251; www.canyouexperience.com; Loch Lomond Shores, Balloch; ⊙ 9am-5.30pm Easter-Oct) Offers a huge range of activities on water and land from various bases around Loch Lomond. Hires mountain bikes (£13/17 per half/full day), canoes and kayaks, and offers a full-day guided canoe safari (£50).

Loch Lomond Seaplanes   SCENIC FLIGHTS
(📞 01436-675030; www.lochlomondseaplanes.com; flights from £129) Leaving from the Cameron House Hotel just north of Balloch, this company offers a variety of scenic flights over the loch and western Scotland.

👉 Tours

Sweeney's Cruises   BOAT TOURS
(📞 01389-752376; www.sweeneyscruises.com; Balloch Rd, Balloch) Offers a range of trips including a one-hour cruise to Inchmurrin and back (adult/child £9.80/6.50, five times daily), and a two-hour cruise (£17/9.50, departs 12.30pm and 3pm May to September) around the islands. The quay is directly opposite Balloch train station, beside the tourist office. It also runs some trips from a dock at Loch Lomond Shores.

Cruise Loch Lomond   BOAT TOURS
(📞 01301-702356; www.cruiselochlomond.co.uk; Tarbet/Luss; ⊙ 8.30am-5.30pm early Apr-late Oct) With departures from Tarbet and Luss, this company offers short cruises and two-hour trips to Arklet Falls and Rob Roy's Cave (adult/child £15/8). You can also be dropped off at Rowardennan to climb Ben Lomond (£15/9), getting picked up in the afternoon, or get picked up at Inversnaid after a 9-mile hike along the West Highland Way (£15/9). It also hires out bikes at Tarbet.

Balmaha Boatyard   BOAT TOURS
(📞 01360-870214; www.balmahaboatyard.co.uk; Balmaha) Runs a lovely old wooden mailboat from Balmaha to loch islands, departing at 11.30am and returning at 2pm, with a one-hour stop on Inchmurrin (£10/5 per adult/child). Trips depart daily (except Tuesday and Sunday) in July and August; and on

Monday, Thursday and Saturday in May, June and September. There are also various other low-priced cruises in summer.

It also hires out rowing boats (£10/40 per hour/day) and motorboats (£20/60).

ℹ Information

Balloch Tourist Office (☎01389-753533; Balloch Rd, Balloch; ☺9.30am-6pm Jun-Aug, 10am-5pm Sep-May) Opposite Balloch train station.

Balmaha National Park Centre (☎01389-722100; www.lochlomond-trossachs.org; Balmaha; ☺9.30am-4.30pm Apr-Sep, 9.30am-4pm Sat & Sun Oct-Mar) Has maps showing local walking routes.

National Park Gateway Centre (☎01389-751035; www.lochlomondshores.com; Loch Lomond Shores, Balloch; ☺10am-6pm Apr-Sep, 10am-5pm Oct-Mar; ☏) Crowded information desk with shop and cafe.

Tarbet Tourist Office (☎01301-702260; Tarbet; ☺10am-4pm Easter & May-Sep) At the junction of the A82 and the A83.

ℹ Getting There & Away

BUS

First Glasgow (☎0141-423 6600; www.firstglasgow.com) bus 1A runs from Argyle St in central Glasgow to Balloch (£4.50, 1½ hours, at least two per hour) and bus C8 to Drymen (£5.20, 1¼ hours, two daily)

Scottish Citylink (☎0871 266-3333; www.citylink.co.uk) coaches from Glasgow stop at Luss (£8.50, 55 minutes, nine daily), Tarbet (£8.50, 65 minutes, nine daily) and Ardlui (£14.90, 1¼ hours, four daily).

TRAIN

Glasgow–Ardlui £14.90, 1½ hours, three or four daily, continuing to Oban and Fort William
Glasgow–Arrochar & Tarbet £11.40, 1¼ hours, three or four daily
Glasgow–Balloch £5.10, 45 minutes, every 30 minutes

ℹ Getting Around

McGill's (☎08000-515651; www.mcgillsbuses.co.uk) bus 309 runs from Balloch to Drymen and Balmaha (£2.90, 25 minutes, nine to 10 daily). An **SPT Daytripper ticket** (www.spt.co.uk) gives a family group unlimited travel for a day on most bus and train services in the Glasgow, Loch Lomond and Helensburgh area. Buy the ticket (£11.20 for one adult and two children, £19.80 for two adults and up to four children) from any train station or Glasgow bus station.

Local buses run from Helensburgh to Arrochar via Luss and Tarbet thrice daily Monday to Saturday.

LOCH LOMOND'S ISLANDS

There are around 60 islands, large and small, in Loch Lomond. Most are privately owned, and only two (Inchcailloch and Inchmurrin) can be reached without your own boat or canoe. Four of the most interesting:

➜ **Inchcailloch** A nature reserve reached by passenger ferry from Balmaha or Luss. The most accessible island, with nature trails and a small bookable campsite. See www.lochlomond-trossachs.org.

➜ **Inchmurrin** Privately owned, reached by passenger ferry from Arden on the loch's western shore. Has walking trails, beaches, self-catering cottages and a restaurant that is open from Easter to October. See www.inchmurrin-lochlomond.com.

➜ **Inchconnachan** Privately owned. Only accessible by boat or canoe. Has an unlikely wallaby population; the rare capercaillie nests here too.

➜ **Island I Vow** Privately owned. Only accessible by boat or canoe. The loch's most northerly island is home to a ruined castle; Wordsworth visited in 1814 and found a hermit living in it, inspiring his poem *The Brownie's Cell*.

Western Shore

Balloch, straddling the River Leven at Loch Lomond's southern end, is the loch's main population centre and transport hub. A Victorian resort once thronged by day trippers transferring between the train station and the steamer quay, it is now a 'gateway centre' for Loch Lomond and the Trossachs National Park. Visitors still arrive in abundance.

⊙ Sights & Activities

Loch Lomond Shores (www.lochlomondshores.com; ☺9.30am-6pm), a major tourism development, sports a park information centre plus various family-friendly visitor attractions, outdoor activities and boat trips. In keeping with the times, the heart of the development is a large shopping mall. Also here is a birds-of-prey exhibition and **Loch Lomond Aquarium** (www.sealife.co.uk; adult £13.20, adult plus child £23.40;

ℹ FERRY UPDATE

By late 2015, some of the ferry prices in this chapter will have been substantially reduced, as the government's Road Equivalent Tariff scheme, designed to make Scotland's islands more accessible and already in action on several routes, is rolled out to cover all Calmac ferry services.

10am-5pm), with an otter enclosure (housing short-clawed Asian otters, not Scottish ones), and a host of sea-life exhibits ranging from sharks to stingrays to turtles. Look for discount vouchers in *Loch Lomond Area Guide,* available in the visitor centre, before entering.

The vintage paddle steamer **Maid of the Loch** (www.maidoftheloch.com; ⊙11am-5pm Easter-Oct) FREE is moored here as she is gradually restored to working order – nip aboard for a look around or stop for tea in the cafe.

Unless it's raining, give Loch Lomond Shores a miss and head for the picture-postcard village of **Luss**. Stroll among the pretty cottages, built by the local laird in the 19th century for his estate workers, and admire the lochside vistas.

Beyond Luss, **Tarbet** sits at the junction where you choose between Argyll and Kintyre or Oban and the Highlands. Following the shore brings you to **Ardlui** and thence Crianlarich.

🛏 Sleeping & Eating

Ardlui Hotel   HOTEL **££**
(☎01301-704243; www.ardlui.co.uk; Ardlui; s/d £55/110; 🅿🛜🐾) This plush pub and hotel has a great lochside location, and a view of Ben Lomond from the breakfast room. The rooms are decorated in fairly classical Scottish country-comfort style and there are self-catering cabins available too.

Glenview   B&B **££**
(☎01436-860606; www.bonniebank.com; Luss; s/d £70/90; 🅿🛜) In the centre of things on the road through the village of Luss, this white house offers a genuine welcome and highly appealing rooms. Both are showroom-spotless, one is plush and cosy, the other contemporary and stylish, with a modish four-poster bed. Both have swish bathrooms and a sitting area.

★**Drover's Inn**   PUB **££**
(☎01301-704234; www.thedroversinn.co.uk; Ardlui; bar meals £8-12; ⊙11.30am-10pm Mon-Sat, to 9.30pm Sun; 🅿🛜) This is one *howff* (drinking den) you shouldn't miss – a low-ceilinged place just north of Ardlui with smoke-blackened stone, barmen in kilts, and walls festooned with moth-eaten stags' heads and stuffed birds. The bar, where Rob Roy allegedly dropped by for pints, serves hearty hill-walking fuel and hosts live folk at weekends. We recommend this more as an atmospheric place to eat and drink than somewhere to stay.

Village Rest   CAFE **££**
(www.the-village-rest.co.uk; Pier Rd, Luss; mains £9-12; ⊙10am-9pm; 🛜) Set in a typically cute Luss cottage, this spot offers appealing outdoor seating for when the sun shines, a sweet interior and tasty, well-proportioned if overpriced dishes that run from pastas and rolls to satisfying posh burgers.

Eastern Shore

The road along the loch's eastern shore runs from the walkers' hub of **Drymen** through attractive **Balmaha**, where you can hire boats or take a cruise. A short but steep climb from the car park leads up **Conic Hill** (361m), a superb viewpoint (2.5 miles round trip, allow two to three hours). The **Millennium Forest Path** is a 40-minute introduction to the area's tree and plant life.

There are several lochside picnic areas: **Millarochy Bay** (1.5 miles north of Balmaha) has a nice gravel beach and superb views across the loch to the Luss hills.

The road ends at **Rowardennan**, but the West Highland Way (p44) hiking trail continues north along the shore of the loch. It's 7 miles to **Inversnaid**, reachable by road from the Trossachs, and 15 miles to **Inverarnan** at the loch's northern end.

🛏 Sleeping & Eating

From March to October, wild camping is banned on the eastern shore of Loch Lomond between Drymen and Ptarmigan Lodge (just north of Rowardennan Youth Hostel). There are campsites at Millarochy, Cashel and Sallochy. See also the hostel at Inversnaid (p51).

★**Rowardennan SYHA**   HOSTEL **£**
(☎01360-870259; www.syha.org.uk; Rowardennan; dm/tw £18/42; ⊙late Mar-early Oct; 🅿🛜)

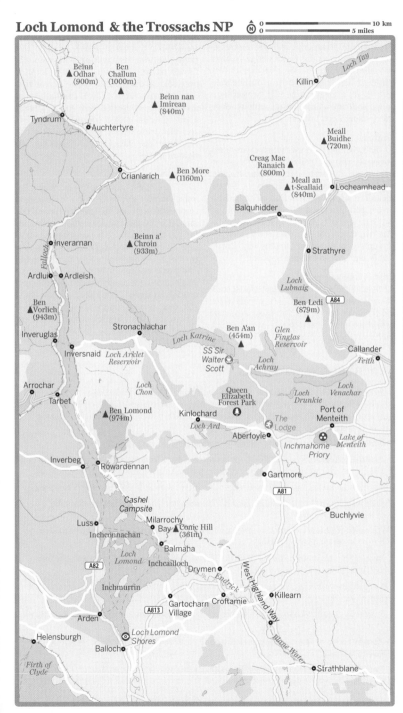

N 0 _____ 10 km
   0 _____ 5 miles

Loch Tay

Beinn Odhar (900m)
Ben Challum (1000m)
Beinn nan Imirean (840m)
Killin

Tyndrum
Auchtertyre

Meall Buidhe (720m)

Creag Mac Ranaich (800m)
Meall an t-Seallaid (840m)
Locheamhead

Crianlarich
Ben More (1160m)

Balquhidder

Beinn a' Chroin (933m)
Strathyre

Inverarnan

Ardlui Ardleish

Loch Lubnaig

Ben Vorlich (943m)
Ben Ledi (879m)
A84

Inveruglas

Stronachlachar
Loch Katrine
Ben A'an (454m)
Glen Finglas Reservoir

Inversnaid
Loch Arklet Reservoir
SS Sir Walter Scott
Loch Achray
Callander
Teith

Arrochar
Loch Chon
Queen Elizabeth Forest Park
Loch Drunkie
Loch Venachar

Tarbet

Ben Lomond (974m)
Kinlochard
Loch Ard
The Lodge
Aberfoyle
Inchmahome Priory
Port of Menteith
Lake of Menteith

Inverbeg Rowardennan

Gartmore

A81

Cashel Campsite
Milarrochy Bay
Conic Hill (361m)
Buchlyvie

Luss
Inchconnachan

Balmaha

Loch Lomond
Inchcailloch
Drymen
West Highland Way

A82
Inchmurrin

Killearn

Gartocharn Village
Croftamie
A813
Endrick

Arden

Helensburgh
Loch Lomond Shores
Balloch
Blane Water

Firth of Clyde
Strathblane

Where the road ends on the eastern side of the loch, this is a wonderful retreat in an elegant ex-hunting lodge with lawns stretching right down to the water's edge. Whether you're walking the West Highland Way, climbing Ben Lomond, or just putting your feet up, it's a great choice with atmosphere, genial staff and a huge lounge with windows overlooking Loch Lomond.

Elmbank
B&B £

(☑01360-661016; www.elmbank-drymen.com; Stirling Rd, Drymen; d £56-70; P🛜) Just off the square, this welcoming, walker-friendly place has an interesting variety of rooms, including self-catering options. The friendly owner runs a relaxed ship and is flexible, so will happily do deals for singles and groups. The two rooms looking over the garden are absolutely fabulous on a sunny day. Breakfast is available in the pub opposite.

Cashel Campsite
CAMPSITE £

(☑01360-870234; www.campingintheforest.co.uk; Rowardennan; sites incl car £20-31, without vehicle £15-17; ⊙Mar-Oct; P🛒) The most attractive campsite in the area is 3 miles north of Balmaha, on the loch shore.

★ Passfoot Cottage
B&B ££

(☑01360-870324; www.passfoot.com; Balmaha; s/d £70/80; ⊙Apr-Sep; P🛜) Passfoot is a pretty whitewashed cottage with colourful flower baskets, enjoying a lovely location overlooking Balmaha Bay. The bright bedrooms have a homely feel, the bathrooms are Scandinavian-style wet rooms, there's a cosy lounge with a wood-burning stove and loch view, and a wee garden down by the shore. The cheery owner makes you feel right at home.

Oak Tree Inn
INN ££

(☑01360-870357; www.oak-tree-inn.co.uk; Balmaha; dm/s/d £30/50/85; P🛜) An attractive traditional inn built in slate and timber, this inn offers bright, modern guest bedrooms for pampered hikers, super-spacious superior chambers, self-catering cottages and two four-bed bunkrooms for hardier souls. The rustic restaurant brings locals, tourists and walkers together and dishes up hearty meals that cover lots of bases (mains £9 to £12, food noon to 9pm). There's lots of outdoor seating and they brew their own beers.

LOCH LOMOND WATER BUS

From April to October a network of boats criss-crosses Loch Lomond, allowing you to explore the loch's hiking and biking trails using public transport. A **Loch Lomond Water Bus** (www.lochlomond-trossachs.org/waterbus) timetable is available from tourist offices and online.

Arden to Inchmurrin (www.inchmurrin-lochlomond.com; return £4) On demand.

Ardlui to Ardleish (☑01307-704243; per person £4 or £ for solo passengers; ⊙9am-7pm May-Sep, to 6pm Apr & Oct) On demand; operated by Ardlui Hotel.

Balloch to Luss (www.sweeneyscruises.com; single/return £10/17; ⊙ Jun-Aug) Three daily.

Balmaha to Inchcailloch (☑01360-870214; www.balmahaboatyard.co.uk; return £5; ⊙9am-8pm) On demand.

Balmaha to Luss (www.cruiselochlomond.co.uk; single/return £8/11.50; ⊙Apr-Sep) Four daily, calls at Inchcailloch island.

Inveruglas to Inversnaid (☑01301-702356; www.cruiselochlomond.co.uk; single/return £8/11.50; ⊙Apr-Oct) Must be booked.

Luss to Inchcailloch (www.cruiselochlomond.co.uk; single/return £8/11.50; ⊙Apr-Oct) Two daily.

Rowardennan to Luss (www.cruiselochlomond.co.uk; single/return £8/11.50; ⊙Apr-Oct) Three daily.

Tarbet to Inversnaid (www.cruiselochlomond.co.uk; single/return £8/11.50; ⊙Apr-Oct) Five to six daily.

Tarbet to Rowardennan (www.cruiselochlomond.co.uk; single/return £8/11.50; ⊙Apr-Oct) One daily

Crianlarich & Tyndrum

POP 400

Surrounded by spectacular hillscapes at the northern edge of the Loch Lomond and the Trossachs National Park, these villages are popular pit stops on the main A82 road, for walkers on the West Highland Way and Munro-baggers. Crianlarich has a train station and more community atmosphere but Tyndrum (*tyne*-drum), 5 miles up the road, has two stations, a bus interchange, petrol station, late-opening motorists' cafes and tourist office (☑01838-400246; 6 Main St, Tyndrum; ⊙10am-5pm Apr-Oct) – a good spot for route information and maps for ascents of Munros Cruach Ardrain (1046m), Ben More (1174m) and magnificent Ben Lui (1130m).

🛏 Sleeping & Eating

Crianlarich makes a more appealing base than Tyndrum: vehicles slow down through town and the views are better.

Crianlarich SYHA　　　　　　　HOSTEL £
(☑01838-300260; www.syha.org.uk; Station Rd, Crianlarich; dm £18; P@🕏) Well-run and comfortable, with a spacious kitchen, dining area and lounge, this is a real haven for walkers or anyone passing through. Dorms vary in size – there are some great en suite family rooms that should be prebooked – but all are clean and roomy.

Strathfillan Wigwams　　　CAMPSITE CABIN £
(☑01838-400251; www.wigwamholidays.com; sites per adult/child £8/3, wigwam d small/large £38/44, lodge d from £60; P@🕏🐾) A working farm off the A82 between Crianlarich and Tyndrum, this has 16 heated 'wigwams' – wooden A-frame cabins with fridge and foam mattresses, that can sleep four at a pinch. More upmarket are the self-contained lodges with their own bathroom and kitchen facilities. There's also camping and decent facilities.

Tigh-na-Fraoch　　　　　　　B&B ££
(☑01838-400354; www.tigh-na-fraoch.com; Lower Station Rd, Tyndrum; d £66; ⊙Jan-Oct; P🕏) The name means 'house of the heather' and Heather is the name of the owner – an alternative therapist offering kinesiology and head massages as well as three bright, clean and comfortable bedrooms, and a breakfast menu that includes (resident anglers' luck

---

CLIMBING BEN LOMOND

Standing guard over the eastern shore of Loch Lomond is Ben Lomond (974m), Scotland's most southerly Munro. It's a popular climb: most follow the Tourist Route up and down from Rowardennan car park. It's a straightforward climb on a well-used and maintained path; allow five hours for the 7 mile (11km) round trip.

The Ptarmigan Route is less crowded and has better views, following a narrow but clearly defined path up the western flank, directly overlooking the loch, to a curving ridge leading to the summit. You can then descend via the tourist route, making a satisfying circuit.

To find the start of the Ptarmigan path, head north from Rowardennan car park 600m, past the youth hostel; cross the bridge after Ben Lomond Cottage and immediately turn right along a path through the trees. The route is then easy to follow.

---

permitting) freshly caught trout as well as the usual bacon and eggs. Walker friendly.

Real Food Café　　　　　　　CAFE £
(☑01838-400235; www.therealfoodcafe.com; Tyndrum; mains £7-10; ⊙11am-9.30pm Sun-Fri, 7.30am-9.30pm Sat, opens at 8.30am Sun-Fri Jul & Aug; 🕏🐾) 🐾 Hungry hill walkers throng the tables in this justifiably popular eatery. The menu looks familiar – with fish and chips, soups, salads and burgers – but the owners make an effort to source sustainably and locally, and the quality shines through. Hours are reduced in winter.

❶ Getting There & Away

Scottish Citylink (www.citylink.co.uk) runs several buses daily to Edinburgh, Glasgow, Oban and Skye from both villages.

Trains run to Tyndrum and Crianlarich from Fort William (£19.30, 1¾ hours, four daily Monday to Saturday, two on Sunday), Oban (£11.70, 1¼ hours, three or four daily) and Glasgow (£18.20, 1¾ hours, three to five daily).

Helensburgh

POP 14,200

With the coming of the railway in the mid-19th century, Helensburgh – named after the

50

SOUTHERN HIGHLANDS & ISLANDS ARROCHAR

wife of Sir James Colquhoun of Luss – became a popular seaside retreat for wealthy Glaswegian families. Their spacious Victorian villas now populate the hillside above the Firth of Clyde, but none can compare with splendid **Hill House** (NTS; ☑ 0844 493-2208; www.nts.org.uk; Upper Colquhoun St; adult/child £10.50/7.50; ☉ 1.30-5.30pm Apr-Oct). Built in 1902 for Glasgow publisher Walter Blackie, it is perhaps architect Charles Rennie Mackintosh's finest creation – its timeless elegance still feels chic today. Mackintosh was keen not to cast his pearls before swine: he once chided Mrs Blackie for putting the wrong-coloured flowers in a vase in the hall. You can stay here – check www.landmark trust.org.uk.

On the eastern side of town, peaceful **Braeholm** (☑ 01436-671880; www.braeholm. org.uk; 31 East Montrose St; s/d £40/60; 🅿🛜) 📶 is a sizeable guesthouse run by a naval charity and managed by a friendly family. Rooms are great value, and on-site facilities include gym, sauna and laundry. Breakfast is very tasty.

Helensburgh has frequent trains to Glasgow (£6, 50 minutes, two per hour). Hill House is near Upper Helensburgh station, but not all trains stop there.

Arrochar

POP 700

The village of Arrochar has a wonderful location, looking across the head of Loch Long to the jagged peaks of the **Cobbler** (Ben Arthur; 884m). The mountain takes its name from the shape of its north peak (the one on the right, seen from Arrochar), which looks like a cobbler hunched over his bench. The village makes a picturesque overnight stop.

If you want to climb the Cobbler, start from the roadside car park at Succoth near the head of Loch Long. A steep uphill hike through woods is followed by an easier section heading into the valley below the triple peaks. Then it's steeply uphill again to the saddle between the north and central peaks. The central peak is higher, but it's awkward to get to – scramble through the hole and along the ledge to reach the airy summit. The north peak to the right is an easy walk. Allow five to six hours for the 5-mile round trip.

The black-and-white, 19th-century **Village Inn** (☑ 01301-702279; www.villageinnarrochar.co.uk; s/d from £55/85; mains £9-15; ☉ food

10am-9pm; 🅿🛜) is a gloriously convivial pub, which boasts a beer garden with a great view of the Cobbler. There are 14 lovely renovated chambers, some with loch views and most with decent bathrooms. Meals – bar standards supplemented by more ambitious blackboard specials – are somewhat overpriced but tasty enough.

Citylink (www.citylink.co.uk) buses from Glasgow to Inveraray and Campbeltown call at Arrochar (£8.50, 1¼ hours, seven daily). There are also three or four trains a day from Glasow to Arrochar & Tarbet station (£11.40, 1¼ hours), continuing to Oban or Fort William.

THE TROSSACHS

The Trossachs region has long been a favourite weekend getaway, offering outstanding natural beauty and excellent walking and cycling routes within easy reach of the southern population centres. With thickly forested hills, romantic lochs, national-park status and an interesting selection of places to stay and eat, its popularity is sure to continue.

The Trossachs first gained popularity in the early 19th century, when curious visitors came from across Britain, drawn by the romantic language of Walter Scott's poem *Lady of the Lake*, inspired by Loch Katrine, and *Rob Roy*, about the derring-do of the region's most famous son.

In summer the Trossachs can be overburdened with coach tours, but many of these are day trippers – peaceful, long evenings gazing at the reflections in the nearest loch are still possible. If you can, it's worth timing your visit not to coincide with a weekend.

Aberfoyle & Around

POP 800

Crawling with visitors on most weekends and dominated by a huge car park, little Aberfoyle is easily overwhelmed by day trippers. Callander or other Trossachs towns appeal more as places to stay, but Aberfoyle has lots to do close at hand and has great accommodation options nearby. It's also a stop on the Rob Roy Way.

◉ Sights

There are also some good (and not too busy) walking trails in the woods south of Loch Ard, west of town.

Inchmahome Priory RUIN

(HS; www.historic-scotland.gov.uk; adult/child incl ferry £5.50/3.30; ⏲10am-5pm Apr-Sep, to 4pm Oct, last ferry to island 1hr before closing) From the **Lake of Menteith** (called lake not loch due to a mistranslation from Gaelic), 3 miles east of Aberfoyle, a ferry takes visitors to these substantial ruins. Mary, Queen of Scots, was kept safe here as a child during Henry VIII's 'Rough Wooing'. Henry attacked Stirling trying to force Mary to marry his son in order to unite the kingdoms.

The Lodge NATURE RESERVE

(David Marshall Lodge; www.forestry.gov.uk; car park £1-3; ⏲10am-4pm Nov-Mar, to 5pm Apr-Jun & Sep-Oct, to 6pm Jul & Aug) FREE Half a mile north of Aberfoyle, this nature centre has info about the many walks and cycle routes in and around the Queen Elizabeth Forest Park. There are live wildlife cameras offering a peek at osprey and barn owl nests among others. The centre is worth visiting solely for the views. Picturesque but busy waymarked trails start from here, ranging from a light 20-minute stroll to a nearby waterfall – with great interactive play options for kids – to a hilly 4-mile circuit.

The centre has a popular cafe. Also here, **Go Ape!** (☎0845 519 3023; www.goape.co.uk; adult/child £30/24; ⏲Sat & Sun Nov & Feb-Easter, Wed-Mon Easter-Oct) will bring out the monkey in you on its exhilarating adventure course of long zip lines, swings and rope bridges through the forest.

Activities

Cycling

An excellent 20-mile circular cycle route links with the boat at Loch Katrine. From Aberfoyle, join the Lochs & Glens Cycle Way on the forest trail, or take the A821 over Duke's Pass. Following the southern shore of Loch Achray, you reach the pier on Loch Katrine. The 10.30am boat (there's also a 2pm sailing in summer) can take you to Stronachlachar (one way with bike £15) on the western shore (or it's an extra 14 miles biking it along the northern shore), from where you can follow the beautiful B829 via Loch Ard back to Aberfoyle.

Sleeping & Eating

Inversnaid Bunkhouse HOSTEL £

(☎01877-386249; www.inversnaid.com; Inversnaid; tent site per person £8.50, dm £17.50-20.50, tw/d without bathroom £44/57; ⏲Apr-Sep; P 📶 🐾) Fifteen miles from Aberfoyle by road, a ferry across Loch Lomond, or an 8-mile walk north from Rowardennan on the West Highland Way, this former church is now a remote welcoming hostel in a peaceful streamside location. It's very popular with walkers and offers simple accommodation in crowded dorms, decent twins, very pleasant doubles and grassy campsites (pre-pitched tents available). A hot tub is great for aching muscles.

It offers simple meals (noon to 4pm and 6pm to 8pm), packed lunches and decent beers in the cafe; you can also self-cater evening meals. It's a 15-minute uphill trudge from the lakeshore and trail, but there are free transfers. A modern self-catering cabin is also available.

Mayfield Guest House B&B ££

(☎01877-382962; www.mayfield-aberfoyle.co.uk; Main St, Aberfoyle; s £40, d £60-65; P 📶 🐾) Nothing is too much trouble for the friendly hosts at this guest house right in the heart of Aberfoyle. It has three compact, comfortable ground-floor rooms, all painted in cheerful colours and very well kept. There's a sweet little conservatory lounge and it's bike and motorbike friendly, with a garage out back.

★**Lake of Menteith Hotel** HOTEL £££

(☎01877-385258; www.lake-hotel.com; s £110, d £130-240; P 📶 🐾) Soothingly situated on a lake (yes, it's the only non-loch in Scotland) 3 miles east of Aberfoyle, this makes a great romantic getaway. Though all rooms are excellent, with a handsome contemporary feel, it's worth the upgrade to the enormous 'lake heritage' ones with a view of the water: it really is a sensational outlook. Even if you're not staying, head down to the waterside bar-restaurant (mains £10 to £15; open noon to 2.30pm and 5.30pm to 9pm). Check the website for packages.

Duchray Castle B&B £££

(☎01877-389333; www.duchraycastle.com; Aberfoyle; d £130-185; P 📶) Splendidly set in secluded rural surrounds, all forest and stream but just three miles from Aberfoyle, this castle is a real treat, with four sumptuous rooms, a noble great hall, and a cosier lounge space with games, DVDs, CDs and books. It's good for a luxurious romantic break, but also for families – children will love the spiral stairs, castle atmosphere and acres to romp around in.

ℹ TROSSACHS TRANSPORT

In a bid to cut public transport costs, 'Demand Responsive Transport' (DRT) now covers the Trossachs area. It sounds complex, but basically it means you get a taxi to where you want to go, for the price of a bus. There are various zones. Taxis should preferably be booked 24 hours in advance; call ☑01877-330496. A cab between Callander and Aberfoyle, for example, costs £5.

Breakfast is a treat, with quality produce served in an atmospheric stone-vaulted chamber. To get here, head across the stone bridge in Aberfoyle, take the third turning on the right (past a post box), and keep going.

Forth Inn   PUB **£**
(☑01877-382372; www.forthinn.com; Main St, Aberfoyle; mains £8-12; ⊙noon-5.30pm & 6-8.30pm; P ⚟ 🖥 ❀) In the middle of the village, locals and visitors alike queue up here for good, honest pub fare; the best bar meal in Aberfoyle. It's got a top selection of Scottish craft beers on tap and drinkers spilling outside into the sunny courtyard. Single (£60) and double (£80 to £90) rooms are available, but they can be noisy at weekends.

ℹ Information

Aberfoyle Tourist Office (☑01877-382352; www.visitscottishheartlands.com; Main St, Aberfoyle; ⊙10am-5pm Apr-Oct, to 4pm Nov-Mar; 🕪) Large office with good selection of walking information.

ℹ Getting There & Away

First (www.firstgroup.com) has six daily buses (Monday to Saturday) from Stirling (£4.60, 40 minutes).

Lochs Katrine & Achray

This rugged area, 7 miles north of Aberfoyle and 10 miles west of Callander, is the heart of the Trossachs. From April to October, two **boats** (☑01877-376315; www.lochkatrine. com; Trossachs Pier; 1hr cruise adult/child £13/8; ⊙Easter-Oct) run cruises from Trossachs Pier at the eastern tip of Loch Katrine. One of these is the fabulous centenarian steamship *Sir Walter Scott;* check the website depar-

tures, as it's worth coinciding with this veteran if you can. There are various one-hour afternoon sailings, and at 10.30am (plus additional summer departures) there's a departure to Stronachlachar at the other end of the loch before returning (single/return adult £13/15.50, child £8/9.50, two hours return). From Stronachlachar (also accessible by car via a 12-mile road from Aberfoyle), you can reach the eastern shore of Loch Lomond at isolated Inversnaid. A tarmac path links Trossachs Pier with Stronachlachar, so you can take the boat out and walk/cycle back (14 miles). At Trossachs Pier, **Katrinewheelz** (☑01877-376366; www.katrinewheelz. co.uk; hire per half-/full day from £15/20; ⊙9am-5pm Apr-Oct, 11am-3pm Sat & Sun Nov, Dec, Feb & Mar) hires out good bikes and even electric buggies. Bring a picnic; the cafe is mediocre.

Two good walks start from nearby Loch Achray. The path to the rocky cone called **Ben A'an** (460m) begins at a car park just east of the Loch Katrine turn-off. It's easy to follow and the return trip is just under 4 miles (allow 2½ hours). A tougher walk is up rugged **Ben Venue** (727m) – there's a path right to the summit. Start walking from the signed car park just south of the Loch Katrine turn-off. The return trip is 7.5 miles – allow around five to six hours.

Between here and Aberfoyle, the **Three Lochs Forest Drive** is a worthwhile 7.5-mile circuit (April to October, £2) through pine forest opening up to picturesque vistas. There are plenty of walks here to stretch your legs.

Callander

POP 3100

Callander, the principal Trossachs town, has been pulling in tourists for over 150 years, and has a laid-back ambience along its main thoroughfare that quickly lulls visitors into lazy pottering. There's an excellent array of accommodation options here, and some intriguing places to eat.

◎ Sights & Activities

The **Hamilton Toy Collection** (☑01877-330004; www.thehamiltontoycollection.co.uk; 111 Main St; adult/child £3/1; ⊙10am-4.30pm Mon-Sat, noon-4.30pm Sun Apr-Oct) is a powerhouse of 20th-century juvenile memorabilia, chock-full of dolls houses, puppets and toy soldiers. It's an amazing collection and a guaranteed nostalgia trip. Phone in winter as it opens some weekends.

Impressive Bracklinn Falls are reached by track and footpath from Bracklinn Rd (30 minutes each way from the car park). Also off Bracklinn Rd, a woodland trail leads up to Callander Crags, with great views over the surroundings; a return trip from the car park is about 4 miles.

The Trossachs is a lovely area to cycle around. On a cycle route, excellent Wheels Cycling Centre (☑01877-331100; www. wheelscyclingcentre.com; bike per hr/day/week from £8/20/90; ☺10am-6pm Mar-Oct) has a wide range of hire bikes. To get there, take Bridge St off Main St, turn right onto Invertrossachs Rd and continue for a mile.

🛏 Sleeping

White Shutters
B&B £

(☑01877-330442; www.incallander.co.uk/white-shutters.htm; 6 South Church St; s/d £26/46; ☎) A cute little house just off the main street, White Shutters offers pleasing rooms with shared bathroom and a friendly welcome. The large double is particularly appealing, but it's all clean and comfortable and offers exceptional value.

Callander Hostel
HOSTEL £

(☑01877-330141; www.callanderhostel.co.uk; 6 Bridgend; dm/d £23/70; ℗☎) ✎ This hostel in a mock-Tudor building run by a youth project has well-furnished dorms and a welcoming and enthusiastic, if not wholly professional, attitude.

Arden House
B&B ££

(☑01877-339405; www.ardenhouse.org.uk; Bracklinn Rd; s from £70, d £85-100; ☺Mar-Oct; ℗☎) This elegant home has a fabulous hillside location with verdant garden and lovely vistas; close to the centre but far from the crowds. The commodious rooms are impeccable, with lots of natural light. They include large upstairs doubles with great views. Welcoming owners, noble architectural features – super bay windows – and a self-catering studio make this a top option.

Abbotsford Lodge
HOTEL ££

(☑01877-330066; www.abbotsfordlodge.com; Stirling Rd; s/d £65/85; ☺Mar-Nov; ℗☎) This friendly Victorian house offers something different to the norm, with tartan and florals consigned to the bonfire, replaced by stylish, comfortable contemporary design

that enhances the building's original features. There are fabulous, spacious superiors with modish grey fabrics (from £125) as well as cheaper top-floor rooms – shared bathroom – with lovably offbeat under-roof shapes. Room-only rates are available.

Callander Meadows
B&B ££

(☑01877-330181; www.callandermeadows.co.uk; 24 Main St; s £55, d £75-85; ℗☎☀) Upstairs at this recommended restaurant are some very appealing rooms, elegantly kitted out with solid furniture and good modern shower rooms. One, which can serve as a family room, has a four-poster bed. The owners are very welcoming.

Roslin Cottage
B&B ££

(☑01877-339787; www.roslincottage.co.uk; Stirling Rd; s £40, d £55-65; ℗☎) A characterful cottage that's a haven of good hospitality holds three snug en suite rooms that make an enticing Trossachs base. They all have charm: we love the Kirtle room with the original 17th-century wall exposed. Other delights include a lovely big back garden, a log fire in the lounge and sociable chef-cooked breakfasts. It's on the right as you enter Callander from the east, before the petrol station.

Highland Guest House
B&B ££

(☑01877-330269; www.thehighlandguesthouse. co.uk; 8 South Church St; s £39, d £65-70; ☎) The cheery welcome from the musical owner here makes up for a few minor quirks in the rooms. It offers solid comfort with a good central location, decent wi-fi and maybe a blast on the bagpipes at breakfast time.

★ Roman Camp Hotel
HOTEL £££

(☑01877-330003; www.romancamphotel.co.uk; Main St; s/d/superior £110/160/210; ℗☎☀) Callander's best hotel is centrally located but feels rural, set by the river in beautiful grounds. Endearing features include a lounge with blazing fire and a library with a tiny secret chapel. It's an old-fashioned warren of a place with four grades of room; standards are certainly luxurious, but superiors are even more appealing, with period furniture, excellent bathrooms, armchairs and fireplace.

The upmarket restaurant is open to the public. Reassuringly, the name refers not to toga parties but to a ruin in the adjacent fields.

Scottish Castles

JONATHAN SMITH / GETTY IMAGES ©

Scotland is home to more than one thousand castles, ranging from meagre 12th-century ruins to magnificent Victorian mansions. They all began with one purpose: to serve as fortified homes for the landowning aristocracy. But as society became more settled and peaceful, defensive features gave way to ostentatious displays of wealth and status.

Curtain Wall Castles

Norman castles of the 12th century were mainly of the 'motte-and-bailey' type, consisting of earthwork mounds and timber palisades. The first wave of stonebuilt castles emerged in the 13th century, characterised by massive curtain walls up to 3m thick and 30m tall to withstand sieges, well seen at Dunstaffnage Castle.

Tower Houses

The appearance of the tower house in the 14th century marks the beginning of the development of the castle as a residence. Clan feuds, cattle raiders and wars between Scotland and England meant that local lords built fortified stone towers in which to live.

Artillery Castles

The arrival of gunpowder and cannon in the 15th century transformed castle design, with features such as gun loops, round towers, bulwarks and bastions making an appearance.

Status Symbols

The Scottish Baronial style of castle architecture, characterised by a profusion of pointy turrets, crenellations and stepped gables, had its origins in 16th- and 17th-century castles such as Craigievar and Castle Fraser, and reached its apotheosis in the royal residences of Glamis and Balmoral.

Balmoral Castle (p134) **2.** Dunstaffnage Castle (p97)
Dunvegan Castle (p204)

3

GAELIC & NORSE PLACE NAMES

Throughout the Highlands and islands of Scotland Gaelic place names are often inter-mixed with Old Norse names. The spelling is now Anglicised, but the meaning is still clear.

Gaelic Place Names

ach, auch – from *achadh* (field)

ard – from *ard* or *aird* (height, hill)

avon – from *abhainn* (river or stream)

bal – from *baile* (village or homestead)

ban – from *ban* (white, fair)

beg – from *beag* (small)

ben – from *beinn* (mountain)

buie – from *buidhe* (yellow)

dal – from *dail* (field or dale)

dow, dhu – from *dubh* (black)

drum – from *druim* (ridge or back)

dun – from *dun* or *duin* (fort or castle)

glen – from *gleann* (narrow valley)

gorm – from *gorm* (blue)

gower, gour – from *gabhar* (goat), eg Ardgour (height of the goats)

inch, insh – from *inis* (island, water-meadow or resting place for cattle)

inver – from *inbhir* (rivermouth or meeting of two rivers)

kil – from *cille* (church), eg Kilmartin (Church of St Martin)

kin, ken – from *ceann* (head), eg Kinlochleven (head of Loch Leven)

kyle, kyles – from *caol* or *caolas* (narrow sea channel)

more, vore – from *mor* or *mhor* (big), eg Ardmore (big height), Skerryvore (big reef)

strath – from *srath* (broad valley)

tarbert, tarbet – from *tairbeart* (portage), meaning a narrow neck of land between two bodies of water, across which a boat can be dragged

tay, ty – from *tigh* (house), eg Tyndrum (house on the ridge)

tober – from *tobar* (well), eg Tobermory (Mary's well)

tom – small hill

Norse Place Names

a, ay, ey – from *ey* (island)

bister, buster, bster – from *bolstaor* (dwelling place, homestead)

geo – from *gja* (chasm)

holm – from *holmr* (small island)

kirk – from *kirkja* (church)

pol, poll, bol – from *bol* (farm)

quoy – from *kvi* (sheep fold, cattle enclosure)

sker, skier, skerry – from *sker* (rocky reef)

ster, sett – from *setr* (house)

vig, vaig, wick – from *vik* (bay, creek)

voe, way – from *vagr* (bay, creek)

✕ Eating & Drinking

★**Callander Meadows**   SCOTTISH ££
(✍ 01877-330181; www.callandermeadows.co.uk;
24 Main St; lunch £10, mains £12-16; ⊙ 9am-9pm
Thu-Sun; 🖥) Informal but smart, this well-
loved restaurant in the centre of Callander
occupies the two front rooms of a house on
the main street. There's a contemporary flair
for presentation and unusual flavour combinations, but a solidly British base under-
pins the cuisine. There's a great beer/coffee
garden out the back, where you can also eat.
Opens daily from June to September.

Mhor Fish   SEAFOOD ££
(✍ 01877-330213; www.mhor.net; 75 Main St;
mains £7-16; ⊙ noon-9pm Tue-Sun) 🌿 This simply decorated spot, with formica tables and
a hodgepodge of chairs, sources brilliant
sustainable seafood. Browse the fresh catch
then eat it pan-seared in the dining area
accompanied by a decent wine selection, or
fried and wrapped in paper with chips to
take away. It's all great – calamari and oysters are wonderfully toothsome starters.

Venachar Lochside   SEAFOOD ££
(Harbour Cafe; ✍ 01877-330011; www.venachar-
lochside.co.uk; Loch Venachar; mains £9-15;
⊙ lunch noon-3pm Jan-Nov, plus dinner 5.30-
8.30pm Fri & Sat Jun-Sep; 🖥) On lovely Loch
Venachar, 4.5 miles west of Callander, this
cafe-restaurant has a stunning waterside
setting and does a nice line in delicious fresh
seafood. It opens from 10am to 5pm daily for
coffees, teas and baked goods. You can also
hire boats here.

Poppies   SCOTTISH ££
(✍ 01877-330329; www.poppieshotel.com; Leny
Rd; mains £10-19; ⊙ noon-2pm & 6-9pm, to 3pm
Sun; 🖥) This is the restaurant of a small
main-road hotel, and offers high-class cuisine based on rigorously sourced quality
Scottish meat and fish in an elegant dining
space. It's a friendly place with an atmosphere that is more quiet clinks of cutlery
than belches and belly laughs. There's a
good-value early-dining special.

Lade Inn   PUB
(www.theladeinn.com; Kilmahog; ⊙ noon-11pm
Mon-Thu, noon-1am Fri & Sat, 12.30-10.30pm
Sun; 🖥🍴) Callander's best pub isn't in
Callander – it's a mile west of town. Staff
pull a good pint (with their own real ales),
and next door is a shop with a dazzling selection of Scottish beers. There's low-key live

music here at weekends. The food (noon to
9pm, from 12.30pm Sunday; mains £9 to
£12) at last visit was overpriced and mediocre.

❶ Information

Callander Visitor Centre (✍ 01877-330342;
www.lochlomond-trossachs.org; 52 Main St;
⊙ 9.30am-5pm Apr-Oct, to 4pm Nov-Mar; 🖥)
Very helpful for information on the region and
national park.

❶ Getting There & Away

First (✍ 0871 200 2233; www.firstgroup.
com) operates buses from Stirling (£5.20, 45
minutes, hourly Monday to Saturday, every two
hours Sunday), while **Kingshouse** (✍ 01877-
384768; www.kingshousetravel.com) buses run
from Killin (£5.70, 45 minutes, five to six Monday
to Saturday). For Aberfoyle, use DRT (see boxed
text, p52) or get off a Stirling-bound bus at
Blair Drummond safari park and cross the road.
There are also **Citylink** (www.citylink.co.uk)
buses via Callander from Edinburgh (£16.20,
1¾ hours, two daily mid-May to mid-October)
to Oban (£21.30, 2¼ hours) or Fort William
(£23.20, 2½ hours).

Balquhidder & Around

North of Callander, you'll skirt past the
shores of gorgeous Loch Lubnaig. Not as
famous as some of its cousins, it's still well
worth a stop for its sublime views of forested
hills. A campsite (£5 per person) with nine
bookable lochside pitches plus motorhome
bays is 4½ miles north of Callander. In the
small village of Balquhidder (ball-whidder),
9 miles north of Callander off the A84,
there's a churchyard with **Rob Roy's grave**.
It's an appropriately beautiful spot in a
deep, winding glen in big-sky country. In the
church is the 8th-century **St Angus' stone**,
probably a marker to the original tomb of St
Angus, an 8th-century monk who built the
first church here.

🛏 Sleeping

★**Monachyle Mhor**   HOTEL £££
(✍ 01877-384622; www.mhor.net; d £195-265;
⊙ Feb-Dec; 🅿🖥🐾) 🌿 Monachyle Mhor
is a luxury hideaway with a fantastically
peaceful location overlooking two lochs. It's
a great fusion of country Scotland and contemporary attitudes to design and food. The
rooms are superb and feature quirkily original decor, particularly the fabulous 'feature

rooms'; you might get your own steam room or a wonderful double bathtub. The restaurant serves soup-and-sandwich deals, delicious lunches and five-course dinners (£50), which are high in quality, sustainably sourced and deliciously innovative. Enchantment lies in its successful combination of top-class hospitality with a relaxed rural atmosphere; dogs and kids happily romp on the lawns, and no one looks askance if you come in flushed and muddy after a day's fishing or walking. It's 4 miles from Balquhidder.

Mhor 84
HOTEL ££

(☎ 01877-384646; www.mhor.net; A84, Kingshouse; r without breakfast £60-70; P ⑤) At the A84 junction, this 18th-century inn has been given a modern-retro revamp and is now a great place with bags of facilities, simple, good-value rooms and a delicious menu of hearty, nourishing meals with the Mhor philosophy of local and sustainable. A great pit stop for drivers, walkers and cyclists.

ⓘ Getting There & Away

Local buses between Callander and Killin stop at the main road turn-off to Balquhidder, as do daily Citylink (www.citylink.co.uk) buses between Edinburgh and Oban/Fort William.

Killin

POP 800

A fine base for the Trossachs or Perthshire, this lovely village sits at the western end of Loch Tay and has a spread-out, relaxed feel, particularly around the scenic Falls of Dochart, which tumble through the centre. On a sunny day people sprawl over the rocks by the bridge, pint or picnic in hand. Killin offers fine walking around the town, and mighty mountains and glens close at hand.

🏃 Activities

Five miles northeast of Killin, Ben Lawers (1214m) rises above Loch Tay. Walking routes abound; one rewarding circular walk heads up into the Acharn forest south of town, emerging above the treeline to great views of Loch Tay and Ben Lawers. Killin Outdoor Centre offers walking advice.

Glen Lochay runs westwards from Killin into the hills of Mamlorn. You can take a mountain bike up the glen; the scenery is

impressive and the hills aren't too difficult. It's possible, on a nice summer day, to climb over the top of Ben Challum (1025m) and descend to Crianlarich, but it's hard work. A potholed road also connects Glen Lochay with Glen Lyon.

Killin is on the Lochs & Glens Cycle Way from Glasgow to Inverness. Hire bikes from helpful Killin Outdoor Centre (☎ 01567-820652; www.killinoutdoor.co.uk; Main St; bike per 24hr £25, kayak/canoe per 2hr £25/30; ⊙ 8.45am-5.45pm), which also has canoes and kayaks or, in winter, crampons and snowshoes.

🛏 Sleeping & Eating

High Creagan
CAMPGROUND £

(☎ 01567-820449; www.highcreagan.co.uk; Aberfeldy Rd; per person tent/caravan site £5/8; ⊙ Apr-Oct; P ⑧) This place has a well-kept, sheltered campsite with plenty of grass set high on the slopes overlooking sparkling Loch Tay, 3 miles east of Killin. Kids under five aren't allowed in the tent area (for insurance reasons) as there's a stream running through it.

Old Smiddy
B&B ££

(Riverview; ☎ 01567-820619; www.theoldsmiddy-killin.co.uk; Main St; s £38, d £65-70; ⊙ Apr-Oct; P ⑤) Three appealing rooms above a decent restaurant here are within hearing distance of the falls. All rooms have modern styling, are en suite and one can fit a family of four. The lively, friendly owner makes guests very welcome and breakfast is a pleasure.

Falls of Dochart Inn
PUB ££

(☎ 01567-820270; www.falls-of-dochart-inn.co.uk; mains £11-14; ⊙ noon-3pm & 6-9pm Mon-Thu, to 9.30pm Fri, noon-9.30pm Sat, noon-8.30pm Sun; P ⑤) In a prime position overlooking the falls, this is a terrific pub, a snug, atmospheric space with a roaring fire, real ales, personable service and decent pub grub, with some Asian flavours adding a dimension to tasty staples and daily specials. The rooms (single/double from £60/80) are handsome but a few glitches like poor heating let some of them down. The outside tables are great spots on a sunny day.

ⓘ Information

Old Mill (☎ 07802-929796; Pier Rd; ⊙ 10am-4pm Mar-Oct; ⑤) This picturesque old mill building by the falls houses a thrift shop with volunteers who also give out tourist information.

❶ Getting There & Away

Two daily **Citylink** (www.citylink.co.uk) buses between Edinburgh (£20.70, 2¼ hours) and Crianlarich/Oban/Fort William stop here; two buses from Dundee (£15.30, two hours) to Oban also pass through. Kingshouse (p57) runs five to six buses Monday to Saturday to Callander (£5.70, 45 minutes), where you can change for Stirling. A summer **bus** (www.breadalbane. org; ☉ Tue, Wed & Sun Jun–mid-Oct, plus Sat Jul-Aug) does a hop-on/hop-off Breadalbane circuit, running to Ben Lawers, Kenmore, Aberfeldy, Crieff and back.

SOUTH ARGYLL

Cowal

The remote and picturesque Cowal peninsula is cut off from the rest of the country by the lengthy fjords of Loch Long and Loch Fyne. It comprises rugged hills and narrow lochs, with only a few small villages and the old-fashioned holiday resort of Dunoon.

From Arrochar, the A83 to Inveraray loops around the head of Loch Long and climbs into spectacular Glen Croe. The pass at the head of the glen is called the Rest and Be Thankful. As you descend Glen Kinglas on the far side, the A815 forks to the left just before Cairndow; this is the main overland route into Cowal. From Glasgow, the most direct route is by ferry from Gourock to Dunoon.

Dunoon & Around

Like Rothesay on the Isle of Bute, Dunoon is a Victorian seaside resort that owes its existence to the steamers that once carried thousands of Glaswegians on pleasure trips 'doon the watter' in the 19th and 20th centuries. Fortunes declined when cheap foreign holidays stole the market and Dunoon is still a bit down in the dumps.

❂ Sights & Activities

The town's main attraction is still, as it was in the 1950s, strolling along the promenade, licking an ice-cream cone and watching the yachts at play in the Firth of Clyde.

Benmore Botanic Garden   GARDENS
(www.rbge.org.uk; adult/child £6/free; ☉ 10am-6pm Apr-Sep, to 5pm Mar & Oct) This garden, 7 miles north of Dunoon, has Scotland's finest collection of flowering trees and shrubs, including impressive displays of rhododendrons and azaleas, and is entered along a spectacular avenue of giant redwoods. A highlight is the Victorian fernery, nestled in an unlikely fold in the crags. The year-round cafe here appeals for lunch or coffee. Buses run between Dunoon and the gardens.

✯ Festivals & Events

Cowal Highland Gathering   HIGHLAND GAMES
(www.cowalgathering.com) Held in Dunoon in late August. The finale features over a thousand bagpipers saluting the chieftain.

⌂ Sleeping & Eating

There are numerous guesthouses arrayed along the waterfront.

Dhailling Lodge   B&B **££**
(☑ 01369-701253; www.dhaillinglodge.com; 155 Alexandra Pde; s/d £45/85; P ❅ ❀) You can experience some of Dunoon's former elegance at this large Victorian villa with stirring views over the bay, pleasantly removed from the

---

ROB ROY
....

Nicknamed Red ('*ruadh*' in Gaelic, anglicised to 'roy') for his ginger locks, Robert MacGregor (1671–1734) was the wild leader of the wildest of Scotland's clans, outlawed by powerful neighbours, hence their sobriquet, Children of the Mist. Incognito, Rob became a prosperous livestock trader, before a dodgy deal led to a warrant for his arrest.

A legendary swordsman, the fugitive from justice then became notorious for daring raids into the Lowlands to carry off cattle and sheep. Forever hiding from potential captors, he was twice imprisoned, but escaped dramatically on both occasions. He finally turned himself in and received his liberty and a pardon from the king. He lies buried – perhaps – in the churchyard at Balquhidder; his uncompromising later epitaph reads 'MacGregor despite them'. His life has been glorified over the years due to Walter Scott's novel and the 1995 film. Many Scots see his life as a symbol of the struggle of the common folk against the inequitable ownership of vast tracts of the country by landed aristocrats.

shabby town centre but within a 10-minute walk. The owners are the essence of Scottish hospitality, and can provide excellent evening meals.

Chatters SCOTTISH ££
(☎01369-706402; www.chattersdunoon.co.uk; 58 John St; mains lunch £5-9, dinner £15-22; ⏲noon-3pm & 6-9.30pm Wed-Sat) This pretty little cottage restaurant has tartan sofas in the sitting room and a few tables in the tiny garden. It serves a mix of lunchtime snacks and more elaborate dinner dishes, and is famous for its open sandwiches and tempting home-made puddings. Booking recommended.

Information

The **tourist office** (☎01369-703785; www.visitcowal.co.uk; 7 Alexandra Pde; ⏲10am-4pm Nov-Mar, 10am-5pm Apr–mid-Jun, Sep & Oct, 9am-5pm mid-Jun–Aug) is on the waterfront.

Getting There & Away

Dunoon is served by two competing ferry services from Gourock – Argyll Ferries is better if you are travelling on foot and want to arrive in the town centre.

McGill's (p45) runs buses from Glasgow to Dunoon (£9.50, 1¾ hours, six to nine daily). Buses around the Cowal Peninsula, to Inveraray (£3.90) and to Bute (£3.50) are operated by **West Coast Motors** (www.westcoastmotors.co.uk).

Tighnabruaich

POP 200

Sleepy little seaside Tighnabruaich (tinna-*broo*-ach) is one of the most attractive villages on the Firth of Clyde.

The village is home to **Royal an Lochan Hotel** (☎01700-811239; www.theroyalanlochan.co.uk; r £100-150; ⏲food 12.30-2.30pm & 6.30-8.30pm; P 📶 🐾), a local institution with a range of rooms that, typically for these venerable buildings, vary markedly in size. Sea views – most rooms have them – cost extra but are worth it. The restaurant serves fine seafoody fare and the cosy snug bar is a temple to the successes of the local shinty side, one of Scotland's finest.

A mile south, excellent **Kames Hotel** (☎01700-811489; www.kames-hotel.com; s £50, d £75-120; ⏲food noon-2.30pm & 6-8.30pm; 📶) has a variety of comfortable rooms, including cute low-bedded ones under the sloping roof on the top floor. The bar downstairs has great atmosphere and serves good-value bar meals (mains £7 to £15) with daily seafood specials.

For hearty homemade grub, go for local mussels and chips at central **Burnside Bistro** (www.burnsidebistro.co.uk; mains £7-13; ⏲10am-5pm Sun-Thu, to 9pm Fri & Sat); the waterside tables are great for a sunny afternoon.

Isle of Bute

POP 6500

Bute lies pinched between the thumb and forefinger of the Cowal peninsula, separated from the mainland by a narrow, scenic strait. The Highland Boundary Fault cuts through the middle of the island so that, geologically speaking, the northern half is in the Highlands and the southern half is in the central Lowlands.

The **Isle of Bute Discovery Centre** (☎01700-502151; www.visitscottishheartlands.com; Victoria St, Rothesay; ⏲9.30am-5.30pm Jul & Aug, 10am-5pm Apr-Jun & Sep, 10am-4pm Mon-Sat, 11am-3pm Sun Oct-Mar) is in Rothesay's restored Winter Gardens.

The five-day **Isle of Bute Jazz Festival** (www.butejazz.com) is held over the first weekend of May.

Rothesay

From the mid-19th century until the 1960s, Rothesay was one of Scotland's most popular holiday resorts, bustling with day trippers disembarking from numerous steamers crowded around the pier. Its hotels were filled with elderly holidaymakers and convalescents taking advantage of the famously mild climate.

Cheap foreign holidays saw Rothesay's fortunes decline, but a nostalgia-fuelled resurgence of interest has seen many Victorian buildings restored. The grassy, flowery waterfront and row of noble villas is a lovely place to be once again.

Sights

Victorian Toilets HISTORIC BUILDING
(Rothesay Pier; adult/child 30p/free; ⏲9am-4.45pm daily Oct-Apr, 8am-5.45pm Tue-Thu, 8am-7.45pm Fri-Mon May-Sep) Dating from 1899, these are a monument to lavatorial luxury – a disinfectant-scented temple of green and black marbled stoneware, glistening white enamel, glass-sided cisterns and gleaming copper pipes. The attendant will escort

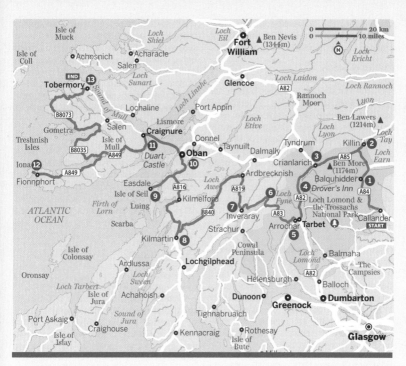

Driving Tour
The Trossachs to Mull

START CALLANDER
FINISH TOBERMORY
DISTANCE 240 MILES
DURATION 2-4 DAYS

Having explored the southern part of the Trossachs, head north out of Callander on the A84, following pretty Loch Lubnaig before optional detours of a few miles to see Rob Roy's grave at ❶ **Balquhidder** and the Falls of Dochart at pretty ❷ **Killin**. Continue on the A85 to ❸ **Crianlarich**, surrounded by Highland majesty, then turn left on the A82 to follow the western shore of Loch Lomond. Stop for a look and/or pint at the quirky ❹ **Drover's Inn** (p46), then deviate right at Tarbet onto the A83 – shortly thereafter, ❺ **Arrochar** makes a scenic lunch stop.

Head through scenic Glen Croe, over the pass and into Glen Kinglas, then follow the shore of ❻ **Loch Fyne** – stops at the brewery and/or oyster bar obligatory! – to picturesque ❼ **Inveraray**. Go right through

the arch here on the A819, then left onto the B840, a lonely road following stiletto-like Loch Awe. You'll eventually reach ❽ **Kilmartin**, with a great museum and evocative pre-historic sights. Follow the A816 north – you may want to deviate to see the ❾ **Isle of Seil** en-route: from here, great boat trips can take you out to the Corryvreckan whirlpool. Then on to ❿ **Oban** where good accommodation options, a handsome harbour and delicious seafood awaits you.

Catch a ferry from Oban to Mull and follow the A849 southwest via ⓫ **Duart Castle** (p88) to the island's tip at Fionnphort, where you cross to the emerald jewel of ⓬ **Iona** and can take a boat trip to the spectacular rock formations of Staffa. Retrace your steps, then follow Mull's winding west coast on the B8035 and B8073 via spectacular coastline and the beach at Calgary to arrive at the colourful shorefront houses of the main town, ⓭ **Tobermory**.

women into the hallowed confines of the gents for a look around when unoccupied. You can shower here too.

Rothesay Castle   CASTLE
(HS; www.historic-scotland.gov.uk; King St; adult/child £4.50/2.70; ⊙9.30am-5.30pm Apr-Sep, to 4.30pm Sat-Wed Oct-Mar) Splendid ruined 13th-century Rothesay Castle, with seagulls and jackdaws nesting in the walls, was once a favourite residence of the Stuart kings. It is unique in Scotland in having a circular plan, with four stocky round towers. The landscaped moat, with manicured turf, flower gardens and lazily cruising ducks, makes a picturesque setting.

🛌 Sleeping

Bute Backpackers Hotel   HOSTEL £
(☎01700-501876; www.butebackpackers.co.uk; 36 Argyle St; r per person £20; P🅿🛜) An appealing budget option on Rothesay's main thoroughfare, this large, well-equipped place offers private rooms of various sizes at a bargain price. Some are en suite, but shared bathrooms are modern and spotless, with power showers. The kitchen is huge, and there's a barbecue too.

Roseland Holiday Park   CAMPSITE, BUNGALOW £
(☎01700-501840; www.roselandlodgepark.co.uk; Roslin Rd; tent sites for two £10, pods s/d £25/30; ⊙Mar-Oct; P🅿🛜🐕) A steep climb up the eccentric hairpins of Serpentine Rd, this campsite has a small but pleasant grassy area for tents amid the static caravans, and a handful of pitches for campervans. Adjacent, the holiday park section (open year-round) has bungalows, and cute little pods for glamping that sleep up to four.

Glendale Guest House   B&B ££
(☎01700-502329; www.glendalebute.com; 20 Battery Pl; s £40, d £64-90, f £120; P🅿🛜) This noble Victorian waterfront villa, complete with turret, offers very commodious rooms with plush furniture and good family options. Front-facing bedrooms have superb sea views from large windows, as does the lavishly elegant lounge and the breakfast room, where you'll find homemade smoked haddock fish cakes on the menu among other interesting options. Genial hosts make for a pleasurable stay.

Boat House   B&B ££
(☎01700-502696; www.theboathouse-bute. co.uk; 15 Battery Pl; s/d from £38/65; 🛜) The Boat House brings a touch of class to

Rothesay's guesthouse scene, with quality fabrics and furnishings and an eye for design that makes it feel a bit like a boutique hotel, without the expensive price tag. Other features include a garden, sea views, a central location and a ground-floor room kitted out for wheelchair users. The owners are helpful, with a great attitude to hospitality.

Moorings   B&B ££
(☎01700-502277; www.themoorings-bute.co.uk; 7 Mountstuart Rd; s/d/f £35/70/85; P🅿🛜🐕) A delightful sandstone lodge with a great outlook over the water from huge windows: request a sea view when booking. All rooms are spacious, with a seating area; there's also an outdoor play area for kids and a high chair in the breakfast room.

🍴 Eating

⭐**Musicker**   CAFE £
(www.musicker.co.uk; 11 High St; mains £3-7; ⊙10am-5pm Mon-Sat; 🍴) This cool little cafe serves Bute's best coffee, alongside a range of home baking and sandwiches with imaginative fillings. It also sells CDs, books and guitars and sports an old-fashioned jukebox.

Harry Haw's   BISTRO ££
(☎01700-505857; www.harryhaws.com; 23 High St; mains £8-12; ⊙11am-9pm; 🛜🍴) Great scenes at this welcoming modern bistro, where clement prices and a brilliant range of deli-style fare plus burgers, local roast meat and tasty pastas make it a standout. Staff are very friendly and so cheerful you wonder if there's something in the water.

Brechin's on Bridgend Street   BRASSERIE ££
(☎01700-502922; www.rothesaymusicshop. com; 2 Bridgend St; light meals £6-8; ⊙10.30am-2.30pm Tue-Sat, plus 7-9.30pm Fri & Sat; 🛜) A friendly neighbourhood eatery and music shop owned by jazz fan Tim, Brechin's serves unpretentious but delicious dinners (£35 for two people including a bottle of wine) at weekends, and light lunchtime fare like jacket potatoes and sandwiches. Hard to miss with its bright yellow-and-blue livery.

ℹ Information

The Isle of Bute's information centre (p60) is in the centre of Rothesay, in the Winter Gardens building, once an entertainment venue.

Around Rothesay

★ Mount Stuart HISTORIC BUILDING

(☑ 01700-503877; www.mountstuart.com; adult/
child £11.50/6.75; ☺ noon-4pm Apr-Oct, grounds
10am-6pm) The family seat of the Stuart Earls
of Bute is one of Britain's more magnificent
19th-century stately homes, the first to have
a telephone, underfloor heating and heated
pool. Its eclectic interior, with a magnificent
central hall and chapel in Italian marble, is
heavily influenced by the third Marquess's
interests in Greek mythology and astrology.
The drawing room has paintings by Titian
and Tintoretto among other masters.

Buy tickets at the visitor centre (last sale
at 3pm), from where it's a 15-minute stroll
through lovely grounds to the house. A shuttle bus runs the route. Private tours (£50) offer glimpses of the pool and more bedrooms.

Mount Stuart is 5 miles south of Rothesay; bus 490 runs hourly. Discounted
ferry-plus-entrance tickets are available
from Calmac.

Around Bute

In the southern part of the island you'll
find the haunting 12th-century ruin of St
Blane's Chapel and a sandy beach at Kilchattan Bay. There are more good beaches: Scalpsie Bay has a fantastic outlook
to Arran, Ettrick Bay is bigger, and has a
tearoom (ugly outside but great chat and
snacks inside).

Cycling is excellent: you can hire a bike
from the Bike Shed (☑ 01700-505515; david.
thebikeshed@btinternet.com; 23-25 East Princes
St; ☺ 9.30am-5.30pm, closed Sun Oct-Mar) for
£6/10 per half-/full day.

❶ Getting There & Away

BOAT

CalMac (www.calmac.co.uk) car ferries serve
Bute from Wemyss Bay in Ayrshire and Colintraive in Cowal.

Colintraive to Rhubodach Passenger/car
£1.60/9.90, five minutes, every 15 to 20
minutes

Wemyss Bay to Rothesay Passenger/car
£5.05/19.85, 35 minutes, hourly

BUS

West Coast Motors (p60) buses run four
or five times a week from Rothesay to Dunoon
(£3.50, 1½ hours) via the ferry and Tighnabruaich. On Monday to Friday a bus goes from
Rothesay to Portavadie (via the Rhubodach–
Colintraive ferry), where there's another ferry to
Tarbert in Kintyre.

Inveraray

POP 600

There's no fifty shades of grey around here:
this historic planned village is all black and
white – even logos of high-street shops con-
form. Spectacularly set on the shores of Loch
Fyne, Inveraray was built by the Duke of Argyll in Georgian style when he revamped his
nearby castle in the 18th century.

◉ Sights

Inveraray Castle CASTLE
(☑ 01499-302203; www.inveraray-castle.com;
adult/child £10/7, parking £2; ☺ 10am-5.45pm Apr-
Oct) This visually stunning castle has been
the seat of the Dukes of Argyll – chiefs of
Clan Campbell – since the 15th century. The
18th-century building, with its fairy tale turrets and fake battlements, houses an impressive armoury hall, its walls patterned with
more than 1000 pole-arms, dirks, muskets
and Lochaber axes. The castle is 500m north
of town, entered from the A819 Dalmally
road.

Inveraray Jail MUSEUM
(☑ 01499-302381; www.inverarayjail.co.uk; Church
Sq; adult/child £9.50/5.25; ☺ 9.30am-6pm Apr-
Oct, 10am-5pm Nov-Mar; ⊕) At this entertaining interactive tourist attraction you can
sit in on a trial, try out a cell and discover
the harsh tortures that were meted out to
unfortunate prisoners. The attention to
detail – including a life-sized model of an
inmate squatting on a 19th-century toilet –
more than makes up for the sometimes tedi-
ous commentary.

🛏 Sleeping & Eating

Claonairigh House B&B £
(☑ 01499-302160; www.inveraraybandb.co.uk;
Bridge of Douglas; s £35-40, d £50-55; P @ ☎)
This attractive 18th-century house, built for
the Duke of Argyll in 1745, is set in 3 hectares
of grounds on the bank of a river complete
with waterfall and salmon-fishing. There
are three homely en suite rooms, one with
a four-poster bed, others compact and cute
with exposed stone and sloping ceiling. It's a
cheerful country home with a resident menagerie of dogs, ducks and chickens, 4 miles
south of town on the A83.

DON'T MISS

FYNE FOOD AND DRINK

Eight miles north of Inveraray, at the head of Loch Fyne, it pays to stop by two great local establishments.

Fyne Ales (☑01499-600120; www.fyneales.com; Achadunan, Cairndow; tours £5; ☺10am-6pm) These friendly folk do a great range of craft beers and have recently upgraded to a shiny new brewery. There's a bar-cafe here where you can taste them all: the light, citrussy Jarl is a standout. Tours run at least twice daily – call for times. A range of walks tackle the pretty glen from a car park nearby.

Loch Fyne Oyster Bar (☑01499-600236; www.lochfyne.com; Clachan, Cairndow; mains £11-22; ☺9am-7pm or 8pm; ☎) The success of this cooperative is such that it now lends its name to dozens of restaurants throughout the UK. But the original's still the best, with salty oysters straight out of the lake, and fabulous salmon dishes. The atmosphere and decor is simple, friendly, and unpretentious; there's also a shop and deli.

Inveraray Hostel   HOSTEL **£**
(☑01499-302454; www.inverarayhostel.co.uk; Dalmally Rd; dm £17-18; ☺Apr-Oct; P☎) To get to this hostel, housed in a comfortable, modern bungalow, go through the right hand one of the two arched entrances on the seafront. Metal bunk beds – rooms sleep only two or four – are comfortable, and there's a wee lounge and kitchen with plenty of stoves.

George Hotel   HOTEL **££**
(☑01499-302111; www.thegeorgehotel.co.uk; Main St E; d £80-100; P☎❀) The George boasts a magnificent choice of opulent, individual rooms complete with four-poster beds, period furniture, Victorian roll-top baths and private jacuzzis (superior rooms cost £145 to £170 per double). Some are in an annexe across the way. The cosy wood-panelled bar, with rough stone walls, flagstone floor and peat fires, is a delightful place for all-day bar meals (mains £9 to £16; noon to 9pm) and has a beer garden.

ℹ Information

Inveraray Tourist Office (☑01499-302063; Front St; ☺9am-5.30pm Jun-Aug, 10am-5pm Apr, May, Sep & Oct, 10am-4pm Nov-Mar; ☎) On the seafront.

ℹ Getting There & Away

Scottish Citylink (www.citylink.co.uk) buses run from Glasgow to Inveraray (£11.90, 1¾ hours, seven daily). Five continue to Campbeltown (£13, 2½ hours); the others to Oban (£9.90, 1¼ hours, two daily). There are also buses to Dunoon (£3.90, 1¼ hours, three daily Monday to Saturday)

Crinan Canal

Completed in 1801, picturesque Crinan Canal runs for 9 miles from Ardrishaig to Crinan allowing seagoing vessels – mostly yachts, these days – to take a short cut from the Firth of Clyde and Loch Fyne to the west coast of Scotland, avoiding the long passage around the Mull of Kintyre. You can easily walk or cycle the canal towpath in an afternoon.

The Crinan end is overlooked by romantic **Crinan Hotel** (☑01546-830261; www.crinan-hotel.com; Crinan; s/d from £110/180; P☎❀), which boasts one of the west coast's most spectacular views. All the bright, light rooms enjoy wonderful perspectives, and the somewhat faded olde-worlde atmosphere is beguiling, with paintings throughout and a top-floor gallery. You're paying for the ambience and view here: don't expect five-star luxury. The hotel offers various eating options: **Westward** (set dinner £35; ☺7-8.30pm) does posh set dinners, the cosy **Seafood Bar** (mains £11-20; ☺noon-2.30pm & 6-8.30pm; ☎) does great fresh food, including excellent local mussels with white wine, thyme and garlic, and the **coffee shop** (snacks £3-7; ☺9am-6pm Apr-Oct) below the hotel has great home baking.

If you want to walk along the canal and take the bus back, buses 425/426 from Lochgilphead run along it Monday to Saturday.

Kilmartin Glen

This magical glen is the focus of one of the biggest concentrations of prehistoric sites in Scotland. Burial cairns, standing stones, stone circles, hill forts and cup-and-ring-marked rocks litter the countryside. Within a 6-mile radius of Kilmartin village there are 25 sites with standing stones and over 100 rock carvings.

In the 6th century, Irish settlers arrived in this part of Argyll and founded the kingdom of Dál Riata (Dalriada), which eventually united with the Picts in 843 to create the first Scottish kingdom. Their capital was the hill fort of Dunadd, on the plain to the south of Kilmartin.

◎ Sights

Your first stop should be Kilmartin House Museum (☑ 01546-510278; www.kilmartin. org; Kilmartin; adult/child £5/2; ☉ 10am-5.30pm Mar-Oct, 11am-4pm Nov-23 Dec), in Kilmartin village. Its a fascinating interpretative centre that provides a context for the ancient monuments you can go on to explore, alongside displays of artefacts recovered from various sites. There's also an excellent cafe (☑ 01546-510278; mains £5-9; ☉ 10am-5pm Mar-Oct, 11am-4pm Nov-Christmas; ☎) and a shop with handcrafts and books on Scotland.

The oldest monuments at Kilmartin date from 5000 years ago and comprise a linear cemetery of burial cairns that runs south 1.5 miles from Kilmartin village. There are also two stone circles at Temple Wood, 0.75 miles southwest of Kilmartin.

Kilmartin Churchyard contains 10th-century Celtic crosses and medieval grave slabs with carved effigies of knights. Some researchers have surmised that these were the tombs of Knights Templar who fled persecution in France in the 14th century.

The hill fort of Dunadd, 3.5 miles south of Kilmartin village, was the seat of power of the first kings of Dál Riata, and may have been where the Stone of Destiny was originally located. Faint rock carvings of a boar and two footprints with an Ogham inscription may have been used in some kind of inauguration ceremony. The prominent little hill rises straight out of the boggy plain of Moine Mhor Nature Reserve. A slippery path leads to the summit where you can gaze out on much the same view that the kings of Dál Riata enjoyed 1300 years ago.

❶ Getting There & Away

Bus 423 between Oban and Ardrishaig (three to five Monday to Friday, two on Saturday) stops at Kilmartin (£5.60, one hour).

You can walk or cycle along the Crinan Canal from Ardrishaig, then turn north at Bellanoch on the minor B8025 road to reach Kilmartin (12 miles one way).

RETURN OF THE BEAVER

Beavers have been extinct in Britain since the 16th century. But in 2009 they returned to Scotland, when a population of Norwegian beavers was released into the hill lochs of Knapdale, Argyll. After a broadly successful five-year trial, a mid-2015 decision will decide on the future of the beaver project.

Meanwhile, you can try and get a glimpse of them on the Beaver Detective Trail. It starts from the Barnluasgan forestry car park on the B8025 road to Tayvallich, about 1.5 miles south of the Crinan Canal. There's an information centre here. The trail is three miles but you might glimpse them at pretty Dubh Loch just half a mile down the track. Rangers offer guided walks (☑ 01546-603346; adult/child £2/1) in summer: phone to book.

Kintyre

The 40-mile long Kintyre peninsula is almost an island, with only a narrow isthmus at Tarbert connecting it to Knapdale. During the Norse occupation of the Western Isles, the Scottish king decreed that the Vikings could claim as their own any island they circumnavigated in a longship. So in 1098 the wily Magnus Barefoot stood at the helm while his men dragged their boat across this neck of land, validating his claim to Kintyre.

Tarbert

POP 1200

The attractive fishing village and yachting centre of Tarbert is the gateway to Kintyre, and the most scenic, with buildings strung around its excellent natural harbour. It's well worth a stopover.

◎ Sights & Activities

The picturesque harbour is overlooked by the crumbling, ivy-covered ruins of Tarbert Castle, rebuilt by Robert the Bruce in the 14th century. You can hike up via a signposted footpath beside Loch Fyne Gallery (www. lochfynegallery.com; Harbour St; ☉ 10am-5pm Mon-Sat, 10.30am-5pm Sun), which showcases the work of local artists.

Tarbert is the starting point for the 100-mile Kintyre Way. The nine-mile first section to Skipness makes a pleasant day hike, climbing through forestry plantations to a high moorland plateau where you can soak up superb views to the Isle of Arran.

🛏 Sleeping & Eating

There are plenty of B&Bs and hotels, but book ahead in summer, as there are regular festivals and events in town.

Knap Guest House   B&B **££**
(☑ 01880-820015;   www.knapguesthouse.co.uk; Campbeltown Rd; s/d from £50/70; @ 🛜) A flight of stairs lit by Edwardian stained glass leads to this 1st-floor flat with three spacious en suite bedrooms sporting an attractive blend of Scottish and Far Eastern decor. The welcome is warm, and there are great harbour views from the lounge (leather sofas, log fire and a small library) and breakfast room.

Moorings   B&B **££**
(☑ 01880-820756;   www.themooringsbb.co.uk; Pier Rd; s £40, d £70-80; **P** 🛜) Follow the harbour just past the centre to this spot which is beautifully maintained and decorated by one man and his dogs, has great views over the water and an eclectic menagerie of ceramic and wooden animals and offbeat artwork.

Springside B&B   B&B **££**
(☑ 01880-820413;   www.scotland-info.co.uk/springside; Pier Rd; s/d £40/70; **P** 🛜 🐾) You can sit in front of this attractive fisherman's cottage, which overlooks the entrance to the harbour, and watch the yachts and fishing boats come and go. There are four comfy rooms, three with en suite, and the house is just five minutes' walk from the village centre. It's run with kind good humour by an older couple who know how to make guests feel welcome.

★ Starfish   SEAFOOD **££**
(☑ 01880-820733; wwwstarfishtarbert.com; Castle St; mains £11-19; ☺ noon-2pm & 6-9pm Tue-Sun) Simple but stylish describes not only the decor in this friendly restaurant, but the seafood too. A great variety of specials – anything from classic French fish dishes to Thai curries – are prepared with whatever's fresh off the Tarbert boats that day. Best to book a table. Reduced hours in the low season.

🛈 Information

Tarbert Tourist Office (☑ 01880-820429; Harbour St; ☺ 10am-5pm Mon-Sat, 11am-5pm Sun Apr-Oct) Some years this opens in the winter months too.

🛈 Getting There & Away

BOAT
CalMac (☑ 0800 066-5000; www.calmac.co.uk) operates a car ferry from Tarbert to Portavadie on the Cowal peninsula (passenger/car £4.30/19, 25 minutes, hourly).

Ferries to Islay and Colonsay depart from Kennacraig ferry terminal, 5 miles southwest.

BUS
Tarbert is served by five daily **Scottish Citylink** (www.citylink.co.uk) coaches between Campbeltown (£7.70, one hour) and Glasgow (£16.20, three hours).

Skipness
POP 100

Tiny Skipness, 13 miles south of Tarbert, is pleasant and quiet with great views of Arran. Beyond the village rise the substantial remains of 13th-century **Skipness Castle** (HS; admission free; ☺ 24hr, tower Apr-Sep only), a former possession of the Lords of the Isles. It's strikingly composed of dark-green local stone trimmed with Arran red-brown sandstone. The tower house was added in the 16th century. From the top you can see roofless, 13th-century **St Brendan's Chapel** by the shore. The kirkyard contains some excellent carved grave slabs. In summer a cabin in the grounds of nearby Skipness House does cracking crab sandwiches.

Local bus 448 runs from Tarbert (£2.80, 35 minutes, two daily Monday to Saturday).

At Claonaig, 2 miles southwest, there's a ferry to Lochranza on Arran (passenger/car return £10.35/47, 30 minutes, seven to nine daily April to September).

Isle of Gigha
POP 160

Gigha (*ghee*-ah; www.gigha.org.uk) is a low-lying island, 6 miles long by about 1 mile wide, famous for sandy beaches, pristine turquoise water and mild climate – sub tropical plants thrive in **Achamore Gardens** (☑ 01583-505254; www.gigha.org.uk/gardens; Achamore House; adult/child £6/3; ☺ dawn-dusk). Other highlights include the ruined **church** at Kilchattan, the **bible garden** at the manse, and Gigha's picturesque northern end. The island was bought by its residents in 2002.

You can hire bikes, as well as sea kayaks and rowing boats from Gigha Boats Activity Centre (☎07876-506520; www.gighaboatsactivitycentre.co.uk; bike hire per half-/full day £8/12; ⊙10am-6pm Easter-Oct) near the ferry slip.

There are several B&B and self-catering options; check the website. Community-owned Gigha Hotel (☎01583-505254; www.gigha.org.uk; s/d £50/90; ⊙food noon-2pm & 6-8pm; [P][☎][☎]) has a dozen rooms and serves bar meals. The friendly island shop, Ardminish Stores (☎01583-505251; www.facebook.com/ardminishstores; ⊙shop 9am-6.30pm Mon-Sat, noon-5pm Sun; [P]), sells petrol, food and hires bikes. There is a bunkhouse with dorms and a family room planned to open by the time you read this. The Boat House Café Bar (☎01583-505123; mains £8-15; ⊙10.30am-9pm; [☎]) does simple dishes as well as quality fresh local seafood. You can also camp here: there's no charge but space is limited, so call in advance.

CalMac (www.calmac.co.uk) runs from Tayinloan in Kintyre (passenger/car return £4.80/14.20, 20 minutes, roughly hourly).

Campbeltown

POP 4900

Blue-collar Campbeltown, set around a beautiful harbour, still suffers from the decline of its fishing and whisky industries and the closure of the nearby air-force base, but is rebounding on the back of golf tourism and a ferry link to Ayrshire. The spruced-up seafront backed by green hills lends the town a distinctly optimistic air.

The Mull of Kintyre Music Festival (☎01583-551053; www.mokfest.com), held in late August, is a popular event featuring traditional Scottish and Irish music.

◉ Sights & Activities

Springbank   DISTILLERY

(☎01586-552009; www.springbankwhisky.com; 85 Longrow; tours from £6.50; ⊙tours 10am & 2pm Mon-Sat) There were once no fewer than 32 distilleries around Campbeltown, but most closed in the 1920s. Today this is one of only three operational. It is also one of the few around that distils, matures and bottles all its whisky on the one site, making for an interesting tour. It's a quality malt, one of Scotland's finest.

WALK KINTYRE

Want to explore Kintyre? The Kintyre Way (www.kintyreway.com) is an appealing 100-mile hike that stretches from Tarbert right the way to the bottom of the peninsula.

Davaar Cave   CAVE

An unusual sight awaits in this cave on the southern side of Davaar island, at the mouth of Campbeltown Loch. On the wall of the cave is an eerie painting of the Crucifixion by local artist Archibald MacKinnon, dating from 1887. You can walk to the island at low tide: check tide times with the tourist office.

Machrihanish Bay   BEACH, GOLF

Five miles northwest of Campbeltown, this bay has a 3-mile-long sandy beach popular with surfers and windsurfers. There are two great golf courses here, both very competitively priced compared to their more famous rivals: Machrihanish Golf Club (☎01586-810213; www.machgolf.com; green fee £65) is a classic links course, designed by Old Tom Morris. Much-newer Machrihanish Dunes (☎01586-810000; www.machrihanishdunes.com; Campbeltown; green fee around £70) offers another impressive seaside experience, commendably light on snobbery: the clubhouse is a convivial little hut, kids play free and there are always website offers.

☞ Tours

Mull of Kintyre Seatours   BOAT TOURS

(☎07785-542811;   www.mull-of-kintyre.co.uk; ⊙Apr-Sep) Operates high-speed boat trips out of Campbeltown harbour to the spectacular sea cliffs of the Mull of Kintyre, Arran, Ailsa Craig (£30; gannet colony and puffins), or Sanda Island (£25; seals, puffins and other seabirds) as well as whale-watching (£30, best late July to early September). Book in advance by phone or at the tourist office.

⌘ Sleeping & Eating

Campbeltown Backpackers   HOSTEL £

(☎01586-551188; www.campbeltownbackpackers.co.uk; Big Kiln St; dm £20; [P][☎]) ✦ This beautiful hostel occupies a central former school building: it's great, with a modern kitchen, disabled access, and state-of-the-art wooden bunks. Profits go to maintain the Heritage Centre that runs it. Rates are £2 cheaper if you prebook.

Redknowe B&B ££

(☑ 01586-550374; www.redknowe.co.uk; Witchburn Rd; s £35, d £60-70; P🞲🛜🐾) An interesting Victorian home that's a short walk from the centre of town but feels rural with a lovely garden and an outlook over green fields. There's a fine welcome from the friendly couple that run it, a very decent breakfast, and comfortable rooms, a couple of which share an immaculate bathroom.

Royal Hotel HOTEL £££

(☑ 01586-810000; www.machrihanishdunes.com; Main St; r £142-152; ☺food noon-9pm Sun-Thu, to 10pm Fri & Sat; P🛜) Historically Campbeltown's best address, this hotel opposite the harbour is looking swish again. It caters mostly to yachties and golfers; though rack rates feel overpriced, there are often online specials and rooms are very spacious and attractive. The restaurant (mains £11 to £30) is the town's best, with fresh seafood and tasty grilled steaks the highlight.

ℹ️ Information

Campbeltown Tourist Office (☑ 01586-552056; www.visitscottishheartlands.com; The Pier; ☺10am-4pm Mon-Fri Nov-Mar, 10am-5pm Mon-Sat Apr & Oct, 10am-5pm Mon-Sat & noon-4pm Sun May, Jun & Sep, 9am-6pm Mon-Sat & 11am-5pm Sun Jul & Aug) Beside the harbour. Very helpful.

ℹ️ Getting There & Away

AIR

Loganair/FlyBe (www.flybe.com) flies six days a week between Glasgow and Campbeltown's mighty runway.

BOAT

Kintyre Express (☑ 01586-555895; www.kintyreexpress.com) operates a small, high-speed passenger ferry from Campbeltown to Ballycastle in Northern Ireland (£35/60 one way/return, 1½ hours, daily May to August, four weekly April and September, two weekly October to March). You must book in advance.

Calmac (☑ 0800 066-5000; www.calmac.co.uk) runs thrice weekly May to September between Ardrossan in Ayrshire and Campbeltown (adult/car £9.80/60, 2¾ hours); the Saturday return service stops at Brodick on Arran.

BUS

Scottish Citylink (www.citylink.co.uk) runs from Campbeltown to Glasgow (£19.80, 4¼ hours, five daily) via Tarbert, Inveraray and Loch Lomond. Change at Inveraray for Oban.

Mull of Kintyre

A narrow winding road, 15 miles long, leads south from Campbeltown to the **Mull of Kintyre**, passing some good sandy beaches near Southend. This remote headland was immortalised in Paul McCartney's famous song – the former Beatle owns a farmhouse in the area. From where the road ends, a 30-minute steep downhill walk leads to a clifftop **lighthouse**, with Northern Ireland, only 12 miles away, visible across the channel. Don't leave the road when the frequent mists roll in as it's easy to become disoriented.

Isle of Arran

POP 4600

Enchanting Arran is a jewel in Scotland's scenic crown. The island is a visual feast, and boasts culinary delights, its own brewery and distillery and stacks of accommodation options. The variations in Scotland's dramatic landscape can all be experienced on this one island, best explored by pulling on the hiking boots or jumping on a bicycle. Arran offers some challenging walks in the mountainous north while the island's circular coastal road is deservedly popular with cyclists.

ℹ️ Information

Brodick Tourist Office (☑ 01770-303774; www.ayrshire-arran.com; Brodick; ☺9am-5pm Mon-Sat) Efficient. Located by Brodick ferry pier; also open Sundays in summer. Slightly reduced hours in winter.

ℹ️ Getting There & Away

CalMac (☑ 0800 066-5000; www.calmac.co.uk) runs between Ardrossan and Brodick (passenger/car return £11.35/70, 55 minutes, four to 10 daily), and from April to late October also runs services between Claonaig on the Kintyre peninsula and Lochranza (passenger/car return £10.35/47, 30 minutes, seven to nine daily).

ℹ️ Getting Around

BICYCLE

Arran Adventure Company (☑ 01770-303479; www.arranadventure.com; Auchrannie Rd, Brodick; day/3 days £15/37) Good mountain bikes.

Arran Bike Hire (☑ 01770-302377; www.arranbikehire.com; The Shorehouse, Shore Rd, Brodick; half-day/full day/week £10/15/50)

On the water front in Brodick. Trail bikes and hybrids and can offer mountain-biking route advice.

CAR

Isle of Arran Car Hire (☑ 01770-302839; The Pier, Brodick; car part-day/24hr £30/40) is at the service station by Brodick ferry pier.

PUBLIC TRANSPORT

Four to seven buses daily go from Brodick pier to Lochranza (£2.95, 45 minutes), and many head to Lamlash (£2.05) and Whiting Bay (£2.95, 30 minutes), then on to Kildonan and Blackwaterfoot. Pick up a timetable from the tourist office. An Arran Dayrider costs £5.40 from the driver, giving a day's travel.

Brodick & Around

Most visitors arrive in Brodick, the beating heart of the island, and congregate along the coastal road to admire the town's long curving bay. Main attractions are just out of town, off the Lochranza road.

◎ Sights

Brodick Castle   CASTLE
(NTS; www.nts.org.uk; castle & park adult/child £12.50/9, park only £6.50/5.50; ☺ castle 11am-4pm May-Sep, 11am-3pm Apr & Oct, park 9.30am-sunset year-round) This elegant castle 2 miles north of Brodick evolved from 13th-century origins into a stately home and hunting lodge for the Dukes of Hamilton and was used until the 1950s. You enter via the hunting gallery, wallpapered with deer heads. The rest of the interior is characterised by fabulous 19th-century wooden furniture and an array of horses and hounds paintings. Helpful guides and laminated sheets – the kids' ones are more entertaining – add info.

The extensive grounds, now a country park with various trails among the rhododendrons, justify the steep entry fee.

Arran Aromatics   SOAP FACTORY
(☑ 01770-302595;   www.arranaromatics.com; ☺ 9.30am-5.30pm or 6pm) Near the castle is this popular shop and visitor centre where you can purchase any number of scented items and watch the production line at work. There's also **Soapworks** (soapmaking from £6.50; ☺ 10am-12.30pm & 1.30-4pm Apr-Oct, 10am-noon & 2-4pm Nov-Mar), a fun little place where kids (and adults…) can experiment by making their own soaps, combining colours and moulds to make weird and wonderful

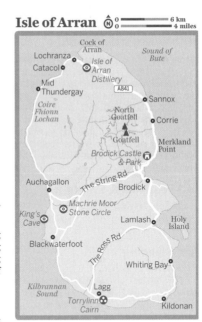

Isle of Arran
0 — 6 km
0 — 4 miles

Cock of Arran
Lochranza
Catacol
Isle of Arran
Mid Thundergay
Isle of Arran Distillery
A841
Coire Fhionn Lochan
Sound of Bute
Sannox
North Goatfell
Corrie
Goatfell
Merkland Point
Brodick Castle & Park
Auchagallon
The String Rd
Brodick
Machrie Moor Stone Circle
King's Cave
Lamlash
Holy Island
Blackwaterfoot
The Ross Rd
Whiting Bay
Kilbrannan Sound
Lagg
Torrylinn Cairn
Kildonan

creations. There's a similar candle-dipping workshop (£3 for two candles).

Isle of Arran Brewery   BREWERY
(☑ 01770-302353; www.arranbrewery.com; tours £4; ☺ 10am-5pm Mon-Sat, 12.30-5pm Sun Apr-Sep, variable hours Oct-Mar) A mile from town off the Lochranza road, this brewery produces the excellent-quality Arran beers, which include the addictive Arran Dark. Tours run daily: call for times as they vary by season. There's a good outdoors shop, **Arran Active** (www.arranactive.co.uk; ☺ 9.30am-5pm Mon-Sat, 10.30am-5pm Sun), here too, if you're heading up Goatfell.

⚡ Activities

The 55-mile coastal circuit is popular with cyclists and has few serious hills – more in the south than the north. There are plenty of walking booklets and maps available and trails are clearly signposted around the island. Several leave from Lochranza, including the spectacular walk to the island's northeast tip, the **Cock of Arran**, finishing in the village of Sannox (8 miles one way).

Tackling **Goatfell** (the island's tallest peak) is 8 miles return (up to eight hours), starting in Brodick. If the weather's fine, there are superb views to Ben Lomond and the coast of Northern Ireland. It can be very cold and windy; take the appropriate maps and waterproof gear.

Arran Adventure Company OUTDOORS
(☑ 01770-303479; www.arranadventure.com; Auchrannie Rd; adult/teen/child £50/40/30) Run out of the Auchrannie Resort (which has an indoor pool and spa), this company offers loads of activities, including gorge walking, sea kayaking, climbing, abseiling and mountain biking. All activities run for about three hours. Drop in to see what's available while you're around.

★✦ Festivals & Events

Arran Folk Festival FOLK MUSIC
(www.arranevents.com) A four-day festival in mid-June.

🛏 Sleeping

Glen Rosa Campsite CAMPSITE £
(☑ 01770-302380; www.arrancamping.co.uk; sites per adult/child £4/2; P 🐾) In a lush glen 2 miles from Brodick, this campsite offers picturesque but basic camping in a large grassy riverside meadow, with cold water and toilets only. Take String Rd, then turn right almost immediately. After 400m, you'll see a white house on the left, where you register; the campground is 400m further.

Glenartney B&B ££
(☑ 01770-302220; www.glenartney-arran.co.uk; Mayish Rd; s/d £52/85; ☺ Easter-Sep; P 🛜 🐾) 🌿 Uplifting bay views and genuine, helpful hosts make this a cracking option. Airy, stylish rooms make the most of the natural light available at the top of the town. Cyclists will appreciate bike wash, repair and storage facilities, while hikers can benefit from drying rooms and expert trail advice. They make big efforts to be sustainable.

Rothwell Lodge B&B ££
(☑ 01770-302208; www.rothwell-lodge.com; s £35-40, d £60-70; P 🛜) Sparklingly clean and luminous, this well-kept place offers an attractive modern environment with state-of-the-art bathrooms and numerous thoughtful touches at breakfast time. The upstairs en suite has heaps of space, and there's a large lounge. There are good discounts for multi-night stays and a self-catering apartment available downstairs. The owner was considering her future at last visit.

Belvedere Guest House B&B ££
(☑ 01770-302397; www.vision-unlimited.co.uk; Alma Rd; s £35, d £70-90; P 🛜) Overlooking town, bay and surrounding mountains, this has pleasant hosts and rooms are well-presented. Rooms are commodious but feel a smidgen overpriced; the two at the front are dearer but are en suite with great views. There's also a self-catering cottage as well as reiki and healing packages available.

★ Kilmichael Country House Hotel HOTEL £££
(☑ 01770-302219; www.kilmichael.com; s £95, d £163-204; ☺ Apr-Oct; P 🛜 🐾) The island's best hotel is also the oldest building – one bit dates from 1650. Luxurious and tastefully decorated, it's a mile outside Brodick but seems a world away in deep countryside. With just eight spacious, very individual rooms and excellent four-course dinners (£45, open to nonguests), it's an ideal, utterly relaxing hideaway, which feels very classy without being overly formal.

In the grounds, patrolled by a sizeable muster of peacocks, there are also five self-catering cottages.

Douglas HOTEL £££
(☑ 01770-302968; www.thedouglashotel.co.uk; d/superior d £149/179; P 🛜 🐾) Opposite the ferry, this hotel is a smart, stylish haven of island hospitality. Views are magnificent and luxurious rooms make the most of them. There are numerous thoughtful touches like binoculars to admire the vistas, and bathrooms are great. The downstairs bar (food served noon to 9pm) and bistro (6pm to 9.30pm) are also recommended. Prices drop midweek and in winter.

🍴 Eating & Drinking

Wineport CAFE £
(☑ 01770-302101; www.wineport.co.uk; Cladach Centre; mains £8-11; ☺ 10am-5pm Apr-Oct) A mile-and-a-half from Brodick, next to the brewery, whose ales are offered on tap, this summer-only cafe-bar has great outdoor tables for sunny days and does a nice line in salads and pub grub. Opening hours are very changeable.

Ormidale Hotel PUB £
(☑ 01770-302293; www.ormidale-hotel.co.uk; Glen Cloy; mains £8-11; ☺ food 5-9pm daily & 12.30-2.30pm Sat & Sun; ☑ 🍴) This hotel has decent bar food. Dishes change regularly, but there are always some good vegetarian options,

and daily specials. Quantities and value for money are high, and Arran beers are on tap.

★ Brodick Bar
BRASSERIE **££**

(☑ 01770-302169; www.brodickbar.co.uk; Alma Rd; mains £9-19; ⊙ noon-2.30pm & 5.30-8.45pm or later Mon-Sat; 🐾) Don't leave Brodick without dropping in here. The regularly changing blackboard menu brings modern French flair to this Arran pub, with great presentation, efficient service and delicious flavour combinations. You'll have a hard time choosing, as it's all brilliant. It's very buzzy on weekend evenings.

Fiddlers' Music Bar
CAFE **££**

(www.facebook.com/fiddlersmusicbar; Shore Rd; mains £9-12; ⊙ meals 9am-9.30pm; 🐾) Newly opened when we last passed by, this place was doing a good job serving decently priced food on gingham tablecloths and putting on live folk several times a week. Check out the appropriate toilet seats.

🛍 Shopping

Arran Cheese Shop
FOOD

(www.arrancheese.com; Duchess Ct, Home Farm; ⊙ 9am-5pm Mon-Sat, 10am-4.30pm Sun) Stop by this place to stock up on the famed local varieties. There are free samples and you can watch them make the stuff.

Corrie to Lochranza

The coast road continues north to small, pretty Corrie, where there's a **Goatfell** trailhead. After **Sannox**, with sandy beach and great mountain views, the road cuts inland. Heading to the very north, on the island's main road, visitors weave through lush glens flanked by Arran's towering mountain splendour.

Pubs in Sannox and Corrie offer accommodation, food and drinks with sea views.

Lochranza

The village of Lochranza has a stunning location in a small bay at the island's north. On a promontory stands ruined 13th-century **Lochranza Castle** (HS; www.historic-scotland.gov.uk; ⊙ 24hr; **FREE**), basically a draughty shell inside.

Isle of Arran Distillery (☑ 01770-830264; www.arranwhisky.com; tours adult/child £6/free) produces a light, aromatic single malt. The tour is a good one; it's a small set-up, and the whisky-making process is thoroughly explained. More expensive tours (£15) include extra tastings.

The Lochranza area bristles with red deer, who wander insouciantly into the village to crop the grass.

🛏 Sleeping & Eating

★ Lochranza SYHA
HOSTEL **£**

(☑ 01770-830631; www.syha.org.uk; dm/d £19/50; ⊙ mid-Mar–Oct plus Sat & Sun year-round; **P @ 🐾 🦮**) An excellent hostel in a charming place, with lovely views. Rooms sport chunky wooden furniture, keycards and lockers. Rainwater toilets, energy-saving heating solutions and an excellent wheelchair-accessible room show thoughtful design, while plush lounging areas, a kitchen you could run a restaurant out of, a laundry, a drying room, red deer in the garden, and welcoming management combine to make this a top option.

Castlekirk
B&B **££**

(☑ 01770-830202; www.castlekirkarran.co.uk; s £35-40, d £60-75; ⊙ Mar-Oct; **P 🐾 🦮**) This unusual and warmly welcoming place to stay is a converted church chock-full of excellent artworks; there's a gallery downstairs, and paintings decorate the passageways and rooms. The breakfast area is dignified by a rose window, and there are great views of the castle opposite. Rooms are cosy under the sloping ceiling.

Apple Lodge
B&B **££**

(☑ 01770-830229; www.applelodgearran.co.uk; s/d/apt £50/78/90; **P 🐾**) Once the village manse, this rewarding choice is dignified and hospitable. Rooms are individually furnished and very commodious. One has a four-poster bed, while another is a self-contained apartment in the garden. The guest lounge is perfect for curling up with a good book, and courteous hosts mean you should book this one well ahead in summer.

Lochranza Hotel
HOTEL **££**

(☑ 01770-830223; www.lochranzahotel.co.uk; s/d £60/99; **P 🐾**) The only place in town for an evening meal (open noon to 9pm), this has somewhat overpriced but comfortable rooms: it's well worth paying the extra fiver for a larger front room, with super views. Showers are pleasingly powerful. The bar does toasties, jacket potatoes and the like, as well as fuller evening plates (dishes £10 to £13).

Catacol Bay Hotel
PUB £

(☑ 01770-830231; www.catacol.co.uk; mains £8-11; ⊙ food noon-8.45pm, to 10pm summer; P 🛜 📶 🐾) Genially run, and with a memorable position overlooking the water, this no-frills, somewhat rundown pub 2 miles south of Lochranza offers unpretentious bar food that comes out in generous portions. There's a Sunday lunch buffet (£13.95), and the beer garden is worth a contemplative pint with spirit-soothing views. Comfortable-enough rooms with shared bathroom are available (single/double £35/60).

West Coast

On the western side of the island is **Machrie Moor Stone Circle**, a pleasant 2-mile stroll (20 to 30 minute) from the parking area on the coastal road. There are actually several separate groups of stones of varying sizes, erected around 4000 years ago. You pass a Bronze Age burial cairn along the path.

Blackwaterfoot is the west coast's largest village, with shop and hotel. You can walk to **King's Cave** from here (6 miles) – Arran is one of several islands that claim the cave where Robert the Bruce had his famous arachnid encounter. This walk can easily be extended to the Machrie stones.

South Coast

The landscape in the south is gentler; the road drops into little wooded valleys, and it's particularly lovely around **Lagg**, where a 10-minute walk goes to **Torrylinn Cairn**, a chambered tomb over 4000 years old. **Kildonan** has pleasant sandy beaches, a gorgeous water outlook, a hotel, a campground and an ivy-clad ruined castle.

In genteel **Whiting Bay**, you'll find small sandy beaches and easy one-hour walks through the forest to the **Giant's Graves** and **Glenashdale Falls**, and back – keep an eye out for golden eagles and other birds of prey.

🛏 Sleeping & Eating

Sealshore Campsite
CAMPSITE £

(☑ 01770-820320; www.campingarran.com; Kildonan; sites per adult/child £6/3, per tent £2-4; ⊙ Apr-Oct; P 🛜 🐾) Living up to its name, this excellent small campsite is right by sea (and the Kildonan Hotel) with one of Arran's finest views from its grassy camping area. There's a good washroom area with heaps of showers, kitchen facilities, and the breeze keeps the midges away. Cosy camping pods cost £30 for two people.

Kildonan Hotel
HOTEL ££

(☑ 01770-820207; www.kildonanhotel.com; Kildonan; s/d/ste £75/99/135; P @ 🛜 🐾) Appealing rooms and a grounded attitude – dogs and kids are made very welcome – combine to make this one of Arran's better options. Oh, and it's right by the water, with seals basking on the rocks. The standard rooms could do with a pep-up but are decent; the suites – with private terrace or small balcony – are great.

Nearly all rooms have sea views; other attractions include great staff, a bar and restaurant serving tasty meals (mains £9 to £17; noon to 3pm and 6pm to 9pm), and live folk music.

Lagg Hotel
INN ££

(☑ 01770-870255; www.lagghotel.com; Lagg, Kilmory; s/d £50/90; ⊙ Apr-Oct; P 🛜 🐾) This 18th-century coaching inn has a beautiful location and is the perfect place for a romantic weekend away from the cares of modern life. Rooms are smart; grab a superior one (£100) with garden views. There's also a cracking beer garden, a fine bar with log fire and an elegant restaurant (mains £9 to £13; noon to 3pm and 5.30pm to 9pm) with good veggie options.

Viewbank House
B&B ££

(☑ 01770-700326; www.viewbank-arran.co.uk; Whiting Bay; s £30-35, d £62-79; P 🛜 🐾) Appropriately named, this friendly place does indeed have tremendous views from its vantage point high above Whiting Bay. Rooms, of which there are a variety with and without bathroom, are tastefully furnished and well kept. It's well signposted from the main road.

Coast
BISTRO ££

(☑ 01770-700308; www.coastarran.co.uk; Shore Rd, Whiting Bay; mains £10-14; ⊙ 10am-4pm daily, plus 6-9pm Thu-Sat; 🛜) Offering a sun-drenched conservatory on the water's edge, this serves grills, seafood and salads in the evening, with lighter offerings during the day. Opens Wednesday and Sunday evenings in summer too.

Lamlash

Lamlash is in a dazzling setting, strung along the beachfront. The bay was used as a safe anchorage by the navy during WWI and WWII.

Just off the coast is Holy Island, owned by the Samye Ling Tibetan Centre and used as a retreat, but day visits are allowed. Depending on tides, the ferry (☑01770-600998; tomin10@btinternet.com; adult/child return £12/6; ☺May-Sep, by arrangement Tue & Fri winter) makes around seven daily trips from Lamlash (15 minutes) between May and September. The same folk also run mackerel-fishing expeditions (£25).

No dogs, bikes, alcohol or fires are allowed on Holy Island. A good walk to the top of the hill (314m) takes two or three hours return. You can stay at the Holy Island Centre for World Peace & Health (☑01770-601100; www.holyisle.org; dm/s/d £28/47/72; ☺Apr-Oct). Prices include full (vegetarian) board.

🛏 Sleeping & Eating

★ Glenisle Hotel   HOTEL ££
(☑01770-600559; www.glenislehotel.com; Shore Rd; s/d/superior d £83/128/167; ☎) This stylish hotel offers great service and high comfort levels. Rooms are decorated with contemporary fabrics; the 'cosy' ones under the sloping ceiling upstairs are a little cheaper. All feel fresh and include binoculars for scouring the seashore; upgrade to a superior for the best views over the water. Downstairs is excellent pub food (mains £10 to £13; 8am to 9pm, reduced hours in winter), with Scottish classics and a good wine list.

Lilybank Guest House   B&B ££
(☑01770-600230; www.lilybank-arran.co.uk; Shore Rd; s/d £50/80; ☐ ☎) Built in the 17th century, Lilybank retains its heritage but has been refurbished for 21st-century needs. Rooms are clean and comfortable, with one adapted for disabled use. The front ones have great views over Holy Island. Breakfast includes organic porridge, oak-smoked kippers and other Arran goodies.

★ Drift Inn   PUB ££
(☑01770-600608; www.driftinnarran.com; Shore Rd; mains £10-18; ☺food noon-9pm; ☒☎) Recently refurbished, this is now the island's best pub, with a plush interior with leather chairs and a fireplace, as well as a fabulous beer garden – enjoy magnificent views from both across to Holy Island. Great bar food is on offer – upmarket fare with thoughtful vegetarian options – as well as Arran ales on tap and soul and blues on the stereo.

Isle of Islay

POP 3200

The home of some of the world's greatest and peatiest whiskies, the names of which reverberate on the tongue like a pantheon of Celtic deities, Islay (eye-lah) is a wonderfully friendly place whose welcoming inhabitants offset its lack of scenic splendour. The distilleries are well-geared up for visits; even if you're not a fan of single malt, the birdlife, fine seafood, turquoise bays and basking seals are ample reason to visit. Locals are among Britain's most genial: a wave or cheerio to passers-by is mandatory, and you'll soon find yourself unwinding to relaxing island pace. The only drawback is that the waves of well-heeled whisky tourists have induced many sleeping and eating options to raise prices to eye-watering levels.

☞ Tours

Islay Sea Safaris   BOAT TOURS
(☑01496-840510; www.islayseasafari.co.uk) Customised tours (£25 to £30 per person per hour) by sea from Port Ellen to spot some or all of Islay and Jura's distilleries in a single day, as well as birdwatching trips, coastal exploration, and trips to Jura's remote west coast and the Corryvreckan whirlpool.

☆ Festivals & Events

Fèis Ìle   MUSIC, WHISKY
(Islay Festival; www.islayfestival.com) A week-long celebration of traditional Scottish music and whisky at the end of May. Events include ceilidhs, pipe-band performances, distillery tours, barbecues and whisky tastings.

Islay Jazz Festival   MUSIC
(www.islayjazzfestival.co.uk) This three-day festival takes place over the second weekend in September. A varied line-up of international talent plays at various venues across the island.

❶ Information

Islay Tourist Office (☑01496-810254; The Square, Bowmore; ☺10am-5pm Mon-Sat, noon-3pm Sun Easter-Oct, 10am-3pm Mon-Fri Nov-Mar)

❶ Getting There & Away

There are two ferry terminals: Port Askaig on the east coast, and Port Ellen in the south. Islay airport lies midway between Port Ellen and Bowmore.

AIR

Loganair/FlyBe (www.loganair.co.uk) flies daily from Glasgow to Islay, while **Hebridean Air Services** (☑ 0845 805 7465; www.hebridean air.co.uk) operates twice daily Tuesday and Thursday from Oban to Colonsay and Islay.

BOAT

CalMac (www.calmac.co.uk) runs ferries from Kennacraig to Port Ellen or Port Askaig (person/car £6.45/32, 2 to 2¼ hours, three to five daily). On Wednesday and Saturdays in summer you can continue to Colonsay (£3.95/16.55, 1¼ hours) and Oban (£11.10/54, four hours).

ⓘ Getting Around

BICYCLE

There are various places to hire bikes, including **Islay Cycles** (☑ 07760-196592; www.islaycycles.co.uk; bikes per day/week from £15/60) in Port Ellen.

BUS

A bus links Ardbeg, Port Ellen, Bowmore, Port Charlotte, Portnahaven and Port Askaig (limited service on Sunday). Pick up a copy of the *Islay & Jura Public Transport Guide* from the tourist office.

CAR

D&N MacKenzie (☑ 01496-302300; www.carhireonislay.co.uk; Islay Airport) offers car hire from £32 a day and can meet ferries.

TAXI

There are various drivers; **Carol** (☑ 01496-302155; www.carols-cabs.co.uk) can take bikes.

Port Ellen & Around

Port Ellen is Islay's principal entry point. The coast stretching northeast is one of the loveliest parts of the island, where within three miles you'll find three of whisky's biggest names: Laphroaig, Lagavulin and Ardbeg (see boxed text, p76).

A pleasant drive or ride leads past the distilleries to ruined Kildalton Chapel, 8 miles from Port Ellen. In the kirkyard is the exceptional late-8th-century Kildalton Cross. There are carvings of biblical scenes on one side and animals on the other.

The kelp-fringed *skerries* (small rocky islands or reefs) of the Ardmore Islands, near Kildalton, are a wildlife haven and home to Europe's second-largest colony of common seals.

🛏 Sleeping & Eating

Kintra Farm   CAMPSITE, B&B £
(☑ 01496-302051; www.kintrafarm.co.uk; tent sites £6-8, plus adult/child £4/2, s/d £50/80; ⓟ Apr-Sep; Ⓟ) At the southern end of Laggan Bay, 3.5 miles northwest of Port Ellen, Kintra is a basic but beautiful campsite on buttercup-sprinkled turf amid the dunes, with a sunset view across the beach. There's also B&B available.

★ Oystercatcher B&B   B&B ££
(☑ 01496-300409; www.islay-bedandbreakfast.com; 63 Frederick Cres; s/d £60/80; 🛜) Two beautifully decorated upstairs rooms with a maritime theme and water views make inviting Islay bases in this excellent B&B. Thoughtful breakfast options and a super-welcoming host add appeal. If you want to dine here, you can organise to order in a seafood platter.

Old Kiln Café   CAFE £
(☑ 01496-302244; www.ardbeg.com; Ardbeg; mains £5-11; ⓟ 10am-4.30pm daily May-Sep, Mon-Sat Apr & Oct, Mon-Fri Nov-Mar) Housed in the former malting kiln at Ardbeg distillery, this cafe serves homemade soups, tasty light meals, heartier daily specials and a range of desserts, including traditional clootie dumpling (a rich steamed pudding filled with currants and raisins).

Bowmore

This attractive Georgian village was built in 1768 to replace the village of Kilarrow, which just had to go – it was spoiling the view from the laird's house. Its centrepieces are the Bowmore distillery (p76) and distinctive Round Church at the top of Main St, built in circular form to ensure that the devil had no corners to hide in. He was last seen in one of Islay's distilleries.

🛏 Sleeping & Eating

Bowmore distillery offers a tempting range of self-catering cottages around the centre.

Lambeth House   B&B ££
(☑ 01496-810597; lambethguesthouse@tiscali.co.uk; Jamieson St; s/d £60/94; 🛜) Cheerily welcoming, and with smart refurbished rooms with top-notch en suite bathrooms, this is a sound option in the centre of town. Breakfasts are reliably good. Rooms vary substantially in size.

Islay, Jura & Colonsay

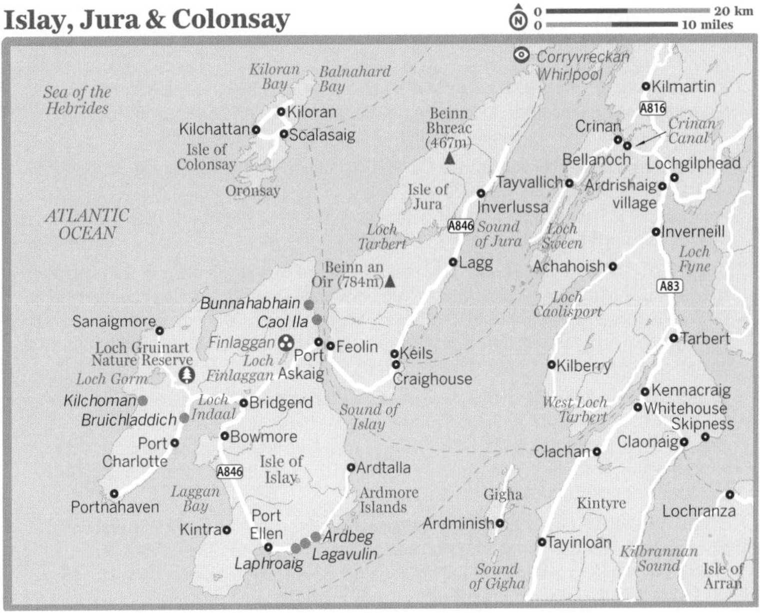

Bowmore House B&B £££
(☎01496-810324; www.thebowmorehouse.co.uk; Shore St; s/d £75/150; P 📶) This stately former bank offers plenty of character and super water views. It's top-level B&B here, with coffee machines in the rooms, an honesty minibar with bottles of wine and local ales, and plush king-sized beds. Rooms are spacious, high-ceilinged and light.

Harbour Inn INN £££
(☎01496-810330; www.harbour-inn.com; The Square; s/d from £110/145; 📶) The plush seven-room Harbour Inn, now owned by Bowmore whisky, is the poshest place in town. The restaurant (mains £19 to £26; open noon to 2pm and 6pm to 9pm) has harbour views and serves fresh local oysters, lobster and scallops, Islay lamb and Jura venison. It's tasty but feels a little overpriced.

Lochside Hotel HOTEL £££
(☎01496-810244; www.lochsidehotel.co.uk; 19 Shore St; s/d £70/140; 📶) Bedrooms at the Lochside are kitted out with chunky pine furniture, including one room adapted for wheelchair users. The conservatory dining room (mains £10 to £18; open 11am to 9pm) provides simple fare in generous portions with sweeping views over Loch Indaal, and the likeably boisterous bar boasts hundreds of single malts, including many rare bottlings.

Taste of Islay BISTRO ££
(www.bowmore.com; School St; dishes £7-13; ⊙9am-5pm Mon-Sat, 11am-4pm Sun; 📶) Alongside and owned by Bowmore distillery, this new spot offers appealing lunchtime fare, including good sandwiches and tasty seafood – local langoustine tails and other tempting morsels.

Port Charlotte and Around

Eleven miles from Bowmore, on the opposite shore of Loch Indaal, is attractive Port Charlotte.

Sights & Activities

Museum of Islay Life MUSEUM
(☎01496-850358; www.islaymuseum.org; Port Charlotte; adult/child £3/1; ⊙10.30am-4.30pm Mon-Fri Apr-Sep), Islay's long history is lovingly recorded in this museum, housed in an old church. Prize exhibits include an illicit still, 19th-century crofters' furniture, and a set of leather boots once worn by the horse that pulled the lawnmower at Islay House (so it wouldn't leave hoof prints on the lawn!).

DON'T MISS

ISLAY'S DISTILLERIES

Islay has eight working distilleries, with a ninth, Gartbreck, on the way. All welcome visitors and run tours. It's worth booking visits by phone, as they have maximum numbers. More expensive, specialised tours let you taste more malts and take you further behind the scenes. Pick up the pamphlet listing tour times from the tourist office.

Ardbeg (www.ardbeg.com; tours from £5; ⊙ 9.30am-5pm Mon-Fri, plus Sat Apr-Oct & Sun May-Sep) Ardbeg's iconic peaty whiskies start with their magnificent 10-year-old. The basic tour is good, and it also offers longer tours involving walks, stories and extended tastings. Three miles northeast of Port Ellen.

Bowmore (☑ 01496-810441; www.bowmore.com; School St; tours from £6; ⊙ 9am-5pm Mon-Fri & 9am-12.30pm Sat Oct-Mar, 9am-5pm Mon-Sat & noon-4pm Sun Apr-Sep) In the centre of Bowmore, this distillery malts its own barley. The tour begins with an overblown marketing video, but is redeemed by a look at (and taste of) the germinating grain laid out in golden billows on the floor of the malting shed.

Bruichladdich (☑ 01496-850190; www.bruichladdich.com; tours £5; ⊙ 9am-6pm Mon-Fri & 9.30am-4pm Sat, plus 12.30-3.30pm Sun Apr-Aug) At the northern edge of Port Charlotte, Bruichladdich (brook-laddy) is an infectiously fun place to visit and produces a mind-boggling range of bottlings; there's always some new experiment cooking. Gin is also made herehere, infused with local herbs.

Bunnahabhain (☑ 01496-840646; www.bunnahabhain.com; tours from £5; ⊙ 10am-5pm Mon-Sat, 11am-4pm Sun Apr-Sep, ring for winter hours) Pronounced 'boona-hah-ven', this distillery is 4 miles north of Port Askaig. It enjoys a wonderful location with great views across to Jura. The standard malt is very lightly peated compared to most of the island's whiskies.

Caol Ila (☑ 01496-302769; www.discovering-distilleries.com; tours from £6; ⊙ 9am-5pm daily mid-Apr–Aug, 9am-5pm Mon-Sat Sep-Oct, 10am-4pm Tue-Sat Nov–mid-Apr) Pronounced 'cull ee-lah', this distillery is a mile north of Port Askaig. It's a big, industrial set-up but enjoys a wonderful location with great views across to Jura. Tours are free if you sign up to Diageo's mailing list.

Kilchoman (☑ 01496-850011; www.kilchomandistillery.com; Rockfield Farm; tours from £6; ⊙ 10am-5pm Mon-Fri, plus Sat Apr-Oct) Likeable Kilchoman, set on a farm, is Scotland's second-smallest distillery, going into production in 2005. It grows and malts some of its own barley here and does its own bottling by hand. The tour is informative and the tasting generous. There's also a good cafe.

Lagavulin (www.discovering-distilleries.com; tours from £6; ⊙ 9am-7pm Mon-Fri, to 5pm Sat & Sun Jun-Sep, 9am-5pm daily Apr-May & Oct, 10am-4pm Mon-Sat Nov-Feb, 10am-4pm daily Mar) Peaty and powerful, this is one of the triumvirate of southern distilleries near Port Ellen. Tours are free if you sign up to Diageo's mailing list.

Laphroaig (www.laphroaig.com; tours from £6; ⊙ 9.45am-5pm daily Mar-Oct, 9.45am-4.30pm daily Nov & Dec, 9.45am-4.30pm Mon-Fri Jan-Feb) Famously peaty whiskies just outside Port Ellen. The 'Water to Whisky' tour (£82) is recommended – you see the water source, dig peat, have a picnic and try plenty of drams.

Islay Natural History Centre NATURE DISPLAY (www.islaynaturalhistory.org; Port Charlotte; adult/child £3/1.50; ⊙ 10am-4.30pm Mon-Fri May-Sep), next to the youth hostel, has displays explaining the island's natural history – with wildlife-watching advice – and hands-on exhibits for kids.

Six miles southwest of Port Charlotte the road ends at Portnahaven, a picturesque fishing village. For seal-spotting, you can't do better; there are frequently dozens of the portly beasts basking in the small harbour.

Seven miles north of Port Charlotte is Loch Gruinart Nature Reserve, where you can hear corncrakes in summer and see huge flocks of migrating ducks, geese and waders in spring and autumn; there's a hide with wheelchair access

🛏 Sleeping & Eating

Islay SYHA HOSTEL £
(☎ 01496-850385; www.syha.org.uk; dm/q £19/80; ☺ Apr-Oct; @ 🛜) This modern and comfortable hostel is housed in a former distillery building with views over the loch.

Port Mòr Campsite CAMPSITE £
(☎ 01496-850441; www.islandofislay.co.uk; tent sites per adult/child £8/4; @ 🛜) The sports field doubles as a campsite with toilets, showers, laundry and a children's play area in the main building. Open all year.

Distillery House B&B ££
(☎ 01496-850495; mamak@btinternet.com; Port Charlotte; s £37.50, d £75-80; P 🛜) For a taste of genuine islander hospitality at a fair price, head directly to this homely B&B on the right as you enter Port Charlotte. Set in part of the former Lochindaal distillery rooms are well-kept and most comfortable, with low beds. The cute single has sea views.

Port Charlotte Hotel HOTEL £££
(☎ 01496-850360; www.portcharlottehotel. co.uk; s/d £115/190; P 🛜 🐾) This lovely old Victorian hotel has stylish bedrooms with sea views, and a candlelit restaurant (mains £21 to £33; open 6.30pm to 9pm) serving local seafood, Islay beef, venison and duck. The bar (mains £10 to £16; meals noon to 2pm and 5.30pm to 8.30pm) also does great food, is well stocked with Islay malts and real ales, and has a nook at the back with a view over the loch towards the Paps of Jura.

Finlaggan

Loch Finlaggan, 3 miles southwest of Port Askaig, was once the most important settlement in the Hebrides, the central seat of power of the Lords of the Isles from the 12th to the 16th centuries. From the little island at the northern end of the loch they administered their island territories and entertained visiting chieftains in their great hall. Little remains now except the tumbled ruins of houses and a chapel, but the setting is beautiful and the history fascinating. A wooden walkway leads over the reeds and water lilies to the island, where information boards describe the remains.

Finlaggan Visitor Centre (www.finlaggan. com; adult/child £3/1; ☺ 10.30am-4.30pm Mon-Sat & 1.30-4.30pm Sun Apr-Sep) explains the site's history and archaeology. The island itself is open at all times.

Buses between Bowmore and Port Askaig stop at the road junction, from where it's a 15-minute walk to the loch.

Port Askaig & Around

Port Askaig is little more than a hotel, shop (with ATM), petrol pump and ferry pier, set in a picturesque nook halfway along the Sound of Islay. There are two distilleries within reach and ferry connections to the mainland and Jura, just across the strait.

Isle of Jura

POP 200

Jura lies long, dark and low off the coast like a vast Viking longship, its billowing sail the distinctive triple peaks of the Paps of Jura. A magnificently wild and lonely island, it's the perfect place to get away from it all – as George Orwell did in 1948. Orwell wrote his masterpiece *1984* while living at the remote farmhouse of Barnhill in the north of the island, describing it in a letter as 'a very un-get-at-able place'.

Jura takes its name from the Old Norse *dyr-a* (deer island) – an apt appellation, as the island supports a population of around 6000 red deer, outnumbering their human cohabitants by about 30 to one.

There's a shop but no ATM; you can get cashback with debit cards at the Jura Hotel.

⊙ Sights

Apart from superb wilderness walking and wildlife-watching, there's not a whole lot to do except visit **Isle of Jura Distillery** (☎ 01496-820385; www.jurawhisky.com; Craighouse; tours from £6; ☺ 9.30am-4.30pm Mon-Sat Apr-Oct, 10am-2pm Mon-Fri Nov-Mar), near Craighouse, which includes a passenger return ferry ticket with each tour.

Jura Music Festival (www.juramusicfestival.com) in late September offers a convivial weekend of traditional Scottish folk music. The other big event is the **Isle of Jura Fell Race** (www.jurafellrace.org.uk) in late May, when around 250 hill runners converge on the island to race over the Paps.

🏃 Activities

There are few proper footpaths, and off-path exploration often involves rough going through giant bracken, knee-deep bogs and thigh-high tussocks. Most of the island is occupied by deer-stalking estates, and hill access may be restricted during the stalking season (July to February); the Jura Hotel can provide details.

Corryvreckan Viewpoint WALKING

A good walk is to a viewpoint for the Corryvreckan Whirlpool. From the northern end of the public road (allow five to six hours for the 16-mile return trip from here) hike past Barnhill to Kinuachdrachd Farm (6 miles). Just before the farm a footpath forks left and climbs before traversing rough and boggy ground, a natural grandstand for viewing the turbulent waters of the Gulf of Corryvreckan.

If you have timed it right (check tide times at the Jura Hotel), you will see the whirlpool as a writhing mass of white water.

Evans Walk WALKING

This is a stalkers' path leading 6 miles from the main road through a pass in the hills to a hunting lodge above the remote sandy beach at Glenbatrick Bay. The path leaves the road 4 miles north of Craighouse (just under a mile north of the bridge over the River Corran). Allow six hours for the 12-mile round trip.

The first 0.75 mile is hard going along an interwoven braid of faint, squelchy trails through lumpy bog; aim just left of the cairn on the near horizon. The path firms up and is easier to follow after you cross a stream. On the descent on the far side of the pass, look out for wild orchids and sundew, and keep an eye out for adders.

Paps of Jura WALKING

Climbing the Paps is a truly tough hill walk over ankle-breaking scree that requires good fitness and navigational skills (allow eight hours for the 11 hard miles). One starting place is by the bridge over the River Corran, 3 miles north of Craighouse. The first peak you reach is Beinn a'Chaolais (734m), the second is Beinn an Oir (784m) and the third is Beinn Shiantaidh (755m). Most also climb Corra Bheinn (569m), before joining Evans Walk to return.

If you succeed in bagging all four, you can reflect on the fact that the record for the annual Paps of Jura fell race is just three hours!

🛏 Sleeping & Eating

Places to stay are very limited, so book ahead – don't rely on just turning up. As well as the hotel, there's a handful of B&B options and several self-catering cottages that are let by the week (see www.juradevelopment.co.uk). One of these is Barnhill (☑ 01786-850274; www.escapetojura.com; per week from £600), where Orwell stayed at the far north of the island. It sleeps eight and is very remote: seven miles from the main road on a rough 4WD track, and 25 miles from the pub.

You can camp (£5 per person) in the field below the Jura Hotel; there's a new toilet and shower (small charge) block that walkers, yachties and cyclists can also use. From July to February, check on the deer-stalking situation before wild camping.

Jura Hotel HOTEL ££

(☑ 01496-820243; www.jurahotel.co.uk; Craighouse; s £50-60, d £94-120; 🅿 �{}) The heart of Jura's community is this hotel, which is warmly welcoming and efficiently run. Rooms vary in size and shape, but all are renovated and feel inviting. The premier rooms – all of which have sea view – are just lovely, with understated elegance and polished modern bathrooms. You can eat (mains £9 to £14; noon to 2.30pm and 6.30pm to 8.30pm) in the elegant restaurant or the convivial pub.

Antlers CAFE ££

(☑ 01496-820496; www.juradevelopment.co.uk; Craighouse; light meals £4-7; ⊙ 10am-5pm Mar-Oct, plus 6.30-8.30pm Fri) 🍴 This community-owned cafe has a craft shop and displays on Jura heritage. It does tasty home baking, sandwiches and the like, and is also open for more elaborate dinners on Fridays. Not licensed – £3 corkage.

ℹ Getting There & Around

A car ferry shuttles between Port Askaig on Islay and Feolin on Jura (passenger/car/bicycle £1.60/8.55/free, five minutes, hourly Monday to Saturday, every two hours Sunday). There is no direct car-ferry connection to the mainland.

From April to September, **Jura Passenger Ferry** (☑ 07768-450000; www.jurapassengerferry. com; one-way £20; ⊙ mid-Apr–Sep) runs from Tayvallich on the mainland to Craighouse on Jura (one hour, one or two daily except Wednesday). Booking recommended.

The island's only **bus service** (☑ 01436-810200; www.garelochheadcoaches.co.uk) runs between the ferry slip at Feolin and Craighouse (20 minutes, three or four a day), timed to coincide with ferry arrivals and departures. One or two of the runs continue north as far as Inverlussa.

THE SCOTTISH MAELSTROM

The Gulf of Corryvreckan – the 1km-wide channel between the northern end of Jura and the island of Scarba – is home to one of the most notorious tidal whirlpools in the world.

On Scotland's west coast, the rising tide – the flood tide – flows northwards. As it moves up the Sound of Jura, to the east of the island, it is forced into a narrowing bottleneck jammed with islands and builds up to a greater height than the open sea to the west of Jura. As a result, millions of tonnes of seawater pour westwards through the Gulf of Corryvreckan at speeds of up to 8 knots – an average sailing yacht is going fast at 6 knots.

The Corryvreckan Whirlpool forms where this mass of moving water hits an underwater pinnacle, which rises from the 200m-deep seabed to within just 28m of the surface, and swirls over and around it. The turbulent waters create a magnificent spectacle, with white-capped breakers, standing waves, bulging boils and overfalls, and countless miniature maelstroms whirling around the main vortex.

Corryvreckan is at its most violent when a flooding spring tide, flowing west through the gulf, meets a westerly gale blowing in from the Atlantic. In these conditions, standing waves up to 5m high can form and dangerously rough seas extend more than 3 miles west of Corryvreckan, a phenomenon known as the Great Race.

You can see the whirlpool by making the long hike to the Corryvreckan Viewpoint at the northern end of Jura or by taking a boat trip from Islay or the Isle of Seil.

For tide times, see www.whirlpool-scotland.co.uk.

Hire bikes from **Jura Bike Hire** (07768-450000; www.jurabikehire.com; per day £12.50) in Craighouse.

Isle of Colonsay

POP 100

Legend has it that when St Columba set out from Ireland in 563, his first landfall was Colonsay. But on climbing a hill he found he could still see the distant coast of his homeland, and pushed on north to Iona, leaving behind only his name (Colonsay means 'Columba's Isle').

Colonsay is a little jewel-box of varied delights, none exceptional but each exquisite – an ancient priory, a woodland garden, a golden beach – set amid a Highland landscape in miniature: rugged, rocky hills, cliffs and sandy strands, machair and birch woods, even a trout loch.

Sights & Activities

If tides are right, don't miss walking across the half-mile of cockleshell-strewn sand that links Colonsay to the smaller island of Oronsay. Here you can explore the 14th-century ruins of Oronsay Priory, one of Scotland's best-preserved medieval priories. There are two beautiful 15th-century stone crosses in the kirkyard, but the highlight is the collection of superb carved grave slabs in the Prior's House. The island is accessible on foot for about 1½ hours either side of low tide; there are tide tables at the ferry terminal and hotel.

The woodland garden (01951-200211; www.colonsayestate.co.uk; Kiloran; gardens dawn-dusk, walled garden 2-5pm Wed & noon-5pm Sat Easter-Sep) FREE at Colonsay House, 1.5 miles north of Scalasaig, is tucked in an unexpected fold of the landscape and is famous for its outstanding collection of hybrid rhododendrons and unusual trees. There's a cafe in the formal walled garden beside the house.

There are several good sandy beaches, but Kiloran Bay in the northwest, a scimitar-shaped strand of dark golden sand, is outstanding.

Back at Scalasaig, the Colonsay Brewery (01951-200190; www.colonsaybrewery.co.uk; Scalasaig; ring for hours) offers you the chance to have a look at how it produces its handcrafted ales – the Colonsay IPA is a grand pint.

You can hire bikes from Archie McConnell (01951-200355; www.colonsaycottage.co.uk; Colnatarun Cottage, Kilchattan; per day/week £7.50/35) – book in advance and he'll deliver to the aerodrome or ferry.

Sleeping & Eating

Accommodation is limited and should be booked before coming to the island. Wild camping is allowed. See www.colonsay.org.uk for self-catering listings.

Backpackers Lodge
HOSTEL £

(☑ 01951-200312; www.colonsayestate.co.uk; Kiloran; dm/tw £19.50/50) Set in a former gamekeeper's house, this lodge is a 30-minute walk from the ferry (you can arrange to be picked up). Rates include use of the tennis court at nearby Colonsay House.

★ Colonsay Hotel
HOTEL ££

(☑ 01951-200316; www.colonsayestate.co.uk; s/d from £70/100; P ☎) 🖋 This wonderfully laid-back hotel is set in an atmospheric old inn dating from 1750, a short walk uphill from the ferry pier. The stylish restaurant (mains £11 to £20) offers down-to-earth cooking using local produce as much as possible, from Colonsay oysters and lobsters to herbs and salad leaves from the Colonsay House gardens. The bar is a convivial melting pot of locals, guests, hikers, cyclists and yachties.

ℹ Information

The ferry pier is at Scalasaig, the main village, with shop but no ATM. General information is available at the ferry waiting room, and at www.colonsay.org.uk.

Tiny **Colonsay Bookshop** (☑ 01951-200320; Scalasaig; ☉ 3-5.30pm Mon-Sat, from noon Wed & Sat), in the same building as the microbrewery, has an excellent range of books on Hebridean history and culture.

ℹ Getting There & Around

AIR

Hebridean Air Services (☑ 0845 805-7465; www.hebrideanair.co.uk) operates flights from Oban Airport (at North Connel) to Colonsay and Islay twice daily Tuesday and Thursday.

BOAT

CalMac (www.calmac.co.uk) runs from Oban to Colonsay (passenger/car £7/35.50, 2¼ hours, six weekly summer, three in winter). From April to October, on Wednesday and Saturdays, the ferry from Kennacraig to Islay continues to Colonsay and on to Oban. A day trip from Islay allows you six to seven hours on the island; the return fare from Islay to Colonsay per passenger/car is £7.90/33.10. A local minibus offers hop-on/hop-off service for day trippers.

OBAN & MULL

Oban

POP 8600

Oban, main gateway to many of the Hebridean islands, is a peaceful waterfront town on a delightful bay, with sweeping views to Kerrera and Mull. OK, that first bit about peaceful is true only in winter; in summer the town centre is jammed with traffic and crowded with holidaymakers and travellers headed for the islands. But the setting is still lovely, and Oban's brilliant seafood restaurants are marvellous places to be as the sun sets over the bay.

◎ Sights

McCaig's Tower
HISTORIC BUILDING

(cnr Laurel & Duncraggan Rds; ☉ 24hr) Crowning the hill above town is this Colosseum-like Victorian folly, commissioned in 1890 by local worthy John Stuart McCaig, with the philanthropic intention of providing work for unemployed stonemasons. To reach it on foot, make the steep climb up Jacob's Ladder (a flight of stairs) from Argyll St; the bay views are worth the effort.

Oban Distillery
DISTILLERY

(☑ 01631-572004; www.discovering-distilleries.com; Stafford St; tours £7.50; ☉ noon-4.30pm Dec-Feb, 9.30am-5pm Mar-Jun & Oct-Nov, 9.30am-7.30pm Mon-Fri & 9.30am-5pm Sat & Sun Jul-Sep) This handsome distillery has been producing since 1794. The standard guided tour leaves regularly (worth booking) and includes a dram and a taste straight from the cask. Specialist tours (£35) run once daily in summer. Even without a tour, it's still worth a look at the small exhibition in the foyer.

Dunollie
CASTLE, MUSEUM

(☑ 01631-570550; www.dunollie.org; Dunollie Rd; adult/child £4/2; ☉ 10am-4pm Mon-Sat & 1-4pm Sun Easter-Oct) A pleasant 1-mile stroll along the coast road leads to Dunollie Castle, built by the MacDougalls of Lorn in the 13th century and unsuccessfully besieged for a year during the 1715 Jacobite rebellion. It's very much a ruin, but the nearby 1745 House – seat of Clan MacDougall – is an intriguing museum of local and clan history. Ongoing improvement works are in progress.

Pulpit Hill VIEWPOINT

An excellent viewpoint to the south of Oban Bay; the footpath to the summit starts by Maridon B&B on Dunuaran Rd.

🏃 Activities

A tourist-office leaflet lists various local bike rides, including a 16-mile route to the Isle of Seil. Hire bikes from **Oban Cycles** (☑ 01631-566033; www.obancycleshop.com; 87 George St; per day/week £15/70; ⊘ 10am-5pm Tue-Sat, plus Sun in summer), which also offers same-day repairs. Various operators offer boat trips to spot seals and other marine wildlife, departing from North Pier (adult/child £10/5).

Puffin Adventures DIVING

(☑ 01631-566088; www.puffin.org.uk; Port Gallanach) If you fancy exploring the underwater world, Puffin Adventures offers a 1½-hour package (£69) for complete beginners.

Sea Kayak Oban KAYAKING

(☑ 01631-565310; www.seakayakoban.com; Argyll St; ⊘ 10am-5pm Mon-Fri, 9am-5pm Sat, 10am-4pm Sun) Has a well-stocked shop, great route advice and sea-kayaking courses, including an all-inclusive two-day intro for beginners (£170 per person). Also full equipment rental for experienced paddlers – trolley your kayak from the shop to the ferry (kayaks carried free) to visit the islands.

👉 Tours

Basking Shark Scotland BOAT TRIP

(☑ 07975-723140; www.baskingsharkscotland. co.uk; ⊘ May-Sep) Runs entertaining boat trips with optional snorkelling, focussed on finding and observing basking sharks – the world's second-largest fish – and other notable marine species.

Coastal Connection BOAT TOURS

(☑ 01631-565833; www.coastal-connection.co.uk) Runs wildlife-spotting trips, fast day trips to Tobermory, and custom excursions to many west coast islands.

West Coast Tours COACH TOURS

(☑ 01631-566809; www.westcoasttours.co.uk; 1 Queens Park Pl; ⊘ Apr-Oct) Offers a Three Isles day trip (adult/child £60/30, 10 hours, daily) from Oban that visits Mull, Iona and Staffa. The crossing to Staffa is weather dependent. Without Staffa, the trip is £40/20 and takes eight hours. Also runs various trips on Mull.

🎊 Festivals & Events

Highlands and Islands Music & Dance Festival TRADITIONAL MUSIC

(www.obanfestival.org) At the beginning of May, this is an exuberant celebration of traditional Scottish music and dance. The town packs out.

West Highland Yachting Week SAILING

(www.whyw.co.uk) In late July/early August, Oban becomes the focus of one of Scotland's biggest yachting events. Hundreds of yachts cram into the harbour and the town's bars are jammed with thirsty sailors.

Argyllshire Gathering HIGHLAND GAMES

(www.obangames.com; adult/child £10/5) Held in late August, this is a key event in the Highland Games calendar and includes a prestigious pipe-band competition.

🛏 Sleeping

Despite having lots of B&B accommodation, Oban's beds can still fill up quickly in July and August, so try to book ahead. If you can't find a bed in Oban, consider Connel, 4 miles north.

Oban SYHA HOSTEL £

(☑ 01631-562025; www.syha.org.uk; Corran Esplanade; dm/tw £21/48; P @ ⑦) Set in a grand Victorian villa on the Esplanade, 0.75 miles north of the train station, this hostel is modernised to a high standard with comfy wooden bunks, lockers, good showers and a lounge with great views across Oban Bay. All dorms are en suite; the neighbouring lodge has three- and four-bedded rooms. Breakfast available

Oban Backpackers HOSTEL £

(☑ 01631-562107; www.obanbackpackers.com; Breadalbane St; dm £15-18; @ ⑦) Simple, colourful, relaxed and casual, this place has plenty of atmosphere. Dorms are cheap and cheerful – price varies according to the number of bunks – and there's a sociable downstairs lounge. Breakfast available for £2. Don't confuse with similarly named (also decent) Backpackers Plus situated across the road.

Jeremy Inglis Hostel HOSTEL £

(☑ 01631-565065; www.jeremyinglishostel.co.uk; 21 Airds Cres; dm/s £17/25; ⑦ ⑧) More eccentric B&B than a hostel – most 'dorms' have only two or three beds, and might come decorated with colourful duvets, original artwork, books, fresh flowers and more. It's

SOUTHERN HIGHLANDS & ISLANDS OBAN

Oban

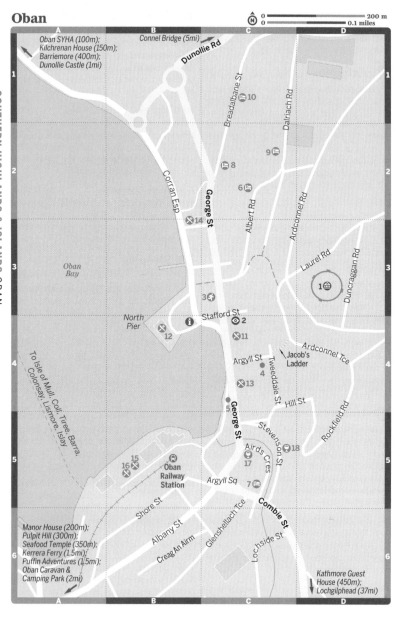

Oban SYHA (100m);
Kilchrenan House (150m);
Barriemore (400m);
Dunollie Castle (1mi)

Connel Bridge (5mi)

Dunollie Rd

Breadalbane St

Dalriach Rd

Corran Esp

George St

Albert Rd

Ardconnel Rd

Oban
Bay

Laurel Rd

Duncraggan Rd

North
Pier

Stafford St

Argyll St

Jacob's
Ladder

Ardconnel Tce

Tweeddale St

Hill St

Rockfield Rd

George St

Stevenson St

To Isle of Mull, Coll, Tiree, Barra,
Colonsay, Lismore, Islay

Airds Cres

Oban
Railway
Station

Argyll Sq

Combie St

Glenshellach Tce

Shore St

Albany St

Creag An Airm

Lochside St

Manor House (200m);
Pulpit Hill (300m);
Seafood Temple (350m);
Kerrera Ferry (1.5mi);
Puffin Adventures (1.5mi);
Oban Caravan &
Camping Park (2mi)

Kathmore Guest
House (450m);
Lochgilphead (37mi)

grungy, friendly, decent value and there's a good kitchen/eating area. It won't be for everyone but the spirit of hospitality thrives here. Breakfast is included and features homemade jams. Wi-fi doesn't reach the rooms.

Oban Caravan & Camping Park

CAMPSITE £

(☑ 01631-562425; www.obancaravanpark.com; Gallanachmore Farm; tent/campervan sites £15/20; ⊙ Apr-Oct; 🐾) This spacious campsite has a superb location overlooking the Sound of

Oban

Kerrera, 2.5 miles south of Oban (two buses on schooldays). A one-person tent with no car is £8. No prebooking – it's first come, first served. There are also bungalows and camping pods that sleep up to four (for two/four £40/50).

★ **Old Manse Guest House** B&B ££
(☑01631-564886; www.obanguesthouse.co.uk; Dalriach Rd; s/d £65/90; P☎) Set on the hillside above town, this B&B commands magnificent views over to Kerrera and Mull. It's run with genuine enthusiasm, and the owners are constantly adding thoughtful new features to the bright, cheerful rooms – think binoculars, DVDs, poetry, corkscrews and tartan hot-water bottles – and breakfast menus, with special diets catered for.

Barriemore GUESTHOUSE ££
(☑01631-566356; www.barriemore-hotel.co.uk; Corran Esplanade; s from £70, d £99-119; ☺Mar-Nov; P☎) With a grand location overlooking the entrance to Oban Bay, this place offers top-notch hospitality with tartan carpets on the stairs and plump Loch Fyne kippers on the breakfast menu. Rooms are all spacious, recently refurbished and full of features. The front ones – pricier but enormous – have fabulous vistas; there's also a great family suite up the back and solicitous service.

Sandvilla Guesthouse B&B ££
(☑01631-564483; www.holidayoban.co.uk; Breadalbane St; s/d £50/70; P☎) Upbeat and modern, the rooms in this welcoming spot – all en suite by the time you read this – are lovely, bright and very well-kept. Enthusiastic owners guarantee a personal welcome and service with a smile. It's our favourite of several options on this street.

Kilchrenan House B&B ££
(☑01631-562663; www.kilchrenanhouse.co.uk; Corran Esplanade; s £50, d £70-110; P☎) You'll get a warm welcome at the Kilchrenan, an elegant Victorian villa built for a textile magnate in 1883. Most of the rooms have views across Oban Bay, but rooms 5 and 9 are the best: room 5 has a huge free-standing bath tub, perfect for soaking weary bones.

Heatherfield House B&B ££
(☑01631-562806; www.heatherfieldhouse.co.uk; Albert Rd; s £50, d £80-115; P☎) Welcoming Heatherfield House occupies a converted 1870s rectory set in extensive grounds and has six spacious rooms. One comes complete with fireplace, sofa and a view over the garden to the harbour.

Kathmore Guest House B&B ££
(☑01631-562104; www.kathmore.co.uk; Soroba Rd; s £35-50, d £60-75; P☎) Warmly welcoming, this B&B combines traditional Highland hospitality and hearty breakfasts with a wee touch of boutique flair in its stylish bedspreads and colourful artwork. It's actually two adjacent houses combined; each has a comfortable lounge and shares an outdoor garden deck where you can enjoy a glass of wine on those long summer evenings. It's a 10-minute stroll from the centre.

Manor House HOTEL £££
(☑01631-562087; www.manorhouseoban.com; Gallanach Rd; r £170-235; P☎) Built in 1780 for the Duke of Argyll, the old-fashioned Manor House is now one of Oban's finest hotels. It has small but elegant Georgian-style rooms – some with sea views – a posh bar frequented by local and visiting yachties, and a fine restaurant serving Scottish and

French cuisine. Children under 12 years are not welcome.

Eating

Oban Seafood Hut
SEAFOOD **£**

(www.obanseafoodhut.co.uk; Railway Pier; mains £3-13; ⊙10am-6pm Mar-Oct) If you want to savour superb Scottish seafood without the expense of an upmarket restaurant, head for Oban's famous seafood stall – it's the green shack on the quayside near the ferry terminal. Here you can buy fresh and cooked seafood to take away – excellent prawn sandwiches (£2.95), dressed crab (£4.95), and fresh oysters (95p each).

Kitchen Garden
DELI, CAFE **£**

(☏01631-566332; www.kitchengardenoban.co.uk; 14 George St; light meals £4-8; ⊙9am-5.30pm Mon-Sat, 10am-4.30pm Sun) A deli packed with delicious picnic food. Also has a great little cafe – good coffee, scones, cakes, homemade soups and sandwiches.

Oban Chocolate Company
SWEETS, CAFE **£**

(☏01631-566099; www.obanchocolate.co.uk; 34 Corran Esplanade; hot chocolate £3; ⊙10am-5pm Mon-Sat, 11am-5pm Sun Easter-Sep, shorter hours in winter, closed Jan; 📶) Specialises in hand-crafted chocolates (you can watch them being made) and also has a cafe serving excellent coffee and hot chocolate (try the chilli chocolate for a kick in the tastebuds), with big leather sofas in a window with a view of the bay. Open to 9pm Thursday to Saturday in July and August.

Waterfront Fishouse Restaurant
SEAFOOD **££**

(☏01631-563110; www.waterfrontoban.co.uk; Railway Pier; mains £12-20; ⊙noon-2.15pm & 5.30-9.30pm Sun-Fri, noon-9.30pm Sat; 📶📶) Housed on the top floor of a converted seamen's mission, the Waterfront's stylish, unfussy decor in burgundy and brown, with dark wooden furniture, does little to distract from the superb seafood freshly landed at the quay just a few metres away. The menu ranges from classic haddock and chips to fresh oysters, scallops and langoustines. Best to book for dinner.

Cuan Mór
BISTRO **££**

(☏01631-565078; www.cuanmor.co.uk; 60 George St; mains £9-14; ⊙10am-10pm; 📶📶) This always-busy bar and bistro brews its own beer, and sports a no-nonsense menu of old favourites – from haddock and chips or homemade lasagne to sausage and mash

with onion gravy – spiced with a few more sophisticated plates such as squat lobster carbonara, and a decent range of vegetarian dishes. And the sticky toffee pudding is not to be missed!

★ Seafood Temple
SEAFOOD **£££**

(☏01631-566000; www.obanseafood.com; Gallanach Rd; mains £16-25; ⊙6.15-8.30pm Apr-Sep, 6.15-8.30pm Wed-Sat Oct-Dec & Feb-Mar) 🌿 Locally sourced seafood is the god that's worshipped at this tiny temple, a former park pavilion with glorious views over the bay. Oban's smallest restaurant serves up whole lobster cooked to order, baked crab, plump langoustines and a seafood platter (£75 for two) which offers a taste of everything. Dinner is in two sittings, at 6.15pm and 8.30pm; bookings essential.

Ee-usk
SEAFOOD **£££**

(☏01631-565666; www.eeusk.com; North Pier; mains £12-24; ⊙noon-3pm & 5.45-9.30pm; 📶) 🌿 Bright and modern Ee'usk (it's how you pronounce *iasg*, Gaelic for 'fish') occupies a prime pier location. Floor-to-ceiling windows allow diners on two levels to enjoy sweeping views while sampling locally caught seafood ranging from fragrant fish cakes to langoustines and succulent fresh fish. A bevy of serving staff make it swift and efficient, and they make an effort to give you the best view available.

It's a little pricey, perhaps, but both food and location are first class. Closes 9pm in winter.

🍷 Drinking & Nightlife

Lorne Bar
PUB

(www.thelornebar.co.uk; Stevenson St; ⊙noon-11pm Mon-Wed, noon-2am Thu-Sun; 📶) A traditional pub with a lovely old island bar, polished brass fittings, stained glass and a beer garden, the Lorne serves local real ales, as well as above-average pub grub. You'll like it better before the disco lights come up on Friday and Saturday nights.

Aulay's Bar
PUB

(☏01631-562596; www.aulaysbar.com; 8 Airds Cres; ⊙11.30am-11pm) An authentic Scottish pub, Aulay's is cosy and low-ceilinged, its walls covered with old photographs of Oban ferries and other ships. It pulls in a mixed crowd of locals and visitors with its warm atmosphere and wide range of malt whiskies.

ℹ Information

Lorn & Islands District General Hospital
(☑01631-567500; Glengallan Rd) Southern end
of town.

Oban Library (www.argyll-bute.co.uk; 77
Albany St; ☉10am-1pm & 2-7pm Mon & Wed, to
6pm Thu, to 5pm Fri, 10am-1pm Sat; 🛜) Free
internet.

Oban Tourist Office (☑01631-563122; www.
oban.org.uk; 3 North Pier; ☉10am-5pm daily,
extended weekday hours Apr-Oct) Helpful; on
the waterfront.

ℹ Getting There & Away

Bus, train and ferry terminals are grouped
conveniently together on the southern edge of
the bay.

AIR

Hebridean Air (☑0845 805 7465; www.hebri-
deanair.co.uk) flies from Connel airfield to the
islands of Coll, Tiree, Colonsay and Islay.

BOAT

CalMac (☑0800 066 5000; www.calmac.co.uk)
ferries link Oban with the islands of Mull, Coll,
Tiree, Lismore, Colonsay, Barra and South Uist.
See each island section for details. Ferries to the
Isle of Kerrera depart from a separate jetty, 2
miles southwest of Oban town centre.

BUS

Scottish Citylink (www.citylink.co.uk) operates
most intercity coaches, while **West Coast Motors** (www.westcoastmotors.co.uk) runs local
and regional services.

Fort William (via Appin and Ballachulish)
£9.40, 1½ hours, two Monday to Saturday

Glasgow (via Inveraray and Arrochar) £23.10,
3¼ hours, three daily

TRAIN

Oban is at the terminus of a scenic route that
branches off the West Highland line at Crianlarich. The train isn't much use for travelling
north – to reach Fort William requires a long
detour (3¾ hours). Take the bus instead.

Glasgow £22, three hours, three daily

Tyndrum/Crianlarich £10.70, one hour, three
daily

ℹ Getting Around

Hazelbank Motors (☑01631-566476; www.
obancarhire.co.uk; Lynn Rd; per day/week from
£40/225; ☉8.30am-5pm Mon-Sat) hires cars.

Around Oban

Isle of Kerrera

POP 50

Some of the area's best walking is on Kerrera, which faces Oban across the bay.
There's a 6-mile circuit (allow three hours),
which follows tracks or paths and offers the
chance to spot wildlife such as Soay sheep,
wild goats, otters, golden eagles, peregrine
falcons, seals and porpoises. At the island's
southern end, there's a ruined castle.

Kerrera Bunkhouse (☑01631-566367;
www.kerrerabunkhouse.co.uk; Lower Gylen; dm £15;
☉Easter-Sep) is a charming seven-bed bothy
in a converted 18th-century stable a 2-mile
walk south from the ferry. Booking ahead
is recommended. You can get snacks and
light meals at the neighbouring **Tea Garden**
(☑01631-570223; www.kerrerabunkhouse.co.uk;
Lower Gylen; light meals £3-9; ☉10.30am-4.30pm
Easter-Sep).

There's a daily **passenger ferry** (☑01631-
563665; www.kerrera-ferry.co.uk; ☉half-hourly
10.30am-12.30pm & 2-6pm Easter-Oct, plus 8.45am
Mon-Sat, 6-7 daily Nov-Easter) from Gallanach,
2 miles southwest of Oban town centre
(adult/child return £4.50/2, bicycle free, 10
minutes). You need to slide a signboard to
summon the ferry.

Isle of Seil

POP 600

The small island of Seil, 10 miles southwest
of Oban, is best known for its connection to
the mainland – the graceful **Bridge over the
Atlantic**, designed by Thomas Telford and
opened in 1793.

⊙ Sights

On the west coast is the pretty conservation
village of **Ellenabeich**, with whitewashed
cottages and rainwater barrels backed by a
wee harbour and rocky cliffs. It was built to
house local slate workers, but the industry
collapsed in 1881 when the sea broke into
the main quarry – the flooded pit can still
be seen. The **Scottish Slate Islands Heritage Trust** (☑01852-300449; www.slateislands.
org.uk; Ellenabeich; ☉10.30am-4.30pm Apr-Oct)
FREE displays fascinating old photographs
illustrating life in the village.

Coach tours flock to Highland Arts (☑01852-300273; www.highlandarts.co.uk; Ellenabeich; admission free; ◷9am-7pm Apr-Sep, 9am-5pm Oct-Mar), a gift shop and a shrine to the eccentric output of the late 'poet, artist and composer' C John Taylor. Please, try to keep a straight face.

Just offshore is small Easdale Island, which has more old slate-workers' cottages and an interesting folk museum (☑01852-300370; www.easdalemuseum.org; adult/child £2.50/50p; ◷11am-4.30pm Apr–mid-Oct, to 5pm Jul & Aug) with displays about the slate industry and social history. Climb to the top of the island (a 38m peak) for great views of the surrounding area. Confusingly, Ellenabeich is also referred to as Easdale, so 'Easdale Harbour', for example, is on the Seil side.

Anyone who fancies their hand at ducks and drakes should attend the World Stone-Skimming Championships (www.stoneskimming.com), held each year in an old quarry on the last Sunday in September.

A ferry hop from Seil's southern end takes you to neighbouring Isle of Luing, a quiet backwater with no real sights but appealing for wildlife walks and easygoing bike rides.

🏃 Activities

Sea Kayak Scotland
KAYAKING
(☑01852-300770; www.seakayakscotland.com; courses per person £80) Hire, instruction and guided sea kayaking trips run by an experienced operator.

👉 Tours

Sea.fari Adventures
BOAT TOURS
(☑01852-300003; www.seafari.co.uk; Ellenabeich; ◷Apr-Oct) Runs a series of exciting boat trips in high-speed rigid inflatables to Corryvreckan whirlpool (adult/child £38/29; call for dates of 'Whirlpool Specials', when the tide is at its strongest), as well as three-hour summer whale-watching trips (£48/36). There are also cruises to Iona and Staffa (£75/55), a weekly day trip to Colonsay (£48/36), plus trips to the remote Garvellach Islands (£48/36). Minimum of six out of season.

Sealife Adventures
BOAT TOURS
(☑01631-571010; www.sealife-adventures.com; 3-/4-/5-hour trip £49/58/65) Exciting boat trips, based on the eastern side of the island near the bridge. It has a large, comfortable boat offering wildlife cruises with knowledgeable guides and trips to the Corryvreckan whirlpool.

🍴 Eating

Oyster Bar
PUB
(www.seilislandpub.co.uk; Ellenabeich; half-dozen oysters £8; ◷food noon-2.15pm & 6-8pm, closed Mon evening; 🐾) This cute pub has a snug interior and a great back deck overlooking the water. With Fyne ales on tap and local oysters and other seafood, it's a great venue for a meal or drink.

ℹ️ Getting There & Around

West Coast Motors (www.westcoastmotors.co.uk) Bus 418 runs four times a day, except Sunday, from Oban to Ellenabeich (£3, 45 minutes) and on to North Cuan (£3, 53 minutes) for the ferry to Luing.

Easdale Ferry (☑01631-562125; http://seil.oban.ws/) Daily passenger-only ferry service from Ellenabeich to Easdale Island (£1.80 return, bicycles free, five minutes, every 30 minutes).

Luing Ferry (http://seil.oban.ws/; ◷return per person/car £1.80/7.20) Departs every 30 minutes for the three-minute trip.

Isle of Mull

POP 2800

From the rugged ridges of Ben More and the black basalt crags of Burg to the blinding white sand, rose-pink granite and emerald waters that fringe the Ross, Mull can lay claim to some of the finest and most varied scenery in the Inner Hebrides. Noble birds of prey soar over mountain and coast, while the western waters provide good whale-watching. Add a lovely waterfront 'capital', an impressive castle, the sacred island of Iona and easy access from Oban, and you can see why it's sometimes impossible to find a spare bed on the island.

👉 Tours

Mull's varied landscapes and habitats offer the chance to spot some of Scotland's rarest and most dramatic wildlife, including sea eagles, golden eagles, otters, dolphins and whales. Numerous operators offer walking or road trips to see them.

Staffa Tours
BOAT TOURS
(☑07831-885985; www.staffatours.com) Runs boat trips from Fionnphort to Staffa (adult/child £30/15, 2½ hours, daily April to October), or Staffa plus the Treshnish Isles (£55/27.50, five hours, Sunday to Friday May to July). It has options ex-Oban.

Mull, Coll & Tiree

Ⓝ 0 ——— 20 km
0 ——— 10 miles

Sea of the
Hebrides

Ardnamurchan • Achosnich   Acharacle•
Point   • Kilchoan   Saleno

Hogh Bay   • Sorisdale
        Coll   Glengorm   Oronsay   Loch
Totamore•   • Arinagour   Castle 🏰   Sunart
RSPB Reserve ◉   **Tobermory** •
                        • Bonnavoulin   A884
Crossapol• 🏰 Breachacha   Calgary•   • Dervaig
            Castles
Tiree   ⚲ •Caolas   Loch
                        Frisa
Sandaig   Gott•   Treshnish   Loch Ballygown   Sound of
        Bay •Scarinish   Isles   Tuath •   Mull   •Lochaline
Crossapoll   • Gruline •Salen •Fishnish
•Hynish   Gometra   Ulva Loch •Killiechronan
                        Ferry na Keal   Craignure•
                Staffa Little B8035   Duart 🏰
                    Colonsay ▲ Mull A849   Castle
                Iona Balmeanach Ben More
ATLANTIC   (966m)   Ben Buie
OCEAN   Baile Mor•   Burg• •Tiroran   ▲ (717m)
            Fionnphort   Loch Scridain Loch •Lochbuie
                Ross of Mull Bule
                •Bunessan   Carsaig Firth of
            •Uisken   Carsaig   ◎   Lorn
                    Arches   Luing

Turus Mara   BOAT TOURS

(☑ 08000 858786; www.turusmara.com) Offers trips from Ulva Ferry in central Mull to Staffa and the Treshnish Isles (adult/child £57.50/29, 6½ hours), with an hour ashore on Staffa and two hours on Lunga, where you can see seals, puffins, kittiwakes, razorbills and many other species of seabird. It will do pick-ups from the Craignure ferry terminal.

Sea Life Surveys   WILDLIFE WATCHING

(☑ 01688-302916; www.sealifesurveys.com; Ledaig) Whale-watching trips head from Tobermory harbour to the waters north and west of Mull. An all-day whale-watch gives up to seven hours at sea (£80), and has a 95% success rate for sightings. The four-hour Wildlife Adventure cruise (adult/child £50/40) is better for young kids. Shorter seal-spotting excursions are also available.

Mull Wildlife Expeditions   WILDLIFE WATCHING

(☑ 01688-500121; www.scotlandwildlife.com; Ulva Ferry) Full-day Land Rover tours of the island with the chance of spotting red deer, golden eagles, peregrine falcons, white-tailed sea eagles, hen harriers, otters and perhaps dolphins and porpoises. Cost includes pick-up from accommodation or ferry, picnic lunch

and binoculars. Possible as a day trip from Oban.

Mull Magic   WALKING TOURS

(☑ 01688-301213; www.mullmagic.com) Offers guided walking tours in the Mull countryside to spot eagles, otters, butterflies and other wildlife, as well as customised tours. Check the website for the different itineraries available.

West Coast Tours   BUS TOURS

(☑ 01631-566809;   www.westcoasttours.co.uk; tours £40-60) Various bus-and-boat day trips from Oban to Mull, with options that include Iona and Staffa.

🎆 Festivals & Events

Mull Music Festival   MUSIC

(www.mishnish.co.uk) Last weekend of April; four days of foot-stomping traditional Scottish and Irish folk music at Tobermory's pubs.

Mendelssohn on Mull   MUSIC

(www.mendelssohnonmull.com)   A   week-long festival of classical music in early July.

Mull Rally   MOTORSPORT

(www.mullrally.org) Part of the Scottish Rally Championship, with around 150 cars involved. Public roads are closed for parts of the early-October weekend.

ℹ Information

There's a bank with ATM in Tobermory, otherwise you can get cashback with a purchase from Co-op food stores.

Craignure Tourist Office (☑ 01680-812377; ◷ 8.30am-5pm Mon-Sat, 10am-5pm Sun, to 7pm Jul & Aug) Opposite the ferry slip.

Explore Mull (☑ 01688-302875; www.explore-mull.com; Ledaig, Tobermory; ◷ 9am-5pm Easter-Oct, to 7pm Jul-Aug; 🛜) In Tobermory car park. Local information, books all manner of island tours, hires bikes and has internet access.

ℹ Getting There & Away

Three **CalMac** (www.calmac.co.uk) car ferries link Mull with the mainland.

Lochaline to Fishnish (£3.30/14.45, 15 minutes, at least hourly) On the east coast of Mull.

Oban to Craignure (passenger/car £5.55/49.50, 40 minutes, every two hours) The busiest route – booking advised for cars.

Tobermory to Kilchoan (£5.30/27.50, 35 minutes, seven daily Monday to Saturday, plus five Sunday May to August) Links to the Ardnamurchan peninsula.

ℹ Getting Around

BICYCLE

You can hire bikes for around £15 per day from various places around the island, including Explore Mull in Tobermory.

BUS

West Coast Motors (☑ 01631-566809; www.westcoastmotors.co.uk) connects ferry ports and main villages. Its Discovery Day Pass (adult/child £15/7.50) is available from April to October and grants a day's unlimited bus travel.

Craignure to Fionnphort (£9/14 single/return, 1¼ hours, three to four Monday to Saturday, one Sunday)

Craignure to Tobermory (single/return £7/10, one hour, four to seven daily)

Tobermory to Dervaig and Calgary (£3/5.10 single/return, two to four Monday to Saturday)

CAR

Almost all of Mull's road network consists of single-track roads. There are petrol stations at Craignure, Fionnphort, Salen and Tobermory. **Mull Self Drive** (☑ 01680-300402; www.mullselfdrive.co.uk) rents small cars for £45/237 per day/week.

Craignure & Around

There's not much to see at Craignure, but three miles south is **Duart Castle** (☑ 01680-812309; www.duartcastle.com; adult/child £5.75/2.85; ◷ 10.30am-5pm daily May–mid-Oct, 11am-4pm Sun-Thu Apr), the ancestral seat of the Maclean clan, enjoying a spectacular position on a rocky outcrop overlooking the Sound of Mull. Originally built in the 13th century, it was abandoned for 160 years before a 1912 restoration. As well as the dungeons, courtyard and battlements with memorable views, there's a lot of clan history – pantomime boos go to Lachlan Cattanach, who took his wife on an outing to an island in the strait, then left her there to drown when the tide came in. A bus to the castle meets the Oban ferry but it's a pretty walk too.

🛏 Sleeping

There's a handful of places to stay within 10 minutes' walk of the ferry.

Shieling Holidays CAMPSITE £ (☑ 01680-812496; www.shielingholidays.co.uk; Craignure; tent sites & 2 people £18, dm/d/d with en suite £13.50/33/49.50, cottages from £66; ◷ mid-Mar–Oct; 🅿🛜🐾) Walking distance from the Oban ferry is this well-equipped campsite with great views. Most of the permanent accommodation, including the hostel dorms and toilet block (dribbly showers), consists of 'cottage tents' made from heavy-duty tarpaulin, which gives the place a bit of a PVC-fetish feel.

Tobermory

POP 1000

Mull's main town is a picturesque little fishing and yachting port with brightly painted houses arranged around a sheltered harbour. The children's TV program *Balamory* was set here, and while the series stopped filming in 2004, regular repeats mean that the town still swarms in summer with toddlers (and nostalgic teenagers) towing parents around (you can get a *Balamory* info sheet from tourist offices).

◎ Sights & Activities

Whale-watching boat trips run out of Tobermory harbour.

WALKING ON MULL

More information on the following walks can be obtained from the tourist offices in Oban, Craignure and Tobermory.

Ben More

Mull's highest peak, and the only island Munro outside Skye, Ben More (966m) offers spectacular views of surrounding islands. A trail leads up the mountain from Loch na Keal, by the bridge on the B8035 eight miles southwest of Salen – see Ordnance Survey (OS) 1:50,000 map sheet 49. Return the same way or continue down the narrow ridge to the eastern top, A'Chioch, then descend to the road via Gleann na Beinn Fhada. The glen can be wet and there's not much of a path. The return trip is 6.5 miles; allow five hours.

Carsaig Arches

One of the most adventurous walks is along the coast west of Carsaig Bay to the natural rock formation of Carsaig Arches at Malcolm's Point. There's a good path below the cliffs most of the way, but near the arches the route climbs and then traverses a very steep slope above a vertical drop into the sea (not for the unfit or faint-hearted). You'll see spectacular rock formations on the way, culminating in the arches themselves: the 'keyhole', a freestanding rock stack, and the 'tunnel', a huge natural arch. The western entrance is hung with curtains of columnar basalt – an impressive place. The return trip is 8 miles – allow three to four hours' walking time plus at least an hour at the arches.

Hebridean Whale & Dolphin Trust WILDLIFE EXHIBITION
(☑ 01688-302620; www.whaledolphintrust.co.uk; 28 Main St; ☉ 10am-5pm Mon-Fri, 11am-4pm Sun Apr-Oct, 11am-5pm Mon-Fri Nov-Mar) ✔FREE
This place has displays, videos and interactive exhibits on whale and dolphin biology and ecology, and is a great place for kids to learn about sea mammals. It also provides information about volunteering and reporting sightings of whales and dolphins. Opening is rather variable.

Mull Museum MUSEUM
(☑ 01688-302603; www.mullmuseum.org.uk; Main St; admission by donation; ☉ 10am-4pm Mon-Fri plus most Sat Easter-Oct) Places to go on a rainy day include Mull Museum, which records the history of the island. There are interesting exhibits on crofting, and on the *Tobermory Galleon*, a ship from the Spanish Armada that sank in Tobermory Bay in 1588 and has been the object of treasure seekers ever since.

Marine Visitor Centre MUSEUM
(www.tobermorymarinevisitorcentre.com; Ledaig; admission by donation; ☉ 9am-5pm Easter-Oct) By the harbour car park, this museum has good information on the local marine environment, and little touch pools with crabs and the like for the kids.

An Tobar Arts Centre GALLERY
(☑ 01688-302211; www.antobar.co.uk; Argyll Tce; ☉ 10am-5pm Mon-Sat May-Sep, 10am-4pm Tue-Sat Mar-Apr & Oct-Dec) FREE An art gallery and exhibition space in a former primary school with a good vegetarian-friendly cafe and top water views.

Tobermory Distillery DISTILLERY
(☑ 01688-302647; www.tobermorymalt.com; Ledaig; tours £6; ☉ 10am-5pm) This bijou distillery was established in 1798. It doesn't always open winter weekends; phone to check or book. There are two lines here, the standard Tobermory and the lightly peated Ledaig.

🛏 Sleeping

Tobermory has dozens of B&Bs, but the place can still be booked solid any time from May through to August, especially at weekends.

Tobermory SYHA HOSTEL £
(☑ 01688-302481; www.syha.org.uk; Main St; dm/q £19/84; ☉ Mar-Oct; @ 🛜) Great location in a Victorian house right on the waterfront, with dorms and good triples and quads for families. Was up for sale at time of writing so its future is uncertain but hopefully will remain a hostel.

Tobermory Campsite
CAMPSITE **£**

(☎01688-302624; www.tobermory-campsite. co.uk; Newdale, Dervaig Rd; tent sites per adult/ child £7.50/3; ☻Mar-Oct; P ✿) ✐ A quiet, family-friendly campsite 1 mile west of town on the road to Dervaig. It also has a self-catering house and static caravans available. Credit/debit cards not accepted.

Cuidhe Leathain
B&B **££**

(☎01688-302504; www.cuidhe-leathain.co.uk; Breadalbane St; r £85; 🛜) A handsome 19th-century house in the upper town, Cuidhe Leathain (coo-lane), which means Maclean's Corner, exudes a cosily cluttered Victorian atmosphere. The rooms are beautifully plush, with plunger coffee and decent teas, breakfasts will set you up for the rest of the day, and the owners are a fount of knowledge about Mull and its wildlife. Minimum two-night stay.

Harbour View
B&B **££**

(☎01688-301111; www.tobermorybandb.com; 1 Argyll Tce; s £65, d £80-90; 🛜) This beautifully renovated fishering cottage is perched on the edge of Tobermory's 'upper town'. Exposed patches of original stone walls add a touch of character, while a new extension provides the family suite (two adjoining rooms with shared bathroom, sleeps four) with an outdoor terrace that enjoys breathtaking views across the harbour.

Sonas House
B&B **££**

(☎01688-302304; www.sonashouse.co.uk; The Fairways, Erray Rd; s/d £110/125, apt from £90; P 🛜✿) Here's a first – a B&B with a heated, indoor 10m swimming pool! Sonas is a large, modern house – follow signs to the golf course – offering luxury B&B in a beautiful setting with superb views over Tobermory Bay; ask for the 'Blue Poppy' bedroom, which has its own balcony. There's also a self-contained studio apartment with double bed.

Harbour Guesthouse
B&B **££**

(☎01688-302209; www.harbourguesthouse-tobermory.com; 59 Main St; s/d £37.50/78; ☻Mar-Nov; 🛜) On the harbourfront, this B&B is friendly and offers rooms that vary in size and shape. The ones with water view are small, those without the vistas larger. It's got more rooms than most so can be a good option when things are booked; also, there aren't too many single beds around Tobermory, but there are a couple of compact ones here.

★ Highland Cottage
HOTEL **£££**

(☎01688-302030; www.highlandcottage.co.uk; Breadalbane St; d £150-165; ☻Apr–mid-Oct; P 🛜✿) Antique furniture, four-poster beds, embroidered bedspreads, fresh flowers and candlelight lend this small hotel (only six rooms) an appealingly old-fashioned cottage atmosphere, but with all mod cons including cable TV, full-size baths and room service. There's also an excellent restaurant here (dinner £39.50), and the personable owners are experts in guest comfort.

✗ Eating & Drinking

Fish & Chip Van
FISH & CHIPS **£**

(☎01688-301109; www.tobermoryfishandchipvan. co.uk; Main St; mains £6-9; ☻12.30-9pm Mon-Sat Apr-Dec, plus Sun Jun-Sep, 12.30-7pm Mon-Sat Jan-Mar) If it's a takeaway you're after, you can tuck into some of Scotland's best gourmet fish and chips down on the waterfront. And where else will you find a chip van selling freshly cooked scallops?

Pier Café
CAFE **£**

(The Pier; light meals £6-9; ☻10am-5pm, to 9pm Fri & Sat) A cosy wee corner with local art on the walls, tucked beneath Café Fish at the north end of the village, the Pier serves great coffee and breakfast rolls, plus tasty lunches such as haddock and chips, pasta and sandwiches.

★ Café Fish
SEAFOOD **££**

(☎01688-301253; www.thecafefish.com; The Pier; mains £13-24; ☻11am-3pm & 5.30-9.30pm mid-Mar–Oct) Seafood doesn't come much fresher than the stuff served at this warm and welcoming little restaurant overlooking Tobermory harbour – as its motto says, 'The only thing frozen here is the fisherman'! Langoustines and squat lobsters go straight from boat to kitchen to join rich Tuscan-style seafood stew, fat scallops, fish pie and catch-of-the-day on the daily-changing menu, where confident use of Asian ingredients adds an extra dimension.

Mishnish Hotel
PUB **££**

(☎01688-302009; www.mishnish.co.uk; Main St; mains £13-18; ☻food noon-2pm & 6-9pm; 🛜) 'The Mish' is a favourite hang-out for visiting yachties and a good place for a pint, or a meal at the restaurant. Wood-panelled and flag-draped, this is a good old traditional pub where you can listen to live folk music, toast your toes by the open fire or challenge the locals to a game of pool.

North Mull

The road from Tobermory west to Calgary cuts inland, leaving most of Mull's north coast wild and inaccessible. It continues through the settlement of Dervaig to the beach at Calgary. From here onwards you are treated to spectacular coastal views; it's worth doing the route in reverse from Grunart for the best vistas.

Sights

Glengorm Castle GALLERY, PARK
(01688-302321; www.glengormcastle.co.uk; Glengorm; 10am-5pm May-Aug) FREE A long, single-track road leads north for 4 miles from Tobermory to majestic Glengorm Castle, with views across the sea to Ardnamurchan, Rum and the Outer Hebrides. The castle outbuildings house an **art gallery** featuring local artists, a **farm shop**, and an excellent cafe (p92). The castle, which offers upmarket B&B, is not open to the public, but you're free to explore the beautiful grounds, where several good walks are signposted.

Old Byre Heritage Centre MUSEUM
(01688-400229; www.old-byre.co.uk; Dervaig; adult/child £4/2; 10.30am-6.30pm Wed-Sun Easter-late Oct) The curious and cheerful Old Byre brings Mull's heritage and natural history to life through a series of tableaux and half-hour film shows. The prize for most bizarre exhibit goes to the 40cm-long model of a midge. The centre's tearoom serves good, inexpensive snacks, and there's a kids' outdoor play area.

Calgary Art in Nature GALLERY
(01688-400256; www.calgaryartinnature.co.uk; 10.30am-5pm) Run with enthusiasm and vision, this place just back from Calgary beach, as well as offering great self-catering accommodation, is an excellent art space. On-site silversmiths and wood sculptors ply their trade in their workshops, while a luminous gallery exhibits high-quality work from local artists. Other pieces dot the woodland ramble on the hill behind. There's also a good **tearoom** (www.calgary.co.uk; light meals £5-9; 10.30am-5pm;).

Calgary Beach BEACH
Mull's best (and busiest) silver-sand beach, flanked by cliffs and with views out to Coll and Tiree, is about 12 miles west of Tobermory. And yes – this is the place from which Canada's more famous Calgary takes its name.

Sleeping & Eating

Calgary Bay Campsite CAMPSITE
FREE You can camp for free in a lovely setting at the southern end of the beach at Calgary Bay. There are no facilities other than the public toilets across the road; water comes from the stream.

Dervaig Hostel HOSTEL £
(01688-400491; www.mull-hostel-dervaig.co.uk; Dervaig; dm/q £18/60;) Basic but very comfortable bunkhouse accommodation in Dervaig's village hall, with self-catering kitchen and sitting room.

★Calgary Farmhouse SELF-CATERING ££
(01688-400256; www.calgary.co.uk; Calgary; per wk summer £400-1275;) This brilliant complex near Calgary beach offers a number of fantastic apartments, cottages and a farmhouse, sleeping from two to nine, beautifully designed and fitted out with timber furniture and wood-burning stoves. The Hayloft is spectacular, with noble oak and

---

THAR SHE BLOWS!

The North Atlantic Drift – a swirling tendril of the Gulf Stream – carries warm water into the cold, nutrient-rich seas off the Scottish coast, resulting in huge plankton blooms. Small fish feed on the plankton, and bigger fish feed on the smaller fish; this huge seafood smorgasbord attracts large numbers of marine mammals, from harbour porpoises and dolphins to minke whales and even – though sightings are rare – humpback and sperm whales.

There are dozens of operators around the coast offering **whale-watching** boat trips lasting from a couple of hours to all day; some have sighting success rates of 95% in summer.

While seals, porpoises and dolphins can be seen year-round, minke whales are migratory. The best time to see them is from June to August, with August being the peak month for sightings. The website of the **Hebridean Whale & Dolphin Trust** (www.whaledolphin-trust.co.uk) has lots of information on the species you are likely to see, and how to identify them.

local art. We loved romantic Kittiwake (one/three days £100/225), a beautiful wooden camping cabin among the trees, with bay views, boat for a ceiling and chemical toilet below decks.

The larger ones go by the week in summer, but smaller ones are available for shorter stays.

Achnadrish   APARTMENT **££**

(☑01688-400388; www.achnadrish.co.uk; Dervaig Rd; 1-bedroom apt per week £300, 3-bedroom apt per week £700; **P**⊚) Achnadrish is a sympathetically restored shooting lodge that offers self-catering accommodation in two units: the cute little one-bedroomed White Cabin sleeps two; the three-bedroom West Wing, a range of former servants' quarters, sleeps six. Both have fully fitted kitchens, while the latter also has a large lounge with woodburning stove. The house is halfway between Tobermory and Calgary beach.

Bellachroy   HOTEL **££**

(☑01688-400225; www.thebellachroy.co.uk; Dervaig; s/d £70/100; **P**⊚⊛) The Bellachroy is an atmospheric 17th-century droving inn with six plain but comfortable bedrooms. The bar is a focus for local social life and serves decent, if somewhat overpriced, food.

Glengorm Castle   B&B, SELF-CATERING **£££**

(☑01688-302321; www.glengormcastle.co.uk; r £165-215; ⊙mid-Feb–mid-Dec; **P**⊚) Bristling with turrets as a real castle should, this special spot enjoys an unforgettable location; huge windows frame green fields sloping down to the water. The interior is very attractive: 20th-century art instead of stags' heads. The five bedrooms are all different, with lots of space and character. The place is run by lively, genuinely friendly owners, and kids will have a ball running around the grounds.There are also various self-catering cottages available (£495 to £920 per week).

Glengorm Coffee Shop   CAFE **£**

(www.glengormcastle.co.uk; Glengorm; light meals £3-8; ⊙10am-5pm May-Aug; ⊚) *⃠* Set in a cottage courtyard in the grounds of Glengorm Castle, this licensed cafe serves superb lunches (from noon to 4.30pm) – the menu changes daily, but includes sandwiches and salads (much of the salad veg is grown on the Glengorm estate), soups and tasty specials.

Am Birlinn   SCOTTISH **££**

(☑01688-400619; www.ambirlinn.com; Penmore, Dervaig; mains £13-23; ⊙6-9pm Wed-Sun, plus noon-2pm Wed-Sun May-Oct) *⃠* Occupying a spacious modern wooden building between Dervaig and Calgary, this is an interesting dining option. Locally caught crustaceans and molluscs are the way to go here, though there are burgers, venison and other meat dishes available. Free pick-up and drop-off from Tobermory or other nearby spots is offered.

Central Mull

The central part of the island, between the Craignure–Fionnphort road and the narrow isthmus between Salen and Gruline, contains the island's highest peak, **Ben More** (966m) and some of its wildest scenery.

In tiny Gruline is the **mausoleum** of Lachlan Macquarie, enlightened fifth governor of New South Wales (Australia) and a Mull native. It's a 500m walk off the main road in attractive farmland.

The narrow B8035 along the southern shore of Loch na Keal squeezes past impressive cliffs before cutting south towards Loch Scridain. About 1 mile along the shore from Balmeanach, where the road climbs away from the coast, is **Mackinnon's Cave**, a deep spooky fissure in basalt cliffs that was once used as a refuge by Celtic monks. A big, flat rock inside, known as **Fingal's Table**, may have been their altar.

There's a very basic **campsite** (☑01680-300403; per person £4) at Killiechronan, 0.5 miles north of Gruline (toilets and water a five-minute walk away), and wild camping options on the south shore of Loch na Keal below Ben More.

South Mull

The road from Craignure to Fionnphort climbs through wild and desolate scenery before reaching the southwestern part of the island, which consists of a long peninsula called the **Ross of Mull**. The Ross has a spectacular south coast lined with black basalt cliffs that give way further west to white-sand beaches and pink granite crags. The cliffs are highest at Malcolm's Point, near the superb **Carsaig Arches**.

The village of **Bunessan** is home to the **Ross of Mull Historical Centre** (☑01681-700659; www.romhc.org.uk; admission £2; ⊙10am-4pm Mon-Fri Easter-Oct, 10am-1pm

Mon-Thu Nov-Easter), a cottage museum by a ruined mill that houses displays on local history, geology, archaeology, genealogy and wildlife.

A minor road leads south from here to the beautiful white-sand bay of **Uisken**, with views of the Paps of Jura.

At the western end of the Ross, 35 miles from Craignure, is **Fionnphort** (*finn*-a-fort) and the Iona ferry. The coast here is a beautiful blend of pink granite rocks, white sandy beaches and vivid turquoise sea.

🛏 Sleeping & Eating

Fidden Farm   CAMPSITE **£**
(☑ 01681-700427; Fidden, Fionnphort; adult/child £7/4; ⊙ Easter-Aug; **P** 🐾) A basic but popular and beautifully situated campground, with views over pink granite reefs to Iona and Erraid. It's 1.25 miles south of Fionnphort. Opening months vary a little year to year.

★**Seaview**   B&B **££**
(☑ 01681-700235; www.iona-bed-breakfast-mull.com; Fionnphort; d £75-90; ⊙ Mar-Oct; **P** 🛜 🐾) 🏊 Just up from the ferry, this place has beautifully decorated bedrooms and a breakfast conservatory with grand views across to Iona. The owners are incredibly helpful and also offer tasty three-course dinners (£25 per person, not in summer), often based around local seafood. Breakfasts include locally sourced produce and the rooms are compact and charming, with gleaming modern bathrooms. Bikes available for guests to hire.

Staffa House   B&B **££**
(☑ 01681-700677; www.staffahouse.co.uk; Fionnphort; s/d £53/76; ⊙ Mar-Oct; **P** 🛜) 🏊 This charming and hospitable B&B is packed with antiques and period features, and offers breakfast in a conservatory with a view of Iona. Solar panels top up the hot-water supply, and the hearty breakfasts and packed lunches (£6 to £8.50) make use of local and organic produce where possible. Rooms are designed for relaxation, with no TVs.

★**Ninth Wave**   SCOTTISH **£££**
(☑ 01681-700757; www.ninthwaverestaurant.co.uk; Fionnphort; 3-/4-course dinner £44/52; ⊙ 6-9pm Tue-Sun May-Oct) 🏊 Based in a former croft, this restaurant is owned and operated by a lobster fisherman and his Canadian wife. The daily menu makes use of locally landed shellfish and crustaceans, and vegetables and salad grown in the croft garden, served

in a stylishly converted bothy. It's excellent. Advance booking essential. No under-12s.

Isle of Iona

POP 200

Like an emerald teardrop off Mull's western shore, enchanting, idyllic Iona, holy island and burial ground of kings, is a magical place that lives up to its lofty reputation. From the moment you embark on the ferry towards its sandy shores and green fields, you'll notice something different about it. To appreciate its charms, spend the night: there are some excellent places to do it. Iona has declared itself a fair-trade island and actively promotes ecotourism.

History

St Columba sailed from Ireland and landed on Iona in 563, establishing a monastic community with the aim of Christianising Scotland. It was here that the *Book of Kells* – the prize attraction of Dublin's Trinity College – is believed to have been transcribed. It was taken to Ireland for safekeeping from 9th-century Viking raids.

The community was refounded as a Benedictine monastery in the early 13th century and prospered until its destruction during the Reformation. The ruins were given to the Church of Scotland in 1899, and by 1910 a group of enthusiasts called the Iona Community Council had reconstructed the abbey. It's still a flourishing spiritual community offering regular courses and retreats.

◎ Sights & Activities

Past the abbey, look for a footpath on the left signposted **Dun I** (dun-ee). An easy 15-minute walk leads to Iona's highest point, with fantastic 360 degree views.

Iona Abbey   HISTORIC BUILDING
(HS; ☑ 01681-700512; adult/child £7.10/4.30; ⊙ 9.30am-5.30pm Apr-Sep, to 4.30pm Oct-Mar) Iona's ancient but heavily reconstructed abbey is the spiritual heart of the island. The spectacular nave, dominated by Romanesque and early Gothic vaults and columns is a powerful space; a door on the left leads to the beautiful cloister, where medieval grave slabs sit alongside modern religious sculptures. Out the back, the new museum displays fabulous carved high crosses and other inscribed stones, along with lots of background information. A replica of the

intricately carved St John's Cross stands outside the abbey

Next to the abbey is an ancient graveyard where there's an evocative Romanesque chapel as well as a mound that marks the burial place of 48 of Scotland's early kings, including Macbeth; the ruined nunnery nearby was established at the same time as the Benedictine abbey.

Iona Heritage Centre MUSEUM
(☑ 01681-700576; adult/child £2.50/1.50; ⊙10.30am-5pm Mon-Sat Easter-Oct) Covers the history of Iona, crofting and lighthouses; there's a craft shop and cafe that serves delicious home baking.

🖝 Tours

Alternative Boat Hire BOAT TOURS
(☑ 01681-700537; www.boattripsiona.com; ⊙Mon-Thu Apr-Oct) Offers cruises in a traditional wooden sailing boat for fishing, birdwatching, picnicking, or just admiring the scenery. Three-hour afternoon trips cost £25/10 per adult/child; on Wednesday there's a full day cruise (10am to 5pm, £45/20). Booking essential.

MV Iolaire BOAT TOURS
(☑ 01681-700358; www.staffatrips.co.uk) Three-hour boat trips to Staffa (adult/child £30/15), departing Iona pier at 9.45am and 1.45pm, and from Fionnphort at 10am and 2pm, with one hour ashore on Staffa.

MV Volante WILDLIFE, FISHING
(☑ 01681-700362; www.volanteiona.com; ⊙Jun-Oct) Four-hour sea-angling trips (£50 per person including tackle and bait), as well as 1½-hour round-the-island wildlife cruises (adult/child £15/8) and 3½-hour whale-watching trips (per person £40).

🛌 Sleeping & Eating

There are B&B options and a supermarket on the island.

★Iona Hostel HOSTEL £
(☑ 01681-700781; www.ionahostel.co.uk; dm adult/child £21/17.50; 🅿 🖃) 🖉 This working ecological croft and environmentally sensitive hostel is one of Scotland's most rewarding and tranquil places to stay. Lovable black Hebridean sheep surround the building, which features pretty, practical and comfy dorms and an excellent kitchen-lounge. There's a fabulous beach nearby, and a hill to climb

for views. It's just over a mile from the ferry, past the abbey.

Iona Campsite CAMPSITE £
(☑ 01681-700112; www.ionacampsite.co.uk; tent sites per adult/child £6.50/3; ⊙Apr-Oct; 🖃) Basic campsite about 1 mile west of the ferry.

★Argyll Hotel HOTEL ££
(☑ 01681-700334; www.argyllhoteliona.co.uk; s £69, d £82-99; ⊙Mar-Oct; @🖃🖃) 🖉 This cute, higgledy-piggledy warren of a hotel has great service and appealing snug rooms (a sea view costs more – £150 for a double), including good-value family options. Most of the rooms look out to the rear, where a huge organic garden supplies the country-house restaurant (lunch £6-8, dinner mains £12-16; ⊙12.15-2pm & 6.30-8pm; 🖃) 🖉 with wooden fireplace and antique tables and chairs. The menu includes home-grown salads, local seafood and Scottish beef and lamb.

❶ Getting There & Away

The passenger ferry from Fionnphort to Iona (£5.10 return, five minutes, hourly) runs daily. There are also various day trips available from Oban to Iona.

Isle of Tiree

POP 700

Low-lying Tiree (tye-*ree*) is a fertile sward of lush, green machair liberally sprinkled with grazing sheep and yellow buttercups, much of it so flat that, from a distance, the houses seem to rise out of the sea. It's one of the sunniest places in Scotland, but also one of the windiest. One major benefit – the constant breeze keeps away the midges.

The surf-lashed coastline here is scalloped with magnificent broad, sweeping beaches of white sand, hugely popular with windsurfers and kitesurfers. Others come for the birdwatching and lonely coastal walks.

◎ Sights

In the 19th century Tiree had a population of 4500, but poverty, food shortages and overcrowding led the Duke of Argyll to introduce a policy of assisted emigration. Between 1841 and 1881, more than 3600 left, many emigrating to Canada, the USA, Australia and New Zealand.

An Iodhlann
LIBRARY, EXHIBITION

(📞01879-220385; www.aniodhlann.org.uk; Scarinish; adult/child £3/free; ⊙9am-1pm Mon & Wed-Thu, 10.30am-3.30pm Tue & Fri) A historical and genealogical library and archive, where some of the tens of thousands of descendants of Tiree emigrants come to trace their ancestry. The centre stages summer exhibitions on island life and history.

Skerryvore Lighthouse Museum
MUSEUM

(www.hebrideantrust.org; Hynish; ⊙9am-5pm) **FREE** The picturesque harbour and hamlet of Hynish, near Tiree's southern tip, was built in the 19th century to house workers and supplies for the construction of lonely Skerryvore Lighthouse, 10 miles offshore. This museum occupies the old workshops by the sand-filled but flushable harbour; up the hill is the signal tower once used to communicate by semaphore with the lighthouse.

🏃 Activities

Reliable wind and big waves have made Tiree one of Scotland's top windsurfing venues. The annual **Tiree Wave Classic** (www.tireewaveclassic.co.uk) competition is held here in October.

Wild Diamond
WATERSPORTS

(📞01879-220399; www.wilddiamond.co.uk; Cornaig) Professional and friendly, this outfit runs courses in windsurfing (£30/100 per session/day), kitesurfing (£70/120 per half-day/full day), surfing, sand-yachting and stand-up paddleboarding, and rents out equipment, including surfboards.

Blackhouse Watersports
WATERSPORTS

(📞07711 807976; www.blackhouse-watersports.co.uk; Gott Bay; ⊙Mar-Nov) Operates out of a beach hut at the far end of Gott Bay. Welcoming set-up that runs kitesurfing (£100) and surf (£35) lessons, hires kayaks (£25 for three hours including wetsuit), lends out fishing tackle and rents bikes (£10 per day).

🛏 Sleeping & Eating

Most of Tiree's accommodation is self-catering; make sure you have booked something before arriving.

Millhouse Hostel
HOSTEL £

(📞01879-220435; www.tireemillhouse.co.uk; Cornaig; dm/s/tw £21/33/46; P🛜) Housed in a converted barn next to an old ruined water mill, this small but comfortable hostel is 5 miles west from the ferry pier. The dorms have beds rather than bunks, there's a com-

WORTH A TRIP

ISLE OF STAFFA

Felix Mendelssohn, who visited the uninhabited island of Staffa in 1829, was inspired to compose his *Hebrides Overture* after hearing waves echoing in the impressive and cathedral-like **Fingal's Cave**. The cave walls and surrounding cliffs are composed of vertical, hexagonal basalt columns that look like pillars (Staffa is Norse for 'Pillar Island'). You can land and walk into the cave via a causeway. Nearby **Boat Cave** can be seen from the causeway, but you can't reach it on foot. Staffa also has a sizeable puffin colony, north of the landing place.

Northwest of Staffa lies a chain of uninhabited islands called the **Treshnish Isles**. The two main islands are curiously shaped **Dutchman's Cap** and **Lunga**. You can land on Lunga, walk to the top of the hill and visit the shag, puffin and guillemot colonies on the west coast at **Harp Rock**.

Unless you have your own boat, the only way to reach Staffa and the Treshnish Isles is on an organised boat trip from Ulva, Fionnphort or Iona.

mon area and it's cheaper if you stay more than one night.

Balinoe Croft Campsite
CAMPSITE £

(📞01879-220399; www.wilddiamond.co.uk; Balinoe; tent sites adult/child £12/6; P🛜🐕) A sheltered site with full facilities in the southwest of the island, near Balemartine, with great views of Mull. It's cheaper for multi-night stays or in the off-season.

Kirkapol House
B&B ££

(📞01879-220729; www.kirkapoltiree.co.uk; Kirkapol; s/d £38/70; ⊙Apr-Sep; P🛜🐕) Set in a converted 19th-century church overlooking the island's biggest beach, the Kirkapol has six homely rooms with soothing sounds of waves, and a big lounge with a leather sofa. It's 2 miles north of the ferry terminal.

Scarinish Hotel
HOTEL ££

(📞01879-220308; www.tireescarinishhotel.com; Scarinish; s/d £70/90; P🛜🐕) The island's main hotel is looking a little tired these days, and the welcome is curtly professional rather than effusive, but it's an acceptable choice. Both the restaurant (two-/three-course dinner £22/26), with pleasant harbour views, and traditional lean-to bar (mains £6 to £9) do food, and you can get a packed lunch too. Food is served noon to 2.30pm and 5pm to 8.30pm.

Ceàbhar SCOTTISH **££**
(☑ 01879-220684; www.ceabhar.com; Sandaig; mains £8-15; ⊙ 7-8.30pm Wed-Sat Easter-Oct, plus Tue Jul & Aug; ⓟ 🎧 🐾) 🍴 At Tiree's western end, this attractive restaurant looks out over the Atlantic towards the sunset. The cordial owners have the right attitude; they grow their own salads, eschew chips and have a nice line in good Fyne ales. The menu runs to handmade pizzas, soups, fish of the day and local lamb. A snug cottage sleeps up to eight people in five bedrooms.

ℹ Information

There's a bank (without ATM), post office and supermarket in Scarinish, the main village, half a mile south of the ferry pier. You can get cashback with debit-card purchases at the Co-op.

Some tourist information is available in the ferry terminal. A useful website is www.isleof tiree.com.

ℹ Getting There & Around

AIR

Loganair/FlyBe (www.loganair.co.uk) flies from Glasgow to Tiree daily. **Hebridean Air** (☑ 0845 805-7465; www.hebrideanair.co.uk) operates from Oban to Tiree via Coll (one-way from Oban/ Coll £65/25, twice daily Monday and Wednesday plus once Friday and Sunday during school term).

BICYCLE & CAR

Rent bicycles (per day £10) and cars (per day £45) from **MacLennan Motors** (☑ 01879-220555; www.maclennanmotors.com; Gott) at the ferry pier. **Tiree Fitness** (☑ 01879-220421; www.tireefitness.co.uk; Sandaig; per day £15) has better bikes and will deliver them to the ferry (£5 extra).

BOAT

A **CalMac** (www.calmac.co.uk) ferry runs from Oban to Tiree (passenger/car £20.30/108 return, four hours, one daily) via Coll, except on Wednesday and Friday when the boat calls at Tiree first (three hours 20 minutes). The one-way fare from Coll to Tiree (one hour) is £3.30/14.90 per passenger/car. On Thursdays, the ferry continues to Barra in the Outer Hebrides (£8.60/44.50 one way, four hours), and stops again on the way back to Oban, allowing a long day trip to Tiree from the mainland.

Isle of Coll

POP 200

More rugged, Coll is Tiree's less populous neighbour. The northern part of the island is a mix of bare rock, bog and lochans (small lochs), while the south is swathed in golden shell-sand beaches and machair dunes up to 30m high. It's a gloriously relaxing place.

The island's main attraction is the peace and quiet – empty beaches, bird-haunted coastlines, and long walks along the shore. The biggest and most beautiful sandy beaches are at Crossapol in the south, and Hogh Bay and Cliad on the west coast.

In summer the corncrake's 'krek-krek' is heard at the RSPB Reserve at Totronald in the southwest of the island. From Totronald a sandy 4WD track runs north past the dunes backing Hogh Bay to the road at Totamore, allowing walkers and cyclists to make a circuit back to Arinagour rather than backtracking.

There are two castles about 6 miles southwest of Arinagour, both known as Breachacha Castle, built by the Macleans. The older, ruined towerhouse was replaced by a mid-18th century palace alongside, now gradually being restored.

🍽 Sleeping & Eating

You can wild camp for free on the hill above the Coll Hotel (no facilities); ask at the hotel first.

Coll Bunkhouse HOSTEL **£**
(☑ 01879-230000; www.collbunkhouse.com; Arinagour; dm/tw £20/48; ⓟ 🎧) The gorgeous modern bunkhouse is in the main settlement, just a 10- to 15-minute walk from the ferry pier.

Tigh-na-Mara B&B **££**
(☑ 01879-230354; www.tighnamara.info; Arinagour; s £50-60, d £70-90; ⓟ 🎧) The first building you reach coming from the ferry is this lovely B&B, with a large front garden and magnificent views over the water. The owners are relaxed and welcoming, and the rooms have bird books and planispheres so you can do some spotting from your window. Wi-fi is fast for the Hebrides, and breakfast very tasty – try the stuffed tomato. There's also a self-catering option.

Coll Hotel HOTEL ££
(☎01879-230334; www.collhotel.com; Arinagour; s £65, d £100-125; P🐾) The island's only hotel is an atmospheric old place. Its quirkily shaped rooms have white-painted, wood-panelled walls, and some have lovely views over the manicured hotel gardens and the harbour. The hotel also has a lively public bar and good restaurant (mains £13 to £22; noon to 2pm and 6pm to 9pm) serving dishes prepared with regional smoked and fresh fish, shellfish and lamb. You can order smaller portions of the mains: not a bad idea, as they're sizeable.

Island Café CAFE ££
(Arinagour; mains £6-13; ⊙11am-2pm & 5-9pm Mon & Thu-Sat, noon-6pm Sun; 🐾) This cheerful spot serves hearty, homemade meals such as sausage and mash, haddock and chips, and vegetarian cottage pie, accompanied by organic beer, wine and cider. Sunday roasts are legendary on the island.

ℹ Information
Arinagour, 0.5 miles from the ferry pier, is Coll's only village, home to a shop, post office (with ATM), craft shops and aged petrol station. Coll has no reliable mobile-phone signal; there are payphones at the pier and in the hotel. For more information see www.visitcoll.co.uk.

ℹ Getting There & Around
AIR
Hebridean Air (☎0845 805-7465; www.hebrideanair.co.uk) operates flights from Connel Airfield (near Oban) to Coll (£65 one way, twice daily Monday and Wednesday plus once daily Friday and Sunday in school term).

BICYCLE
There is no public transport. Mountain bikes can be hired from the post office in Arinagour for £10 per day.

BOAT
CalMac (www.calmac.co.uk) runs from Oban to Coll (passenger/car £20.30/108 return, 2¾ hours, one daily) and continues to Tiree (one hour), except on Wednesday and Friday when the boat calls at Tiree first. The one-way fare from Coll to Tiree is £3.30/14.90 per passenger/car.

On Thursdays, you can take a ferry to Barra in the Outer Hebrides (£8.60/44.50 one way, four hours); it stops again on the way back to Oban, allowing a long day trip to Coll from the mainland.

NORTH ARGYLL

Loch Awe
Loch Awe is one of Scotland's most beautiful lochs, with rolling forested hills around its southern end and spectacular mountains in the north. It lies between Oban and Inveraray and is the longest loch in Scotland – about 24 miles – but is less than 1 mile wide for most of its length. At its northern end, it escapes to the sea through the narrow Pass of Brander, where Robert the Bruce defeated the MacDougalls in 1309. Here you can visit Cruachan power station (☎01866-822618; www.visitcruachan.co.uk; adult/child £7.50/2.50; ⊙9.30am-4.45pm Easter-Oct, 11am-3.45pm Mon-Fri Nov-Dec, Feb & Mar). Electric buses take you deep inside Ben Cruachan, allowing you to see the pump-storage hydroelectric scheme which occupies a vast cavern hollowed out of the mountain.

Also at the northern end of Loch Awe, a half-mile walk off the A85 are the scenic ruins of Kilchurn Castle (HS; ⊙9am-5pm Apr-Sep) FREE, built in 1440, which enjoys one of Scotland's finest settings; you can climb to the top of the four-storey castle tower.

Citylink (www.citylink.co.uk) buses from Glasgow to Oban go via Dalmally, Lochawe village and Cruachan power station. Trains from Glasgow to Oban stop at Dalmally and Lochawe village.

Connel & Taynuilt
Hemmed in by dramatic mountain scenery, Loch Etive stretches 17 miles from Connel to Kinlochetive (accessible by road from Glencoe). At Connel Bridge, 5 miles north of Oban, the loch joins the sea via a narrow channel partly blocked by an underwater rock ledge. When the tide flows in and out water pours through this bottleneck, creating spectacular white-water rapids known as the Falls of Lora. Park near the north end of the bridge and walk back into the middle to have a look.

Dunstaffnage Castle (HS; ☎01631-562465; www.historic-scotland.gov.uk; adult/child £4.50/2.70; ⊙9.30am-5.30pm Apr-Sep, to 4.30pm Oct), 2 miles west of Connel, looks like a schoolkid's drawing of what a castle should be – square and massive, with towers at the corners, perched on top of a rocky outcrop. It was built around 1260 and was captured by Robert the Bruce during the Wars of Independence. The haunted ruins of the nearby chapel contain lots of Campbell tombs. You reach the castle through a smart new European marine-research complex.

One of the region's most unusual historical sights is Bonawe Iron Furnace (HS; ☑ 01866-822432; www.historic-scotland.gov.uk; adult/child £4.50/2.70; ⊙ 9.30am-5.30pm Apr-Sep), near Taynuilt. Dating from 1753, it felled the local birchwoods to make charcoal, needed for smelting. To produce Bonawe's annual output of 700 tons of pig iron took 10,000 acres of woodland. A fascinating self-guided tour leads you around the site.

From the nearby jetty, Loch Etive Cruises (☑ 01866-822430; 2-/3-hour cruises £10/15; ⊙ 2-3 cruises Sun-Fri Easter-Oct) runs boat trips to the head of Loch Etive and back. You may spot eagles, otters, seals and deer, and at the head of the loch you can see the famous Etive slabs. Bookings essential.

Buses between Oban and Fort William or Glasgow, and trains between Oban and Glasgow, all stop in Connel and Taynuilt.

Appin & Around

The Appin region, once ruled over by the Stewarts from their stronghold at Castle Stalker, stretches north from the rocky shores of Loch Creran to the hills of Glencoe.

The Scottish Sea Life Sanctuary (☑ 01631-720386; www.sealsanctuary.co.uk; Barcaldine; adult/child £13.20/10.80; ⊙ 10am-4pm Nov-Mar, 10am-5pm Apr-Oct) ✈, 10 miles north of Oban, provides a haven for orphaned seal pups. As well as seals there are tanks with herrings, rays and flatfish, touch pools for children, an otter sanctuary and displays on Scotland's marine environment. An outdoor nature trail is aimed at young 'uns.

North of Loch Creran, at Portnacroish, there's a wonderful view of Castle Stalker (www.castlestalker.com; adult/child £15/7; ⊙ check website for summer guided tours) perched on a tiny offshore island. This spectacular tower house is only open for five weeks or so per year: book ahead. Port Appin, a couple of miles off the main road, is a pleasant spot with a passenger ferry to Lismore.

Scottish Citylink (www.citylink.co.uk) buses between Oban and Fort William stop at the Sea Life Sanctuary and Appin village.

🛏 Sleeping & Eating

Pierhouse Hotel HOTEL **£££**
(☑ 01631-730302; www.pierhousehotel.co.uk; Port Appin; s/d from £75/140; ℗ 🛜) The quaint Pierhouse Hotel sits on the waterfront above the pier and has stylish modern rooms, a sauna and an excellent restaurant (mains £13-28; ⊙ noon-2.30pm & 6.9pm; 🛜) with views to Lismore, and specialises in local seafood and game. The bar offers cheaper fishy fare.

Lismore

POP 200

The island of Lismore (in Gaelic Lios Mor means 'Big Garden') is all lush grassland sprinkled with wildflowers. It's limestone that's the secret – it's rare in the Highlands, but it weathers to a very fertile soil.

In the middle of the island, Lismore Gaelic Heritage Centre (☑ 01631-760300; www.lismoregaelicheritagecentre.org; admission by donation; ⊙ 11am-4pm Apr-Oct) ✈ has a museum with a fascinating exhibition on Lismore's history and culture; alongside stands a reconstruction of a crofter's cottage. The cafe (☑ 01631-760020; light meals £4-8; ⊙ 11am-4pm Apr-Oct; 🍴) ✈ has an outdoor deck with a stunning view of the mainland mountains.

The romantic ruins of 13th-century Castle Coeffin have a lovely setting on the west coast. Tirefour Broch, a defensive tower with double walls reaching 4m in height, is directly opposite on the east coast. There is very little short-stay accommodation on Lismore. However, there are several self-catering options advertised on www.isleoflismore.com. Lismore is long and narrow – 10 miles long by 1 mile wide – with a road running almost its full length. There's a shop.

❶ Getting There & Around

BICYCLE

You can hire **bikes** (☑ 01631-730391; per day adult/child £15/10) in Port Appin to bring across on the ferry.

BOAT

A **CalMac** (www.calmac.co.uk) car ferry runs from Oban to Achnacroish, with four to five sailings Monday to Saturday, two on Sunday (passenger/car return £6.60/55, 50 minutes).

Argyll & Bute Council (☑ 01631-569160; www.argyll-bute.gov.uk) operates the passenger ferry from Port Appin to Point (£1.60, 10 minutes, hourly). Bicycles are free.

Walking the West Highland Way

Includes

Best Viewpoints

➡ Conic Hill (p102)

➡ Inversnaid (p103)

➡ Above Crianlarich (p104)

➡ Mam Carraigh (p105)

Best Wild Camping

➡ Inversnaid Boathouse (p101)

➡ Garadhban (p102)

➡ Doune Bothy (p104)

➡ Inveroran (p105)

Why Go?

From the outskirts of Glasgow, Scotland's biggest city, the West Highland Way leads through fertile, populous lowland countryside to the shores of Loch Lomond, on the threshold of the Highlands. From there it carries you north, through rugged glens, beside fast-flowing streams and past wild moorland where magnificent mountains are never out of sight. The very names have an alluring ring: Rannoch Moor, Glen Coe, Devil's Staircase.

Not only is the West Highland Way a rich sensory experience, it's also steeped in history. The route follows long stretches of drove roads, along which cattle were once taken to market; the flat beds of old railway lines; roads along which coaches and horses once jolted; and the 18th-century military road built to subdue rebellious Highlanders.

This is the most popular long-distance path in Scotland (and Britain for that matter); something like 15,000 walkers go the full distance each year, so you'll rarely be short of like-minded company from around the world.

When to Go

Tyndrum

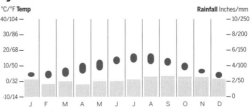

Feb Experienced walkers can have spectacular snow-covered scenery almost to themselves.

May The woods along Loch Lomond's shores are a purple blaze of Scottish bluebells.

Oct Not as busy as summer, the midges are gone and autumn colours start to appear.

PLANNING

The walk begins at Milngavie, easing you into things with the two least strenuous days before you hit the harder going north of Rowardennan. Spreading it over seven days means only one long day (between Tyndrum and Kings House) and a majority of comfortable days; don't overlook the fact that it's not only horizontal distance that matters – the Way involves a total of 3500m (11,500ft) of ascent.

Of course, you can take much longer, by doing shorter days, or by taking time out to knock off some of the nearby Munros – Ben Lomond and Ben Nevis are the two obvious candidates. Or you can do a one-day hike on a part of the way – recommended sections include Inversnaid to Inverarnan (7 miles), and Kings House to Glen Nevis (19 miles).

Navigation is generally straightforward: the route is clearly waymarked with the official thistle-and-hexagon logo, and there's a shelf-full of guidebooks and maps

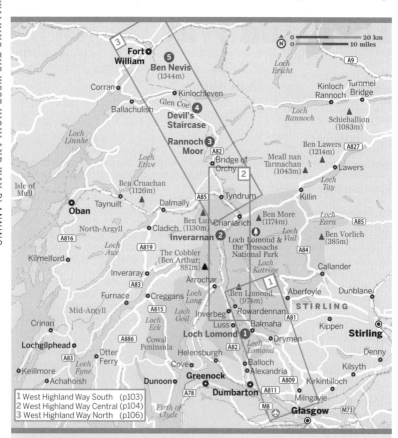

1 West Highland Way South (p103)
2 West Highland Way Central (p104)
3 West Highland Way North (p106)

West Highland Way Highlights

❶ Soaking up the gorgeous scenery along the bonnie banks of lovely **Loch Lomond** (p102)

❷ Enjoying a well-earned pint of ale in the atmospheric **Drover's Inn** (p46) at Inverarnan

❸ Reveling in the wild open spaces of bleak but beautiful **Rannoch Moor** (p105)

❹ Taking in the dramatic views from the **Devil's Staircase** (p106), the highest point of the walk

❺ Rounding off your achievement with an ascent of **Ben Nevis** (p153), Britain's highest summit

to enlighten and entertain you along the way. By the time you reach Fort William you might even be supremely fit and ready to climb Ben Nevis, or continue along the Great Glen Way to Inverness.

ⓘ Maps & Books

Four OS Landranger 1:50,000 maps – No 64 *Glasgow*, No 56 *Loch Lomond & Inveraray*, No 50 *Glen Orchy & Loch Etive* and No 41 *Ben Nevis* – cover the Way, although it's much easier to use a purpose-designed, all-in-one route map. Both the excellent Harvey 1:40,000 Route map *West Highland Way* and the superbly designed Rucksack Readers guide *The West Highland Way* are more than adequate, and include lots of practical information for walkers.

Trailblazer's *West Highland Way*, by Charlie Loram, is the most comprehensive guidebook, with detailed trail maps and information on accommodation, places to eat and tourist attractions in Glasgow, Fort William and all the villages along the way.

The *West Highland Way Pocket Companion*, a free booklet listing accommodation and facilities along the route (updated annually), can be picked up at most tourist offices in the region; it can also be downloaded for free from the official website.

ⓘ Accommodation

If you're planning to rely on serviced accommodation (hotels, B&Bs and hostels) it's essential to book rooms in advance; the official website lists accommodation along the route. Note that Kings House is an accommodation 'bottleneck' with just the one hotel. Public transport here is limited to one bus every two hours (last bus westbound 8.13pm) and taxis are expensive, so plan ahead and don't get caught out.

There are several fully serviced campgrounds along the way, as well as two official backpacker campgrounds (free, no facilities, one-night stay only) at Garadhban Forest and Inversnaid Boathouse. Local bylaws forbid camping on the eastern shore of Loch Lomond between Drymen and Rowardennan, except at recognised campsites.

ⓘ Guided Walk & Baggage Services

Rather than doing all the organising, you can take advantage of the services offered by a few small companies who can arrange your accommodation and carry your luggage between overnight stops. Some outfits go a step further and provide you with sheaves of information about the Way and the places through which you pass, or can provide a guide to lead you on the walk.

ⓘ PRACTICALITIES

Duration seven days

Distance 96 miles (154km)

Difficulty moderate

Start Milngavie

Finish Fort William

Transport train, bus

Summary Scotland's most popular long-distance path, passing through some of the country's finest landscapes, from suburban Glasgow to the foot of the highest mountain in Britain.

Easyways (☑ 01324-714132; www.easyways. com) has years of experience organising accommodation and baggage transfer; **Transcotland** (☑ 01887-820848 ; www.transcotland.com) also has a good track record and can provide reams of directions and background information. **C-n-Do Scotland** (☑ 01786-445703; www. cndoscotland.com) offer guided walks along the West Highland Way.

ⓘ Information

The official West Highland Way website (www. west-highland-way.co.uk) is a comprehensive resource, covering pretty much everything you need to know: from the route itself, equipment and planning to weather, accommodation, food and public transport.

There are ATMs at Milngavie, Drymen, Crianlarich, Tyndrum, Kinlochleven and Fort William.

ⓘ Getting There & Away

The official start of the West Highland Way is a granite obelisk (unveiled in 1992) beside the bridge over the Allander Water on Douglas St, Milngavie, but for most people the journey begins at Milngavie train station. Buses stop here and there's a car park near the station, just off Station Rd. To reach the obelisk from the station, go through the underpass and up a flight of steps to the pedestrianised centre of Milngavie. Bear left at the underpass exit to join Douglas St, passing through a shopping precinct before reaching the Allander Water and the official start point.

Fort William, at the end of the walk, has frequent rail and bus connections to other parts of Scotland, including an overnight sleeper train to London.

If you plan to walk just a section of the Way, Crianlarich, Tyndrum and Bridge of Orchy are well served by trains; contact ScotRail (p290) for details. **Scottish Citylink** (☑ 0871 266 33 33; www.citylink.co.uk) buses on the Glasgow–Fort William route stop at Crianlarich, Tyndrum and Bridge of Orchy. Traveline Scotland (p288) provides a journey planner and timetable information for all public transport in Scotland.

From April to October a network of passenger ferries criss-crosses Loch Lomond, linking the main A82 road on the western shore with various locations along the West Highland Way on the eastern shore. A **Loch Lomond Water Bus** (www.lochlomond-trossachs.org/waterbus) timetable is available from tourist offices and online.

THE WALK

Day One: Milngavie to Drymen

➡ **Duration** 4½ to 5½ hours

➡ **Distance** 12 miles (19km)

From the obelisk on Douglas St, descend the ramp beneath the huge West Highland Way sign, pass through a small car park and follow a path along a disused railway, then upstream beside Allander Water, to **Mugdock Wood**. At the end of the wood, paths and a track take you past a couple of small lochs to the B821. Turn left and follow the road for about 300m to a stile giving onto a path to the right. As you skirt **Dumgoyach Hill** watch out for Bronze Age standing stones to

DISCLAIMER

Although the authors and publisher have done their utmost to ensure the accuracy of all information in this guide, they cannot accept any responsibility for any loss, injury or inconvenience sustained by people using this book. They cannot guarantee that the paths and routes described here have not become impassable for any reason in the interval between research and publication. The fact that a walk is described in this guidebook does not mean that it is safe for you and your walking party. You are ultimately responsible for judging your own capabilities in the conditions you encounter.

your right, just before the hill. A mile past Dumgoyach Bridge you pass **Glengoyne Distillery**; 800m further on you reach the **Beech Tree Inn** (☑ 01360-550297; www.the beechtreeinn.co.uk; mains £9-19; ⊙ food noon-9pm daily Apr-Sep, noon-9pm Thu-Sun, to 4pm Mon-Wed Oct-Mar) at Dumgoyne. In the village of **Killearn**, 1.5 miles to the right, there's accommodation, shops, pubs and a post office.

Follow the old railway track to **Gartness**, from where you're on a road most of the way to the edge of Drymen. A mile beyond Gartness there's camping available at **Easter Drumquhassle Farm** (Drymen Camping; ☑ 01360-660597; www.drymencamping.co.uk; Gartness Rd; sites per person £5, wigwams per night £30), from where a view of Loch Lomond makes its first appearance. Pass a quarry and continue along the road; just past a sharp left bend, the Way leaves the road and follows a path to the right. If you're going to Drymen, continue along the road and cross the A811 to enter the village.

Drymen

Drymen is a pretty village with a central green and lots of character. There are plenty of accommodation and eating options, an excellent pub, several shops and a small supermarket.

Day Two: Drymen to Rowardennan

➡ **Duration** five to 6½ hours

➡ **Distance** 14 miles (22.5km)

From near the A811 just outside Drymen, a forest track gradually climbs to **Garadhban Forest** (backpacker campground, no facilities). Just over an hour from Drymen, a side path runs left to the village of **Milton of Buchanan**; it's also the alternative route when Conic Hill is closed to dog walkers during the lambing season (late April to early May). There are a couple of B&Bs in the village but no pubs or shops.

The Way climbs then contours north of the summit of **Conic Hill** (358m), but it's worth the short detour to the top for the wonderful panorama over **Loch Lomond**. This viewpoint also has a special, even unique significance: from the summit you can make out the unmistakable line of the Highland Boundary Fault, separating the lowlands from the Highlands – so from this point on you really are in the Highlands.

Descend to **Balmaha**, a small lakeside village usually thronged with people messing about in boats. As well as the National Park Centre there's also a small shop and the Oak Tree Inn (p48), which offers accommodation, food and a bar.

Continue along the shore of Loch Lomond, passing a marker commemorating the Way's opening in 1980, to **Milarrochy** (one hour from Balmaha; campground available). From **Critreoch**, about 800m further on, the path dives into a dark forest and emerges to follow the road for about 1 mile. Just after you join the road is the Cashel Caravan and Camping Site (p48). A mile beyond Sallochy House, the Way climbs through **Ross Wood**, its magnificent oaks making it one of Scotland's finest natural woodlands, to Rowardennan.

Rowardennan

Rowardennan is little more than a hamlet, but it has a **hotel** (☏ 01360-870273; www.rowardennanhotel.co.uk; s/d £70/98; ☺ Feb-Dec; P 🛜 🐾) and a youth hostel (p46), and Rowchoish Bothy (free, no facilities) is 2.5 miles north. Rowardennan is also the starting point for the ascent of **Ben Lomond** (974m; see p49).

Day Three: Rowardennan to Inverarnan

→ **Duration** six to 7½ hours

→ **Distance** 14 miles (22.5km)

From Rowardennan follow the unsealed road that parallels the loch shore. Just past private Ptarmigan Lodge an alternative path branches left and follows the shoreline; it's more interesting, but much rougher going (not recommended with a heavy backpack) than the upper route, which follows a track higher up the hillside. The lower path leads past a natural rock cell in a crag about 1.5 miles north of Ptarmigan Lodge, which is known as **Rob Roy's prison**: the famous outlaw is said to have kept kidnap victims here (for more on Rob Roy see p59). From both routes you can reach **Rowchoish Bothy**, a simple stone shelter.

Not far beyond the bothy the forestry track gives way to a path, which dives down to the loch for a stretch of difficult walking

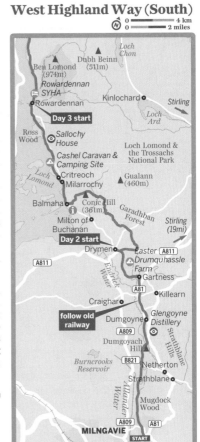

West Highland Way (South)

to **Cailness**. From here the going improves to **Inversnaid**, shortly before which the path crosses Snaid Burn just above the impressive **Inversnaid Falls**. The huge Inversnaid Hotel could be a good place to stop for refreshments before you tackle the next and toughest section of all.

For a couple of miles north from Inversnaid, the path twists and turns around large boulders and tree roots, a good test of balance and agility. A mile or so into this, the Way passes close to **Rob Roy's cave**, where he is alleged to have hidden from the authorities, although it's little

West Highland Way (Central)

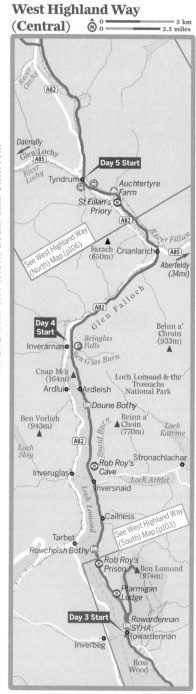

more than a gap beneath fallen blocks of rock. Further on, Doune Bothy provides basic accommodation (no facilities). Almost 1 mile beyond the bothy, at Ardleish, there's a landing stage used by the ferry across to the Ardlui Hotel (p46).

From Ardleish, you leave the loch and climb to a col below Cnap Mór (164m), where on a clear day there are good views north towards the Highlands and south over Loch Lomond. The path descends into Glen Falloch; a footbridge over Ben Glas Burn heralds your arrival at Inverarnan. Just upstream is the spectacular Beinglas Falls, a cascade of 300m (1000ft) – very impressive after heavy rain.

Inverarnan

There's a choice of B&B and camping accommodation in Inverarnan, as well as an excellent country pub, the Drover's Inn (p46), which also offers food and lodging.

Day Four: Inverarnan to Tyndrum

➠ **Duration** 4½ to 5½ hours

➠ **Distance** 13 miles (21km)

From Inverarnan the route follows the attractive River Falloch most of the way to Crianlarich, the approximate halfway point of the Way. About 4 miles along, it crosses the river and joins an old military road. This track climbs out of Glen Falloch, and then at a stile into the forest, a path leads down to the right towards Crianlarich. There's no real need to go to Crianlarich, though there are B&Bs, a youth hostel, a bar and restaurant and a small shop with an ATM.

The Way climbs to the west from the stile, offering good views east to Ben More (1174m), and continues through the trees for about 2 miles. Next, it crosses under the railway line, goes over the road and crosses a wooden bridge over the River Fillan. Pass the remains of St Fillan's Priory, turn left and go on to Strathfillan Wigwams (p49) at Auchtertyre Farm. The route crosses the A82 once more and, in less than an hour, you make it to Tyndrum.

Tyndrum

Tyndrum, originally a lead-mining settlement and now a popular staging point between Glasgow and Fort William, is

LOCH LOMOND

Loch Lomond fills a trough that was gouged by a glacier flowing south from the ice sheet that covered Rannoch Moor during the last Ice Age. It straddles the boundary between the Highlands and the lowlands, so that two distinct environments can be seen along its shores.

The southern part of the loch is broad, shallow and dotted with 38 islands, and bordered by relatively flat, low-lying arable land. This part of the loch freezes over during severe winters, and it has been possible to reach the islands on foot on several occasions over the last 50 years.

The northern end of the loch is deep and narrow (at its deepest, just south of Inversnaid, the water depth is 190m), generally less than 1 mile wide, and enclosed by steep mountains rising to 900m. The slopes at the loch shore are covered by Scotland's largest remnant of native oak woodland, mixed with newer conifer plantations. Botanical studies have found that 25% of all known British flowering plants and ferns can be found along the West Highland Way on the eastern shore, which is famous for its display of Scottish bluebells in spring.

strung out along the A82. It has a tourist office (p49), shops (including one selling outdoor equipment), hotels, B&Bs and campgrounds, and is well served by train and bus. Eating places include the Real Food Cafe (p49).

Day Five: Tyndrum to Kings House Hotel

→ **Duration** 6½ to eight hours

→ **Distance** 19 miles (30.5km)

From Tyndrum the route soon rejoins the old military road and crosses the railway line, affording easy walking with lovely views. Three miles from Tyndrum, you cross a burn at the foot of Beinn Dòrain (1074m), the hill that dominates this section of the path.

The path climbs gradually to pass the entrance to Glen Orchy, crossing the railway again, heralding the beginning of the really mountainous scenery. The hamlet of Bridge of Orchy is dominated by the Bridge of Orchy Hotel (01838-400208; www.bridgeoforchy.co.uk; mains £6-13; food 8am-9pm daily). Cross the old bridge (built in 1750) that gives the settlement its name and climb through the trees to the crest of Mam Carraigh, from where there are superb views across to Rannoch Moor. The path then winds down to the secluded Inveroran Hotel. It's possible to camp wild (no facilities) beside a stone bridge 400m west of the hotel (caution: this area is subject to flooding after heavy rains).

The Way follows the minor road, which soon becomes a track, climbing gently past some plantations and out onto Rannoch Moor. There's no shelter for about 7 miles, and Bà Bridge, about 3 miles beyond the plantations, is the only real marker point. It can be very wild and windy up here, and there's a real sense of isolation. A cairn marks the summit at 445m and from here there's a wonderful view down into Glen Coe. As the path descends from the moor to join the road again, you can see the chairlift of the Glencoe Mountain Resort (p146) to the left. There's a cafe at the base station, about 500m off the West Highland Way. Kings House Hotel is just over 1 mile ahead, across the A82.

Kings House Hotel

Dating from the 17th century, the Kings House Hotel (p147) was originally used as barracks for George III's troops (hence the name). If you can't get a bed here you can catch a bus to Glencoe village, 11 miles west, where there's a wider selection of accommodation. It's possible to camp for free across the bridge behind the hotel.

Day Six: Kings House Hotel to Kinlochleven

→ **Duration** three to four hours

→ **Distance** 9 miles (14.5km)

From Kings House Hotel the route follows the old military road and then goes alongside the A82 to a parking area at

West Highland Way (North)

Mallaig
A830 Corpach B8004
River Lochy
A861 END A830 A82
Loch Linnhe Fort William West Highland Railway Inverness (60mi)
A82
Glen Nevis Aonach
Dùn Deardail Ben Nevis Mór
(1344m) (1221m)
Blar a' Chaorainn
Tigh-na-sleubhaich Aonach Beag
(1234m)
Sgurr a' Mhaim
(1097m)
Loch Leven Binnein
Pap of Mór
Glencoe (1127m)
(740m) Kinlochleven
Glen Coe Glas Bheinn
(788m)
River Leven
Bidean
nam Bian Devil's Blackwater
(1148m) Staircase Reservoir
Buachaille Etive
Beag Altnafeadh Meall nan
Glen Etive Ruadhag
River Etive Buachaille Etive (646m)
Mor (1022m) Kings House
Stob Dubh Glencoe Hotel
(884m) Mountain
Resort
River Bá
Stob Ghabhar
(1086m) Bà Bridge Loch
Loch Bá
Dochard Rannoch
Beinn Sùileag Moor
(674m) Water of Tulla
Inveroran Loch Tulla A82
Hotel
Bridge of Beinn
Glen Orchy Orchy Achaladair
(1038m)
River Orchy
See West Highland Way
(Central) Map (p104)
Beinn
Dòrain
Glen Lochy (1074m) A82
A85
River Lochy
Tyndrum Day 5 Start
Auchtertyre
Farm
A82

0 — 5 km
0 — 2.5 miles

Day 7 Start
Day 6 Start

Altnafeadh. This is a wonderful vantage point from which to appreciate the mountainous scenery of Glen Coe. The conical peak to your left is Buachaille Etive Mor (1022m).

From here the Way turns right, leaving the road to begin a steep, zigzagging climb up the Devil's Staircase. The cairn at the top is at 548m and marks the highest point of the Way. The views are stunning, especially on a clear day, and you may even be able to see Ben Nevis (1344m). The path now winds gradually down towards Kinlochleven, hidden below in the glen. As you descend you join the Blackwater Reservoir access track, and meet the pipes that carry water from there down to the town's hydroelectric power station. It's not a particularly pretty sight but was essential for the now-defunct aluminium smelter, the original reason for the town's establishment in 1907; the electricity generated is now used to power Fort William's aluminium works.

Kinlochleven

Kinlochleven eases you back into 'civilisation' before you arrive at Fort William and experience the sensory onslaught that one feels after returning from the wilderness. There's plenty of B&B, hostel and camping accommodation, including the Blackwater Hostel (p149), as well as a village store and small supermarket.

The Ice Factor (p149), housed in part of the former smelting plant, has the world's largest indoor ice-climbing wall (plus a 'normal' climbing wall), so you can watch people performing amazing vertical feats while you tuck into a large pizza in the centre's cafe.

Day Seven: Kinlochleven to Fort William

➜ **Duration** six to 7½ hours

➜ **Distance** 15 miles (24km)

From Kinlochleven follow the road north out of town and turn off opposite the school. The path climbs through woodland to the old military road, from which you get a grand view along Loch Leven to the Pap of Glencoe (740m). Climb gradually to the crest, just beyond which are the ruins of several old farm buildings at Tigh-na-sleubhaich. From here the Way

Top: Buachaille Etive
Mor and Rannoch Moor

Bottom: Walker
descending Ben Nevis

THE DEVIL'S STAIRCASE

The steep zigzags on the West Highland Way where it climbs out of Glen Coe were given the name 'Devil's Staircase' by the soldiers who built them back in 1750 as part of a military road linking Stirling Castle to Fort William. It was superseded by Thomas Telford's road through Glen Coe in the early 19th century (and by the modern A82 in 1933), but the name Devil's Staircase was again used during the building of the Blackwater Reservoir above Kinlochleven in 1905–09, when the navvies working on the dam used the route to go drinking at the Kings House Hotel – in harsh winter weather, many perished in the snow on the way back.

continues gently downhill and into conifer plantations 2 miles further on. You emerge at **Blar a' Chaorainn**, which is nothing more than a bench and an information board.

The Way leads on and up, through more plantations; occasional breaks in the trees provide fine views of Ben Nevis. After a few miles, a sign points to nearby **Dùn Deardail**, an Iron Age fort with walls that have been partly vitrified (turned to glass) by fire.

A little further on, cross another stile and follow the forest track down towards **Glen Nevis**. Across the valley the huge bulk of Ben Nevis fills the view. A side track leads down to Glen Nevis, which can make a good base for an ascent of 'the Ben'.

Continue along the path if you're heading for Fort William, passing a small graveyard just before you meet the road running through Glen Nevis. Turn left here; soon after, there's a large visitor centre (p152) on the right. Continue along the roadside into Fort William. The official end of the West Highland Way is in Gordon Sq, at the far end of Fort William's pedestrianised main street, marked by a bronze sculpture of a weary hiker rubbing his feet. After a rest on one of the benches thoughtfully provided here, you can look forward to an end-of-walk celebration in one of the town's several restaurants and bars.

Fort William

Fort William promotes itself as the 'Outdoor Capital of the UK' (www.outdoorcapital. co.uk), and has good rail and bus connections to the rest of the country. There's a wide range of hostel and B&B accommodation, including Fort William Backpackers (p150) and No 6 Caberfeidh (p151), and lots of places to eat – the Grog & Gruel (p151) does great Mexican grub. If you're camping, be aware that the nearest campsite is back in Glen Nevis (p152), 2.5 miles before you reach Fort William, as is the SYHA hostel (p152); both are signposted off the Way above Glen Nevis.

Inverness & the Central Highlands

Best Places to Eat

➡ Lime Tree (p151)

➡ Café 1 (p115)

➡ Cross (p132)

➡ Lochleven Seafood Cafe (p149)

➡ Old Forge (p160)

Best Places to Stay

➡ Rocpool Reserve (p115)

➡ Lime Tree (p150)

➡ Lovat (p125)

➡ Eagleview Guest House (p132)

➡ Trafford Bank (p114)

Why Go?

From the subarctic plateau of the Cairngorms to the rolling hills of Highland Perthshire and the rugged, rocky peaks of Glen Coe, the central mountain ranges of the Scottish Highlands are testimony to the sculpting power of ice and weather. Here the landscape is at its grandest, with soaring hills of rock and heather bounded by wooded glens and rushing waterfalls.

Not surprisingly, this part of the country is an adventure playground for outdoor-sports enthusiasts. Aviemore, Glen Coe and Fort William draw hill walkers and climbers in summer, and skiers, snowboarders and ice climbers in winter. Inverness, the Highland capital, provides urban rest and relaxation, while nearby Loch Ness and its elusive monster add a hint of mystery.

From Fort William, base camp for climbing Ben Nevis, the Road to the Isles leads past the beaches of Arisaig and Morar to Mallaig, jumping-off point for the isles of Eigg, Rum, Muck and Canna.

When to Go
Inverness

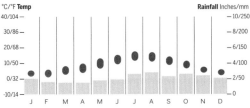

Apr–May Mountain scenery is at its most spectacular, with snow lingering on the higher peaks.

Jun Fort William hosts the UCI Mountain Bike World Cup, pulling huge crowds.

Sep Ideal for hiking and hill walking: midges are dying off, but weather is still reasonably good.

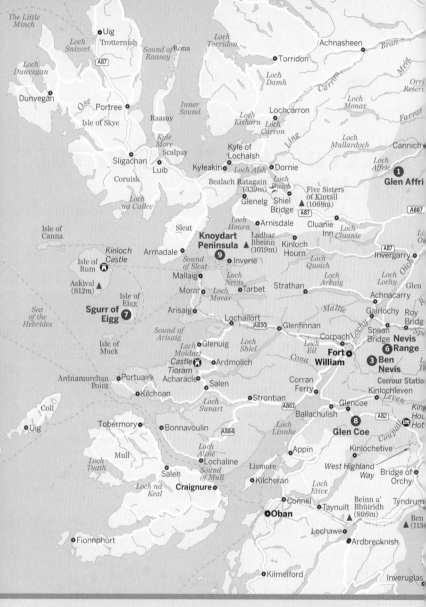

Inverness & the Central Highlands Highlights

1 Hiking among the hills, lochs and forests of beautiful **Glen Affric** (p118)

2 Wandering through the ancient Caledonian forest

at **Rothiemurchus Estate** (p126)

3 Making it to the summit of **Ben Nevis** (153) – and being able to see the view

4 Exploring the hills around gorgeous **Glen Lyon** (p145)

5 Keeping right on to the end of the road at bleak but beautiful **Rannoch Moor** (p142)

6 Rattling your teeth loose on the championship downhill mountain-bike course at **Nevis Range** (p153)

7 Taking in the stunning panorama from the summit of the **Sgurr of Eigg** (p162)

8 Soaking up the scenery (when you can see it!) in moody but magnificent **Glen Coe** (p146)

9 Venturing into the remote and rugged wilderness of the **Knoydart Peninsula** (p159)

ⓘ Getting Around

For timetable information, call **Traveline Scotland** (☑ 0871 200 2233; www.travelinescotland.com).

BUS

Scottish Citylink (☑ 0871 266 3333; www.citylink.co.uk) Runs buses from Perth and Glasgow to Inverness and Fort William, and links Inverness to Fort William along the Great Glen.

Stagecoach (www.stagecoachbus.com) The main regional bus company, with offices in Aviemore, Inverness and Fort William. Dayrider tickets are valid for a day's unlimited travel on Stagecoach buses in various regions, including Inverness (£3.40), Aviemore and around (£6.50) and Fort William (£3.20).

TRAIN

Two railway lines serve the region: the Perth–Aviemore–Inverness line in the east, and the Glasgow–Fort William–Mallaig line in the west.

INVERNESS & THE GREAT GLEN

Inverness, one of the fastest growing towns in Britain, is the capital of the Highlands. It's a transport hub and jumping-off point for the central, western and northern Highlands, the Moray Firth coast and the Great Glen.

The Great Glen is a geological fault running in an arrow-straight line across Scotland from Fort William to Inverness. The glaciers of the last ice age eroded a deep trough along the fault line, which is now filled by a series of lochs – Linnhe, Lochy, Oich and Ness. The glen has always been an important communication route – General George Wade built a military road along the southern side of Loch Ness in the early 18th century, and in 1822 the various lochs were linked by the Caledonian Canal to create a cross-country waterway. The modern A82 road along the glen was completed in 1933 – a date that coincides neatly with the first modern sightings of the Loch Ness Monster.

Inverness

POP 61,235

Inverness has a great location astride the River Ness at the northern end of the Great Glen. In summer it overflows with visitors intent on monster hunting at nearby Loch Ness, but it's worth a visit in its own right for a stroll along the picturesque River Ness, a cruise on Loch Ness, and a meal in one of the city's excellent restaurants.

Inverness was probably founded by King David in the 12th century, but thanks to its often violent history few buildings of real age or historical significance have survived – much of the older part of the city dates from the period following the completion of the Caledonian Canal in 1822. The broad and shallow River Ness, famed for its salmon fishing, runs through the heart of the city.

⊙ Sights & Activities

★ Ness Islands   PARK

The main attraction in Inverness is a leisurely stroll along the river to the Ness Islands. Planted with mature Scots pine, fir, beech and sycamore, and linked to the river banks and each other by elegant Victorian footbridges, the islands make an appealing picnic spot. They're a 20-minute walk south of the castle – head upstream on either side of the river (the start of the Great Glen Way), and return on the opposite bank.

On the way you'll pass the red-sandstone towers of **St Andrew's Cathedral** (11 Ardross St), dating from 1869, and the modern Eden Court Theatre (p116), which hosts regular art exhibits, both on the west bank.

Inverness Museum & Art Gallery   MUSEUM

(☑ 01463-237114; www.inverness.highland.museum; Castle Wynd; ⊙ 10am-5pm Tue-Sat Apr-Oct, Thu-Sat Nov-Mar) **FREE** Inverness Museum & Art Gallery has wildlife dioramas, geological displays, period rooms with historic weapons, Pictish stones and exhibitions of contemporary Highland arts and crafts.

Victorian Market   MARKET

(www.invernessvictorianmarket.co.uk; Academy St; ⊙ 9am-5pm Mon-Sat) If the rain comes down, you could opt for a spot of retail therapy in the Victorian Market, a shopping mall that dates from the 1890s and has rather more charm than its modern equivalents.

Inverness Castle   CASTLE

(Castle St) The hill above the city centre is topped by the picturesque Baronial turrets of Inverness Castle, a pink-sandstone confection dating from 1847 that replaced a medieval castle blown up by the Jacobites in 1746; it serves today as the Sheriff's Court. It's not open to the public, but there are good views from the surrounding gardens.

Inverness

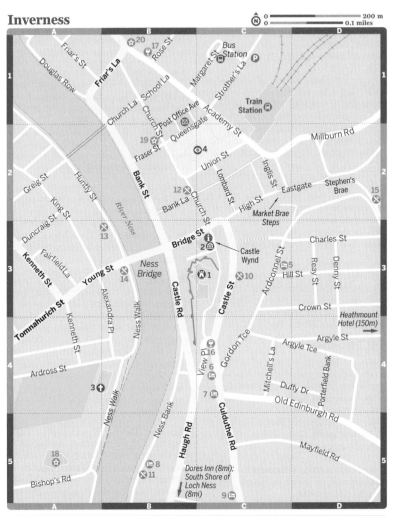

N 0 —————————— 200 m
   0 —————————— 0.1 miles

Inverness

⊙ Sights

1 Inverness Castle	C3
2 Inverness Museum & Art Gallery	C3
3 St Andrew's Cathedral	A4
4 Victorian Market	C2

🛏 Sleeping

5 Ardconnel House	C3
6 Bazpackers Backpackers Hotel	C4
Glenmoriston Town House Hotel	(see 11)
7 Inverness Student Hotel	C4
8 MacRae Guest House	B5
9 Rocpool Reserve	C5

⊗ Eating

10 Café 1	C3
11 Contrast Brasserie	B5
12 Joy of Taste	B2
13 Kitchen Brasserie	B3
14 Rocpool	B3
15 Velocity Cafe	D2

🍷 Drinking & Nightlife

| 16 Castle Tavern | C4 |
| 17 Phoenix | B1 |

✪ Entertainment

18 Eden Court Theatre	A5
19 Hootananny	B2
20 Ironworks	B1

INVERNESS & THE CENTRAL HIGHLANDS INVERNESS

👉 Tours

Jacobite Cruises BOAT TOURS
(📞 01463-233999; www.jacobite.co.uk; Glenurquhart Rd; adult/child £31.50/25; ☺ daily Apr-Sep)
Boats depart from Tomnahurich Bridge at 2pm for a 1½-hour 'Discovery' cruise along Loch Ness, followed by a visit to Urquhart Castle and a return to Inverness by coach. You can buy tickets at the tourist office and catch a free minibus to the boat. Other cruises and combined cruise/coach tours, from one to 6½ hours, are also available.

Happy Tours WALKING TOURS
(📞 07828 154683; www.happy-tours.biz; per person £6) Offers 1¼-hour guided walks exploring the town's history and legends. City history tours begin outside the tourist office at 11am, 1pm and 3pm daily, while 'crime and punishment' tours start at 7pm and 8.30pm.

Inverness Taxis TOURS
(📞 01463-222900; www.inverness-taxis.co.uk)
Wide range of day tours to Urquhart Castle, Loch Ness, Culloden and even Skye. Fares per car (up to four people) range from £60 (two hours) to £240 (all day).

🛏 Sleeping

Inverness has a good range of backpacker accommodation, and also has some excellent boutique hotels. There are lots of guesthouses and B&Bs along Old Edinburgh Rd and Ardconnel St on the east side of the river, and on Kenneth St and Fairfield Rd on the west bank; all are within 10 minutes' walk of the city centre.

The city fills up quickly in July and August, so you should either prebook your accommodation or get an early start looking for somewhere to stay.

Bazpackers Backpackers Hotel HOSTEL £
(📞 01463-717663; www.bazpackershostel.co.uk; 4 Culduthel Rd; dm/tw £17/44; @ 📶) This may be Inverness' smallest hostel (34 beds), but it's hugely popular. It's a friendly, quiet place – the main building has a convivial lounge centred on a wood-burning stove, and a small garden and great views (some rooms are in a separate building with no garden). The dorms and kitchen can be a bit cramped, but the showers are great.

Inverness Student Hotel HOSTEL £
(📞 01463-236556; www.scotlands-top-hostels. com; 8 Culduthel Rd; dm £18; P @ 📶) Set in a rambling old house with comfy beds and

views across the River Ness, this hostel has a party atmosphere, and runs organised pub crawls in town. It's a 10-minute walk from the train station, just past the castle.

Inverness Millburn SYHA HOSTEL £
(SYHA; 📞 01463-231771; www.syha.org.uk; Victoria Dr; dm/tw £19/54; ☺ Apr-Dec; P @ 📶) Inverness' modern 166-bed hostel is 10 minutes' walk northeast of the city centre. With its comfy beds and flashy stainless-steel kitchen, some reckon it's the best SYHA hostel in the country. Booking is essential, especially at Easter and in July and August.

Bught Caravan Park & Campsite CAMPSITE £
(📞 01463-236920; www.invernesscaravanpark. com; Bught Lane; sites per person £10, campervan £16; ☺ Easter-Sep; 📶) A mile southwest of the city centre near Tomnahurich Bridge, this camping ground is hugely popular with backpackers.

★**Trafford Bank** B&B ££
(📞 01463-241414; www.traffordbankguesthouse. co.uk; 96 Fairfield Rd; d £120-132; P 📶) Lots of word-of-mouth rave reviews for this elegant Victorian villa, which was once home to a bishop, just a mitre-toss from the Caledonian Canal and 10 minutes' walk west from the city centre. The luxurious rooms include fresh flowers and fruit, bathrobes and fluffy towels – ask for the Tartan Room, which has a wrought-iron king-size bed and Victorian roll-top bath.

Ardconnel House B&B ££
(📞 01463-240455; www.ardconnel-inverness.co.uk; 21 Ardconnel St; r per person £35-40; 📶) The six-room Ardconnel is one of our favourites – a terraced Victorian house with comfortable en suite rooms, a dining room with crisp white table linen, and a breakfast menu that includes Vegemite for homesick Antipodeans. Kids under 10 not allowed.

Ach Aluinn B&B ££
(📞 01463-230127; www.achaluinn.com; 27 Fairfield Rd; r per person £25-35; P) This large, detached Victorian house is bright and homely, and offers all you might want from a B&B:a a private bathroom, TV, reading lights, comfy beds with two pillows each and an excellent breakfast. Less than 10 minutes' walk west from the city centre.

Heathmount Hotel BOUTIQUE HOTEL ££
(📞 01463-235877; www.heathmounthotel.com; Kingsmills Rd; s/d from £75/115; P 📶) Small and friendly, the Heathmount combines a

popular local bar and restaurant with eight designer hotel rooms, each one different, ranging from a boldly coloured family room in purple and gold to a slinky black velvet four-poster double. Five minutes' walk east of the city centre.

MacRae Guest House
B&B ££

(☑ 01463-243658; joycemacrae@hotmail.com; 24 Ness Bank; s/d from £45/64; P ⬚) This pretty, flower-bedecked Victorian house on the eastern bank of the river has smart, tastefully decorated bedrooms (one is wheelchair accessible), and vegetarian breakfasts are available. Minimum two-night bookings in July and August.

★ Rocpool Reserve
BOUTIQUE HOTEL £££

(☑ 01463-240089; www.rocpool.com; Culduthel Rd; s/d from £185/220; P ⬚) Boutique chic meets the Highlands in this slick and sophisticated little hotel, where an elegant Georgian exterior conceals an oasis of contemporary cool. A gleaming white entrance hall lined with red carpet and contemporary art leads to designer rooms in shades of chocolate, cream and gold; a restaurant by Albert Roux completes the luxury package.

Expect lots of high-tech gadgetry in the more expensive rooms, from iPod docks to balcony hot tubs with aquavision TV.

Glenmoriston Town House Hotel
BOUTIQUE HOTEL £££

(☑ 01463-223777; www.glenmoristontownhouse. com; 20 Ness Bank; r from £180; P ⬚) Luxurious boutique hotel on the banks of the River Ness. Can organise golfing and fishing for guests.

✗ Eating

Velocity Cafe
CAFE £

(☑ 01463-419956; http://velocitylove.co.uk; 1 Crown Ave; mains £4-7; ⊙ 9am-5pm Fri-Mon & Wed, 10am-5pm Tue, 9am-9pm Thu; ⬚) 🖉 This cyclists' cafe serves soups, sandwiches and salads prepared with organic, locally sourced produce, as well as yummy cake and coffee. There's also a workshop where you can repair your bike or book a session with a mechanic.

★ Café 1
BISTRO ££

(☑ 01463-226200; www.cafe1.net; 75 Castle St; mains £10-24; ⊙ noon-2.30pm & 5-9.30pm Mon-Fri, noon-2.30pm & 6-9.30pm Sat) 🖉 Café 1 is a friendly and appealing bistro with candle-lit tables amid elegant blonde-wood and wrought-iron decor. There is an international menu based on quality Scottish produce,

from Aberdeen Angus steaks to crisp pan-fried sea bass and meltingly tender pork belly. The set lunch menu (two courses for £8) is served noon to 2.30pm Monday to Saturday.

Contrast Brasserie
BRASSERIE ££

(☑ 01463-227889; www.glenmoristontownhouse. com; 22 Ness Bank; mains £17-26) Book early for what we think is one of the the best-value restaurants in Inverness: a dining room that drips designer style, with smiling professional staff and truly delicious food prepared using fresh Scottish produce. The two-course lunch menu (£11) and three-course early-bird menu (£16, 5pm to 6.30pm) are bargains.

Joy of Taste
BRITISH ££

(☑ 01463-241459; www.thejoyoftaste.co.uk; 25 Church St; mains £15-19; ⊙ noon-3pm & 5.30-10.30pm Mon-Sat, 5.30-9.30pm Sun) 🖉 Here's a novel concept – a restaurant run by a head chef and 25 volunteers who work a shift a week just for 'the love of creating a beautiful restaurant' (plus a share of the profits). And a very good job they have made of it, with a menu of classic British cuisine and a growing fan club of satisfied customers.

Rocpool
MEDITERRANEAN ££

(☑ 01463-717274; www.rocpoolrestaurant.com; 1 Ness Walk; mains £18-25; ⊙ noon-2.30pm & 5.45-10pm Mon-Sat) 🖉 Lots of polished wood, crisp white linen and leather booths and banquettes lend a nautical air to this relaxing bistro, which offers a Mediterranean-influenced menu that makes the most of quality Scottish produce, especially seafood. The two-course lunch is £15.

Kitchen Brasserie
MODERN SCOTTISH ££

(☑ 01463-259119; www.kitchenrestaurant.co.uk; 15 Huntly St; mains £8-19; ⊙ noon-10pm; ⬚) This spectacular glass-fronted restaurant offers a great menu and a view over the River Ness – try to get a table upstairs. Great value two-course lunch (£7, noon to 3pm) and early-bird menu (£12, 5pm to 7pm).

🍺 Drinking & Nightlife

Clachnaharry Inn
PUB

(☑ 01463-239806; www.clachnaharryinn.co.uk; 17-19 High St; ⊙ 11am-11pm, to midnight Fri & Sat) Just over a mile northwest of the city centre, on the bank of the Caledonian Canal just off the A862, this is a delightful old coaching inn (with beer garden out back) serving an excellent range of real ales and good pub grub.

Castle Tavern
PUB

(☑ 01463-718718; www.castletavern.net; 1-2 View Pl; ⊘ 11am-11pm) With a tasty selection of real ales, this pub has a wee suntrap of a terrace out the front. It's a great place for a pint on a summer afternoon.

Phoenix
PUB

(☑ 01463-233685; 108 Academy St; ⊘ 11am-11pm) Recently refurbished, this is the most traditional of the pubs in the city centre, with a mahogany horseshoe bar and several real ales on tap, including beers from the Cairngorm, Cromarty and Isle of Skye breweries.

☆ Entertainment

Hootananny
LIVE MUSIC

(☑ 01463-233651; www.hootananny.com; 67 Church St) Hootananny is the city's best live-music venue, with traditional folk- and/ or rock-music sessions nightly, including big-name bands from all over Scotland (and, indeed, the world). The bar is well stocked with a range of beers from the local Black Isle Brewery.

Eden Court Theatre
THEATRE

(☑ 01463-234234; www.eden-court.co.uk; Bishop's Rd) The Highlands' main cultural venue (with theatre, art-house cinema and conference centre), Eden Court stages a busy program of drama, dance, comedy, music, film and children's events, and has a good bar and restaurant. Pick up a program from the foyer or check the website.

Ironworks
LIVE MUSIC, COMEDY

(☑ 0871 789 4173; www.ironworksvenue.com; 122 Academy St) With live bands (rock, pop, tribute) and comedy shows two or three times a week, the Ironworks is the town's main venue for big-name acts.

ℹ Information

Inverness Tourist Office (☑ 01463-252401; www.visithighlands.com; Castle Wynd; internet access per 20min £1; ⊘ 9am-6pm Mon-Sat, 9.30am-5pm Sun Jul & Aug, 9am-5pm Mon-Sat, 10am-4pm Sun Jun, Sep & Oct, 9am-5pm Mon-Sat Apr & May) Bureau de change and accommodation-booking service; also sells tickets for tours and cruises. Opening hours limited November to March.

ℹ Getting There & Away

AIR

Inverness Airport (INV; ☑ 01667-464000; www.hial.co.uk/inverness-airport) At Dalcross, 10 miles east of the city, off the A96 towards Aberdeen. There are scheduled flights to Amsterdam, London, Manchester, Orkney, Shetland and the Outer Hebrides, as well as other places in the British Isles.

BUS

Services depart from **Inverness bus station** (Margaret St).

Aberdeen £12.50, 3¾ hours, hourly
Aviemore £9.80, 45 minutes, eight daily
Edinburgh £30, 3½ to 4½ hours, hourly
Fort William £11.20, two hours, five daily
Glasgow £30, 3½ to 4½ hours, hourly
London £45, 13 hours, one daily; more frequent services requiring a change at Glasgow. Operated by **National Express** (☑ 08717 81 81 78; www.gobycoach.com).
Portree £25, 3¼ hours, three daily
Thurso £19, three hours, three to five daily
Ullapool £12.80, 1½ hours, two daily except Sunday

If you book far enough in advance, **Megabus** (☑ 0871 266 3333; www.megabus.com) offers fares from as little as £1 for buses from Inverness to Glasgow and Edinburgh, and £10 to London.

TRAIN

Aberdeen £27, 2¼ hours, eight daily
Edinburgh £41, 3½ hours, eight daily
Glasgow £41, 3½ hours, eight daily
Kyle of Lochalsh £22, 2½ hours, four daily Monday to Saturday, two Sunday; one of Britain's great scenic train journeys
London £100, eight to nine hours, one daily direct; others require a change at Edinburgh
Wick £19, 4½ hours, four daily Monday to Saturday, one or two on Sunday; via Thurso

ℹ Getting Around

TO/FROM THE AIRPORT

Stagecoach Jet (www.stagecoachbus.com) Buses run from the airport to Inverness bus station (£3.90, 20 minutes, every 30 minutes).

BICYCLE

Ticket to Ride (☑ 01463-419160; www.ticket-toridehighlands.co.uk; Bellfield Park; per day from £22; ⊘ 9am-6pm Apr-Oct) Hire mountain bikes, hybrids and tandems; can be dropped off in Fort William. Will deliver bikes free to local hotels and B&Bs.

BUS

City services and buses to places around Inverness, including Nairn, Forres, the Culloden battlefield, Beauly, Dingwall and Lairg, are operated by Stagecoach (p289). An Inverness City Dayrider ticket costs £3.40 and gives unlimited travel for a day on buses throughout the city.

CAR

Focus Vehicle Rental (☑ 01463-709517; www. focusvehiclerental.co.uk; 6 Harbour Rd) The big boys charge from around £50 to £60 per day, but Focus has cheaper rates starting at £38 per day.

TAXI

Highland Taxis (☑ 01463-222222; www. highlandtaxisinverness.co.uk)

Around Inverness

Culloden Battlefield

The Battle of Culloden in 1746, the last pitched battle ever fought on British soil, saw the defeat of Bonnie Prince Charlie and the end of the Jacobite dream when 1200 Highlanders were slaughtered by government forces in a 68-minute rout. The Duke of Cumberland, son of the reigning King George II and leader of the Hanoverian army, earned the nickname 'Butcher' for his brutal treatment of the defeated Jacobite forces. The battle sounded the death knell for the old clan system, and the horrors of the Clearances soon followed. The sombre moor where the conflict took place has scarcely changed in the ensuing 260 years.

Culloden is 6 miles east of Inverness. Bus No 2 runs from Queensgate in Inverness to Culloden battlefield (£2.40, 30 minutes, hourly).

Culloden Visitor Centre INTERPRETATION CENTRE
(NTS; www.nts.org.uk/culloden; adult/child £11/8.50; ⊙ 9am-6pm Jun-Aug, to 5.30pm Apr, May, Sep & Oct, 10am-4pm Nov-Mar) This impressive visitor centre has everything you need to know about the Battle of Culloden in 1746, including the lead-up and the aftermath, with perspectives from both sides. An innovative film puts you on the battlefield in the middle of the mayhem, and a wealth of other audio presentations must have kept Inverness' entire acting community in business for weeks. The admission fee includes an audioguide for a self-guided tour of the battlefield itself.

Fort George

The headland guarding the narrows in the Moray Firth opposite Fortrose is occupied by the magnificent and virtually unaltered 18th-century artillery fortification of Fort George.

Fort George FORTRESS
(HS; ☑ 01667-462777; adult/child £8.90/5.40; ⊙ 9.30am-5.30pm Apr-Sep, to 4.30pm Oct-Mar) One of the finest artillery fortifications in Europe, Fort George was established in 1748 in the aftermath of the Battle of Culloden, as a base for George II's army of occupation in the Highlands. By the time of its completion in 1769 it had cost the equivalent of around £1 billion in today's money. It still functions as a military barracks; public areas have exhibitions on 18th-century soldiery, and the mile-plus walk around the ramparts offers fine views out to sea and back to the Great Glen.

Given its size, you'll need at least two hours to do the place justice. The fort is off the A96 about 11 miles northeast of Inverness; there is no public transport.

Nairn

POP 9775

Nairn is a popular golfing and seaside resort with a good sandy beach. The most interesting part of town is the old fishing village of **Fishertown**, down by the harbour, a maze of narrow streets lined with picturesque cottages. **Nairn Museum** (☑ 01667-456791; www.nairnmuseum.co.uk; Viewfield House; adult/ child £3/50p; ⊙ 10am-4.30pm Mon-Fri, to 1pm Sat Apr-Oct), a few minutes' walk from the tourist office, has displays on the history of Fishertown, as well as on local archaeology, geology and natural history.

You can spend many pleasant hours wandering along the **East Beach**, one of the finest in Scotland.

The big event in the town's calendar is the **Nairn Highland Games** (www.nairnhighlandgames.co.uk; ⊙ mid-Aug), and there's also the **Nairn Book and Arts Festival** (www.nairnfestival.co.uk; ⊙ Sep).

🛏 Sleeping & Eating

Glebe End B&B ££
(☑ 01667-451659; www.glebe-end.co.uk; 1 Glebe Rd; r per person £35-45; 🅿🛜) It's people as much as place that make a good B&B, and the owners here are all you could wish for –

helpful and welcoming. The house is lovely too, a spacious Victorian villa with home-away-from-home bedrooms and a sunny conservatory where breakfast is served.

Boath House Hotel HOTEL **£££**
(☑01667-454896; www.boath-house.com; Auldearn; s/d from £190/260; P☎) This beautifully restored Regency mansion, set in private woodland gardens 2 miles east of Nairn on the A96, is one of Scotland's most luxurious country-house hotels, and includes a spa offering holistic treatments and a Michelin-starred restaurant (three-/six-course dinner £45/70).

Classroom GASTROPUB **££**
(☑01667-455999; www.theclassroombistro.com; 1 Cawdor St; mains £14-25; ☺noon-4.30pm & 5-10pm) ✍ Done up in an appealing mixture of modern and traditional styles (lots of richly glowing wood with designer detailing) the Classroom doubles as cocktail bar and gastropub with a tempting menu that goes from Cullen skink (soup made with smoked haddock, potato, onion and milk) to Highland steak with peppercorn sauce.

❶ Information

Nairn has a **tourist information point** (☑01667-453476; Nairn Community Centre, King St; ☺9am-5pm), banks with ATMs and a post office.

❶ Getting There & Away

Buses run hourly (less frequently on Sunday) from Inverness to Nairn (£5.50, 35 minutes) and on to Aberdeen. The bus station is just west of the town centre. The town also lies on the Inverness–Aberdeen railway line; there are five to seven trains a day from Inverness (£5.80, 15 minutes).

Cawdor Castle

Cawdor Castle CASTLE
(☑01667-404615; www.cawdorcastle.com; adult/child £10/6.50; ☺10am-5.30pm May-Sep) This was the 14th-century home of the thanes of Cawdor, one of the titles prophesied by the three witches for Shakespeare's Macbeth. But Macbeth couldn't have lived here, since the oldest part of the castle dates from the 14th century (the wings were 17th-century additions) and he died in 1057. The tour gives an insight into the 18th- and 19th-century lives of the Scottish

aristocracy; the castle is 5 miles southwest of Nairn.

Cawdor Tavern (www.cawdortavern.co.uk; bar meals £9-21; ☺11am-11pm Mon-Thu, 11am-midnight Fri & Sat, noon-11pm Sun, food served noon-9pm Mon-Sat, 12.30-9pm Sun) in the nearby village is worth a visit, though it can be difficult deciding what to drink as it stocks more than 100 varieties of whisky. There's also good pub food, with tempting daily specials.

West of Inverness

Beauly

POP 1365

Mary, Queen of Scots is said to have given this village its name in 1564 when she exclaimed, in French: *'Quel beau lieu!'* (What a beautiful place!). Founded in 1230, the red-sandstone **Beauly Priory** is now an impressive ruin, haunted by the cries of rooks nesting in a magnificent centuries-old sycamore tree.

The central **Priory Hotel** (☑01463-782309; www.priory-hotel.com; The Square; s/d £65/110; P☎) has bright, modern rooms and serves good bar meals. However, the best place for lunch is across the street at the **Corner on the Square** (www.corneronthesquare.co.uk; 1 High St; mains £7-13; ☺8.30am-5.30pm Mon-Fri, 8.30am-5pm Sat, 9.30am-5pm Sun), a superb little delicatessen and cafe that serves breakfast (till 11.30am), daily lunch specials (11.30am to 4.30pm) and excellent coffee.

Buses 28 and 28A from Inverness run to Beauly (£4.80, 30 to 45 minutes, hourly Monday to Saturday, five on Sunday), and the town lies on the Inverness–Thurso railway line.

Strathglass & Glen Affric

The broad valley of Strathglass extends about 18 miles inland from Beauly, followed by the A831 to **Cannich** (the only village in the area), where there's a grocery store and a post office.

Glen Affric (www.glenaffric.org), one of the most beautiful glens in Scotland, extends deep into the hills beyond Cannich. The upper reaches of the glen, now designated as **Glen Affric National Nature Reserve** (www.nnr-scotland.org.uk/glen-affric), is a scenic wonderland of shimmering lochs, rugged mountains and native Scots pine, home to pine martens, wildcats, otters, red squirrels and golden eagles.

About 4 miles southwest of Cannich is **Dog Falls**, a scenic spot where the River Affric squeezes through a narrow, rocky gorge. A circular walking trail (red waymarks) leads from Dog Falls car park to a footbridge below the falls and back on the far side of the river (2 miles, allow one hour).

The road continues beyond Dog Falls to a parking area and picnic site at the eastern end of **Loch Affric** where there are several short walks along the river and the loch shore. The circuit of Loch Affric (10 miles, allow five hours walking, two hours by mountain bike) follows good paths right around the loch and takes you deep into the heart of some very wild scenery.

It's possible to walk all the way from Cannich to **Glen Shiel** on the west coast (35 miles) in two days, spending the night at the remote Glen Affric SYHA Hostel. The route is now part of the newly waymarked **Affric-Kintail Way** (www.glenaffric.info), a 56-mile walking or mountain-biking trail leading from Drumnadrochit to Kintail via Cannich.

The minor road on the east side of the River Glass leads to the pretty little conservation village of **Tomich**, 3 miles southwest of Cannich, built in Victorian times as accommodation for estate workers. The road continues (unsurfaced for the last 2 miles) to a forestry car park, the starting point for a short (800m) walk to pretty **Plodda Falls**. A restored Victorian viewing platform extends over the top of the falls like a diving board, giving a dizzying view straight down the cascade into a remote and thickly forested river gorge. Keep your eyes peeled to see red squirrels and crossbills.

🛏 Sleeping & Eating

Glen Affric SYHA HOSTEL £
(📞bookings 0845 293 7373; www.syha.org.uk; Allt Beithe; dm £22; ⊙Apr–mid-Sep) This remote and rustic hostel is set amid magnificent scenery at the halfway point of the cross-country walk from Cannich to Glen Shiel, 8 miles from the nearest road. Facilities are basic and you'll need to take all supplies with you (and all litter away).

Book in advance. There is no phone, internet or mobile-phone signal at the hostel.

BCC Loch Ness Hostel HOSTEL £
(📞01456-476296; www.bcclochnesshostel.co.uk; Glen Urquhart; s/d £25/45, tent sites per person £5, 2-person pods £30; ℗🛜) Clean, modern, high-quality budget accommodation located halfway between Cannich and Loch Ness; advance booking recommended. There's also a good campsite with the option of luxury glamping pods.

Cannich Caravan & Camping Park CAMPSITE £
(📞01456-415364; www.highlandcamping.co.uk; sites per person £7.50, pods s/d £22/30; 🛜) Good, sheltered site, with option of wooden camping 'pods' and on-site cafe. Mountain bikes for hire at £17 a day.

★ Kerrow House B&B ££
(📞01456-415243; www.kerrow-house.co.uk; Cannich; per person £40-45; ℗) 🍽 This wonderful Georgian hunting lodge has bags of old-fashioned character – it was once the home of Highland author Neil M Gunn – and has spacious grounds with 3.5 miles of private trout fishing. It's a mile south of Cannich on the minor road along the east side of the River Glass.

Tomich Hotel HOTEL ££
(📞01456-415399; www.tomichhotel.co.uk; Tomich; s/d from £70/110; ℗🛜🏊) About 3 miles southwest of Cannich on the southern side of the river, this Victorian hunting lodge has a blazing log fire, a Victorian restaurant, eight comfortable en suite rooms and – a bit of a surprise out here in the wilds – a small, heated indoor swimming pool.

ℹ Getting There & Away

Stagecoach (www.stagecoachbus.com) buses 17 and 117 run from Inverness to Cannich (£5.40, one hour, three a day Monday to Saturday) via Drumnadrochit, and continue from Cannich to Tomich (10 minutes).

Ross's Minibuses (www.ross-minibuses.co.uk) From the first Monday in July to the 2nd Friday in September, runs a minibus from Inverness bus station to the Glen Affric car park via Drumnadrochit and Cannich (1½ hours, once daily Monday, Wednesday and Friday only). It shuttles between Cannich and Glen Affric (30 minutes) twice more on the same days. Check the website for the latest timetables.

Black Isle

The Black Isle – a peninsula rather than an island – is linked to Inverness by the Kessock Bridge.

Fortrose & Rosemarkie

At **Fortrose Cathedral** you'll find the vaulted crypt of a 13th-century chapter house and sacristy, and the ruinous 14th-century south aisle and chapel. **Chanonry Point**, 1.5 miles to the east, is a favourite dolphin-spotting vantage point; there are one-hour **dolphin-watching cruises** (☑ 01381-622383; www.dolphintripsavoch.co.uk; adult/child £14/9) departing from the harbour at Avoch (pronounced 'auch'), 3 miles southwest.

In Rosemarkie, the **Groam House Museum** (☑ 01381-620961; www.groamhouse.org.uk; High St; ☺ 11am-4.30pm Mon-Fri, 2-4.30pm Sat & Sun Easter-Oct) **FREE** has a superb collection of Pictish stones engraved with designs similar to those on Celtic Irish stones.

From the northern end of Rosemarkie's High St, a short but pleasant signposted walk leads you through the gorges and waterfalls of the **Fairy Glen**.

Once you've worked up a thirst, retire to the bar at the **Anderson Hotel** (☑ 01381-620236; www.theanderson.co.uk; Union St) to sample its range of real ales (including Belgian beers and Somerset cider) and more than 200 single malt whiskies.

Cromarty

POP 725

The pretty village of Cromarty at the northeastern tip of the Black Isle has lots of 18th-century red-sandstone houses, and a lovely green park beside the sea for picnics and games. An excellent walk, known as the **100 Steps**, leads from the north end of the village to the headland viewpoint of South Sutor (4 miles round trip).

The 18th-century **Cromarty Courthouse** (☑ 01381-600418; www.cromarty-courthouse.org.uk; Church St; ☺ noon-4pm daily Jul & Aug, Sun-Thu Easter-Jun & Sep) **FREE** details the town's history using contemporary references. Kids will enjoy the talking mannequins.

Near the courthouse is **Hugh Miller's Cottage & Museum** (www.hughmiller.org; Church St; adult/child £6.50/5; ☺ noon-5pm daily Apr-Sep, Tue, Thu & Fri only Oct), the thatchroofed birthplace of Hugh Miller (1802–56), a local stonemason and amateur geologist who later moved to Edinburgh and became a famous journalist and newspaper editor. The Georgian villa next door is home to a museum celebrating his life and achievements.

From Cromarty harbour, **Ecoventures** (☑ 01381-600323; www.ecoventures.co.uk; Cromarty Harbour; adult/child £26/20) runs 2½-hour boat trips into the Moray Firth to see bottlenose dolphins and other wildlife.

Also at the harbour, **Sutor Creek** (☑ 01381-600855; www.sutorcreek.co.uk; 21 Bank St; mains lunch £7-12, dinner £15-22; ☺ 11am-9pm Wed-Sun) 🍽 is an excellent little cafe-restaurant serving wood-fired pizzas and fresh local seafood – if you can't get a table here, try its sister cafe, **Couper's Creek** (☑ 01381-600729; www.sutorcreek.co.uk; 20 Church St; mains £5-9; ☺ 10am-5pm).

For something lighter, there are good tea and scones at the **Pantry** (1 Church St; ☺ 10am-5pm Easter-Sep), or delicious filled rolls and savoury pies at the **Cromarty Bakery** (8 Bank St; ☺ 9am-5pm Mon-Sat).

❶ Getting There & Away

Stagecoach buses 26 and 26A run from Inverness to Fortrose and Rosemarkie (£3.30, 30 to 40 minutes, twice hourly Monday to Saturday); half of them continue to Cromarty (£4.70, one hour).

Loch Ness

Deep, dark and narrow, Loch Ness stretches for 23 miles between Inverness and Fort Augustus. Its bitterly cold waters have been extensively explored in search of Nessie, the elusive Loch Ness monster, but most visitors see her only in cardboard-cutout form at Drumnadrochit's monster exhibitions. The busy A82 road runs along the northwestern shore, while the more tranquil and picturesque B862 follows the southeastern shore. A complete circuit of the loch is about 70 miles – travel anticlockwise for the best views.

🏃 Activities

The 79-mile **Great Glen Way** (www.greatglenway.com) long-distance footpath stretches from Inverness to Fort William, where walkers can connect with the **West Highland Way**. It is described in detail in *The Great Glen Way*, a guide by Jacquetta Megarry and Sandra Bardwell.

MONSTERS, MYTHS & LOCH NESS

Highland folklore is filled with tales of strange creatures living in lochs and rivers, notably the kelpie (water horse) that lures unwary travellers to their doom. The use of the term 'monster', however, is a relatively recent phenomenon, the origins of which lie in an article published in the *Inverness Courier* on 2 May 1933, entitled 'Strange Spectacle on Loch Ness'.

The article recounted the sighting of a disturbance in the loch by Mrs Aldie Mackay and her husband: 'There the creature disported itself, rolling and plunging for fully a minute, its body resembling that of a whale, and the water cascading and churning like a simmering cauldron.'

The story was taken up by the London press and sparked off a rash of sightings that year, including a notorious on-land encounter with London tourists Mr and Mrs Spicer on 22 July 1933, again reported in the *Inverness Courier*:

It was horrible, an abomination. About 50 yards ahead, we saw an undulating sort of neck, and quickly followed by a large, ponderous body. I estimated the length to be 25 to 30 feet, its colour was dark elephant grey. It crossed the road in a series of jerks, but because of the slope we could not see its limbs. Although I accelerated quickly towards it, it had disappeared into the loch by the time I reached the spot. There was no sign of it in the water. I am a temperate man, but I am willing to take any oath that we saw this Loch Ness beast. I am certain that this creature was of a prehistoric species.

The London newspapers couldn't resist. In December 1933 the *Daily Mail* sent Marmaduke Wetherall, a film director and big-game hunter, to Loch Ness to track down the beast. Within days he found 'reptilian' footprints in the shoreline mud (soon revealed to have been made with a stuffed hippopotamus foot). Then in April 1934 came the famous 'long-necked monster' photograph taken by the seemingly reputable Harley St surgeon Colonel Kenneth Wilson. The press went mad and the rest, as they say, is history.

In 1994, however, Christian Spurling – Wetherall's stepson, by then 90 years old – revealed that the most famous photo of Nessie ever taken was in fact a hoax, perpetrated by his stepfather with Wilson's help. Today, of course, there are those who claim that Spurling's confession is itself a hoax. And, ironically, the researcher who exposed the surgeon's photo as a fake still believes wholeheartedly in the monster's existence.

There have been regular sightings of the monster through the years (see www.lochnesssightings.com), with a peak in 1996–97 (the Hollywood movie *Loch Ness* was released in 1996), but reports have tailed off in recent years – there were no sightings at all in 2013.

Hoax or not, the bizarre mini-industry that has grown up around Loch Ness and its mysterious monster since that eventful summer three-quarters of a century ago is a spectacle in itself.

The Great Glen Way can also be ridden (strenuous!) by mountain bike, while the **Great Glen Mountain Bike Trails** at Nevis Range and Abriachan Forest offer challenging cross-country and downhill trails. (You can hire a mountain bike in Fort William and drop it off in Inverness, and vice versa.)

The **South Loch Ness Trail** (www.visitlochness.com/south-loch-ness-trail), opened in 2011, links a series of footpaths and minor roads along the less-frequented southern side of the loch. The 28 miles from Loch Tarff near Fort Augustus to Torbreck on the fringes of Inverness can be done on foot, by bike or on horseback.

There's also the option of the **Great Glen Canoe Trail** (www.greatglencanoetrail.info), a series of access points, waymarks and informal campsites that allow you to travel the length of the glen by canoe or kayak.

The climb to the summit of **Meallfuarvonie** (699m), on the northwestern shore of Loch Ness, makes an excellent short hill walk: the views along the Great Glen from the top are superb. It's a 6-mile round trip, so allow about three hours. Start from the car park at the end of the minor road leading south from Drumnadrochit to Bunloit.

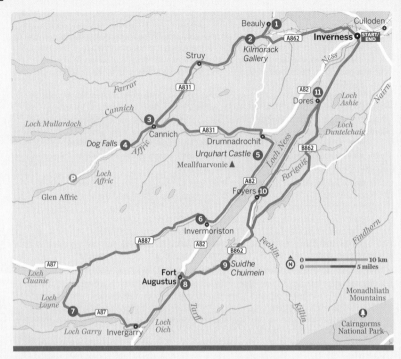

Driving Tour
A Loch Ness Circuit

START INVERNESS
FINISH INVERNESS
DISTANCE 130 MILES
DURATION 4 HOURS

Head out of Inverness on the A862 to Beauly, arriving in time for breakfast at **1 Corner on the Square** (p118) in Beauly. Backtrack a mile and turn right on the A831 to Cannich, passing **2 Kilmorack Gallery**, which exhibits contemporary art in a converted church. The scenery gets wilder as you approach **3 Cannich**; turn right and follow the single-track road to the car park at **4 Dog Falls**. Take a stroll along the rushing river, or hike to the viewpoint (about a one-hour round trip; 2 miles) for a glimpse of remote Glen Affric.

Return to Cannich and turn right on the A831 to Drumnadrochit, then right on the A82 past picturesque **5 Urquhart Castle** (p124) and along the shores of Loch Ness. At **6 Invermoriston**, pause to look at the old bridge, built by engineer Thomas Telford

in 1813, then head west on the A887 towards Kyle of Lochalsh; after 16 miles go left on the A87 towards Invergarry. You are now among some of the finest mountain scenery in the Highlands; as the road turns east above Loch Garry, stop at the famous **7 viewpoint** (layby on right, signposted Glengarry Viewpoint). By a quirk of perspective, the lochs to the west appear to form the map outline of Scotland.

At Invergarry, turn left on the A82 to reach **8 Fort Augustus** and a late lunch at the Lovat or Lock Inn. Take the B862 out of town, following the line of General Wade's 18th-century military road, to another viewpoint at **9 Suidhe Chuimein**. A short (800m) walk up the well-worn path to the summit affords an even better panorama.

Ahead, you can choose the low road via the impressive **10 Falls of Foyers**, or stay on the the high road (B862) for more views; both converge on Loch Ness at the **11 Dores Inn** (p123), where you can sip a pint with a view along Loch Ness, and even stay for dinner before returning to Inverness.

✦ Festivals & Events

RockNess Music Festival MUSIC
(www.rockness.co.uk; ☉Jun) A vast lochside field at the village of Dores hosts this annual festival, a three-day smorgasbord of the best in Scottish and international DJs and bands. Recent headliners include Fat Boy Slim, Basement Jaxx and Ellie Goulding.

Drumnadrochit

POP 1100

Seized by monster madness, its gift shops bulging with Nessie cuddly toys, Drumnadrochit is a hotbed of beastie fever, with two monster exhibitions battling it out for the tourist dollar.

◉ Sights & Activities

Urquhart Castle CASTLE
(HS; ☏01456-450551; adult/child £7.90/4.80; ☉9.30am-6pm Apr-Sep, to 5pm Oct, to 4.30pm Nov-Mar; P) Commanding a brilliant location 1.5 miles east of Drumnadrochit, with outstanding views (on a clear day), Urquhart Castle is a popular Nessie-watching hot spot. A huge visitor centre (most of which is beneath ground level) includes a video theatre (with a dramatic 'unveiling' of the castle at the end of the film) and displays of medieval items discovered in the castle.

The castle was repeatedly sacked and rebuilt (and sacked and rebuilt) over the centuries; in 1692 it was blown up to prevent the Jacobites from using it. The five-storey tower house at the northern point is the most impressive remaining fragment and offers wonderful views across the water. The site includes a huge gift shop and a restaurant, and is often very crowded in summer.

Loch Ness Centre & Exhibition INTERPRETATION CENTRE
(☏01456-450573; www.lochness.com; adult/child £7.45/4.95; ☉9.30am-6pm Jul & Aug, to 5pm Easter-Jun, Sep & Oct, 10am-3.30pm Nov-Easter; P) This Nessie-themed attraction adopts a scientific approach that allows you to weigh the evidence for yourself. Exhibits include the original equipment – sonar survey vessels, miniature submarines, cameras and sediment coring tools – used in various monster hunts, as well as original photographs and film footage of sightings. You'll find out about hoaxes and optical illusions, as well as learning a lot about the ecology of Loch Ness – is there enough food in the loch to support even one 'monster', let alone a breeding population?

Nessieland EXHIBITION
(www.nessieland.co.uk; adult/child £6/3; ☉9am-7pm Apr-Oct, to 5pm Nov-Mar; P) This attraction is a miniature theme park aimed squarely at the kids, though we suspect its main function is to sell you Loch Ness monster souvenirs.

Nessie Hunter BOAT TOURS
(☏01456-450395; www.lochness-cruises.com; adult/child £15/10; ☉Easter-Oct) One-hour monster-hunting cruises, complete with sonar and underwater cameras. Cruises depart from Drumnadrochit hourly (except 1pm) from 9am to 6pm daily.

WORTH A TRIP

DORES INN

While crowded tour coaches pour down the west side of Loch Ness to the hot spots of Drumnadrochit and Urquhart Castle, the narrow B862 road along the eastern shore is relatively peaceful. It leads to the village of Foyers, where you can enjoy a pleasant hike to the **Falls of Foyers**.

But it's worth making the trip just for the **Dores Inn** (☏01463-751203; www.thedoresinn.co.uk; Dores; mains £10-14; ☉pub 10am-11pm, food served noon-2pm & 6-9pm; P☏), a beautifully restored country pub furnished with recycled furniture, local landscape paintings and fresh flowers. The menu specialises in quality Scottish produce, from haggis, turnips and *tatties* (potatoes), and haddock and chips, to steaks, scallops and seafood platters.

The pub garden enjoys a stunning view along Loch Ness, and even has a dedicated monster-spotting vantage point. The nearby campervan, emblazoned with Nessie-Serry Independent Research, has been home to dedicated Nessie hunter Steve Feltham (www.nessiehunter.co.uk) since 1991; he sells clay models of the monster, and is a font of fascinating stories about the loch.

LOCAL KNOWLEDGE

LOCH NESS & AROUND

The leader of the Loch Ness Project, and designer of the Loch Ness Centre & Exhibition, Adrian Shine, offers his recommendations for the Loch Ness area.

Urquhart Castle

If, having learned some of the inner secrets of the loch at the Loch Ness Centre & Exhibition (p123), you want to see it through new eyes, you cannot do better than visit Urquhart Castle (p123). Perched on a rocky promontory jutting into Loch Ness, its exhibits recount the castle's history from a vitrified Pictish fort to its role in the Scottish Wars of Independence. The view from the Grant Tower is truly breathtaking.

Fort Augustus Locks

At the southern end of the loch there is a flight of locks on the Caledonian Canal (p125) built by the great engineer Thomas Telford. It is always interesting to watch vessels being worked up this 'staircase' of water. British Waterways have a fascinating exhibition beside the locks.

Waterfall Walks

Starting from the car park at Invermoriston, cross the road to find a magnificent waterfall, then go back to take the path down the river through a mature beech wood to the shores of the loch. There is another famous waterfall at Foyers on the southeastern shore of Loch Ness, and Divach Falls up Balmacaan Rd at Drumnadrochit.

🛏 Sleeping & Eating

Loch Ness Backpackers Lodge   HOSTEL £
(☎ 01456-450807; www.lochness-backpackers.com; Coiltie Farmhouse, East Lewiston; per person from £16; P🐕) This snug, friendly hostel housed in a cottage and barn has six-bed dorms, one double and a large barbecue area. It's about 0.75 miles from Drumnadrochit, along the A82 towards Fort William; turn left where you see the sign for Loch Ness Inn, just before the bridge.

Loch Ness SYHA   HOSTEL £
(☎ 01320-351274; www.syha.org.uk; Glenmoriston; dm £20; ☺ Apr-Sep, closed 10am-5pm daily; @) This hostel is housed in a big lodge overlooking Loch Ness, and many dorms have loch views. It's located on the A82 road, 13 miles southwest of Drumnadrochit, and 4 miles northeast of Invermoriston. Buses from Inverness to Fort William stop nearby.

Borlum Farm   CAMPSITE £
(☎ 01456-450220; www.borlum.co.uk; sites per adult/child £6/4; ☺ Mar-Oct) Basic campsite beside the main road 800m southeast of Drumnadrochit.

Loch Ness Inn   INN ££
(☎ 01456-450991; www.staylochness.co.uk; Lewiston; d/f £90/120; P🐕) The Loch Ness Inn ticks all the weary traveller's boxes, with comfortable bedrooms (the family suite

sleeps two adults and two children), a cosy bar pouring real ales from the Cairngorm and Isle of Skye breweries, and a rustic restaurant (mains £9 to £19) serving hearty, wholesome fare such as whisky-flambéed haggis, and roast rump of Scottish lamb.

It's conveniently located in the quiet hamlet of Lewiston, between Drumnadrochit and Urquhart Castle.

Drumbuie Farm   B&B ££
(☎ 01456-450634; www.loch-ness-farm.co.uk; Drumnadrochit; s/d from £44/68; P) Drumbuie is a B&B in a modern house on a working farm – the surrounding fields are full of sheep and highland cattle – with views over Urquhart Castle and Loch Ness. Walkers and cyclists are welcome.

**Fiddler's Coffee Shop &
Restaurant**   CAFE, RESTAURANT ££
(www.fiddledrum.co.uk; mains £11-18; ☺ 11am-11pm; 🐕) The coffee shop does cappuccino and croissants, while the restaurant serves traditional Highland fare, such as venison and haggis, and a wide range of bottled Scottish beers. There's also a whisky bar with huge range of single malts.

ⓘ Getting There & Away

Scottish Citylink (p112) and Stagecoach buses from Inverness to Fort William run along the shores of Loch Ness (six to eight daily, five on

Sunday); those headed for Skye turn off at Invermoriston. There are bus stops at Drumnadrochit (£3.20, 30 minutes), Urquhart Castle car park (£3.50, 35 minutes) and Loch Ness Youth Hostel (£9, 45 minutes).

Fort Augustus

POP 620

Fort Augustus, at the junction of four old military roads, was originally a government garrison and the headquarters of General George Wade's road-building operations in the early 18th century. Today it's a neat and picturesque little place, often overrun by coach-tour crowds in summer.

◉ Sights & Activities

Caledonian Canal CANAL
(www.scottishcanals.co.uk) At Fort Augustus, boats using the Caledonian Canal are raised and lowered 13m by a 'ladder' of five consecutive locks. It's fun to watch, and the neatly landscaped canal banks are a great place to soak up the sun or compare accents with fellow tourists. The **Caledonian Canal Visitor Centre** (☑ 01320-366493; Ardchattan House, Canalside; ⊙ 10am-1.30pm & 2-5.30pm Apr-Oct) **FREE**, beside the lowest lock, showcases the history of the canal (p155).

Clansman Centre MUSEUM
(www.scottish-swords.com; ⊙ 10am-6pm Apr-Oct) This exhibition of 17th-century Highland life has live demonstrations of how to put on a plaid (the forerunner of the kilt) and how the claymore (Highland sword) was made and used. There is also a workshop where you can purchase handcrafted reproduction swords, dirks and shields.

Cruise Loch Ness BOAT TOURS
(☑ 01320-366277; www.cruiselochness.com; adult/child £13.50/8; ⊙ hourly 10am-4pm Apr-Oct, 1 & 2pm only Nov-Mar) One-hour cruises on Loch Ness accompanied by the latest high-tech sonar equipment so you can keep an underwater eye open for Nessie. There are also one-hour evening cruises, departing 8pm daily (except Friday) April to August, and 90-minute speedboat tours.

⌅ Sleeping & Eating

Morag's Lodge HOSTEL £
(☑ 01320-366289; www.moragslodge.com; Bunoich Brae; dm/tw/f from £21/50/69; P@🤝) This large and well-run hostel is based in a big Victorian house with great views of Fort Au-

gustus' hilly surrounds, and has a convivial bar with open fire. It's hidden away in the trees up the steep side road just north of the tourist-office car park.

Cumberland's Campsite CAMPSITE £
(☑ 01320-366257; www.cumberlands-campsite.com; Glendoe Rd; sites per adult/child £8/3; ⊙ Apr-Sep) Southeast of the village on the B862 towards Whitebridge; entrance beside Stravaigers Lodge.

Lorien House B&B ££
(☑ 01320-366576; www.lorien-house.co.uk; Station Rd; s/d £60/74) Lorien is a cut above your usual B&B: the bathrooms come with bidets and the breakfasts with smoked salmon, and there's a library of walking, cycling and climbing guides in the lounge. No children under 12.

★ Lovat HOTEL £££
(☑ 01456-459250; www.thelovat.com; Main Rd; d from £121; P🤝) 🍃 A boutique-style makeover has transformed this former huntin'-and-shootin' hotel into a luxurious but ecoconscious retreat set apart from the tourist crush around the canal. The bedrooms are spacious and stylishly furnished, while the lounge is equipped with a log fire, comfy armchairs and grand piano. It has an informal brasserie and a highly acclaimed restaurant (five-course dinner £50), which serves top-quality cuisine.

Lock Inn PUB ££
(Canal Side; mains £9-14; ⊙ meals noon-8pm) A superb little pub right on the canal bank, the Lock Inn has a vast range of malt whiskies and a tempting menu of bar meals, which includes Orkney salmon, Highland venison and daily seafood specials; the house speciality is beer-battered haddock and chips.

ℹ Information

There's an ATM and bureau de change in the post office beside the canal.

Fort Augustus Tourist Office (☑ 01320-366367; ⊙ 9am-6pm Mon-Sat & to 5pm Sun Easter-Oct) In the central car park.

ℹ Getting There & Away

Scottish Citylink (www.citylink.co.uk) and **Stagecoach** (www.stagecoachbus.com) buses from Inverness to Fort William stop at Fort Augustus (£6 to £10.20, one hour, five to eight daily Monday to Saturday, five on Sunday).

THE CAIRNGORMS

The Cairngorms National Park (www.cairngorms.co.uk) encompasses the highest landmass in Britain: a broad mountain plateau, riven only by the deep valleys of the Lairig Ghru and Loch Avon, with an average altitude of over 1000m and including five of the six highest summits in the UK. This wild mountain landscape of granite and heather has a sub-Arctic climate and supports rare alpine tundra vegetation and high-altitude bird species, such as snow bunting, ptarmigan and dotterel.

The harsh mountain environment gives way lower down to scenic glens softened by beautiful open forests of native Scots pine, home to rare animals and birds such as pine martens, wildcats, red squirrels, ospreys, capercaillies and crossbills.

This is prime hill-walking territory, but even couch potatoes can enjoy a taste of the high life by taking the Cairngorm Mountain Railway up to the edge of the Cairngorm plateau.

Aviemore

POP 3150

The gateway to the Cairngorms, Aviemore is the region's main centre for transport, accommodation, restaurants and shops. It's not the prettiest town in Scotland by a long stretch – the main attractions are in the surrounding area – but when bad weather puts the hills off limits, Aviemore fills up with hikers, cyclists and climbers (plus skiers and snowboarders in winter) cruising the outdoor-equipment shops or recounting their latest adventures in the cafes and bars. Add in tourists and locals and the eclectic mix makes for a lively little town.

Aviemore is on a loop off the A9 Perth-Inverness road; almost everything of note is to be found along the main drag, Grampian Rd; the train station and bus stop are towards its southern end.

The Cairngorm skiing area and funicular railway lie 9 miles southeast of Aviemore along the B970 (Ski Rd) and its continuation, past Coylumbridge and Glenmore.

◎ Sights

Strathspey Steam Railway   HERITAGE RAILWAY
(☑ 01479-810725;   www.strathspeyrailway.co.uk; Station Sq; return ticket per adult/child £13.95/6.98) Strathspey Steam Railway runs steam trains on a section of restored line be-

tween Aviemore and Broomhill, 10 miles to the northeast, via Boat of Garten. There are four or five trains daily from June to August, and a more limited service in April, May, September, October and December, with the option of enjoying afternoon tea, Sunday lunch or a five-course dinner on board.

An extension to Grantown-on-Spey is under construction (see www.railstograntown.org); in the meantime, you can continue from Broomhill to Grantown-on-Spey by bus.

★ **Rothiemurchus Estate**   FOREST
(www.rothiemurchus.net) The Rothiemurchus Estate, which extends from the River Spey at Aviemore to the Cairngorm summit plateau, is famous for having Scotland's largest remnant of **Caledonian forest**, the ancient forest of Scots pine that once covered most of the country. The forest is home to a large population of red squirrels, and is one of the last bastions of the Scottish wildcat.

The **Rothiemurchus Estate visitor centre** (☑ 01479-812345; ◎ 9.30am-5.50pm) **FREE**, a mile southeast of Aviemore along the B970, sells an *Explorer Map* detailing more than 50 miles of footpaths and cycling trails, including the wheelchair-accessible 4-mile trail around **Loch an Eilein**, with its ruined castle and peaceful pine woods.

Craigellachie Nature Reserve   NATURE RESERVE
(www.nnr-scotland.org.uk/craigellachie; Grampian Rd; 🚶) A trail leads west from Aviemore Youth Hostel and passes under the A9 into the Craigellachie Nature Reserve, a great place for short hikes across steep hillsides covered in natural birch forest. Look out for wildlife, including the peregrine falcons that nest on the crags from April to July.

🏃 Activities

Bothy Bikes   MOUNTAIN BIKING
(☑ 01479-810111; www.bothybikes.co.uk; 5 Granish Way, Dalfaber; per half-/full day £16/20; ◎ 9am-5.30pm) Located in northern Aviemore on the way to the golf course, this place rents out mountain bikes and can also advise on routes and trails; a good choice for beginners is the **Old Logging Way**, which runs from Aviemore to Glenmore, where you can make a circuit of Loch Morlich before returning. For experienced bikers, the whole of the Cairngorms is your playground. Booking recommended.

The Cairngorms

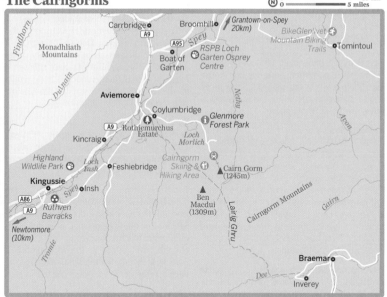

Rothiemurchus Fishery   FISHING

(🖅 01479-810703; www.rothiemurchus.net; Rothiemurchus Estate; ⊘9.30am-5pm Sep-May, to dusk Jun-Aug) Cast for rainbow trout at this loch at the southern end of the village; buy permits (from £10 for two hours to £30 per day, plus £5 for tackle hire) at the Fish Farm Shop. If you're a fly-fishing virgin, there's a beginner's package, including tackle hire, one hour's instruction and one hour's fishing, for £45 per person.

For experienced anglers, there's also salmon and sea-trout fishing on the River Spey – a day permit costs around £20; numbers are limited, so it's best to book in advance.

Cairngorm Sled-Dog Centre   DOG SLEDDING

(🖅 07767-270526; www.sled-dogs.co.uk; Ski Rd) This outfit will take you on a 30-minute sled tour of local forest trails in the wake of a team of huskies (adult/child £60/40), or a three-hour sled-dog safari (£175 per person). The sleds have wheels, so snow's not necessary. There are also one-hour guided tours of the kennels (adult/child £8/4). The centre is 3 miles east of Aviemore, signposted off the road to Loch Morlich.

Alvie & Dalraddy Estate   QUAD BIKING

(🖅 01479-810330; www.alvie-estate.co.uk; Dalraddy Holiday Park; per person £45) Join an hour-

long cross-country quad-bike trek at this estate, 3 miles south of Aviemore on the B9152 (call first).

🛏 Sleeping

Aviemore Bunkhouse   HOSTEL £

(🖅 01479-811181; www.aviemore-bunkhouse.com; Dalfaber Rd; dm/d/f from £19/50/65; P@🛜) This independent hostel provides accommodation in bright, modern six- or eight-bed dorms, each with private bathroom, and one twin/family room. It has a drying room, secure bike storage and wheelchair-accessible dorms. From the train station, cross the pedestrian bridge over the tracks, turn right and walk south on Dalfaber Rd.

Aviemore SYHA   HOSTEL £

(🖅 01479-810345; www.syha.org.uk; 25 Grampian Rd; dm £20; P@🛜) Upmarket hostelling in a spacious, well-equipped building, five minutes' walk south of the village centre. There are four- and six-bed rooms, and a comfortable lounge with views of the mountains.

**Rothiemurchus Camp &
Caravan Park**   CAMPSITE £

(🖅 01479-812800; www.rothiemurchus.net; Coylumbridge; sites per adult/child £11/2) The nearest camping ground to Aviemore is this year-round park, beautifully sited among

Scots pines at Coylumbridge, 1.5 miles along the B970.

Old Minister's House B&B ££

(☑ 01479-812181; www.theoldministershouse.co.uk; Rothiemurchus; s/d £70/110; P 🕿) This former manse dates from 1906 and has four rooms with a homely, country-farmhouse feel. It's in a lovely setting amid Scots pines on the banks of the River Druie, just 0.75 miles southeast of Aviemore.

Ardlogie Guest House B&B ££

(☑ 01479-810747; www.ardlogie.co.uk; Dalfaber Rd; s/d from £40/62, Bothy per 3 nights £165; P 🕿) Handy to the train station, the five-room Ardlogie has great views over the River Spey towards the Cairngorms. There's also self-catering accommodation in the Bothy, a cosy, two-person timber cabin. Facilities include a boules pitch in the garden, and guests can get free use of the local country club's pool, spa and sauna.

Ravenscraig Guest House B&B ££

(☑ 01479-810278; www.aviemoreonline.com; Grampian Rd; s/d £48/82; P 🕿) Ravenscraig is a large, flower-bedecked Victorian villa with six spacious en suite rooms, plus another six in a modern chalet at the back (one wheelchair accessible). It serves traditional and veggie breakfasts in an attractive conservatory dining room.

Cairngorm Hotel HOTEL ££

(☑ 01479-810233; www.cairngorm.com; Grampian Rd; s/d from £61/104; P 🕿) Better known as 'the Cairn', this long-established hotel is set in the fine old granite building with the pointy turret opposite the train station. It's a welcoming place with comfortable rooms and a determinedly Scottish atmosphere, all tartan carpets and stags' antlers. There's live music on weekends, so it can get a bit noisy – not for early-to-bedders.

✖ Eating & Drinking

★ Mountain Cafe CAFE £

(www.mountaincafe-aviemore.co.uk; 111 Grampian Rd; mains £4-10; ⊙ 8.30am-5pm Tue-Thu, to 5.30pm Fri-Mon; P ☑ 👶) The Mountain Cafe offers freshly prepared local produce with a Kiwi twist (the owner is from New Zealand): healthy breakfasts of muesli, porridge and fresh fruit (till 11.30am), hearty lunches of seafood chowder, burgers and imaginative salads, and home-baked breads, cakes and biscuits. Vegan, coeliac and nut-allergic diets catered for.

Ski-ing Doo STEAKHOUSE ££

(☑ 01479-810392; 9 Grampian Rd; mains £8-13, steaks £18-21; ⊙ noon-9.30pm; 🕿 👶) A long-standing Aviemore institution, the child-friendly Ski-ing Doo (it's a pun...ask the waiter!) is a favourite with family skiers and hikers. It's an informal place offering a range of hearty, homemade burgers, chicken dishes and juicy steaks; the Doo Below cafe-bar is open from 3pm to 11pm.

Winking Owl PUB

(www.thewinkingowl.net; Grampian Rd; ⊙ 11am-11pm) Lively local pub, popular with hikers and climbers, serving a good range of real ales and malt whiskies.

Old Bridge Inn PUB

(☑ 01479-811137; www.oldbridgeinn.co.uk; 23 Dalfaber Rd; ⊙ noon-midnight Sun-Thu, to 1am Fri & Sat; 🕿) The Old Bridge has a snug bar, complete with roaring log fire in winter, and a cheerful, chalet-style restaurant (mains £10-24; ⊙ noon-2pm & 6-9pm, to 10pm Fri & Sat) at the back serving quality Scottish cuisine.

❶ Information

There are ATMs outside the Tesco supermarket, and currency exchange at the post office and the tourist office, all located on Grampian Rd.

Aviemore Tourist Office (☑ 01479-810930; www.visitaviemore.com; The Mall, Grampian Rd; ⊙ 9am-6pm Mon-Sat, 9.30am-5pm Sun Jul & Aug, 9am-5pm Mon-Sat, 10am-4pm Sun Easter-Jun, Sep & Oct) Hours are limited from October to Easter.

❶ Getting There & Away

BUS

Buses stop on Grampian Rd opposite the train station; buy tickets at the tourist office. Services include the following:

Edinburgh £26, four hours, five daily

Glasgow £26, 2¾ hours, five daily

Grantown-on-Spey £3.50, 35 minutes, five daily weekdays, two Saturday; bus 33 via Carrbridge (15 minutes)

Inverness £9.80, 45 minutes, eight daily

Perth £19.20, 2¼ hours, five daily

TRAIN

The train station is on Grampian Rd.

Edinburgh £40, three hours, six daily

Glasgow £40, three hours, six daily

Inverness £11.70, 40 minutes, 12 daily

ⓘ Getting Around

BICYCLE

Several places in Aviemore, Rothiemurchus Estate and Glenmore have mountain bikes for hire. An off-road cycle track links Aviemore with Glenmore and Loch Morlich.

Bothy Bikes (☑ 01479-810111; www.bothy-bikes.co.uk; 5 Granish Way, Dalfaber; ☉ 9am-5.30pm) Charges £20 a day for a quality bike with front suspension and disc brakes.

BUS

Bus 31 links Aviemore to Cairngorm car park (£2.50, 30 minutes, hourly) via Coylumbridge and Glenmore. A Strathspey Dayrider/Megarider ticket (£6.50/17) gives one/seven days unlimited bus travel from Aviemore as far as Cairngorm, Carrbridge and Kingussie (buy from the bus driver).

Around Aviemore

Cairngorm Mountain

Cairngorm Mountain Railway   FUNICULAR RAILWAY
(☑ 01479-861261; www.cairngormmountain.org; adult/child return £10.50/6.80; ☉ every 20min, 10am-4pm May-Nov, 9am-4.30pm Dec-Apr) The region's most popular attraction is a funicular railway that will whisk you to the edge of the Cairngorm plateau (1085m) in just eight minutes. The bottom station is at the Coire Cas car park at the end of Ski Rd; at the top is an exhibition, a shop (of course) and a restaurant. Unfortunately, for environmental and safety reasons, you're not allowed out of the top station in summer unless you book a guided walk or mountain-bike descent.

From May to October, a 90-minute guided walk to the summit of Cairn Gorm (per person £6) departs twice a day, while a five-hour guided hill-walk runs twice a week. There's also the option of a guided mountain-bike descent (per person £25 to £35 including bike hire), Thursday to Sunday only. Check the website for details.

Cairngorm Mountain Ski Area   SNOW SPORTS
(www.cairngormmountain.org; 1-day ski pass per adult/child £33.50/20) Aspen or Val d'Isère it ain't, but with 19 runs and 23 miles of piste Cairngorm is Scotland's biggest ski area. When the snow is at its best and the sun is shining you can close your eyes and imagine you're in the Alps; sadly, low cloud, high winds and horizontal sleet are more common. Ski or snowboard hire is around £23/17 per adult/child per day; there are lots of hire outlets at Coire Cas, Glenmore and Aviemore.

The season usually runs from December until the snow melts, which may be as late as the end of April, but snowfall here is unpredictable – in some years the slopes can be open in November, but closed for lack of snow in February. During the season the tourist office in Aviemore displays snow conditions and avalanche warnings. You can check the latest snow conditions at http://ski.visitscotland.com and www.winterhighland.info.

Loch Morlich

Six miles east of Aviemore, Loch Morlich is surrounded by some 8 sq miles of pine and spruce forest that make up the **Glenmore Forest Park**. Its attractions include a sandy beach (at the east end).

◉ Sights & Activities

The park's visitor centre at Glenmore has a small exhibition on the Caledonian forest and sells the *Glenmore Forest Park Map*, detailing local walks. The **circuit of Loch Morlich** (one hour) makes a pleasant outing; the trail is pram- and wheelchair-friendly.

★ **Glenmore Lodge**   ADVENTURE SPORTS
(☑ 01479-861256; www.glenmorelodge.org.uk) One of Britain's leading adventure-sports training centres, offering courses in hill walking, rock climbing, ice climbing, canoeing, mountain biking and mountaineering. The centre's comfortable **B&B accommodation** (tw £76) is available to all, even if you're not taking a course, as is the indoor-climbing wall, gym and sauna.

Cairngorm Reindeer Centre   GUIDED TOURS
(www.cairngormreindeer.co.uk; adult/child £12/6) The warden here will take you on a guided walk to see and feed Britain's only herd of reindeer, who are very tame and will even eat out of your hand. Walks take place at 11am daily year-round (weather-dependent), plus another at 2.30pm from May to September, and 3.30pm Monday to Friday in July and August.

Loch Morlich Watersports Centre   WATER SPORTS
(☑ 01479-861221; www.lochmorlich.com; ☉ 9am-5pm May-Oct) This popular outfit rents out

Canadian canoes (£21 an hour), kayaks (£8), sailboards (£17.50), sailing dinghies (£25) and rowing boats (£21), and also offers instruction.

🛏 Sleeping

There is also accommodation at Glenmore Lodge (p129).

Cairngorm Lodge SYHA HOSTEL £
(☑ 01479-861238; dm/tw £17/45; ☺ closed Nov & Dec; @ 🛜) Set in a former shooting lodge that enjoys a great location at the east end of Loch Morlich; prebooking is essential.

Glenmore Campsite CAMPSITE £
(☑ 01479-861271; www.campingintheforest.co.uk; tent & campervan sites £27) Campers can set up base at this attractive lochside site with pitches amid the Scots pines; rates include up to four people per tent/campervan.

ℹ Getting There & Away

Bus 31 links Aviemore with Glenmore (£1.95, 30 minutes, hourly) .

Kincraig & Glen Feshie

Highland Wildlife Park WILDLIFE PARK
(☑ 01540-651270; www.highlandwildlifepark.org; adult/child £14.50/10.50; ☺ 10am to 6pm Jul & Aug, to 5pm Apr-Jun & Sep-Oct, to 4pm Nov-Mar) It features a drive-through safari park and animal enclosures offering the chance to view rarely seen native wildlife, such as Scottish wildcats, capercaillies, pine martens and red squirrels, as well as species that once roamed the Scottish hills but have long since disappeared, including wolves, lynx, wild boars,

beavers and European bison. Visitors without cars get driven around by staff (at no extra cost). It's near Kincraig, 6 miles southwest of Aviemore, and last entry is two hours before closing. Stagecoach bus 32 runs from Aviemore to Kincraig (10 minutes, five daily Monday to Saturday).

At Kincraig the Spey widens into Loch Insh, home of the **Loch Insh Watersports Centre** (☑ 01540-651272; www.lochinsh. com; Kincraig; day ticket per adult/child £32/25; ☺ 8.30am-5.30pm), which offers canoeing, windsurfing, sailing, bike hire and fishing, as well as B&B accommodation. The food here is good, especially after 6.30pm when the lochside cafe becomes a cosy restaurant.

Beautiful, tranquil Glen Feshie extends south from Kincraig, deep into the Cairngorms, with Scots pine woods in its upper reaches surrounded by big, heathery hills. The 4WD track to the head of the glen makes a great mountain-bike excursion (25-mile round trip).

Carrbridge

POP 700

Carrbridge, 7 miles northeast of Aviemore, is a good alternative base for exploring the region. It takes its name from the graceful old bridge (spotlit at night), built in 1717, over the thundering rapids of the Dulnain.

The **Landmark Forest Adventure Park** (☑ 01479-841613; www.landmarkpark.co.uk; adult/child £15.50/13.50; ☺ 10am-7pm mid-Jul–Aug, to 5 or 6pm Apr–mid-Jul & Sep, to 5pm Oct-Mar), set in a forest of Scots pines, is a theme park with a difference – the theme is timber. The main attractions are the Ropeworx high-wire adventure course, the Treetops Trail (a raised

INVERNESS & THE CENTRAL HIGHLANDS AROUND AVIEMORE

MOUNTAIN WALKS IN THE CAIRNGORMS

The climb from the car park at the Coire Cas ski area to the summit of **Cairn Gorm** (1245m) is 2 miles and takes about two hours (one way). From there, you can continue south across the high-level plateau to Ben Macdui (1309m), Britain's second-highest peak. From the car park to the peak and then back is 12 miles and takes eight to 10 hours. It's a serious undertaking, and is for experienced and well-equipped walkers only.

The **Lairig Ghru trail**, which can take eight to 10 hours, is a demanding 24-mile walk from Aviemore through the Lairig Ghru pass (840m) to Braemar. An alternative to doing the full route is to make the six-hour return hike up to the summit of the pass and back to Aviemore. The path starts from Ski Rd, a mile east of Coylumbridge, and involves some very rough going.

Warning: the Cairngorm plateau is a sub-Arctic environment where navigation is difficult and weather conditions can be severe, even in midsummer. Hikers must have proper hill-walking equipment, and know how to use a map and compass. In winter it is a place for experienced mountaineers only. Trip durations are estimates only.

walkway through the forest canopy that allows you to view red squirrels, crossbills and crested tits), and the steam-powered sawmill.

Bus 34 runs from Inverness to Carrbridge (£4.65, 45 minutes, six daily Monday to Friday, three on Saturday) and onwards to Grantown-on-Spey (£2.50, 20 minutes) and Aviemore.

Boat of Garten

Boat of Garten is known as the Osprey Village because these rare and beautiful birds of prey nest nearby at the **RSPB Loch Garten Osprey Centre** (01479-831694; www.rspb.org.uk/lochgarten; Tulloch; osprey hide adult/child £5/2; ⊙osprey hide 10am-6pm Apr-Aug). The ospreys migrate here each spring from Africa and nest in a tall pine tree – you can watch from a hide as the birds feed their young. The centre is signposted about 2 miles east of the village.

There is flexible, good-quality home-stay accommodation at **Fraoch Lodge** (01479-831331; www.scotmountainholidays.com; Deshar Rd; per person £21-25; P🐾), along with a wide range of outdoor activities, while the **Boat Hotel** (01479-831258; www.boathotel.co.uk; r from £100; P🐾🐕) offers luxurious accommodation and a superb restaurant.

Boat of Garten is 6 miles northeast of Aviemore. The most interesting way to get here is on the Strathspey Steam Railway (p126) from Aviemore.

Grantown-on-Spey

POP 2430

Grantown (*gran*-ton) is an elegant Georgian town on the banks of the Spey, a favoured haunt of anglers and the tweed-cap-and-green-wellies brigade. Thronged with tourists in summer, it reverts to a quiet backwater in winter. Most hotels can kit you out for a day of fly-fishing or put you in touch with someone who can.

Sleeping & Eating

⭐**Brooklynn** B&B ££
(01479-873113; www.woodier.com; Grant Rd; r per person £38-44; P🐾) This beautiful Victorian villa features original stained glass and wood panelling, and seven spacious, luxurious rooms (all doubles have en suites). The food – dinner is available as well as breakfast – is superb too.

Chaplin's Coffee House & Ice Cream Parlour CAFE £
(High St; ⊙10am-5pm May-Sep, closed Sun Oct-Apr) Traditional family cafe selling delicious homemade ice cream.

ℹ️ Getting There & Away

Bus 34 runs from Inverness to Aviemore via Grantown-on-Spey (£5.90, 1¼ hours, six daily Monday to Friday, three on Saturday).

Kingussie & Newtonmore

The gracious old Speyside towns of Kingussie (kin-*yew*-see) and Newtonmore sit at the foot of the great heather-clad humps known as the Monadhliath Mountains. Newtonmore is best known as the home of the excellent Highland Folk Museum; the road west from Newtonmore to Spean Bridge passes Ardverikie Estate and Loch Laggan, famous as the setting for the BBC TV series *Monarch of the Glen*.

👁️ Sights & Activities

Highland Folk Museum MUSEUM
(01540-673551; www.highlandfolk.museum; Kingussie Rd, Newtonmore; ⊙10.30am-5.30pm Apr-Aug, 11am-4.30pm Sep & Oct) **FREE** The open-air Highland Folk Museum comprises a collection of historical buildings and artefacts revealing many aspects of Highland culture and lifestyle. Laid out like a farming township, it has a community of traditional thatch-roofed cottages, a sawmill, a schoolhouse, a shepherd's bothy (hut) and a rural post office. Actors in period costume give demonstrations of woodcarving, wool-spinning and peat-fire baking. You'll need at least two to three hours to make the most of a visit here.

Ruthven Barracks RUIN
(HS; ⊙24hr) **FREE** Ruthven Barracks was one of four garrisons built by the British government after the first Jacobite rebellion of 1715, as part of a Hanoverian scheme to take control of the Highlands. Ironically, the barracks were last occupied by Jacobite troops awaiting the return of Bonnie Prince Charlie after the Battle of Culloden. Perched dramatically on a river terrace and clearly visible from the main A9 road near Kingussie, the ruins are spectacularly floodlit at night.

Laggan Wolftrax   MOUNTAIN BIKING

(http://scotland.forestry.gov.uk/visit/laggan-wolf-trax; Strathmashie Forest; trails free, parking £3; ⊙10am-6pm Mon, 9.30am-5pm Tue, Thu & Fri, 9.30am-6pm Sat & Sun) Ten miles southwest of Newtonmore, on the A86 road towards Spean Bridge, this is one of Scotland's top mountain-biking centres, with purpose-built trails ranging from open-country riding to black-diamond downhills with rock slabs and drop-offs. By the time you read this, there will be a new centre with a cafe and bike shop or similar.

Highland All Terrain   ADVENTURE TOUR

(✆0845 094 5513; http://quadbiketours.co.uk; Kinloch Laggan; from per person £45) Join an off-road quad-bike tour of Ardverikie Estate, which appears as Glen Bogle in the TV series *Monarch of the Glen*. Tours range from one hour to 3½ hours, and take in many of the TV locations.

🛏 Sleeping & Eating

⭐**Eagleview Guest House**   B&B ££

(✆01540-673675; www.eagleviewguesthouse. co.uk; Perth Rd, Newtonmore; r per person £39-40; P🛜) Welcoming Eagleview is one of the best places to stay in the area, with beautifully decorated bedrooms, super-king-size beds, spacious bathrooms with power showers (except room 4, which has a Victorian slipper bath!), and nice little touches such as cafetières (coffee plungers) with real coffee – and fresh milk – on your hospitality tray, and Scottish kippers on the breakfast menu.

Hermitage   B&B ££

(✆01540-662137; www.thehermitage-scotland. com; Spey St, Kingussie; s/d from £40/70; P🛜) The five-bedroom Hermitage is a lovely old house with plenty of character, filled with Victorian period features – ask for room 5 (superior king), with double bed, Chesterfield sofa, and a view of the hills. The lounge has deep sofas arranged by a log fire, and there are good views of the Cairngorms from the breakfast room and garden.

⭐**Cross**   SCOTTISH £££

(✆01540-661166; www.thecross.co.uk; Tweed Mill Brae, off Ardbroilach Rd, Kingussie; 2-course lunch £23, 3-course dinner £60; ⊙noon-2pm & 7-8.30pm; P🛜) 🍴 Housed in a converted water mill, the Cross is one of the finest restaurants in the Highlands. The intimate, low-raftered dining room has an open fire and a patio overlooking the stream, and

serves a daily-changing menu of fresh Scottish produce accompanied by a superb wine list. If you want to stay the night, there are eight stylish rooms (double or twin £100 to £180) to choose from.

❶ Getting There & Away

BUS

Kingussie and Newtonmore are served by **Scottish Citylink** (✆0871 266 3333; www.citylink. co.uk) buses:

Aviemore £7.70, 25 minutes, five to seven daily

Inverness £13.40, one hour, six to eight Monday to Saturday, three Sunday

Perth £16.30, 1¾ hours, five daily

TRAIN

Kingussie's train station is at the southern end of town. Kingussie and Newtonmore are served by the following:

Edinburgh £35, 2½ hours, seven a day Monday to Saturday, two Sunday

Inverness £11.70, 50 minutes, eight a day Monday to Saturday, four Sunday

Eastern Cairngorms

Tomintoul & Around

This high-altitude (345m) village was built by the Duke of Gordon in 1775 on the old military road that leads over the Lecht pass from Corgarff, a route now followed by the A939 (usually the first road in Scotland to be blocked by snow when winter closes in). The duke hoped that settling the dispersed population of his estates in a proper village would help to stamp out cattle stealing and illegal distilling.

Tomintoul (tom-in-*towel*) is a pretty, stone-built village with a grassy, tree-lined main square (the museum here was closed at the time of writing, but it is hoped that it will reopen soon).

The surrounding Glenlivet Estate (now the property of the Crown) has lots of walking and cycling trails – the estate's **tourist office** (✆01479-870070; www.glenlivetestate. co.uk; Main St; ⊙9am-5pm Mon-Fri) distributes free maps of the area – and a spur of the **Speyside Way** long-distance footpath runs between Tomintoul and Ballindalloch, 15 miles to the north.

There's excellent mountain biking at the new **BikeGlenlivet** (www.glenlivetestate.co.uk; trails free, parking £3) trail centre, 4.5 miles north of Tomintoul, off the B9136 road. Custom-built trails range from the 9km blue run for beginners to the 22km red route for more experienced riders. Cafe, showers and bike hire on site.

🛏 Sleeping & Eating

Accommodation for walkers includes the **Smugglers Hostel** (☑01807-580364; www.thesmugglershostel.co.uk; Main St; dm £15-18; 🐾), housed in the old village school; the highly recommended **Argyle Guest House** (☑01807-580766; www.argyletomintoul.co.uk; 7 Main St; d/f £64/110) is a more comfortable alternative (best porridge in the Cairngorms!).

For something to eat, try the **Clockhouse Restaurant** (The Square; mains £10-13; ☺noon-2pm & 6-8pm), which serves light lunches and bistro dinners, or the **Coffee Still** (☑07599 973845; BikeGlenlivet Trail Centre; mains £6-8; ☺11am-5pm Tue-Fri, 10am-5.30pm Sat & Sun; 🅿), which specialises in home baking and mouth-watering homemade burgers.

ℹ Getting There & Away

There is a very limited bus service to Tomintoul, once a week from Elgin via Aberlour (£6, 1½ hours, one a day, Thursday only), and from Keith via Dufftown (£4.50, one hour, one a day, Tuesday only); check with the tourist office in Elgin for the latest timetables. Outside these times, there is a **Dial-a-Bus** service (call ☑01343-562533 Monday to Friday to book a seat).

Cockbridge-Tomintoul Road

The A939, known as the Cockbridge–Tomintoul road – a magnificent rollercoaster of a route much loved by motorcyclists – crosses the Lecht pass (637m), where there's a small skiing area with lots of short easy and intermediate runs.

Corgarff Castle CASTLE
(HS; ☑01975-651460; adult/child £5.50/3.30; ☺9.30am-5.30pm Apr-Sep) In the wild hills of the eastern Cairngorms, near the A939 from Cockbridge to Tomintoul, is the impressive fortress of Corgarff Castle. The tower house dates from the 16th century, but the star-shaped defensive curtain wall was added in 1748 when the castle was converted to a military barracks in the wake of the Jacobite rebellion.

Lecht 2090 WINTER SPORTS
(www.lecht.co.uk) In winter, you can hire skis, boots and poles for £20 a day; a one-day lift

pass is £29. In summer (weekends only), the chairlift serves mountain-biking trails (day ticket £29); there are no bike-hire facilities, though, so you'll need to bring your own.

Southern Cairngorms

Royal Deeside

The upper valley of the River Dee stretches west from Aboyne to Braemar, closely paralleled by the A93 road. Made famous by its long association with the monarchy (today's royal family still holiday at Balmoral Castle, built for Queen Victoria in 1855) the region is often called Royal Deeside.

The River Dee, renowned around the world for its **salmon fishing**, has its source in the Cairngorm Mountains west of Braemar, the starting point for long walks into the hills. The **FishDee website** (www.fishdee.co.uk) has all you need to know about fishing on the river.

BALLATER
POP 1530
The attractive little village of Ballater owes its 18th-century origins to the curative waters of nearby Pannanich Springs (now bottled commercially as Deeside Natural Mineral Water), and its prosperity to nearby Balmoral Castle.

The **tourist office** (☑01339-755306; Station Sq; ☺9am-6pm Jul & Aug, 10am-5pm Sep-Jun) is in the Old Royal Station.

◉ Sights & Activities

When Queen Victoria travelled to Balmoral Castle she would alight from the royal train at Ballater's **Old Royal Station** (☑01339-755306; Station Sq; admission £2; ☺10am-6pm Jul & Aug, to 5pm Sep-Jun). The station has been beautifully restored and now houses the tourist office, a cafe and a museum with a replica of Victoria's royal coach (the original is in the National Railway Museum in York).

Also on Station Sq is **Dee Valley Confectioners** (☑01339-755499; www.dee-valley.co.uk; Station Sq; admission free; ☺9am-noon & 2-4.30pm Mon-Thu Apr-Oct), where you can drool over the manufacture of traditional Scottish sweeties. Note the crests on the shop fronts along the main street proclaiming 'By Royal Appointment' – the village is a major supplier of provisions to Balmoral.

As you approach Ballater from the east the hills start to close in, and there are many pleasant walks in the surrounding area. The steep woodland walk up **Craigendarroch** (400m) takes just over one hour. **Morven** (871m) is a more serious prospect, taking about six hours, but offers good views from the top; ask at the tourist office for more info.

You can hire bikes from **CycleHighlands** (☑ 01339-755864; www.cyclehighlands. com; The Pavilion, Victoria Rd; bicycle hire per day £18; ☺ 9am-6pm) and **Bike Station** (☑ 01339-754004; www.bikestationballater.co.uk; Station Sq; bicycle hire per 3hr/day £12/18; ☺ 9am-6pm), which also offers guided bike rides and advice on local trails.

🛏 Sleeping & Eating

Habitat HOSTEL £
(☑ 01339-753752; www.habitat-at-ballater.com; Bridge Sq; dm/tw from £20/45; ☏) ◢ Tucked up a lane near the bridge over the River Dee, Habitat is an attractive and ecofriendly hostel with three eight-bed bunk rooms (with personal lockers and reading lamps), and a comfortable lounge with big, soft sofas and a wood-burning stove.

★ Auld Kirk HOTEL ££
(☑ 01339-755762; www.theauldkirk.com; Braemar Rd; s/d from £65/100; P☏☺) Here's something a little out of the ordinary – a seven-bedroom hotel housed in a converted 19th-century church. The interior blends original features with sleek modern decor – the pulpit now serves as the reception desk, while the breakfast room is bathed in light from leaded gothic windows.

Rock Salt & Snails CAFE £
(☑ 07834 452583; 2 Bridge St; mains £4-8; ☺ 10am-5pm Mon-Sat, 11am-5pm Sun; ☏☺) A great litte cafe serving excellent coffee, and tempting lunch platters composed of locally sourced deli products (cheese, ham, salads etc), including a kids' platter.

ℹ Getting There & Away

Bus 201 runs from Aberdeen to Ballater (£11, 1¾ hours, hourly Monday to Saturday, six on Sunday) via Crathes Castle, and continues to Braemar (£5.60, 30 minutes) every two hours.

BALMORAL CASTLE

Eight miles west of Ballater lies **Balmoral Castle** (☑ 01339-742334; www.balmoralcastle. com; adult/child £11/5; ☺ 10am-5pm Apr-Jul, last admission 4.30pm), the Queen's Highland holiday home, screened from the road by a thick curtain of trees. Built for Queen Victoria in 1855 as a private residence for the royal family, it kicked off the revival of the Scottish Baronial style of architecture that characterises so many of Scotland's 19th-century country houses.

The admission fee includes an interesting and well thought-out audioguide, but the tour is very much an outdoor one through garden and grounds; as for the castle itself, only the ballroom, which displays a collection of Landseer paintings and royal silver, is open to the public. Don't expect to see the Queen's private quarters! The main attraction is learning about Highland estate management, rather than royal revelations.

You can buy a booklet that details several waymarked walks within Balmoral Estate; the best is the climb to **Prince Albert's Cairn**, a huge granite pyramid that bears the inscription 'To the beloved memory of Albert the great and good, Prince Consort. Erected by his broken hearted widow Victoria R. 21st August 1862'.

The massive pointy-topped mountain that looms to the south of Balmoral is **Lochnagar** (1155m), immortalised in verse by Lord Byron, who spent his childhood years in Aberdeenshire:

England, thy beauties are tame and domestic
To one who has roamed o'er the mountains
afar.
Oh! for the crags that are wild and majestic:
The steep frowning glories of dark Lochnagar.

Lord Byron, Lochnagar

Balmoral is beside the A93 at Crathie and can be reached on the Aberdeen–Braemar bus.

BRAEMAR
POP 450

Braemar is a pretty little village with a grand location on a broad plain ringed by mountains where the Dee valley and Glen Clunie meet. In winter this is one of the coldest places in the country – temperatures as low as -29°C have been recorded – and during spells of severe cold, hungry deer wander the streets looking for a bite to eat. Braemar is an excellent base for hill walking, and there's also skiing at nearby Glenshee.

The **tourist office** (✉ 01399-741600; The Mews, Mar Rd; ☺ 9am-6pm Aug, 9am-5pm Jun, Jul, Sep & Oct, 10am-5pm Mon-Sat, 2-5pm Sun Nov-May), opposite the Fife Arms Hotel, has lots of useful info on walks in the area. There's a bank with an ATM in the village centre, an outdoor equipment shop and a **grocery store** (☺ 7.30am-9pm Mon-Sat, 9am-6pm Sun).

◉ Sights & Activities

Just north of the village, turreted **Braemar Castle** (www.braemarcastle.co.uk; adult/child £8/4; ☺ 10am-4pm Sat & Sun Jun-Sep, also Wed Jul-mid-Sep, daily Aug, 11am-3pm Sat-Sun May & Oct) dates from 1628 and served as a government garrison after the 1745 Jacobite rebellion. It was taken over by the local community in 2007, and now offers guided tours of the historic castle apartments.

An easy walk from Braemar is up **Creag Choinnich** (538m), a hill to the east of the village above the A93. The 1-mile route is waymarked and takes about 1½ hours. For a longer walk (4 miles; about three hours) and superb views of the Cairngorms, head for the summit of **Morrone** (859m), southwest of Braemar. Ask at the tourist office for details of these and other walks.

You can hire mountain bikes from **Braemar Mountain Sports** (✉ 01339-741242; www.braemarmountainsports.com; 5 Invercauld Rd; bike hire per day £18; ☺ 9am-6pm) for £18 per 24 hours. It also rents skiing and mountaineering equipment.

⌂ Sleeping

★ Rucksacks Bunkhouse
HOSTEL £

(✉ 01339-741517; 15 Mar Rd; bothies £7, dm £12-15, tw £36; P) An appealing cottage with a comfy dorm, and cheaper beds in an alpine-style bothy (shared sleeping platform for 10 people; bring your own sleeping bag). Extras include a drying room (for wet-weather gear), a laundry and even a sauna (£10 an hour). The friendly owner is a font of knowledge about the local area.

Braemar SYHA
HOSTEL £

(✉ 01339-741659; www.syha.org.uk; 21 Glenshee Rd; dm/tw £18.50/44; ☺ Feb-Oct; @) This hostel is housed in a grand former shooting lodge just south of Braemar village centre on the A93 to Perth. It has a comfy lounge with pool table, and a barbecue in the garden.

Braemar Caravan & Camping Park
CAMPSITE £

(✉ 01339-741373; www.braemarcaravansite.co.uk; tent sites incl 2 people £12.50; ☺ closed mid-Oct–mid-Dec; ☎) There is good camping here, or you can camp wild (no facilities) along the minor road on the east bank of the Clunie Water, 3 miles south of Braemar.

Craiglea
B&B ££

(✉ 01339-741641; www.craigleabraemar.com; Hillside Dr; d/f from £74/105; P ☎) Craiglea is a homely B&B set in a pretty stone cottage with three en suite bedrooms. Vegetarian breakfasts are available and the owners can give advice on local walks.

St Margarets
B&B ££

(✉ 01339-741697; soky37@hotmail.com; 13 School Rd; s/tw £34/56; ☎) Grab this place if you can, but there's only one room, a twin with a serious sunflower theme. The genuine warmth of the welcome is delightful. It's tucked behind the church on the south side of the A93 road.

Braemar Lodge Hotel
HOTEL, BUNKHOUSE ££

(✉ 01339-741627; www.braemarlodge.co.uk; Glenshee Rd; dm from £12, s/d £75/120; P) This Victorian shooting lodge on the southern outskirts of Braemar has bags of character, not least in the wood-panelled Malt Room bar, which is as well stocked with mounted deer heads as it is with single malt whiskies. There's a good restaurant with views of the hills, plus a 12-berth hikers' bunkhouse in the hotel grounds.

✕ Eating

Taste
CAFE £

(✉ 01339-741425; www.taste-braemar.co.uk; Airlie House, Mar Rd; mains £4-7; ☺ 10am-5pm Tue-Sat; ⊡) ✐ Taste is a relaxed little cafe with armchairs in the window, serving homemade soups, sandwiches, coffee and cakes.

★ Gathering Place
BISTRO ££

(✉ 01339-741234; www.the-gathering-place.co.uk; 9 Invercauld Rd; mains £12-19; ☺ 6-9pm Tue-Sat; ☎) This bright and breezy bistro is an unexpected corner of culinary excellence, with a welcoming dining room and sunny conservatory, tucked below the main road junction at the entrance to Braemar village.

ⓘ Getting There & Away

Bus 201 runs from Aberdeen to Braemar (£11, 2¼ hours, every two hours Monday to Saturday,

INVERNESS & THE CENTRAL HIGHLANDS SOUTHERN CAIRNGORMS

five on Sunday). The 50-mile drive from Perth to Braemar is beautiful, but there's no public transport on this route.

MAR LODGE ESTATE

West of Braemar spreads the National Trust for Scotland's **Mar Lodge Estate** (NTS; www. nts.org.uk/property/mar-lodge-estate; ⊙24hr year round) `FREE`, one of the country's most important nature conservation areas, covering 7% of the Cairngorms National Park. The £4-million legacy that allowed the trust to purchase the property in 1995 stipulated that, as well as promoting conservation and public access, the trust should continue to run Mar Lodge as a sporting estate. So, alongside walking trails and forest regeneration there is salmon fishing and deer stalking.

Several easy, waymarked walks start from the Linn of Dee car park, 6.5 miles west of Braemar, including the **Linn of Dee**, a narrow gorge that extends downstream from the road bridge, and **Glen Lui**. Numerous long mountain walks (for experienced hill walkers only) also start from here, including the adventurous 24-mile walk through the **Lairig Ghru** pass to Aviemore.

Another short walk (3 miles, 1½ hours) begins 4 miles beyond the Linn of Dee at the **Linn of Quoich** – a waterfall that thunders through a narrow slot in the rocks. Head uphill on a footpath on the east bank of the stream, past the **Punch Bowl** (a giant pothole) to a modern bridge that spans the narrow gorge, and return via a 4WD road on the far bank. A longer walk (10 miles) is to follow the 4WD road up Glen Quoich to a beautiful remnant of Caledonian pine forest (return the same way).

GLENSHEE

The route along the A93 from Braemar to Blairgrowrie through Glenshee is one of the most scenic drives in the country. It's fantastic walking country in summer, and there's skiing in winter. Blairgowrie and Braemar are the main accommodation centres for the Glenshee resort, although there is a small settlement 5 miles south of the ski runs at **Spittal of Glenshee** with a couple of good sleeping options.

Glenshee Ski Resort   SNOW SPORTS
(☑01339-741320; www.ski-glenshee.co.uk; 1-day lift pass £29) With 22 lifts and 36 runs Glenshee is one of Scotland's largest skiing areas. When the sun burns through the clouds after a good fall of snow, you'll be in a unique position to drink in the beauty of the country; the skiing isn't half bad either. The chairlift, which also opens in July and August for walkers and mountain bikers, can whisk you up to 910m, near the top of the **Cairnwell** (933m).

The Angus Glens

Five scenic glens – Isla, Prosen, Clova, Lethnot and Esk – cut into the hills along the southern fringes of the Cairngorms National Park, accessible from Kirriemuir in Angus. All have attractive scenery, though each glen has its own distinct personality: Glen Clova and Glenesk are the most beautiful, while Glen Lethnot is the least frequented. You can get detailed information on walks in the Angus Glens from the tourist office in Kirriemuir and from the Glen Clova Hotel in Glen Clova.

There is no public transport to the Angus Glens other than a limited school-bus service along Glen Clova; ask at the tourist office in Kirremuir for details.

GLEN ISLA

At Bridge of Craigisla at the foot of the glen is a spectacular, 24m waterfall called **Reekie Linn**; the name Reekie (Scottish for 'smoky') comes from the billowing spray that rises from the falls.

A 5-mile walk beyond the road end at Auchavan leads into the wild and mountainous upper reaches of the glen, where the **Caenlochan National Nature Reserve** protects rare alpine flora on the high plateau.

GLEN PROSEN

Near the foot of Glen Prosen, 6 miles north of Kirriemuir, there's a good forest walk up to the **Airlie monument** on Tulloch Hill (380m); start from the eastern road, about a mile beyond Dykehead.

From Glenprosen Lodge, at the head of the glen, a 9-mile walk along the **Kilbo Path** leads over a pass between Mayar (928m) and Driesh (947m), and descends to Glendoll Lodge at the head of Glen Clova (allow five hours).

Prosen Hostel (☑01575-540238; www. prosenhostel.co.uk; dm £20; ⊙year round; P@) is an 18-bed bunkhouse with excellent facilities (including a red squirrel viewing area in the lounge). It's 7 miles up the glen, just beyond Prosen village (no public transport).

GLEN CLOVA

The longest and loveliest of the Angus Glens stretches north from Kirriemuir for 20 miles, broad and pastoral in its lower reaches but growing narrower and craggier as the steep, heather-clad Highland hills close in around its head.

The minor road beyond the Glen Clova Hotel ends at a Forestry Commission car park at Glen Doll with a **visitor centre** (☑ 01575-550233; Glen Doll; ◷ 9am-6pm Apr-Sep, to 4.30 Oct-Mar) and **picnic area**, which is the trailhead for a number of strenuous walks through the hills to the north.

Jock's Road is an ancient footpath that was much used by cattle drovers, soldiers, smugglers and shepherds in the 18th and 19th centuries; 700 Jacobite soldiers passed this way during their retreat in 1746, en route to defeat at Culloden. From the car park the path strikes west along Glen Doll, then north across a high plateau (900m) before descending steeply into Glen Callater and on to Braemar (15 miles; allow five to seven hours). The route is hard going and should not be attempted in winter; you'll need OS 1:50,000 map numbers 43 and 44.

An easier walk leads from Glen Doll car park to **Corrie Fee**, a spectacular glacial hollow in the edge of the mountain plateau (4.5 miles round trip, waymarked).

Glen Clova Hotel (☑ 01575-550350; www.clova.com; s/d from £65/90, bunkhouse per person £17; P) is a lovely old drover's inn near the head of the glen and a great place to get away from it all. As well as 10 comfortable, country-style, en suite rooms (one with a four-poster bed), it has a bunkhouse out the back, a rustic, stone-floored climbers' bar with a roaring log fire, and a bay-windowed **restaurant** (mains £9-16; ◷ noon-8.15pm Sun-Thu, to 8.45pm Fri & Sat, shorter hr Nov-Mar; ♿) with views across the glen. The menu includes haggis, venison casserole and vegetarian lasagne, and there's a separate children's menu.

GLEN LETHNOT

This glen is noted for the **Brown & White Caterthuns** – two extraordinary Iron Age hill forts, defended by ramparts and ditches, perched on twin hilltops at its southern end. A minor road crosses the pass between the two summits, and it's an easy walk to either fort from the parking area in the pass; both are superb viewpoints.

GLENESK

The most easterly of the Angus Glens, Glenesk runs for 15 miles from Edzell to lovely **Loch Lee**, surrounded by beetling cliffs and waterfalls. Ten miles up the glen from Edzell is **Glenesk Folk Museum** (www.gleneskretreat.co.uk; ◷ 10am-5pm Mon-Fri, to 6pm Sat & Sun Apr-Oct) FREE, an old shooting lodge that houses a fascinating collection of antiques and artefacts documenting the local culture of the 17th, 18th and 19th centuries. It also has a tearoom, restaurant and gift shop, and has public internet access.

Five miles further on, the public road ends at **Invermark Castle**, an impressive ruined tower guarding the southern approach to the Mounth, a hill track to Deeside.

HIGHLAND PERTHSHIRE

ⓘ Getting Around

Away from the main A9 Perth to Inverness road public transport is thin on the ground, and often geared to the needs of local schools. On Tuesdays, Wednesdays and Sundays from June to mid-October, the **Ring of Breadalbane Explorer** (☑ 01828-626262; www.facebook.com/breadalbaneexplorer) bus service operates on a circular route taking in Crieff, Comrie, Lochearnhead, Killin, Kenmore and Aberfeldy, with four circuits a day in each direction. It also runs on Saturdays in July and August. The £10 fare allows unlimited hop-on/hop-off travel for one day.

Dunkeld to Blair Atholl

There are a number of major sights strung along the busy but scenic A9, the main route north from Perth to the Cairngorms and Inverness.

Dunkeld & Birnam

POP 1005

The Tay runs like a story-book river between the twin towns of Dunkeld and Birnam, nestled in the heart of Perthshire's Big Tree Country. As well as Dunkeld's lovely cathedral, there's much walking to be done in this area of magnificent forested hills. These same walks were one of the inspirations for Beatrix Potter to create her children's tales.

◉ Sights & Activities

Dunkeld Cathedral
CHURCH
(HS; www.dunkeldcathedral.org.uk; High St; ⊙9.30am-6.30pm Apr-Sep, to 4pm Oct-Mar) **FREE** Situated on the grassy banks of the River Tay, Dunkeld Cathedral is one of the most beautifully sited churches in Scotland; don't miss it on a sunny day, when there are few lovelier places to be. Half the cathedral is still in use as a church; the rest is in ruins. It partly dates from the 14th century, having suffered damaged during the Reformation and the battle of Dunkeld (Jacobites vs government) in 1689.

The Wolf of Badenoch, a fierce 14th-century noble who burned towns and abbeys to the ground in protest at his excommunication, is buried here – undeservedly – in a fine medieval tomb behind the wooden screen in the church.

Dunkeld House Grounds
GARDENS
(⊙24hr) **FREE** Waymarked walks lead upstream from Dunkeld Cathedral through the gorgeous grounds of Dunkeld House Hotel, formerly a seat of the dukes of Atholl. In the 18th and early 19th centuries the 'planting dukes', as they became known, planted more than 27-million conifers on their estates 'for beauty and profit', introducing species such as larch, Douglas fir and sequoia, and sowing the seeds of Scottish forestry.

The abundance of vast, ancient trees here has given rise to the nickname Big Tree Country (www.perthshirebigtreecountry.co.uk). Just west of the cathedral is the 250-year-old 'parent larch', the lone survivor of several planted in 1738, and said to have provided the seed stock for all Scottish larch trees. On the far side of the river is Niel Gow's Oak, another ancient tree said to have provided inspiration for legendary local fiddler Niel Gow (1727–1807).

Birnam
VILLAGE
Across the bridge from Dunkeld is Birnam, a name made famous by *Macbeth*. There's not much left of Birnam Wood, but there is a small, leafy Beatrix Potter Park (the children's author, who wrote the evergreen story of *Peter Rabbit*, spent childhood holidays in the area). Next to the park, in the Birnam Arts Centre (www.birnaminstitute.com; Station Rd; admission £1.50; ⊙10am-5pm mid-Mar–Nov, 10am-4.30pm Mon-Sat, 11am-4.30pm Sun Dec–mid-Mar), is a small exhibition on Potter and her characters.

Loch of the Lowes Wildlife Centre
WILDLIFE RESERVE
(☑01350-727337; www.swt.org.uk; adult/child £4/50p; ⊙10am-5pm Mar-Oct, 10.30am-4pm Fri-Sun Nov-Feb) Loch of the Lowes, 2 miles east of Dunkeld off the A923, has a visitor centre devoted to red squirrels and the majestic osprey. There's a birdwatching hide (with binoculars provided), where you can see the birds nesting during breeding season (late April to August).

⌸ Sleeping & Eating

★ Jessie Mac's
HOSTEL, B&B £
(☑01350-727324; www.jessiemacs.co.uk; Murthly Tce, Birnam; dm/d £18/70; 🛜) 🧼 Set in a Victorian manse complete with baronial turret, Jessie Mac's is a glorious cross between B&B and luxury hostel, with three gorgeous doubles and five shared rooms with bunks. Guests make good use of the country-style lounge, sunny dining room and well-equipped kitchen, and breakfasts are composed of local produce, from organic eggs to Dunkeld smoked salmon.

Erigmore Estate
LODGE £££
(☑01350-727236; www.erigmore.co.uk; Birnam; d for 2 nights from £380; 🅿🖾🐾) Scattered around the wooded, riverside grounds of Erigmore House, the former country retreat of a wealthy clipper ship's captain, these luxury timber lodges provide cosseted comfort complete with outdoor deck and – at the more expensive end of the range – a private hot tub. The house itself contains shared facilities, including a bar, restaurant and swimming pool.

★ Taybank
PUB £
(☑01350-727340; www.thetaybank.co.uk; Tay Tce; mains £6-9; ⊙11am-11pm Mon-Thu, to midnight Fri & Sat, 12.30-11pm Sun) Top choice for a sun-kissed pub lunch by the river is the Taybank, a regular meeting place and performance space for musicians of all creeds and a wonderfully welcoming bar serving ales from the local Strathbraan Brewery. There's live music several nights per week, and the menu runs to burgers and stovies (stewed potato and onion with meat or other ingredients).

❶ Information

Dunkeld Tourist Office (☑01350-727688; www.dunkeldandbirnam.org.uk; The Cross; ⊙9am-5pm Apr-Oct, Fri-Sun Nov-Mar) Has information on local hiking and biking trails.

ℹ Getting There & Away

Dunkeld is 15 miles north of Perth. Citylink buses running between Glasgow/Edinburgh (£16.60, two hours, five daily) and Inverness stop at the Birnam Hotel. **Stagecoach** (www.stage-coachbus.com) runs hourly buses (only five on Sunday) between Perth and Dunkeld (£2.50, 40 minutes), continuing to Aberfeldy.

There are also buses from Dunkeld to Blair-gowrie (£2.50, 35 minutes), twice daily on Tuesday, Thursday and Saturday only.

Pitlochry

POP 2780

Pitlochry, with the scent of the Highlands already in the air, is a popular stop on the way north. In summer the main street can be a conga line of tour groups, but linger a while and it can still charm – on a quiet spring evening it's a pretty place with salmon leaping in the Tummel and good things brewing at the Moulin Hotel.

◉ Sights

One of Pitlochry's attractions is its beautiful riverside; the River Tummel is dammed here, and if you're lucky you might see salmon swimming up the fish ladder to Loch Faskally above (May to November, best month is October).

★ Edradour Distillery DISTILLERY
(☑ 01796-472095; www.edradour.co.uk; tours adult/child £7.50/2.50; ☉ 10am-5pm Mon-Sat Apr-Oct; P ♿) This is proudly Scotland's smallest and most picturesque distillery and one of the best to visit: you can see the whole process, easily explained, in one building. It's 2.5 miles east of Pitlochry by car, along the Moulin road, or a pleasant 1-mile walk.

Bell's Blair Athol Distillery DISTILLERY
(☑ 01796-482003; www.discovering-distilleries. com; Perth Rd; standard tour £6.50; ☉ 10am-5pm Apr-Oct, to 4pm Nov-Mar, closed Sun Jan-Mar) Tours here focus on whisky making and the blending of this well-known dram. More detailed private tours give you greater insights and superior tastings.

Explorers Garden GARDENS
(☑ 01796-484600; www.explorersgarden.com; Foss Rd; adult/child £4/1; ☉ 10am-5pm Apr-Oct) This gem of a garden is based around plants brought to Scotland by 18th- and 19th-century Scottish botanists and explorers such as David Douglas (after whom the Douglas fir is named), and celebrates 300 years of collecting and the 'plant hunters' who tracked down these exotic species.

Wild Space GALLERY
(www.jmt.org/wildspace.asp; Tower House, Station Rd; ☉ 10am-4.30pm Mon-Fri, 10.30am-4.30pm Sat, 11am-4pm Sun May-Sep, shorter hr winter) FREE This combined art gallery, interpretation centre and bookshop is run by environmental charity the John Muir Trust. It stages exhibitions of contemporary landscape art, and sells maps, walking guides and wildlife- and evironment-related books.

✦ Festivals & Events

Winter Words LITERATURE
(www.pitlochry.org/whats_on; ☉ Feb) A 10-day literary festival, with a packed program of talks by authors, poets and broadcasters. Past guests have included novelist Louis de Bernieres and mountaineer/author Sir Chris Bonington.

Étape Caledonia CYCLING
(www.etapecaledonia.co.uk; ☉ mid-May) This 81-mile charity cycling event brings competitors of all standards to the beautiful Highland roads between Pitlochry and Tummel Bridge. It's grown into a huge event, with more than 5000 participants; you'll have to prebook accommodation when its on.

Enchanted Forest LIGHT SHOW
(www.enchantedforest.org.uk; adult £14-18, child £7-9; ☉ Oct) This spectacular three-week sound-and-light show staged in a forest near Pitlochry is a major family hit.

🛏 Sleeping

Ashleigh B&B £
(☑ 01796-470316; www.realbandbpitlochry.co.uk; 120 Atholl Rd; s/d £30/57; ☎) Genuine welcomes don't come much better than Nancy's, and her place on the main street makes a top Pitlochry pit stop. Two comfortable doubles share an excellent bathroom, and there's an open kitchen stocked with goodies where you make your own breakfast in the morning. A home away from home and a standout budget choice. Cash only; no kids.

She also has a good self-catering apartment with great views, available by the night.

Pitlochry Backpackers Hotel HOSTEL £
(☑ 01796-470044; www.scotlands-top-hostels. com; 134 Atholl Rd; dm/tw/d £18/47/52; ☉ Apr–mid-Nov; P @ ☎) Friendly, laid-back and very comfortable, this is a cracking hostel smack

bang in the middle of town, with three- to eight-bed dorms that are in mint condition. There are also good-value en suite twins and doubles, with beds, not bunks. Cheap breakfast and a pool table add to the convivial party atmosphere. No extra charge for linen.

Pitlochry SYHA HOSTEL £

(☑ 01796-472308; www.syha.org.uk; Knockard Rd; dm/tw £17/45; ☺ Mar-Oct; P @ 🛜) Great location overlooking the town centre. Popular with families and walkers.

★ Craigatin House B&B ££

(☑ 01796-472478; www.craigatinhouse.co.uk; 165 Atholl Rd; s £80, d standard/deluxe £90/100; P @ 🛜) Several times more tasteful than the average Pitlochry lodging, this elegant house and garden is set back from the main road. Chic contemporary fabrics covering expansive beds offer a standard of comfort above and beyond the reasonable price; the rooms in the converted stable block are particularly inviting. A fabulous breakfast and lounge area gives views over the lush garden.

Breakfast choices include whisky-laced porridge, smoked-fish omelettes and apple pancakes. Kids not allowed.

Tir Aluinn B&B ££

(☑ 01796-473811; www.tiraluinn.co.uk; 10 Higher Oakfield Rd; per person £35-37; P 🛜) Tucked away above the main street, this is a little gem of a place with bright rooms and easy-on-the-eye furniture, and a warm personal welcome. Breakfasts are a pleasure too.

Knockendarroch House HOTEL £££

(☑ 01796-473473; www.knockendarroch.co.uk; Higher Oakfield; d incl dinner from £208; P 🛜 🌞) Top of the town and boasting the best views, this genteel, well-run hotel has a range of luxurious rooms with huge windows that take advantage of the Highland light. The standard rooms have better views than the larger, slightly pricier superior ones. A couple of rooms have great little balconies, perfect for a sundowner. Meals are highly commended.

🍴 Eating & Drinking

★ Moulin Hotel PUB ££

(☑ 01796-472196; www.moulinhotel.co.uk; Kirkmichael Rd; mains £8-12; P 🛜 🍴) A mile away from town but a world apart, this atmospheric inn was trading centuries before the tartan tack came to Pitlochry. With its low ceilings, ageing wood and booth seats, the Moulin is a wonderfully romantic spot for a house-brewed ale and a portion of Highland comfort food: try the mince and tatties, or venison stew. It's a pleasant uphill stroll from Pitlochry, and an easy roll down afterwards.

Port-na-Craig Inn BAR, BISTRO ££

(☑ 01796-472777; www.portnacraig.com; Port Na Craig; mains £13-22, 2-/3-course lunch £13/15; ☺ 11am-8.30pm; P 🍴) Across the river from the town centre, this cute little cottage sits in what was once a separate hamlet. Top-quality main meals are prepared with confidence and panache; there are also simpler sandwiches, kids' meals and light lunches. Or you could just sit outdoors by the river with a pint and watch the anglers.

McKay's PUB

(www.mckayshotel.co.uk; 138 Atholl Rd; ☺ 11am-11pm Sun-Thu, to 12.30am Fri-Sat) This is the place to go to meet locals and have a big night out. Live music at weekends, weekly karaoke and DJs make this Pitlochry's most popular place. The action moves from the spacious front bar (which serves food) to the boisterous dance floor out the back.

☆ Entertainment

★ Pitlochry Festival Theatre THEATRE

(☑ 01796-484626; www.pitlochryfestivaltheatre. com; Port-na-Craig; tickets £26-35) Founded in 1951 (in a tent!), this famous and much-loved theatre is the focus of Highland Perthshire's cultural life. The summer season, from May to mid-October, stages a different play each night of the week except Sunday.

ℹ Information

Pitlochry Tourist Office (☑ 01796-472215; www.perthshire.co.uk; 22 Atholl Rd; ☺ 9am-5pm Mar-Oct, Mon-Sat Nov-Feb) Good information on local walks.

ℹ Getting There & Away

Citylink (www.citylink.co.uk) Buses run every two hours to Inverness (£16.60, 2¼ hours), Perth (£10.70, 40 minutes), Edinburgh (£16.60, two to 2½ hours) and Glasgow (£16.60, 2¼ hours).

Megabus (☑ 0871 266 3333; www.megabus. com) Offers discounted fares to Inverness, Perth, Edinburgh and Glasgow.

Stagecoach (www.stagecoachbus.com) Buses run to Aberfeldy (£2, 30 minutes, hourly Monday to Saturday, three Sunday), Dunkeld (£2, 30 minutes, hourly Monday to Saturday) and Perth (£3.40, 1¼ hours, hourly Monday to Saturday).

Pitlochry is on the main railway line from Perth (£13.20, 30 minutes, nine daily Monday to Saturday, five on Sunday) to Inverness.

ⓘ Getting Around

Escape Route (☑ 01796-473859; www.escape-route.co.uk; 3 Atholl Rd; bike hire per half-/full day from £16/24; ☉ 9am-5.30pm Mon-Sat, 10am-5pm Sun) Rents out bikes and provides advice on local trails; it's worth booking ahead at weekends.

Killiecrankie

The beautiful, rugged pass of Killiecrankie, 3.5 miles north of Pitlochry, where the River Garry tumbles through a narrow gorge, was the site of the 1689 battle that ignited the Jacobite rebellion. The **Killiecrankie visitor centre** (NTS; ☑ 01796-473233; www.nts.org.uk; admission free, parking £2; ☉ 10am-5.30pm Apr-Oct) has great interactive displays on Jacobite history and local flora and fauna. There's plenty to touch, pull and open – great for kids. There are some stunning walks into the wooded gorge too; keep an eye out for red squirrels. Also here, **Highland Fling** (☑ 0845 366 5844; www.bungeejumpscotland.co.uk; per person £75, repeat jumps £30) offers breathtaking 40m bungee jumps off the bridge over the gorge at weekends, plus Wednesday and Friday from May to September.

A standout choice, the **Killiecrankie House Hotel** (☑ 01796-473220; www.killiecrankiehotel.co.uk; d standard/superior dinner, bed & breakfast £240/290; ☉ Mar-Dec; P ⑳ ⑳ ⑳) offers faultless hospitality in a peaceful setting. There's interesting art on the walls, and rooms are relaxing retreats with views over the lovely gardens. The best things about the Scottish country-house experience are here without the musty feel that sometimes goes with it; the food is also excellent. Two-night minimum stay at busy times; B&B-only rates are sometimes available.

Local buses between Pitlochry and Blair Atholl stop at Killiecrankie (£1.50, 10 minutes, three to seven daily).

Blair Castle & Blair Atholl

One of the most popular tourist attractions in Scotland, magnificent **Blair Castle** (☑ 01796-481207; www.blair-castle.co.uk; adult/child/family £9.90/5.95/26.75; ☉ 9.30am-5.30pm

Apr-Oct, 10am-4pm Sat & Sun Nov-Mar; P ⑳), and the 108 sq miles it sits on, is the seat of the duke of Atholl, head of the Murray clan. It's an impressive white building set beneath forested slopes above the River Garry. Thirty rooms are open to the public and they present a wonderful picture of upper-class Highland life from the 16th century on.

The original tower was built in 1269, but the castle has undergone significant remodelling since. The dining room is sumptuous – check out the nine-pint wine glasses – and the ballroom is a vaulted chamber that's a virtual stag cemetery. The current duke visits the castle every May to review the **Atholl Highlanders**, Britain's only private army.

For a great walk, drive or cycle (strenuous!), take the steep, winding road to **Glenfender** and Loch Moraig from Blair Atholl. It's about 3 miles on a long, narrow uphill road to a farmhouse; the view of the peaks Beinn a'Ghlo at the top is spectacular.

The **Atholl Arms Hotel** (☑ 01796-481205; www.athollarms.co.uk; s/d from £70/86; P ⑳ ⑳), near the castle, is a traditional place with darkish rooms and comfortably old-fashioned decor. The Bothy Bar here is the sibling pub of the Moulin Hotel in Pitlochry, snug with booth seating, low-slung roof, bucketloads of character and an enormous fireplace.

Blair Atholl is 6 miles northwest of Pitlochry, and the castle a further mile beyond it. Local buses run between Pitlochry and Blair Atholl (£2, 25 minutes, three to seven daily). Four buses a day (Monday to Saturday) go directly to the castle. There are trains from Perth (£13.20, 40 minutes, nine daily Monday to Saturday, five on Sunday).

Lochs Tummel & Rannoch

The scenic route along Lochs Tummel and Rannoch (www.rannochandtummel.co.uk) is worth doing any way you can – by foot, bicycle or car. Hillsides shrouded with ancient birchwoods and forests of spruce, pine and larch make up the fabulous **Tay Forest Park**. These wooded hills roll into the glittering waters of the lochs; a visit in autumn is recommended, when the birch leaves are at their finest.

The **Queen's View Visitor Centre** (www.forestry.gov.uk; admission free, parking £2; ☉ visitor centre 10am-6pm late Mar–mid-Nov) at the eastern end of Loch Tummel provides access to a magnificent viewpoint along the loch to

RANNOCH MOOR

Beyond Rannoch Station, civilisation fades away and Rannoch Moor begins. This is the largest area of moorland in Britain, stretching west for eight barren, bleak and uninhabited miles to the A82 Glasgow–Fort William road. A triangular plateau of blanket bog occupying more than 50 sq miles, the moor is ringed by high mountains and puddled with countless lochs, ponds and peat hags. Water covers 10% of the surface, and it has been canoed across, swum across and even skated across in winter.

Despite the appearance of desolation, the moor is rich in wildlife, with curlews, golden plovers and snipe darting among the tussocks, black-throated divers, goosanders and mergansers on the lochs, and – if you're lucky – ospreys and golden eagles overhead. Herds of red deer forage alongside the railway, and otters patrol the loch shores. And keep an eye out for the sundew, a tiny, insect-eating plant with sticky-fingered leaves.

A couple of excellent (and challenging) walks start from Rannoch Station: north to Corrour Station (11 miles, four to five hours), from where you can return by train; and west along the northern edge of the moor to the King's House Hotel at the eastern end of Glen Coe (11 miles, four hours).

the conical peak of **Schiehallion** (1083m). A new cafe and shop was under construction here at the time of writing.

Waterfalls, mountains and a shimmering loch greet visitors in **Kinloch Rannoch**. It's a great base for walks and cycle trips around **Loch Rannoch**, including the hike up Schiehallion (6.5 miles return), a relatively straightforward climb from Braes of Foss rewarded by spectacular views. See www.jmt.org/east-schiehallion-estate.asp for more information. Loch Rannoch can be fished for brown trout, Arctic char and pike; you can get permits (£8 per day) at the Country Store in Kinloch Rannoch.

Eighteen miles west, the road ends at romantic, isolated **Rannoch Station**, which is on the Glasgow–Fort William railway line. Beyond is desolate, intriguing **Rannoch Moor**. There's a tearoom on the platform, and a welcoming small hotel alongside.

Rannoch Station is a dead end, and there's no petrol in this area; the closest pumps are at Aberfeldy, Pitlochry, and Blair Atholl.

🛏 Sleeping & Eating

Kilvrecht Campsite CAMPSITE £
(☑ 01350-727284; tent sites with/without car £8/5; ⊙ Apr–mid-Oct) This basic but beautiful campsite (toilet block, but no hot water) is 2 miles west of Kinloch Rannoch on the south shore of the loch. Hiking and mountain-biking trails begin from the site.

Moor of Rannoch Hotel HOTEL ££
(☑ 01882-633238; www.moorofrannoch.co.uk; Rannoch Station; s/d £80/114; ⊙ mid-Feb–Oct; 🅿 🐾) At the end of the road beside Rannoch train station, this is one of Scotland's most isolated places (no internet, no TV, only fleeting mobile-phone reception), but luckily this hotel is here to keep your spirits up with cosy rooms and great walks right from the doorstep – a magical getaway. It does good dinners (three courses £29), and can prepare a packed lunch.

Gardens B&B B&B ££
(☑ 01882-632434; www.thegardensdunalastair.co.uk; Dunalastair; per person £40-45; 🅿) Off the beaten track between Kinloch Rannoch and Tummel Bridge, this place has just two rooms – a double and a twin. But what rooms they are: effectively suites, each with their own bathroom and sitting room. The conservatory space is great for soaking up the sun and contemplating the stunning view of Schiehallion.

Loch Tummel Inn PUB ££
(☑ 01882-634272; www.lochtummelinn.co.uk; dinner mains £10-17; ⊙ 12.15-2.30pm & 5.30-8.30pm Tue-Sat, 12.15-8pm Sun Apr-Oct; 🅿 🐾) This old coaching inn is a snug spot for a decent feed, the menu ranging from pub classics to more ambitious meat and game dishes. The friendly bar serves locally brewed beer and is a top spot for a quiet pint at the outdoor tables with a view over Loch Tummel. The inn is about 3 miles east of the village of Tummel Bridge

❶ Getting There & Away

Broons Buses (☑ 01882-632331) Runs between Kinloch Rannoch and Rannoch Station

(£2.50, 35 minutes, two to four a day Monday to Friday).

Elizabeth Yule Coaches (☑ 01796-47229) From April to October operates a bus service from Pitlochry to Kinloch Rannoch (£3.50, 50 minutes, three to five a day Monday to Saturday) via Queen's View and Loch Tummel Inn

There are two to four trains daily from Rannoch station north to Fort William (£10.10, one hour) and Mallaig, and south to Glasgow (£23.10, 2¾ hours).

Strathtay

From Ballinluig, south of Pitlochry, the valley of the River Tay arcs westward through Aberfeldy towards the scenic delights of Kenmore and Loch Tay. This is the heart of Highland Perthshire.

Aberfeldy

POP 1895

Aberfeldy is a peaceful, pretty place on the banks of the Tay; adventure sports, art and castles all feature on the menu here, but if it's moody lochs and glens that steal your heart, you may want to push a little further west.

◉ Sights & Activities

The Birks of Aberfeldy, made famous by a Robert Burns poem, offer a great short walk from the centre of town, following a vigorous burn upstream past several picturesque cascades. The B846 road towards Fortingall crosses the Tay via the elegant Wade's Bridge, built in 1733 as part of the

network of military roads designed to tame the Highlands.

Dewar's World of Whisky   DISTILLERY (www.dewarsworldofwhisky.com; tours adult/child £7/4; ☉ 10am-6pm Mon-Sat & noon-4pm Sun Apr-Oct, 10am-4pm Mon-Sat Nov-Mar) At the eastern end of Aberfeldy, this home of the famous blend offers a good tour, fully 90 minutes long. After the usual overblown film, there's a museum section with audioguide, and an entertaining interactive blending session, as well as the tour of the whisky-making process. More expensive tours allow you to try venerable Aberfeldy single malts and others.

Watermill   GALLERY, BOOKSHOP (www.aberfeldywatermill.com; Mill St; ☉ 10am-5pm Mon-Sat, 11am-5pm Sun, to 5.30pm daily May-Sep) **FREE** You could while away several hours at this converted watermill, which houses a cafe, bookshop and art gallery exhibiting contemporary works of art. The shop has the biggest range of titles in the Highlands, with a great selection of books on Scottish history, landscape and wildlife.

Castle Menzies   CASTLE (www.castlemenzies.org; adult/child £6/2.50; ☉ 10.30am-5pm Mon-Sat, 2-5pm Sun Easter-Oct; ℗) Castle Menzies is the 16th-century seat of the chief of Clan Menzies (*ming*-iss), magnificently set against a forest backdrop. Inside it reeks of authenticity, despite extensive restoration work. Check out the fireplace in the dungeon-like kitchens, and the gaudy great hall with windows revealing a ribbon of lush, green countryside extending into wooded hills beyond the estate. You get

---

SALMON FISHING ON THE TAY

The Tay is Scotland's longest river (117 miles) and the most powerful in Britain, discharging more water into the sea each year than the Thames and Severn combined. It is also Europe's most famous salmon river, attracting anglers from all over the world (the season runs from 15 January to 15 October). The British record rod-caught salmon, weighing in at 64lb (29kg), was hooked in the Tay near Dunkeld in 1922, by local girl Georgina Ballantine.

Salmon fishing has an air of exclusivity, and can be expensive, but anyone, even complete beginners, can have a go. There is lots of information on the FishTay website (www.fishtay.co.uk), but novices will do best to hire a guide.

Fishinguide Scotland (☑ 07714 598848; www.fishinguide.co.uk; ⊞) A lifetime's experience of exploring his native rivers, lochs and coastline means there isn't much that professional guide Duncan Pepper doesn't know about Scottish fishing. Though based near the Tay, he leads fishing trips all over Scotland for salmon, trout, pike, pollack and more. Packages cost from £200 per person per day, including travel, instruction, permits, tackle and a lavish picnic lunch.

in for free if you share a surname with the castle. It's about 1.5 miles west of Aberfeldy, off the B846.

Highland Safaris
TOURS

(☑ 01887-820071; www.highlandsafaris.net; ☉ 9am-5pm, closed Sun Nov-Jan; 🚗) This outfit offers an ideal way to spot some wildlife or simply enjoy Perthshire's magnificent countryside. Standard trips include the 2½-hour Mountain Safari (adult/child £40/20), which includes whisky and shortbread in a mountain bothy; and the four-hour Safari Trek (adult/child £65/45), culminating with a walk in the mountains and a picnic. You may spot wildlife such as golden eagles, osprey and red deer. There's also gold panning for kids (£5) and mountain-bike hire (per day £20).

Splash
RAFTING

(☑ 01887-829706; www.rafting.co.uk; Dunkeld Rd; ☉ 9am-9pm; 🚗) Splash offers family-friendly white-water rafting on the River Tay (adult/child £40/30, Wednesday to Sunday year-round) and more advanced adult trips on the Tummel (grade 3/4, June to September) and the Orchy (grade 3/5, October to March). It also offers pulse-racing descents on river bugs (£60), canyoning (£55) and mountain-bike hire (per half/full day £15/20).

🛌 Sleeping & Eating

Tigh'n Eilean Guest House
B&B ££

(☑ 01887-820109; www.tighneilean.com; Taybridge Dr; s/d £48/75; 🅿 🛜 🐾) Everything about this property screams comfort. It's a gorgeous place overlooking the Tay, with individually designed rooms: one has a jacuzzi, while another is set on its own in a cheery yellow summer house in the garden, giving you a bit of privacy. The garden itself is fabulous, with hammocks for lazing in, and the riverbank setting is delightful.

Balnearn Guest House
B&B ££

(☑ 01887-820431; www.balnearnhouse.com; Crieff Rd; s/d/f from £48/69/80; 🅿 🛜 🐾) Balnearn is a sedate, refined and luxurious mansion near the centre of town, with space to spare. Most rooms have great natural light, and there's a particularly good family room downstairs. Breakfast has been lavishly praised by readers, and the attentive, cordial hosts are helpful while respecting your privacy.

ℹ Information

Aberfeldy Tourist Office (☑ 01887-829010; The Square; ☉ 9.30am-5pm Apr-Oct, closed Thu & Sun Nov-Mar) In an old church on the central square.

ℹ Getting There & Away

Stagecoach (www.stagecoachbus.com) bus 23 runs from Perth to Aberfeldy (1½ hours, hourly Monday to Saturday, fewer on Sunday) via Dunkeld; from Pitlochry (£3.40, 40 minutes), you'll need to change buses at Ballinluig. There's no regular bus link west to Killin, but see also the Ring of Breadalbane Explorer (p137).

Local buses run a circular route from Aberfeldy through Kenmore, Fortingall and back to Aberfeldy once each way on school days only.

Kenmore

The picturesque village of Kenmore lies at Loch Tay's eastern end, 6 miles west of Aberfeldy. Dominated by a striking archway leading to **Taymouth Castle** (not open to the public), it was built by the third Earl of Breadalbane in 1760 to house his estate workers.

Kenmore is a good activity base, and **Loch Tay Boat House** (☑ 07923 540826; www.loch-tay.co.uk; Pier Rd; ☉ mid-Mar–mid-Oct) can have you speeding off on a mountain bike (per half/full day £15/20) or out on the loch itself, in anything from a canoe to a cabin cruiser that'll sleep a whole family.

The heart of the village, **Kenmore Hotel** (☑ 01887-830205; www.kenmorehotel.com; The Square; r from £89; 🅿 @ 🛜 🐾) has a bar with a roaring fire and some verses scribbled on the chimneypiece by Robert Burns in 1787, when the inn was already a couple of centuries old. There's also a riverbank beer garden, great views from the restaurant and a wide range of accommodation.

Loch Tay

Loch Tay is the heart of the ancient region known as Breadalbane (from the Gaelic *Bràghad Albainn,* 'the heights of Scotland') – mighty **Ben Lawers** (1214m), looming over the loch, is the highest peak outside the Ben Nevis and Cairngorms regions. Much of the land to the north of Loch Tay falls within the **Ben Lawers National Nature Reserve** (www.nnr-scotland.org.uk/ben-lawers), known for its rare alpine flora. The minor road along the south shore is narrow and twisting (unsuitable for large vehicles), but offers great views of the hills to the north.

The main access point for the ascent of Ben Lawers is the car park 1½ miles off the A827, on the minor road from Loch Tay to Bridge of Balgie. The climb is 6.5 miles and can take up to five hours (return): pack wet-weather gear, water and food, and a map and compass. There's also an easier nature trail here.

Less than a mile south of Kenmore is the fascinating Scottish Crannog Centre (☑01887-830583; www.crannog.co.uk; tours adult/child £8/6; ☉10am-5.30pm Apr-Oct), perched on stilts above the loch. Crannogs – effectively artificial islands – were a favoured form of defensive dwelling from the 3rd millennium BC onwards. This superb re-creation (based on studies of Oakbank crannog, one of 18 discovered in Loch Tay) offers a guided tour that includes an impressive demonstration of fire making and Iron Age crafts.

Culdees Bunkhouse (☑01887-830519; www.culdeesbunkhouse.co.uk; dm/tw/f £18/50/69; ⓟ@☞☎) is a wonderfully offbeat hostel with majestic vistas: the whole of the loch stretches out below you. It's fine base for hill walking or for mucking in with the volunteers who help run the sustainable farm here. It's half a mile above the village of Fearnan, 4 miles west of Kenmore.

Fortingall

Fortingall is one of the prettiest villages in Scotland, with 19th-century thatched cottages in a tranquil setting. The church has impressive wooden beams and a 7th-century monk's bell; in the churchyard, there's a 2000-year-old yew tree that was around when the Romans camped in the meadows by the River Lyon. Popular if unlikely tradition says that Pontius Pilate was born here. Today the tree is a shell of its former self – at its zenith it had a girth of over 17m, but souvenir hunters have reduced it to two much smaller trunks.

Fortingall Hotel (☑01887-830367; www.fortingall.com; s/d £120/165; ⓟ☞☎) ✐ is a peaceful, old-fashioned country hotel furnished with quiet good taste. The spotless bedrooms have huge beds, modern bathrooms and thoughtful little extras, and look out over green meadows; in all, a perfect spot for doing very little except enjoying the clean air and excellent food.

WORTH A TRIP

UPPER STRATHEARN

The Highland villages of Comrie and St Fillans in upper Strathearn are surrounded by forests and bare, craggy hilltops where deer and mountain hares live in abundance. St Fillans enjoys an excellent location at the eastern end of Loch Earn, which reflects the silhouettes of distant peaks.

The Four Seasons (☑01765-685333; www.thefourseasonshotel.co.uk; St Fillans; d from £122; ☉Mar-Dec; ⓟ☞☎) is a historic hotel – the Beatles stayed here while on tour in 1964 – that has been given a classy modern makeover. Two beautifully appointed lounges and an atmospheric wee bar enjoy great views over the loch. The superior rooms – worth the upgrade – have the best vistas, and there are many activities to choose from, including waterskiing, quad biking and pony trekking. There are also six chalets nestled in the slopes behind the hotel, plus a noted fine-dining restaurant.

Comrie is 24 miles west of Perth, and St Fillans is about 5 miles further west. Buses run from Perth via Crieff to Comrie (£3.60, one hour, roughly hourly Monday to Saturday, every two hours Sunday) and St Fillans (£6.20, 1½ hours, five daily Monday to Saturday).

Glen Lyon

This remote and romantic glen stretches for 34 unforgettable miles of rickety stone bridges, Caledonian pine forest and heather-clad peaks. It becomes wilder and more uninhabited as it snakes its way west, and is proof that hidden treasures still exist. The ancients believed it to be a gateway to Faerieland, and even the most sceptical of visitors will be entranced by the valley's magic.

From Fortingall, a narrow road winds up the glen, while another from Loch Tay crosses the hills to Bridge of Balgie, halfway along. The road continues as far as the dam on Loch Lyon, passing a memorial to Robert Campbell (1808–94; a Canadian explorer and fur trader, who was born in the glen). Cycling through Glen Lyon is a wonderful way to experience this special place.

There are no villages in the valley – the majestic and lonely scenery is the main reason to be here – just a cluster of houses at Bridge of Balgie, where the **Bridge of Balgie Tearoom** (☏ 01887-866221; Bridge of Balgie; snacks £3-5; ☺ 10am-5pm Apr-Oct) serves homemade cakes, sandwiches and soups to hungry walkers and cyclists.

★**Milton Eonan** (☏ 01887-866337; www.miltoneonan.com; Bridge of Balgie; per person £43; P ☏ 🐾) is a must for those seeking tranquillity in a glorious natural setting. On a bubbling stream where a watermill once stood, it's a working rare-breed croft with a romantic one-bedroom self-catering cottage (breakfast available) at the bottom of the garden. The lively owners offer packed lunches and evening meals (£20) using local and home-grown produce. It's signposted to the right a short distance beyond Bridge of Balgie, on the road towards Loch Tay.

There is no public transport in the glen.

WEST HIGHLANDS

This region extends from the bleak blanket bog of the Moor of Rannoch to the west coast beyond Glen Coe and Fort William, and includes the southern reaches of the Great Glen. The scenery is grand throughout, with high and wild mountains dominating the glens. Great expanses of moor alternate with lochs and patches of commercial forest. Fort William, at the inner end of Loch Linnhe, is the only sizeable town in the area.

Since 2007 the region has been promoted as **Lochaber Geopark** (www.lochabergeopark.org.uk), an area of outstanding geology and scenery.

Glen Coe

Scotland's most famous glen is also one of the grandest and – in bad weather – the grimmest. The approach to the glen from the east, watched over by the rocky pyramid of **Buachaille Etive Mor** – the Great Shepherd of Etive – leads over the Pass of Glencoe and into the narrow upper valley. The southern side is dominated by three massive, brooding spurs, known as the **Three Sisters**, while the northern side is enclosed by the continuous steep wall of the knife-edged **Aonach Eagach** ridge, a classic mountaineering challenge. The main road threads its lonely way through the middle of all this mountain grandeur, past deep gorges and crashing waterfalls, to the more pasto-

ral lower reaches of the glen around Loch Achtriochtan and Glencoe village.

Glencoe was written into the history books in 1692 when the resident MacDonalds were murdered by Campbell soldiers in what became known as the Glencoe Massacre.

🏃 Activities

There are several short, pleasant walks around **Glencoe Lochan**, near the village. To get there, turn left off the minor road to the youth hostel, just beyond the bridge over the River Coe. There are three walks (40 minutes to an hour), all detailed on a signboard at the car park. The artificial lochan was created by Lord Strathcona in 1895 for his homesick Canadian wife Isabella and is surrounded by a North American–style forest.

A more strenuous hike, but well worth the effort on a fine day, is the climb to the **Lost Valley**, a magical mountain sanctuary still haunted by the ghosts of the murdered MacDonalds (only 2.5 miles round trip, but allow three hours). A rough path from the car park at Allt na Reigh (on the A82, 6 miles east of Glencoe village) bears left down to a footbridge over the river, then climbs up the wooded valley between Beinn Fhada and Gearr Aonach (the first and second of the Three Sisters). The route leads steeply up through a maze of giant, jumbled, moss-coated boulders before emerging – quite unexpectedly – into a broad, open valley with an 800m-long meadow as flat as a football pitch. Back in the days of clan warfare, the valley – invisible from below – was used for hiding stolen cattle; its Gaelic name, Coire Gabhail, means 'corrie of capture'.

The summits of Glen Coe's mountains are for experienced mountaineers only. The Cicerone guidebook *Ben Nevis & Glen Coe* by Ronald Turnbull, available in most bookshops and outdoor-equipment shops, details everything from short easy walks to challenging mountain climbs.

East of the Glen

Glencoe Mountain Resort   OUTDOORS
(☏ 01855-851226; www.glencoemountain.com; Kingshouse; ☺ 9am-8.30pm) A few miles east of Glen Coe proper is the Glencoe Mountain Resort, where commercial skiing in Scotland first began back in 1956. The **chairlift** (adult/child £10/5; ☺ 9am-4.30pm Mon-Fri, 8.30am-4.30pm Sat & Sun) continues to operate in summer – there's a grand view over the

Moor of Rannoch from the top – providing access to mountain-biking trails. The **Lodge Café-Bar** has comfy sofas where you can soak up the view through the floor-to-ceiling windows. In winter a lift pass costs £30 a day; equipment hire is £25.

Two miles west of the ski centre, a minor road leads along peaceful and beautiful **Glen Etive**, which runs southwest for 12 miles to the head of Loch Etive. On a hot summer's day the River Etive contains many tempting pools for swimming in, and there are lots of good picnic sites.

Kings House Hotel   HOTEL, PUB **££**
(☑ 01855-851259; www.kingy.com; Kingshouse; s/d £45/100; **P**) This remote hotel claims to be one of Scotland's oldest licensed inns, dating from the 17th century. It has long been a favourite meeting place for climbers, skiers and walkers (it's on the West Highland Way); accommodation is basic, but there is good pub grub and real ale. The rustic **Climbers Bar** (bar meals £8-12; ☺ 11am-11pm) round the back is more relaxed than the lounge.

The hotel lies on the old military road from Stirling to Fort William, and after the Battle of Culloden it was used as a Hanoverian garrison – hence the name.

Glencoe Village

POP 360

The little village of Glencoe stands on the south shore of Loch Leven at the western end of the glen, 16 miles south of Fort William.

◉ Sights & Activities

Glencoe Folk Museum   MUSEUM
(☑ 01855-811664; www.glencoemuseum.com; adult/child £3/free; ☺ 10am-4.30pm Mon-Sat Easter-Oct) This small, thatched museum houses a varied collection of military memorabilia, farm equipment, and tools of the woodworking, blacksmithing and slate-quarrying trades.

Glencoe Visitor Centre   INTERPRETATION CENTRE
(NTS; ☑ 01855-811307; www.glencoe-nts.org.uk; adult/child £6.25/5; ☺ 9.30am-5.30pm Easter-Oct, 10am-4pm Thu-Sun Nov-Easter; **P**) ✍ The centre provides comprehensive information on the geological, environmental and cultural history of Glencoe via high-tech interactive and audiovisual displays, charts the history of mountaineering in the glen, and

tells the story of the Glencoe Massacre in all its gory detail. It's 1.5 miles east of Glencoe village.

Steven Fallon Mountain Guides   OUTDOORS
(☑ 07795 146400; www.stevenfallon.co.uk; per person from £50) If you lack the experience or confidence to tackle Glen Coe's challenging mountains alone, then you can join a guided hill walk or hire a private guide from this outfit.

🛏 Sleeping

Glencoe Independent Hostel   HOSTEL **£**
(☑ 01855-811906; www.glencoehostel.co.uk; dm £13-16.50, bunkhouse £12.50-14.50; **P @ 🛜**) This handily located hostel, just 1.5 miles southeast of Glencoe village, is set in an old farmhouse with six- and eight-bed dorms, and a bunkhouse with another 16 bed spaces in communal, alpine-style bunks. There's also a cute little wooden cabin that sleeps up to three (£19 to £25 per person per night).

Glencoe SYHA   HOSTEL **£**
(☑ 08155-811219; www.syha.org.uk; dm/tw £21/56; **P @ 🛜 🐾**) Very popular with hikers, though the atmosphere can be a little institutional. It's a 1.5-mile walk from the village along the minor road on the northern side of the river.

Invercoe Caravan &
Camping Park   CAMPSITE **£**
(☑ 01855-811210; www.invercoe.co.uk; tent sites without car per person £9, campervan sites £22) Our favourite official camping ground in Glencoe, this place has great views of the surrounding mountains and is equipped with antimidge machines and a covered area for campers to cook in.

Clachaig Inn   HOTEL **££**
(☑ 01855-811252; www.clachaig.com; per person from £51; **P 🛜**) The Clachaig has long been a favourite haunt of hill walkers and climbers. As well as comfortable en suite accommodation, there's a smart, wood-panelled lounge bar with lots of sofas and armchairs, mountaineering photos, and climbing magazines to leaf through.

Climbers usually head for the lively **Boots Bar** (mains £9-18) on the other side of the hotel – it has log fires, serves real ale and good pub grub, and has live Scottish music on Saturday nights. It's 2 miles southeast of Glencoe village.

THE GLENCOE MASSACRE

Glen Coe – Gleann Comhann in Gaelic – is sometimes (wrongly) said to mean 'the glen of weeping', a romantic mistranslation that gained popularity in the wake of the brutal murders that took place here in 1692 (the true origin of the name is pre-Gaelic, its meaning lost in the mists of time).

Following the Glorious Revolution of 1688, in which the Catholic King James VII/II (VII of Scotland, II of England) was replaced on the British throne by the Protestant King William II/III, supporters of the exiled James – known as Jacobites, most of them Highlanders – rose up against William in a series of battles. In an attempt to quash Jacobite loyalties, King William offered the Highland clans an amnesty on the condition that all clan chiefs took an oath of loyalty to him before 1 January 1692.

Maclain, the elderly chief of the MacDonalds of Glencoe, had long been a thorn in the side of the authorities. Not only was he late in setting out to fulfil the king's demand, but he mistakenly went first to Fort William before travelling slowly through winter mud and rain to Inveraray, where he was three days late in taking the oath before the Sheriff of Argyll.

The secretary of state for Scotland, Sir John Dalrymple, decided to use the fact that Maclain had missed the deadline to punish the troublesome MacDonalds, and at the same time set an example to other Highland clans, some of whom had not bothered to take the oath.

A company of 120 soldiers, mainly from the Campbell territory of Argyll, were sent to the glen under cover of collecting taxes. It was a long-standing tradition for clans to provide hospitality to travellers and, since their commanding officer was related to Maclain by marriage, the troops were billeted in MacDonald homes.

After they'd been guests for 12 days, the government order came for the soldiers to 'fall upon the rebels the MacDonalds of Glencoe and put all to the sword under 70. You are to have a special care that the Old Fox and his sons do upon no account escape'. The soldiers turned on their hosts at 5am on 13 February, killing Maclain and 37 other men, women and children. Some of the soldiers alerted the MacDonalds to their intended fate, allowing them to escape; many fled into the snow-covered hills, where another 40 people perished in the cold.

The ruthless brutality of the incident caused a public uproar, and after an inquiry several years later Dalrymple lost his job. There's a monument to Maclain in Glencoe village, and members of the MacDonald clan still gather here on 13 February each year to lay a wreath.

✕ Eating

★ Glencoe Café   CAFE £

(☑01855-811168; www.glencoecafe.com; mains £4-8; ☺10am-4pm, to 5pm May-Sep, closed Nov) This friendly cafe is the hub of Glencoe village, serving breakfast fry-ups till 11.30am (including vegetarian versions), light lunches based around local produce (think Cullen skink, smoked salmon quiche, venison burgers) and the best cappuccino in the glen.

Crafts & Things   CAFE £

(☑01855-811325; www.craftsandthings.co.uk; Annat; mains £3-7; ☺10am-5pm Mon-Fri, 9.30am-5pm Sat & Sun; ℗♿) Just off the main road between Glencoe village and Ballachulish, the coffee shop in this craft shop is a good spot for a lunch of homemade lentil soup with crusty rolls, ciabatta sandwiches, or just coffee and carrot cake. There are tables outdoors and a box of toys to keep the little ones occupied.

ℹ Getting There & Away

Scottish Citylink (☑0871 266 3333; www.citylink.co.uk) Buses run between Fort William and Glencoe (£7.80, 30 minutes, eight daily) and from Glencoe to Glasgow (£21, 2½ hours, eight daily). Buses stop at Glencoe village, Glencoe Visitor Centre and Glencoe Mountain Resort.

Stagecoach (www.stagecoachbus.com) Bus 44 links Glencoe village with Fort William (£3.70, 35 minutes, hourly Monday to Saturday, three on Sunday) and Kinlochleven (£2, 25 minutes).

Kinlochleven

POP 900

Kinlochleven is hemmed in by high mountains at the head of beautiful Loch Leven, about 7 miles east of Glencoe village. The aluminium smelter that led to the town's development in the early 20th century has long since closed, and the opening of the Ballachulish Bridge in the 1970s allowed the main road to bypass the town completely. Decline was halted by the opening of the West Highland Way, which now brings a steady stream of hikers through the village.

The final section of the West Highland Way stretches for 14 miles from Kinlochleven to Fort William. The village is also the starting point for easier walks up the glen of the River Leven, through pleasant woods to the Grey Mare's Tail waterfall, and harder mountain hikes into the Mamores.

Activities

Ice Factor ADVENTURE SPORTS
(☑01855-831100; www.ice-factor.co.uk; Leven Rd; ⊙9am-10pm Tue & Thu, to 7pm Mon, Wed & Fri-Sun; ⊞) If you fancy trying your hand at ice climbing, even in the middle of summer, the world's biggest indoor ice-climbing wall offers a one-hour beginner's 'taster' session for £30. You'll also find a rock-climbing wall, an aerial adventure course, a sauna and steam room, and a cafe and bar-bistro.

Via Ferrata ADVENTURE SPORTS
(☑01397-747111; www.verticaldescents.com; per person £65) Scotland's first via ferrata – a 500m climbing route equipped with steel ladders, cables and bridges – snakes through the crags around the Grey Mare's Tail waterfall, allowing nonclimbers to experience the thrill of climbing (you'll need a head for heights, though!).

⏸ Sleeping & Eating

Blackwater Hostel HOSTEL, CAMPSITE £
(☑01855-831253; www.blackwaterhostel.co.uk; Lab Rd; dm/tw £16.50/40, tent sites per person £7, pods from £35; ☎) This 40-bed hostel has spotless dorms with en suite bathrooms and TV, and a level, well-sheltered camping ground with the option of wooden 'glamping' pods.

★**Lochleven Seafood Cafe** SEAFOOD ££
(☑01855-821048; www.lochlevenseafoodcafe.co.uk; mains £11-22, whole lobster £40; ⊙noon-3pm & 6-9pm Apr-Oct; ℗) This outstanding place serves superb shellfish freshly plucked from live tanks – oysters on the half shell, razor clams, scallops, lobster and crab – plus a daily fish special and some nonseafood dishes. For warm days, there's an outdoor terrace with a view across the loch to the Pap of Glencoe, a distinctive conical mountain.

❶ Getting There & Away

Stagecoach (www.stagecoachbus.com) bus 44 runs from Fort William to Kinlochleven (£4.70, 50 minutes, hourly Monday to Saturday, three on Sunday) via Ballachulish and Glencoe village.

Fort William

POP 9910

Basking on the shores of Loch Linnhe amid magnificent mountain scenery, Fort William has one of the most enviable settings in the whole of Scotland. If it wasn't for the busy dual carriageway crammed between the town centre and the loch, and one of the highest rainfall records in the country, it would be almost idyllic. Even so, the Fort has carved out a reputation as 'Outdoor Capital of the UK' (www.outdoorcapital.co.uk), and easy access by rail and bus makes it a good place to base yourself for exploring the surrounding mountains and glens.

Magical Glen Nevis begins near the northern end of the town and wraps itself around the southern flanks of Ben Nevis (1344m), Britain's highest mountain and a magnet for hikers and climbers. The glen is also popular with movie makers – parts of *Braveheart*, *Rob Roy* and the *Harry Potter* movies were filmed there.

History

There is little left of the fort from which the town derives its name. The first castle here was constructed by General Monck in 1654 and called Inverlochy, but the meagre ruins by the loch are those of the fort built in the 1690s by General Mackay and named after King William II/III. In the 18th century it became part of a chain of garrisons (along with Fort Augustus and Fort George) that controlled the Great Glen in the wake of the Jacobite rebellions; it was pulled down in the 19th century to make way for the railway.

Originally a tiny fishing village called Gordonsburgh, the town adopted the name of the fort after the opening of the railway in 1901 (in Gaelic it is known as An Gearasdan, 'the garrison'). The juxtaposition of the railway and the Caledonian Canal saw the town grow into a major tourist centre. Its position has been consolidated in the last three decades by the huge increase in popularity of climbing, skiing, mountain biking and other outdoor sports.

◎ Sights

Jacobite Steam Train
HERITAGE RAILWAY

(☏ 0844 850 4685; www.westcoastrailways.co.uk; day return adult/child £34/19; ⊙ daily Jul & Aug, Mon-Fri mid-May–Jun & Sep-Oct) The Jacobite Steam Train, hauled by a former LNER K1 or LMS Class 5MT locomotive, travels the scenic two-hour run between Fort William and Mallaig. Classed as one of the great railway journeys of the world, the route crosses the historic Glenfinnan Viaduct, made famous in the *Harry Potter* films – the Jacobite's owners supplied the steam locomotive and rolling stock used in the film.

Trains depart from Fort William train station in the morning and return from Mallaig in the afternoon. There's a brief stop at Glenfinnan station, and you get 1½ hours in Mallaig.

West Highland Museum
MUSEUM

(☏ 01397-702169; www.westhighlandmuseum.org.uk; Cameron Sq; ⊙ 10am-5pm Mon-Sat Apr-Oct, to 4pm Mar & Nov-Dec, closed Jan & Feb) FREE This small but fascinating museum is packed with all manner of Highland memorabilia. Look out for the secret portrait of Bonnie Prince Charlie – after the Jacobite rebellions all things Highland were banned, including pictures of the exiled leader, and this tiny painting looks like nothing more than a smear of paint until viewed in a cylindrical mirror, which reflects a credible likeness of the prince.

☞ Tours

Crannog Cruises
CRUISE

(☏ 01397-700714; www.crannog.net/cruises; adult/child £14/7) Operates four daily 1½-hour wildlife cruises on Loch Linnhe, visiting a seal colony and a salmon farm.

✯ Festivals & Events

UCI Mountain Bike World Cup
MOUNTAIN BIKING

(www.fortwilliamworldcup.co.uk) In June, Fort William pulls in crowds of more than 18,000 spectators for this World Cup downhill mountain-biking event. The gruelling downhill course is at nearby Nevis Range ski area.

🛏 Sleeping

It's best to book well ahead in summer, especially for hostels.

Calluna
APARTMENT £

(☏ 01397-700451; www.fortwilliamholiday.co.uk; Heathercroft, Connochie Rd; dm/tw £16/36, 6- to 8-person apt per week £550; P �) Run by well-known mountain guide Alan Kimber and wife Sue, the Calluna offers self-catering apartments geared to groups of hikers and climbers, but also takes individual travellers prepared to share; there's a fully equipped kitchen and an excellent drying room for your soggy hiking gear.

Bank Street Lodge
HOSTEL £

(☏ 01397-700070; www.bankstreetlodge.co.uk; Bank St; dm/tw from £17/55; P) Part of a modern hotel and restaurant complex, the Bank Street Lodge offers the most central budget beds in town, only 250m from the train station. It has kitchen facilities and a drying room.

Fort William Backpackers
HOSTEL £

(☏ 01397-700711; www.scotlands-top-hostels.com; Alma Rd; dm/tw £18/47; P @ ſ) A 10-minute walk from the bus and train stations, this lively and welcoming hostel is set in a grand Victorian villa, perched on a hillside with great views over Loch Linnhe.

★ Grange
B&B ££

(☏ 01397-705516; www.grangefortwilliam.com; Grange Rd; r per person £65-70; P ſ) An exceptional 19th-century villa set in its own landscaped grounds, the Grange is crammed with antiques and fitted with log fires, chaise longues and Victorian roll-top baths. The Turret Room, with its window seat in the turret overlooking Loch Linnhe, is our favourite. It's 500m southwest of the town centre. No children.

★ Lime Tree
HOTEL ££

(☏ 01397-701806; www.limetreefortwilliam.co.uk; Achintore Rd; s/d from £100/110; P) Much more interesting than your average guesthouse, this former Victorian manse overlooking Loch Linnhe is an 'art gallery with rooms', decorated throughout with the artist-owner's atmospheric Highland landscapes. Foodies rave about the restaurant, and the gallery space – a triumph of sensitive design – stages everything from serious exhibitions (works by David Hockney and Andy Goldsworthy have appeared) to folk concerts.

St Andrew's Guest House
B&B **££**

(☑ 01397-703038; www.standrewsguesthouse.
co.uk; Fassifern Rd; s/d £55/68; ℗ 🛜) Set in a
lovely 19th-century building that was once a
rectory and choir school, St Andrew's retains
period features, such as carved masonry,
wood panelling and stained-glass windows.
It has six spacious bedrooms those at the
front have stunning views.

No 6 Caberfeidh
B&B **££**

(☑ 01397-703756; www.6caberfeidh.com; Fassifern
Rd, 6 Caberfeidh; d/f £70/110; 🛜) Friendly owners and comfortable accommodation make
a great combination; add a good central
location and you're all set. Choose from
one of two family rooms (one double and
one single bed) or a romantic double with
four-poster. Freshly prepared breakfasts include scrambled egg with smoked salmon.

Crolinnhe
B&B **£££**

(☑ 01397-703795; www.crolinnhe.co.uk; Grange
Rd; r £130-140; ☺ Easter-Oct; ℗) This grand
19th-century villa enjoys a lochside location,
beautiful gardens and sumptuous accommodation – a welcome dose of luxury at the
end of the West Highland Way. Breakfast
porridge comes with cream and a wee jug
of whisky!

✖ Eating & Drinking

Sugar and Spice
CAFE **£**

(☑ 01397-705005; 147 High St; mains £8-11;
☺ 11am-4pm Mon-Wed, to 9pm Thu-Sat; 🛜🖶)
Enjoy what is probably the best coffee in
town at this colourful cafe, just a few paces
from the official finishing line of the West
Highland Way. In the evening (Thursday to
Saturday only) it serves authentic Thai dishes (BYOB).

Crannog Seafood Restaurant
SEAFOOD **££**

(☑ 01397-705589; www.crannog.net; Town Pier;
mains £15-20; ☺ noon-2.30pm & 6-9pm) ✦ The
Crannog wins the prize for best location in
town – perched on the Town Pier, giving
window-table diners an uninterrupted view
down Loch Linnhe. Informal and unfussy,
it specialises in fresh local fish – there are
three or four daily fish specials plus the
main menu – though there are lamb, venison and vegetarian dishes too. Two-course
lunch £15.

Grog & Gruel
MEXICAN **££**

(☑ 01397-705078; www.grogandgruel.co.uk; 66
High St; mains £9-18; ☺ bar meals noon-9pm, restaurant 5-9pm; 🛜🖶) Upstairs from the Grog
& Gruel real-ale pub is a lively Tex-Mex
restaurant, with a crowd-pleasing menu of
tasty enchiladas, burritos, fajitas, burgers,
steaks and pizza.

★ Lime Tree
SCOTTISH **£££**

(☑ 01397-701806; www.limetreefortwilliam.co.uk;
Achintore Rd; mains £14-23; ☺ 6.30-9.30pm; ℗)
✦ Fort William is not overendowed with
great places to eat, but the restaurant at
this small hotel and art gallery has put the
UK's Outdoor Capital on the gastronomic
map. The chef turns out delicious dishes
built around fresh Scottish produce, ranging
from partan bree (crab soup) to roast cod to
venison sausage.

Ben Nevis Bar
PUB

(☑ 01397-702295; 105 High St; ☺ 11am-11pm) The
lounge here enjoys a good view over the
loch, and the bar exudes a relaxed, jovial atmosphere where climbers and tourists can
work off leftover energy jigging to live music
(Thursday and Friday nights).

❶ Information

Belford Hospital (☑ 01397-702481; Belford
Rd) Opposite the train station.

Fort William Tourist Office (☑ 01397-703781;
www.visithighlands.com; 15 High St; internet
per 20min £1; ☺ 9am-6pm Mon-Sat, 10am-5pm
Sun Apr-Sep, limited hours Oct-Mar) Internet
access.

Post Office (☑ 0845 722 3344; 5 High St)

❶ Getting There & Away

Both bus and train station are next to the huge
Morrisons supermarket, reached from the town
centre via an underpass next to the Nevisport
shop.

BUS

Scottish Citylink (☑ 0871 266 3333; www.
citylink.co.uk) buses link Fort William with other
major towns and cities:

Edinburgh £34, 4½ hours, one daily direct,
seven with a change at Glasgow; via Glencoe
and Crianlarich

Glasgow £23, three hours, eight daily

Inverness £11.20, two hours, six daily

Oban £9.40, 1½ hours, three daily

Portree £30, three hours, three daily

Shiel Buses (☑ 01397-700700; www.shielbus-
es.co.uk) service no 500 runs to Mallaig (£6.10,
1½ hours, three daily Monday to Friday) via Glenfinnan (30 minutes) and Arisaig (one hour).

CAR

Easydrive Car Hire (☑ 01397-701616; www.easydrivescotland.co.uk; Unit 36a, Ben Nevis Industrial Estate, Ben Nevis Dr) Hires out small cars from £32/175 a day/week, including tax and unlimited mileage, but not Collision Damage Waiver (CDW).

TRAIN

The spectacular West Highland line runs from Glasgow to Mallaig via Fort William. The overnight **Caledonian Sleeper** (www.scotrail.co.uk/sleeper) service connects Fort William and London Euston (from £113 sharing a twin-berth cabin, 13 hours).

There's no direct rail connection between Oban and Fort William – you have to change at Crianlarich, so it's faster to use the bus.

Edinburgh £42, five hours; three daily, two on Sunday; change at Glasgow's Queen St station

Glasgow £28, 3¾ hours, three daily, two on Sunday

Mallaig £11.80, 1½ hours, four daily, three on Sunday

ⓘ Getting Around

BICYCLE

Alpine Bikes (☑ 01397-704008; www.lochaberbikehire.com; 117 High St; ⊙ 9am-5.30pm Mon-Sat, 10am-5.30pm Sun) Mountain-bike rental from £20 a day; bikes can be hired here and dropped off in Inverness. Also hires out full-suspension downhill bikes and body armour for use on Nevis Range trails.

BUS

The Fort Dayrider ticket (£3.20) gives unlimited travel for one day on Stagecoach bus services in the Fort William area. Buy from the bus driver.

TAXI

There's a taxi rank on the corner of High St and the Parade.

Around Fort William

Glen Nevis

You can walk the 3 miles from Fort William to scenic Glen Nevis in about an hour or so. The **Glen Nevis Visitor Centre** (☑ 01397-705922; www.bennevisweather.co.uk; ⊙ 8.30am-6pm Jul-Aug, 9am-5pm Apr-Jun & Sep-Oct, 9am-3pm Nov-Mar) FREE is situated 1.5 miles up the glen, and provides information on walking, weather forecasts and specific advice on climbing Ben Nevis.

From the car park at the far end of the road along Glen Nevis, there is an excellent 1.5-mile walk through the spectacular Nevis Gorge to **Steall Meadows**, a verdant valley dominated by a 100m-high bridal-veil waterfall. You can reach the foot of the falls by crossing the river on a wobbly, three-cable wire bridge: one cable for your feet and one for each hand – a real test of balance!

🛏 Sleeping & Eating

★ Ben Nevis Inn HOSTEL £

(☑ 01397-701227; www.ben-nevis-inn.co.uk; Achintee; dm £15.50; ⊙ pub noon-11pm daily Apr-Oct, Thu-Sun only Nov-Mar; ℙ) This great barn of a pub serves real ale and tasty bar meals (mains £9 to £15, food served noon to 9pm), and has a comfy 24-bed bunkhouse downstairs. It's at the start of the path from Achintee up Ben Nevis, and only a mile from the end of the West Highland Way.

Achintee Farm B&B, HOSTEL £

(☑ 01397-702204; www.achinteefarm.com; Achintee; per person hostel £21, B&B £39-45; ℙ🕱) This attractive farmhouse offers excellent B&B accommodation and also has a small hostel attached. It's at the start of the path up Ben Nevis.

Glen Nevis SYHA HOSTEL £

(SYHA; ☑ 01397-702336; www.syha.org.uk; dm/tw £22/55; @🕱) Large, impersonal and reminiscent of a school camp, this hostel is 3 miles from Fort William, right beside one of the starting points for the tourist track up Ben Nevis.

Glen Nevis Caravan

& Camping Park CAMPSITE £

(☑ 01397-702191; www.glen-nevis.co.uk; tent sites £7.20, incl car £11, campervan £12.10, plus per person £3.50; ⊙ mid-Mar–Oct; 🕱) This big, well-equipped site is a popular base camp for Ben Nevis and the surrounding mountains. The site is 2.5 miles from Fort William, along the Glen Nevis road.

ⓘ Getting There & Away

Bus 41 runs from Fort William bus station to the Glen Nevis SYHA (£2, 15 minutes, two daily year round, five daily Monday to Saturday June to September). Check at the tourist office for the latest timetable, which is liable to alteration.

Nevis Range

Nevis Range OUTDOORS
(☎01397-705825; www.nevisrange.co.uk; gondola return trip per adult/child £11.50/6.75; ⊘10am-5pm summer, 9.30am-dusk winter, closed mid-Nov-mid-Dec) The Nevis Range ski area, 6 miles north of Fort William, spreads across the northern slopes of Aonach Mor (1221m). The gondola that gives access to the bottom of the ski area at 655m operates year round (15 minutes each way). At the top there's a restaurant and a couple of hiking trails through nearby Leanachan Forest, as well as excellent mountain-biking trails.

During the **ski season** a one-day lift pass costs £30/18.50 per adult/child; a one-day package, including equipment hire, lift pass and two hours' instruction, costs £64.

Bus 41 runs from Glen Nevis youth hostel and Fort William bus station to Nevis Range (£1.95, 20 minutes, five daily Monday to Saturday, three on Sunday, limited service October to April). Check at the tourist office for the latest timetable, which is liable to alteration.

**Nevis Range Downhill &
Witch's Trails** MOUNTAIN BIKING
(☎01397-705825; bike.nevisrange.co.uk; single/multitrip ticket £13/31; ⊘10.15am-3.45pm mid-May–mid-Sep) A world championship **downhill mountain-bike trail** – for experienced riders only – runs from the Snowgoose restaurant at the Nevis Range ski area to the base station; bikes are carried up on a rack on the gondola cabin. A multitrip ticket gives unlimited uplift for a day; full-suspension bike hire costs from £40/70 per single run/full day.

There's also a 4-mile **XC red trail** that begins at the Snowgoose, and the **Witch's Trails**, 25 miles of waymarked forest road and singletrack in the nearby forest, including a 5-mile world-championship loop.

CLIMBING BEN NEVIS

As the highest peak in the British Isles, Ben Nevis (1344m) attracts many would-be ascensionists who would not normally think of climbing a Scottish mountain – a staggering (often literally) 100,000 people reach the summit each year.

Although anyone who is reasonably fit should have no problem climbing Ben Nevis on a fine summer's day, an ascent should not be undertaken lightly. Every year people have to be rescued from the mountain. You will need proper walking boots (the path is rough and stony, and there may be snow on the summit), warm clothing, waterproofs, a map and compass, and plenty of food and water. And don't forget to check the weather forecast (see www.bennevisweather.co.uk).

Here are a few facts to mull over before you go racing up the tourist track: the summit plateau is bounded by 700m-high cliffs and has a sub-Arctic climate; at the summit it can snow on any day of the year; the summit is wrapped in cloud nine days out of 10; in thick cloud, visibility at the summit can be 10m or less; and in such conditions the only safe way off the mountain requires careful use of a map and compass to avoid walking over those 700m cliffs.

The tourist track (the easiest route to the top) was originally called the Pony Track. It was built in the 19th century for the pack ponies that carried supplies to a meteorological observatory on the summit (now in ruins), which was manned continuously from 1883 to 1904.

There are three possible starting points for the tourist track ascent – Achintee Farm; the footbridge at Glen Nevis SYHA; and, if you have a car, the car park at Glen Nevis Visitor Centre. The path climbs gradually to the shoulder at Lochan Meall an t-Suidhe (known as the Halfway Lochan), then zigzags steeply up beside the Red Burn to the summit plateau. The highest point is marked by a trig point on top of a huge cairn beside the ruins of the old observatory; the plateau is scattered with countless smaller cairns, stones arranged in the shape of people's names and, sadly, a fair bit of litter.

The total distance to the summit and back is 8 miles; allow at least four or five hours to reach the top, and another 2½ to three hours for the descent. Afterwards, as you celebrate in the pub with a pint, consider the fact that the record time for the annual Ben Nevis Hill Race is just under 1½ hours – up *and* down. Then have another pint.

Corpach to Loch Lochy

Corpach lies at the southern entrance to the Caledonian Canal, 3 miles north of Fort William; there's a classic picture-postcard view of Ben Nevis from the mouth of the canal. Nearby is the award-winning Treasures of the Earth (☑ 01397-772283; www.treasuresoftheearth.co.uk; Corpach; adult/child £5/3; ⊙ 9.30am-6pm Jul-Sep, 10am-5pm Apr-Jun & Oct, shorter hours Nov-Feb) exhibition, a rainy-day diversion with a great collection of gemstones, minerals, fossils and other geological curiosities.

A mile east of Corpach, at Banavie, is Neptune's Staircase, an impressive flight of eight locks that allows boats to climb 20m to the main reach of the Caledonian Canal. The B8004 road runs along the west side of the canal to Gairlochy at the south end of Loch Lochy, offering superb views of Ben Nevis; the canal towpath on the east side makes a great walk or bike ride (6.5 miles).

From Gairlochy the B8005 continues along the west side of Loch Lochy to Achnacarry and the Clan Cameron Museum (☑ 01397-712480; www.clan-cameron.org; Achnacarry; adult/child £3.50/free; ⊙ 11am-5pm Jul & Aug, 1.30-5pm Easter-Jun & Sep–mid-Oct), which records the history of the clan and its involvement with the Jacobite rebellions, including items of clothing that once belonged to Bonnie Prince Charlie.

From Achnacarry the Great Glen Way continues along the roadless western shore of Loch Lochy, and a dead-end minor road leads west along remote but lovely Loch Arkaig.

There are a couple of backpacker hostels in Corpach. At Farr Cottage Lodge (☑ 01397-772315; www.farrcottage.com; Corpach; dm/tw £16.50/50; P@☎) bike hire is also available, while the folk at Blacksmiths Backpackers Hostel (☑ 01397-772467; www.highland-mountain-guides.co.uk; Corpach; dm £17; P☎) can organise courses in climbing, kayaking and other sports.

Glen Spean & Glen Roy

Near Spean Bridge, at the junction of the B8004 and A82, 2.5 miles east of Gairlochy, stands the Commando Memorial, which commemorates the WWII special forces soldiers who trained in this area.

Four miles further east, at Roy Bridge, a minor road leads north up Glen Roy, which is noted for its intriguing, so-called parallel roads. These prominent horizontal terraces contouring around the hillside are actually ancient shorelines formed during the last ice age by the waters of an ice-dammed glacial lake. The best viewpoint is at a car park just over 3 miles up Glen Roy, where there's an interpretation board explaining the landscape features you can see.

Ardnamurchan

Ten miles south of Fort William, a car ferry (car £7.60, bicycle & foot passenger free; ⊙ 5 min, every 30min) makes the short crossing to Corran Ferry. The drive from here to Ardnamurchan Point (www.ardnamurchan. com), the most westerly point on the British mainland, is one of the most beautiful in the western Highlands, especially in late spring and early summer when much of the narrow, twisting road is lined with the bright pink and purple blooms of rhododendrons.

The road clings to the northern shore of Loch Sunart, going through the pretty villages of Strontian – which gave its name to the element strontium, first discovered in ore from nearby lead mines in 1790 – and Salen.

The mostly single-track road from Salen to Ardnamurchan Point is only 25 miles long, but it'll take you 1½ hours each way. It's a dipping, twisting, low-speed roller coaster of a ride through sun-dappled native woodlands draped with lichen and fern. Just when you're getting used to the views of Morvern and Mull to the south, it makes a quick detour to the north for a panorama over the islands of Rum and Eigg.

◉ Sights

Nádurra Visitor Centre   WILDLIFE CENTRE
(☑ 01972-500209; www.nadurracentre.co.uk; Glenmore; adult/child £4.50/2.25; ⊙ 10am-5.30pm Mon-Sat, 11am-5.30pm Sun Apr-Oct, 10am-4pm Tue-Fri, 11.30am-4pm Sun Nov-Mar; ♿) This fascinating centre – midway between Salen and Kilchoan – was originally devised by a wildlife photographer and tries to bring you face to face with the flora and fauna of the Ardnamurchan peninsula. The Living Building exhibit is designed to attract local wildlife, with a mammal den that is occasionally occupied by hedgehogs or pine martens, an owl nest-box, a mouse nest and a pond.

If the beasties are not in residence, you can watch recorded video footage of the animals. There's also seasonal live CCTV coverage of local wildlife, ranging from nesting herons to a golden eagle feeding site.

Ardnamurchan Distillery   DISTILLERY
(www.adelphidistillery.com; Glenbeg) A brand-new whisky distillery went into production on the shores of Loch Sunart in summer 2014, complete with visitor centre and tasting room. Although you will be able to see the whisky-making process, the finished product will be matured in casks until at least 2020 before being bottled as a single malt.

Ardnamurchan Lighthouse   HISTORIC BUILDING
(☑ 01972-510210; www.ardnamurchanlighthouse. com; Ardnamurchan Point; visitor centre adult/ child £3/2, guided tours £6/4; ⊙ 10am-5pm Apr-Oct; 🚗) The final 6 miles of road from Kilchoan to Ardnamurchan Point end at the 36m-high, grey granite tower of Ardnamurchan Lighthouse, built in 1849 by the 'Lighthouse Stevensons' – family of Robert Louis – to guard the westernmost point of the British mainland. There's a tearoom, and the visitor centre will tell you more than you'll ever need to know about lighthouses, with lots of hands-on stuff for kids.

The guided tour (every half-hour 11am to 4.30pm) includes a trip to the top of the lighthouse. But the main attraction here is the expansive view over the ocean – this is a superb sunset viewpoint, provided you don't mind driving back in the dark.

Kilchoan   VILLAGE
The scattered crofting village of Kilchoan, the only village of any size west of Salen, is best known for the scenic ruins of 13th-century **Mingary Castle**. The village has a **tourist office** (☑ 01972-510222; Pier Rd, Kilchoan; ⊙ 9am-5pm Mon-Sat Easter-Oct), a shop, a hotel and a campsite, and there's a ferry to Tobermory on the Isle of Mull.

🍽 Sleeping & Eating

Ardnamurchan Campsite   CAMPSITE £
(☑ 01972-510766; www.ardnamurchanstudycentre. co.uk; Kilchoan; sites per adult/child £8/3; ⊙ May-Sep; 🐾) Basic but beautifully situated campsite, with the chance of seeing otters from your tent. It's along the Ormsaig road, 2 miles west of Kilchoan village.

Salen Hotel   INN ££
(☑ 01967-431661; www.salenhotel.co.uk; Salen; r £70-100; 🅿 🐾) A traditional Highland inn with views over Loch Sunart, the Salen Hotel has three rooms in the pub (two with sea views) and another three rooms (all en suite) in a modern chalet out the back. The cosy lounge has a roaring fire and comfy

---

THE CALEDONIAN CANAL
....

Running for 59 miles from Corpach, near Fort William, to Inverness via Lochs Lochy, Oich and Ness, the Caledonian Canal links the east and west coasts of Scotland, avoiding the long and dangerous sea passage around Cape Wrath and through the turbulent Pentland Firth. Designed by Thomas Telford and completed in 1822 at a cost of £900,000 – a staggering sum then – the canal took 20 years to build, including 29 locks, four aqueducts and 10 bridges.

Conceived as a project to ease unemployment and bring prosperity to the Highlands in the aftermath of the Jacobite rebellions and the Clearances, the canal proved to be a commercial failure – the locks were too small for the new breed of steamships which came into use soon after its completion. But it proved to be a success in terms of tourism, especially after it was popularised by Queen Victoria's cruise along the canal in 1873. Today the canal is used mainly by yachts and pleasure cruisers, though since 2010 it has also been used to transport timber from west-coast forestry plantations to Inverness.

Much of the Great Glen Way (p120) follows the line of the canal; it can be followed on foot, by mountain bike or on horseback, and 80% of the route has even been done on mobility scooters. An easy half-day hike or bike ride is to follow the canal towpath from Corpach to Gairlochy (10 miles), which takes you past the impressive flight of eight locks known as **Neptune's Staircase**, and through beautiful countryside with grand views to the north face of Ben Nevis.

If you're cycling the length of the Great Glen Way, you can hire mountain bikes from Alpine Bikes (p152) in Fort William and drop them off at Ticket to Ride (p116) in Inverness, or vice versa.

sofa, and the bar meals, including seafood, venison and other game dishes, are very good.

Inn at Ardgour   INN **££**
(☑ 01855-841225; www.ardgour.biz; Corran Ferry; d/tw/f £100/120/140; ℗) This pretty, white-washed coaching inn, draped in colourful flower baskets, makes a great place for a lunch break or overnight stop. The restaurant (mains £9 to £17) is set in the row of cottages once occupied by the Corran ferrymen, and serves traditional, homemade Scottish dishes.

Antler Tearoom   CAFE **£**
(Nádurra Visitor Centre, Glenmore; mains £4-7; ⊙ 10am-5.30pm Mon-Sat, 11am-5.30pm Sun Apr-Oct, 10am-4pm Tue-Fri, 11.30am-4pm Sun Nov-Mar; ℗ 🛜 🚼) The cafe at this wildlife centre serves coffee, home baking and lunch dishes, including fresh salads and sandwiches and homemade soup.

ⓘ Getting There & Away

Shiel Buses (☑ 01397-700700; www.shielbuses.co.uk) bus 506 runs from Fort William to Acharacle, Salen and Kilchoan (£7.50, 3½ hours, one daily Monday to Saturday) via Corran Ferry. There's a car ferry between Kilchoan and Tobermory on the Isle of Mull.

Salen to Lochailort

The A861 road from Salen to Lochailort passes through the low, wooded hills of Moidart. A minor road (signposted Dorlin) leads west from the A861 at Shiel Bridge to a parking area looking across to the picturesque roofless ruin of 13th-century **Castle Tioram**. The castle sits on a tiny island in Loch Moidart, connected to the mainland by a narrow strand that is submerged at high tide (the castle's name, pronounced *chee*-ram, means 'dry'). It was the ancient seat of the Clanranald Macdonalds, but the Clanranald chief ordered it to be burned (to prevent it falling into the hands of Hanoverian troops) when he set off to fight with the Jacobites in the 1715 rebellion. You can walk to the island at low tide, but signs warn that the castle is dangerous to enter.

As the A861 curls around the north shore of Loch Moidart you will see a line of three huge beech trees (one badly damaged) and two obvious stumps between the road and the shore. Known as the **Seven Men of Moidart** (four have been blown down by

gales and replaced with saplings), they were planted in the late 18th century to commemorate the seven local men who accompanied Bonnie Prince Charlie from France and acted as his bodyguards at the start of the 1745 rebellion.

Road to the Isles

The 46-mile A830 road from Fort William to Mallaig is traditionally known as the Road to the Isles, as it leads to the jumping-off point for ferries to the Small Isles and Skye, itself a stepping stone to the Outer Hebrides. This is a region steeped in Jacobite history, having witnessed both the beginning and the end of Bonnie Prince Charlie's doomed attempt to regain the British throne in 1745–46.

The final section of this scenic route, between Arisaig and Mallaig, has been upgraded to a fast straight road. Unless you're in a hurry, opt instead for the more scenic old road (signposted Alternative Coastal Route).

Between the A830 and the A87 far to the north lie Knoydart and Glenelg – forming Scotland's 'Empty Quarter' – a rugged landscape of wild mountains and lonely sea lochs roughly 20 miles by 30 miles in size, mostly uninhabited and penetrated only by two minor roads (along Lochs Arkaig and Quoich). If you want to get away from it all, this is the place to go.

ⓘ Getting Around

BUS

Shiel Buses (☑ 01397-700700; www.shielbuses.co.uk) Bus 500 runs from Fort William to Mallaig (£6.10, 1½ hours, three daily Monday to Friday, one on Saturday) via Glenfinnan (30 minutes) and Arisaig (one hour).

TRAIN

The Fort William–Mallaig railway line has four trains a day (three on Sunday), with stops at many points along the way, including Corpach, Glenfinnan, Lochailort, Arisaig and Morar.

Glenfinnan

POP 100

Glenfinnan is hallowed ground for fans of Bonnie Prince Charlie; the monument here marks where he raised his Highland army. It is also a place of pilgrimage for steam-train enthusiasts and *Harry Potter* fans – the famous railway viaduct features in the films, and is regularly traversed by the Jacobite Steam Train (p150).

◉ Sights & Activities

Glenfinnan Monument   MONUMENT
This tall column, topped by a statue of a kilted Highlander, was erected in 1815 on the spot where Bonnie Prince Charlie first raised his standard and rallied the Jacobite clans on 19 August 1745, marking the start of his ill-fated campaign, which would end in disaster at Culloden 14 months later. The setting, at the north end of Loch Shiel, is hauntingly beautiful.

**Glenfinnan Visitor
Centre**   INTERPRETATION CENTRE
(NTS; adult/child £3.50/2.50; ☺9.30am-5pm Jul & Aug, 10am-5pm Easter-Jun, Sep & Oct) This centre recounts the story of the '45, as the Jacobite rebellion of 1745 is known, when Bonnie Prince Charlie's loyal clansmen marched and fought their way from Glenfinnan south via Edinburgh to Derby, then back north to final defeat at Culloden.

Glenfinnan Station Museum   MUSEUM
(www.glenfinnanstationmuseum.co.uk; admission 80p; ☺9am-5pm May-Oct; P) This fascinating little museum is dedicated to the great days of steam on the West Highland line. The famous 21-arch **Glenfinnan Viaduct**, just east of the station, was built in 1901, and featured in several *Harry Potter* movies. A pleasant walk of around 0.75 miles east from the station (signposted) leads to a viewpoint for the viaduct and for Loch Shiel.

Loch Shiel Cruises   CRUISE
(☑07801 537617; www.highlandcruises.co.uk; ☺Apr-Sep) Offers boat trips along Loch Shiel, with the opportunity of spotting golden eagles and other wildlife. There are one- to 2½-hour cruises (£10 or £18 per person) daily except Saturday and Wednesday. On Wednesday the boat goes the full length of the loch to **Acharacle** (£17/25 one way/return), calling at Polloch and Dalilea, allowing for a range of walks and bike rides using the forestry track on the eastern shore. The boat departs from a jetty near Glenfinnan House Hotel.

🛏 Sleeping & Eating

Sleeping Car Bunkhouse   HOSTEL £
(☑01397-722295; www.glenfinnanstationmuseum.co.uk; Glenfinnan Station; per person £14, entire coach £120; ☺May-Oct; P) Two converted railway carriages at Glenfinnan Station house this unusual 10-berth bunkhouse and the atmospheric **Dining Car Tearoom** (snacks £3-5; ☺9am-4.30pm May-Oct), which serves scones with cream and jam and pots of tea. There are superb views of the mountains above Loch Shiel.

★Prince's House Hotel   INN £££
(☑01397-722246; www.glenfinnan.co.uk; s/d from £80/130; P) A delightful old coaching inn from 1658, the Prince's House is a great place to pamper yourself – ask for the spacious, tartan-clad Stuart Room (£190), complete with four-poster bed, if you want to stay in the oldest part of the hotel. The relaxed but well-regarded restaurant specialises in Scottish produce (four-course dinner £43.50).

There's no documentary evidence that Bonnie Prince Charlie actually stayed here in 1745, but it was the only sizeable house in Glenfinnan at that time, so...

Arisaig & Morar

The five miles of coast between Arisaig and Morar is a fretwork of rocky islets, inlets and gorgeous silver-sand beaches backed by dunes and machair, with stunning sunset views across the sea to the silhouetted peaks of Eigg and Rum. The **Silver Sands of Morar**, as they are known, draw crowds of bucket-and-spade holidaymakers in July and August, when the many camping grounds scattered along the coast are filled to overflowing.

◉ Sights & Activities

Camusdarach Beach   BEACH
Fans of the movie *Local Hero* still make pilgrimages to Camusdarach Beach, just south of Morar, which starred in the film as Ben's beach. To find it, look for the car park 800m north of Camusdarach campsite; from here, a wooden footbridge and a 400m walk through the dunes lead to the beach. (The village that featured in the film is on the other side of the country, at Pennan.)

**Land, Sea & Islands
Visitor Centre**   MUSEUM
(www.arisaigcentre.co.uk; Arisaig; ☺10am-6pm Mon-Fri, 10-4pm Sat, 2-5pm Sun Apr-Oct, shorter hours Sat-Mon only Nov-Mar; P) **FREE** This centre in Arisaig village houses exhibits on the cultural and natural history of the region, plus a small but fascinating exhibition on the part played by the local area as a base for training spies for the Special Operations Executive (SOE, forerunner of MI6) during WWII.

WORTH A TRIP

INN PEACE

Glenuig Inn (☎ 01687-470219; www.glenuig.com; Glenuig; bunkhouse per person £28, B&B s/d/q from £65/105/145; P ☎) Set on a peaceful bay on the Arisaig coast, halfway between Lochailort and Acharacle on the A830, the Glenuig Inn is a great place to get away from it all. As well as offering comfortable accommodation, good food (served noon to 9pm), and real ale on tap, it's a great base for exploring Arisaig, Morar and the Loch Shiel area.

Arisaig Marine   CRUISE
(☎ 01687-450224; www.arisaig.co.uk; Arisaig Harbour; ☉ Apr-Sep) Runs cruises from Arisaig harbour to Eigg (£18 return, one hour, six a week), Rum (£25 return, 2½ hours, two or three a week) and Muck (£20 return, two hours, three a week), with four hours ashore on Eigg, or two to three hours on Rum or Muck. The trips include whale-watching, with up to an hour for close viewing.

🛏 Sleeping & Eating

There are at least a half-dozen camping grounds between Arisaig and Morar; all are open in summer only, and are often full in July and August, so book ahead. Several are listed on www.road-to-the-isles.org.uk.

Garramore House   B&B ££
(☎ 01687-450268; r per person £25-35; P ☻) Built as a hunting lodge in 1840, this house served as an HQ for the SOE during WWII. Today it's a wonderfully atmospheric, old-fashioned guest-house set in lovely woodland gardens with resident peacocks and great views to the Small Isles and Skye. Garramore is signposted off the coastal road, 4 miles north of Arisaig village.

Camusdarach Campsite   CAMPSITE £
(☎ 01687-450221; Arisaig; tent/campervan sites £8/15, plus per person £3; ☉ Mar-Oct; ☎) 🏴 A small and nicely landscaped site with good facilities, only three minutes' walk from the *Local Hero* beach (via gate in northwest corner).

Old Library Lodge & Restaurant SCOTTISH ££
(☎ 01687-450651; www.oldlibrary.co.uk; Arisaig; mains £10-19; P ☎) 🏴 The Old Library is a charming restaurant with rooms (B&B

single/double £75/120) set in converted 200-year-old stables overlooking the waterfront in Arisaig village. The lunch menu concentrates on soups, burgers and smoked fish or meat platters, while dinner is a more sophisticated affair offering local seafood, beef and lamb.

Mallaig

POP 800

If you're travelling between Fort William and Skye, you may find yourself overnighting in the bustling fishing and ferry port of Mallaig (*mahl*-ig). Indeed, it makes a good base for a series of day trips by ferry to the Small Isles and Knoydart.

◉ Sights & Activities

Loch Morar   LAKE
(www.lochmorar.org.uk) A minor road from Morar village, 2.5 miles south of Mallaig, leads to scenic 11-mile-long Loch Morar, which at 310m is the deepest body of water in the United Kingdom. Reputed to be inhabited by its own version of Nessie – Morag, the Loch Morar monster – the loch and its surrounding hills are the haunt of otters, wildcats, red deer and golden eagles.

A 5-mile signposted footpath leads along the north shore of the loch from the road-end at Bracorina, 3 miles east of Morar village, to Tarbet on Loch Nevis, from where you can catch a passenger ferry (p160) back to Mallaig (departs 3.40pm June to September).

Mallaig Heritage Centre INTERPRETATION CENTRE
(☎ 01687-462085; www.mallaigheritage.org.uk; Station Rd; ☉ 11am-4pm Tue-Fri, noon-4pm Sat) **FREE** The village's rainy-day attractions are limited to this heritage centre, which covers the archaeology and history of the region, including the heart-rending tale of the Highland Clearances in Knoydart.

MV Grimsay Isle   FISHING, BOAT TOURS
(☎ 07780 815158; Apr-Sep; adult/child £20/10) The MV *Grimsay Isle* provides entertaining, two-hour customised sea-fishing trips and wildlife-watching tours (book at the tourist office).

🛏 Sleeping & Eating

Seaview Guest House   B&B ££
(☎ 01687-462059; www.seaviewguesthousemallaig.com; Main St; r per person £30-38; ☉ Mar–mid-Nov; P) This comfortable five-bedroom B&B

has grand views over the harbour, not only from the upstairs bedrooms but also from the breakfast room. There's also a cute little cottage next door that offers self-catering accommodation (www.selfcateringmallaig. com; one double and one twin room) for £400 to £495 a week.

Springbank Guest House
B&B ££

(☑ 01687-462459; www.springbank-mallaig.co.uk; East Bay; s/d £35/65; [P] [🛜]) The Springbank is a traditional West Highland house with six homely guest bedrooms, with superb views across the harbour to the Cuillin of Skye.

Fish Market Restaurant
SEAFOOD ££

(☑ 01687-462299; Station Rd; mains £10-21) 🍴 At least half-a-dozen signs in Mallaig advertise 'seafood restaurant', but this bright, modern bistro-style place next to the harbour is our favourite, serving simply prepared scallops, smoked salmon, mussels, and fresh Mallaig haddock fried in breadcrumbs, as well as the tastiest Cullen skink on the west coast.

Upstairs is a **coffee shop** (mains £6-7; ⊘11am-5pm) that serves delicious hot roast-beef rolls with horseradish sauce, and scones with clotted cream and jam.

Tea Garden
CAFE £

(☑ 01687-462764; www.mallaigteagarden.co.uk; Harbour View; mains £6-12; ⊘9am-6pm, to 9pm May-Sep) On a sunny day the Tea Garden's terrace cafe, with its flowers, greenery and cosmopolitan backpacker staff, can feel more like the Med than Mallaig. The coffee is good, and the speciality of the house is a pint glass full of Mallaig prawns with dipping sauce (£12.50). From late May to September the cafe opens in the evening with a bistro menu.

Jaffy's
FISH & CHIPS £

(www.jaffys.co.uk; Station Rd; mains £4-8; ⊘noon-2.30pm & 5-8pm daily May-Oct, 5-8pm Thu-Sat only Nov-Apr) Owned by a third-generation fish-merchant's family, Mallaig's chippy serves superbly fresh fish and chips, as well as kippers, prawns and other seafood.

ℹ️ Information

Mallaig has a **tourist office** (☑ 01687-462170; East Bay; ⊘10am-5.30pm Mon-Fri, 10.15am-3.45pm Sat, noon-3.30pm Sun), a post office, a bank with ATM and a **co-op supermarket** (⊘8am-10pm Mon-Sat, 9am-9pm Sun).

ℹ️ Getting There & Away

BOAT

Ferries run from Mallaig to the Small Isles, the Isle of Skye, Knoydart and South Uist. See the relevant sections for details.

BUS

Shiel Buses (☑ 01397-700700; www.shielbus-es.co.uk) bus 500 runs from Fort William to Mallaig (£6.10, 1½ hours, three daily Monday to Friday, one on Saturday) via Glenfinnan (30 minutes) and Arisaig (one hour).

TRAIN

The West Highland line runs between Fort William and Mallaig (£11.80, 1½ hours) four times a day (three on Sunday).

Knoydart Peninsula

POP 150

The Knoydart peninsula is the only sizeable area in Britain that remains inaccessible to the motor car, cut off by miles of rough country and the embracing arms of Lochs Nevis and Hourn – Gaelic for the lochs of Heaven and Hell. No road penetrates this wilderness of rugged hills – **Inverie**, its sole village, can only be reached by ferry from Mallaig, or on foot from the remote road's end at Kinloch Hourn (a tough 16-mile hike).

The main reasons for visiting are to climb the remote 1020m peak of **Ladhar Bheinn** (*laar*-ven), which affords some of the west coast's finest views, or just to enjoy the feeling of being cut off from the rest of the world. There are no shops, no TV and no mobile-phone reception (although there *is* internet access); electricity is provided by a private hydroelectric scheme – truly 'off the grid' living! For more information and full accommodation listings, see www.knoydart-foundation.com.

🛏️ Sleeping & Eating

Knoydart Foundation Bunkhouse
HOSTEL £

(☑ 01687-462163; www.knoydart-foundation. com; Inverie; dm adult/child £17/10; [@] [🛜]) 🍴 A 15-minute walk east of Inverie ferry pier, this is a cosy hostel with wood-burning stove, kitchen and drying room.

Long Beach
CAMPSITE £

(Long Beach; per tent & 1 person £4, per extra person £3) Basic but beautiful campsite, a 10-minute walk east of the ferry; water supply and composting toilet, but no showers. Ranger comes around to collect fees.

Knoydart Lodge B&B ££

(☑01687-460129; www.knoydartlodge.co.uk; Inverie; s/d £68/95; ⓢⓧ) This must be some of the most spacious and luxurious B&B accommodation on the whole west coast, let alone in Knoydart. On offer are five large, stylish bedrooms in a fantastic, modern timber-built lodge reminiscent of an Alpine chalet, just a short stroll from the beach.

★ **Old Forge** PUB, RESTAURANT ££

(☑01687-462267; www.theoldforge.co.uk; Inverie; mains £10-20; ⓢfood served 12.30-3pm & 6.30-9.30pm; ⓢⓐ) ✿ The Old Forge is listed in the *Guinness Book of Records* as Britain's most remote pub. It's surprisingly sophisticated – as well as having real ale on tap, there's an Italian coffee machine for those wilderness lattes and cappuccinos. The house special is a seafood platter (£30), all ingredients sourced within 7 miles of the pub.

In the evening you can sit by the fire, pint of beer in hand and join the impromptu *ceilidh* (an evening of traditional Scottish entertainment including music, song and dance) that seems to take place just about nightly.

❶ Getting There & Away

Sea Bridge Knoydart (☑01687-462916; www.knoydartferry.com; one way/return £11/20) From April to October this fast passenger ferry service runs from Mallaig to Inverie eight times daily Monday to Friday, four times Saturday and Sunday (25 minutes), and will carry bikes, canoes and kayaks at no extra charge. From November to March, there are four crossings on weekdays, two on weekends.

Western Isles Cruises (☑01687-462233; westernislescruises.co.uk; 1 way/day return £10/15) Passenger ferry linking Mallaig to Inverie (45 minutes) twice daily Monday to Saturday from April to October. Taking the morning boat gives you up to 5½ hours ashore in Knoydart before the return trip. There's also an afternoon sailing between Inverie and Tarbet on the south side of Loch Nevis, allowing walkers to hike along the northern shore of Loch Morar to Tarbet and return by boat (£15 Tarbet–Inverie–Mallaig).

It's also possible to join the boat just for the cruise, without going ashore (£20 for Mallaig–Inverie–Tarbet–Mallaig).

SMALL ISLES

The scattered jewels of the Small Isles – Rum, Eigg, Muck and Canna – lie strewn across the silvery-blue cloth of the Cuillin Sound to the south of the Isle of Skye. Their distinctive outlines enliven the glorious views from the beaches of Arisaig and Morar.

Rum is the biggest and boldest of the four, a miniature Skye of pointed peaks and dramatic sunset silhouettes. Eigg is the most pastoral and populous, dominated by the miniature sugarloaf mountain of the Sgurr. Muck is a botanist's delight with its wildflowers and unusual alpine plants, and Canna is a craggy bird sanctuary made of magnetic rocks.

If your time is limited and you can only visit one island, choose Eigg; it has the most to offer on a day trip.

❶ Getting There & Away

The main ferry operator is **CalMac** (www.calmac.co.uk), which operates the passenger-only ferry from Mallaig:

Canna £23.75 return, two hours, six a week

Eigg £12.80 return, 1¼ hours, four a week

Muck £19.50 return, 1½ hours, five a week

Rum £18.90 return, 1¼ hours, five a week

You can also hop between the islands without returning to Mallaig, but the timetable is complicated and it requires a bit of planning – you would need at least five days to visit all four. Bicycles are carried for free.

In summer Arisaig Marine (☑01687-450224; www.arisaig.co.uk; Arisaig Harbour; ⓢApr-Sep) operates day cruises from Arisaig harbour to Eigg (£18 return, one hour, six a week), Rum (£25 return, 2½ hours, two or three a week) and Muck (£20 return, two hours, three a week). The trips include whale-watching, with up to an hour for close viewing. Sailing times allow four or five hours ashore on Eigg, two or three hours on Muck or Rum.

Isle of Rum

POP 22

The Isle of Rum – the biggest and most spectacular of the Small Isles – was once known as the Forbidden Island. Cleared of its crofters in the early 19th century to make way for sheep, from 1888 to 1957 it was the private sporting estate of the Bulloughs, a nouveau riche Lancashire family who made their fortune in the textile industry. Curious outsiders who ventured too close to the island were liable to find themselves staring down the wrong end of a gamekeeper's shotgun.

The island was sold to the Nature Conservancy in 1957 and has since been a reserve noted for its deer, wild goats, ponies, golden and white-tailed eagles, and a 120,000-strong nesting colony of Manx shearwaters. Its dramatic, rocky mountains, known as the Rum Cuillin for their similarity to the peaks on neighbouring Skye, draw hill walkers and climbers.

◉ Sights & Activities

★ Kinloch Castle   CASTLE
(☑ 01687-462037; www.isleofrum.com; adult/child £9/4.50; ☺ guided tours daily Apr-Oct, to coincide with ferry times) When George Bullough – a dashing, Harrow-educated cavalry officer – inherited Rum along with half his father's fortune in 1891, he became one of the wealthiest bachelors in Britain. Bullough blew half his inheritance on building his dream bachelor pad – the ostentatious Kinloch Castle. Since the Bulloughs left, the castle has survived as a perfect time capsule of upper-class Edwardian eccentricity – the guided tour should not be missed.

Bullough shipped in pink sandstone from Dumfriesshire and 250,000 tonnes of Ayrshire topsoil for the gardens, and paid his workers a shilling extra a day to wear tweed kilts – just so they'd look more picturesque. Hummingbirds were kept in the greenhouses and alligators in the garden, and guests were entertained with an orchestrion, the Edwardian equivalent of a Bose hi-fi system (one of only six that were ever made).

Nature Trails   WALKING
There's some great coastal and mountain walking on the island, including a couple of easy, waymarked nature trails in the woods around Kinloch. The first path on the left after leaving the pier leads to an otter hide (signposted).

Glen Harris is a 10-mile round trip from Kinloch, on a rough 4WD track; allow four to five hours' walking. The climb to the island's highest point, Askival (812m), is a strenuous hike and involves a bit of rock scrambling (allow six hours for the round trip from Kinloch).

You can hire bikes from the Craft Shop (☑ 01687-462744; www.rumbikehire.co.uk; per day £15) near Kinloch Castle.

🛏 Sleeping

Accommodation on Rum is strictly limited – at the time of writing there was only the Castle Hostel, one B&B and the campsite; a new bunkhouse should be open by the time you read this. Booking is essential for the hostel, though not for campers. There are also two bothies (unlocked cottages with no facilities, for the use of hikers) on the island, and wild camping is permitted.

Kinloch Castle Hostel   HOSTEL £
(☑ 01687-462037; www.isleofrum.com; dm/d £19.50/74; ☺ Mar-Oct; 🛜) The castle hostel has 32 beds in four-bed dorms. There are two self-catering kitchens and a comfortable lounge.

Kinloch Village Campsite   CAMPSITE £
(☑ 01687-460328; www.isleofrum.com; sites per adult/child £6/3) Situated between the pier and Kinloch Castle, this basic camping ground has toilets, a water supply and hot showers (from April to October). There are also two wooden camping cabins (£22 for two persons), which must be booked in advance.

ℹ Information

Kinloch, where the ferry lands, is the island's only settlement; it has a small **grocery shop** (☺ 5-7pm), post office and public telephone, and a **tourist office** (☺ 8.30am-5pm Apr-Oct) near the pier where you can get information and leaflets on walking and wildlife. There's a **tearoom** (☺ noon-6pm Mon-Sat Apr-Sep; 🛜) in the village hall, with wi-fi and internet access. The hall itself is open at all times for people to shelter from the rain (or the midges!). For more information see www.isleofrum.com.

Isle of Eigg

POP 83

The Isle of Eigg made history in 1997 when it became the first Highland estate to be bought out by its inhabitants. The island is now owned and managed by the Isle of Eigg Heritage Trust (www.isleofeigg.org), a partnership among the islanders, Highland Council and the Scottish Wildlife Trust.

◉ Sights & Activities

The island takes its name from the Old Norse *egg* (edge), a reference to the Sgurr of Eigg (393m), an impressive minimountain that towers over Galmisdale. Ringed by vertical cliffs on three sides, it's composed of pitchstone lava with columnar jointing similar to that seen on the Isle of Staffa and at the Giant's Causeway in Northern Ireland.

The climb to the summit of the **Sgurr of Eigg** (4.5 miles round trip; allow three to four hours) begins on the road that leads steeply uphill from the pier, which continues through the woods to a red-roofed cottage. Go through the gate to the right of the cottage and turn left; just 20m along the road a cairn on the right marks the start of a boggy footpath that leads over the eastern shoulder of the Sgurr, then traverses beneath the northern cliffs until it makes its way up onto the summit ridge.

On a fine day the views from the top are magnificent – Rum and Skye to the north, Muck and Coll to the south, Ardnamurchan Lighthouse to the southeast and Ben Nevis shouldering above the eastern horizon. Take binoculars – on a calm summer's day there's a good chance of seeing minke whales feeding down below in the Sound of Muck.

A shorter walk (2 miles; allow 1½ hours round trip, and bring a torch) leads west from the pier to the spooky and claustrophobic **Uamh Fraing** (Massacre Cave). Start as for the Sgurr of Eigg, but 800m from the pier turn left through a gate and into a field. Follow the 4WD track and fork left before a white cottage to pass below it. A footpath continues across the fields to reach a small gate in a fence; go through it and descend a ridge towards the shore.

The cave entrance is tucked inconspicuously down to the left of the ridge. The entrance is tiny – almost a hands-and-knees job – but the cave opens out inside and runs a long way back. Go right to the back, turn off your torch, and imagine the cave packed shoulder to shoulder with terrified men, women and children. Then imagine the panic as your enemies start piling firewood into the entrance. Almost the entire population of Eigg – around 400 people – sought refuge in this cave when the MacLeods of Skye raided the island in 1577. In an act of inhuman cruelty, the raiders lit a fire in the narrow entrance and everyone inside died of asphyxiation. There are more than a few ghosts floating around in here.

🛏 Sleeping & Eating

All accommodation should be booked in advance. For a full listing of self-catering accommodation, see www.iseleofeigg.org.

Glebe Barn   HOSTEL **£**
(☑ 01687-482417; www.glebebarn.co.uk; dm/tw £17/40; @�🎧) Excellent bunkhouse accommodation in the middle of the island, with a smart, maple-floored lounge with central fireplace, modern kitchen, laundry, drying room, and bright, clean dorms and bedrooms.

Sue Holland's Croft   CAMPSITE **£**
(☑ 01687-482480;   www.eiggorganics.co.uk; Cleadale; per tent £5, yurt £35-40; 🎧) This organic croft in the north of the island has a campsite with basic facilities, and also offers accommodation for two in a Mongolian yurt.

Lageorna   B&B **££**
(☑ 01687-460081; www.lageorna.co.uk; Cleadale; per person incl dinner £65; 🎧) 🍽 This converted croft house and lodge in the island's northwest is Eigg's most luxurious accommodation. Rooms are fitted with beautiful, locally made, 'driftwood-style' timber beds, and even have iPod docks (but no mobile-phone reception). Evening meals are part of the package, with the menu heavy on locally grown vegetables, seafood and venison.

Galmisdale Bay   CAFE **£**
(www.galmisdale-bay.com; Galmisdale; mains £4-9; ⊙10am-5pm Mon-Sat, 11am-4.30pm Sun May-Sep, longer hours Jul-Aug, shorter hous Oct-Apr) 🍽 There's a good cafe-bar above the ferry pier. Winter opening hours coincide with ferry arrivals and departures.

ℹ Information

The ferry landing is at Galmisdale in the south.
An Laimhrig (www.isleofeiggshop.co.uk; ⊙10am-5pm Mon-Wed & Fri, 10am-3pm Thu, 11am-5pm Sat, noon-1pm & 3.30-5pm Sun May–mid-Oct, shorter hours winter) An Laimhrig, the building above the pier, houses a grocery store, post office, craft shop and cafe. You can hire **bikes** (☑ 07833 701493; www.eiggadventures.co.uk; per day £15) here too.

Isle of Muck

POP 27

The tiny island of Muck (www.isleofmuck.com), measuring just 2 miles by 1 mile, has exceptionally fertile soil, and the island is carpeted with wildflowers in spring and early summer. It takes its name from the Gaelic *muc* (pig), and pigs are still raised here.

Ferries call at the southern settlement of Port Mor. There's a **tearoom and craft** shop (11am-4pm Jun-Aug, shorter hours May & Sep) above the pier, which also acts as a tourist office.

It's an easy 15-minute walk along the island's only road from the pier to the sandy beach at Gallanach on the northern side of the island. A longer and rougher hike (3.5 miles; 1½ hours round trip) goes to the top of Beinn Airein (137m) for the best views. Puffins nest on the cliffs at the western end of Camas Mor, the bay to the south of the hill.

The cosy six-bed Isle of Muck Bunkhouse (01687-462042; dm £15), with self-catering kitchen, is just above the pier, while the gorgeous, new Gallanach Lodge (01687-462365; lodge@isleofmuck.com; per person incl dinner £85;) enjoys stunning views over Gallanach Bay on the west side of the island.

You can camp on the island for free – but ask at the craft shop first. For a full accommodation listings see www.isleofmuck.com.

Isle of Canna

POP 12

The island of Canna (www.theisleofcanna.com) is a moorland plateau of black basalt rock, just 5 miles long and 1.25 miles wide; it was gifted to the National Trust for Scotland in 1981 by its owner, the Gaelic scholar and author John Lorne Campbell. Compass Hill

(143m), at the northeastern corner, contains enough magnetite (an iron oxide mineral) to deflect the navigation compasses in passing yachts.

The ferry arrives at the hamlet of A'Chill at the eastern end of the island, where visiting yachts people have left extensive graffiti on the rock face south of the harbour. There's a tearoom and craft shop by the harbour, and a tiny post office in a hut. There is no mobile-phone reception.

You can walk to An Coroghon, just east of the ferry pier, a medieval stone tower perched atop a sea cliff, and continue to Compass Hill, or take a longer hike along the southern shore past Canna House (guided tour £5; 1-2.30pm Wed, 4-5.30pm Sat Apr-Sep), the former home of John Lorne Campbell, and an ornately decorated early Christian stone cross. In 2012 a *bullaun* (cursing stone), with an inscribed cross was discovered nearby; these are common in Ireland, but this was the first to be found in Scotland.

Accommodation is very limited. Tighard (01687-462474; www.tighard.co.uk; s/d £80/120;) is the only B&B, and cafe-restaurant Gille Brighde (1687 482488; www.cafecanna. co.uk; mains £9-18; 12.30-8.30pm Wed-Mon Apr-Oct, longer hours Jun-Aug) the only eating place (booking recommended for dinner). Check www.theisleofcanna.co.uk for self-catering accommodation. Wild camping is allowed.

164

1. Loch Awe (p97) **2.** Caledonian Canal (p125) and Ben Nevis (p153) **3.** Loch Ness (p120) **4.** Schiehallion (p142)

SIMON BUTTERWORTH / GETTY IMAGES ©

Lochs & Mountains

Since the 19th century, when the first tourists started to arrive, the Scottish Highlands have been famed for their wild nature and majestic scenery, and today the country's biggest draw remains its magnificent landscape. At almost every turn is a vista that will stop you in your tracks – keep your camera close at hand.

Ben Nevis

Scotland's highest peak is a perennial magnet for hillwalkers and ice climbers, but it's also one of the country's most photographed mountains. The classic viewpoints for the Ben include Corpach Basin at the entrance to the Caledonian Canal, and the B8004 road between Banavie and Gairlochy, from where you can see the precipitous north face.

Loch Ness

Scotland's largest loch by volume (it contains more water than all the lakes in England and Wales added together) may be most famous for its legendary monster, but it is also one of Scotland's most scenic. The minor road along the southeastern shore reveals a series of classic views.

Schiehallion

From the Gaelic *Sìdh Chailleann* (Fairy Hill of the Caledonians), this is one of Scotland's most distinctive mountains, its conical peak a prominent feature of views along Loch Tummel and Loch Rannoch. It's also one of the easier Munros, and a hike to the summit is rewarded with a superb panorama of hills and lochs.

Loch Awe

Loch Awe is a little off the beaten track, but is well worth seeking out for its gorgeous scenery. Dotted with islands and draped with native woodlands of oak, birch and alder, its northern end is dominated by the evocative ruins of Kilchurn Castle, with the pointed peaks of mighty Ben Cruachan reflected in its shifting waters.

Northern Highlands & Islands

Best Places to Eat

➡ Albannach (p184)

➡ Three Chimneys (p205)

➡ Côte du Nord (p180)

➡ Plockton Shores (p192)

Best Places to Stay

➡ The Torridon (p190)

➡ Gearrannan Holiday Cottages (p212)

➡ Toravaig House Hotel (p200)

➡ Pennyland House (p178)

➡ Mackays Rooms (p182)

➡ Mey House (p177)

Why Go?

Scotland's vast and melancholy soul is here: an epic land with a stark beauty that imprints the hearts of those who journey through it. Mist and mountains, rock and heather; long summer evenings are the pay-off for so many days of horizontal rain. It's simply magical.

The chambered cairns of Caithness and structures of the Western Isles are testament to the skills of prehistoric builders; cragtop castles and broken walls of abandoned crofts tell of the Highlands' turbulent history.

Outdoors is the place to be, whatever the weather; there's nothing like comparing windburn or mud-ruined boots over a well-deserved dram by the fire of a Highland pub. The landscape lends itself to activity, be it woodland strolls, thrilling mountain-bike descents, sea-kayaking, Munro-bagging, beachcombing or birdwatching. Best are the locals, big-hearted and straight-talking; make it your business to get to know them.

When to Go?
Portree

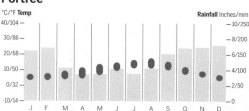

Jun Long evenings bathe achingly sublime landscapes in dreamy light.

Jul The Hebridean Celtic Festival is a top time to experience the culture of the Outer Hebrides.

Sep Less busy than summer, the midges have gone and temperatures are (maybe!) still OK.

EAST COAST

The east coast landscapes of the old counties of Ross and Sutherland unfold real wilderness and Highland character. While the interior is dominated by mournful moor-and-mountain landscapes, along the coast great heather-covered hills heave themselves out of the wild North Sea. Rolling farmland drops suddenly into icy waters, and small, historic towns are moored precariously alongside.

Strathpeffer

POP 1100

Strathpeffer is a charming old Highland spa town, creaking pavilions and grandiose hotels dripping with faded grandeur. It rose to prominence during Victorian times, when the fashionable flocked here in huge numbers to bathe in, wash with and drink the sulphurous waters. The tourist influx led to the construction of grand buildings and architectural follies.

Sights & Activities

Locals have put together excellent interactive tours of Strathpeffer: download them to your phone at www.strathpeffer.org, or pick up a tablet from participating places around town.

The **Eagle Stone** (follow signs from the main drag) is well worth a look. It's a pre-7th-century Pictish stone connected to a figure from local history – the Brahan Seer, who predicted many future events.

There are many good signposted walking trails around Strathpeffer.

The **Strathpeffer & District Pipe Band** plays in the town square every Saturday from 8.30pm, mid-May to mid-September. There's Highland dancing and a festive air.

Highland Museum of Childhood   MUSEUM
(☑01997-421031; www.highlandmuseumof-childhood.org.uk; Old Train Station; adult/child £2.50/1.50; ☺10am-5pm Mon-Sat, 2-5pm Sun Apr-Oct) Strathpeffer's former train station houses a wide range of social-history displays about childhood, and also has activities for children, including a dressing-up box and toy train. There's a good gift shop for presents for a little somebody, and a peaceful cafe.

Spa Pavilion & Upper Pump Room   HISTORIC BUILDINGS
(www.strathpefferpavilion.org; Golf Course Rd; ☺Pump Room 10am-5pm Jun-Aug, 1-5pm Tue-Thu & Sat-Sun Sep-May) FREE In Strathpeffer's heyday, the Pavilion was the social centre, venue for dances, lectures and concerts. These days it's been renovated as a performing arts venue. Alongside, the Upper Pump Room has some splendid displays showing the bizarre lengths Victorians went to for a healthy glow, and exhibitions of local art, as well as artisanal sweets and tourist information in the friendly shop.

Square Wheels Cycles   BICYCLE RENTAL
(☑01997-421000; www.squarewheels.biz; The Square; half-/full day £12/20; ☺10am-6pm Tue-Sat, noon-4pm Sun) Hires out mountain bikes and gives route information; prices decrease with multiday hire.

🛏 Sleeping & Eating

There are a couple of large hotels geared to coach tours of retirees.

★Craigvar   B&B ££
(☑01997-421622; www.craigvar.com; The Square; s/d £60/90; 🅿🖥) Luxury living with a refined touch is what you'll find in this delightful Georgian house in the village's heart. Classy little extras are all here, such as a welcome drink, Highland-Belgian chocolates, bathrobes and fresh fruit. The owner offers a wonderfully genuine welcome. Light, elegant rooms are great, with fabulous new bathrooms. One double has a particularly pleasing outlook and a sensational bed – you'll need to collapse back into it after the gourmet breakfast.

Coul House Hotel   HOTEL £££
(☑01997-421487; www.coulhouse.com; s/d £95/170; 🅿🖥🐾) At Contin, south of Strathpeffer on the A835, Coul House dates from 1821 but has a light, airy feel in contrast to many country houses of this vintage. It's family run, and very cordial. Beautiful dining and lounge areas are complemented by elegant rooms with views over the lovely gardens; superiors look out to the mountains beyond. There are forest trails for walking or mountain biking right on the doorstep and a good restaurant. You can often find lower prices on the website.

Northern Highlands & Islands Highlights

1 Gorging on fresh, succulent seafood in the delightful town of **Ullapool** (p186), with its picture-perfect harbour

2 Dipping your toes in the water at some of the world's most beautiful beaches on **Harris** (p213)

3 Shouldering the challenge of the **Cuillin Hills** (p201), with their rugged silhouettes brooding over the skyscape of Skye

4 Picking your jaw up off the floor as you marvel at the epic Highland scenery of the **far northwest** (p182)

5 Taking the trip out to **Cape Wrath** (p184), Britain's gloriously remote northwestern shoulder

6 Relaxing in postcard-pretty **Plockton** (p191), where the Highlands meet the Caribbean

7 Launching yourself in a sea kayak to explore the otter-rich waters around the **Isle of Skye** (p194)

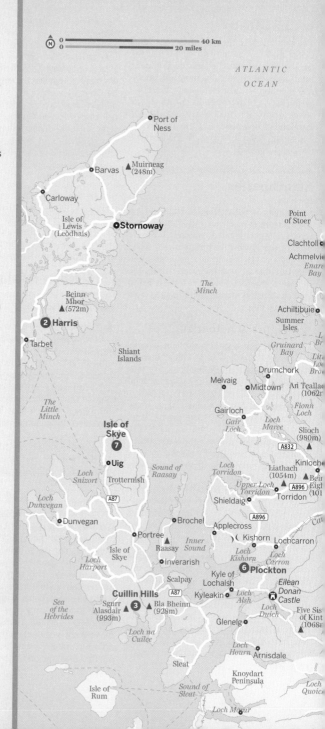

To Stromness (Orkney)

NORTH SEA

Pentland Firth

Dunnet Head

Scrabster

Dunnet Bay

Meye

Gills Bay

John O'Groats

Cape Wrath **5**

Kyle of Durness

Durness

Thurso

Melvich

Strathy Point

Bettyhill

Melness

Coldbackie

Loch Eriboll

Tongue

Loch Hope

Naver

Forss Water

Loch Calder

Halkirk

Watten

A882

Kinlochbervie

Ben Hope (927m)

Ben Loyal (764m)

A871

CAITHNESS

A9

Wick

Laxford Bridge

ourie

Loch More

A894

A836

Strathy

Halladale

Forsinard

Achavanich

A99

Lybster

achillis Bay

Kylesku

Loch Glencoul

SUTHERLAND

Loch Rimsdale

Kinbrace

Berriedale Water

Dunbeath

4 **Far Northwest**

Ben Klibreck (961m)

Skinsdale

Helmsdale

Badbea

chinver

Suilven (731m)

Ben More Assynt (998m)

Loch Shin

Black Water

Brora

Brora

Helmsdale

Helmsdale

NORTH SEA

tac ollaidh 312m)

Knockan

Tirry

Cassley

Lairg

Loch Brora

Invercassley

A837

Dunrobin Castle

Golspie

Ullapool

Culrain

An Uidh

Dornoch Firth

Croick

Ardgay

Bonar Bridge

Dornoch

ndonnell

Braemore

Beinn Dearg (1084m)

A835

Tain

Portmahomack

Ben Wyvis (1046m)

Loch Glass

Invergordon

Cromarty Firth

Moray Firth

A832

Garve

Dingwall

Black Isle

Nairn

Elgin

Lossie

nnasheen

Loch Luichart

Strathpeffer

ROSS

Bran

Meig

Orrin

Loch Monar

Farrar

Glass

A82

Inverness

Spey

Loch ullardoch

Loch Ness

A9

Grantown-on-Spey

Avon

Fiddich

Livet

Loch Affric

Monadhliath Mountains

Nethy

Cairngorm Mountains

anie

A87

Fort Augustus

Aviemore

Cairngorms National Park

ch anie

Loch Oich

Kingussie

Spey

Cairn Gorm (1245m)

Invergarry

Newtonmore

Braemar

Loch Lochy

Red Poppy
BISTRO ££

(☎ 01997-423332; www.redpoppyrestaurant.co.uk; Main Rd; mains £14-20; ⊙ 11.30am-9pm Tue-Sat, noon-3.30pm Sun; 🛜) On the main road opposite the spa buildings, this is comfortably Strathpeffer's best eatery. The casual modern interior with its bright red chairs is the venue for confident, well-presented dishes covering game and other classic British ingredients. It's a little cheaper at lunchtime, when set-priced menus are available.

❶ Getting There & Around

BUS
Stagecoach (www.stagecoachbus.com) operates from Inverness to Strathpeffer (£5.20, 45 minutes, hourly Monday to Saturday, four on Sunday). Inverness to Gairloch and Durness services, plus some Inverness to Ullapool buses, also drop in.

Tain
POP 3700

Scotland's oldest royal burgh, Tain is a proud sandstone town that rose to prominence as pilgrims descended to venerate the relics of St Duthac, who is commemorated by the 12th-century ruins of St Duthac's Chapel, and St Duthus Church.

◉ Sights

Tain Through Time
MUSEUM

(☎ 01862-894089; www.tainmuseum.org.uk; Tower St; adult/child £3.50/2.50; ⊙ 10am-5pm Mon-Fri Apr-Oct, also Sat Jun-Aug) Set in the grounds of St Duthus Church is Tain Through Time, an entertaining heritage centre with a colourful and educational display on St Duthac, King James IV and key moments in Scottish history. Another building focuses on the town's fine silversmithing tradition. Admission includes an audioguided walk around town.

Glenmorangie
DISTILLERY

(www.glenmorangie.com; tours £5; ⊙ 10am-5pm Mon-Fri, plus 10am-4pm Sat & noon-4pm Sun Jun-Aug) Located on Tain's northern outskirts, Glenmorangie (emphasis on the second syllable) produces a fine lightish malt, subjected to a number of different cask finishes for variation. The tour is less in-depth than some but finishes with a free dram. A special tour is £30.

🛏 Sleeping & Eating

Golf View House
B&B ££

(☎ 01862-892856; www.bedandbreakfasttain.co.uk; 13 Knockbreck Rd; s/d £60/85; 🅿🛜) Set in an old manse in a secluded location just off the main drag, this spot offers magnificent views over fields and water. Impeccable rooms are very cheerful and bright, and there's an upbeat feel, with delicious breakfasts and welcoming hospitality. It's worth the extra for a room with a view.

Royal Hotel
HOTEL ££

(☎ 01862-892013; www.royalhoteltain.co.uk; High St; s/d £55/90; 🛜🐾) So much the heart of town that the main street has to detour around it, the refurbished Royal has good-sized spruce rooms. For only a tenner more, you get a four-poster room in the older wing; these have a choice of colour schemes, and are well worth the upgrade. The restaurant is the best in town and bar meals are also decent.

❶ Getting There & Away

Stagecoach (www.stagecoachbus.com) buses run from Inverness (£9.70, 50 minutes, roughly hourly); some continue north as far as Thurso.

Trains run daily to Inverness (£13.50, 1¼ hours) and Thurso (£16.50, 2¾ hours).

Portmahomack
POP 600

Portmahomack is a former fishing village in a flawless spot – off the beaten track, gazing across the water at sometimes snowcapped peaks.

Tarbat Discovery Centre
MUSEUM

(☎ 01862-871351; www.tarbat-discovery.co.uk; Tarbatness Rd; adult/child £3.50/1; ⊙ 10am-5pm Mon-Sat May-Sep, 2-5pm Mon-Sat Apr & Oct, plus 2-5pm Sun Jun-Oct) This intruiging museum has great carved Pictish stones. The foundations of an Iron Age settlement were discovered around the village church; ongoing investigation revealed a Pictish monastery with evidence of manuscript production. The exhibition is excellent and includes the church's spooky crypt.

Oystercatcher Restaurant
SEAFOOD ££

(☎ 01862-871560; www.the-oystercatcher.co.uk; Main St; lunch mains £8-14, dinner mains £15-20; ⊙ 12.15-2.45pm Thu-Sun, plus 6.30-8.30pm Wed-Sat Mar-Oct; 🅿🛜🚲). Seafood aficionados shouldn't miss this bright and cheerful place where a lunchtime bistro menu lets you choose your serving size, and a classy brasserie evening menu includes lots of lobster among other temptations. Fourteen-course tasting menus (£60) are a delight, with invention and quality given levity by the whimsical dish names. It also offers three cosy rooms (single/double £52/108). Rates include what has to be Scotland's most amazing breakfast, with numerous gourmet options.

Stagecoach (www.stagecoachbus.com) runs from Tain to Portmahomack (£1.95, 25 minutes, four to five Monday to Friday).

Bonar Bridge & Around

The A9 crosses Dornoch Firth by bridge and causeway, near Tain. An alternative route goes around the firth via Ardgay and Bonar Bridge, where the A836 to Lairg branches west.

◉ Sights & Activities

Croick VILLAGE
From Ardgay, a single-track road leads 10 miles up Strathcarron to Croick, the scene of notorious evictions during the 1845 Clearances. You can still see the evocative messages scratched by refugee crofters from Glencalvie on the eastern windows of **Croick Church**.

Kyle of Sutherland Trails MOUNTAIN BIKING
(☎01408-634063; scotland.forestry.gov.uk/visit/carbisdale) Mountain bikers will find two networks of forest trails around Bonar Bridge. From the car park below Carbisdale Castle, there's a red and a blue trail with great views. At Balblair, a mile from Bonar Bridge off the Lairg road, 7 miles of black track will test expert bikers.

⌕ Sleeping

Carbisdale Castle SYHA HOSTEL £
(☎01549-421232; www.syha.org.uk; ⊘mid-Mar–Oct; P@🛜) This castle, 10 minutes' walk north of Culrain train station, was Scotland's most opulent hostel, but its future was in doubt at time of writing, as spiralling maintenance costs had closed it. It may or may not reopen: check the website.

❶ Getting There & Away

Trains from Inverness to Thurso stop at Culrain (£15.20, 1½ hours), half a mile from Carbisdale Castle.

THE RIGHT SIDE OF THE TRACKS

Sleeperzzz.com (☎01408-641343; www.sleeperzzz.com; dm £16-20; ⊘Mar–Sep; P) Scotland has some unusual hostels and this is one of them. Set in three caringly converted railway carriages, an old bus and a beautiful wooden caravan parked up in a siding by Rogart station, it has cute two-person bedrooms, kitchenettes and tiny lounges. The owners make an effort to run the hostel on sustainable lines.

There's a local pub that does food, as well as beautifully lonely Highland scenery in the vicinity. It's on the A839, 10 miles east of Lairg, but is also easily reached by train on the Inverness–Wick line (10% discount if you arrive this way or by bike).

Lairg & Around
POP 900

Lairg is an attractive village, although the tranquillity can be rudely interrupted by the sound of military jets roaring overhead (Loch Shin valley is frequently used by the RAF for low-flying exercises). Located at the southern end of Loch Shin, it's a remote but important Highlands crossroad, gateway to central Sutherland's remote mountains and loch-speckled bogs.

◉ Sights & Activities

Ferrycroft Visitor Centre MUSEUM
(☎01549-402160; www.highland.gov.uk/ferrycroft; ⊘10am-4pm Apr-Oct; 🚻) On the opposite side of the the river from the town centre, this visitor centre has displays on local history, wildlife and a tourist information desk. A short walk leads from the centre to the **Ord Hut Circles and Chambered Cairns**, a collection of prehistoric roundhouses and tombs.

Falls of Shin WATERFALL
(www.fallsofshin.co.uk; 🚻) **FREE** Four miles south of Lairg, the picturesque Falls of Shin is one of the best places in the Highlands to see salmon leaping on their way upstream to spawn (June to September). A short and easy footpath leads to a viewing terrace overlooking the waterfall. There are waymarked forest trails here; other attractions

were closed at last research after the visitor centre burned down.

🛏 Sleeping

Lochview B&B ££

(☎ 01549-402578; www.lochviewlairg.co.uk; Lochside; s/d £40/84; P 🛜) Years of experience have made the kindly owners here absolute experts in ensuring guest comfort. Huge rooms with seating areas and great facilities overlook the loch; the lounge gives onto the grassy garden that stretches down to it. Bathrooms are modern and sparklingly clean: in all, it's a very impressive set-up.

ⓘ Getting There & Away

Trains from Inverness to Thurso stop at Lairg (£16.30, 1¾ hours). Four buses run Monday to Saturday to Tain via Bonar Bridge and Ardgay (one via the Falls of Shin). Three buses run Monday to Friday to Helmsdale via Rogart and Golspie.

Dornoch

POP 1200

On the north shore of Dornoch Firth, two miles off the A9, this attractive old market town is one of the east coast's most pleasant settlements. Dornoch is best known for its championship golf course, but there's a fine cathedral among other noble buildings. Other historical oddities: the last witch to be executed in Scotland was boiled alive in hot tar here in 1722 and Madonna married Guy Ritchie here in 2000.

◉ Sights & Activities

Have a walk along Dornoch's golden-sand beach, which stretches for miles. South of Dornoch, seals are often visible on the sandbars of Dornoch Firth.

Dornoch Cathedral CHURCH

(www.dornoch-cathedral.com; St Gilbert St; ⊙9am-7pm or later) FREE Consecrated in the 13th century, Dornoch Cathedral is an elegant Gothic edifice with an interior softly illuminated through modern stained-glass windows. The controversial first Duke of Sutherland, whose wife restored the church in the 1830s, lies in a sealed burial vault beneath the chancel.

By the western door is the sarcophagus of Sir Richard de Moravia, who died fighting the Danes at the battle of Embo in the 1260s. Until he met his maker, the battle had been going rather well for him; he'd managed to slay the Danish commander with the unattached leg of a horse that was to hand.

Historylinks MUSEUM

(www.historylinks.org.uk; The Meadows; adult/child £2.50/free; ⊙10am-4pm daily Jun-Sep, Mon-Fri Apr, May & Oct, Wed & Thu only Nov-Mar; 📶) Historylinks is a child-friendly museum focusing on local history. Displays cover geology, the Picts, the building of the cathedral and the development of the golf course – and you can add to your background knowledge of the area through a selection of audiovisuals.

Royal Dornoch GOLF

(☎ 01862-810219; www.royaldornoch.com; Golf Rd, Dornoch; summer green fee £120) One of Scotland's most famous links, described by Tom Watson as 'the most fun I have ever had on a golf course'. It's public, and you can book a slot online. Twilight rates are the most economical. A golf pass (www.dornochfirthgolf.co.uk) lets you play several courses in the area at a good discount.

🛏 Sleeping

★ **Dornoch Castle Hotel** HOTEL ££

(☎01862-810216; www.dornochcastlehotel.com; Castle St; s/d £73/125, superior/deluxe d £169/250; P 🛜) This 16th-century former bishop's palace makes a wonderful place to stay, particularly if you upgrade to one of the superior rooms, which have views, space, whisky and chocolates on the welcome tray and (some) a four-poster bed; the deluxe rooms are unforgettable. Cheaper rooms (single/double £50/65), simpler, without the historic atmosphere, are also available in adjoining buildings.

2 Quail B&B ££

(☎01862-811811; www.2quail.com; Castle St; s £80, d £90-100; 🛜) Intimate and upmarket, 2 Quail offers a warm main-street welcome. Tasteful, spacious chambers are full of old-world comfort, with sturdy metal bedframes, plenty of books and plump duvets. The downstairs guest lounge is an absolute delight. It's best to book ahead, especially in winter. It also offers a self-catering cottage sleeping six.

Trevose Guest House B&B ££

(☎01862-810269; jamackenzie@tiscali.co.uk; Cathedral Sq; s/d £40/64; ⊙May-Sep; 🛜🐾) First impressions deceive at Trevose Guest House, a lovely stone cottage right by the cathedral. It looks compact but actually boasts very spacious rooms with significant comfort and well-loved old wooden furnishings. Character oozes from every pore of the place and a benevolent welcome is a given.

Eating

Luigi   ITALIAN **£**
(www.luigidornoch.com; Castle St; light meals £5-9; ◷10am-5pm daily, plus 6.45-9pm Fri & Sat, dinner daily in summer) The clean lines of this contemporary Italian-American cafe make a break from the omnipresent heritage and history of this coastline. Ciabattas and salads stuffed with tasty deli ingredients make it a good lunch stop; more elaborate dinners (£14 to £19) usually include fine seafood choices.

Eagle Hotel   PUB **£**
(☑ 01862-810008; www.eagledornoch.co.uk; Castle St; bar meals £8-11; ◷food noon-9pm) Nobody on the streets of Dornoch after 7pm? You'll find most of them in this cosy, welcoming pub, which looks after its customers with good service and a menu of very solid fare – reliably tasty burgers, haggis sausages, fish and chips or daily roasts – at fair prices. It packs out at weekends so book.

Dornoch Castle Hotel   SCOTTISH **£££**
(☑ 01862-810216; www.dornochcastlehotel.com; Castle St; mains £18-22; ◷noon-2.30pm & 6-9pm) In the evening, toast your toes in the cosy bar, which has decent real ales and a substantial malt selection, before dining in style at this hotel restaurant, tucking into dishes featuring plenty of game and seasonal produce. Bar meals are also available during the day.

❶ Information

Tourist Office (☑ 01862-810594; Castle St; ◷9am-12.30pm & 1.30-4pm Mon-Fri, plus 10am-4pm Sat May-Aug & 10am-4pm Sun Jul & Aug) In the council building alongside Dornoch Castle Hotel.

❶ Getting There & Away

There are buses roughly hourly from Inverness (£10.20, 1¼ hours), with some services continuing north to Wick or Thurso.

Golspie
POP 1400

Golspie is a pretty little village most visited for nearby Dunrobin Castle. There are good facilities and a pleasant beach: it's a congenial place to spend a day or two.

◉ Sights & Activities

There are several good local walks, including the classic 3.75 mile (return) hike climbing steeply to the summit of **Ben Bhraggie** (394m), crowned by a massive monument to the Duke of Sutherland, notorious for his leading role in the Highland Clearances.

★Dunrobin Castle   CASTLE
(☑ 01408-633177; www.dunrobincastle.co.uk; adult/child £10.50/5.75; ◷10.30am-4.30pm Mon-Sat & noon-4.30pm Sun Apr, May & Sep–mid-Oct, 10am-5pm daily Jun & Aug) Magnificent Dunrobin Castle, a mile past Golspie, is the Highlands' largest house. Although it dates to 1275, most of what you see was built in French style between 1845 and 1850. A home of the dukes of Sutherland, it's richly furnished and offers an intriguing insight into the aristocratic lifestyle. The beautiful castle inspires mixed feelings locally; it was once the seat of the first Duke of Sutherland, notorious for some of the cruellest episodes of the Highland Clearances.

The duke's estate was, at over 6000 square kilometres, the largest privately owned area of land in Europe. He evicted around 15,000 people from their homes to make way for sheep.

This classic fairy-tale castle is adorned with towers and turrets, but only 22 of its 187 rooms are on display, with hunting trophies much to the fore. Beautiful formal gardens, where impressive falconry displays take place two or three times a day, extend down to the sea. In the gardens is a museum with an eclectic mix of archaeological finds, natural-history exhibits, more non-PC animal remains and an excellent collection of Pictish stones.

Highland Wildcat   MOUNTAIN BIKING
(www.highlandwildcat.com; ◷dawn-dusk) `FREE` The expert-only black trail at Highland Wildcat is famous for having the highest single-track descent in the country (a 390m drop over 7km). There's plenty for beginners and families too, with a scenic blue trail and easy forest routes. No facilities; grab the map off the website.

⏟ Sleeping

Blar Mhor   B&B **££**
(☑ 01408-633609; www.blarmhor.co.uk; Drummuie Rd; s/d/f £35/60/80; P🐾🅿) On the

approach into Golspie from Dornoch, this excellent guesthouse has large, beautifully kept rooms with swish modern bathrooms in a towering Victorian mansion. There are beautifully landscaped gardens and cheerful hosts will brighten your stay with little extras like chocolates on the bed.

ⓘ Getting There & Away

Both trains (£18.20, 2¼ hours, two or three daily) and buses (£11.60, 1½ hours) between Inverness and Wick/Thurso stop in Golspie and at Dunrobin Castle.

Helmsdale

POP 700

Surrounded by breathtaking coastline and gorse-covered hills that explode mad-yellow in spring, this sheltered fishing town, like many on this coast, was a major emigration point during the Clearances and a booming herring port.

Timespan Heritage Centre (www. timespan.org.uk; Dunrobin St; adult/child £4/2; ☺10am-5pm Easter-Oct, 10am-3pm Sat & Sun & 2-4pm Tue Nov-Easter) has an impressive display covering local history (including the 1869 gold rush) and Barbara Cartland, queen of romance novels, who was a Helmsdale regular. There are also local art exhibitions, a geology garden and a cafe.

The River Helmsdale offers some of the best Highland salmon fishing. Permits, tackle and advice can be obtained from **Helmsdale Tackle Company** (☑01431-821372; www.helmsdalecompany.com; 15-17 Dunrobin St; ☺9am-5pm Mon-Sat), which also hires rods and boots.

🛏 Sleeping & Eating

Helmsdale Hostel HOSTEL £
(☑07971-516287, 01431-821636; www.helmsdalehostel.co.uk; Stafford St; dm/tw/f £19/45/60; ☺Apr-Sep; 🛜🐾) This caringly run hostel is in very good nick, well-equipped and spotlessly clean; it makes a cheerful, comfortable budget base for exploring Caithness. Dorms have mostly cosy single beds rather than bunks, and en suite rooms are great for families. The lofty central space has a lounge with wood stove and good kitchen.

Customs House B&B £
(☑01431-821648; Shore St; r per person £22; P) Old-fashioned, cordial and top value, this has a great location opposite the little har-

bour, and fluffy, comfortable rooms with heaps of cushions and big cosy beds. Breakfast is great, with fresh fruit, cheese, abundant coffee and juice, plus cooked options.

La Mirage BISTRO £
(☑01431-821615; www.lamirage.org; 7 Dunrobin St; mains £7-12; ☺11am-8.45pm Mon-Sat, noon-8.45pm Sun; 🛜) Created in homage to Barbara Cartland, this is a '70s throwback with pink walls, kitschy installations and a retro menu. Meals aren't gourmet – think chicken Kiev – but portions are huge. Fish and chips are also available takeaway; eat 'em by the pretty harbour.

ⓘ Getting There & Away

Buses from Inverness (£11.60, 1¾ hours) and Thurso stop in Helmsdale, as do trains (from Inverness £18.20, 2½ hours, two to three daily).

CAITHNESS

Once you pass Helmsdale, you are entering Caithness, a place of jagged gorse-and-grass-topped cliffs hiding tiny fishing harbours. Scotland's top corner was once Viking territory, historically more connected to Orkney and Shetland than the rest of the mainland. It's a mystical, ancient land peopled by wise folk with long memories who are fiercely proud of their Norse heritage.

Helmsdale to Lybster

Seven miles north of Helmsdale is **Badbea**, an abandoned crofting village established during the Highland Clearances in the early 19th century. The village of **Dunbeath** is spectacularly set in a deep glen; the **Heritage Centre** (☑01593-731233; www.dunbeath-heritage.org.uk; The Old School, Dunbeath; adult/child £2.50/free; ☺10am-5pm Sun-Fri Apr-Sep, 11am-3pm Mon-Fri Oct-Mar) has a stone carved with runic graffiti, and a display on Neil Gunn, whose wonderful novels evoke the Caithness of his boyhood.

Two miles north is **Laidhay Croft Museum** (☑0756-370 2321; www.laidhay.co.uk; adult/child £2.50/50p; ☺10am-5pm Mon-Sat Jun-Sep), which recreates crofting life from the mid-1800s to WWII. At **Clan Gunn Heritage Centre** (☑01593-741700; www.clangunnsociety.org; Latheron; adult/child £2.50/50p; ☺11am-1pm & 2-4pm Mon-Sat Jun-Sep) in **Latheron**, a mile beyond, there's information on the Gunn

NORTHERN HIGHLANDS & ISLANDS HELMSDALE

clan, from its Viking origins to the present day. It's worth pulling into the car park on a fine day to admire the stunning views.

Lybster & Around

Lybster is a purpose-built fishing village dating from 1810, with a stunning harbour area surrounded by grassy cliffs. In its heyday, it was Scotland's third-busiest port. Things have changed – now there are only a couple of boats – but there are several interesting prehistoric sites in the area.

◉ Sights & Activities

Waterlines   MUSEUM
(☑ 01593-721520; The Harbour; adult/child £2.50/50p; ◷ 11am-5pm May-Oct) At the picturesque harbour in Lybster, this museum has an exhibition on the town's fishing heritage, a smokehouse and a cafe.

Whaligoe Steps   CLIFFS
At Ulbster, 5 miles north of Lybster, this staircase cut into the cliff provides access to a tiny natural harbour, with an ideal grassy picnic spot, ringed by vertical cliffs and echoing with the cackle of nesting fulmars. The path begins at the end of the minor road opposite the road signposted 'Cairn of Get'. There's a cafe at the top.

Cairn o'Get   PREHISTORIC SITE
The Cairn o'Get, a prehistoric burial cairn, is signposted off the road in Ulbster. It's a mile's boggy walk from the car park.

Achavanich Stone Setting   PREHISTORIC SITE
Six miles to the northwest of Lybster and a mile off the A9, these 30 standing stones date from around 2000 BC. These crumbling monuments of the distant past still capture the imagination with their desolate location. Nearby are the remains of a burial cairn, another millennium older.

Grey Cairns of Camster   PREHISTORIC SITE
Dating from between 4000 BC and 2500 BC, these burial chambers are hidden in long, low mounds rising from an evocatively lonely moor. The Long Cairn measures 60m by 21m. You can enter the main chamber, but must first crawl into the well-preserved Round Cairn, which has a corbelled ceiling.

From a turn-off a mile east of Lybster on the A99, the cairns are 4 miles north. You can continue 7 further miles to approach Wick on the A882.

Hill o'Many Stanes   PREHISTORIC SITE
Two miles beyond the Camster turn-off on the A99 is a curious, fan-shaped arrangement of 22 rows of small stones, probably from around 2000 BC. Staggeringly, there were 600 in the original pattern. On a sunny day, the views from this hill are stunning.

❶ Getting There & Away

Stagecoach buses between Thurso and Inverness run via Lybster and Dunbeath. The Wick–Helmsdale service also stops at these places.

Wick

POP 7200
More gritty than pretty, Wick has been down on its luck since the collapse of the herring industry. It was once the world's largest fishing port for the 'silver darlings', but when the market dropped off after WWII, job losses were huge and the town hasn't totally recovered. It's worth a visit though, particularly for its excellent museum and attractive, spruced-up harbour area.

◉ Sights & Activities

A path leads a mile south to the ruined 12th-century Old Wick Castle (◷ 24hr) FREE, with spectacular cliffs a little further south. In good weather, it's a fine coastal walk, but take care on the final approach. Three miles northeast of Wick is the magnificently located clifftop ruin of Castle Sinclair (◷ 24hr).

★ **Wick Heritage Centre**   MUSEUM
(☑ 01955-605393; www.wickheritage.org; 20 Bank Row; adult/child £4/50p; ◷ 10am-5pm Apr-Oct, last entry 3.45pm) Tracking the rise and fall of the herring industry, this great town museum displays everything from fishing equipment to complete herring boats. It's absolutely huge inside, and is crammed with memorabilia and extensive displays describing Wick's heyday in the mid-19th century.

The Johnston collection is the star exhibit. From 1863 to 1977, three generations photographed everything that happened around Wick; the 70,000 photographs are an amazing record.

Old Pulteney   DISTILLERY
(☑ 01955-602371; www.oldpulteney.com; Huddart St; tours £6; ◷ 10am-4pm Mon-Fri Oct-Apr, 10am-5pm Mon-Fri & 10am-4pm Sat May-Sep) The most northerly distillery on mainland Scotland

runs excellent tours twice daily, with more expensive visits available for aficionados.

Tours

Caithness Seacoast BOAT TOURS
(☑ 01955-609200; www.caithness-seacoast.co.uk; ☺ Apr-Oct) This outfit will take you out to sea to inspect the rugged coastline of the northeast. Various options include a half-hour jaunt (adult/child £17/11) to a three-hour return trip down to Lybster (adult/child £45/35).

🛏 Sleeping & Eating

Seaview B&B £
(☑ 01955-602735; www.wickbb.co.uk; 14 Scalesburn; s/d £40/60; P🖭🛜🐾) On the water, though not in its prettiest part, this offers genuine, bend-over-backwards hospitality from cheerful June. It's reliably comfortable, with compact rooms, two of which share a bathroom. The little conservatory lounge is a top spot for lazy moments with river views.

Mackays Hotel HOTEL ££
(☑ 01955-602323; www.mackayshotel.co.uk; Union St; s/d £89/119; 🛜) Hospitable Mackays is Wick's best hotel by a long stretch. Attractive, mostly refurbished rooms vary in layout and size, so ask to see a few; prices are usually lower than these rack rates. On-site **No 1 Bistro** (Union St; mains £11-17; ☺ noon-2pm & 5-9pm; 🛜) is a fine option for lunch or dinner. The world's shortest street, 2.06m-long Ebenezer Place, is on one side of the hotel.

Bord de l'Eau FRENCH ££
(☑ 01955-604400; 2 Market St; mains £14-19; ☺ noon-2.30pm & 6-9pm Tue-Sat, 6-9pm Sun) This serene, relaxed French restaurant is Wick's best place to eat. It overlooks the river and serves a changing menu of mostly meat-and-game French classics, backed up by daily fish specials. Starters are great value, and mains include a huge assortment of vegetables, so you won't go hungry. The conservatory dining room with water views is lovely on a sunny evening.

❶ Information

Wick Tourist Office (☑ 01955-602547; www.visithighlands.com; 66 High St; ☺ 9am-5.30pm Mon-Sat) Good selection of information; upstairs in McAllans Clothing Store.

❶ Getting There & Away

AIR
Wick is a Caithness transport gateway. **Flybe/Loganair** (☑ 0871 700 2000; www.flybe.com) flies from Edinburgh; **Eastern Airways** (☑ 0870 366 9100; www.easternairways.com) from Aberdeen.

BUS
Stagecoach (p171) and Citylink (www.citylink.co.uk) operate to/from Inverness (£19, three hours, six daily) and Stagecoach to Thurso (£3.30, 35 minutes, hourly). There's also connecting service to John O'Groats and Gills Bay (£3.30, 40 minutes, two to three daily) for the passenger and car ferries to Orkney.

TRAIN
Trains service Wick from Inverness (£19.30, 4¼ hours, four daily).

John O'Groats

POP 300

Though not the northernmost point of the British mainland (that's Dunnet Head), John O'Groats still serves as the end point of the 874-mile trek from Land's End in Cornwall, a popular if arduous route for cyclists and walkers, many of whom raise money for charitable causes. There's a passenger ferry from here to Orkney. Most of the settlement is taken up by a stylish modern self-catering complex, which has given a dose of new life to the once-tawdry locale.

◎ Sights & Activities

Ninety-minute wildlife cruises to the island of Stroma or Duncansby Head cost £18 (late June to August).

Duncansby Head LOOKOUT
Two miles east, Duncansby Head has a small lighthouse and 60m-high cliffs sheltering nesting fulmars. A 15-minute walk through a sheep paddock yields spectacular views of the sea-surrounded monoliths known as Duncansby Stacks.

🛏 Sleeping & Eating

There's a campsite and several B&Bs in and around John O'Groats.

Natural Retreats SELF-CATERING ££
(☑ 0844 384-3166; www.naturalretreats.com; apt £125-250; P🛜🐾) Nearly all of John O'Groats is now taken up by this company, which has erected a series of modern wooden holiday

chalets offering spectacular views, and transformed the old hotel – with the addition of some eye-catchingly colourful giant Scandi-modern 'fish warehouses' – into self-catering apartments. All are stylish and well-equipped. There's a minimum two-night stay.

Teuchters   B&B **££**
(☑01955-611323; www.teuchtersbandb.co.uk; Gills; s/d £40/60; P🖥🛜🐕) By the Gills Bay ferry, 3 miles west of John O'Groats, this purpose-built B&B offers excellent rooms, plenty of space, modern comfort and stunning water views across to Stroma and Orkney. It has a lock-up shed for bikes and motorbikes.

Storehouse   CAFE **£**
(www.naturalretreats.com; light meals £5-10; ⊙8am-5pm; 🛜) The best of the eating options, this modern cafe does pizzas, panini, sandwiches on tasty thick-cut bread, and deli platters with Arran cheeses and local smoked salmon.

ℹ Information

John O'Groats Tourist Office (☑01955-611373; www.visithighlands.com; ⊙11am-3pm Nov-Mar, 10am-4pm Apr, 10am-5pm May & Sep-Oct, 9am-6pm Jun-Aug) Has a fine selection of local novels and nonfiction.

ℹ Getting There & Away

BOAT

From May to September, a passenger ferry (p409) shuttles across to Burwick in Orkney. Three miles west, a car ferry (p409) runs from Gills Bay to St Margaret's Hope in Orkney.

BUS

Stagecoach (p171) runs between John O'Groats and Wick (£3.30, 40 minutes, two to three daily) or Thurso (£4, 40 minutes, regular Monday to Saturday).

Mey

The **Castle of Mey** (www.castleofmey.org.uk; adult/child £11/6.50; ⊙10.20am-5pm May-Sep, last admission 4pm), a big crowd-puller for its Queen Mother connections, is 6 miles west of John O'Groats. The exterior is grand but inside it feels domestic and everything is imbued with the Queen Mum's character. The highlight is the genteel guided tour, with various anecdotes recounted by staff who once worked for her. In the grounds

there's a farm zoo, an unusual walled garden that's worth a stroll and lovely views over the Pentland Firth. The castle normally closes for a couple of weeks at the end of July for royal visits.

On the main road nearby, excellent **Hawthorns** (☑01847-851710; www.thehawthornsbnb.co.uk; s/d £50/75; P🛜🐕) is a modern, easygoing B&B with contemporary artistic flair, a genuine welcome and very spruce, super-spacious ground floor rooms with mini-fridges. There are good options for families. Also just off the main road, **Mey House** (☑01847-851852; www.meyhouse.co.uk; East Mey; r £100-120; ⊙Easter-Oct; P🛜) is beautifully situated among green fields running down to the water with majestic views of Orkney and Dunnet Head. This modern top-drawer sleep is a welcoming, sumptuous place to stay. They've thought it all through: huge, luxurious rooms have arty designer decor, excellent custom-made beds, Nespresso machines, big flatscreens, sound bar and stunning modern bathrooms with shower and tub. There's fast satellite wi-fi and transfers: free for nearby ferries and inexpensive for Wick or Thurso. No toddlers are allowed, as there's an interior balcony.

Dunnet Head

Eight miles east of Thurso a minor road leads to dramatic Dunnet Head, the most northerly point on the British mainland. There are majestic cliffs dropping into the turbulent Pentland Firth, inspiring views of Orkney, basking seals and nesting seabirds below, and a lighthouse built by Robert Louis Stevenson's grandad. Also on the headland, near the main road, is **Mary-Ann's Cottage** (adult/child £3/0.50; ⊙2-4.30pm Jun-Sep). Mary-Ann lived in this 19th-century croft for nigh on a century; in-depth guided tours take you round her humble but cosy farm and house: a fascinating back-in-time experience.

Just west, **Dunnet Bay** offers one of Scotland's finest beaches, backed by high dunes, as well as **Seadrift** (☑01847-821531; ⊙2-5pm Sun-Tue, Thu & Fri May-Sep, from 10.30am Jul & Aug) FREE a small wildlife display, and a caravan-dominated **campsite** (☑01847-821319; www.caravanclub.co.uk; site £5.10, plus adult member/nonmember £6.20/16.20; ⊙Apr-Sep; P) backing the beach.

Thurso

POP 7900

Britain's most northerly mainland town, Thurso makes a handy overnight stop if you're heading west or across to Orkney. There's a pretty town beach, riverbank strolls and a good museum. Ferries for Orkney leave from Scrabster, 2.5 miles away.

◉ Sights

Caithness Horizons   MUSEUM
(www.caithnesshorizons.co.uk; High St; ⊙10am-6pm Mon-Sat, also 11am-4pm Sun Apr-Sep) `FREE` This museum brings Caithness history and lore to life through excellent displays. Fine Pictish cross-slabs greet the visitor downstairs; the main exhibition is a wide-ranging look at local history using plenty of audiovisuals – check out the wistful account of the now-abandoned island of Stroma. There's also a gallery space, an exhibition on the Dounreay nuclear reactor, tourist information and a cafe.

🏌 Activities

Thurso is an unlikely surfing centre but the nearby coast has arguably the best and most regular surf on mainland Britain. There's an excellent right-hand reef break on the eastern side of town, directly in front of the castle (closed to the public), and another shallow reef break 5 miles west at **Brimms Ness**. Pack a drysuit: this is no Hawaii. **Thurso Surf** (☑ 0844 802 5750; www.thursosurf.com; half-day lessons £35-50) gives lessons, normally at Dunnet Bay east of town.

🛏 Sleeping

Sandra's Hostel   HOSTEL £
(☑01847-894575; www.sandras-backpackers.co.uk; 24 Princes St; dm/d/f £16/38/60; [P][@][🛜]) In the heart of town above a chip shop, this budget backpacker option offers en suite dorms, mostly four-berthers with elderly mattresses, a spacious kitchen and traveller-friendly facilities such as internet and help-yourself cereals and toast. It's not luxurious but it's a reliable cheap sleep.

★ Pennyland House   B&B ££
(☑01847-891194; www.pennylandhouse.co.uk; s/d/tr £60/80/90; [P][🛜][🐾]) A super conversion of an historic house, this is a standout B&B choice. It offers phenomenal value for this level of accommodation, with huge oak-furnished rooms named after golf courses: we especially loved St Andrews – superspacious, with a great chessboard-tiled bathroom. Hospitality is enthusiastic and helpful, and there's an inviting breakfast space, garden and terraced area with views across to Hoy. Two-night minimum stay in summer.

Marine   B&B ££
(☑01847-890676; www.themarinethurso.co.uk; 38 Shore St, s £75, d £90-99; [P][🛜]) Tucked away in Thurso's most appealing corner you'll find a top spot right by the pretty town beach, offering spectacular vistas over it and across to Orkney. Surfers can study the breakers from the stunning conservatory-lounge, and rooms are just fabulous, with a designer's touch and a subtle maritime feel. Two rooms in the adjacent house make a great family option.

Murray House   B&B ££
(☑01847-895759; www.murrayhousebb.com; 1 Campbell St; s/d/f £35/70/80; [P][🛜]) A solid, handsome 19th-century town house on a central corner, Murray House gives a good first impression with a genuine welcome and ample dimensions. It continues with smart rooms with solid wooden furniture and modern bathrooms, two of which offer secluded sloping-ceiling spaces on the top floor. No credit cards.

Forss House Hotel   HOTEL £££
(☑01847-861201; www.forsshousehotel.co.uk; s/d/superior d £99/135/175; [P][🛜][🐾]) Tucked into trees 5 miles west of Thurso is a Georgian mansion offering elegant accommodation with both character and style. Sumptuous upstairs rooms are preferable to basement rooms as they have lovely garden views. There are also beautifully appointed suites in the garden itself, providing both privacy and tranquillity. Thoughtful extras like CDs and books in every room add appeal. It's right alongside a beautiful salmon river – the hotel can sort out permits and equipment – and if you've had a chilly day in the waders, some 300 malt whiskies await in the hotel bar.

🍴 Eating

Cups   CAFE £
(www.cups-scrabster.co.uk; Scrabster; light meals £4-8; ⊙10am-4pm Mon-Sat, 11am-4pm Sun) Set in a converted chapel, it's all about teas and delicious home-baked scones and cakes at

this place near the ferry. It also does a nice line in baked potatoes and sandwiches.

Y-Not   PUB £
(www.facebook.com/Ynotthurso; Meadow Lane; mains £7-12; ⊙food 11.30am-9pm; 🐾) Just off the pedestrian strip, this looks grim from outside but gets better once you're in, offering a cavernous split-level eating and lounging space with live music at weekends, and a cosier lounge bar. Food is pretty decent, with good-value pub standards and a few more ambitious daily specials. It also offers accommodation.

Holborn Hotel   BISTRO, PUB ££
(☑01847-892771; www.holbornhotel.co.uk; 16 Princes St; bar meals £8-11, restaurant mains £13-20; ⊙noon-2pm & 6-8pm or 9pm; 🐾) A trendy, comfortable place decked out in light wood, the Holborn contrasts starkly with more traditional Thurso watering holes. In the bar, uncomplicated but decent meals are available, while quality seafood – including delicious home-smoked salmon – is the mainstay of a short but solid menu fleshed out by specials at Red Pepper restaurant, where desserts are excellent too. Service can be slow when busy.

Le Bistro   BISTRO ££
(☑01847-893737; 2 Traill St; lunch £6-10, dinner mains £11-17; ⊙10am-3pm Tue-Sat, 5-9pm Thu-Sat) This eatery buzzes with chatter on weekend evenings as locals of all ages chow down on its simple meat-and-carb creations. What it does, it does well: respectably sized steaks come on a sizzling platter and service has a smile.

★Captain's Galley   SEAFOOD £££
(☑01847-894999; www.captainsgalley.co.uk; Scrabster; 5-course dinner £49; ⊙7-9pm Tue-Sat) 🐟 By the Scrabster ferry, this is classy but friendly, offering a short, seafood-based menu featuring local and sustainably sourced produce prepared in relatively simple ways, letting natural flavours shine through. The chef picks the best fish off the local boats, and the menu describes exactly which fishing grounds your morsel came from. Cheaper, quality fish 'n' chips are also available to take away from 4.30pm until 6.30pm.

❶ Information

Thurso Tourist Office (☑01847-893155; www.visithighlands.com; High St; ⊙10am-6pm Mon-Sat, plus 11am-4pm Sun Apr-Sep) In the Caithness Horizons museum.

❶ Getting There & Around

It's a 2-mile walk from Thurso train station to the ferry at Scrabster; there are buses from Olrig St.

BUS

From Inverness, Stagecoach/Citylink run to Thurso/Scrabster (£19, three hours, five daily). There are buses roughly hourly to Wick, as well as every couple of hours to John O'Groats (£4, 40 minutes, Monday to Saturday). There's one bus on Tuesdays and Fridays westwards to Tongue via Bettyhill; it also runs some Saturdays.

TRAIN

There are four daily trains from Inverness (£19.30, 3¾ hours), with a connecting bus to Scrabster.

NORTH & WEST COAST

Quintessential wilderness such as this, marked by single-track roads, breathtaking emptiness and a wild, fragile beauty, makes this perhaps Scotland's most evocative region. The scenic majesty is never forgotten.

Thurso to Durness

It's 80 winding – and utterly spectacular – coastal miles from Thurso to Durness.

Dounreay & Melvich

Ten miles west of Thurso, Dounreay nuclear power station was the first in the world to supply mains electricity; it's currently being decommissioned. The clean-up is planned to be finished by 2023; it's still a major employment source for the region.

Beyond, Melvich overlooks a fine beach and there are great views from Strathy Point (a 2-mile drive from the coast road, then a 15-minute walk).

Bettyhill
POP 500

Bettyhill is a crofting community of resettled tenant farmers kicked off their land during the Clearances; the spectacular panorama of a sweeping, sandy beach backed by velvety green hills with rocky outcrops makes a sharp contrast to that sad history.

Strathnaver Museum (☑01641-521418; www.strathnavermuseum.org.uk; adult/child £2/1; ☺10am-5pm Mon-Sat Apr-Oct), housed in an old church, tells the story of the Strathnaver Clearances through posters written by local kids. The museum contains Clan Mackay memorabilia, crofting equipment and a boat-shaped container that was used by St Kildans to send messages to the mainland. Outside the back door is the **Farr Stone**, a fine carved Pictish cross-slab.

A good B&B option is **Farr Cottage** (☑01641-521755; www.bettyhillbedandbreakfast. co.uk; Farr; s/d £40/64; **P** ☎), a welcoming white bungalow amid the bleating of sheep and beautiful scenery a mile off the main road (follow signs to Farr). Rooms are modern and compact, with sparkling bathrooms. Good dinners (£16 for two courses) as well as packed lunches are available.

An extraordinary place to eat, **Côte du Nord** (☑01641-521773; www.cotedunord.co.uk; The School House, Kirtomy; degustation £39; ☺7-9pm Wed, Fri & Sat Apr-Oct) 🥢, is in the nearby village of Kirtomy. Brilliantly innovative cuisine, local ingredients and wonderfully whimsical presentation are the highlights of the excellent degustation menu here. It's an unlikely spot to find such a gourmet experience and the chef is none other than the local GP who forages for wild herbs and flavours in between patients. Top value. It's tiny, so reserve well ahead.

Bettyhill **tourist office** (☑01641-521244; www.visithighlands.com; ☺10.45am-4.30pm Mon-Thu, 10.45am-4pm Fri, 11am-4pm Sat) has information on the area and the **cafe** (☑01641-521244; mains £5-9; ☺10.30am-4pm Mon-Thu, 10.30am-4pm & 5-7.30pm Fri, 11am-4pm & 5-7.30pm Sat) here serves home baking and light meals.

Tongue & Around

POP 500

Coldbackie has outstanding views over sandy beaches, turquoise waters and offshore islands. Two miles further is Tongue, with the evocative 14th-century ruins of Castle Varrich, once a Mackay stronghold. To get to the castle, take the trail next to the Royal Bank of Scotland – it's an easy stroll.

🛏 Sleeping & Eating

Kyle of Tongue Hostel & Holiday Park HOSTEL, CAMPSITE £
(☑01847-611789; www.tonguehostelandholiday-park.co.uk; dm £18, d £42-50; **P** ☎) In a won-

derful spot right by the causeway across the Kyle of Tongue, a mile west of town, this is the top budget option in the area, with clean, spacious dorms, great family rooms, views, a decent kitchen and a cosy lounge. It's bright and helpful, and there's a bike shed as well as camping (£7 per person).

Cloisters B&B ££
(☑01847-601286; www.cloistertal.demon.co.uk; Talmine; s/d £38/65; **P** ☎ ☺) Superbly located, this has three en suite twin rooms and absolutely brilliant views over the Kyle of Tongue and offshore islands. Breakfast is in the artistically converted church alongside, and it can do evening meals at weekends. From Tongue, cross the causeway and take the right-hand turn to Melness; Cloisters is a couple of miles down this road.

Tongue Hotel HOTEL ££
(☑01847-611206; www.tonguehotel.co.uk; s/d/superior d £75/110/130; **P** ☎) A stalwart of the north coast, this former hunting lodge is looking very spruce again and offers attractive, roomy chambers, including plush superiors with top views, and classic standards, some with recently renovated bathrooms. It has a restaurant, plus bar meals in the snug Brass Tap basement bar, a good spot to chat with locals. Food is served noon to 2pm and 6pm to 9pm.

Tigh-nan-Ubhal B&B ££
(☑01847-611281; www.tigh-nan-ubhal.com; Main St; d £60-70; **P** ☎ ☺) In the middle of Tongue, and within stumbling distance of two pubs, is this charming B&B. There are snug, loft-style rooms with plenty of natural light, but the basement double with spa is the pick of the bunch – it's the biggest en suite we've seen in northern Scotland. There's also a caravan in the garden and a cheaper room (£50) that shares a bathroom.

Craggan Hotel SCOTTISH ££
(☑01847-601278; www.thecraggan.co.uk; Talmine; mains £10-21; ☺11am-9.15pm) On the side road to Melness, across the causeway from Tongue village, the Craggan Hotel doesn't look much from outside, but go in and you'll find smart, formal service and a menu ranging from exquisite burgers to classy game and local scallops, crab and langoustines, presented beautifully. It also does pizzas and curries to take away and the wine list's not bad either.

ⓘ Getting There & Away

One bus runs to Tongue Tuesday and Friday to/ from Thurso. A postbus runs Monday to Saturday to Lairg. For Durness a bus runs schooldays from Talmine, stopping just west of the causeway across the kyle. It also goes on to Lairg.

Tongue to Durness

From Tongue it's 30 miles to Durness – the main road follows a causeway across the **Kyle of Tongue**, while the old road goes around the head of the kyle, with beautiful views of **Ben Loyal**. Continuing west, you cross a desolate moor to the northern end of freshwater **Loch Hope**. Beyond Loch Hope, as the main road descends towards the sea, there are stunning views over **Loch Eriboll**, Britain's deepest sea inlet and a shelter for ships during WWII.

Durness

POP 400

Scattered Durness (www.durness.org) is wonderfully located, strung out along cliffs rising from a series of pristine beaches. When the sun shines, the effects of blinding white sand, the cry of seabirds and the spring-green-coloured seas combine in a magical way. There are shops, an ATM, petrol and plenty of accommodation options.

◎ Sights & Activities

Walking around the sensational sandy coastline is a highlight, as is a visit to Cape Wrath. Durness' beautiful beaches include Rispond to the east, Sango Sands below town and Balnakeil to the west. At **Balnakeil**, under a mile beyond Durness, a craft village occupies a onetime early-warning radar station. A walk along the beach to the north leads to **Faraid Head**, where you can see puffin colonies in early summer. You can hire bikes from a shed on the square.

Smoo Cave — CAVE

(www.smoocave.org) A mile east of the centre is a path down to Smoo Cave. From the vast main chamber, you can head through to a smaller flooded cavern where a waterfall sometimes cascades from the roof. There's evidence the cave was inhabited about 6000 years ago. You can take a **boat trip** (☑01971-511704; adult/child £4/2; ⊙11am-4pm Apr-May & Sep, 10am-5pm Jun-Aug) to explore a little further into the interior.

OFF THE BEATEN TRACK

DETOUR – FORSINARD & STRATHNAVER

••

Though it's tough to tear yourself away from the coast, we recommend plunging down the A897 just east of Melvich. After 14 miles you reach the railway at **Forsinard**. On the platform is **Forsinard Flows Visitor Centre** (☑01641-571225; www.rspb.org.uk; ⊙9am-5pm Apr-Oct) FREE, with a small nature exhibition. There's a live hen-harrier cam, plus guided walks and 4x4 excursions available – phone for dates. A 1-mile trail introduces you to the Flows peatland; 4 miles north is a 4-mile trail crossing golden plover and dunlin nesting grounds. The deep peat blanket bog is a rare and important habitat, at risk from climate change. A larger visitor centre is in the works.

Past here, the epic peaty moorscapes stir the heart with their desolate beauty. Take a right at Kinbrace onto the B871, which covers more jaw-dropping scenery before arriving at Syre. Turn right to follow the Strathnaver (valley) back to the coast near Bettyhill. Strathnaver saw some of the worst of the Clearances; the **Strathnaver Trail** is a series of numbered points of interest along the valley relating to both this and various prehistoric sites.

Accommodation options on this lonely detour include **Cornmill Bunkhouse** (☑01641-571219; www.achumore. co.uk; dm £15; 🅿), a comfortable, modern hostel occupying a picturesque old mill on a working croft in the middle of nowhere; it's on the A897 4 miles south of the coast road. Turning left instead of right at Syre, you'll eventually reach the remote **Altnaharra Hotel** (☑01549-411222; www.altnaharra.com; s/d/superior d £65/130/150; ⊙Mar-Dec; 🅿🛜🐾).

🛌 Sleeping

Lazy Crofter Bunkhouse — HOSTEL £

(☑01971-511202; www.durnesshostel.com; dm £17.50; 🛜) Durness' best budget accommodation is here, opposite the supermarket. A bothy vibe gives it a very Highland feel. Inviting dorms have plenty of room and lockers, and there's also a sociable shared table for meals and board games, and a great wooden deck with sea views, perfect for midge-free evenings.

Sango Sands Oasis CAMPSITE **£**
(☑ 01971-511222; www.sangosands.com; sites per adult/child £7/5; P 🐾) You couldn't imagine a better location for a campsite: great grassy areas on the edge of cliffs, descending to two lovely sandy beaches. Facilities are good and very clean and there's a pub next door. Electric hookup is an extra £4. You can camp free from November to March but don't complain about the cold.

★ Mackays Rooms HOTEL **££**
(☑ 01971-511202; www.visitdurness.com; d standard/deluxe £125/139; ☉ Easter-Oct; P 🛜 🐾) You really feel you're at the furthest corner of Scotland here, where the road turns through 90 degrees. But whether heading south or east, you'll go far before you find a better place to stay than this haven of Highland hospitality. With big beds, contemporary colours and soft fabrics, it's a romantic spot with top service and numerous boutique details. The same owners run **Croft 103** (☑ 01971-511202; www.croft103.com; Port na Con, Laid; per week £1600; P 🛜), a stunning, modern self-catering option for couples 6 miles east, right on Loch Eriboll. There are two cottages, both immaculate.

Morven B&B **££**
(☑ 01971-511252; s/d £40/60; P 🐾) Cheery owners, a handy next-to-pub location and a serious border collie theme to the decor are key features of this ultra-cosy place. Rooms, which are upstairs and share a downstairs bathroom, have been recently renovated and feel new and super-comfortable. One is especially spacious and has a top coastal vista.

Glengolly B&B B&B **££**
(☑ 01971-511255; www.glengolly.com; d £72-76; ☉ Apr-Oct; P 🛜) This working croft provides comfortable rooms with good space in a traditional B&B atmosphere. Apart from the handy central location, there are other advantages: a superior breakfast menu, with smoked fish and fortified porridge options, and a chance to see a demonstration of sheepdogs at work.

✖ Eating

★ Cocoa Mountain CAFE **£**
(☑ 01971-511233; www.cocoamountain.co.uk; Balnakeil; hot chocolate £3.75, 10 truffles £9.50; ☉ 9am-6pm high season, 10am-5pm low season) 🌊 At the Balnakeil craft village, this up-beat cafe and chocolate maker offers handmade treats including a chilli, lemongrass and coconut white-chocolate truffle, plus many more unique flavours. Tasty espresso and hot chocolate warm the cockles on those blowy horizontal-drizzle days. It offers light lunches and home-baking too, plus chocolate-making workshops.

Sango Sands Oasis PUB FOOD **£**
(www.sangosands.com; mains £7-12; ☉ food noon-2.30pm & 6.30-8pm Mon-Sat, 12.30-3pm & 6.30-8pm Sun) On the clifftops in the centre of town, this pub by the campsite offers great views from its window tables. A cosy restaurant area does decent bar food in generous quantities.

Smoo Cave Hotel PUB **££**
(www.smoocavehotel.co.uk; mains £9-15; ☉ food 11.30am-9.30pm; 🛜) Signposted off the main road at the eastern end of town, this amiable local offers quality bar food in hefty portions. Haddock or daily seafood specials are an obvious and worthwhile choice; there's also a restaurant area with clifftop views.

ℹ Information

Durness Tourist Office (☑ 01971-511368; www.visithighlands.com; ☉ 10am-4.30pm Mon-Sat & 10am-3pm Sun Easter-Jun & Sep, 9.30am-5.30pm Mon-Sat & 10am-4pm Sun Jul-Aug, 10am-4.30pm Mon-Sat Oct) Very helpful. Phone for possible winter opening.

ℹ Getting There & Away

From mid-May to mid-September, one **bus** (☑ 01463-222444; www.decoaches.co.uk) runs daily Monday to Saturday from Durness to Inverness (£16.70) via Ullapool (£12.50). You can take bikes (£6) but they must be booked ahead (during office hours). Another, year-round **bus** (☑ 07782-110007; www.thedurnessbus.com) heads daily Monday to Saturday to Lairg (£7.85), which has a train station. On Saturday a bus heads to either Inverness or Thurso.

Durness to Ullapool

Perhaps Scotland's most spectacular road, the 69 miles connecting Durness to Ullapool is a smorgasbord of dramatic scenery, almost too much to take in. From Durness you pass through a broad heathered valley with the looming grey bulk of Foinaven and Arkle to the southeast. Heather gives way to a rockier landscape of Lewisian gneiss pockmarked with hundreds of small lochans, and gorse-covered hills prefacing the magnificent Torridonian sandstone mountains of Assynt and Coigach, including Suilven's distinctive sugarloaf, ziggurat-like Quinag and pinnacled Stac Pollaidh. The area has been named **Northwest Highlands Geopark** (www.nwhgeopark.com).

Scourie & Handa Island

Scourie (www.scourie.co.uk) is a pretty crofting community halfway between Durness and Ullapool. A few miles north lies **Handa Island** (www.scottishwildlifetrust.org.uk), a nature reserve run by the Scottish Wildlife Trust. The island's western cliffs support important seabird breeding populations. The **boat** (📞07775-625890; adult/child £13.50/7; ⊙outbound 9am-2pm Mon-Sat Apr-Aug, last ferry back 5pm) to Handa leaves from Tarbet Pier, 5.5 miles north of Scourie.

Scourie Lodge (📞01971-502248; www.scourielodge.co.uk; s/d £55/90; ⊙Apr-Oct; 🅿🐾), in a gorgeous building overlooking the bay, has old-style comfort and hospitality in a lovely setting. The welcoming owners have been doing this for decades so they know all about guests' comfort. Rooms are traditionally styled and good-sized. The separate 'coach-house' twin is a lovely space. Best is the spectacular walled garden, a gloriously peaceful haven; palm trees are proof of the Gulf Stream's good works. Cards aren't taken.

Kylesku & Loch Glencoul

Hidden away on the shores of Loch Glencoul, tiny Kylesku served as a ferry crossing on the route north until it was made redundant by beautiful Kylesku Bridge in 1984. It's a good base for walks; you can hire bikes too.

⊙ Sights & Activities

Eas a'Chuil Aluinn   WATERFALL
Five miles southeast of Kylesku, in wild, remote country lies 213m-high Eas a'Chuil Aluinn, Britain's highest waterfall. You can hike to the top of the falls from a parking area at a sharp bend in the main road 3 miles south of Kylesku (6 miles return; allow five hours).

Kylesku Boat Tours   BOAT TOURS
(📞01971-502239; www.rachaelclare.com; adult/child £25/18; ⊙mid-May–Sep) By the Kylesku Hotel, this little boat runs trips out to see

the Eas a'Chuil Aluinn waterfall and local seal colonies.

🛏 Sleeping & Eating

⭐**Kylesku Hotel**   INN ££
(📞01971-502231; www.kyleskuhotel.co.uk; s £68-89, d £97-120; ⊙Mar-Oct; 🛜🐾) 🍴 Run with pride and enthusiasm, this is a great place to stay, or to gorge yourself on delicious sustainable seafood in the convivial bar (mains £10 to £19; food served noon to 9pm). Local langoustines and mussels are a speciality. There's a variety of rooms; the small extra charge for loch views is well worthwhile.

Achmelvich & Around

Not far south of Kylesku, a 30-mile detour on the narrow B869 rewards with spectacular views and fine beaches. From the lighthouse at Point of Stoer, a one-hour cliff walk leads to the **Old Man of Stoer**, a spectacular sea stack. On this stretch is **Clachtoll Beach Campsite** (📞01571-855377; www.clachtollbeachcampsite.co.uk; tent site £6-14, plus per adult/child £4/1; ⊙Apr-Sep; 🅿🛜🐾), a great coastal spot, and **Achmelvich Beach SYHA** (📞01571-844480; www.syha.org.uk; dm/tw £18/46; ⊙Apr-Sep), a whitewashed cottage beside a great beach. Dorms are simple with privacy curtains separating bunks, and there's a sociable common kitchen/eating area. It does breakfasts and sells heat-up dinners; there's a basic summer shop and chip van at the adjacent campsite. It's a 4-mile walk from Lochinver; some buses from Ullapool and Lochinver stop here.

Lochinver & Assynt

With its otherworldly scenery of isolated peaks rising above a sea of crumpled, lochan-spattered gneiss, Assynt epitomises

WORTH A TRIP

CAPE WRATH

Though its name actually comes from the Norse word for 'turning point', there is something daunting and primal about Cape Wrath, the remote north-western point of the British mainland, crowned by a lighthouse built by the famous Stevenson family of engineers and close to the seabird colonies of Clo Mor, Britain's highest coastal cliffs. Getting to Cape Wrath involves a boat ride (☏01971-511284; www.capewrathferry.co.uk; single/return £4/6; ☺Easter–Oct) – passengers and bikes only – across the Kyle of Durness (10 minutes), connecting with a minibus (☏01971-511284; www.visitcapewrath.com; single/return £7/12; ☺Easter–Oct) running 11 miles to the cape (40 minutes). This combination is a friendly but eccentric, sometimes shambolic service with limited capacity, so plan on waiting in high season, and ring beforehand to make sure the ferry is running. The ferry leaves from two miles southwest of Durness, and runs twice or more daily from April to September. If you eschew the minibus, it's a spectacular 11-mile ride or hike from boat to cape over bleak scenery occasionally used by the Ministry of Defence as a firing range. A cafe at the lighthouse serves soup and sandwiches.

An increasingly popular walking route, the Cape Wrath Trail (www.capewrathtrail.co.uk), runs from Fort William up to Cape Wrath (200 miles). It's unmarked, so you may want to do it guided – C-n-Do (www.cndoscotland.com) is one operator – or buy the *Cape Wrath Trail* guidebook (www.cicerone.co.uk).

the northwest's wild magnificence. Glaciers have sculpted the hills of Suilven (731m), Canisp (846m), Quinag (808m) and Ben More Assynt (998m) into strange, wonderful silhouettes.

Lochinver is the main settlement, a busy little fishing port that's a popular port of call with its laid-back atmosphere, good facilities and striking scenery.

🏃 Activities

NorWest Sea Kayaking
KAYAKING

(☏01571-844281; www.norwestseakayaking.com) This outfit offers three-day introductory sea-kayaking courses and guided kayaking tours around the Summer Isles and in the Lochinver/Ullapool area. It also hires kayaks in Lochinver.

🛏 Sleeping & Eating

Veyatie
B&B ££

(☏01571-844424; www.veyatie-scotland.co.uk; Lochinver; s/d £70/90; ☐🐾📶) This choice, at the end of the road across the bay, has perhaps the finest views of all, best enjoyed from the grassy garden or conservatory lounge on a sunny day. There are two enormous rooms with lovely plush beds, great en suites, flatscreens and iPod docks. Breakfast is highly recommended.

★ Albannach
HOTEL £££

(☏01571-844407 www.thealbannach.co.uk; Lochinver; s/d/ste incl dinner £220/300/380; ☺Tue-Sun Mar-Dec; ☐📶) 🍴 One of the Highlands' top places to stay and eat, this hotel combines old-fashioned country-house elements – steep creaky stairs, stuffed animals, fireplaces, and noble antique furniture – with strikingly handsome showroom-class rooms that range from a sumptuous four-poster to more modern spaces with things like underfloor heating and, in one case, a private deck with outdoor spa.

The restaurant serves a table d'hôte (tailored to your needs) that's famed throughout Scotland (£68 for nonresidents); the welcoming owners grow lots of their own produce and focus on organic and local ingredients. Glorious views, spacious grounds and great walks in easy striking distance make this a perfect base.

Lochinver Larder & Riverside Bistro
CAFE, BISTRO ££

(☏01571-844356; www.lochinverlarder.co.uk; 3 Main St, Lochinver; pies £5, mains £11-20; ☺10am-7.45pm, to 8.30pm Jun-Sep; 📶) This offers an outstanding menu of inventive food made with local produce. The bistro turns out delicious seafood dishes in the evening, while the takeaway counter (open till 7pm) sells delicious pies with a wide range of gourmet fillings: try the wild boar and apricot. It also does quality meals to take away and heat up: great for hostellers and campers.

Caberfeidh
PUB ££

(☑01571-844321; www.caberfeidhlochinver.co.uk; Main St, Lochinver; tapas £6-8; ⊘food noon-2.30pm & 6-8.45pm; 🕿) ⊘ This convivial pub (with riverside beer garden) serves a range of real ales and some excellent food. The menu is based around tapas-sized portions like venison meatballs or local langoustines. A sustainable, low food-mile philosophy is at work and the quality shines through.

🛍 Shopping

Highland Stoneware
CERAMICS

(www.highlandstoneware.com; Lochinver; ⊘9am-5.30pm Mon-Fri Jan-Easter, 9am-6pm Mon-Fri & 9am-5pm Sat Easter-Oct, plus 11am-3pm Sun Jun-Sep) Using local landscapes as inspiration, Highland Stoneware ensures you can relive the northwest's majesty every time you have a cuppa. Even better are the mosaics outside, especially the car. You can watch the potters at work here on weekdays.

ℹ Information

Assynt Visitor Centre (☑01571-844194; www.discoverassynt.co.uk; Main St; ⊘10am-4.30pm Mon-Sat & 11am-3pm Sun Easter-Jun, Sep &Oct, 9.30am-5pm Mon-Sat & 10am-4pm Sun Jul & Aug) Has leaflets on hill walks in the area and a display on the story of Assynt.

ℹ Getting There & Away

There are usually one to three bus services of some sort between Ullapool and Lochinver (50 minutes to 1½ hours) Mondays to Saturdays, including a summer bus that goes on to Durness.

Coigach

The region south of Assynt, west of the main A835 road from Ullapool to Ledmore Junction, is known as Coigach (www.coigach.com). A lone, single-track road penetrates this wilderness, leading through gloriously wild scenery to remote settlements. At the western end of Loch Lurgainn, a branch leads north to Lochinver, a scenic backroad so narrow and twisting that it's nicknamed the **Wee Mad Road**.

Coigach is a wonderland for walkers and wildlife enthusiasts, with a patchwork of sinuous silver lochs dominated by the isolated peaks of Cul Mor (849m), Cul Beag (769m), Ben More Coigach (743m) and Stac Pollaidh (613m). The main settlement is the straggling township of **Achiltibuie**,

15 miles from the main road, with the gorgeous Summer Isles moored just off the coast, and silhouettes of mountains skirting the bay.

👁 Sights & Activities

Stac Pollaidh
WALKING

Despite its diminutive size, Stac Pollaidh provides one of the most exciting hill walks in the Highlands, with some good scrambling on its narrow sandstone crest. Begin at the car park overlooking Loch Lurgainn, 5 miles west of the A835, and follow a clearly marked and well-made footpath around the eastern end of the hill to ascend from the far side; return by the same route (3 miles return, two to four hours).

☞ Tours

Summer Isles Seatours
BOAT TOURS

(☑07927-920592; www.summerisles-seatours.co.uk; adult/child £25/15; ⊘Mon-Sat May-Sep) Three cruises daily to the Summer Isles from Achiltibuie, with time ashore on Tanera Mor, where the post office issues its own Summer Isles stamps.

🛏 Sleeping & Eating

Achininver SYHA
HOSTEL £

(☑01854-622482; www.syha.org.uk; dm £18; ⊘May-Aug) The rudimentary 20-bed Achininver hostel, a half-mile walk off the main road, is designed for walkers and outdoor enthusiasts. Its remote, serene location has to be one of the country's best.

★ Summer Isles Hotel
HOTEL £££

(☑01854-622282; www.summerisleshotel.co.uk; Achiltibuie; s £125-190, d £165-240; ⊘Easter-Oct; P🕿🐾) This is a special place, with wonderfully romantic, commodious rooms – one themed on Charlie Chaplin, who stayed here, others suites in separate cottages – plus cracking views and a snug bar with outdoor seating. 'Courtyard view' rooms are darkish: it's worth upgrading to one with vistas. It's the perfect spot for a romantic getaway or some quality time off life's treadmill.

The restaurant (noon to 3pm and 6pm to 9pm; dinner £59) is of high quality, with local lobster usually featuring, plus the renowned cheese and dessert trolleys – and there's a great wine list considering you're in the middle of nowhere.

ⓘ Getting There & Around

There are one to two daily buses Monday to Saturday from Ullapool to Badenscallie (half a mile from Achininver SYHA) and Achiltibuie (1¼ hours).

Ullapool

POP 1500

This pretty port on the shores of Loch Broom is the largest settlement in Wester Ross and one of the most alluring spots in the Highlands, a wonderful destination in itself as well as a gateway to the Western Isles. Offering a row of whitewashed cottages arrayed along the harbour and special views of the loch and its flanking hills, the town has a very distinctive appeal. The harbour served as an emigration point during the Clearances, with thousands of Scots watching Ullapool recede behind them as the diaspora cast them across the world.

◉ Sights & Activities

Ullapool is a great centre for walking. Good walking books and leaflets are available at the tourist office.

Ullapool Museum MUSEUM
(www.ullapoolmuseum.co.uk; 7 West Argyle St; adult/child £3.50/free; ⏱10am-5pm Mon-Sat Apr-Oct) Housed in a converted Telford church, this museum relates the prehistoric, natural and social history of the town and Loch-broom area, with a particular focus on the emigration to Nova Scotia and other places. There's also a genealogy section if you want to trace your Scottish roots.

An Talla Solais GALLERY
(☎01854-612310; www.antallasolais.org; Market St; ⏱10am-4pm Wed-Sun mid-Apr–mid-Oct) FREE This community-run gallery stages changing exhibitions of works by Highland artists, from paintings and photography to ceramics and textiles. Opening hours vary, so check the website for exhibition dates and times. There's a decent cafe here.

☞ Tours

Seascape BOAT TOURS
(☎01854-633708; www.sea-scape.co.uk; adult/child £30/20; ⏱Jun-Aug) Runs enjoyable two-hour tours out to the Summer Isles in an orange rigid inflatable boat (RIB).

Summer Queen BOAT TOURS
(☎01854-612472; www.summerqueen.co.uk; ⏱Mon-Sat May-Sep) The stately *Summer Queen* takes you out (weather permitting) around Isle Martin (£20/10 per adult/child, two hours) or to the Summer Isles (£30/15, four hours), with a stop on Tanera Mor.

✫ Festivals & Events

Ullapool Guitar Festival MUSIC
(www.ullapoolguitarfestival.com) Held in early October, this features a series of concerts and workshops over a weekend, with late-night club sessions and some high-quality musicians on show.

🛏 Sleeping

Note that during summer Ullapool is very busy and finding accommodation can be tricky – book ahead.

Ullapool SYHA HOSTEL £
(☎01854-612254; www.syha.org.uk; Shore St; dm/tw/q £20/45/88; ⏱Apr-Oct; 🛜) You've got to hand it to the SYHA; it's chosen some very sweet locations for its hostels. This is as close to the water as it is to the town's best pub: about four seconds' walk. The front rooms have harbour views but the busy dining area and little lounge are also good spots for contemplating the water.

Ceilidh Clubhouse HOSTEL £
(☎01854-612103; www.theceilidhplace.com; West Lane; s/tw/f £23-30/58/68; 🅿🛜) Opposite the Ceilidh Place, which runs it, this annexe offers no-frills accommodation for walkers, journeyers and staff. A big building, it has hostel-style rooms with sturdy bunks and basins. Though shared showers and toilets are a little institutional, rooms are private: if you're woken by snores, at least they'll be familiar ones. Prices drop substantially outside high summer.

Broomfield Holiday Park CAMPSITE £
(☎01854-612020; www.broomfieldhp.com; West Lane; tent sites £15-19, sites solo campers £8-12; ⏱Apr-Sep; 🅿🛜🐾) Great grassy headland location, very close to centre. Midge-busting machines in action.

★ West House B&B ££
(☎01854-613126; www.ullapoolaccommodation. net; West Argyle St; s £60, d £75-85; 🅿🛜) 🍃 Slap bang in the centre, this solid white house, once a manse, offers excellent rooms with contemporary style and great bathrooms.

Breakfast is continental: rooms come with a fridge stocked with fresh fruit, cheeses, yoghurts, homemade bread, proper coffee and juice so you can eat at your leisure in your own chamber. Most rooms have great views, as well as iPod docks and other conveniences. The owners also have tempting self-catering options in the Ullapool area.

★**Tamarin Lodge**   B&B **££**
(☑ 01854-612667; www.tamarinullapool.com; The Braes; s/d £42/84; P 🕏 🌶) Effortlessly elegant modern architecture in this hilltop house is noteworthy in its own right, but the glorious vistas over the hills opposite and water far below are unforgettable. All rooms face the view; some have a balcony, and all are very spacious, quiet and utterly relaxing, with unexpected features and gadgets. The great lounge and benevolent hosts are a delight. Follow signs for Braes from the Inverness road.

Point Cottage   B&B **££**
(☑ 01854-335062; www.pointcottagebandb.co.uk; 22 West Shore St; d £70; P 🕏) If you've just arrived by ferry, you've probably already admired Ullapool's line of shorefront cottages; this is one of them. It's a romantic option for couples, with impeccable modernised rooms with plush bedding, preserving their cottage feel. An upmarket continental breakfast is served in-room: it's a pleasure to eat at your little window table with loch views.

★**Ceilidh Place**   HOTEL **£££**
(☑ 01854-612103; www.theceilidhplace.com; 14 West Argyle St; s £58-92, d £140-164; ⊙ Feb-Dec; P 🕏 🌶) This hotel, which includes a bookshop, is a celebration of Scottish culture: we're talking literature and traditional music, not tartan and Nessie dolls. It's one of the Highlands' more unusual and delightful places to stay. Rooms go for character over modernity: instead of TV they come with a selection of books chosen by Scottish literati, eclectic artwork and cosy touches. The sumptuous lounge has sofas, chaises longues and an honesty bar.

✕ **Eating & Drinking**

Arch Inn   PUB **££**
(☑ 01854-612454; www.thearchinn.co.uk; West Shore St; mains £10-18; ⊙ food noon-2.30pm & 5-9pm Mon-Sat, 12.30-2.30pm & 5-9pm Sun; 🕏) There's pleasing pub food to be had at this shorefront establishment, where the cosy bar and restaurant area dishes up generous well-presented mains that range from tender chicken and fish dishes to more advanced blackboard specials with local seafood a highlight. Service is helpful and efficient. The outdoor tables right beside the lapping water are a top spot for a pint.

Ceilidh Place   SCOTTISH **££**
(☑ 01854-612103; 14 West Argyle St; mains £10-18; ⊙ 8am-9pm Feb-Dec; 🕏) Serves up inventive dishes that focus on fresh local seafood backed up by stews, plus lighter meals like pies and burgers during the day. Presentation and quality are high, and it's an atmospheric place, cosy with outdoor seating, good wines by the glass and regular live music and events.

Ferry Boat Inn   PUB **££**
(☑ 01854-612431; www.ferry-boat-inn.com; Shore St; mains £9-15; ⊙ food 7.30am-9.30pm; 🕏) Known as the FBI, this character-laden waterfront inn is a little less traditional looking these days with its bleached wood and nonstained carpet, but it's still a place where locals and visitors mingle. Management and chefs seem to change frequently, but if things are going well it's an atmospheric venue for local seafood. Drop by for a drink either way.

ℹ️ **Information**

Ullapool Bookshop (☑ 01854-612918; www.ullapoolbookshop.co.uk; Quay St; ⊙ 9am-6pm Mon-Sat, 10am-5pm Sun) Lots of books on Scottish topics and local maps. Internet access £1 per 15 minutes.

Ullapool Tourist Office (☑ 01854-612486; ullapool@visitscotland.com; Argyle St; ⊙ 9.30am-5pm Mon-Sat Easter-Oct, plus 10am-3pm Sun Jun-Aug) Can book ferries and buses.

Ullapool Library (☑ 01854-612543; Mill St; ⊙ 9am-5pm Mon-Fri, plus 6-8pm Tue & Thu, closed Mon & Wed during holidays; 🕏) Free internet access.

ℹ️ **Getting There & Around**

Citylink (www.citylink.co.uk) has one to three daily buses from Inverness to Ullapool (£12.80, 1½ hours), connecting with the Lewis ferry (p209).

Ullapool to Kyle of Lochalsh

Although it's less than 50 miles as the crow flies from Ullapool to Kyle of Lochalsh, it's more like 150 miles along the circuitous coastal road – but don't let that put you off. It's a deliciously remote region and there are fine views of beaches and bays backed by mountains all the way along.

If you're hurrying to Skye, head inland on the A835 (towards Inverness) and catch up with the A832 further south, near Garve.

Braemore & Around

Twelve miles southeast of Ullapool at Braemore, the A832 doubles back towards the coast as it heads for Gairloch (the A835 continues southeast across the wild, sometimes snowbound, **Dirrie More** pass to Garve and Inverness).

Just west of the junction, a car park gives access to the **Falls of Measach**, which spill 45m into spectacularly deep and narrow **Corrieshalloch Gorge**. You can cross the gorge on a swaying suspension bridge, and walk west for 250m to a viewing platform that juts out dizzyingly above a sheer drop. The thundering falls and misty vapours rising from the gorge are very impressive.

Gairloch & Around

POP 1000

Gairloch is a group of villages (comprising Achtercairn, Strath and Charlestown) around the inner end of a loch of the same name. Gairloch is a good base for whale- and dolphin-watching excursions and the surrounding area has beautiful sandy beaches, good trout fishing and birdwatching.

◉ Sights & Activities

The B8056 runs along Loch Gairloch's southern shore, past the cute little harbour of **Badachro**, to end at the gorgeous pink-sand beach of **Red Point** – a perfect picnic spot. Another coastal road leads north from Gairloch 11 miles to the settlement of **Melvaig**. From here a private road (open to walkers and cyclists) continues 3 miles to **Rua Reidh Lighthouse** (building and grounds off limits to non-guests).

Gairloch Heritage Museum   MUSEUM
(www.gairlochheritagemuseum.org; adult/child £4/1; ⊙10am-5pm Mon-Fri & 11am-3pm Sat Apr-Oct) This has interesting displays on life in the West Highlands from Pictish times to the present, including locally built fishing boats and a faithful re-creation of a crofter's cottage.

Inverewe Garden   GARDENS
(NTS; www.nts.org.uk; adult/concession £10.50/7.50; ⊙10am-3pm Nov-Mar, to 5pm Apr & Sep, to 5.30pm May, to 6pm Jun-Aug, to 4pm Oct) Six miles north of Gairloch, this splendid garden is a welcome splash of colour on this otherwise bleak coast. The climate here is warmed by the Gulf Stream, which allowed Osgood MacKenzie to create this exotic woodland garden in 1862. There are free guided tours on weekdays at 1.30pm (March to October). The cafe has great cakes.

Gairloch Marine Wildlife Centre   NATURE DISPLAY
(☑01445-712636; www.porpoise-gairloch.co.uk; Pier Rd; ⊙10am-4pm Easter-Oct) 🐾 FREE This has audiovisual and interactive displays, lots of charts, photos and knowledgeable staff. **Cruises** (☑01445-712636; www.porpoise-gairloch.co.uk; adult/child £20/15) run from the centre up to three times daily (weather permitting); during the two-hour trips you may see basking sharks, porpoises and minke whales. The crew collects data on water temperature and conditions, and monitors cetacean populations, so you are subsidising important research.

Gairloch Trekking Centre   HORSE RIDING
(☑01445-712652; www.gairlochtrekkingcentre.co.uk; Flowerdale Mains; ⊙Fri-Wed Mar-Oct) Offers riding lessons, pony trekking and guided treks in the ample grounds of Gairloch Estate.

🚩 Tours

Hebridean Whale Cruises   BOAT TOURS
(☑01445-712458; www.hebridean-whale-cruises.com; Pier Rd; cruises 2½/4hr £45/75) Based at the harbour, this set-up runs close-in trips to see seals, otters and seabirds, or trips further out to feeding grounds where you might see dolphins, minke whales or orca. It operates two boats, one a cabin cruiser, the other a zippy rigid inflatable.

🛏 Sleeping

Wayside Guest House   B&B £
(☑01445-712008; issmith@msn.com; Strath; s/d £40/60; 🐾) Cosy and compact, this offers comfortable and welcoming accommodation in Strath, the spiritual heart of Gairloch. The spotless rooms come with either en suite bathroom or fabulous view; you decide what's more important. It offers excellent value and hosts full of kind thoughts.

Rua Reidh Lighthouse LODGE ££

(☎ 01445-771263; www.stayatalighthouse.co.uk; d/f £60/110; ☺ Easter–Oct; P ﹖ ☻) Three miles down a private road beyond Melvaig (11 miles north of Gairloch), this simple, excellent lodge gives a taste of a lighthouse keeper's life. It's a wild, lonely location great for walking and birdwatching. Breakfast is included and tasty evening meals are available. It's open Easter to October, but there's a self-catering apartment open almost year-round. Book well ahead.

Gairloch View Guest House B&B ££

(☎ 01445-712666; www.gairlochview.com; s/d £55/80; P ﹖) The unique selling point of this unassuming modern house is a patio with a stunning view over the sea to Skye – a view you can also enjoy from your breakfast table. The three bedrooms, with plenty of natural light, are comfortably furnished in classic country style, and the residents' lounge has satellite TV and a small library of books and games.

✗ Eating

Mountain Coffee Company CAFE £

(Strath Sq, Strath; light meals £4-7; ☺ 9am-5.30pm, shorter hours low season; ﹖) ✦ More the sort of place you'd expect to find on the gringo trail in the Andes, this offbeat and cosy spot is a shrine to all things mountaineering and travelling. It sells tasty savoury bagels, home baking and a range of decadent coffees and hot chocolates. The conservatory is the place to lap up the sun, while the attached Hillbillies Bookshop is worth a browse.

Badachro Inn PUB ££

(☎ 01445-741255; www.badachroinn.com; Badachro; light meals £5-8, mains £11-16; ☺ food noon-3pm & 6-9pm, from 12.30pm Sun; P) ✦ Set in an enchanting location, overlooking a sheltered yacht harbour at Badachro, 5 miles southwest of Gairloch, this old Highland inn serves local real ales and platters of fresh local seafood: crab, scallops and langoustines, some landed right alongside. There are also tasty panini and sandwiches; eating out on the deck on a sunny day here is a real treat.

Na Mara BISTRO ££

(www.namararestaurant.co.uk; Strath Sq, Strath; mains £10-18; ☺ 5-8pm Thu-Tue; ♿) On the square in Strath, this brings a light, cheery smile to west-coast eating with its inclusive menu that starts at burgers, pastas and curries and includes steaks and seafood dishes

in classic bistro style with a range of influences. Good value, but check opening times ahead.

ⓘ Information

Gairloch Tourist Office (☎ 01445-712071; ☺ 10am-4pm Mon-Sat Oct–Apr, 10am-5pm Mon-Sat & 10am-4pm Sun May-Sep) In the wooden Gale Centre, on the road through town, this has good walking pamphlets. Opening hours are slightly variable.

ⓘ Getting There & Away

Public transport to Gairloch is very limited. **Westerbus** (☎ 01445-712255) runs Monday to Saturday to/from Inverness (£10, 2¼ hours), and Thursday to/from Ullapool.

Loch Maree & Around

Stretching 12 miles between Poolewe and Kinlochewe, **Loch Maree** is considered one of Scotland's prettiest lochs. At its southern end, tiny **Kinlochewe** makes a good base for outdoor activities. **Beinn Eighe Visitor Centre** (☎ 01445-760254; www.nnr-scotland.org.uk/beinn-eighe; ☺ 9am-5pm Easter-Oct; ♿) FREE, a mile north, has interactive kid-friendly displays on local geography, ecology, flora and fauna, and provides information on local walking routes, including the **Beinn Eighe Mountain Trail**. This is a waymarked 4-mile return walk to a plateau and cairn on the side of Beinn Eighe, offering magnificent views over Loch Maree.

Kinlochewe Hotel (☎ 01445-760253; www.kinlochewehotel.co.uk; Kinlochewe; dm £15.50, s £50, d £90-98; P ﹖ ☻) ✦ is a well-run, welcoming place that's very walker-friendly. As well as comfortable, spotless rooms – 'economy' ones share a bathroom – there are nice features like a handsome lounge well stocked with books, a great bar with real ales on tap and a thoughtful menu of locally sourced food. There's also a bunkhouse with one no-frills 12-bed dorm (BYO sleeping bag and towels), a decent kitchen and clean bathrooms.

The **Whistle Stop Cafe** (Kinlochewe; meals £6-13; ☺ 9am-9pm Mon-Sat Apr-Oct, to 6pm midweek Mar & Nov; ﹖), a colourful presence in the former village hall, is a tempting place to drop by for anything from a coffee to enticing bistro fare. It's very friendly, and used to pumping life back into chilled walkers and cyclists. Unlicensed, but you can take your own wine.

Torridon & Around

The road southwest from Kinlochewe passes through Glen Torridon, amid some of Britain's most beautiful scenery. Carved by ice from massive layers of ancient sandstone that takes its name from the region, the mountains here are steep, shapely and imposing, whether flirting with autumn mists, draped in dazzling winter snows, or reflected in the calm blue waters of Loch Torridon on a summer day.

The road reaches the sea at spectacularly sited Torridon village, then continues westwards to lovely Shieldaig, which boasts an attractive main street of whitewashed houses right on the water, before turning south to Applecross, Lochcarron and Kyle of Lochalsh.

⊙ Sights & Activities

The Torridon Munros – Liathach (1054m; pronounced 'lee-agakh', Gaelic for 'the Grey One'), Beinn Eighe (1010m; 'ben ay', 'the File') and Beinn Alligin (986m; 'the Jewelled Mountain') – are big, serious mountains for experienced hill walkers only. Though not technically difficult, their ascents are long and committing, often over rough and rocky terrain. Information is available at the NTS Countryside Centre (NTS; ☑ 01445-791221; www.nts.org.uk; ☉ 10am-5pm Sun-Fri Easter-Sep) FREE in Torridon; rangers offer guided mountain walks (£25 per person, weekdays only, advance booking necessary) in July and August. You can buy food here for a nearby red-deer herd.

Torridon Sea Tours   BOAT TRIPS
(☑ 01520-755353; www.torridonseatours.com) Runs various trips from Shieldaig, including 90-minute morning or evening cruises on Loch Torridon (adult/child £25/15) and half- or full-day cruises around offshore islands.

🛏 Sleeping & Eating

There's a free campsite at the entrance to Torridon village and a decent shop and cafe in the village itself.

Torridon SYHA   HOSTEL £
(☑ 01445-791284; www.syha.org.uk; dm £20, tw £45-49; ☉ Mar-Oct, plus weekends Nov-Feb; P @ 🛜 🐾) This spacious hostel has enthusiastic, can-do management and sits in a magnificent location, surrounded by spectacular mountains. Spacious dorms and privates (twins have single beds) are allied to a huge

kitchen and convivial lounge area, with ales on sale. It's a very popular walking base, with great advice from the in-house mountain rescue team, so book ahead. As well as breakfasts, packed lunches and heat-up dinners are offered.

Ferroch   B&B ££
(☑ 01445-791451; www.ferroch.co.uk; s/d £75/98; P 🛜) Just outside town, on the road to Shieldaig, this offers most memorable vistas from its pleasant garden and top-floor double. All rooms are very spacious and comfortable, and it's a welcoming place, with a lounge with fire and music, afternoon tea served on the grass and excellent breakfasts and dinners featuring homemade yoghurt, cheese and bread, among other goodies. No cards.

Torridon Inn   INN ££
(☑ 01445-791242; www.thetorridon.com; s/d/q £100/110/175; ☉ daily May-Oct, Thu-Sun Nov, Dec, Mar & Apr, closed Jan & Feb; P 🛜 🐾) Adjacent to The Torridon hotel, this convivial but upmarket walkers' hang-out offers excellent modern rooms that vary substantially in size and layout, and a sociable bar offering all-day food. Rooms for groups (up to six) offer more value.

★ The Torridon   HOTEL £££
(☑ 01445-791242; www.thetorridon.com; r standard/superior/master £235/290/440; ☉ closed Jan, plus Mon & Tue Nov, Dec, Feb & Mar; P @ 🛜 🐾) If you prefer the lap of luxury to the sound of rain beating on your tent, head for this lavish Victorian shooting lodge with a romantic lochside location. Sumptuous contemporary rooms with awe-inspiring views and top bathrooms and a cheery Highland cow atop the counterpane couldn't be more inviting. This is one of Scotland's top country hotels, always luxurious but never pretentious.

Master suites are lavish in size and comfort, with a more classic decor and bay windows making the most of the panoramas. Service is excellent, with muddy boots positively welcomed, and dinners are sumptuous affairs, open to non-residents (£55). Friendly staff can organise any number of activities on land or water.

Tigh an Eilean Hotel   HOTEL £££
(☑ 01520-755251; www.tighaneilean.co.uk; Shieldaig; s/d £80/160; ☉ Feb-Dec; 🛜) With a lovely waterfront position, this is an appealing destination for a relaxing stay, offering not luxury but comfortable old-style rooms.

You'll feel it offers better value if you manage to get a loch-view one – the vistas are gloriously soothing. Service is very helpful, and there's a cosy lounge with honesty bar. Dinner (£45) features regional produce, local seafood and delicious Scottish cheeses. Book ahead in winter.

Shieldaig Bar and Coastal Kitchen SEAFOOD ££

(www.shieldaigbarandcoastalkitchen.co.uk; Shieldaig; mains £9-17; ⊘ noon-2.30pm & 6-9pm Sep-May, noon-9pm Jun-Aug) This attractive pub has real ales and waterside tables plus a great upstairs dining room and outdoor deck for more casual dining, with an emphasis on local seafood and bistro-style meat dishes like steak-frites or sausages and mash. Blackboard specials feature the daily catch.

Applecross

POP 200

The delightfully remote seaside village of Applecross feels like an island retreat due to its isolation and the magnificent views of Raasay and the hills of Skye that set the pulse racing, particularly at sunset. On a clear day it's an unforgettable place, though the campsite and pub fill to the brim in school holidays.

A road leads here 25 winding miles from Shieldaig, but more spectacular (accessed from further south on the A896) is the magnificent **Bealach na Ba** (626m; Pass of the Cattle), the third-highest motor road in the UK, and the longest continuous climb. Originally built in 1822, it climbs steeply and hair-raisingly via hairpin bends perched over sheer drops, with gradients up to 25%, then drops dramatically to the village with views of Skye. **Mountain & Sea Guides** (☑ 01250-744394; www.applecross.uk.com) runs short sea-kayaking, hill-walking and mountaineering excursions, as well as more serious expeditions.

🛏 Sleeping & Eating

Applecross Campsite CAMPSITE £

(☑ 01520-744268; www.applecross.uk.com; sites per adult/child £9/4.50, 2-person hut £45; ⊘ Mar-Oct; ᴾ ᴬ ᴬ) Offers green grassy plots, cute little wooden cabins and a good greenhouse-like cafe.

★ **Applecross Inn** INN ££

(☑ 01520-744262; www.applecross.uk.com; Shore St; s/d £85/130, mains £9-18; ⊘ food noon-9pm;

ᴾ ᴬ ᴬ) 🍴 The hub of the spread-out community and the perfect shoreside location for a sunset pint, this inn is famous for its food – mostly daily blackboard specials concentrate on local seafood and venison – and sports seven snug bedrooms. All have a view of the Skye hills and the sea.

Lochcarron

POP 900

Appealing, whitewashed Lochcarron is a veritable metropolis in these parts, with good services and a long lochside shoreline.

The **Old Manse** (☑ 01520-722208; www.the-oldmaselochcarron.com; Church St; s/d £40/65, tw with loch view £75; ᴾ ᴬ ᴬ) is a top-notch Scottish guesthouse, beautifully appointed and in a prime lochside position. Rooms are traditional in style and simply gorgeous with elegant furniture. Those overlooking the water are larger and well worth the extra tenner. Evening meals (£12 for two courses) are available. Take the road towards Strome.

On the main waterfront road through town, **Rockvilla** (☑ 01520-722379; www.therockvilla.com; Main St; s £61, d £72-86; ⊘ Easter-Sep; ᴾ ᴬ) has very welcoming hosts and lovely modernised rooms with heaps of space and dreamy views over the water. The restaurant here serves inventive bistro fare at fair prices.

Four miles west of town on the A896, **Kishorn Seafood Bar** (☑ 01529-733240; www.kishornseafoodbar.co.uk; A896, Kishorn; mains £10-16; ⊘ 10am-5pm Mar-Nov, to 9pm Fri & Mon-Sat Jul-Sep) 🍴 is a cute pale-blue bungalow which serves the freshest of local seafood simply and well, with very fair prices. Views are spectacular, and you've got the satisfaction of knowing that much of your meal was caught in Loch Kishorn just below.

Plockton

POP 400

Idyllic little **Plockton** (www.plockton.com), with its perfect cottages lining a perfect bay, looks like it was designed as a film set. And it has indeed served as just that – scenes from *The Wicker Man* (1973) were filmed here, and the village became famous as the location for the 1990s TV series *Hamish Macbeth*.

With all this picture-postcard perfection, it's hardly surprising that Plockton is a tourist hot spot, crammed with day trippers and holidaymakers in summer. But there's no denying its appeal, with 'palm trees' (actually hardy New Zealand cabbage palms) lining the waterfront, a thriving small-boat sailing scene and several good places to stay, eat and drink. The big event of the year is the **Plockton Regatta** (www.plockton-sailing.com), a fortnight of boat races culminating in a concert and *ceilidh*.

🏃 Activities

Hire canoes and rowboats on the waterfront to explore the bay.

Sea Kayak Plockton   KAYAKING
(☑ 01599-544422; www.seakayakplockton.co.uk) Offers everything from beginners' lessons to multi-day trips around Skye to highly challenging odysseys right out to St Kilda.

👉 Tours

Calum's Seal Trips   BOAT TOURS
(☑ 01599-544306; www.calums-sealtrips.com; adult/child £10/6; ⊙ Apr-Oct) Runs seal-watching cruises – there are swarms of the slippery fellas just outside the harbour, and the trip comes with an excellent commentary. Trips leave several times daily. You may even spot otters, and there's a longer dolphin-watching trip available.

🛏 Sleeping

The village has some excellent places to stay, but it's popular. Best to book ahead.

Tigh Arran   B&B £
(☑ 01599-544307; www.plocktonbedandbreakfast. com; Duirinish; s/d £50/60; P 🛜 🐾) It's hard to decide which is better at this sweet spot in Duirinish, two miles from the Plockton shorefront. The warm personal welcome is a highlight, but it's matched by absolutely stunning views across to Skye. All three of the en suite rooms – with appealing family options – enjoy them, as does the comfy lounge. A top spot, far from stress and noise; and great value.

Plockton Station Bunkhouse   HOSTEL £
(☑ 01599-544235; mickcoe@btInternet.com; dm £15; P 🛜) Airily set in the former train station (the new one is opposite), this has cosy four-bed dorms, a garden and kitchen-lounge with plenty of light and good perspectives over the frenetic comings-and-goings (OK, that last bit's a lie) of the platforms below. It can get a bit cramped when there are lots of folk in. The owners also do good-value B&B

(single/double £30/50) next door in inaccurately named 'Nessun Dorma'.

Plockton Hotel   INN ££
(☑ 01599-544274; www.plocktonhotel.co.uk; 41 Harbour St; s/d £90/130, cottage s/d £55/80; 🛜 🐾) Black-painted Plockton Hotel is one of those classic Highland spots that manages to make everyone happy, whether it's thirst, hunger or fatigue that brings you knocking. Assiduously tended rooms are a delight, with excellent facilities and thoughtful touches. Those without a water view are consoled with more space and a balcony with rock-garden perspectives. The cottage nearby offers simpler comfort. The cosy bar, or wonderful beer garden on a sunny day, are memorable places for a pint, and food ranges from sound-value bar meals to seafood platters and local langoustines brought in on the afternoon boat (mains £6 to £12).

Shieling   B&B ££
(☑ 01599-544282; jane@shieling282.freeserve. co.uk; s/d £40/65; ⊙ late May-late Sep; P 🛜) A short stroll across the little causeway from the waterfront strip, characterful Shieling is surrounded by an expertly trimmed garden and has pleasing rooms with views and big beds as well as a lovely lounge with water outlook. Next door is an historic thatched blackhouse. A kindly welcome is guaranteed.

Duncraig Castle   B&B ££
(☑ 01599-544295; www.duncraigcastle.co.uk; P) Duncraig Castle offers luxurious, offbeat hospitality, as long as stuffed animals don't offend you. At time of research it was closed for substantial renovation, but should open for the 2016 season. It's very close to Plockton but has its own train station.

🍴 Eating

⭐ **Plockton Shores**   SEAFOOD ££
(☑ 01599-544263; www.plocktonshoresrestaurant.com; 30 Harbour St; mains £11-18; ⊙ noon-2.30pm & 6-8.30pm Mon-Sat, from 11am Sun; 🐾) 🐾 This welcoming restaurant attached to a shop sports a tempting menu of local seafood, including good-value platters with langoustines, mussels, crab, squat lobster and more, or succulent hand-dived tempura scallops. There's also a very tasty line in venison, steaks and a small selection of tasty vegetarian dishes that are more than an afterthought. Breakfast, teas and snacks from morning until night are served.

Plockton Inn

SEAFOOD ££

([phone] 01599-544222; www.plocktoninn.co.uk; mains £10-18; [clock] noon-2.15pm & 6-9pm; [wifi]) Offering a wide range from haggis to local langoustines (Plockton prawns) and daily seafood specials, this offers welcoming service. A range of rooms – some substantially more spacious than others, and some in an annexe – are available at a decent price.

Kyle of Lochalsh

POP 700

Before the bridge was opened in 1995, this was Skye's main ferry port. Visitors now tend to buzz through town, but Kyle has some good boat trips if you're interested in marine life.

[icon] Sights & Activities

Seaprobe Atlantis

BOAT TOURS

([phone] 0800 980 4846; www.seaprobeatlantis.com; adult/child from £13/7; [clock] Easter-Oct) A glass-hulled boat takes you on a spin around the kyle to spot seabirds, seals and maybe an otter. The basic trip includes entertaining commentary and plenty of beautiful jellyfish; longer trips also take in a WWII shipwreck. Book at the tourist office.

[icon] Sleeping & Eating

There's a string of B&Bs just outside of town on the road to Plockton.

Buth Bheag

SEAFOOD £

(salads £3-6; [clock] 10am-5pm Tue-Fri, 10am-3pm Sat) This tiny place by the water, near the tourist office, has great takeaway fresh seafood salads and rolls for a pittance. Munch them sitting by the harbour.

Waverley

SCOTTISH ££

([phone] 01599-534337; www.waverleykyle.co.uk; Main St; mains £12-21; [clock] 5.30-9.30pm Fri-Tue) This is an intimate place with excellent service; try the Taste of Land and Sea, combining Aberdeen Angus fillet steak with fresh local prawns, or one of several other reliably good fish options. Blackboard specials offer a dinner deal if you eat before 7pm.

[icon] Information

Kyle of Lochalsh Tourist Office ([phone] 01599-534276; [clock] 9.30am-4.30pm Easter-Oct) Beside the main seafront car park; stocks information on Skye. Next to it is one of Scotland's most lavishly decorated public toilets.

[icon] Getting There & Away

Citylink runs two to three daily buses from Inverness (£19.90, two hours) and three from Glasgow (£36.20, five to six hours).

The train route between Inverness and Kyle of Lochalsh (£22, 2½ hours, up to four daily) is marvellously scenic.

Kyle to the Great Glen

It's 55 miles southeast via the A87 from Kyle to Invergarry, which lies between Fort William and Fort Augustus, on Loch Oich.

Eilean Donan Castle

Photogenically sited at the entrance to Loch Duich, near Dornie, **Eilean Donan** ([phone] 01599-555202; www.eileandonancastle.com; adult/child/family £6.50/5.50/16; [clock] 10am-6pm Feb-Dec, from 9am Jul & Aug) is one of Scotland's most evocative castles, and must be represented in millions of photo albums. It's on an islet linked to the mainland by a stone-arched bridge. It's very much a re-creation inside, with an excellent introductory exhibition. Keep an eye out for the photos of castle scenes from *Highlander;* there's also a sword that was used at Culloden in 1746. The castle, though built in the early 13th century by the Mackenzies, was bombarded into ruins by government ships in 1719 when Jacobite forces were defeated at the Battle of Glenshiel. It was rebuilt between 1912 and 1932 by the Macraes, who own it.

Citylink buses to or from Skye will stop opposite the castle.

Glen Shiel & Glenelg

From Eilean Donan Castle, the A87 follows Loch Duich into spectacular Glen Shiel, with 1000m-high peaks soaring on either side of the road. Here in 1719, a Jacobite army was defeated by Hanoverian government forces. Among those fighting on the rebel side were clansmen led by famous outlaw Rob Roy MacGregor, and 300 soldiers loaned by the king of Spain; the mountain above the battlefield is still called Sgurr nan Spainteach (Peak of the Spaniard).

At Shiel Bridge, home to a famous wild-goat colony, a narrow side road goes over the Bealach Ratagain (pass), with great views of the Five Sisters of Kintail peaks, to Glenelg, where there's a community-run ferry to Skye. From palindromic Glenelg round

MADDENING MIDGES

Forget Nessie; the Highlands have a real monster. A voracious bloodsucking female fully 3mm long named *culicoides impunctatus*, or the Highland midge. The bane of campers and as much a symbol of Scotland as the kilt or dram, they drive sane folk to distraction, descending in biting clouds.

Though normally vegetarian, the female midge needs a dose of blood in order to lay her eggs. And, like it or not, if you're in the Highlands between June and August, you just volunteered as a donor. Midges especially congregate near water, and are most active in the early morning, though squadrons also patrol in the late evening.

Repellents and creams are reasonably effective, though some walkers favour midge veils. Light-coloured clothing also helps. Many pubs and campsites have midge-zappers. Check www.midgeforecast.co.uk for activity levels by area, but don't blame us: we've been eaten alive when the forecast said moderate too.

to the road-end at Arnisdale, the scenery becomes even more spectacular, with great views across Loch Hourn to the remote Knoydart peninsula. Along this road are two fine ruined Iron Age brochs.

🏃 Activities

There are several good walks in the area, including the two-day, cross-country hike from Morvich to Cannich via scenic **Gleann Lichd** and Glen Affric SYHA (35 miles). A traverse of the **Five Sisters of Kintail** is a classic but seriously challenging hill-walking expedition, taking in three Munro summits; start at the parking area just east of the Glen Shiel battlefield and finish at Morvich (eight to 10 hours).

🛏 Sleeping & Eating

Ratagan SYHA   HOSTEL £
(☑ 01599-511243; www.syha.org.uk; Ratagan; dm £18.50; ☺ mid-Mar–Oct; 🅿 @ 🛜) This hostel has excellent facilities and a to-die-for spot on the south shore of Loch Duich. Cheap meals are on offer, and there's a licensed bar. A bus runs Monday to Friday from Kyle of

Lochalsh, otherwise it's a 2-mile walk from Shiel Bridge on the main road.

Kintail Lodge Hotel   INN, BOTHY ££
(☑ 01599-511275; www.kintaillodgehotel.co.uk; Shiel Bridge; dm/s/d £16/95/130; 🅿 🛜) With most of the fine rooms here facing the loch, you'd be unlucky not to get a decent outlook. Tasty bar meals (£9 to £16), including local venison and seafood, are available for lunch (noon to 2.30pm) and dinner (6pm to 9pm). There are also two bunkhouses with self-catering facilities, each sleeping six; linen is £6 extra.

Glenelg Inn   INN ££
(☑ 01599-522273; www.glenelg-inn.com; Glenelg; mains £11-19; ☺ food 12.30-2.30pm & 6.30-9pm; 🅿 🛜 🐾) One of the Highlands' most picturesque places for a pint or a romantic away-from-it-all stay (doubles £120), the Glenelg Inn has tables in a lovely garden with cracking views of Skye. The elegant dining room and cosy bar area serves up posh fare, with the local catch always featuring. Service variable.

ℹ Getting There & Away

BOAT

At Glenelg, a picturesque community-owned vehicle **ferry** (www.skyeferry.com; foot passenger/bike/car with passengers £3/4/15; ☺ 10am-6pm Easter–mid-Oct) runs across to Kylerhea on Skye. This is a highly recommended way of reaching the island; it runs every 20 minutes and doesn't need booking.

BUS

Citylink buses between Fort William/Inverness and Skye travel along the A87. A bus runs Monday to Friday from Kyle of Lochalsh to Arnisdale, via Shiel Bridge, Ratagan and Glenelg. Check www.skyeways.co.uk for new Glenelg services.

ISLE OF SKYE

POP 10,000

The Isle of Skye (an t-Eilean Sgiathanach in Gaelic) takes its name from the old Norse *sky-a*, meaning 'cloud island', a Viking reference to the often-mist-enshrouded Cuillin Hills. It's the second-largest of Scotland's islands, a 50-mile-long patchwork of velvet moors, jagged mountains, sparkling lochs and towering sea cliffs. The stunning scenery is the main attraction, but when the mist closes in there are plenty of castles, crofting museums and cosy pubs and restaurants;

there are also dozens of art galleries and craft studios (ask at Portree tourist office for the free *Gallery & Studio Trails* booklet).

Along with Edinburgh and Loch Ness, Skye is one of Scotland's top-three tourist destinations. However, the hordes tend to stick to Portree, Dunvegan and Trotternish – it's almost always possible to find peace and quiet in the island's further-flung corners. Come prepared for changeable weather: when it's fine it's very fine indeed, but all too often it isn't.

Activities

Walking

Skye offers some of the finest – and in places, the roughest and most difficult – walking in Scotland. There are many detailed guidebooks available, including a series of four walking guides by Charles Rhodes, available from the Aros Experience (p202) and the tourist office in Portree. You'll need Ordnance Survey (OS) 1:50,000 maps 23 and 32. Don't attempt the longer walks in bad weather or in winter.

Easy, low-level routes include: through **Strath Mor** from Luib (on the Broadford–Sligachan road) and on to Torrin (on the Broadford–Elgol road; allow 1½ hours, 4 miles); from **Sligachan to Kilmarie** via Camasunary (four hours, 11 miles); and from **Elgol to Kilmarie** via Camasunary (2½ hours, 6.5 miles). The walk from **Kilmarie to Coruisk** and back via Camasunary and the 'Bad Step' is superb but slightly harder (11 miles round trip, allow five hours). The **Bad Step** is a rocky slab poised above the sea that you have to scramble across; it's easy in fine, dry weather, but some walkers find it intimidating.

Skye Wilderness Safaris   WALKING
(✆01470-552292; www.skye-wilderness-safaris. com; per person £295; ☉May-Sep) Runs two-day guided hiking trips through the Cuillin Hills or along the Trotternish ridge; meals and luxury camping accommodation included.

Climbing

The Cuillin Hills is a playground for rock climbers, and the two-day traverse of the Cuillin Ridge is the finest mountaineering expedition in the British Isles. There are several mountain guides in the area who can provide instruction and safely introduce inexperienced climbers to the more difficult routes.

Skye Guides   ROCK CLIMBING
(✆01471-822116; www.skyeguides.co.uk) A two-day introduction-to-rock-climbing course costs around £380, and a private mountain guide can be hired for £200 a day (both rates are for two clients).

Sea Kayaking

The sheltered coves and sea lochs around the coast of Skye provide water lovers with magnificent sea-kayaking opportunities. The centres listed here can provide kayaking instruction, guiding and equipment hire for both beginners and experts. It costs around £40 to £50 for a half-day kayak hire with instruction.

Whitewave Outdoor Centre   KAYAKING
(✆01470-542414; www.white-wave.co.uk; 19 Linicro, Kilmuir; ☉Mar-Oct) Provides kayaking instruction, guiding and equipment hire for both beginners and experts.

Skyak Adventures   KAYAKING
(✆01471-820002; www.skyakadventures.com; 29 Lower Breakish, Breakish) Expeditions and courses to take both beginners and experienced paddlers to otherwise inaccessible places.

Tours

There are several operators who offer guided tours of Skye, covering history, culture and wildlife. Rates are from £150 to £200 for a six-hour tour for up to six people.

Skye Tours   BUS TOURS
(✆01471-822716; www.skye-tours.co.uk; adult/child £35/30; ☉Mon-Sat) Five-hour sightseeing tours of Skye in a minibus, departing from the tourist office car park in Kyle of Lochalsh (close to Kyle of Lochalsh train station).

Skye Light Images   4WD TOURS
(✆07909-706802; www.skyejeepsafaris.co.uk; ☉Oct-Easter) Offers 4WD winter safaris in the wilder areas of Skye with tuition on landscape and wildlife photography.

Information

INTERNET ACCESS

The Portree Tourist Office (p197) has internet access for £1 per 20 minutes.

Columba 1400 Community Centre (Staffin; per hr £1; ☉10am-8pm Mon-Sat Apr-Oct; 🛜)
Seamus's Bar (Sligachan Hotel; per 15min £1; ☉11am-11pm; 🛜)

NORTHERN HIGHLANDS & ISLANDS ISLE OF SKYE

Skye & Outer Hebrides

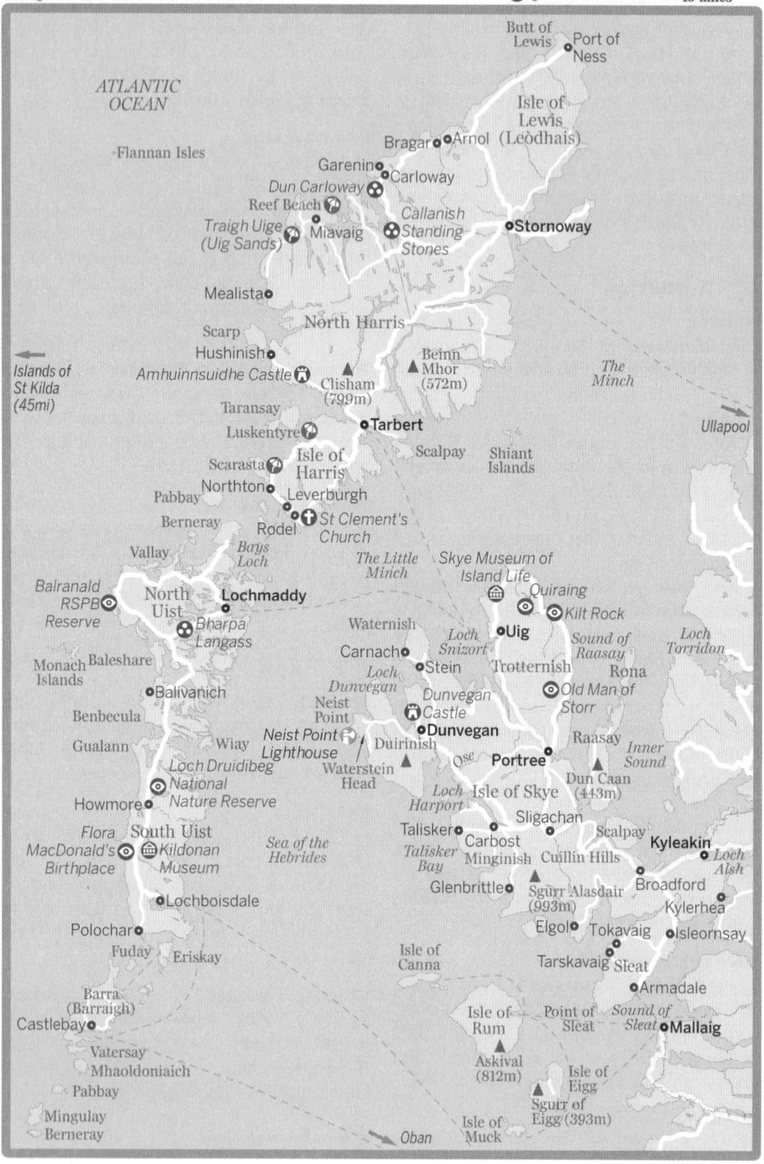

Map features and labels:

- 0 — 30 km
- 0 — 15 miles
- N

ATLANTIC OCEAN

- Flannan Isles
- Butt of Lewis
- Port of Ness
- Isle of Lewis (Leòdhais)
- Bragar
- Arnol
- Garenin
- Carloway
- Dun Carloway
- Reef Beach
- Callanish Standing Stones
- Stornoway
- Traigh Uige (Uig Sands)
- Miavaig
- Mealista
- North Harris
- Scarp
- Hushinish
- Beinn Mhor (572m)
- *The Minch*
- Amhuinnsuidhe Castle
- Clisham (799m)
- Islands of St Kilda (45mi)
- Taransay
- Luskentyre
- Tarbert
- Scalpay
- Shiant Islands
- *Ullapool*
- Scarasta
- Isle of Harris
- Northton
- Leverburgh
- Pabbay
- Berneray
- Rodel
- St Clement's Church
- Vallay
- *Bays Loch*
- *The Little Minch*
- Skye Museum of Island Life
- Quiraing
- Kilt Rock
- Balranald RSPB Reserve
- North Uist
- Lochmaddy
- Bharpa Langass
- Waternish
- *Loch Snizort*
- Uig
- Trotternish
- *Sound of Raasay*
- Rona
- *Loch Torridon*
- Monach Islands
- Baleshare
- Carnach
- Stein
- *Loch Dunvegan*
- Dunvegan
- Old Man of Storr
- Balivanich
- Benbecula
- Neist Point
- Dunvegan Castle
- Dunvegan
- Raasay
- *Inner Sound*
- Gualann
- Wiay
- Neist Point Lighthouse
- Duirinish
- Portree
- Loch Druidibeg National Nature Reserve
- Waterstein Head
- *Loch Harport*
- Isle of Skye
- Dun Caan (443m)
- Howmore
- *Sea of the Hebrides*
- Sligachan
- Flora MacDonald's Birthplace
- South Uist
- Kildonan Museum
- Talisker
- Carbost
- Scalpay
- Kyleakin
- *Talisker Bay*
- Minginish
- Cuillin Hills
- *Loch Alsh*
- Lochboisdale
- Glenbrittle
- Sgurr Alasdair (993m)
- Broadford
- Kylerhea
- Polochar
- Fuday
- Eriskay
- Isle of Canna
- Elgol
- Tokavaig
- Isleornsay
- Barra (Barraigh)
- Tarskavaig
- Sleat
- Castlebay
- Armadale
- Vatersay
- Mhaoldoniaich
- Isle of Rum
- Point of Sleat
- *Sound of Sleat*
- Pabbay
- Askival (812m)
- Isle of Eigg
- Mallaig
- Mingulay
- Berneray
- Sgurr of Eigg (393m)
- *Oban*
- Isle of Muck

MEDICAL SERVICES

Portree Community Hospital (☏ 01478-613200; Fancyhill) There's a casualty department and dental surgery here.

MONEY

Only Portree and Broadford have banks with ATMs, and Portree's tourist office has a currency exchange desk.

Portree Tourist Office (☑ 01478-612137;
Bayfield Rd, Portree; internet per 20min £1;
☺ 9am-6pm Mon-Sat & 10am-4pm Sun Jun-
Aug, 9am-5pm Mon-Fri & 10am-4pm Sat Apr,
May & Sep, shorter hours Oct-Mar) The only
tourist office on the island; provides internet
access (£1 per 20 minutes) and currency
exchange.

🛈 Getting There & Away

BOAT

Despite the bridge, there are still a couple of
ferry links between Skye and the mainland.
Ferries also operate from Uig on Skye to the
Outer Hebrides.

Mallaig to Armadale (www.calmac.co.uk;
per person/car £4.65/23.90) The Mallaig to
Armadale ferry (30 minutes, eight daily Monday
to Saturday, five to seven on Sunday) is very
popular on weekends and in July and August,
so book ahead if you're travelling by car.

Glenelg to Kylerhea (www.skyeferry.co.uk;
car with up to four passengers £15; ☺ Easter-
mid-Oct) Runs a tiny vessel (six cars only) on
the short Kylerhea to Glenelg crossing (five
minutes, every 20 minutes). The ferry operates from 10am to 6pm daily (till 7pm June to
August).

BUS

Glasgow to Portree £41, seven hours, three
daily

Glasgow to Uig £41, 7½ hours, two daily; via
Crianlarich, Fort William and Kyle of Lochalsh

Inverness to Portree £24, 3¼ hours, three
daily

CAR & MOTORCYCLE

The Isle of Skye became permanently tethered
to the Scottish mainland when the Skye Bridge
opened in 1995. The controversial bridge tolls
were abolished in 2004 and the crossing is now
free.

There are petrol stations at Broadford (open
24 hours), Armadale, Portree, Dunvegan and
Uig.

🛈 Getting Around

Getting around the island by public transport
can be a pain, especially if you want to explore
away from the main Kyleakin–Portree–Uig road.
Here, as in much of the Highlands, there are
fewer buses on Saturday and only a handful of
Sunday services.

BUS

Stagecoach (p170) operates the main bus
routes on the island, linking all the main villages
and towns. Its **Skye Dayrider/Megarider** ticket

gives unlimited bus travel for one day/seven
days for £8/32. For timetable info, call **Traveline**
(☑ 0871 200 22 33).

TAXI

Kyle Taxi Company (☑ 01599-534323; www.
skyecarhire.co.uk) You can order a taxi or hire
a car from Kyle Taxi Company. Car hire costs
from around £40 a day, and you can arrange
for the car to be waiting at Kyle of Lochalsh
train station.

Kyleakin (Caol Acain)

POP 100

Poor wee Kyleakin had the carpet pulled
from under it when the Skye Bridge opened –
it went from being the gateway to the island
to a backwater bypassed by the main road.
It's now a pleasant, peaceful little place, with
a harbour used by yachts and fishing boats.

The community-run **Bright Water Visitor Centre** (☑ 01599-530040; www.eileanban.
org; The Pier; adult/child £1/free; ☺ 10am-4pm
Mon-Fri Easter-Sep) serves as a base for tours
of **Eilean Ban** – the island used as a stepping stone by the Skye Bridge – where
Gavin Maxwell (author of *Ring of Bright
Water*) spent the last 18 months of his life
in 1968–69, living in the lighthouse keeper's
cottage. The island is now a nature reserve
and tours (£7 per person) are available in
summer (must be booked in advance). The
visitor centre also houses a child-friendly
exhibition on Maxwell, the lighthouse and
the island's wildlife. Tours run twice daily on
weekdays, at 11am and 2pm.

There are two hostels and a couple of
B&Bs in the village. The friendly **Skye
Backpackers** (☑ 01599-534510; www.skye-
backpackers.com; dm/tw £18/47; @ ☎) is our
favourite, with even cheaper beds (£13) in
caravans out back. For something to eat,
Harry's Coffee Shop (The Pier; mains £3-
6; ☺ 10am-8pm May-Sep, shorter hours winter)
serves great coffee and cake, breakfast rolls
and hot lunches.

About 3 miles southwest of Kyleakin, a
minor road leads southwards to **Kylerhea**,
where there's a 1½-hour nature trail to a
shorefront **otter hide**, where you stand a
good chance of seeing these elusive creatures. A little further on is the jetty for the
car ferry to Glenelg on the mainland.

A shuttle bus runs half-hourly between
Kyle of Lochalsh and Kyleakin (£1.20, five
minutes), and there are eight to 10 buses
daily (except Sunday) to Broadford (£2.40,

15 minutes), and three or four to Portree (£6.20, one hour).

Broadford (An T-Ath Leathann)

POP 750

Broadford is a service centre for the scattered communities of southern Skye. The long, straggling village has a 24-hour petrol station, a large **Co-op supermarket** (⊙8am-10pm Mon-Sat, 9am-6pm Sun) with an ATM, a laundrette and a bank.

There are lots of B&Bs in and around Broadford and the village is well placed for exploring southern Skye by car.

🛏️ Sleeping & Eating

⭐ **Tigh an Dochais** B&B **££**
(☎01471-820022; www.skyebedbreakfast.co.uk; 13 Harrapool; d £90; P) 🌐 A cleverly designed modern building, Tigh an Dochais is one of Skye's best B&Bs – a little footbridge leads to the front door, which is on the 1st floor. Here you'll find the dining room (gorgeous breakfasts) and lounge offering a stunning view of sea and hills; the bedrooms (downstairs) open onto an outdoor deck with that same wonderful view.

Berabhaigh B&B **££**
(☎01471-822372; www.isleofskye.net/berabhaigh; 3 Lime Park; r per person £38; ⊙Mar-Oct; P📶) This is a lovely old croft house with bay views located just off the main road at the east end of the village, not far from Creelers.

Luib House B&B **££**
(☎01471-820334; www.luibhouse.co.uk; Luib; r per person £33-35; P📶) This is a large, comfortable and well-appointed B&B 6 miles north of Broadford.

Broadford Hotel HOTEL **£££**
(☎01471-822204; www.broadfordhotel.co.uk; Torrin Rd; s/d from £120/140; P📶) The Broadford Hotel is a stylish retreat with luxury fabrics and designer colour schemes. There's a formal restaurant and the more democratic **Gabbro Bar** (mains £7-12; ⊙food served noon-9pm), where you can enjoy a bar meal of smoked haddock chowder or steak pie washed down with Isle of Skye Brewery ale.

Creelers SEAFOOD **££**
(☎01471-822281; www.skye-seafood-restaurant.co.uk; Lower Harrapool; mains lunch £10, dinner £14-19; ⊙noon-9.30pm Mon-Sat Mar-Nov; 🍴) 🌐

Broadford has several places to eat but one really stands out: Creelers is a small, bustling, no-frills restaurant that serves some of the best seafood on Skye. The house speciality is a rich, spicy seafood gumbo. Best to book ahead.

Cafe Sia CAFE, PIZZERIA **££**
(☎01471-822616; www.cafesia.co.uk; mains £6-12; ⊙9.30am-9pm Sun-Thu, to 10pm Fri-Sat; 📶📡) 🌐 Serving everything from eggs Benedict and cappuccino to cocktails and seafood specials, this appealing new cafe specialises in wood-fired pizzas (also available to take away) and artisan coffee (yes, that's a coffee roaster sitting in the corner). There's also an outdoor deck with great views of the Red Cuillin.

Sleat

If you cross over the sea to Skye on the ferry from Mallaig you arrive in Armadale, at the southern end of the long, low-lying peninsula known as Sleat (pronounced 'slate'). The landscape of Sleat itself is not exceptional, but it provides a grandstand for ogling the magnificent scenery on either side – take the steep and twisting minor road that loops through Tarskavaig and Tokavaig for stunning views of the Isle of Rum, the Cuillin Hills and Bla Bheinn.

Armadale

Armadale, where the ferry from Mallaig arrives, is little more than a store, a post office and a couple of houses. There are six or seven buses a day Monday to Saturday (three on Sunday) from Armadale to Broadford (£3.50, 30 minutes) and Portree (£6.80, 1¼ hours).

◉ Sights & Activities

Museum of the Isles MUSEUM
(☎01471-844305; www.clandonald.com; adult/child £8/6.50; ⊙9.30am-5.30pm Apr-Oct, occasionally shorter hours Oct; P) Just along the road from Armadale pier is the part-ruined **Armadale Castle**, former seat of Lord Macdonald of Sleat. The neighbouring museum will tell you all you ever wanted to know about Clan Donald, as well as providing an easily digestible history of the Lordship of the Isles. Prize exhibits include rare portraits of clan chiefs, and a wine glass that was once used by Bonnie Prince Charlie. The

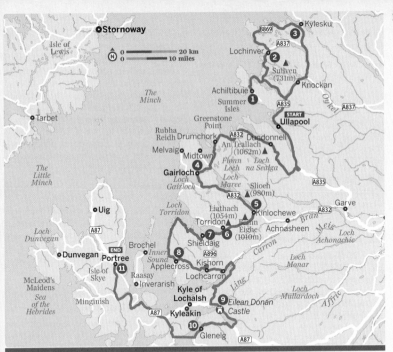

Driving Tour
Wee Roads & Mighty Mountains

START ULLAPOOL
FINISH PORTREE
DISTANCE 320 MILES
DURATION 3-4 DAYS

Starting in Ullapool, this drive takes in some of the lesser-known roads and the most majestic Highland scenery, leaving you on the Isle of Skye in summer, or in Glenelg in winter.

Leave your bags in the hotel, because the first day is a long round trip from Ullapool. Head north on the A835, and left turn to **1 Achiltibuie**, where after gaping at impressive lochside Stac Pollaidh en route, you can admire the outlook over the Summer Isles. From here, backtrack 6 miles then turn left up the Wee Mad Road, a narrow, tortuous but scenic drive north to pretty **2 Lochinver**. From here, the B869 winds north past spectacular beaches at Achmelvich and Clachtoll to **3 Kylesku**, where the hotel makes a great lunch stop. Return south to Ullapool on the main road (A894-A837-A835), with classic northwestern scenery and things to see such as Inchnadamph Caves, Ardvreck Castle and Knockan Crag along the way.

The next day head inland along the A835 before taking the A832 **4 Gairloch** turn-off, following the long, circuitous coast road with plenty of options from whale-watching trips to a botanic garden to hill walking around scenic Loch Maree. At **5 Kinlochewe** turn back coastwards on the A896, descending a spectacular pass to **6 Torridon**, where the rugged beauty is simply breathtaking. There are good overnight stops all along this route.

From **7 Shieldaig**, take the coastal road to sublime little **8 Applecross**, then brave the Bealach na Ba pass to get you back to the main road. A loop around Loch Carron will eventually bring you to the A87. Turn left, passing **9 Eilean Donan Castle** (p193) and, reaching Glen Shiel, take the right turn to **10 Glenelg**, a scenic, out-of-the-way place with a wonderfully rustic summer ferry crossing to Skye. Disembark at Kylerhea and enjoy the vistas on one of the island's least-trafficked roads before hitting the A87 again. From here, **11 Portree** is an easy drive, but numerous picturesque detours – to Sleat or Elgol for example – mean you might take a while to reach it yet.

ticket also gives admission to the lovely castle gardens.

Aird Old Church Gallery   GALLERY
(📞 01471-844291; www.airdoldchurchgallery.co.uk; Aird; ⊙ 10am-5pm Mon-Sat Easter-Sep) FREE At the end of the narrow road that leads southwest from Armadale through Ardvasar village, this small gallery exhibits the powerful landscape paintings of Peter McDermott, along with handmade jewellery and other crafts.

Armadale Bikes   CYCLING
(📞 01471-844421; armadalebikes.co.uk; Ardvasar; per day adult/child £15/10) Bike hire place close to the Mallaig–Armadale ferry.

🛏 Sleeping & Eating

Flora MacDonald Hostel   HOSTEL £
(📞 01471-844272; www.skye-hostel.co.uk; The Glebe; dm/tw/q £18/38/72; P🛜) Rustic accommodation 3 miles north of the Mallaig–Armadale ferry, on a farm full of Highland cattle and Eriskay ponies.

Shed   CAFE ££
(📞 01471-844222; The Pier; mains £7-15; ⊙ 9am-6pm) A cute little wooden shed with some outdoor tables, that serves good seafood salads, pizzas, fish and chips, and coffees – you can sit in or take away.

Isleornsay

This pretty harbour, 8 miles north of Armadale, is opposite Sandaig Bay on the mainland, where Gavin Maxwell lived and wrote his much-loved memoir *Ring of Bright Water.*

⊙ Sights

Gallery An Talla Dearg   GALLERY
(www.eileaniarmain.co.uk; ⊙ 10am-6pm Mon-Fri, to 4pm Sat & Sun Apr-Oct) FREE This gallery exhibits the works of artists who were inspired by Scottish landscapes and culture.

🛏 Sleeping & Eating

★ Toravaig House Hotel   HOTEL ££
(📞 01471-820200; www.skyehotel.co.uk; d £99-130; P🛜) This hotel, 3 miles south of Isleornsay, is one of those places where the owners know a thing or two about hospitality – as soon as you arrive you'll feel right at home, whether relaxing on the sofas by the log fire in the lounge or admiring the view across the Sound of Sleat from the lawn chairs in the garden.

The spacious bedrooms – ask for room 1 (Eriskay), with its enormous sleigh bed – are luxuriously equipped, from the crisp bed linen to the huge, high-pressure shower heads. The elegant restaurant serves the best of local fish, game and lamb. After dinner you can retire to the lounge with a single malt and flick through the yachting magazines – you can even arrange a day trip aboard the owners' 42ft sailing yacht.

Hotel Eilean Iarmain   HOTEL £££
(📞 01471-833332; www.eilean-iarmain.co.uk; s/d from £110/170; P) A charming old Victorian hotel with log fires, a candlelit restaurant and 12 luxurious rooms, many with sea views. The hotel's cosy, wood-panelled **Praban Bar** (mains £9-16) serves delicious, upmarket pub grub.

Elgol (Ealaghol)

On a clear day, the journey along the road from Broadford to Elgol is one of the most scenic on Skye. It takes in two classic postcard panoramas – the view of Bla Bheinn across **Loch Slapin** (near Torrin), and the superb view of the entire Cuillin range from **Elgol pier**.

Just west of Elgol is the **Spar Cave**, famously visited by Sir Walter Scott in 1814 and mentioned in his poem *Lord of the Isles*. The 80m-deep cave is wild, remote and filled with beautiful flowstone formations. It is a short walk from the village of Glasnakille, but the approach is over seaweed-covered boulders and is only accessible for one hour either side of low water. Check tide times and route information at the tearoom in Elgol.

Bus 55 runs from Broadford to Elgol (£3.20, 45 minutes, three daily Monday to Friday, two Saturday).

👉 Tours

Bella Jane   BOAT TOURS
(📞 0800 731 3089; www.bellajane.co.uk; ⊙ Apr-Oct) Bella Jane offers a three-hour cruise (adult/child £24/13, three daily) from Elgol harbour to the remote **Loch na Cuilce**, an impressive inlet surrounded by soaring peaks. On a calm day, you can clamber ashore here to make the short walk to Loch Coruisk in the heart of the Cuillin Hills. You

get 1½ hours ashore and visit a seal colony en route.

Aquaxplore BOAT TOURS
(☑ 0800 731 3089; www.aquaxplore.co.uk; ☺ Apr-Oct) Runs 1½-hour high-speed boat trips from Elgol to an abandoned shark-hunting station on the island of Soay (adult/child £28/20), once owned by *Ring of Bright Water* author Gavin Maxwell. There are longer trips (adult/child £54/44, four hours) to Rum, Canna and Sanday to visit breeding colonies of puffins, with the chance of seeing minke whales on the way.

Misty Isle BOAT TOURS
(☑ 01471-866288; www.mistyisleboattrips.co.uk; adult/child £20/10; ☺ Apr-Oct) The pretty, traditional wooden launch *Misty Isle* offers cruises to Loch Coruisk with 1½ hours ashore (no Sunday service).

Cuillin Hills

The Cuillin Hills are Britain's most spectacular mountain range (the name comes from the Old Norse *kjöllen,* meaning 'keel-shaped'). Though small in stature (Sgurr Alasdair, the highest summit, is only 993m), the peaks are near-alpine in character, with knife-edge ridges, jagged pinnacles, scree-filled gullies and hectares of naked rock. While they are a paradise for experienced mountaineers, the higher reaches of the Cuillin are off limits to the majority of walkers.

The good news is that there are also plenty of good low-level hikes within the ability of most walkers. One of the best (on a fine day) is the steep climb from Glenbrittle campsite to Coire Lagan (6 miles round trip; allow at least three hours). The impressive upper corrie contains a lochan for bathing (for the hardy!), and the surrounding cliffs are a playground for rock climbers – bring your binoculars.

Even more spectacular, but much harder to reach on foot, is Loch Coruisk (from the Gaelic Coir'Uisg, the Water Corrie), a remote loch ringed by the highest peaks of the Cuillin. Accessible by boat trip (p200) from Elgol, or via an arduous 5.5-mile hike from Kilmarie, Coruisk was popularised by Sir Walter Scott in his 1815 poem *Lord of the Isles.* Crowds of Victorian tourists and landscape artists followed in Scott's footsteps, including JMW Turner, whose watercolours were used to illustrate Scott's works.

There are two main bases for exploring the Cuillin – Sligachan to the north (on the Kyle of Lochalsh–Portree bus route), and Glenbrittle to the south (no public transport).

🛏️ Sleeping & Eating

Sligachan Bunkhouse HOSTEL £
(☑ 01478-650458; www.sligachanselfcatering.co.uk; Sligachan; dm £18; ℙ) Comfortable and modern bunkhouse opposite the Sligachan Hotel. Bed linen £4 extra.

Sligachan Campsite CAMPSITE £
(Sligachan; sites per person £6; ☺ Apr-Oct) Across the road from the Sligachan Hotel is this basic campsite; be warned – this spot is a midge magnet. No bookings.

Glenbrittle SYHA HOSTEL £
(☑ 01478-640278; Glenbrittle; dm £18.50; ☺ Apr-Sep) Scandinavian-style timber hostel that quickly fills up with climbers on holiday weekends.

Glenbrittle Campsite CAMPSITE £
(☑ 01478-640404; Glenbrittle; sites per adult/child incl car £8/5; ☺ Apr-Sep) Excellent site, close to mountains and sea, with a shop selling food and outdoor kit; the midges can be diabolical, though.

Sligachan Hotel HOTEL £££
(☑ 01478-650204; www.sligachan.co.uk; Sligachan; per person £68-78; ℙ@🛜) The Slig, as it has been known to generations of climbers, is a near village in itself, encompassing a comfortable hotel, a microbrewery, self-catering cottages, a small mountaineering museum, a big barn of a pub – Seamus's Bar – and an adventure playground.

Seamus's Bar PUB £
(Sligachan Hotel; mains £8-13; ☺ food served 11am-9.30pm; 🛜♿) This place dishes up decent bar meals, including haggis, neeps and tatties, and fish and chips, and serves real ales from its own microbrewery. It also has a range of 200 malt whiskies in serried ranks above the bar.

Minginish

Loch Harport, to the north of the Cuillin, divides the Minginish Peninsula from the rest of Skye. On its southern shore lies the village of Carbost, home to Talisker malt whisky, produced at Talisker Distillery. Magnificent Talisker Bay, 5 miles west of

Carbost, is framed by a sea stack and a waterfall.

◉ Sights

Talisker Distillery DISTILLERY
(☑01478-614308; www.discovering-distilleries.com; guided tour £7; ⊘9.30am-5pm Mon-Sat Apr-Oct, 11am-5pm Sun Jul & Aug, 10am-4.30pm Mon-Fri Nov-Mar) Skye's only distillery produces smooth, sweet and smoky Talisker single-malt whisky; the guided tour includes a free dram.

⌷ Sleeping & Eating

Skyewalker Independent Hostel HOSTEL £
(☑01478-640250; www.skyewalkerhostel.com; Fiskavaig Rd, Portnalong; dm £17; ℗) Three miles northwest of Carbost, this excellent hostel is housed in the old village school, with cosy lounge, well-equipped kitchen, and superb gardens with glass-domed outdoor seating area. No wi-fi or mobile phone signal.

Old Inn B&B, HOSTEL ££
(☑01478-640205; www.theoldinnskye.co.uk; Carbost; s/d £48/76; ℗) The Old Inn is an atmospheric wee pub, offering accommodation in bright B&B bedrooms and an appealing chalet-style bunkhouse (from £17 per person). The bar is a favourite with walkers and climbers from Glenbrittle, and serves excellent pub grub (£10 to £16, noon to 10pm), from fresh oysters to haddock and chips. There's an outdoor patio at the back with great views over Loch Harport.

Oyster Shed SEAFOOD £
(www.skyeoysterman.co.uk; Carbost; mains £4-8; ⊘11am-6pm Mon-Fri, noon-6pm Sat Apr-Oct, shorter hours winter) 🍴 A farm shop selling fresh local seafood to take away, including oysters, cooked mussels and scallops, and seafood platters.

❶ Getting There & Away

There's one bus a day (school days only) from Portree to Carbost (£3.70, 40 minutes) via Sligachan.

Portree (Port Righ)

POP 2320

Portree is Skye's largest and liveliest town. It has a pretty harbour lined with brightly painted houses, and there are great views of the surrounding hills. Its name (from the Gaelic for King's Harbour) commemorates James V, who came here in 1540 to pacify the local clans.

◉ Sights & Activities

Aros Centre INTERPRETATION CENTRE
(☑01478-613649; www.aros.co.uk; Viewfield Rd, Portree; sea-eagle exhibition £4.75; ⊘9am-5.30pm; ℗ 🍴) On the southern edge of Portree, the Aros Centre is a combined visitor centre, book and gift shop, restaurant, theatre and cinema. The visitor centre (Easter to October) offers a look at fascinating, live CCTV images from local sea-eagle nests, and a wide-screen video of Skye's impressive scenery (it's worth waiting for the aerial shots of the Cuillin).

The centre is a useful rainy-day retreat, with an indoor, soft play area for children.

MV Stardust BOAT TOURS
(☑07798 743858; www.skyeboat-trips.co.uk; Portree Harbour; adult/child £18/9) MV *Stardust* offers one- to two-hour boat trips to the Sound of Raasay, with the chance to see seals, porpoises and – if you're lucky – white-tailed sea eagles. On Saturday there are longer cruises to the Isle of Rona (£30 per person). You can also arrange to be dropped off for a hike on the Isle of Raasay and picked up again later.

✸ Festivals & Events

Isle of Skye Highland Games HIGHLAND GAMES
(www.skye-highland-games.co.uk) These annual games are held in Portree in early August.

⌷ Sleeping

Portree is well supplied with B&Bs, but accommodation fills up fast in July and August, so be sure to book ahead.

Bayfield Backpackers HOSTEL £
(☑01478-612231; www.skyehostel.co.uk; Bayfield; dm £18; ℗ @ 🛜) Clean, central and modern, this hostel provides the best backpacker accommodation in town. The owner really makes you feel welcome, and is a fount of advice on what to do and where to go in Skye.

Torvaig Campsite CAMPSITE £
(☑01478-612209; www.portreecampsite.co.uk; Torvaig; per adult/child £7/3; ⊘Apr-Oct; 🛜) An attractive, family-run campsite located 1.5 miles north of Portree, on the road to Staffin.

Ben Tianavaig B&B B&B ££
(☑01478-612152; www.ben-tianavaig.co.uk; 5 Bosville Tce; r £75-88; ℗ 🛜) 🍴 A warm welcome

awaits from the Irish-Welsh couple who run this appealing B&B bang in the centre of town. All four bedrooms have a view across the harbour to the hill that gives the house its name and breakfasts include free-range eggs and vegetables grown in the garden. Two-night minimum stay April to October; no credit cards.

Woodlands
B&B ££

(☑ 01478-612980; www.woodlands-portree.co.uk; Viewfield Rd; r £70; ☺ Mar-Oct; P 🛜) A great location, with views across the bay, and un-stinting hospitality make this modern B&B, a half-mile south of the town centre, a good choice.

Rosedale Hotel
HOTEL ££

(☑ 01478-613131; www.rosedalehotelskye.co.uk; Beaumont Cres; s/d from£60/90; ☺ Easter-Oct; 🛜) The Rosedale is a cosy, old-fashioned ho-tel – you'll be welcomed with a glass of whis-ky or sherry when you check in – delightfully situated down by the waterfront. Its three converted fishermen's cottages are linked by a maze of narrow stairs and corridors, and the restaurant has a view of the harbour.

Peinmore House
B&B £££

(☑ 01478-612574; www.peinmorehouse.co.uk; r £135-145; P 🛜) Signposted off the main road about 2 miles south of Portree, this former manse has been cleverly converted into a guest house that is more stylish and luxurious than most hotels. The bedrooms and bathrooms are huge (one bathroom has an armchair in it!), as is the choice of breakfast (kippers and smoked haddock on the menu), and there are panoramic views to the Old Man of Storr.

Cuillin Hills Hotel
HOTEL £££

(☑ 01478-612003; www.cuillinhills-hotel-skye.co.uk; Scorrybreac Rd; r £210-310; P 🛜) Located on the eastern fringes of Portree, this luxury hotel enjoys a superb outlook across the harbour towards the Cuillin mountains. The more expensive rooms cosset guests with four-poster beds and panoramic views, but everyone can enjoy the scenery from the glass-fronted restaurant and well-stocked whisky bar.

✖ Eating & Drinking

Café Arriba
CAFE £

(☑ 01478-611830; www.cafearriba.co.uk; Quay Brae; mains £5-10; ☺ 7am-6pm daily May-Sep, 8am-5pm Thu-Sat Oct-Apr; 🗐) 🍴 Arriba is a funky little cafe, brightly decked out in primary colours and offering delicious flat-bread melts (bacon, leek and cheese is our favourite) as well as the best choice of veg-etarian grub on the island, ranging from a veggie breakfast fry-up to falafel wraps with hummus and chilli sauce. Also serves excel-lent coffee.

★ Harbour View Seafood Restaurant
SEAFOOD ££

(☑ 01478-612069; www.harbourviewskye.co.uk; 7 Bosville Tce; mains £14-19; ☺ noon-3pm & 5.30-11pm Tue-Sun) 🍴 The Harbour View is Por-tree's most congenial place to eat. It has a homely dining room with a log fire in win-ter, books on the mantelpiece and bric-a-brac on the shelves. And on the table, superb Scottish seafood such as fresh Skye oysters, seafood chowder, king scallops, langoustines and lobster.

Sea Breezes
SEAFOOD ££

(☑ 01478-612016; www.seabreezes-skye.co.uk; 2 Marine Buildings, Quay St; mains £12-20; ☺ noon-2pm & 5-9.30pm Apr-Oct) 🍴 Sea Breezes is an informal, no-frills restaurant specialising in local fish and shellfish fresh from the boat – try the impressive seafood platter, a small mountain of langoustines, crab, oysters and lobster (£48 for two). Book early, as it's often hard to get a table.

L'Incontro
CAFE

(The Green; ☺ 4-11pm Tue-Sun May-Sep) This ad-junct to a popular pizza restaurant (upstairs beside the Royal Hotel) serves excellent Ital-ian espresso, and also has an extensive range of Italian wines.

Isles Inn
PUB

(☑ 01478-612129; Somerled Sq; ☺ 11am-11pm Mon-Thu, 11am-midnight Fri-Sat, 12.30-11pm Sun; 🎱) Portree's pubs are nothing special, but the Isles Inn is more atmospheric than most. The Jacobean bar, with its flagstone floor and open fires, pulls in a lively mix of young locals, backpackers and tourists.

ℹ Getting There & Around

BICYCLE

Island Cycles (☑ 01478-613121; www.island-cycles-skye.co.uk; The Green; ☺ 9am-5pm Mon-Sat) You can hire bikes here for £8.50/15 per half/full day.

BUS

The main bus stop is in Somerled Sq. There are six Scottish Citylink buses every day from Kyle of Lochalsh to Portree (£6.50, one hour) continuing to Uig.

Local buses (mostly six to eight Monday to Saturday, three on Sunday) run from Portree to:

Armadale (£6.80, 1¼ hours) Connecting with the ferry to Mallaig

Broadford (£5.20, 40 minutes)

Dunvegan Castle (£4.65, 40 minutes, one daily)

There are also three buses a day on a circular route around Trotternish (in both directions), taking in Flodigarry (£4.65, 45 minutes), Kilmuir (£4.65, 45 minutes) and Uig (£3.50, 30 minutes).

Dunvegan (Dun Bheagain)

Skye's most famous historic building, and one of its most popular tourist attractions, is **Dunvegan Castle** (☑ 01470-521206; www. dunvegancastle.com; adult/child £10/7; ☺ 10am-5.30pm Apr–mid-Oct; ℗), seat of the chief of Clan MacLeod. It has played host to Samuel Johnson, Sir Walter Scott and, most famously, Flora MacDonald. The oldest parts are the 14th-century keep and dungeon but most of it dates from the 17th to 19th centuries.

In addition to the usual castle stuff – swords, silver and family portraits – there are some interesting artefacts, most famous being the Fairy Flag, a diaphanous silk banner that dates from some time between the 4th and 7th centuries. Bonnie Prince Charlie's waistcoat and a lock of his hair, donated by Flora MacDonald's granddaughter, share a room with Rory Mor's Drinking Horn, a beautiful 16th-century vessel of Celtic design that could hold 2.2L of claret. Upholding the family tradition, in 1956, John MacLeod – the 29th chief, who died in 2007 – downed the contents in one minute and 57 seconds 'without setting down or falling down'.

From the end of the minor road beyond Dunvegan Castle entrance, an easy 1-mile walk leads to the **Coral Beaches** – a pair of blindingly white beaches composed of the bleached exoskeletons of coralline algae known as *maerl*.

On the way to Dunvegan from Portree you'll pass **Edinbane Pottery** (☑ 01470-582234; www.edinbane-pottery.co.uk; ☺ 9am-6pm daily Easter-Oct, Mon-Fri Nov-Easter), one of the island's original craft workshops, established in 1971, where you can watch potters at work creating beautiful and colourful stoneware.

Duirinish & Waternish

The Duirinish peninsula to the west of Dunvegan, and Waternish to the north, boast some of Skye's most atmospheric hotels and restaurants, plus an eclectic range of artists' studios and crafts workshops.

◉ Sights & Activities

The sparsely populated Duirinish peninsula is dominated by the distinctive flat-topped peaks of Helabhal Mhor (469m) and Helabhal Bheag (488m), known locally as **MacLeod's Tables**. There are some fine walks from Orbost, including the summit of Helabhal Bheag (allow 3½ hours return) and the 5-mile trail from Orbost to **MacLeod's Maidens**, a series of pointed sea stacks at the southern tip of the peninsula.

It's worth making the long drive beyond Dunvegan to the west side of the Duirinish Peninsula to see the spectacular sea cliffs of **Waterstein Head**, and to walk down to **Neist Point lighthouse** with its views to the Outer Hebrides.

🛏 Sleeping & Eating

★ **Red Roof Café** CAFE £

(☑ 01470-511766; www.redroofskye.co.uk; Glendale; mains £6-9; ☺ 11am-5pm Sun-Fri Apr-Oct; ℗ 🐾) Tucked away up a glen, a mile off the main road, this restored 250-year-old byre is a wee haven of home-grown grub. As well as great coffee and cake, there are lunch platters (noon to 3pm) of Skye seafood, game or cheese served with salad leaves and edible flowers grown just along the road.

Stein Inn PUB ££

(☑ 01470-592362; www.steininn.co.uk; Stein; mains £8-18; ☺ food noon-4pm & 6-9.30pm Mon-Sat, 12.30-4pm & 6.30-9pm Sun Easter-Oct; ℗) This old country inn dates from 1790 and has a handful of bedrooms (per person £37 to £55), all with sea views, a lively little bar and a delightful beer garden beside the loch – a real suntrap on warm summer afternoons. The bar serves real ales from the Isle of Skye Brewery and excellent bar meals. Food is served in winter too, but call ahead to check.

Lochbay Seafood Restaurant SEAFOOD ££

(☑ 01470-592235; www.lochbay-seafood-restaurant.co.uk; Stein; 3-course dinner £33, lobster £11 extra; ☺ 6.30-9pm Wed-Sat Easter–mid-Oct; ℗) This is one of Skye's most romantic restaurants, a cosy farmhouse kitchen of a place with terracotta tiles and a wood-burning stove, and a menu that includes most things that either swim in the sea or live in a shell. Best to book ahead.

★ **Three Chimneys** MODERN SCOTTISH **£££**
(☑ 01470-511258; www.threechimneys.co.uk; Colbost; 3-course lunch/dinner £37/60; ☺ 12.15-1.45pm Mon-Sat mid-Mar–Oct, plus Sun Easter-Sep, 6.15-9pm daily year-round; P) ✿ Halfway between Dunvegan and Waterstein, the Three Chimneys is a superb romantic retreat combining a gourmet restaurant in a candlelit crofter's cottage with sumptuous five-star rooms (double £345) in the modern house next door. Book well in advance, and note that children are not welcome in the restaurant in the evenings.

🛍 Shopping

Dandelion Designs ARTS & CRAFTS
(www.dandelion-designs.co.uk; Captain's House, Stein; ☺ 11am-5pm Easter-Oct, shorter hours Nov-Mar; 🐾) At Stein on the Waternish Peninsula, Dandelion Designs is an interesting little gallery with a good range of colour and monochrome landscape photography, lino prints by Liz Myhill and a range of handmade arts and crafts.

Shilasdair Yarns KNITWEAR
(www.theskyeshilasdairshop.co.uk; Carnach; ☺ 10am-6pm Apr-Oct) The couple who run this place, a few miles north of Stein, moved to Skye in 1971 and now raise sheep, hand-spin woollen yarn, and hand-dye a range of wools and silks using natural dyes. You can see the dyeing process and try hand-spinning in the exhibition area behind the studio, which sells finished knitwear as well as yarns.

Trotternish

The Trotternish Peninsula to the north of Portree has some of Skye's most beautiful – and bizarre – scenery. A loop road allows a circular driving tour of the peninsula from Portree, passing through the village of Uig, where the ferry to the Outer Hebrides departs. The following sights are described travelling anticlockwise from Portree.

◉ Sights & Activties

Old Man of Storr ROCK FORMATION
The 50m-high, pot-bellied pinnacle of crumbling basalt known as the Old Man of Storr is prominent above the road 6 miles north of Portree. Walk up to its foot from the car park in the woods at the northern end of Loch Leathan (round trip 2 miles). This seemingly unclimbable pinnacle was first scaled in 1955 by English mountaineer Don Whillans, a feat that has been repeated only a handful of times since.

Quiraing ROCK FORMATION
Staffin Bay is dominated by the dramatic basalt escarpment of the Quiraing: its impressive land-slipped cliffs and pinnacles constitute one of Skye's most remarkable landscapes. From a parking area at the highest point of the minor road between Staffin and Uig you can walk north to the Quiraing in half an hour.

Duntulm Castle CASTLE
Near the tip of the Trotternish Peninsula is the ruined MacDonald fortress of Duntulm Castle, which was abandoned in 1739, reputedly because it was haunted. From the red telephone box 800m east of the castle, a faint path leads north for 1.5 miles to **Rubha Hunish coastguard lookout**, now restored as a tiny but cosy bothy overlooking the northernmost point of Skye.

Skye Museum of Island Life MUSEUM
(☑ 01470-552206; www.skyemuseum.co.uk; adult/child £2.50/50p; ☺ 9.30am-5pm Mon-Sat Easter-Oct; P) The peat-reek of crofting life in the 18th and 19th centuries is preserved in the thatched cottages, croft houses, barns and farm implements of the Skye Museum of Island Life. Behind the museum is Kilmuir Cemetery, where a tall Celtic cross marks the **grave of Flora MacDonald**; the cross was erected in 1955 to replace the original monument, of which 'every fragment was removed by tourists'.

Fairy Glen NATURAL FORMATION
Just south of Uig, a minor road (signposted 'Sheader and Balnaknock') leads in a mile or so to the Fairy Glen, a strange and enchanting natural landscape of miniature conical hills, rocky towers, ruined cottages and a tiny roadside lochan.

🛏 Sleeping & Eating

Dun Flodigarry Hostel HOSTEL **£**
(☑ 01470-552212; www.hostelflodigarry.co.uk; Flodigarry; dm/tw £18/40, tent sites per person £9; P @ ✿) A bright and welcoming hostel that enjoys a stunning location above the sea, with views across Raasay to the mainland

MICHAEL FOLLAN · MGFOTO.UK.COM / GETTY IMAGES ©

1. Puffin on Staffa (p95) 2. Glenbrittle, Isle of Skye (p201)
3. Cliffs between Silwick and Westerwick, Shetland (p239) 4. Iona
Abbey (p93)

JOHN LAWSON, BELHAVEN / GETTY IMAGES ©

Scotland's Islands

Scotland's sweeping array of islands – 790 at last count, around a hundred of which are inhabited – defines the country's complex coastline. Ruins, from prehistoric religious centres to staunch castles, overlook landscapes where sheep crop lush grass, the scant remaining fisherfolk take on powerful seas, and urban professionals looking for a quieter life battle with unreliable wi-fi.

Geography & History

Though in the modern world these islands might seem remote outposts, Scotland's complex geography has meant that, from Celts through to Vikings and the Lords of the Isles, transport, trade and power are intimately tied to the sea. Today's lonely island stronghold was yesteryear's hub of connections spreading right across western and northern Britain and beyond.

Sights & Activities

For the visitor, there's bewildering scope. The once-Norse islands of Orkney and Shetland are Britain's northernmost parts, while the Hebrides guard the west coast like a storm shield against the mighty Atlantic. The choice is yours: for scenic splendour with hills to climb and memorable walks you might choose spectacular Skye, diverse Mull, accessible Arran or lonely Jura. Neolithic villages, standing stones, evocative prehistoric monuments? Head to far-flung Orkney, Shetland or the Outer Hebrides. Abbeys, castles or stately homes? Magical Iona, Bute, Coll, Barra or Westray. Beaches? Pick Harris or Tiree. Birdlife? Unst, the Uists, Fair Isle, Noss, North Ronaldsay or Staffa. Whisky? It's got to be Islay. A convivial pub, local seafood and a warm welcome? Take your pick of any and find yourself a snug cottage with a scent of the salty breeze and call it home for a day or three.

mountains. A nearby hiking trail leads to the Quiraing (2.5 miles away), and there's a hotel bar barely 100m from the door. You can also camp nearby and use all the hostel facilities.

Uig SYHA
HOSTEL £

(☑ 01470-542746; Uig; dm £18.50; ⊙ Mar-Sep; ℗ @ 🛜) Sociable hostel with fantastic sunset views over Uig Bay. You have to vacate the place between 10.30am and 5pm, even when it's raining!

Flodigarry Hotel
HOTEL £££

(☑ 01470-552203; www.hotelintheskye.co.uk; Flodigarry; r £130-250; ℗ 🛜) From 1751 to 1759 Flora MacDonald lived in a cottage which is now part of this atmospheric hotel. You can stay in the cottage itself (there are four bedrooms here), or in the more spacious rooms in the main hotel; nonresidents are welcome at the stylish bar and restaurant, with great views over the sea.

Isle of Raasay
POP 160

Raasay (www.raasay.com) is the rugged, 10-mile-long island that lies off Skye's east coast. The island's fascinating history is recounted in the book *Calum's Road* by Roger Hutchinson.

There are several good walks here, including one to the flat-topped conical hill of **Dun Caan** (443m), and another to the extraordinary ruin of **Brochel Castle**, perched on a pinnacle at the northern end of Raasay. The Forestry Commission publishes a free leaflet (available in the ferry waiting room) with suggested walking trails.

Set in a rustic cottage high on the hill overlooking Skye, **Raasay SYHA** (☑ 01478-660240; Creachan Cottage; dm £17.50; ⊙ May-Aug) is a 1.5-mile walk from the ferry pier and makes a good base for exploring the island. Beautifully renovated **Raasay House** (☑ 01478-660266; www.raasay-house.co.uk; dm £25, s/d £105/125; ℗ 🛜) provides outdoor-activity courses, and accommodation ranging from hostel bunks to luxury B&B. It also has the island's only bar and restaurant (mains £12 to £20), serving quality pub grub and locally brewed beers.

A **CalMac ferry** (www.calmac.co.uk; return passenger/car £6.45/24.80) runs from Sconser, on the road from Portree to Broadford, to Raasay (25 minutes, nine daily Monday to Saturday, twice daily Sunday). There are no petrol stations on the island.

OUTER HEBRIDES
POP 27,670

The Western Isles, or Na h-Eileanan an Iar in Gaelic – also known as the Outer Hebrides – are a 130-mile-long string of islands lying off the northwest coast of Scotland. There are 119 islands in total, of which the five main inhabited islands are Lewis and Harris (two parts of a single island, although often described as if they are separate islands), North Uist, Benbecula, South Uist and Barra. The middle three (often referred to simply as 'the Uists') are connected by road-bearing causeways.

The ferry crossing from Ullapool or Uig to the Western Isles marks an important cultural divide – more than a third of Scotland's registered crofts are in the Outer Hebrides, and no less than 60% of the population are Gaelic speakers. The rigours of life in the old island blackhouses are still within living memory.

Religion still plays a prominent part in public and private life, especially in the Protestant north, where shops and pubs close their doors on Sundays and some accommodation providers prefer guests not to arrive or depart on the Sabbath. The Roman Catholic south is a little more relaxed about these things.

If your time is limited, head straight for the west coast of Lewis with its prehistoric sites, preserved blackhouses and beautiful beaches. As with Skye, the islands are dotted with arts and crafts studios – the tourist offices can provide a list.

ℹ Information

INTERNET RESOURCES

CalMac (www.calmac.co.uk) Ferry timetables.
Visit Hebrides (www.visithebrides.com)

MEDICAL SERVICES

Uist & Barra Hospital (☑ 01870-603603; Balivanich, Benbecula)
Western Isles Hospital (☑ 01851-704704; MacAulay Rd, Stornoway, Lewis)

MONEY

There are banks with ATMs in Stornoway (Lewis), Tarbert (Harris), Lochmaddy (North Uist), Balivanich (Benbecula), Lochboisdale (South Uist) and Castlebay (Barra). Elsewhere, some hotels and shops offer cash-back facilities.

TOURIST INFORMATION

Castlebay Tourist Office (☑ 01871-810336; Main St, Castlebay; ⊙ 9am-1pm & 2-5pm Mon-Sat & noon-4pm Sun Apr-Oct)

Lochboisdale Tourist Office (☑ 01878-700286; Pier Rd, Lochboisdale, South Uist; ⊙ 9am-5pm Mon-Sat Apr-Oct)

Stornoway Tourist Office (☑ 01851-703088; www.visithebrides.com; 26 Cromwell St, Stornoway; ⊙ 9am-6pm Mon-Sat year-round)

Tarbert Tourist Office (☑ 01859-502011; Pier Rd, Tarbert; ⊙ 9am-5pm Mon-Sat Apr-Oct)

❶ Getting There & Away

AIR

There are airports at Stornoway (Lewis), Benbecula and Barra. Flights operate to Stornoway from Edinburgh, Inverness, Glasgow and Aberdeen. There are also two flights a day (Tuesday to Thursday only) between Stornoway and Benbecula.

There are daily flights from Glasgow to Barra, from Tuesday to Thursday only to Benbecula. At Barra, the planes land on the hard-sand beach at low tide, so the timetable depends on the tides.

Eastern Airways (☑ 0870 366 9100; www.easternairways.com)

FlyBe/Loganair (☑ 01857-873457; www.loganair.co.uk)

BOAT

There are two or three ferries a day to Stornoway, one or two a day to Tarbert and Lochmaddy, and one a day to Castlebay and Lochboisdale. You can also take the ferry from Lochboisdale to Castlebay (car/passenger £22.90/7.95, 1½ hours, one daily Monday, Tuesday and Thursday) and from Castlebay to Lochboisdale (one daily Wednesday, Friday and Sunday).

Standard one-way fares on CalMac (p215) ferries:

CROSSING	DURATION (HOURS)	CAR	DRIVER/ PASSENGER
Ullapool–Stornoway	2¾	£48	£9.15
Uig–Lochmaddy	1¾	£29	£6
Uig–Tarbert	1½	£29	£6
Oban–Castlebay	4¾	£65	£14.25
Oban–Lochboisdale	6¾	£65	£14.25

Advance booking for cars is recommended (essential in July and August); foot and bicycle passengers should have no problems. Bicycles are carried free.

❶ Getting Around

Despite their separate names, Lewis and Harris are actually one island. Berneray, North Uist, Benbecula, South Uist and Eriskay are all linked by road bridges and causeways. There are car ferries between Leverburgh (Harris) and Berneray; Tarbert (Harris) and Lochmaddy (North Uist); Eriskay and Castlebay (Barra); and Lochboisdale (South Uist) and Castlebay (Barra).

The local council publishes timetables of all bus and ferry services within the Outer Hebrides, available at tourist offices. Or look online at www.cne-siar.gov.uk/travel.

BICYCLE

Bikes can be hired for around £10 to £15 a day or £60 to £80 a week in Stornoway (Lewis), Uig (Lewis), Leverburgh (Harris), Howmore (South Uist) and Castlebay (Barra).

Harris Outdoor Adventure (☑ 07788 425157; www.harrisoutdoor.co.uk; Pier Rd, Leverburgh) Can deliver bikes to your accommodation.

Rothan Cycles (☑ 07740 364093; www.rothan.com; Howmore, South Uist) Offers a delivery and pick-up service at various points between Eriskay and Stornoway.

BUS

The bus network covers almost every village in the islands, with around four to six buses a day on all the main routes; however, there are no buses at all on Sunday. You can pick up timetables from tourist offices, or call **Stornoway bus station** (☑ 01851-704327) for information.

CAR & MOTORCYCLE

Apart from the fast, two-lane road between Tarbert and Stornoway, most roads are single track. The main hazard is posed by sheep wandering about or sleeping on the road. Petrol stations are far apart (almost all of those on Lewis and Harris are closed on Sunday), and fuel is about 10% more expensive than on the mainland.

There are petrol stations at Stornoway, Barvas, Borve, Uig, Breacleit (Great Bernera), Ness, Tarbert and Leverburgh on Lewis and Harris; Lochmaddy and Cladach on North Uist; Balivanich on Benbecula; Howmore, Lochboisdale and Daliburgh on South Uist; and Castlebay on Barra.

Cars can be hired from around £35 per day.

Arnol Motors (☑ 018510-710548; www.arnolmotors.com; Arnol, Lewis; ⊙ 8am-5pm Mon-Sat)

Lewis Car Rentals (☑ 01851-703760; www.lewis-car-rental.co.uk; 52 Bayhead St, Stornoway; ⊙ 8am-5pm Mon-Sat)

Lewis (Leodhais)

POP 21,000 (INCLUDING HARRIS)

The northern part of Lewis is dominated by the expanse of the Black Moor, a vast, undulating peat bog dimpled with glittering lochans, seen clearly from the Stornoway–Barvas road. But Lewis' finest scenery is on the west coast, from Barvas southwest to Mealista, where the rugged landscape of hill, loch and sandy strand is reminiscent of the northwestern Highlands. The Outer Hebrides' most evocative historic sites – Callanish Standing Stones, Dun Carloway and Arnol Blackhouse Museum – are also here.

Stornoway (Stornabhagh)

POP 5715

Stornoway is the bustling 'capital' of the Outer Hebrides. The only real town in the whole archipelago, it's a surprisingly busy little place. Though set on a beautiful natural harbour, the town isn't going to win any prizes for beauty or atmosphere, but it's a pleasant introduction to this remote corner.

⊙ Sights

Lews Castle CASTLE

The Baronial mansion across the harbour from Stornoway town centre was built in the 1840s for the Matheson family, then owners of Lewis; it was gifted to the community by Lord Leverhulme in 1923. A major redevelopment sees the new **Museum nan Eilean** (Museum of the Isles) opening here from summer 2015, covering the history of the Outer Hebrides and exploring traditional island life. The beautiful wooded grounds are open to the public and host the Hebridean Celtic Festival in July.

An Lanntair Arts Centre ARTS CENTRE

(☑ 01851-703307; www.lanntair.com; Kenneth St; ⊙ 10am-9pm Mon-Wed, to 10pm Thu, to midnight Fri & Sat) FREE The modern, purpose-built An Lanntair (Gaelic for 'lighthouse'), complete with art gallery, theatre, cinema and restaurant, is the centre of the town's cultural life; it hosts changing exhibitions of contemporary art and is a good source of information on cultural events.

Lewis Loom Centre MUSEUM

(☑ 01851-704500; 3 Bayhead; adult/child £1/50p; ⊙ 9.30am-5.30pm Mon-Sat) This appealingly ramshackle exhibition records the history of Harris Tweed; the 40-minute guided tour (£2.50 extra) includes wool-spinning and weaving demonstrations.

✯ Festivals & Events

Hebridean Celtic Festival MUSIC

(www.hebceltfest.com) A four-day extravaganza of folk/rock/Celtic music held in the second half of July.

🛏 Sleeping

Heb Hostel HOSTEL £

(☑ 01851-709889; www.hebhostel.co.uk; 25 Kenneth St; dm £18; @ 🛜) The Heb is a friendly, easygoing hostel close to the ferry, with comfy wooden bunks, a convivial living room with peat fire and a welcoming owner who can provide all kinds of advice on what to do and where to go.

Laxdale Holiday Park CAMPSITE £

(☑ 01851-703234; www.laxdaleholidaypark.com; 6 Laxdale Lane; tent sites £8-10, plus per person £3.50; ⊙ Mar-Oct; 🛜) This campsite, 1.5 miles north of town off the A857, has a sheltered woodland setting, though the tent area is mostly on a slope – get there early for a level pitch. There are also wooden camping pods (per night £32 to £40), and a bunkhouse (£17 per person) that stays open year-round.

Hal o' the Wynd B&B ££

(☑ 01851-706073; www.halothewynd.com; 2 Newton St; s/d from £60/80; 🛜) Touches of tartan and Harris Tweed lend a tradtional air to this welcoming B&B, conveniently located directly opposite the ferry pier. Most rooms have views over the harbour to Lews Castle. There's also a cafe on the premises.

Park Guest House B&B ££

(☑ 01851-702485; www.theparkguesthouse.co.uk; 30 James St; s/d from £58/110; @ 🛜) A charming Victorian villa with a conservatory and eight luxurious rooms (mostly en suite), the Park Guest House is comfortable and central and has the advantage of an excellent **restaurant** specialising in Scottish seafood, beef and game plus one or two vegetarian dishes (3-course dinner £30). Rooms overlooking the main road can be noisy on weekday mornings.

Royal Hotel HOTEL ££

(☑ 01851-702109; www.royalstornoway.co.uk; Cromwell St; s/d from £79/99; P 🛜) The 19th-century Royal is the most appealing of Stornoway's hotels – the rooms at the front retain period features such as wood panelling, and enjoy a view across the harbour to Lews Castle. Ask to see your room first, though, as some are a bit cramped.

Braighe House B&B £££
(☑ 01851-705287; www.braighehouse.co.uk; 20 Braighe Rd; s/d from £115/130; [P]) This spacious and luxurious guesthouse, 3 miles east of the town centre on the A866, has stylish, modern bedrooms and a great seafront location. Good bathrooms with powerful showers, hearty breakfasts and genuinely hospitable owners round off the perfect package.

 Eating

Thai Café THAI £
(☑ 01851-701811; www.thai-cafe-stornoway.co.uk; 27 Church St; mains £5-10; ☺ noon-2.30pm & 5.30-11pm Mon-Sat; ☎) Here's a surprise – authentic, inexpensive Thai food in the heart of Stornoway. This spick-and-span, no-frills restaurant has a genuine Thai chef and serves some of the most delicious, best-value Asian food in the Hebrides. If you can't get a table, it does takeaway.

An Lanntair Arts Centre BISTRO ££
(Kenneth St; mains lunch £6-12, dinner £13-19; ☺ cafe 10am-late, restaurant noon-2.30pm Mon-Sat, 5-8.30pm Thu-Sat; ☎ ☑ ▦) The stylish and family-friendly cafe and restaurant at the arts centre serves a broad range of freshly prepared dishes, from tasty bacon rolls at breakfast to burgers, salads or fish and chips for lunch, and char-grilled steaks or local scallops for dinner.

★ **Digby Chick** BISTRO £££
(☑ 01851-700026; www.digbychick.co.uk; 5 Bank St; mains £17-25, 2-course lunch £13.50; ☺ noon-2pm & 5.30-9pm Mon-Sat; ▦) ◢ A modern restaurant that dishes up bistro cuisine such as haddock and chips, slow-roast pork belly or roast vegetable panini at lunchtime. The Digby Chick metamorphoses into a candlelit gourmet restaurant in the evening, serving dishes such as grilled langoustines, seared scallops, venison and steak. Three-course early-bird menu (5.30pm to 6.30pm) for £19.

🔒 **Shopping**

Baltic Bookshop BOOKS
(☑ 01851-702802; 8-10 Cromwell St; ☺ 9am-5.30pm Mon-Sat) Good for local history books and maps.

Sandwick Road Petrol Station FOOD & DRINK
(Engebret Ltd; ☑ 01851-702304; Sandwick Rd; ☺ 6am-11pm Mon-Sat, 10am-4pm Sun) The only shop in town that's open on a Sunday, selling groceries, alcohol, hardware, fishing tackle and outdoor kit; the Sunday papers arrive around 2pm.

ⓘ Getting There & Away

The bus station is on the waterfront, next to the ferry terminal (left luggage desk £1.50 per piece). Bus W10 runs from Stornoway to Tarbert (£4.40, one hour, four or five daily Monday to Saturday) and Leverburgh (£6.20, two hours).

The Westside Circular bus W2 runs a circular route from Stornoway through Callanish (£2.50, 30 minutes), Carloway, Garenin and Arnol; the timetable means you can visit one or two of the sites in a day.

Butt of Lewis (Rubha Robhanais)

The Butt of Lewis – the extreme northern tip of the Hebrides – is windswept and rugged, with a very imposing lighthouse, pounding surf and large colonies of nesting fulmars on the high cliffs. There's a bleak sense of isolation here, with nothing but the grey Atlantic between you and Canada.

Just before the turn-off to the Butt at Eoropie (Eoropaidh), you'll find **St Moluag's Church** (Teampull Mholuidh), an austere, barnlike structure believed to date from the 12th century but still used by the Episcopal Church. The main settlement here is **Port of Ness** (Port Nis) with an attractive harbour. To the west of the village is the sandy beach of **Traigh**, which is popular with surfers and has a kids' adventure playground nearby.

Arnol

One of Scotland's most evocative historic buildings, the **Arnol Blackhouse** (HS; ☑ 01851-710395; adult/child £4.50/2.70; ☺ 9.30am-5.30pm Mon-Sat Apr-Sep, to 4.30pm Oct-Mar; [P]) is not so much a museum as a perfectly preserved fragment of a lost world. Built in 1885, this traditional blackhouse – a combined byre, barn and home – was inhabited until 1964 and has not been changed since the last inhabitant moved out. The staff faithfully rekindle the central peat fire every morning so you can experience the distinctive peat-reek; there's no chimney, and the smoke finds its own way out through the turf roof, windows and door – spend too long inside and you might feel like you've been kippered! The museum is just off the A858, about 3 miles west of Barvas.

NORTHERN HIGHLANDS & ISLANDS LEWIS (LEODHAIS)

At nearby **Bragar**, a pair of whalebones forms an arch by the road, with the rusting harpoon that killed the whale dangling from the centre.

Garenin (Na Gearrannan)

The picturesque and fascinating **Gearrannan Blackhouse Village** is a cluster of nine restored thatch-roofed blackhouses perched above the exposed Atlantic coast. One of the cottages is home to the **Blackhouse Museum** (☑ 01851-643416; www.gearrannan.com; adult/child £3/1; ⊗ 9.30am-5.30pm Mon-Sat Apr-Sep), a traditional 1955 blackhouse with displays on the village's history, while another houses the **Taigh an Chocair Cafe** (mains £3-6; ⊗ 9.30am-5.30pm Mon-Sat).

The other blackhouses in the village are let out as self-catering **holiday cottages** (☑ 01851-643416; www.gearrannan.com; 2-person cottage for 3 nights £226), offering the chance to stay in a unique and luxurious modernised blackhouse with attached kitchen and lounge. There's a minimum five-night stay from June to August.

Carloway (Carlabagh)

Dun Carloway (Dun Charlabhaigh) is a 2000-year-old, dry-stone broch, perched defiantly above a beautiful loch with views to the mountains of North Harris. The site is clearly signposted along a minor road off the A858, a mile southwest of Carloway village. One of the best-preserved brochs in Scotland, its double walls (with internal staircase) still stand to a height of 9m and testify to the engineering skills of its Iron Age architects.

The tiny, turf-roofed **Doune Broch Centre** (☑ 01851-643338; ⊗ 10am-5pm Mon-Sat Apr-Sep) FREE nearby has interpretative displays and exhibitions about the history of the broch and the life of the people who lived there.

Callanish (Calanais)

The **Callanish Standing Stones**, 15 miles west of Stornoway on the A858 road, form one of the most complete stone circles in Britain. It is one of the most atmospheric prehistoric sites anywhere; its ageless mystery, impressive scale and undeniable beauty leave a lasting impression. Sited on a wild and secluded promontory overlooking Loch Roag, 13 large stones of beautifully banded gneiss are arranged, as if in worship, around a 4.5m-tall central monolith. Some 40 smaller stones radiate from the circle in the shape of a cross, with the remains of a chambered tomb at the centre. Dating from 3800 to 5000 years ago, the stones are roughly contemporary with the pyramids of Egypt.

The nearby **Calanais Visitor Centre** (☑ 01851-621422; www.callanishvisitorcentre.co.uk; admission free, exhibition £2.50; ⊗ 9.30am-8pm Mon-Sat Jun-Aug, 10am-6pm Mon-Sat Apr, May, Sep & Oct, 10am-4pm Tue-Sat Nov-Mar; P) is a tour de force of discreet design. Inside is a small exhibition that speculates on the origins and purpose of the stones, and an excellent **cafe** (mains £4-7).

If you plan to stay the night, you have a choice of **Eshcol Guest House** (☑ 01851-621357; www.eshcol.com; 21 Breascleit; r per person £43; P) and neighbouring **Loch Roag Guest House** (☑ 01851-621357; www.lochroag.com; 22a Breascleit; r per person £39-55; P 🛜), half a mile north of Callanish. Both are modern bungalows with the same friendly owner, who is very knowledgeable about the local area (evening meals available).

Great Bernera

This rocky island is connected to Lewis by a bridge built by the local council in 1953 – the islanders had originally planned to blow up a small hill with explosives and use the material to build their own causeway. On a sunny day, it's worth making the long detour to the island's northern tip for a picnic at the perfect little sandy beach of **Bosta** (Bostadh).

In 1996 archaeologists excavated an entire Iron Age village at the head of Bosta beach. Afterwards, the village was reburied for protection, but a reconstruction of an **Iron Age house** (☑ 01851-612331; Bosta; adult/child £3/1; ⊗ noon-4pm Mon-Fri May-Sep; P) now sits nearby. Stand around the peat fire, with strips of mutton being smoked above, while the custodian explains the domestic arrangements – truly fascinating, and well worth the trip.

There are five buses a day between Stornoway and the hamlet of Breacleit (£3.10, one hour) on Great Bernera; two or three a day will continue to Bosta on request. Alternatively, there's a signposted 5-mile coastal walk from Breacleit to Bosta.

Miavaig (Miaghaig) & Mealista (Mealasta)

The B8011 road (signposted Uig, on the A858 Stornoway–Callanish road) from Garrynahine to Timsgarry (Timsgearraidh) meanders through scenic wilderness to some of Scotland's most stunning beaches. At **Miavaig**, a loop road detours north through the Bhaltos Estate to the pretty, mile-long white strand of **Reef Beach**; there's a basic but spectacular **campsite** (Traigh na Beirigh; tent sites £10; ☉ Apr-Oct) in the machair behind the beach.

From April to September, SeaTrek (www. seatrek.co.uk) runs two-hour boat trips (adult/child £35/25, Monday to Saturday) in a high-speed RIB to spot seals and nesting seabirds. In June and July it also runs more adventurous, all-day trips (£95 per person, two per month) in a large motor boat to the **Flannan Isles**, a remote group of tiny, uninhabited islands 25 miles northwest of Lewis. Puffins, seals and a ruined 7th-century chapel are the main attractions, but the isles are most famous for the mystery of the three lighthouse keepers who disappeared without trace in December 1900. There's also a 12-hour round trip to remote **St Kilda** (£180, once or twice weekly, May to September, weather permitting).

From Miavaig, the road continues west through a rocky defile to Timsgarry and the vast, sandy expanse of **Traigh Uige** (Uig Sands). The famous 12th-century **Lewis chess pieces**, made of walrus ivory, were discovered in the sand dunes here in 1831. Of the 78 pieces, 67 are in the British Museum in London, with 11 in Edinburgh's National Museum of Scotland; you can buy replicas at various outlets on the isle of Lewis.

There's a basic **campsite** (sites per person £2) on the south side of the bay (signposted 'Ardroil Beach') and a superb guesthouse, **Baile-na-Cille** (☏ 01851-672242; www. bailenacille.co.uk; Timsgarry, Uig; per person £55; ℗ ☎), on the north side.

At the southwestern end of Traigh Uig is **Auberge Carnish** (☏ 01851-672459; www. aubergecarnish.co.uk; Carnais; s/d from £85/120; ℗), a beautifully designed timber building that houses a luxury B&B and restaurant (3-course dinner £35; booking essential) with a stunning outlook over the sands.

The minor road that continues south from Timsgarry to **Mealista** passes a few smaller, but still spectacular, white-sand and boulder beaches on the way to a remote dead end; on a clear day you can see St Kilda on the horizon.

There are two or three buses a day from Stornoway to Uig (£4.40, 50 minutes).

Harris (Na Hearadh)

Harris, to the south of Lewis, is the scenic jewel in the necklace of islands that comprise the Outer Hebrides. It has a spectacular blend of rugged mountains, pristine beaches, flower-speckled machair and barren rocky landscapes. The isthmus at Tarbert splits Harris neatly in two: North Harris is dominated by mountains that rise forbiddingly above the peat moors to the south of Stornoway – Clisham (799m) is the highest point. South Harris is lower-lying, fringed by beautiful white-sand beaches in the west and a convoluted rocky coastline to the east.

Harris is famous for Harris Tweed, a high-quality woollen cloth still hand-woven in islanders' homes. The industry employs around 400 weavers; staff at Tarbert tourist office can tell you about weavers and workshops you can visit.

Tarbert (An Tairbeart)

POP 480

Tarbert is a harbour village with a spectacular location, tucked into the narrow neck of land that links North and South Harris. It has ferry connections to Uig on Skye. Under construction beside the ferry pier at the time of research, the **Isle of Harris Distillery** will be open to visitors daily (except Sunday) from spring 2015. Village facilities include two petrol stations, a bank, ATM and two general stores.

🛏 Sleeping & Eating

Tigh na Mara　　　　　　　　　　B&B £
(☏ 01859-502270; East Tarbert; per person £25-30; ℗) Excellent-value B&B (though the single room is a bit cramped) just five minutes from the ferry – go up the hill above the tourist office and turn right. The owner bakes fresh cakes every day, to enjoy in the conservatory with a view over the bay.

Harris Hotel　　　　　　　　　HOTEL ££
(☏ 01859-502154; www.harrishotel.com; s/d from £70/98; ℗ @ ☎) Run since 1903 by four generations of the Cameron family, Harris Hotel is a 19th-century sporting hotel, built in 1865 for visiting anglers and deer stalkers, and re-

tains a distinctly old-fashioned atmsophere. It has spacious, comfy rooms and a decent restaurant; look out for JM Barrie's initials scratched on the dining-room window (the author of *Peter Pan* visited in the 1920s).

Hotel Hebrides　　　　　　　HOTEL **£££**
(☑ 01859-502364; www.hotel-hebrides.com; Pier Rd; s/d/f £75/150/180; 🛜) The location and setting don't look promising – a nondescript building squeezed between ferry pier and car park – but this modern establishment brings a dash of urban glamour to Harris, with flashy fabrics and wall coverings, luxurious towels and toiletries, and a stylish restaurant and lounge bar.

Hebscape　　　　　　　　　　CAFE **£**
(www.hebscapegallery.co.uk; Ardhasaig; mains £3-7; ⊙ 10am-4.30pm Mon-Sat Apr-Oct; P🛜) 🖋 This stylish new cafe-cum-art gallery, a couple of miles outside Tarbert on the road north towards Stornoway, occupies a hilltop site with breathatking views over Loch A Siar. Enjoy home-baked cakes or scones with Suki tea or freshly brewed espresso, or a hearty bowl of homemade soup, while admiring the gorgeous landscape photography of co-owner Darren Cole.

First Fruits　　　　　　　　　CAFE **£**
(☑ 01880-502439; www.firstfruits-tearoom.co.uk; Pier Rd; mains £3-10; ⊙ 10.30am-4pm Mon, Wed & Fri, 10am-4pm Tue & Thu & 10am-3pm Sat Apr-Sep) A cosy little cottage tearoom near the tourist office – handy while you wait for a ferry.

North Harris

Magnificent North Harris is the most mountainous region of the Outer Hebrides. There are few roads here, but many opportunities for climbing, walking and birdwatching.

The B887 leads west, from a point 3 miles north of Tarbert, to **Hushinish**, where there's a lovely silver-sand beach. Along the way the road passes an old whaling station, one of Lord Leverhulme's failed development schemes, and the impressive shooting lodge of **Amhuinnsuidhe Castle**, now an exclusive hotel. Between the two, at Miavaig, a parking area and gated track gives hikers access to a golden eagle observatory, a 1.3-mile walk north from the road. On Wednesdays from April to September, local rangers lead a 3½-hour **guided walk** (£5 per person) in search of eagles; details from Tarbert tourist office or www.north-harris.org.

South Harris

The west coast of South Harris has some of the most beautiful beaches in Scotland. The blinding white sands and turquoise waters of **Luskentyre** and **Scarasta** would be major holiday resorts if they were transported to somewhere with a warm climate; as it is, they're usually deserted.

The east coast is a complete contrast to the west – a strange, rocky moonscape of naked gneiss pocked with tiny lochans, the bleakness lightened by the occasional splash of green around the few crofting communities. Film buffs will know that the psychedelic sequences depicting an alien landscape in *2001: A Space Odyssey* were shot from an aircraft flying low over the east coast of Harris.

The narrow, twisting road that winds its way along this coast is known locally as the **Golden Road**, because of the vast amount of money it cost per mile. It was built in the 1930s to link all the tiny communities known as 'The Bays'.

🔘 Sights & Activities

Clò Mòr　　　　　　　　　　　MUSEUM
(☑ 01859-511189; Old School, Drinishader; ⊙ 9am-5.30pm Mon-Sat; P) **FREE** The Campbell family has been making Harris Tweed for 90 years, and this exhibition (behind the family shop) celebrates the history of the fabric known in Gaelic as *clò mòr* (the 'big cloth'); ask about live demonstrations of tweed weaving on the 70-year-old Hattersley loom. Drinishader is 5 miles south of Tarbert on the east coast road.

Seallam! Visitor Centre　　　　MUSEUM
(www.seallam.com; Northton; adult/child £2.50/2; ⊙ 10am-5pm Mon-Sat; P) The culture and landscape of the Hebrides are celebrated in the fascinating exhibition (*Seallam* is Gaelic for 'Let me show you'). The centre, which is in Northton, 3 miles north of Leverburgh, also has a genealogical research centre for people who want to trace their Hebridean ancestry.

St Clement's Church　　　HISTORIC BUILDING
(Rodel; ⊙ 9am-5pm Mon-Sat) **FREE** At the southernmost tip of the east coast of Harris stands the impressive 16th-century St Clement's Church, built by Alexander MacLeod of Dunvegan between the 1520s and 1550s, only to be abandoned after the Reformation. There are several fine tombs inside, includ-

ing the **cenotaph of Alexander MacLeod**, finely carved with hunting scenes, a castle, a birlinn (the traditional longboat of the islands) and various saints, including St Clement clutching a skull.

🛏 Sleeping & Eating

Am Bothan   HOSTEL £
(☎ 01859-520251; www.ambothan.com; Ferry Rd, Leverburgh; dm £20; P 🏠) An attractive, chalet-style hostel, Am Bothan has small, neat dorms and a great porch where you can enjoy morning coffee with views over the creek. The hostel offers bike hire and can arrange wildlife-watching boat trips.

Lickisto Blackhouse Camping   CAMPSITE £
(☎ 01859-530485; www.freewebs.com/vanvon; Liceasto; tent sites per adult/child £12/6, yurt £70) Remote and rustic campsite on an old croft, with pitches set among heather and outcrops with chickens running wild. Campers can use a communal kitchen/lounge in a converted blackhouse, and there are two yurts with woodburning stove and gas cooker (no electricity). Bus W13 from Tarbert to Leverburgh stops at the entrance.

Carminish House   B&B ££
(☎ 01859-520400; www.carminish.com; 1a Strond, Leverburgh; s/d £60/80; P 🏠) One of the few B&Bs in Harris that is open all year, the welcoming Carminish is a modern house with three comfy bedrooms. There's a view of the ferry from the dining room, and lots of nice little touches such as handmade soaps, a carafe of drinking water in the bedroom and fresh fruit salad at breakfast.

Sorrel Cottage   B&B ££
(☎ 01859-520319; www.sorrelcottage.co.uk; 2 Glen, Leverburgh; s/d from £48/72; 🐾) Sorrel Cottage is a pretty crofter's house, about 1.5 miles west of the ferry at Leverburgh. Vegetarians and vegans are happily catered for. Bike hire available.

Rodel Hotel   INN £££
(☎ 01859-520210; www.rodelhotel.co.uk; Rodel; s/d from £85/130; ⊙ Apr-Oct; P 🏠🐾) Don't be put off by the rather grey and grim-looking exterior of this remote hotel – the interior has been refurbished to a high standard and offers four large, luxurious bedrooms; the one called Iona (a twin room) has the best view, across the little harbour towards Skye. The hotel **restaurant** (mains lunch £9-11, dinner £15-20; ⊙ noon-3pm & 5.30-9.30pm) serves delicious local seafood, steak and venison.

Skoon Art Café   CAFE £
(☎ 01859-530268; www.skoon.com; Geocrab; mains £4-7; ⊙ 10am-4.30pm Tue-Sat Apr-Sep, shorter hours Oct-Mar; P) Set halfway along the Golden Road, this neat little art gallery doubles as an excellent cafe serving delicious homemade soups, sandwiches, cakes and desserts (try the marmalade and ginger cake).

ℹ Getting There & Around

A **CalMac** (☎ 0800 066 5000; www.calmac. co.uk) car ferry zigzags through the reefs of the Sound of Harris from Leverburgh to Berneray (pedestrian/car £7.35/33.50, one hour, three or four daily Monday to Saturday, two or three Sunday).

There are two to four buses a day (except Sunday) from Tarbert to Leverburgh; W10 takes the main road along the west coast (£2.90, 40 minutes), while W13 winds along the Golden Road on the east (one hour).

Berneray (Bearnaraigh)

POP 138

Berneray was linked to North Uist by a causeway in October 1998, but that hasn't altered the peace and beauty of the island. The beaches on its west coast are some of the most beautiful and unspoilt in Britain, and seals and otters can be seen in Bays Loch on the east coast.

The basic but atmospheric **Gatliff Hostel** (www.gatliff.org.uk; dm adult/child £12/7, camping per person £8), housed in a pair of restored blackhouses right by the sea, is the place to stay. You can camp outside, or on the grass above the gorgeous white-sand beach just to the north.

The **Nurse's Cottage** (www.isleofberneray. com; ⊙ 11am-3pm Mon-Fri Jun-Aug) provides tourist information and internet access.

Bus W19 runs from Berneray (Gatliff Hostel and Harris ferry) to Lochmaddy (£2.10, 20 to 30 minutes, eight daily Monday to Saturday). There are daily ferries to Leverburgh (Harris).

North Uist (Uibhist A Tuath)

POP 1255

North Uist, an island half-drowned by lochs, is famed for its trout fishing but also has some magnificent beaches on its north and west coasts. For birdwatchers this is paradise, with regular sightings of waders and wildfowl ranging from redshank to red-throated diver to red-necked phalarope. The landscape is less wild and mountainous than Harris but it has a sleepy, subtle appeal. Little Lochmaddy is the first village you hit after arriving on the ferry from Skye. There's a tourist office, a couple of stores, a bank with an ATM, a petrol station, a post office and a pub.

⊙ Sights

Balranald RSPB Reserve   WILDLIFE RESERVE
FREE Birdwatchers flock to this RSPB nature reserve, 18 miles west of Lochmaddy, in the hope of spotting the rare red-necked phalarope or hearing the distinctive call of the corncrake. There's a **visitor centre** (admission free; ⊘ 9am-6pm Apr-Aug) with a resident warden who offers 1½-hour guided walks (£5, depart visitor centre 10am Tuesday, May to September).

Taigh Chearsabhagh   ARTS CENTRE, MUSEUM
(☑ 01876-500293; www.taigh-chearsabhagh.org; Lochmaddy; arts centre free, museum £3; ⊘ 10am-5pm Mon-Sat; P) Taigh Chearsabhagh is a museum and arts centre that preserves and displays the history and culture of the Uists, and is also a thriving community centre, post office and meeting place. The centre's **cafe** (mains £3 to £7) dishes up homemade soups, sandwiches and cakes.

Bharpa Langass & Pobull Fhinn   HISTORIC SITES
A waymarked circular path beside the Langass Lodge Hotel (just off the A867, 6 miles southwest of Lochmaddy) leads to the chambered Neolithic burial tomb of **Bharpa Langass** and the stone circle of **Pobull Fhinn** (Finn's People); both are reckoned to be around 5000 years old. There are lovely views over the loch, where you may be able to spot seals and otters.

🛏 Sleeping & Eating

Rushlee House   B&B ££
(☑ 01876-500274; www.rushleehouse.co.uk; Lochmaddy; s/d £50/75; P) A lovely modern bungalow with three luxuriously appointed bedrooms and great views of the hills to the south. No evening meals, but it's just a short walk to the restaurant at Hamersay House. The B&B is 0.75 miles from the ferry pier; take the first road on the right, then first left.

Langass Lodge Hotel   HOTEL ££
(☑ 01876-580285; www.langasslodge.co.uk; Locheport; s/d from £80/109; P 🛜) The delightful Langass Lodge Hotel is a former shooting lodge set in splendid isolation overlooking Loch Langais. Refurbished and extended, it now offers a dozen appealing rooms, many with sea views, and one of the Hebrides' best **restaurants** (mains £13-23; ⊘ noon-2pm & 6-9pm), noted for its fine seafood and game.

Hamersay House   HOTEL £££
(☑ 01876-500700; www.hamersayhouse.co.uk; Lochmaddy; s/d £95/135; P 🛜) Hamersay is Lochmaddy's most luxurious accommodation, with eight designer bedrooms, a lounge with sofas around an open fire, and a good restaurant with sea views from the terrace.

❶ Getting There & Around

Buses from Lochmaddy to Lochboisdale (£4.80, 1¾ hours), Eriskay Pier (£5.60, 2½ hours), Berneray, Langass, Clachan na Luib, Benbecula and Daliburgh run five to eight times a day Monday to Saturday.

Benbecula (Beinn Na Faoghla)

POP 1305
Benbecula is a low-lying island with a flat, lochan-studded landscape that's best appreciated from the summit of **Rueval** (124m), the island's highest point. There's a path around the south side of the hill (signposted from the main road; park beside the landfill site) that is said to be the route taken to the coast by Bonnie Prince Charlie and Flora MacDonald during the prince's escape in 1746. The main village, Balivanich, has a bank with an ATM, a post office, a large **Co-op supermarket** (⊘ 8am-8pm Mon-Sat, 11am-6pm Sun) and a petrol station (open on Sunday). It is also the location of **Benbecula airport**.

South Uist (Uibhist A Deas)

POP 1755
South Uist is the second-largest island in the Outer Hebrides and saves its choicest corners for those who explore away from the main north–south road. The low-lying west coast is an almost unbroken stretch of white-sand beach and flower-flecked machair – a waymarked hiking trail, the **Machair Way**,

follows the coast – while the multitude of inland lochs provide excellent trout fishing. The east coast, riven by four large sea lochs, is hilly and remote, with spectacular **Beinn Mhor** (620m) the highest point.

Driving south from Benbecula you cross from the predominantly Protestant northern half of the Outer Hebrides into the mostly Roman Catholic south, a religious transition marked by the granite statue of **Our Lady of the Isles** on the slopes of Rueval (the hill with the military radomes on its summit) and the presence of many roadside shrines.

The ferry port of **Lochboisdale** is the island's largest settlement, with a tourist office, a bank with an ATM, a grocery store and a petrol station.

Sights & Activties

Loch Druidibeg National Nature Reserve
WILDLIFE RESERVE

FREE Loch Druidibeg National Nature Reserve is an important breeding ground for birds such as dunlin, redshank, ringed plover, greylag goose and corncrake; you can take a 5-mile self-guided walk through the reserve. Ask for details at the Scottish Natural Heritage office on the main road beside the loch.

Kildonan Museum
MUSEUM

(☑01878-710343; www.kildonanmuseum.co.uk; Kildonan; adult/child £2/free; ⊙10am-5pm Apr-Oct; P) Six miles north of Lochboisdale, Kildonan Museum explores the lives of local crofters through its collection of artefacts, an absorbing exhibition of black-and-white photography and first-hand accounts of harsh Hebridean conditions. There's also an excellent **tearoom** (mains £3-8; ⊙11am-4pm) and craft shop.

Amid Milton's ruined blackhouses, half a mile south of the museum, a cairn marks the site of **Flora MacDonald's birthplace**.

Sleeping & Eating

Tobha Mor Crofters' Hostel
HOSTEL £

(www.gatliff.org.uk; Howmore; dm adult/child £12/7) Atmospheric hostel housed in a restored thatched blackhouse, about 12 miles north of Lochboisdale.

Wireless Cottage
B&B £

(☑01878-700660; www.wirelesscottage.co.uk; Lochboisdale; per person from £25; ☎) This pretty little cottage, which once housed the local telephone exchange, is now a welcoming and good-value B&B a short (300m) walk

from the ferry, with just two bedrooms (one double, one family).

★Polochar Inn
INN ££

(☑01878-700215; www.polocharinn.com; Polochar; s/d from £70/90; P☎) This 18th-century inn has been transformed into a stylish, welcoming hotel with a stunning location looking out across the sea to Barra. The excellent restaurant and bar menu (mains £14 to £18) includes fish chowder, haddock and chips, local salmon and Uist lamb. Polochar is 7 miles southwest of Lochboisdale, on the way to Eriskay.

Lochside Cottage
B&B ££

(☑01878-700472; www.lochside-cottage.co.uk; Lochboisdale; r per person £30; P☎) Lochside Cottage is a friendly B&B, 1.5 miles west of the ferry, and has rooms with views and a sun lounge barely a fishing-rod's length from its own trout loch.

Getting There & Around

CalMac (p215) ferries run between Lochmaddy and Uig (Skye), and Lochboisdale and Oban.

Bus W17 runs about four times a day (not Sunday) between Berneray and Eriskay via Lochmaddy, Balivanich and Lochboisdale. The trip from Lochboisdale to Lochmaddy (£4.80) takes 1¾ hours.

Eriskay (Eiriosgaigh)

POP 143

In 1745 Bonnie Prince Charlie first set foot in Scotland on the west coast of Eriskay, on the sandy beach (immediately north of the ferry terminal) still known as **Prince's Strand** (Coilleag a'Phrionnsa).

More recently the SS *Politician* sank just off the island in 1941. The islanders salvaged much of its cargo of around 250,000 bottles of whisky and, after a binge of dramatic proportions, the police intervened and a number of the islanders landed in jail. The story was immortalised by Sir Compton Mackenzie in his comic novel *Whisky Galore,* later made into a famous film.

A car ferry links Eriskay with Ardmhor at the northern end of Barra.

Barra (Barraigh)

POP 1175

With its beautiful beaches, wildflower-clad dunes, rugged little hills and strong sense of community, diminutive Barra – just 14 miles

CROFTING & THE CLEARANCES

The wild empty spaces up here are among Europe's least populated zones, but this wasn't always so. Ruins of cottages in desolate areas are mute witnesses to one of the most heartless episodes of Scottish history: the Highland Clearances.

Until the 19th century the most common form of farming settlement here was the baile, a group of a dozen or so families who farmed the land granted to them by the local chieftain in return for military service and a portion of the harvest. The arable land was divided into strips called rigs, which were allocated to different families by annual ballot so that each took turns at getting the poorer soils; this system was known as runrig. The families worked the land communally and their cattle shared grazing land.

After Culloden, however, the king banned private armies and new laws made the clan chiefs actual owners of their traditional lands, often vast tracts of territory. With the prospect of unimagined riches allied to a depressing failure of imagination, the lairds decided that sheep were more profitable than agriculture and proceeded to evict tens of thousands of farmers. These desperate folk were forced to head for the cities in the hope of finding work or to emigrate to the Americas or southern hemisphere. Those who stayed were forced to eke a living from narrow plots of marginal agricultural land, often close to the coast. This form of smallholding became known as crofting. The small patch of land barely provided a living and had to be supplemented by other work such as fishing and kelp-gathering. It was always precarious, as rights were granted on a year-by-year basis, so at any moment a crofter could lose not only the farm but also the house they'd built on it.

The late 19th-century economic depression meant many couldn't pay their rent. This time, however, they resisted expulsion, instead forming the Highland Land Reform Association and their own political party. Their resistance led the government to accede to several demands, including security of tenure, fair rents and eventually the supply of land for new crofts. Crofters now have the right to purchase their farmland and 2004 laws finally abolished the feudal system, which created so much misery.

in circumference – is the Outer Hebrides in miniature. For a great view of the island, walk up to the top of **Heaval** (383m), a mile northeast of Castlebay. **Castlebay** (Bagh a'Chaisteil), in the south, is the largest village. There's a tourist office (p209), a bank with an ATM, a post office and two grocery stores.

◉ Sights

Kisimul Castle CASTLE
(HS; ☑ 01871-810313; Castlebay; adult/child incl ferry £5.50/3.30; ◷ 9.30am-5.30pm Apr-Sep) Castlebay takes its name from the island fortress of Kisimul Castle, first built by the MacNeil clan in the 11th century. A short boat trip takes you out to the island, where you can explore the fortifications. The castle was restored in the 20th century by American architect Robert MacNeil, who became the 45th clan chief; he gifted the castle to Historic Scotland in 2000 for an annual rent of £1 and a bottle of whisky (Talisker single malt, if you're interested).

Traigh Mor BEACH
This vast expanse of firm golden sand (the name means 'Big Strand') serves as Barra's airport (a mile across at low tide, and big enough for three 'runways'), the only beach airport in the world that handles scheduled flights. Watching the little Twin Otter aircraft come and go is a popular spectator sport. In between flights, locals gather cockles, a local seafood speciality, from the sands.

Barra Heritage Centre MUSEUM
(☑ 01871-810413; www.barraheritage.com; Castlebay; adult/child £3/1; ◷ 10.30am-4.30pm Mon-Sat Apr-Oct) This heritage centre has Gaelic-themed displays about the island, local art exhibitions and a tearoom.

🛏 Sleeping & Eating

Accommodation on Barra is limited, so make a reservation before committing to a night on the island. Wild camping (on foot or by bike) is allowed almost anywhere; campervans and car campers are restricted to official sites – check www.isleofbarra.com.

Dunard Hostel
HOSTEL **£**

(☏ 01871-810443; www.dunardhostel.co.uk; Castlebay; dm/tw from £18/40; P) Dunard is a friendly, family-run hostel just five minutes' walk from the ferry terminal. The owners can organise sea-kayaking tours for £35/65 a half-/full day.

Borve Camping & Caravan Site
CAMPSITE **£**

(www.barracamping.co.uk; Borve; sites 2-person tent £14, campervan £18; ☉ Mar-Oct) An attractive campsite on the west coast of the island, close to Barra's best sandy beaches.

Castlebay Hotel
HOTEL **££**

(☏ 01871-810223; www.castlebayhotel.com; Castlebay; s/d from £65/110; P ☎) The Castlebay Hotel offers spacious bedrooms decorated with a subtle tartan motif – it's worth paying a bit extra for a sea view – and there's a comfy lounge and conservatory with grand views across the harbour to the islands south of Barra. The hotel bar is the hub of island social life, with regular sessions of traditional music, and the restaurant specialises in local seafood and game.

Tigh na Mara
B&B **££**

(☏ 01871-810304; www.tighnamara-barra.co.uk; Castlebay; per person from £35; ☉ Apr-Oct; P ☎) A lovely cottage B&B with a brilliant location just above the ferry pier, looking out over the bay and Kisimul Castle. Ask for the en suite double bedroom with bay view.

Deck
CAFE **£**

(Castlebay; mains £4-6; ☉ 10am-6pm Mon-Sat & noon-5pm Sun May-Sep) There are only outdoor seats at this cafe (attached to a toffee factory), on a wooden deck overlooking the bay, but it's worth waiting for a fine day to sample the freshly baked scones and homemade cakes.

ℹ Getting There & Around

AIR

There are two daily flights from Glasgow to Barra airport.

BOAT

A CalMac (p215) car ferry (pedestrian/car £8/22.90, 40 minutes, three to five daily) links Eriskay with Ardmhor at the northern end of Barra. Ferries also run from Castlebay to Oban and Lochboisdale.

BICYCLE

You can hire bikes from **Barra Cycle Hire** (☏ 01871-810284; Castlebay; per day £12), at the east end of Castlebay.

BUS

A bus service links ferry arrivals and departures at Ardmhor with Castlebay (£1.60, 20 minutes). Bus W32 makes a circuit of the island up to five times daily (not Sunday), and also connects with flights at the airport.

Orkney & Shetland

Best Places to Eat

➡ Creel (p229)
➡ Foveran (p227)
➡ Hay's Dock (p242)

Best Places to Stay

➡ Scalloway Hotel (p244)
➡ Brinkies Guest House (p233)
➡ Albert Hotel (p226)
➡ West Manse (p238)
➡ Almara (p247)
➡ Busta House Hotel (p246)

Why Go?

Up here at Britain's top end it can feel more Scandinavian than Scottish, and no wonder. For the Vikings, the jaunt across the North Sea from Norway was as easy as a stroll down to the local mead hall and they soon controlled these windswept, treeless archipelagos, laying down longhouses alongside stony remains of ancient prehistoric settlements.

An ancient magic hovers in the air above Orkney and Shetland, endowing them with an allure that lodges firmly in the soul. It's in the misty seas, where seals, whales and porpoises patrol lonely coastlines; it's in the air, where squadrons of seabirds wheel above huge nesting colonies; and it's on land, where standing stones catch late summer sunsets and strains of folk music disperse in the air before the wind gusts shut the pub door. These islands reward the journey.

When to Go
Lerwick

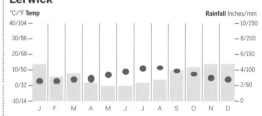

Jan Shetland's Up Helly Aa (p243): horned helmets and burning Viking ships on the beach.

Jun Orkney rocks to the St Magnus Festival (p225): book accommodation ahead.

Jul Summer sunlight and Scotland's longest daylight hours.

ORKNEY

There's a magic to Orkney that you begin to feel as soon as the Scottish mainland slips astern. Only a few short miles of ocean separate Stromness from Scrabster, but the Pentland Firth is one of Europe's most dangerous waterways, a graveyard of ships that adds an extra mystique to these islands shimmering in the sea mists.

An archipelago of mostly flat, green-topped islands stripped bare of trees and ringed with red sandstone cliffs, its heritage dates back to the Vikings whose influence is still strong today. Famed for ancient standing stones and prehistoric villages, for sublime sandy beaches and spectacular coastal scenery, it's a region whose ports tell of lives shared with the blessings and rough moods of the sea, and a destination where seekers can find melancholy wrecks of warships and the salty clamour of remote seabird colonies.

Tours

Orkney Archaeology Tours GUIDED TOURS
(01856-721450; www.orkneyarchaeologytours.co.uk) Specialises in all-inclusive multi-day tours focusing on Orkney's ancient sites with an archaeologist guide. Also runs private full-day (£420 for up to four) tours.

Wildabout Orkney GUIDED TOURS
(01856-877737; www.wildaboutorkney.com) Operates tours covering Orkney's history, ecology, folklore and wildlife. Day trips operate year-round and cost £59, with pick-ups in Stromness and Kirkwall.

John O'Groats Ferries BUS TOURS
(01955-611353; www.jogferry.co.uk; ⊙May-Sep) For the hurried; runs a one-day tour of the main sites for £58, including the ferry from John O'Groats. You can do the whole thing as a long day trip from Inverness.

Getting There & Away

AIR
Flybe (0871 700 2000; www.flybe.com) flies daily from Kirkwall to Aberdeen, Edinburgh, Glasgow, Inverness and Sumburgh (Shetland). Most summers it also serves Bergen (Norway).

BOAT
During summer, book car spaces ahead. Peak season fares are quoted here.

John O'Groats Ferries (01955-611353; www.jogferry.co.uk; single £15, incl bus to Kirkwall £17; ⊙May-Sep) Passenger-only service from John O'Groats to Burwick, on the southern tip of South Ronaldsay, with connecting bus to Kirkwall. Two to three departures daily.

Northlink Ferries (0845 6000 449; www.northlinkferries.co.uk) Operates ferries from Scrabster to Stromness (passenger/car £19.15/58, 1½ hours, two to three daily), from Aberdeen to Kirkwall (passenger/car £31/110, six hours, three or four weekly) and from Kirkwall to Lerwick (passenger/car £24.30/101, six to eight hours, three or four weekly) on Shetland. Fares are up to 30% lower off-season.

Pentland Ferries (01856-831226, 0800 688-8998; www.pentlandferries.co.uk; adult/child/car/bike £15/7/35/free) Leave from Gills Bay, 3 miles west of John O'Groats, and head to St Margaret's Hope on South Ronaldsay three to four times daily.

BUS
Citylink (www.citylink.co.uk) runs daily from Inverness to Scrabster, connecting with the Stromness ferries. John O'Groats Ferries has summer-only 'Orkney bus' service from Inverness to Kirkwall. Tickets (one-way/return £40/55, five hours) include bus-ferry-bus travel from Inverness to Kirkwall. There are two daily from June to August.

Getting Around

The *Orkney Transport Guide* details all island transport and is free from tourist offices.

The largest island, Mainland, is linked by causeways to four southern islands; others are reached by air and ferry.

AIR
Loganair (01856-873457; www.loganair.co.uk) operates interisland flights from Kirkwall.

BICYCLE
Various locations on Mainland hire bikes, including **Cycle Orkney** (01856-875777; www.cycleorkney.com; Tankerness Lane, Kirkwall; per day/3 days/week £15/30/60; ⊙9am-5.30pm Mon-Sat) and **Orkney Cycle Hire** (01856-850255; www.orkneycyclehire.co.uk; 54 Dundas St, Stromness; per day £10-12.50). Both offer out-of-hours pick-ups.

BOAT
Orkney Ferries (01856-872044; www.orkneyferries.co.uk) Operates car ferries from Mainland to the islands. See individual islands for details. An Island Explorer pass costs £42 for a week's passenger travel. Bikes are carried free.

BUS
Stagecoach (01856-878014; www.stagecoachbus.com) Runs buses on Mainland and connecting islands. Most don't operate on Sunday. Dayrider (£8.30) and 7-Day Megarider (£18.55) tickets allow unlimited travel.

Orkney & Shetland Highlights

1 Shaking your head in astonishment at extraordinary **Skara Brae** (p231) and **Maes Howe** (p230), prehistoric perfection that predates the pyramids

2 Soaking up the glorious scenery of **Hoy** and make the hike to the spectacular **Old Man of Hoy** (p234)

3 Island-hopping the magical **Northern Islands** of Orkney (p234), where crystal azure waters lap against glittering white-sand beaches

4 Diving the sunken warships of **Scapa Flow** (p230)

5 Discovering your inner Viking at Lerwick's **Up Helly Aa** (p243) festival

6 Capering with puffins and dodging dive-bombing skuas at Shetland's nature reserves of **Hermaness** (p248), **Fetlar** (p250) or **Noss** (p243)

7 Staying in one of Shetland's romantic **lighthouse cottages** (p244); one of the best is at spectacular **Sumburgh**

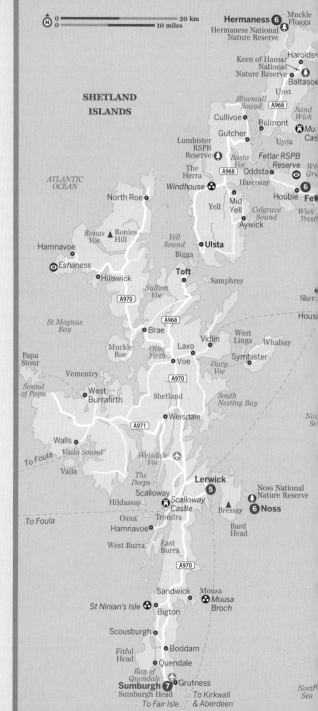

SHETLAND ISLANDS

0 ___ 20 km
0 ___ 10 miles

Hermaness **6** Muckle Flugga
Hermaness National Nature Reserve

Harolds

Keen of Hamar National Nature Reserve

Unst

Baltaso

Bluemull Sound A968

Sand Wick

Cullivoe

Belmont

Mu Cas

Gutcher

Uyea

Lumbister RSPB Reserve

Basta Voe

Fetlar RSPB Reserve

The Herra

A968

Oddsta

W Gre

ATLANTIC OCEAN

Windhouse

Hascosay

6

North Roe

Yell

Mid Yell

Houbie

Fet

Wick Trest

Aywick

Colgrave Sound

Ronies Hill

Ronas Voe

Yell Voe

Hamnavoe

Eshaness

Bigga

Yell Sound

Ulsta

Sker

Hillswick

Toft

Samphrey

Hous

Sullom Voe

A970

St Magnus Bay

A968

Brae

Vidlin

West Linga

Whalsay

Papa Stour

Muckle Roe

Olna Firth

Laxo

Symbister

Vementry

Voe

Dury Voe

Sound of Papa

A970

Shetland

South Nesting Bay

West Burrafirth

Weisdale

No Se

Walls

Vaila Sound

Weisdale Voe

A971

To Foula

Vaila

The Deeps

Lerwick
5

Noss National Nature Reserve

Scalloway

Scalloway Castle

Bressay **6** **Noss**

Hildasay

To Foula

Oxna

Trondra

Bard Head

Hamnavoe

West Burra

East Burra

A970

Sandwick

Mousa

St Ninian's Isle

Bigton

Mousa Broch

Scousburgh

Fitful Head

Boddam

Quendale

Bay of Quendale

Sumburgh **7**

Grutness

Sumburgh Head

To Kirkwall & Aberdeen

North Sea

To Fair Isle

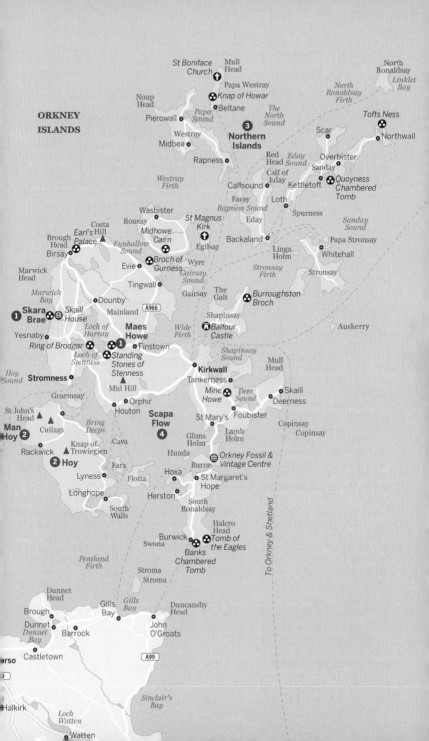

CAR

Small-car rates begin at around £35/190 per day/week, although there are specials for as low as £30 per day.

Orkney Car Hire (☑ 01856-872866; www.orkneycarhire.co.uk; Junction Rd, Kirkwall) Recommended. Close to Kirkwall bus station.

WR Tullock (☑ 01856-875500; www.orkney-carrental.co.uk; Castle St, Kirkwall) Opposite Kirkwall bus station.

Kirkwall

POP 7000

Orkney's capital is a bustling market town on a wide bay. Kirkwall's long, winding, paved main street and twisting wynds (lanes) are very atmospheric, and the town has a magnificent cathedral. Founded in the early 11th century, when Earl Rognvald Brusason established his kingdom here, the original part of Kirkwall is one of the best examples of an ancient Norse town.

◎ Sights

★ **St Magnus Cathedral** CATHEDRAL
(☑ 01856-874894; www.stmagnus.org; Broad St; ⊘9am-6pm Mon-Sat, 1-6pm Sun Apr-Sep, 9am-1pm & 2-5pm Mon-Sat Oct-Mar) **FREE** Constructed from local red sandstone, Kirkwall's centrepiece, dating from the early 12th century, is among Scotland's most interesting cathedrals. The powerful atmosphere of an ancient faith pervades the impressive interior. Lyrical and melodramatic epitaphs of the dead line the walls and emphasise the serious business of 17th- and 18th-century bereavement. Tours of the upper level (£7.25) run on Tuesdays and Thursdays; phone to book.

Earl Rognvald Brusason commissioned the cathedral in 1137 in the name of his martyred uncle, Magnus Erlendsson, who was killed by Earl Hakon Paulsson on Egilsay in 1117. Magnus remains are entombed in an interior pillar. Another notable interment is that of the Arctic explorer John Rae.

Earl's Palace & Bishop's Palace RUIN
(HS; ☑ 01856-871918; www.historic-scotland.gov.uk; Watergate; adult/child £4.50/2.70; ⊘9.30am-5.30pm Apr-Sep, to 4.30pm Oct) These two adjacent ruined palaces are worth poking around. The more intriguing, the **Earl's Palace**, was once known as the finest example of French Renaissance architecture in Scotland. One room features an interesting history of its builder, Earl Patrick Stewart,

THE BA'

Every Christmas Day and New Year's Day, Kirkwall holds a staggering spectacle: a crazy ball game known as The Ba'. Two enormous teams, the Uppies and the Doonies, fight their way, no holds barred, through the streets, trying to get a leather ball to the other end of town. The ball is thrown from the Market Cross to the waiting crowd; the Uppies have to get the ba' to the corner of Main St and Junction Rd, the Doonies must get it to the water. Violence, skulduggery and other stunts are common and the event, fuelled by plenty of strong drink, can last hours.

executed in Edinburgh for treason. He started ed construction in about 1600, but ran out of money and never completed it.

The **Bishop's Palace** was built in the mid-12th century for Bishop William the Old. There's a good cathedral view from the tower.

Orkney Museum MUSEUM
(☑ 01856-873191; www.orkney.gov.uk; Broad St; ⊘10.30am-12.30pm & 1.30-5pm Mon-Sat) **FREE** In a former merchant's house is this labyrinthine display. It has an overview of Orcadian history and prehistory, including Pictish carvings and a display on the Ba'. Most engaging are the last rooms, covering 19th- and 20th-century social history. Note, the museum is open 10.30am to 5.30pm in summer.

★ **Highland Park Distillery** DISTILLERY
(☑ 01856-874619; www.highlandpark.co.uk; Holm Rd; tour adult/child £7.50/free; ⊘10am-5pm Mon-Sat, noon-5pm Sun May-Aug, 10am-5pm Mon-Fri Apr & Sep, 1-5pm Mon-Fri Oct-Mar) South of the centre, this distillery is great to visit. They malt their own barley; you can see it and the peat kiln used to dry it on the excellent, well-informed hour-long tour. The standard 12-year-old is a soft, balanced malt, great for novices and aficionados alike; the 18-year-old is among the world's finest drams. This and older whiskies can be tasted on more specialised tours (£20 to £75), which you can prearrange.

Kirkwall

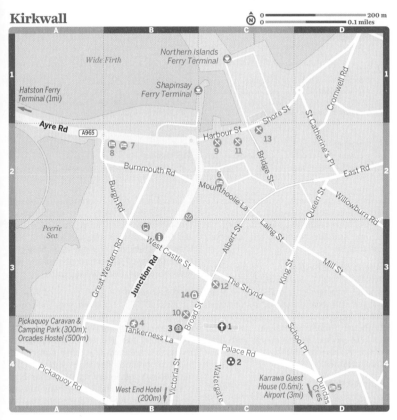

⭐ Festivals & Events

St Magnus Festival ARTS, MUSIC

(☏ 01856-871445; www.stmagnusfestival.com) A colourful celebration of music and the arts in late June.

🛏 Sleeping

Orcades Hostel HOSTEL £

(☏ 01856-873745; www.orcadeshostel.com; Muddisdale Rd; dm/s/d £20/40/52; 🅿 @ 🛜) Book ahead to get a bed in this cracking hostel on the western edge of town. It's a guesthouse conversion so there's a very smart kitchen and lounge, and great-value doubles. Comfortable dorms with just four bunks make for sound sleeping; young, enthusiastic owners give the place spark.

Kirkwall Peedie Hostel HOSTEL £

(☏ 01856-875477; www.kirkwallpeediehostel.com; Ayre Rd; dm/s/d £15/20/30; 🅿 🛜) Nestling into a corner at the end of the Kirkwall water-

front, this cute hostel set in former fisher-folk's cottages squeezes in all the necessary features for a comfortable stay. Despite the compact appearance, the dorms actually have plenty of room – and there are three tiny kitchens so you should find some elbow room. A separate 'bothy' sleeps four.

Pickaquoy Caravan & Camping Park CAMPSITE £

(☏ 01856-879900; www.pickaquoy.co.uk; Muddisdale Rd; sites per adult/child/tent £9.95/4.95/4.85; ☉ Apr-Oct; 🅿 🛜 ⛱ 🐕) No view, but plenty of grass and excellent modern facilities. If unattended, check in at the adjacent leisure centre.

2 Dundas Crescent B&B ££

(☏ 01856-874805; www.twodundas.co.uk; 2 Dundas Cres; s/d £40/75; 🅿 🛜) This former manse is a magnificent building with four enormous rooms blessed with large windows and sizeable beds. There are plenty of period

Kirkwall

features, but the en suite bathrooms are not among them: they're sparklingly new, and one has a free-standing bathtub. Both the welcome and the breakfast will leave you most content.

Karrawa Guest House   GUESTHOUSE **££**
(☑ 01856-871100; www.karrawaguesthouseorkney.co.uk; Inganess Rd; s/d £64/68; P � ☎) In a peaceful location on the southeastern edge of Kirkwall, this enthusiastically-run guesthouse offers significant value for well-kept modern double rooms with comfortable mattresses. Breakfast is generously proportioned.

Lynnfield Hotel   HOTEL **££**
(☑ 01856-872505; www.lynnfieldhotel.com; Holm Rd; s £90-100, d £115-155; P ☎ ☎) South of the centre, this sizeable yet intimate hotel is run with a professional touch. Rooms are individually decorated, and feature handsome furniture and plenty of character. Deluxe rooms have enormous bathrooms and opulent four-posters; others might showcase a Jacuzzi or antique desk. Public areas include a cosy dark-wood drawing room and large, well-regarded **restaurant** (dinner mains £16 to £19; noon to 1.45pm and 6pm to 8.45pm).

Ayre Hotel   HOTEL **££**
(☑ 01856-873001; www.ayrehotel.co.uk; Ayre Rd; s/d £90/120; P ☎) Right on the waterfront, this 200-year-old hotel has been recently renovated, leaving its low-ceilinged, large-bedded rooms looking very spruce. It's definitely worth paying the extra few pounds to grab one with a sea view.

Lerona   B&B **££**
(☑ 01856-874538; Cromwell Cres; s/d £33/66; P) Guests come first here, but the wee folk –

a battalion of garden gnomes and clans of dolls with lifelike stares – are close behind. The rooms, some en suite, are a good size, and friendly owners give an easygoing welcome. It's cheaper if you stay more than one night. Cromwell Crescent comes off the waterfront road just east of the centre.

West End Hotel   HOTEL **££**
(☑ 01856-872368; www.westendkirkwall.co.uk; Main St; s/d £72/105; P ☎ ☎) Run with gentle courtesy, this attractive pale-blue-and-yellow hotel has a series of old-fashioned rooms that are gradually being modernised by the proprietors. The attic rooms are cute but hobbit-sized; other updated chambers offer plenty of comfort and a teddy to cuddle. The fabulous but faded suite has an antique-filled sitting room, reminiscent of stays at some great-uncle's place.

★ Albert Hotel   HOTEL **£££**
(☑ 01856-876000; www.alberthotel.co.uk; Mounthoolie Lane; s/d £96/135; ☎) Stylishly refurbished in plum and grey, this central but peaceful hotel is Kirkwall's finest address. Comfortable contemporary rooms in a variety of categories sport superinviting beds and smart bathrooms. A great Orkney base, with the more-than-decent Bothy Bar downstairs. Walk-in prices often cheaper.

✗ Eating & Drinking

Reel   CAFE **£**
(www.facebook.com/thereelkirkwall; Albert St; sandwiches £3-6; ☉9am-6pm Mon-Sat; ☎) Part music shop and part cafe, Kirkwall's best coffee-stop sits alongside the cathedral, and bravely puts tables outside at the slightest threat of sunshine. It's a relaxed spot, good for morning-after debriefing, a quiet Orkney ale, or lunchtime panini and musically

named sandwiches (plus the cheese-and-mushroom Skara Brie). It's a local folk musicians' centre, with regular evening sessions.

Judith Glue Real Food Cafe CAFE £

(www.judithglue.com; 25 Broad St; light meals £5-10; ⊙ 9am-6pm Mon-Sat, 10am-6pm Sun year-round, to 10pm Fri & Sat May plus Mon-Sat Jun-Sep; 🐾) 🍴 At the back of a lively craft shop opposite the cathedral, this cafe serves toothsome sandwiches and salads, as well as daily specials and succulent seafood platters. There's an open kitchen and a strong emphasis on sustainable and organic ingredients, but put the feel-good factor aside for a moment and fight for a table. Check Facebook for regular events.

Bothy Bar PUB £

(☑ 01856-876000; www.alberthotel.co.uk; Mounthoolie Lane; mains £7-12; ⊙ noon-2pm & 5-9pm; 🐾) In the Albert Hotel, the Bothy looks very smart these days with its modish floor and B&W photos of old-time Orcadian farming, but its low tables provide old-time cheer and sustaining food. Think sausages, haddock and stews: good pub grub.

★ Foveran ORCADIAN ££

(☑ 01856-872389; www.thefoveran.com; St Ola; mains £15-23; ⊙ 6.30-8.30pm mid-Apr–mid-Oct, Fri & Sat only plus other days by arrangement off-season; 🐾) 🍴 Three miles down the Orphir road, one of Orkney's best dining options is surprisingly affordable for the quality. Tranquilly located, with a cosy eating area overlooking the sea, it shines presenting classic Orcadian ingredients – the steak with haggis and whisky sauce is feted throughout, while North Ronaldsay lamb comes in four different, deliciously tender cuts.

A medley of toothsome vegetables accompanies the mains, and interesting wines complement the dishes. If you like the spot – and why wouldn't you? – there are compact, comfortable, Laura Ashley-decorated rooms available (single/double £78/116).

Shore GASTROPUB ££

(www.theshore.co.uk; 6 Shore St; bar meals £8-10, restaurant mains £12-18; ⊙ food 11am-9.30pm; 🐾) This popular harbourside eatery offers bar meals combined with more adventurous evening fare in the restaurant section. It's run with a customer-comes-first attitude, and the seafood is especially good.

Kirkwall Hotel PUB, SCOTTISH ££

(☑ 01856-872232; www.kirkwallhotel.com; Harbour St; mains £8-16; ⊙ noon-2pm & 6-9pm; 🐾) This grand old waterfront hotel is one of Kirkwall's better dining places. The elegant bar and eating area packs out; it's a favourite spot for an evening out with the clan. A fairly standard pub-food list is complemented by a seasonal menu featuring local seafood and meat – the lamb is delicious. The more modern bar down the side, Skippers, also does food.

Helgi's PUB ££

(www.helgis.co.uk; 14 Harbour St; mains £10-12; ⊙ food noon-9pm, from 12.30pm Sun; 🐾) There's a traditional cosiness about this place, but the decor has moved beyond the time-honoured beer-soaked carpet to a comfortable contemporary slate floor and quotes from the *Orkneyinga Saga* plastering the walls. It's more find-a-table than jostle-at-the-bar and serves cheerful, well-priced comfort food – light bites only between 2pm and 5pm. Take your pint upstairs for quiet harbour contemplation.

🛍 Shopping

Kirkwall has some gorgeous jewellery and crafts along Albert St. The **Longship** (☑ 01856-888790; www.olagoriejewellery.com; 7 Broad St; ⊙ 10am-5pm Mon-Sat Sep-May, 9am-5.30pm daily Oct-Apr), established in 1859, has Orkney-made crafts, food, gifts and exquisite designer jewellery across adjacent shops.

ℹ Information

Balfour Hospital (☑ 01856-888000; www.ohb.scot.nhs.uk; New Scapa Rd) Follow Junction Road south out of town and you'll see it on your right.

Kirkwall Tourist Office (☑ 01856-872856; kirkwall@visitscotland.com; West Castle St; ⊙ 9am-6pm daily Jun-Sep, 9am-5pm Mon-Fri & 10am-2pm Sat Oct-Apr, 9am-6pm Mon-Sat & 10am-2pm Sun May) Has a good range of Orkney info. Shares building with the bus station.

ℹ Getting There & Away

AIR

Flybe (p221) and Loganair (p221) services use **Kirkwall Airport** (www.hial.co.uk), located a few miles east of town and served by bus 4.

BOAT

Ferries to the Northern Islands depart from the town harbour; however, ferries to Aberdeen and

Shetland use the Hatston terminal, 1 mile northwest. Bus X10 shuttles out there regularly.

BUS

All services leave from the **bus station** (West Castle St):

Bus X1 Stromness (£3, 30 minutes, hourly, seven Sunday); St Margaret's Hope (£2.80)

Bus 2 Orphir and Houton (£2.70, 20 minutes, four or five daily Monday to Saturday)

Bus 5 Evie (£2.70, 30 minutes, three to five daily Monday to Saturday), Tingwall (Rousay ferry) and Birsay.

East Mainland to South Ronaldsay

After a German U-boat sank battleship HMS *Royal Oak* in 1939, Winston Churchill had causeways of concrete blocks erected across the channels on the eastern side of Scapa Flow, linking Mainland to the islands of Lamb Holm, Glims Holm, Burray and South Ronaldsay. The Churchill Barriers, flanked by rusting wrecks of blockships, now support the main road from Kirkwall to Burwick.

ℹ Getting There & Away

Bus 3 from Kirkwall runs to Deerness in East Mainland (£2.70, 30 minutes, three to five Monday to Saturday), some via Tankerness. Bus X1 goes to South Ronaldsay's St Margaret's Hope (£2.80, 30 minutes, almost hourly Monday to Saturday).

East Mainland

At Tankerness is the mysterious Iron Age site of **Mine Howe** (☑ 01865-861234; www.minehowe.com; adult/child £4/2; ☉ 10am-4pm daily Jun-Aug, 11am-3pm Tue & Fri Sep & May), an eerie underground construction of unknown function. In the centre of an earthen mound ringed by a ditch, a claustrophobic, precarious flight of narrow steps descends steeply to a stone-lined chamber about 1.5m in diameter and 4m high. At the time of research it was closed due to storm damage but will hopefully reopen.

Lamb Holm

This tiny island's **Italian Chapel** (☑ 01865-781268; ☉ 9am-dusk) FREE was once in a POW camp housing Italian soldiers working on the Churchill Barriers. They built the chapel in their spare time, using Nissen huts, scrap metal and considerable artistic skills. It's an extraordinary monument to human ingenuity.

Alongside is the enthusiastic shop of **Orkney Wine Company** (☑ 01856-781736; www.orkneywine.co.uk; ☉ 10am-5pm Mon-Sat May-Sep, plus noon-4pm Sun Jul & Aug, reduced hours Mar-Apr & Oct-Dec, closed Jan & Feb), which produces handmade wines made from berries, flowers and vegetables, all naturally fermented. Get stuck into some strawberry-rhubarb wine or blackcurrant port – unusual flavours but surprisingly delicious.

Burray

POP 400

This small island has a fine beach at Northtown on the east coast, where you may see seals.

◉ Sights

Orkney Fossil & Vintage Centre MUSEUM
(☑ 01865-731255; www.orkneyfossilcentre.co.uk; adult/child £4/2.50; ☉ 10am-5pm mid-Apr–Sep) A quirky collection of household and farming relics, 360-million-year-old Devonian fish fossils found locally and galleries devoted to the world wars, including a display on the Churchill Barriers. There's an excellent coffee shop here. It's on the left half a mile after crossing to Burray, coming from Kirkwall.

🛏 Sleeping & Eating

Sands Hotel HOTEL **££**
(☑ 01856-731298; www.thesandshotel.co.uk; s/d/ste £90/115/165; P 🛜) This commodious refurbished 19th-century herring station is right on the pier in Burray village. Rooms have stylish furnishings, and all have great water views. Families and groups should consider a suite: brilliant two-level self-contained flats that sleep four and have a kitchen. There's a good restaurant (noon to

---

BLACKENINGS

Some attractive Orcadian caught your eye? Think twice, because weddings up here are traditionally preceded by a 'blackening'. The groom (and these days, often the bride) is stripped naked by friends, painted with treacle, floured, feathered and paraded around town before being bound to the Mercat Cross with clingfilm. You have been warned.

2pm and 6pm to 9pm) with a genteel nautical feel.

South Ronaldsay

POP 900

South Ronaldsay's main village, pristine **St Margaret's Hope**, was named after the Maid of Norway, who died here in 1290 on her way to marry Edward II of England (strictly a political affair: Margaret was only seven years old). The ferry from Gills Bay on mainland Scotland docks here, while the passenger ferry from John O'Groats lands at Burwick, at the island's southern tip.

◉ Sights & Activities

★ **Tomb of the Eagles** ARCHAEOLOGICAL SITE
(01865-831339; www.tomboftheeagles.co.uk; Liddel; adult/child £7.50/3.50; ⊙9.30am-5.30pm Apr-Sep, 10am-noon Mar, 9.30am-12.30pm Oct) Two significant archaeological sites were found here by a farmer on his land. The first is a Bronze Age stone building with a firepit, indoor well and plenty of seating: a communal cooking site or the original Orkney pub? Beyond, in a spectacular clifftop position, the neolithic tomb (wheel yourself in prone on a trolley) is an elaborate stone construction which held the remains of up to 340 people who died some five millennia ago.

An excellent personal explanation is given to you at the visitor centre; you meet a few spooky skulls and can handle some of the artefacts found, plus absorb information on the mesolithic period. It's about a mile's airy walk to the tomb from the centre, which is near Burwick.

Banks Chambered Tomb ARCHAEOLOGICAL SITE
(Tomb of the Otters; www.bankschamberedtomb.co.uk; Cleat; adult/child £6/free; ⊙10am-5pm Apr-Oct) Discovered while digging a car park, this 5000-year-old chambered tomb is still being investigated but has yielded a vast quantity of human bones, well preserved thanks to the saturation of the earth. The

tomb is dug into bedrock and makes for an atmospheric if claustrophobic visit. The guided tour from the guy who found it mixes homespun archaeological theories with astute observations.

In the **visitor centre**, which is a good bistro too, you can handle finds of stones and bones, including the remains of otters, who presumably used this as a den. Follow signs for Tomb of the Eagles.

🛏 Sleeping & Eating

St Margaret's Hope Backpackers HOSTEL £
(01856-831225; www.orkneybackpackers.com; dm £15; 🅿) Just a stroll from the Gills Bay ferry, this hostel is a lovely stone cottage offering small, simple rooms with up to four berths – great for families. There's a lounge, kitchen, laundry and good, hot showers. Book in at the Trading Post shop next door.

★ **Bankburn House** B&B ££
(01856-831310; www.bankburnhouse.co.uk; A961; s/d £52/68, without bathroom £41/62; 🅿@🛜🐾) 🍴 This large rustic house does everything right, with smashing good-sized rooms and engaging owners who put on quality breakfasts and take pride in constantly innovating to improve guests' comfort levels. The huge lawn overlooks St Margaret's Hope and the bay – perfect for sunbathing on shimmering Orkney summer days. Prices drop substantially for multinight stays.

Skerries Bistro SEAFOOD ££
(01856-831605; www.skerriesbistro.co.uk; Cleat; lunches £5-9, dinner mains £10-18; ⊙11am-5pm & 6-9pm Apr-Oct) Helpful and friendly, this cafe-bistro occupies a smart, modern glass-walled building with great clifftop views near the island's southern tip. Meals range from soups and sandwiches to daily fish and shellfish specials. It's all delicious. Dinner should be booked ahead. A romantic little separate pod is available for seafood feasts.

★ **Creel** SEAFOOD £££
(01856-831311; www.thecreel.co.uk; Front Rd, St Margaret's Hope; 2-/3-course dinner £33/40; ⊙7-9pm Tue-Sat Apr–mid-Oct; 🛜) 🍴 On the waterfront in an unassuming house, on unpretentious wooden tables, some of Scotland's best seafood has been served up for well over 20 years. Upstairs, three most comfortable **rooms** (singles/doubles £75/110) face the spectacular sunset over the water. Wooden ceilings and plenty of space give

ORKNEY & SHETLAND EAST MAINLAND TO SOUTH RONALDSAY

ℹ ORKNEY EXPLORER PASS

The **Orkney Explorer Pass** covers all Historic Scotland sites in Orkney, including Maes Howe, Skara Brae, the Broch of Gurness, the Brough of Birsay and the Bishop's Palace and Earl's Palace in Kirkwall; it costs £18/10.80/36 per adult/child/family.

them an airy feel. It was up for sale at the time of research, so fingers crossed.

West & North Mainland

This part of the island is sprinkled with outstanding prehistoric monuments: the journey to Orkney is worth it for these alone. It would take the best part of a day to see all of them – if pushed for time, visit Skara Brae then Maes Howe, but book your visit to the latter in advance.

◉ Sights

★ **Maes Howe** ARCHAEOLOGICAL SITE
(HS; ☎ 01856-761606; www.historic-scotland.gov.uk; adult/child £5.50/3.30; ☺ tours hourly 10am-4pm) Egypt has pyramids, Scotland has Maes Howe. Constructed about 5000 years ago, it's an extraordinary place, a Stone Age tomb built from enormous sandstone blocks, some of which weighed many tonnes and were brought from several miles away. Creeping down the long stone passageway to the central chamber, you feel the indescribable gulf of years that separate us from the architects of this mysterious place. Though nothing is known about who and what was interred here, the scope of the project suggests it was a structure of great significance.

In the 12th century, the tomb was broken into by Vikings searching for treasure. A couple of years later, another group sought shelter in the chamber from a three-day blizzard. Waiting out the storm, they carved runic graffiti on the walls. As well as the some-things-never-change 'Olaf was 'ere' and 'Thorni bedded Helga', there are also more intricate carvings, including a particularly fine dragon and a knotted serpent.

Buy tickets in Tormiston Mill across the road. Entry is by 45-minute guided tours on the hour: reserve your tour slot ahead by phone. Oversized groups mean guides tend to only show a couple of the Viking inscriptions, but they'll happily show more if asked.

Standing Stones of Stenness ARCHAEOLOGICAL SITE
(HS; www.historic-scotland.gov.uk; ☺ 24hr) **FREE** Within sight of Maes Howe, four mighty stones remain of what was once a circle of 12. Recent research suggests they were perhaps erected as long ago as 3300 BC and they impose by their sheer size; the tallest measures 5.7m in height. The narrow strip of land they're on, the Ness of Brodgar, separates the Harray and Stenness lochs and was the site of a large settlement, inhabited throughout the neolithic period (3500–1800 BC).

Barnhouse Neolithic Village RUIN
(HS; www.historic-scotland.gov.uk; ☺ 24hr) **FREE** Alongside the Standing Stones of

---

DIVING SCAPA FLOW

One of the world's largest natural harbours, Scapa Flow has been in near-constant use by fleets from the Vikings onwards. After WWI, 74 German ships were interned here; when the armistice dictated a severely reduced German navy, Admiral von Reuter, in charge of the fleet, took matters into his own hands. A secret signal was passed around and the British watched incredulously as every German ship began to sink. Fifty-two of them went to the bottom, with the rest left aground in shallow water.

Most were salvaged, but seven vessels remain to attract divers. There are three battleships – the *König*, the *Kronprinz Wilhelm* and the *Markgraf*. The first two were partially blasted for scrap, but the *Markgraf* is undamaged and considered one of Scotland's best dives.

Numerous other ships rest on the sea bed. HMS *Royal Oak*, sunk by a German U-boat in October 1939 with the loss of 833 crew, is a war grave and diving is prohibited.

It's worth prebooking diving excursions far in advance. **Scapa Scuba** (☎ 01856-851218; www.scapascuba.co.uk; Lifeboat House, Stromness; beginner's try dive £80, 2 guided dives £125-145; ☺ noon-7pm Mon-Fri & 3-6pm Sat & Sun May-Sep) is an excellent operator that caters for both beginners – with 'try dives' around the Churchill barriers – and tried-and-tested divers. You'll need plenty of experience to dive the wrecks, some of which are 47m deep, plus have recent drysuit experience: this can be organised for you. **Diving Cellar** (☎ 01856-850055; www.divescapaflow.co.uk; Pierhead, Stromness; week diving incl B&B £485) offers intensive week-long packages, including accommodation, for experienced divers.

NESS OF BRODGAR

Ongoing excavations on the **Ness of Brodgar**, between the Stenness standing stones and the Ring of Brodgar, are rapidly revealing that this was a neolithic site of huge importance. Probably a major power and religious centre and used for over a millennium, the settlement had a mighty wall, a large building (a temple or palace?) and as many as 100 other structures, some painted. Each dig season reveals new, intriguing finds. During the season, mid-July to late August, free guided tours of the excavation run at 11am, 1pm and 3pm.

Stenness are the excavated remains of a village thought to have been inhabited by the builders of Maes Howe. Don't skip this: it brings the area to life. The houses are well preserved and similar to Skara Brae with their stone furnishings. One of the buildings was entered by crossing a fireplace: possibly of ritual significance.

Ring of Brodgar ARCHAEOLOGICAL SITE
(HS; www.historic-scotland.gov.uk; ⊘24hr) **FREE**
A mile north of Stenness is this wide circle of standing stones, some over 5m tall. The last of the three Stenness monuments to be built (2500–2000 BC), it remains a most atmospheric location. Twenty-one of the original 60 stones still stand among the heather. On a grey day with dark clouds thudding low across the sky, the stones are a spine-tingling sight.

Orkney Folklore & Storytelling Visitor Centre FOLKLORE
(☑01856-841207; www.orkneyattractions.com) Located between Brodgar and Skara Brae, this offbeat centre focuses on the islands' folkloric tradition. The best way to experience it is on one of its atmospheric storytelling evenings, Peatfire Tales of Orkney (Sunday, Tuesday and Friday at 8.30pm March to October, adult/child £10/6) when local legends are told with musical accompaniment around a peat fire. It also runs interesting guided walks of the coastline and of Stromness (£7) and offers B&B.

★**Skara Brae** ARCHAEOLOGICAL SITE
(HS; www.historic-scotland.gov.uk; joint ticket with Skaill House adult/child £7.10/4.30; ⊘9.30am-5.30pm Apr-Sep, to 4.30pm Oct-Mar)

Idyllically situated by a sandy bay 8 miles north of Stromness, and predating Stonehenge and the pyramids of Giza, extraordinary Skara Brae is northern Europe's best-preserved neolithic village. Even the stone furniture – beds, boxes and dressers – has survived the 5000 years since a community lived and breathed here. It was hidden under dunes until an 1850 storm exposed the houses underneath.

There's an excellent interactive exhibit and short video, arming visitors with facts and theory, which will enhance the impact of the site. You then enter a reconstructed house, giving the excavation, which you head on to next, more meaning.

The joint ticket also gets you into **Skaill House** (HS; ⊘Apr-Sep), a mansion built for the bishop in 1620. It's a bit anticlimactic catapulting straight from the neolithic to the 1950s decor, but you can see a smart hidden compartment in the library as well as the bishop's original 17th-century four-poster bed.

Buses run to Skara Brae from Kirkwall and Stromness a few times weekly in summer, but not all are useful to visit the site. It's possible to walk along the coast from Stromness to Skara Brae (9 miles), or it's an easy taxi (£15), hitch or cycle from Stromness. If you ring before 3pm the day before, you can book **Octobus** (☑01856-871536; www.octocic.co.uk) from Kirkwall (£3.20 each way).

Orkney Brewery BREWERY
(☑01856-841777; www.orkneybrewery.co.uk; Quoyloo; tour adult/child £6/3.50; ⊘10am-4.30pm Mon-Sat & 11am-4.30pm Sun Apr-Oct plus most of Dec, winter opening by arrangement) These folk have been producing their brilliant Orcadian beers – Dark Island is a standout, while Skullsplitter lives up to its name – for years now, but this new visitor centre is a great place to come and try them. Tours run regularly and explain the brewing process, while, fashionably decked out in local stone, the cafe-bar is atmospheric.

Birsay

The small village of Birsay is 6 miles north of Skara Brae.

◉ Sights & Activities

Earl's Palace RUIN
(⊘24hr) **FREE** The ruins of this palace, built in the 16th century by the despotic Robert Stewart, earl of Orkney, dominate the village

ORKNEY & SHETLAND WEST & NORTH MAINLAND

of Birsay. Today it's a mass of half walls and crumbling columns; the size of the palace is impressive, matching the reputed ego and tyranny of its former inhabitant.

Brough of Birsay   ARCHAEOLOGICAL SITE
(HS;   www.historic-scotland.gov.uk;   adult/child £4.50/2.70; ⊙9.30am-5.30pm mid-Jun–Sep) At low tide – check tide times at any Historic Scotland site – you can walk out to this windswept island, site of extensive Norse ruins, including a number of longhouses and 12th-century **St Peter's Church**. There's also a replica of a Pictish stone found here. St Magnus was buried here after his murder on Egilsay in 1117, and the island became a pilgrimage place. The attractive lighthouse has fantastic views. Take a picnic, but don't get stranded...

🛏 Sleeping & Eating

Birsay Hostel   HOSTEL, CAMPSITE £
(🖉after hours 01856-721470, office hours 01856-873535; www.orkney.gov.uk; tent sites 1/2 people £6.45/10.25, dm/tw £16.60/46; P🐾) A former activity centre and school now has dorms that vary substantially in spaciousness – go for two- or four-bedded ones. There's a big kitchen and a grassy camping area; kids and families sleep substantially cheaper. It's on the A967 south of Birsay village.

Birsay Bay Tearoom   CAFE £
(www.birsaybaytearoom.co.uk; Birsay; light meals £3-6; ⊙11am-3.30pm Fri-Sun Oct-Mar, 11am-4.30pm Wed-Sun Apr, 11am-6pm Wed-Mon May-Sep; 🔊) A pleasant spot with sweeping views over green grass, black cows and blue-grey sea, this serves teas, coffees, home-baking and light meals. It's a good spot to wait for the tide to go out before crossing the Brough, in plain sight.

Evie

On an exposed headland at Aikerness, 1.5 miles northeast from the village of Evie, the **Broch of Gurness** (HS; www.historic-scotland.gov.uk; adult/child £5.50/3.30; ⊙9.30am-12.30pm & 1.30-5.30pm Apr-Sep) is a fine example of the drystone fortified towers that were both a status symbol for powerful farmers and useful protection from raiders some 2200 years ago. The imposing entranceway and sturdy stone walls – originally 10m high – are impressive; inside you can see the hearth and where a mezzanine floor would have fitted. Around the broch are a number of well-pre-

served outbuildings, including a curious shamrock-shaped house. The visitor centre has some interesting displays on the culture that built these remarkable fortifications.

Stromness

POP 1800

This appealing grey-stone port has a narrow, elongated, flagstone-paved main street and tiny alleys leading down to the waterfront between tall houses. It lacks Kirkwall's size but makes up for that with bucketloads of character, having changed little since its heyday in the 18th century, when it was a busy staging post for ships avoiding the troublesome English Channel during European wars. Stromness is ideally located for trips to Orkney's major prehistoric sites.

⊙ Sights

The main recreation in Stromness is simply strolling up and down the narrow, atmospheric main street, where cars and pedestrians move at the same pace.

★Stromness Museum   MUSEUM
(🖉01856-850025; www.stromnessmuseum.co.uk; 52 Alfred St; adult/child £4.50/1; ⊙10am-5pm daily Apr-Sep, 11am-3.30pm Mon-Sat Oct-Mar) A superb museum full of knick-knacks from maritime and natural-history exhibitions covering whaling, the Hudsons Bay Company and the sunk German fleet. You can happily nose around for a couple of hours. Across the street is the house where local poet and novelist George Mackay Brown lived.

Pier Arts Centre   GALLERY
(🖉01856-850209; www.pierartscentre.com; 30 Victoria St; ⊙10.30am-5pm Tue-Sat, plus Mon Jun-Aug) FREE This gallery has really rejuvenated the Orkney modern-art scene with its sleek lines and upbeat attitude. It's worth a look as much for the architecture as its high-quality collection of 20th-century British art and the changing exhibitions.

✸ Festivals & Events

Orkney Folk Festival   MUSIC
(www.orkneyfolkfestival.com) A four-day event in late May, with folk concerts, *ceilidhs* and casual pub sessions. Stromness packs out, and late-night buses from Kirkwall are laid on. Book tickets and accommodation ahead.

🛏 Sleeping

Hamnavoe Hostel
HOSTEL **£**

(☎01856-851202; www.hamnavoehostel.co.uk; 10a North End Rd; dm/s/tw £20/22/44; 🛜) This well-equipped hostel is efficiently run and boasts excellent facilities, including a fine kitchen and a lounge room with great perspectives over the water. The dorms are very commodious, with duvets, decent mattresses and reading lamps (bring a pound coin for the heating), and the showers are good. Ring ahead as the owner lives off-site.

Brown's Hostel
HOSTEL **£**

(☎01856-850661; www.brownsorkney.co.uk; 45 Victoria St; s £20, d £36-45; @🛜) On the main street, this handy, sociable place has cosy private rooms – no dorms, no bunks – at a good price. There's an inviting common area, where you can browse the free internet or swap pasta recipes in the open kitchen. There are en suite rooms in a house up the street, with self-catering options available.

Point of Ness Caravan & Camping Park
CAMPSITE **£**

(☎office hrs 01856-873535, site 01856-850532; www.orkney.gov.uk; Ness Rd; tent sites 1/2 people £7.20/11.20; ⏱Apr-Sep; P🛜🐾) This breezy, fenced-in campground has a super location overlooking the bay at the southern end of town and is as neat as a pin. There's free wi-fi.

★Brinkies Guest House
B&B **££**

(☎01856-851881; www.brinkiesguesthouse.co.uk; s £50, d £75-80; P🛜) Just a short walk from the centre, but with a lonely, king-of-the-castle position overlooking the town and bay, this exceptional place offers five-star islander hospitality. Compact, modern rooms are handsome, stylish and comfortable, public areas are done out most attractively in wood, but above all it's the charming owner's flexibility and can-do attitude that makes this so special.

Breakfast is 'continental Orcadian' – a stupendous array of quality local cheese, smoked fish and homemade bere bannocks. Want a lie-in? No problem, saunter down at 10am. Don't want breakfast? How about packed lunch instead? Take Outertown Rd off Back Rd, turn right on to Brownstown Rd, and keep going.

Burnside Farm
B&B **££**

(☎01856-850723; www.burnside-farm.com; North End Rd; s £50, d £80-95; P🛜) A most pleasing option on a working dairy farm on the edge of Stromness, this offers lovely views over green fields, the town and harbour. Rooms are elegant, and maintain the style from when the house was built in the late 1940's, with elegant period furnishings. The top-notch bathrooms, however, are sparklingly contemporary. Breakfast is served with vistas, and the kindly owner couldn't be more welcoming.

Ferry Inn
INN **££**

(☎01856-850280; www.ferryinn.com; 10 John St; s £52, d £70-90; 🛜) With a wide variety of rooms divided between the pub itself and a guesthouse opposite, the Ferry is a useful accommodation option in Stromness, which can fill up fast. New owners have renovated the chambers, and they are mostly a good size, with attractive modern decor and OK bathrooms.

🍴 Eating & Drinking

Ferry Inn
PUB **£**

(☎01856-850280; www.ferryinn.com; 10 John St; mains £7-14; ⏱food noon-2pm & 5-9pm Mon-Fri, noon-9pm Sat & Sun; 🛜) Every port has its pub, and in Stromness it's the Ferry. Convivial and central, it warms the cockles with folk music, local beers and characters, and pub food that offers plenty of value in a dining area done out like the deck of a ship. The fish 'n' chips are excellent, and a few blackboard specials fill things out. It's also open for breakfasts.

Hamnavoe Restaurant
SEAFOOD **££**

(☎01856-850606; 35 Graham Pl; mains £15-22; ⏱6-9pm Tue-Sun Jun-Aug) Tucked away off the main street, this Stromness favourite specialises in excellent local seafood in an intimate, cordial atmosphere. There's always something good off the boats, and the chef prides himself on his lobster. Booking is a must. It usually opens weekends off-season.

Stromness Hotel
SEAFOOD, PUB **££**

(☎01856-850298; www.stromnesshotel.com; 15 Victoria St; mains £10-19; ⏱6-9pm daily, plus noon-2pm Sat & Sun; 🛜) This central hotel does decent local seafood dishes plus a few Indian curries and skewers, with some vegetarian options. There's a lounge bar with harbour views, or the earthier, convivial Flattie Bar downstairs.

ℹ️ Information

Stromness Tourist Office (☎01856-850716; www.visitorkney.com; Ferry Rd; ⊙10am-4pm Mon-Fri & 8.30am-2.30pm Sat Apr-May, 9am-5pm daily Jun-Oct) In the ferry terminal.

ℹ️ Getting There & Around

BOAT

Northlink Ferries (p221) runs services from Stromness to Scrabster on the mainland (high season passenger £19.15, car £58, 1½ hours, two to three daily).

BUS

Bus X1 runs regularly to Kirkwall (£3, 30 minutes) and on to St Margaret's Hope.

Hoy

POP 400

Orkney's second-largest island, Hoy (meaning 'High Island'), got the lion's share of the archipelago's scenic beauty. Shallow turquoise bays lace the east coast and massive sea cliffs guard the west, while peat and moorland cover Orkney's highest hills. Much of the north is a reserve for breeding seabirds. Book ahead for the car ferry to Hoy.

👁 Sights & Activities

Scapa Flow Visitor Centre MUSEUM
(☎01856-791300; www.orkney.gov.uk; Lyness; admission by donation; ⊙9am-4.30pm Mon-Fri Mar-Oct, plus 9am-4.30pm Sat May-Oct, 1st ferry arrival to 4pm Sun May-Sep) Lyness was an important naval base during both world wars, when the British Grand Fleet was based in Scapa Flow. This fascinating museum and photographic display, located in an old pumphouse that once fed fuel to the ships, is a must-see for anyone interested in Orkney's military history. Take your time to browse the exhibits and have a look at the folders of supplementary information: letters home from a seaman lost when the *Royal Oak* was torpedoed are particularly moving.

Old Man of Hoy ROCK FORMATION
Hoy's best-known sight is this spectacular 137m-high rock stack jutting from the ocean off the tip of an eroded headland. It's a tough ascent for experienced climbers only but a great walk from Rackwick (6 miles return). You can see it from the Scrabster–Stromness ferry.

🛏 Sleeping & Eating

Hoy Centre HOSTEL £
(☎office hours 01856-873535, warden 01856-791315; www.orkney.gov.uk; dm/tw £18/49; ℙ) This clean, bright modern hostel has an enviable location, around 15 minutes' walk from Moaness Pier, at the base of the rugged Cuilags. Rooms are all en suite and include good-value family options; there's also a spacious kitchen and DVD lounge. The same people run a simpler hostel at Rackwick, five miles away.

Wild Heather B&B ££
(☎01856-791098; www.wildheatherbandb.co.uk; Lyness; s/d £43/69; ℙ) Turn right from the Lyness ferry to reach this great place right on the bay. The lovely room is frilly and spotless, with soul-soothing water views from your own wee conservatory, where you also tuck into breakfast. Packed lunches and three-course dinners (£16.50) are available, as well as cycle storage and a genuine welcome. The owners' daughter runs a cute craft shop alongside.

Stromabank Hotel PUB ££
(☎01856-701494; www.stromabank.co.uk; Longhope; ⊙6-9pm Sat, 12.30-2pm & 6-9pm Sun Sep-May, plus 6-9pm Mon-Wed & Fri Jun-Aug; ℙ🛜) Perched on the hill above Longhope, the small atmospheric Stromabank has very acceptable, refurbished en suite rooms (s/d £45/70), as well as tasty home-cooked meals, including seafood and steaks (£7 to £14) using lots of local produce. The owners were looking to sell, so details may change.

ℹ️ Getting There & Away

Orkney Ferries (p221) runs a passenger/bike ferry (adult £4.25, 30 minutes, two to six daily) between Stromness and Moaness at Hoy's northern end, and a car ferry to Lyness from Houton on Mainland (passenger/car £4.25/13.60, 40 minutes, up to seven daily Monday to Friday, two or three Saturday and Sunday); book cars in advance. Sunday service is May to September only.

A bus meets the ferries and runs to Hoy's main settlements.

Northern Islands

The group of windswept islands north of Mainland is a haven for birds, rich in archaeological sites, and blessed with wonderful white-sand beaches and azure seas. Some give a real sense of what Orkney was like before the modern world infringed upon island life.

Note that the 'ay' at the end of island names (from the Old Norse for 'island') is pronounced 'ee'.

ⓘ Getting There & Away

Orkney Ferries (☑ 01856-872044; www.orkneyferries.co.uk) and **Loganair** (☑ 01857-873457; www.loganair.co.uk) enable you to make day trips to many of the islands from Kirkwall. That said, it's really best to stay and soak up the slow, easy pace of life.

Shapinsay

POP 300

Just a short ferry hop from Kirkwall, Shapinsay is an intensively cultivated island whose southern end is dominated by 19th-century **Balfour Castle** and good beaches along its western edge. About 4 miles from the pier, at the island's northeastern corner, Iron Age **Burroughston Broch** is one of the best preserved of these defensive towers in Orkney.

ⓘ Getting There & Away

Orkney Ferries (p221) operates a ferry from Kirkwall (passenger/car £4.25/13.60, 25 minutes). Services are limited in winter.

Rousay

POP 200

Off the north coast of Mainland, Rousay makes a great day trip, but you'll feel like staying longer. This hilly island is famous for its numerous excellent archaeological sites.

◉ Sights & Activities

You can hire a bike (£7 per day) at Trumland Farm and make the hilly 14-mile circuit of the island. You can walk from the ferry pier to Midhowe Broch, taking in all the main historic sites (12 miles return, allow six hours).

The major archaeological sites are clearly labelled from the road ringing the island. Heading west from the ferry, you soon come to **Taversoe Tuick**, an intriguing burial cairn constructed on two levels, with separate entrances – perhaps a joint tomb for different families; a semidetached solution in posthumous housing. Not far beyond are two other significant cairns: **Blackhammer**,

then **Knowe of Yarso**, the latter a fair walk up the hill but with majestic views.

★ Midhowe Cairn & Broch
ARCHAEOLOGICAL SITES

(HS; www.historic-scotland.gov.uk; ⊙ 24hr) FREE

Six miles from the ferry, mighty **Midhowe Cairn** has been dubbed the 'Great Ship of Death'. Built around 3500 BC and enormous, it's divided into compartments, in which the remains of 25 people were found. Covered by a protective stone building, it's nevertheless memorable. Adjacent **Midhowe Broch**, whose sturdy stone lines echo the rocky shoreline's striations, is a muscular Iron Age fortified compound with a mezzanine floor. The sites are on the water, a 10-minute walk downhill from the main road.

🛏 Sleeping & Eating

Trumland Farm
HOSTEL **£**

(☑ 01856-821252; trumland@btopenworld.com; sites £5, dm £12-14; P 🐾) 🍃 An easy stroll from the ferry (turn left at the main road), this organic farm has a wee hostel with two dorms and a pretty little kitchen and common area. You can pitch tents and use the facilities; there's also well-equipped self-catering in a cottage and various farm buildings.

Taversoe Hotel
HOTEL **££**

(☑ 01856-821325; www.taversoehotel.co.uk; s/d £50/80; P) Two miles west from the ferry pier, the island's only hotel is a low-key place, with neat, simple doubles with water vistas that share a bathroom and a twin with en suite but no view. The best views are from the dining room, which serves good-value meals (noon to 5pm Monday, noon to 9pm Tuesday to Saturday and noon to 7.30pm Sunday in summer). The friendly owners will collect you from the ferry.

ⓘ Getting There & Around

BOAT

A small **ferry** (☑ 01856-751360; www.orkneyferries.co.uk) connects Tingwall on Mainland with Rousay (return passenger/bicycle/car £8.50/free/27.20, 30 minutes, up to six daily) and the nearby islands of Egilsay and Wyre. Vehicle bookings are compulsory.

TAXI

Rousay Tours (☑ 01856-821234; www.rousaytours.co.uk; adult/child £30/10) offers taxi service and recommended guided tours of the island, including wildlife-spotting (seals and otters), visits to the prehistoric sites and optional tasty packed lunch.

Stronsay

POP 350

Stronsay attracts walkers and cyclists for its lack of serious inclines and the beautiful landscapes of its four curving bays. You can spot wildlife here: chubby seals basking on the rocks, puffins and other seabirds.

🛏 Sleeping & Eating

Stronsay Hotel   HOTEL ££
(☑ 01857-616213; www.stronsayhotelorkney.co.uk; s/d £50/79; 🛜🐾) The island's watering hole is near the ferry and has immaculate refurbished rooms. There's also recommended pub grub in the bar.

ℹ Getting There & Away

AIR

Loganair (p235) flies from Kirkwall to Stronsay (£37 one way, 20 minutes, one or two daily).

BOAT

A **ferry** (☑ 01856-872044; www.orkneyferries. co.uk) links Kirkwall with Stronsay (passenger/car £8.35/19.70, 1½ hours, two to three daily) and Eday.

Eday

POP 150

This slender island was extensively cut for peat to supply the surrounding islands. The interior is hilly and covered in peat bog, while the coast and the north of the island are low-lying and green.

⊙ Sights

Eday Heritage & Visitor Centre   MUSEUM
(☑ 01857-622283; www.visiteday.com; ⊙ 9am-5.30pm daily May-Sep, 10am-5pm Sun Oct-Apr) **FREE** Has a range of local history exhibits, as well as an audiovisual about tidal energy initiatives: there's a big test project just offshore.

☞ Tours

Eday Minibus Tour   GUIDED TOURS
(☑ 01857-622206; adult/child £14/12) Offers taxi service and 2¼-hour guided tours from the ferry pier on Monday, Wednesday and Friday from May to mid-September.

OFF THE BEATEN TRACK

OUT TO THE ISLANDS

It's well worth getting out to explore Orkney's further-flung islands, accessible by reasonably priced ferry or plane. Though you can see 'the sights' in a matter of hours, the key is to stay a day or two and relax into the pace of island life.

Though some are hillier than others, all offer a broadly similar landscape of flattish green farmland running down to scenic coastline.

Nearly all have places where you can camp, hire bikes and sleep cheaply. Most islands offer a bus service that meets ferries: you may have to call to book this. The *Islands of Orkney* magazine, available from tourist offices, has detailed listings and maps for every island.

🛏 Sleeping & Eating

Eday Hostel   HOSTEL £
(☑ 07977-281084; dm £12-15; 🅿@🛜) Four miles north of the ferry pier, this recently renovated, community-run hostel is a simple but comfortable place to stay. You can camp alongside too at no cost and there are bikes available to hire.

ℹ Getting There & Away

AIR

There's a Monday and Wednesday flight from Kirkwall (one-way £37, 30 minutes) to London airport – that's London, Eday.

BOAT

Ferries sail from Kirkwall, sometimes via Stronsay or Sanday (passenger/car £8.35/19.70, two hours, two to three daily).

Sanday

POP 500

Aptly named, blissfully quiet flat Sanday is ringed by Orkney's best beaches – with dazzling-white sand of the sort you'd expect in the Caribbean. It's a peaceful, green, pastoral landscape with the sea revealed at every turn.

ORKNEYINGA SAGA

Written around 1200, this saga is a rich tale of sorcery, political intrigue, and cunning and unscrupulous acts among the Viking earls of Orkney. Part myth and part historical fact, it begins with the capture of the islands by the king of Norway and recounts the tumultuous centuries until they become part of Scotland. It's a wonderful piece of medieval literature and well worth a read. Head to the **Orkneyinga Saga Centre** (⊙9am-6pm late May–late Oct) FREE in the south coast village of Orphir for more background.

◉ Sights

Quoyness Chambered Tomb
ARCHAEOLOGICAL SITE

(⊙24hr) FREE There are several archaeological sites on Sanday, the most impressive being the Quoyness chambered tomb, similar to Maes Howe and dating from the 3rd millennium BC. It has triple walls, a main chamber and six smaller cells.

Sanday Heritage Centre
MUSEUM

(Lady; entry by donation; ⊙9am-5pm Mar–Oct) This new museum in the former temperance hall has intriguing displays on various aspects of island history, including fishing, the wars, archaeology and shipwrecks. In an adjacent field, a typical croft house is preserved.

⊨ Sleeping & Eating

Two adjacent pubs in the main settlement, **Kettletoft**, offer accommodation and basic bar meals.

Ayre's Rock Hostel & Campsite
HOSTEL, CAMPSITE £

(☑01857-600410; www.ayres-rock-hostel-orkney.com; tent sites 1-/2-person £7/9, pods per person £10, dm/s/tw £15/18/30; P 🛜 🏠) This super-friendly spot six miles north of the ferry by a beach offers a cosy hostel with three rooms sleeping two or four in beds, and a sweet grassy campsite by the water. As well as tent pitches, there are heated two-person pods and a static caravan. There's a craft shop and Saturday chip shop on-site, and the hosts are extremely helpful.

Backaskaill
B&B ££

(☑01857-600305; www.bedandbreakfastsanday-orkney.com; s/d £45/75; P 🛜) Set on a working cattle farm by the sea, this offers comfortable accommodation in a noble stone farmhouse. The polished interior features an eclectic collection of art and curios and cordial, professional hospitality. Rooms feel light and modern, and there's a fabulous guest lounge. The island's best meals (mains £9 to £16) are here and can be booked by non-guests.

❶ Getting There & Away

AIR

There are flights from Kirkwall to Sanday (one way £37, 20 minutes, once or twice daily).

BOAT

Ferries run from Kirkwall (passenger/car £8.35/19.70, 1½ hours), with a link to Eday. A bus meets the boat.

Westray

POP 600

If you've time to visit only one of Orkney's Northern Islands, make Westray (www.westraypapawestray.co.uk) the one. The largest of the group, it has rolling farmland, handsome sandy beaches, great coastal walks and several appealing places to stay.

◉ Sights & Activities

Noup Head
NATURE RESERVE

FREE This bird reserve at Westray's northwestern tip is a dramatic area of sea cliffs with vast numbers of breeding seabirds from April to July. You can walk here along the clifftops from a car park, passing the impressive chasm of **Ramni Geo**, and return via the lighthouse access road (4 miles).

Westray Heritage Centre
MUSEUM

(☑01857-677414; www.westrayheritage.co.uk; Pierowall; adult/child £3/50p; ⊙10am-noon Tue-Sat & 2-5pm Sun May–Sep) This has displays on local history, nature dioramas and archaeological finds, with some famous neolithic carvings (including the 5000-year-old 'Westray Wife'). These small sandstone figurines are the oldest known depictions of the human form so far found in the British Isles.

★ Noltland Castle
CASTLE

(⊙8am-8pm) FREE A half-mile west of Pierowall stands this sturdy ruined towerhouse, built in the 16th century by Gilbert Balfour, aide to Mary, Queen of Scots. The castle is super-atmospheric and bristles with shot holes, part of the defences of the deceitful Balfour, who plotted to murder Cardinal Beaton and, after being exiled, the king of Sweden. Like a pantomime villain, he met a sticky end.

Tours

Westraak GUIDED TOURS
(☑ 01857-677777; www.westraak.co.uk; Quarry Rd, Pierowall) Runs informative and engaging trips around the island, covering everything from Viking history to puffin mating habits.

🛏 Sleeping & Eating

★ West Manse B&B £
(☑ 01857-677482; www.westmanse.co.uk; Westside; r per person £20; P 🐾 🖲) 🖉 No timetables reign at this imposing house with arcing coastal vistas; make your own breakfast when you feel like it. Your welcoming hosts have introduced a raft of green solutions for heating, fuel and more. Kids will love this unconventional place, its play nooks and hobbit house, while art exhibitions, cooking and blacksmithing classes, venerably comfortable furniture and clean air are drawcards for parents.

Chalmersquoy & The Barn B&B, HOSTEL £
(☑ 01857-677214; http://chalmersquoywestray.co.uk; Pierowall; dm £20, apt per night £60-100, tent sites £5-8 plus per adult/child £2/1; P 🖲) This excellent, intimate, modern hostel is an Orcadian gem. It's heated throughout and has pristine kitchen facilities and an inviting lounge; rooms sleep two or three in comfort. Out the front, the lovely owners have top self-catering apartments with great views, and three spacious en suite B&B rooms. There's also a campground on-site. A recommended all-round choice.

Bis Geos SELF-CATERING £
(☑ 01857-677420; www.bisgeos.co.uk; per week from £350; P) Stunning views at this spectacular, quirky and cosy self-catering option between Pierowall and Noup Head.

Braehead Manse B&B, SELF-CATERING ££
(☑ 01857-677861; www.braeheadmanse.co.uk; Braehead; s/d £65/90; P 🖲) 🖉 A top-notch conversion of a former village hall behind the church in the middle of the island, this has two luminous, high-ceilinged rooms with modern en suite bathrooms and a swish open-plan kitchen/living/dining area.

You can either take it as self-catering – perfect for a family of four – or B&B.

Pierowall Hotel PUB £
(☑ 01857-677472; www.pierowallhotel.co.uk; Pierowall; mains £8-11; ⊙ food noon-1.30pm & 5-8.30pm; 🖲) The heart of this island community, the refurbished local pub is famous throughout Orkney for its popular fish and chips – whatever has turned up in the day's catch by the hotel's boats is displayed on the blackboard. There are also some curries available, but the sea is the way to go here. It also has rooms, hires bikes and offers internet access.

ℹ Getting There & Around

AIR
There are daily flights from Kirkwall to Westray (one way £37, 20 minutes).

BOAT
A ferry (p221) links Kirkwall with Rapness (passenger/car £8.35/19.70, 1½ hours, daily). A bus to the main town, Pierowall, meets the ferry.

Papa Westray
POP 90

Known locally as Papay, this exquisitely peaceful, tiny island (4 miles by 1 mile) is home to possibly Europe's oldest domestic building, the **Knap of Howar** (⊙ 24hr) FREE (5500 years old), and largest arctic tern colony. Plus the two-minute hop from Westray is the world's shortest scheduled air service. The island was the cradle of Christianity in Orkney – **St Boniface Kirk** (⊙ 24hr) FREE was founded in the 8th century, though most of it dates to the 12th.

🛏 Sleeping & Eating

Beltane House GUESTHOUSE, HOSTEL £
(☑ 01857-644224; www.papawestray.co.uk; dm/s/d £17/25/35; P 🐾 🖲) Owned by the local community co-op, this comprises a 20-bed hostel and a guesthouse with four simple and immaculate rooms with en suite and self-catering kitchen access. It's just over a mile north of the ferry. You can camp here (£5/3 per adult/child).

ℹ Getting There & Away

AIR
There are daily flights to Papa Westray (£18, 15 minutes) from Kirkwall, and a special £21 return fare if you stay overnight. Some of the Kirkwall flights go via Westray (£17, 2 minutes) or North Ronaldsay (£17, 10 minutes).

BOAT

A passenger-only ferry runs from Pierowall on Westray to Papa Westray (£4.15, 25 minutes, three to six daily in summer); the crossing is free if you travel direct from the Rapness ferry from Westray. From October to April the boat sails by arrangement (01857-677216).

North Ronaldsay

POP 70

North Ronaldsay is a real outpost surrounded by rolling seas and big skies. Delicious peace-and-quiet and excellent birdwatching lure visitors. There are enough semiferal sheep to seize power, but a 13-mile drystone wall running around the island keeps them off the grass; they make do with seaweed, which gives their meat a unique flavour.

Tours

North Ronaldsay Tour   GUIDED TOURS
(07703-112224; lighthouse or mill adult/child £6/4, combined £9/7) Offers excellent tours of one of North Ronaldsay's two lighthouses and a wool mill.

Sleeping

Observatory Guest House HOSTEL, CAMPSITE **££**
(01857-633200; www.nrbo.co.uk; sites £4.50, dm/s/d £17.50/40.50/81; P @) Powered by wind and solar energy, this offers first-rate accommodation and ornithological activities next to the ferry pier. There's a cafe-bar with lovely coastal views and convivial communal dinners (£14.50) in a sun-kissed (sometimes) conservatory; if you're lucky, local lamb might be on the menu. You can also camp here.

Getting There & Away

AIR

There are two or three daily flights to North Ronaldsay (£18, 20 minutes) from Kirkwall. The £21 return offer (you must stay overnight) is great value.

BOAT

A ferry runs from Kirkwall on Tuesday and Friday (passenger/car £8.35/19.70, 2½ hours).

SHETLAND

Close enough to Norway geographically and historically to make nationality an ambiguous concept, the Shetland Islands are Britain's most northerly outpost. There's a Scandinavian lilt to the local accent, and streets named King Haakon or St Olaf remind that Shetland was under Norse rule until 1469, when it was gifted to Scotland in lieu of the dowry of a Danish princess.

Though the stirringly bleak setting still feels uniquely Scottish, Shetland is far from a backwater: offshore oil makes it quite a busy, well-heeled place, with hotels frequently block-booked for workers. Nevertheless, nature still rules the seas and islands, and the birdlife is spectacular: pack binoculars.

Getting There & Away

AIR

The main **airport** (LSI; 01950-461000; www.hial.co.uk) is at Sumburgh, 25 miles south of Lerwick. **Flybe** (0871 700 2000; www.flybe.com) runs daily services to Aberdeen, Kirkwall, Inverness, Edinburgh and Glasgow, and summer services to Bergen (Norway).

BOAT

Northlink Ferries (0845 600 0449; www.northlinkferries.co.uk;) runs daily overnight car ferries between Aberdeen and Lerwick (high-season one-way passenger/car £41/144, 12 to 15 hours), some stopping at Kirkwall, Orkney. With a basic ticket you can sleep in recliner chairs or the bar area. It's £36 for a berth in a shared cabin and up to £137 for a comparatively luxurious double cabin. Sleeping pods (£18) are comfortable, reclinable seats. There's a cafe, bar, paid lounge and cinema on-board plus slow wi-fi.

Getting Around

AIR

Interisland flights are operated by **DirectFlight** (01595-840246; www.directflight.co.uk) from Tingwall airport, 6.5 miles northwest of Lerwick. There are big discounts for under-25s.

BOAT

Ferry services run by **Shetland Islands Council** (www.shetland.gov.uk/ferries) link Mainland to other islands.

BICYCLE

You can hire bikes from several places, including Grantfield Garage (p240; per day/week £12.50/50) in Lerwick.

BUS

An extensive bus network, coordinated by **ZetTrans** (www.zettrans.org.uk), radiates from Lerwick to all corners of Mainland, and on (via ferry) to the islands of Yell and Unst. Schedules aren't great for day tripping from Lerwick.

ORKNEY & SHETLAND NORTHERN ISLANDS

CAR & MOTORCYCLE

Shetland has broad, well-made roads (think 'oil money'). Car hire is fuss-free, and vehicles can be delivered to transport terminals. Prices are usually around £35/180 for a day/week.

Bolts Car Hire (☑ 01595-693636; www.boltscarhire.co.uk; 26 North Rd, Lerwick) Also has an office at Sumburgh airport.

Grantfield Garage (☑ 01595-692709; www.grantfieldgarage.co.uk; North Rd, Lerwick; ⊙ 9am-5.30pm Mon-Sat) The cheapest. A short walk towards town from the Northlink ferry terminal.

Star Rent-a-Car (☑ 01595-692075; www.starrentacar.co.uk; 22 Commercial Rd, Lerwick) Opposite the bus station. Has an office at Sumburgh airport.

Lerwick

POP 7000

Built on the herring trade, Lerwick is Shetland's only real town, home to a third of the islands' population. It has a solidly maritime feel, with aquiline oilboats competing for space in the superb natural harbour with the dwindling fishing fleet. Wandering along atmospheric Commercial St is a delight, and the excellent museum provides cultural background.

⊙ Sights

★ **Shetland Museum** MUSEUM
(☑ 01595-695057; www.shetland-museum.org.uk; Hay's Dock; ⊙ 10am-5pm Mon-Sat, noon-5pm Sun) **FREE** This is an impressive recollection of 5000 years' worth of culture, people and their interaction with this ancient landscape. Comprehensive but never dull, the display covers everything from the archipelago's geology to its fishing industry, via local mythology – find out about scary *nyuggles* (ghostly horses) or detect *trows* (fairies). Pictish carvings and replica jewellery are among the finest pieces; the museum also includes a working lighthouse mechanism, small gallery, boat-building workshop, and archive for tracing Shetland ancestry.

Böd of Gremista MUSEUM
(Shetland Textile Museum; www.shetlandtextilemuseum.com; Gremista Rd; admission £2; ⊙ noon-5pm Tue-Sat, to 7pm Thu May–mid-Oct) A mile north of the centre, this house, birthplace of P&O founder Arthur Anderson, was also once a fish-curing station. It now holds a display on the knitted and woven textiles

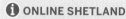

ⓘ ONLINE SHETLAND

The excellent website www.visit.shetland.org has good info on accommodation, activities and more.

and patterns that take their name from the islands.

Clickimin Broch ARCHAEOLOGICAL SITE
FREE This fortified site, just under a mile southwest of the town centre, was occupied from the 7th century BC to the 6th century AD. It's impressively large, and its setting on a small loch gives it a feeling of being removed from the present day.

Fort Charlotte FORTRESS
(Charlotte St; ⊙ 9.30am-sunset) **FREE** Built in 1781, this occupies the site of an earlier fortification built in 1665 to protect the harbour from the Dutch navy. The five-sided fortress never saw action, but today houses local volunteer units and provides excellent views over the harbour.

☞ Tours

Shetland Geotours GUIDED TOURS
(☑ 01595-859218; www.shetlandgeotours.com; per person from £45) Runs daily excursions and guided walks, focusing on geology, history and archaeology, but including some nature-watching. Check the website for the schedule.

⚑ Festivals & Events

Shetland Folk Festival MUSIC
(www.shetlandfolkfestival.com) Held in late April or early May.

⮡ Sleeping

Lerwick has very average hotels but excellent B&Bs. It fills year-round; book ahead. There's no campsite within 15 miles.

Islesburgh House Hostel HOSTEL £
(☑ 01595-745100; www.islesburgh.org.uk; King Harald St; dm/tw/q £20/40/60; ⊙ Apr-Sep; ℗ @ 🖻) This typically grand Lerwick mansion houses an excellent hostel, with comfortable dorms, a shop, a laundry, a cafe and an industrial kitchen. Electronic keys offer excellent security and no curfew. It's wise to book ahead, and ask about winter availability as it sometimes opens for groups.

Lerwick

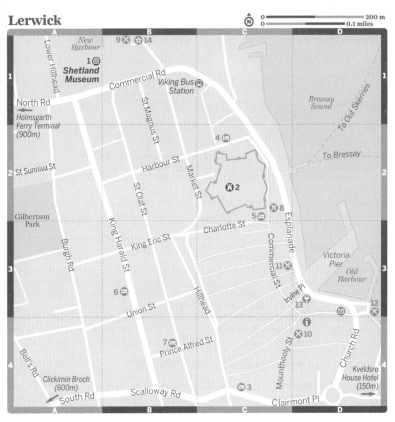

ORKNEY & SHETLAND LERWICK

Woosung B&B **£**
(☏01595-693687; conroywoosung@hotmail.com; 43 St Olaf St; s without bathroom £30-35, d without bathroom £50-55; 🛜🐾) A budget gem in the heart of Lerwick B&B-land, this has a wise and welcoming host, and comfortable, clean, good-value rooms that share a bathroom. The solid stone house dates from the 19th century, built by a clipper captain who traded tea out of the Chinese port it's named after.

★Alder Lodge Guesthouse B&B **££**
(☏01595-695705; www.alderlodgeguesthouse. com; 6 Clairmont Pl; s/d £35/75; 🅿🛜) This stone former bank is a delightful place to stay. Imbued with a sense of space and light, the rooms are large and very well furnished, with good en suites, fridges and DVD player. Excellent hosts really make the effort to help you feel at home, and do a great breakfast, with a smoked fish option and special di-

ets catered for. There is also a self-catering house nearby.

★Fort Charlotte Guesthouse B&B **££**
(☏01595-692140; www.fortcharlotte.co.uk; 1 Charlotte St; s/d £35/70; 🛜🐾) Sheltering under the fortress walls, this friendly place offers summery en suite rooms, including great singles. Views down the pedestrian street are on offer in some; sloping ceilings and oriental touches add charm to others. There's a bike shed and local salmon for breakfast. Very popular; book ahead.

Brentham House B&B **££**
(☏01950-460201; www.brenthamhouse.com; 7 Harbour St; s/d/apt £65/80/130; 🛜) This staffless place – pick up the keys from the restaurant on the corner – offers attractive rooms with comfy seats, decent bathrooms – big towels and powerful showers – and limited harbour views. There's a posh self-catering apartment (the Bressay Suite) also. Conti-

Lerwick

◉ Top Sights	
1 Shetland Museum	A1

◎ Sights	
2 Fort Charlotte	C2

🛌 Sleeping	
3 Alder Lodge Guesthouse	C4
4 Brentham House	C2
Eddlewood Guest House	(see 3)
5 Fort Charlotte Guesthouse	C2
6 Islesburgh House Hostel	B3
7 Woosung	B4

❌ Eating	
8 Fort Café	C2
Hay's Dock	(see 1)
9 Mareel Cafe	B1
10 Monty's Bistro	D4
11 Peerie Shop Cafe	C3
12 Queen's Hotel	D3

◎ Drinking & Nightlife	
13 Captain Flint's	D3

◎ Entertainment	
14 Mareel	B1

nental breakfast is left in the fridge in your room. It could do with a little TLC, but the central location is a plus.

Kveldsro House Hotel HOTEL ££
(☑ 01595-692195; www.shetlandhotels.com; Greenfield Pl; s/d £110/135; P ☎) Lerwick's best hotel overlooks the harbour and has a quiet but central setting. It's a dignified small set-up that will appeal to older visitors or couples. All doubles cost the same, but some are markedly better than others, with four-poster beds or water views. All boast new stylish bathrooms and iPod docks. The bar area is elegant and has fine perspectives.

Eddlewood Guest House B&B ££
(☑ 01595-696734; http://eddlewood.wordpress.com; 8 Clairmont Pl; s/d £50/70; ☎) Cheerfully run, this sound selection has spacious, very well-kept en suite rooms with good showers. The top-floor rooms have plenty of character, with a cosy attic feel and good sea views. The friendly owner runs a welcoming, relaxed ship.

✕ Eating

Peerie Shop Cafe CAFE £
(☑ 01595-692816; www.peerieshopcafe.com; Esplanade; light meals £3-8; ☺ 9am-6pm Mon-Sat; ☎) If you've been craving proper espresso since leaving the mainland, head to this gem, with art exhibitions, wire-mounted halogens and industrial-gantry chic. Newspapers, scrumptious cakes and sandwiches, hot chocolate that you deserve after that blasting wind outside, and – more rarely – outdoor seating give everyone a reason to be here.

Mareel Cafe CAFE £
(Mareel; light meals £3-5; ☺ 10am-11pm Sun-Thu, 10am-1am Fri & Sat; ☎) Buzzy, arty and colour-

ful, this cheery venue in Mareel overlooks the water and does sandwiches and baked potatoes by day, and some cute Shetland tapas in the evenings. The coffee is decent, too, and it's a nice place for a cocktail.

Fort Café CAFE, TAKEAWAY £
(☑ 01595-693125; 2 Commercial St; fish & chips £6-8; ☺ 11am-10.30pm Mon-Fri, 11am-7pm Sat, 4-10.30pm Sun) Lerwick's salty air often creates fish-and-chip cravings. Eat in (until 8pm), or munch down on the pier if you don't mind the seagulls' envious stares.

★ Hay's Dock CAFE, SEAFOOD ££
(☑ 01595-741569; www.haysdock.co.uk; Hay's Dock; mains lunch £7-11, dinner £15-22; ☺ 10.30am-3.30pm Mon-Sat, noon-4.30pm Sun, plus 6.30-9pm Fri & Sat year-round & Tue-Thu Jun-Aug; ☎ ⬛)
🖉 Upstairs in the Shetland Museum, this sports a wall of picture windows and a fair-weather balcony that overlooks the harbour. Clean lines and pale wood recall Scandinavia, but the menu relies on carefully selected local and Scottish produce. Lunch ranges from delicious fish and chips to chowder, while evening menus concentrate on seafood and steak.

Queen's Hotel SCOTTISH ££
(☑ 01595-692826; www.kgqhotels.co.uk; Commercial St; mains £15-22; ☺ noon-2pm & 5.30-9.30pm; ☎) The dining room in this slightly run-down hotel wins marks for its harbour views – book one of the window tables. It's best visited for beautifully presented, classy local seafood dishes.

Monty's Bistro BRITISH ££
(☑ 01595-696555; www.montys-shetland.co.uk; 5 Mounthooly St; mains lunch £8-10, dinner £13-17; ☺ 5-9pm Mon, noon-2pm & 5-9pm Tue-Sat, noon-9.30pm Sun; ☎) 🖉 Though well hidden away

behind the tourist office, Monty's is far from a secret and Shetlanders descend on it with alacrity. The upstairs dining room, with proper floorboards and an upbeat atmosphere, is a cheerful venue for good-quality British bistro fare.

Drinking & Entertainment

Check what's on at **Mareel** (☑ 01595-745555; www.mareel.org), a swish new arts venue near the museum.

Captain Flint's   PUB
(2 Commercial St; ⊘ 11am-1am; 🐾) This portside bar – Lerwick's liveliest – throbs with happy conversation, loud music and has a distinctly nautical, creaky-wooden feel. There's a cross-section of young 'uns, tourists, boat folk and older locals. There's live music some nights and a pool table upstairs.

Shopping

Best buys are the woollen cardigans and sweaters for which Shetland is world famous. Check www.shetlandsartsandcrafts.co.uk for outlets around the islands, or grab the *Shetland Craft Trail* brochure from the tourist office.

ℹ Information

There are several free wi-fi networks around the centre.

Gilbert Bain Hospital (☑ 01595-743000; www.shb.scot.nhs.uk/; South Rd)
Lerwick Tourist Office (☑ 01595-693434; lerwick@visitscotland.com; cnr Commercial St & Mounthooly St; ⊘ 9am-5pm Mon-Sat & 10am-4pm Sun Apr-Sep, 10am-4pm Mon-Sat

---

UP HELLY AA!!

Shetland's long Viking history has rubbed off in more ways than just street names and square-shouldered locals. Most villages have a fire festival, a continuation of Viking midwinter celebrations of the rebirth of the sun. The most spectacular happens in Lerwick.

Up Helly Aa (www.uphellyaa.org) takes place on the last Tuesday in January. Squads of *guizers* dress in Viking costume and march through the streets with blazing torches, dragging a replica longship, which they then surround and burn, bellowing out Viking songs from behind bushy beards.

Oct-Mar) Helpful, with a good range of books and maps.

ℹ Getting There & Away

BOAT
Northlink Ferries (p239) dock at Holmsgarth terminal, a 15-minute walk northwest from the town centre.

BUS
From **Viking bus station** (☑ 01595-694100; Commercial Rd), buses service various corners of the archipelago, including regular services to/from Sumburgh Airport.

Bressay & Noss
POP 400

These islands lie across Bressay Sound just east of Lerwick. Bressay (*bress*-ah) has interesting walks, especially along the cliffs and up Ward Hill (226m), which has good views of the islands. Much smaller Noss is a nature reserve.

◉ Sights & Activities

★**Isle of Noss**   NATURE RESERVE
(☑ 0800-107-7818; www.nnr-scotland.org.uk/noss; boat adult/child £3/1.50; ⊘ 10am-5pm Tue, Wed & Fri-Sun mid-Apr–Aug) Little Noss, 1.5 miles wide, lies just east of Bressay. High sea cliffs harbour over 100,000 pairs of breeding seabirds, while inland heath supports hundreds of pairs of great skua.

Access is by dinghy from Bressay; phone in advance to check that it's running. Walking anticlockwise around Noss is easier, with better cliff viewing. There's a small visitor centre by the dock.

Seabirds & Seals   CRUISE
(☑ 07595-540224; www.seabirds-and-seals.com; adult/child £45/25; ⊘ 10am & 2pm mid-Apr–mid-Sep) Runs three-hour wildlife cruises around Bressay and Noss, departing from Lerwick. Includes underwater viewing. Trips run year-round, weather permitting; book by phone or at Lerwick tourist office.

🛏 Sleeping & Eating

Northern Lights Holistic Spa   B&B ££
(☑ 01595-820257; www.shetlandspa.com; Uphouse; s/d £75/125; 🅿🐾) Offering huge, colourful rooms and marvellous views back over the sound towards Lerwick, this unusual place is appealingly decorated with Asian art. Room rates include sauna, steam

room and jacuzzi; massages and elaborate dinners (£37.50; BYOB) are available. Head for Uphouse; it's the big yellow building near the crest of the hill.

ℹ️ Getting There & Away

Ferries (passenger/car return £5.20/12.80, seven minutes, frequent) link Lerwick and Bressay. The Noss crossing is 2.5 miles across the island.

Central & West Mainland

Scalloway

POP 1200

Surrounded by bare, rolling hills, Scalloway (*scall*-o-wah) – Shetland's former capital – is a busy fishing and yachting harbour with a thriving seafood-processing industry. It's 6 miles from Lerwick.

There are pretty beaches and pleasant walks on the nearby islands, linked by bridges, of Trondra and East and West Burra.

◉ Sights & Activities

Scalloway Museum   MUSEUM
(www.scallowaymuseum.org; Castle St; adult/child £3/1; ⊙11am-4pm Mon-Sat, 2-4pm Sun May-Sep; 🅿️) This enthusiastic modern museum has an excellent display on Scalloway life and history, with prehistoric finds, witch-burnings and local lore all featuring. There's a detailed section on the Shetland Bus, and a fun area for kids.

Scalloway Castle   CASTLE
(HS; www.historic-scotland.co.uk; ⊙24hr) FREE
The town's most promient landmark is Scalloway Castle, built around 1600 by Earl Patrick Stewart. The turreted and corbelled tower house is fairly well preserved. If locked, get keys from Scalloway Museum or Scalloway Hotel.

Shetland Bus Memorial   MONUMENT
(Main St) During WWII a fleet of small boats – the Shetland Bus – shuttled from Scalloway to occupied Norway, carrying agents and supplies for the Norwegian resistance, and returning with refugees, recruits for Free Norwegian forces and Christmas trees. The memorial, built of stones from both countries, is a moving tribute.

OFFBEAT ACCOMMODATION

Shetland offers intriguing options for getting off the beaten accommodation track. There's a great network of *böds* – simple rustic cottages or huts with peat fires. They cost £10 per person, or £8 for the ones without electricity, and are available March to October. Contact and book via **Shetland Amenity Trust** (☑️01595-694688; www.camping-bods.com; ⊙9am-5pm Mon-Thu, 9am-4pm Fri).

The same organisation runs three **Lighthouse Cottages** (☑️01595-694688; www.shetlandlighthouse.com; per three days £277-320, per week £600-700), commanding dramatic views of rugged coastline: one, recently renovated and classy, at Sumburgh, one on the island of Bressay near Lerwick, and one at Eshaness. They sleep six to seven, and prices drop substantially off-season.

🛏️ Sleeping & Eating

⭐ **Scalloway Hotel**   HOTEL ££
(☑️01595-880444; www.scallowayhotel.com; Main St; s/d £80/115; 🅿️🛜) One of Shetland's best, this energetically run waterfront place has very stylish rooms featuring sheepskins, local tweeds and other fabrics, and views over the harbour. Some are larger than others; the best is the fabulous superior, with handmade furniture, artworks and a top-of-the-line mattress on its four-poster bed. The restaurant (mains £11 to £15) is good for quality seafood and Scottish cheeses.

ℹ️ Getting There & Away

Buses run from Lerwick (£1.90, 20 minutes, roughly hourly Monday to Saturday, two Sunday) to Scalloway, stopping on Main St.

South Mainland

From Lerwick, it's 25 miles down this narrow, hilly tail of land to Sumburgh Head. The lapping waters are an inviting turquoise – if it weren't for the raging Arctic gales, you'd be tempted to have a dip.

Sandwick & Around

Opposite scattered Sandwick is the small isle of **Mousa**, an RSPB reserve protecting some 7000 breeding pairs of storm petrels.

SEA KAYAKING

Paddling is great for exploring Shetland's tortuous coastline, and allows you to get up close to seals and bird life. **Sea Kayak Shetland** (01595-840272; www.seakayakshetland.co.uk; beginner session/half-day/day £25/40/75) is a reliable operator catering for beginners and experts alike, and offering various guided trips.

It's also home to rock-basking seals and impressive **Mousa Broch**. Rising to 13m, it's an imposing double-walled structure with a spiral staircase to access a 2nd floor. It features in Viking sagas as a hideout for eloping couples.

Tours

Mousa Boat　　　　　　　　BOAT TOURS

(☑07901-872339; www.mousa.co.uk; ☺Apr–mid-Sep) This operator runs daily boat trips to Mousa (adult/child return £16/7, 15 minutes) from Sandwick, allowing three hours ashore on the island. It also offers night petrel-viewing trips (dates on website).

Bigton & Around

Three buses from Lerwick (not Sunday) stop in Bigton, whence it's another couple of miles to the largest shell-and-sand tombolo (sand or gravel isthmus) in Britain. Walk across to beautiful, emerald-capped **St Ninian's Isle**, where you'll find the ruins of a 12th-century church where a famous hoard of silver Pictish treasure was found. The treasure is now kept in Edinburgh's Museum of Scotland, with replicas in Lerwick's Shetland Museum (p240).

Boddam & Scousburgh

From small Boddam a side road leads to the **Shetland Crofthouse Museum** (☑01950-460557; www.shetlandheritageassociation.com; ☺10am-1pm & 2-5pm May-Sep) FREE, a restored, rethatched 19th-century dwelling furnished with period fittings and utensils. The Lerwick–Sumburgh bus stops right outside.

West of Boddam, Shetland's best beach is gloriously white **Scousburgh Sands**. The nearby **Spiggie Hotel** (☑01950-460409; www.thespiggiehotel.co.uk; s/d £70/130, self-catering s/d from £80/100; P✶) has compact rooms, self-catering annexes and tasty seafood and bar meals (lunch Wednesday to Sunday, dinner daily; mains £9 to £19). The rooms and dining room boast great views down over the local loch.

Sumburgh

With sea cliffs, and grassy headlands jutting out into sparkling blue waters, Sumburgh is one of the most scenic places on the island, with a far greener landscape than the peaty north.

◉ Sights

★**Old Scatness**　　　ARCHAEOLOGICAL SITE

(☑01595-694688; www.shetland-heritage.co.uk; adult/child £5/4; ☺10am-5pm Mon mid-May–Aug; ♿) This dig brings Shetland's prehistory vividly to life; it's a must-see for archaeology buffs, but fun for kids, too. Clued-up guides in Iron Age clothes show you the site, which has provided important clues on the Viking takeover and dating of Shetland material. There's an impressive broch from around 300 BC, roundhouses and later wheelhouses. Best of all is the reconstruction with peat fire and working loom. At time of research, lack of funding had restricted opening to Mondays.

Jarlshof　　　　　　　ARCHAEOLOGICAL SITE

(HS; ☑01950-460112; www.historic-scotland.gov.uk; adult/child £5.30/3.30; ☺9.30am-5.30pm Apr-Sep, 9.30am-4.30pm Oct-Mar) Old and new collide here, with Sumburgh airport right by this picturesque, instructive archaeological site. Various periods of occupation from 2500 BC to AD 1500 can be seen; the complete change upon the Vikings' arrival is obvious: their rectangular longhouses present a marked contrast to the preceding brochs, roundhouses and wheelhouses. Atop the site is 16th-century Old House, named 'Jarlshof' in a novel by Sir Walter Scott. There's an informative audio tour included with admission.

★**Sumburgh Head Visitor Centre**　　　LIGHTHOUSE, MUSEUM

(☑01595-694688; www.sumburghhead.com; adult/child £6/2; ☺10am-4pm May-Aug) High on the cliffs at Sumburgh Head, this excellent new attraction is set across several buildings. Displays explain about the lighthouse, foghorn and radar station that operated here, while there's a good exhibition on the local marine life and bird life. You can visit the lighthouse itself on a guided tour.

Sumburgh Head
BIRDWATCHING

(www.rspb.org.uk) At Mainland's southern tip, these spectacular cliffs offer a good chance to get up close to puffins, and huge nesting colonies of fulmars, guillemots and razorbills. If you're lucky, you might spot dolphins, minke whales or orcas. Also here is an excellent visitor centre, in the lighthouse buildings.

🛏 Sleeping & Eating

Betty Mouat's
BÖD £

(☑ 01595-694688; www.camping-bods.com; Dunrossness; dm £10; ⊘ Mar-Oct; ℗) This is a simple and comfortable hostel run by the Shetland Amenity Trust, with fridge, peat fire (£5 a bag), power and decent hot-water bathrooms.

Sumburgh Hotel
HOTEL ££

(☑ 01950-460201; www.sumburghhotel.com; s/d £85/110; ℗ @ 🛜 🐾) A reliable country-style hotel. Rooms have been recently renovated and feature soft duvets, attractive colour schemes and big towels. Larger sea-view rooms looking out to Fair Isle cost a tenner more. This is handy for the airport or Sumburgh Head birdwatching, though food is mediocre.

Another option is Sumburgh Lighthouse Cottage (p244).

ℹ Getting There & Away

To get to Sumburgh from Lerwick, take the airport bus (£2.60 to Sumburgh, £3 to the airport; 45 minutes, four to six daily).

North Mainland

Northern Mainland is very photogenic – jumbles of cracked, peaty brown hills, blending with grassy pastureland, extend like bony fingers into the icy grey waters of the North Sea.

Brae & Around

The crossroads settlement of Brae has several accommodation options. Book in advance, as they fill with oil workers.

🛏 Sleeping & Eating

★ Busta House Hotel
HOTEL ££

(☑ 01806-522506; www.bustahouse.com; s/d £99/115; ℗ @ 🛜 🐾) 🖉 This genteel, characterful hotel has a long, sad history and inevitable rumours of a (friendly) ghost. Built in the late 18th century (though the oldest part dates from 1588), its refurbished rooms – all individually decorated – are compact and retain a classy but homey charm. Sea views and/or four-poster bed cost a bit more. There are excellent dinners with local produce for £35. Food is served noon to 2.30pm and 6pm to 9pm.

Frankie's Fish & Chips
CAFE, TAKEAWAY £

(☑ 01806-522700; www.frankiesfishandchips.com; mains £6-9; ⊘ 9.30am-8pm Mon-Sat, noon-8pm Sun; 🛜) 🖉 This famous Shetland chippie

---

WESTERN ISLANDS

Off West Mainland is **Papa Stour** (population 15), home to huge colonies of auks, terns and skuas. Buckled volcanic strata have been wonderfully eroded to dramatic caves, arches and stacks. There's limited self-catering accommodation, and a small campsite. The island is served by Tuesday-only flights (p239) from Tingwall (return £65, day return possible) and **ferries** (☑ 01595-745804; www.shetland.gov.uk/ferries/) from West Burrafirth (passenger/car single £5.20/1.50, one hour).

Fifteen miles out in the Atlantic stands windswept **Foula**, perhaps Britain's most isolated community. Thirty-eight people are joined by 500,000 seabirds, including the rare Leach's petrel and Manx shearwater, and the world's largest colony of great skuas. There's no shop, but **Leraback** (☑ 01595-753226; www.originart.eu/leraback/leraback.html; Foula; B&B incl dinner per person £40; ℗) offers B&B and evening meals.

DirectFlight (p239) flies to Foula from Tingwall (£74.50 return), with day trips possible from March to mid-October. There are **ferries** (☑ 01595-840208; www.bkmarine.co.uk) from Walls (person/car single £5.20/19.60); bookings are essential. You can day trip to Foula from Scalloway with **Cycharters** (☑ 01595-696598; www.cycharters.co.uk).

uses only locally sourced and sustainable seafood. As well as chip-shop standards, the menu runs to plump Shetland mussels in garlicky sauces and, when available, scallops. It also does breakfast rolls and fry-ups. Eat in or take away.

❶ Getting There & Away

Buses from Lerwick to North Roe and Mossbank stop in Brae (£2.70, 45 minutes, four to seven daily Monday to Saturday).

Eshaness & Hillswick

Eleven miles northwest of Brae the road ends at the red basalt cliffs of Eshaness, some of Shetland's most impressive coastal scenery. When the wind subsides there is superb walking and panoramic views from the headland lighthouse.

A mile east, a side road leads to **Tangwick Haa Museum** (☑01806-503389; ◷11am-5pm mid-Apr–Sep; FREE), in a restored 17th-century house. The wonderful collection of ancient black-and-white photos captures the sense of community here.

🛏 Sleeping & Eating

Braewick Cafe & Caravan Park   CAMPSITE **£**
(☑01806-503345; www.eshaness.shetland.co.uk; sites for 1/2/wigwams £6/8/42; ◷mid-Mar–mid-Sep; P🐕🛜🐾) 🐾 Decent tent pitches and tasty light meals served in a cafe (dishes £4 to £10; 10am to 5pm Thursday to Monday mid-March to mid-September, daily in July and August) with stunning views over St Magnus Bay's weird and wonderful rock formations, are on offer here. Much food is sourced from the owners' croft next door. It also has 'wigwams' – wooden huts with fridge and kettle that sleep four (six at a pinch). It's on the road between Hillswick and Eshaness.

Johnnie Notions'   BÖD **£**
(☑office 01595-694688, warden 01806-503362; www.camping-bods.co.uk; dm £8; ◷Mar-Oct) There are four spacious berths in this cute wee stone *böd*, 3.5 miles east of Eshaness, with its challengingly low door. It's very basic, with no showers or electricity. This was the birthplace of Johnnie 'Notions' Williamson, an 18th-century blacksmith who inoculated several thousand people against smallpox using a self-devised serum.

★**Almara**   B&B **££**
(☑01806-503261; www.almara.shetland.co.uk; s/d £35/70; P🛜) 🐾 Follow the puffin signpost a mile short of Hillswick to find Shetland's finest welcome. With sweeping views over the bay, this house has a great lounge, unusual features in the excellent rooms and bathrooms (including thoughtful extras such as USB chargers) and a good eye on the environment. You'll feel completely at home and appreciated; this is B&B at its best.

St Magnus Bay Hotel   HOTEL **££**
(☑01806-503372; www.stmagnusbayhotel.co.uk; Hillswick; s/d £80/95; P🛜🐕) This hotel in Hillswick occupies a wonderful wooden mansion built in 1896. The owners are involved in an ongoing renovation process – a major job – to return it to former glories, so availability of rooms is variable, but if you can grab a renovated one, they are great. There's a sauna plus bar and restaurant meals.

❶ Getting There & Away

An evening bus from Lerwick (Monday to Saturday) runs to Hillswick (£2.90, 1¼ hours), Eshaness (1½ hours) and North Roe (1½ hours). Two morning buses run the return route.

The North Isles

Yell, Unst and Fetlar make up the North Isles, connected by ferry, as is Yell to Mainland. All are great for nature-watching; Unst has the most to offer overall. If you're going to spend a night on both Yell and Fetlar/Unst, do Yell on the way back, as the second ferry is free if you are coming from Mainland that same day.

Yell

POP 1000

Yell if you like but nobody will hear; the desolate peat moors here are typical Shetland scenery. The bleak landscape has an undeniable appeal.

◉ Sights & Activities

Lumbister RSPB Reserve   NATURE RESERVE
(www.rspb.org.uk) At this nature reserve red-throated divers, merlins, skuas and other bird species breed. The area is home to a large otter population, too, best viewed around Whale Firth, where you may also spot common and grey seals.

Old Haa Museum
MUSEUM

(☑01957-702431; ☺10am-4pm Tue-Thu & Sat & 2-5pm Sun Apr-Sep) **FREE** This has a medley of curious objects (pipes, piano, dolls-in-cradles, tiny bibles, ships in bottles and a sperm-whale jaw) as well as an archive of local history, and a tearoom. It's in Burravoe, 4 miles east of the southern ferry terminal in Ulsta.

Shetland Gallery
GALLERY

(www.shetlandgallery.com; Sellafirth, Yell; ☺11am-5pm Tue-Sat & 2-5pm Sun Easter-Sep) Not far from the ferry to Unst and Fetlar, this has rotating exhibitions of Shetland artists.

Windhouse
RUIN

Northwest of the small settlement of Mid Yell, on the hillside above the main road, stand the reputedly haunted ruins of Windhouse, dating from 1707. It's been uninhabited since the 1920s, although there are plans to refurbish it. Look out for the Lady in Silk, the most famous of the ruins' several ghostly presences.

🛏 Sleeping & Eating

Lots of excellent self-catering cottages are dotted around the island; check www.visit-scotland.com for options.

Windhouse Lodge
BÖD £

(☑office 01595-694688, warden 01957-702350; www.camping-bods.co.uk; dm £10) Below the haunted ruins of Windhouse, and on the A968, you'll find this well-kept, clean, snug camping *böd* with power and a pot-belly stove to warm your toes. It's one of the cosiest, with a modern interior. Mattresses are thin. Book via phone or the website.

Pinewood House
B&B ££

(☑01957-702092; www.pinewoodhouseshetland.co.uk; Aywick; s/d £35/70; P🅟🛜🐾) Next to Aywick shop, this three-roomer boasts glorious water views from the lounge and bedrooms, and offers a warm welcome and optional, very tasty evening meals (£16).

ⓘ Getting There & Away

BOAT

Yell is connected with Mainland by **ferries** (☑01595-745804; www.shetland.gov.uk/ferries) between Toft and Ulsta (passenger/car return £5.20/7.60, 20 minutes, frequent). It's wise to book car space in summer.

OFF THE BEATEN TRACK

FAIR ISLE

Halfway to Orkney, remote Fair Isle is best known for birdwatching and its patterned knitwear, still produced in the island's cooperative. Smart **Fair Isle Lodge & Bird Observatory** (☑01595-760258; www.fairislebirdobs.co.uk; s/d incl full board £70/130; ☺May-Oct; 🅟@🛜) offers good en suite rooms. Rates are full board, and there are free guided walks and other bird-related displays and activities. From Tingwall, Direct-Flight (p239) operates flights to Fair Isle (£79 return, 25 minutes). Ferries sail from Grutness (near Sumburgh) and some from Lerwick (one-way person/car £5.20/19.60, three hours) two to three times weekly.

BUS

Buses run Monday to Saturday from Lerwick to Yell (£4.60), connecting with ferries to Fetlar and Unst; connecting services cover other parts of the island.

Unst

POP 600

You're fast running out of Scotland once you cross to rugged Unst (www.unst.org). Scotland's most northerly inhabited island is prettier than Yell, with bare, velvety-smooth hills and settlements clinging to waterside locations, fiercely resisting the buffeting winds.

◉ Sights & Activities

Muness Castle
CASTLE

(Muness; ☺24hr) **FREE** This picturesque, sturdy 16th-century tower-house in the island's southeastern corner was built by Laurence Bruce, *foud* (magistrate) of Shetland, who was, by all accounts, a nasty piece of work, overtaxing locals and replacing their elected officials with his cronies. It's an atmospheric visit; grab a torch from under the information panel to explore.

★Hermaness Nature Reserve
NATURE RESERVE

(www.nnr-scotland.org.uk) At marvellous Hermaness headland, a 4.5-mile round walk takes you to cliffs where gannets, fulmars and guillemots nest, and numerous puffins frolic. You can see Scotland's most northerly

ORKNEY & SHETLAND THE NORTH ISLES

point, the rocks of Out Stack, and Muckle Flugga, with its lighthouse built by Robert Louis Stevenson's uncle. Duck into the visitor centre (☑ 01595-711278; ⊙ 9am-5pm May-early Sep) FREE, with its poignant story about long-time resident Albert Ross. To visit Muckle Flugga, you can charter boats (☑ 01806-522447; www.muckleflugga.co.uk; 2-hr charter £150; ⊙ Jun-Aug) in summer.

The path to the cliffs is guarded by a squadron of great skuas who nest in the nearby heather, and dive-bomb at will if they feel threatened. They're damn solid birds too, but don't usually make contact.

★ **Unst Bus Shelter** LANDMARK
(www.unstbusshelter.shetland.co.uk; Baltasound) At the turn-off to Littlehamar, just past Baltasound, is Britain's most impressive bus stop. Enterprising locals, tired of waiting in discomfort, decided to do a job on it, and it now boasts posh seating, novels, numerous decorative features and a visitors' book to sign. The theme and colour scheme changes yearly.

Unst Heritage Centre MUSEUM
(☑ 01957-755244, 01957-711528; www.unstheritage.com; Haroldswick; adult/child £3/free, combined ticket with Unst Boat Haven £5; ⊙ 11am-4pm May-Sep) This heritage centre houses a modern museum with a history of the Shetland pony and a re-creation of a croft house.

Unst Boat Haven MUSEUM
(☑ 01957-755282, 01957-711528; Haroldswick; adult/child £3/free, combined ticket with Unst Heritage Centre £5; ⊙ 11am-4pm May-Sep) This large shed is a boaty's delight, packed with a beautifully cared-for collection of Shetland rowing and sailing boats, all with a backstory. Old photos and maritime artefacts speak of the glory days of Unst fishing.

Skidbladner Longship MUSEUM
(☑ 01595-694688; www.vikingshetland.com; Haroldswick; ⊙ 24hr) FREE Unst has the highest concentration of Viking longhouse sites in the country. The Viking Unst project manages three excavation sites, and has as its centrepiece this replica Viking longship. A recreated longhouse is alongside.

🛏 Sleeping & Eating

★ **Gardiesfauld Hostel** HOSTEL £
(☑ 01957-755279; www.gardiesfauld.shetland.co.uk; 2 East Rd, Uyeasound; tent sites per adult/child £6/2, dm £15; ⊙ Apr-Sep; P 🛜) This spotless hostel has very spacious dorms with lockers, family rooms, a garden, an elegant lounge and a wee conservatory dining area with great bay views. You can camp here too, with separate areas for tents and vans. The bus stops right outside. Bring 20p for a shower.

Saxa Vord HOSTEL £
(☑ 01957-711711; www.saxavord.com; Haroldswick; s/d £21/42; ⊙ late May-early Sep; P 🛜) This former RAF base is not the most atmospheric lodging, but the barracks-style rooms offer great value. The restaurant dishes out reasonable local food, and there's a bar – Britain's northernmost, by our reckoning – and a friendly, helpful atmosphere. Self-catering houses (£450 to £595 per week) are good for families and available year-round.

Prestegaard B&B ££
(☑ 01957-755234; prestegaard@postmaster.co.uk; Uyeasound; s/d £34/60; ⊙ May-Sep; P 🛜) This solid old manse near the water makes a great base. Rooms are spacious and comfy, with sea views and separate (but private) bathroom – we particularly like the upstairs one. The breakfast room with Up Helly Aa memorabilia will bring out the Viking in you, and the kindly owner is helpful. Continental breakfast (and porridge!) only.

Baltasound Hotel   HOTEL, PUB **££**

(☑ 01957-711334;   www.baltasoundhotel.co.uk;
Baltasound; s £45-60, d £90-100; ☺May–mid-
Oct; P ☎) Brightly decorated, commodious rooms – some bigger than others – are
complemented by wooden chalets arrayed
around the lawn. It's worth the tenner upgrade to the 'large doubles', which sport
good modern bathrooms. There's a lovely
country outlook, and evening bar meals
(mains £7 to £12; food served 6pm to 8pm)
in a dining room dappled by the setting sun.

❶ Getting There & Around

BICYCLE

Hire **bikes** (☑ 01957-711393; www.unstcy-
clehire.co.uk; Haroldswick; per day/week
£7.50/30; ☺11.30am-5pm Mon-Sat, 1-4pm Sun,
can hire out of hours) in the chocolate shop at
the Saxa Vord complex in Haroldswick.

BOAT

Unst is connected with Yell and Fetlar by a small
ferry (p248) between Gutcher and Belmont
(free if coming from Mainland that day, otherwise passenger/car £5.20/7.60 return, 10
minutes, frequent).

BUS

Buses run Monday to Saturday from Lerwick
to the Unst ferry (£4.60, 2½ hours). There are
connecting services around Unst itself (£1.70
to £1.80).

Fetlar

POP 60

Fetlar is the smallest but most fertile of the
North Isles. Its name is derived from the Viking term for 'fat land'.

◉ Sights & Activities

There's great birdwatching – Fetlar is home
to three-quarters of Britain's breeding population of red-necked phalaropes, which nest
around the **Loch of Funzie** (pronounced
'finnie') in the southeast of the island. From
April to October, you can view them from an
RSPB hide.

Excellent **Fetlar Interpretive Centre**
(☑ 01957-733206; www.fetlar.com; adult/child £3/
free; ☺11am-4pm Mon-Fri & noon-4pm Sat & Sun
May-Sep) has photos, audio recordings and
videos on the island and its history. You'll
find it right in the middle of the island, 4½
miles from the ferry.

🛏 Sleeping

Friendly **Gord B&B** (☑ 01957-733227; nic-
boxall@btinternet.com; r per person incl dinner
£50; P) has terrific sea views and two
twin rooms and one double, all with en
suite. There's also Aithbank **camping böd**
(☑ 01595-694688; www.camping-bods.com; dm
£10) by the water, handily close to the Loch
of Funzie.

❶ Information

There's no petrol on Fetlar, but there's a part-
time shop in Houbie.

❶ Getting There & Away

Four to nine daily ferries (p248; free if coming
from Mainland that day, otherwise passenger/
car £5.20/7.60 return, 25 minutes) connect
Fetlar with Gutcher on Yell and Belmont on Unst.

Understand Scotland's Highlands & Islands

Scotland's Highlands & Islands Today

Although an integral part of Great Britain since 1707, Scotland has maintained a separate and distinct identity throughout the last 300 years, which strengthened with the return of a devolved Scottish parliament to Edinburgh in 1999. Since then, Scottish politics has diverged significantly from Westminster, culminating in 2011 when the Scottish National Party (SNP) won a landslide victory in the Scottish elections and pledged to hold a referendum on whether Scotland should become an independent country.

Best in Print

Raw Spirit (Iain Banks; 2003) An enjoyable jaunt around the Highlands and islands in search of the perfect whisky.

Mountaineering in Scotland (WH Murray; 1947) Classic account of climbing in the Highlands in the 1930s, when just getting to Glen Coe was an adventure in itself.

The Poor Had No Lawyers (Andy Wightman; 2010) A penetrating, and fascinating, analysis of who owns the land in the Highlands, and how they got it.

The Scottish Islands (Hamish Haswell-Smith; 1996) A comprehensive and beautifully illustrated guide to the geography and history of 162 Scottish islands.

Best on Film

Local Hero The 1983 film that started a tourist stampede to the Highlands in search of Ben's Beach.

Whisky Galore! Classic 1949 comedy about islanders plundering a shipwrecked cargo of whisky under the nose of the authorities.

Scottish Independence

The hot topic of 2014 was the Scottish independence referendum, which was fiercely debated across the Highlands and islands (which voted overwhelmingly for the SNP in the 2011 election). Would the Scots need a new currency, or be able to keep using the pound? Would there be border controls with England? Would Scotland be able to remain in the EU? How would North Sea oil revenues be divided? Would the Queen still be head of state? The referendum took place on 18 September 2014, posing the question: 'Should Scotland be an independent country?' The result was that 55% voted to maintain the status quo (with a turnout of 85%). What this means for the future of Scotland remains unclear. Will there be increased powers for the Scottish parliament in Edinburgh? Will there be a collapse in support for the SNP? The closeness of the result promises that there will be wrangling for years to come.

Renewable Energy

One of the central planks of the SNP's vision for an independent Scotland was its energy policy. The party leader, Alex Salmond, said that he wanted the country to be the 'Saudi Arabia of renewable energy' – becoming self-sufficient in energy by 2020, and a net exporter of 'clean' electricity.

The Highlands and islands are central to this plan. In the first half of the 20th century it was one of the first regions in the world to develop hydroelectric power on a large scale, and since 2000 wind turbines have sprung up all over the place. By 2009 renewables provided 27% of Scotland's energy consumption, a figure that rose to 40% in 2013; the government's target is to reach 100% by 2020.

But the future of Scotland's energy industry lies not on land, but in the sea: Scotland has access to 25% of Europe's available tidal energy and 10% of its wave power. The Highlands and islands are at the leading edge of developing wave, tidal and offshore wind power, and in 2012 the waters around Orkney and the Pentland Firth were designated as a Marine Energy Park.

Development vs Conservation

In 2010 the Scottish government gave the go-ahead to a 135-mile, high-voltage overhead power line from Beauly (near Inverness) to Denny in Stirlingshire, to connect wind- and marine-generated electricity from the north to the heart of the national grid. Construction is underway on 600 giant pylons marching through some of the Highlands' most scenic areas, including Strathglass, Fort Augustus and Bridge of Tummel.

Supporters point out that the scheme also involves the removal of almost 60 miles of low-voltage pylons from the Cairngorms National Park; opponents claim that a seabed cable, while more expensive, would be a better alternative. The debate reflects a larger tension that exists across the Highlands and islands – between those keen to develop the region's resources and conservationists who want to keep the area unspoiled.

Land Reform

Crofting and land ownership are important issues in the Gaelic-speaking areas of northwest Scotland, especially since a headline-grabbing clause in the Land Reform (Scotland) Act (2003) allowed crofting communities to buy out the land that they live on with the aid of taxpayers' money, in the hope of reversing the gradual depopulation of the Highlands.

Several estates have followed Eigg, Gigha, Knoydart and North Harris into community ownership; in 2006 South Uist saw the biggest community buyout yet. The latest case to make the headlines is the Pairc estate on Lewis, where a Warwickshire-based accountant, whose family has owned the estate since 1920, leased the land to a power company who planned to erect a £200 million wind farm. Local residents voted in favour of a community buy-out (which was approved by the government), and after a 10-year legal battle finally took over the estate in 2014.

POPULATION: **APPROX 500,000 (WHOLE OF SCOTLAND 5.25 MILLION)**

AREA: **APPROX 17,548 SQ MI (WHOLE OF SCOTLAND 30,414 SQ MI)**

ANNUAL WHISKY EXPORT: **1 BILLION BOTTLES**

if Scotland were 100 people

98 would be white
1 would be South Asian
1 would be other

belief systems
(% of population)

Church of Scotland — 43
Nonreligious — 28
Roman Catholic — 16
Other Christian — 6.8
Other — 1.2

population per sq mile

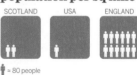

SCOTLAND USA ENGLAND

≈ 80 people

History

From the decline of the Vikings onwards, Scottish history has been predictably and often violently bound to that of its southern neighbour. Battles and border raids were commonplace until shared kingship, then political union, drew the two together. However, there has often been as much – if not more – of a cultural divide between Highland and Lowland Scotland than ever between Lowland Scotland and England.

Stories in Stone

Scotland's Neolithic period (3200 to 2200 BC) has left behind an astonishing record of human development, most impressively at Skara Brae in Orkney and Jarlshof in Shetland – some of the world's best-preserved prehistoric villages – but also in the cairns and stone circles of Lewis, Caithness and Kilmartin. All aspects of early life are represented, from primitive field systems and houses to ceremonial structures such as standing stones, tombs and tribal halls.

Crannogs (artificial islands built on stilts or heaped stones) were a favoured form of defensible dwelling through the Bronze Age (2200 BC to 750 BC), while the Iron Age (750 BC to AD 500) saw the construction of a remarkable series of defence-minded structures of a different sort: the drystone defensive towers known as brochs, which are unique to Scotland. The best preserved examples are Mousa in Shetland, Dun Carloway in Lewis and Dun Telve in Glenelg.

Picts & Romans

The origins of the people known as the Picts is a mystery, but they may have emerged as a confederation of northern Celtic tribes in reaction to the Roman invasion of Scotland in AD 80. Their territory (Pictland, or Pictavia) extended north through the Highlands from the Forth and Clyde estuaries to Orkney and the Western Isles.

Much of what we know about the Picts comes from the Romans, who attempted to conquer northern Scotland but failed to occupy any territory north of the Antonine Wall. This includes their name (from the Latin pictus, meaning 'painted', or possibly 'tattooed'). The main material

TIMELINE	4000–2200 BC	2200–500 BC	AD 43
	Neolithic farmers move to Scotland from mainland Europe; stone circles and tombs from these ancient times dot the Highlands and islands; the best are concentrated in Orkney.	The Bronze Age produces swords and shields, and the construction of hill forts, crannogs and burnt mounds. Impressive stone towers known as brochs are built during the Iron Age.	Claudius begins the Roman conquest of Britain, almost a century after Julius Caesar first invaded. By AD 80 a string of forts is built from the Clyde to the Forth.

evidence of Pictish culture is their fabulous carved symbol stones, found in many parts of northern and eastern Scotland.

The Kingdom of Dalriada

By AD 500 another Celtic tribe, the Scots (from Scotti, a derogatory name given to them by the Romans), had begun to colonise western Scotland from northern Ireland, establishing a kingdom called Dalriada. From their ceremonial headquarters at the hill fort of Dunadd, these seafaring Celts conquered a territory that stretched from Kintyre and the Antrim coast of Ireland to the Isle of Skye and Wester Ross.

Their influence lives on in the districts of Lorn and Cowal, which take their names from Dalriadan chiefs, and the county name of Argyll (from *earra gael,* meaning 'the seaboard of the Gael') – and of course, they eventually gave their name to the kingdom of Scotland. But perhaps their most important legacy is that they brought Christianity and the Gaelic language to the western Highlands and islands of Scotland.

In the 6th century, St Columba, Scotland's most famous missionary, arrived in the west. Columba was an Irish scholar and monk exiled, tradition has it, after involvement in a bloody battle. After fleeing Ireland in 563 he established a monastery on Iona and also travelled northeast to take his message to the Picts. By the late 8th century most of Scotland had converted.

In 843 the Dalriadan king Kenneth MacAlpin, who was the son of a Pictish princess, used the Pictish custom of matrilineal succession to take over the Pictish throne, uniting Scotland north of the Firth of Forth into a single kingdom. Thereafter the Scots gained complete cultural and political ascendancy.

Viking Invaders

The first Viking longboats were spotted off the shores of Orkney in the 780s, and must have inspired terror in those who saw them. The marauders struck without warning, ransacking entire villages, butchering the occupants and carting anything of value back to Norway. For the next 500 years the Norsemen pillaged the Scottish coast and islands, eventually taking control of Orkney, Shetland, the Outer Hebrides and all the islands off the west coast of Scotland from Skye to Arran, plus the mainland districts of Cowal and Kintyre.

Eventually the Viking colonies returned to Scottish rule, but they always retained a distinctively Scandinavian-tinged culture, especially Orkney and Shetland, which – unlike the Western Isles – were taken over by nobles from the Lowlands and ended up speaking a mixture of Scots and Norn (an ancient Viking dialect), rather than Gaelic.

Adomnan (627–704) succeeded St Columba as the abbot of Iona. His book, *Vita Columbae* (Life of Columba), is one of our most important sources of information on the Picts and the kingdom of Dalriada.

HISTORY THE KINGDOM OF DALRIADA

A well-presented and easily absorbed introduction to Scottish history is at www.bbc.co.uk/scotland/history. The accompanying videos help to bring the past to life.

AD 142	Early 500s	6th century	7th century
Building of Antonine Wall marks northern limit of Roman Empire; it's patrolled for about 40 years until the Romans decide the Highlands are too difficult to conquer.	A Celtic tribe, known as the Scots, cross the sea from northern Ireland and establish a kingdom in Argyll called Dalriada.	St Columba establishes a Christian mission on Iona. By the late 8th century the mission is responsible for the conversion of most of pagan Scotland.	The Pictish king Bridei defeats the Northumbrians at Nechtansmere in Angus. Golden age of Pictish culutre sees the creation of hundreds of carved stones, decorated with beautiful but mysterious symbols.

The west coast was returned to the Scottish king Alexander III after the Battle of Largs in 1263. Three years later the Western Isles were ceded to Scotland by the Treaty of Perth, in exchange for an annual rent to the King of Norway. Orkney and Shetland remained Norwegian possessions until 1468 and 1469 respectively, when they were mortgaged to King James III of Scotland in lieu of a dowry for his bride, Margaret, daughter of the king of Denmark.

Clan vs Crown

The dynasty founded by Kenneth MacAlpin tightened its grip on the Highland mainland during the 10th century, but it wasn't until the reign of Malcolm II (1005–18) that the Scots extended their control south of the Forth–Clyde line, creating a single Scottish kingdom extending as far as the River Tweed. This was the beginning of a drift that saw the centre of royal power move southward from Scone to Stirling and Dunfermline, and then to Edinburgh, which eventually emerged as the capital of Scotland by the early 16th century.

However, the cultural and linguistic divide between Highlands and Lowlands had its origins at the other end of Britain, in the Norman invasion of 1066. Malcolm II's great-grandson Malcolm Canmore (1058–93) took a Saxon queen. His youngest son David I (1124–53) had been raised in England and introduced the Anglo-Norman feudal system to Scotland, granting lands and titles (mostly in the south and east) to English-speaking Norman noblemen.

But in the remote Highland glens the Gaelic language and the clan system still held sway: loyalty and military service were based on ties of blood rather than feudal superiority. The clan was led by a chief who was granted his position through the ancient Dalriadan system of tanistry, in which the heir to the chief was nominated from a pool of eligible candidates whose great-grandfathers had been chiefs before them. This ensured that a chief never died without a potential heir, but resulted in many bloody feuds and murders instigated by those who felt their claim to the title had been denied.

The history of the Highlands from the 12th to the 16th centuries was volatile and violent. Robert the Bruce's struggle to win the Scottish crown involved not only fighting the English, but also vanquishing his foes in the Highlands. In 1306 Bruce famously murdered John Comyn, his main rival as king, making Bruce a blood enemy of the powerful Macdougalls of Lorne, whose chief Alexander was related to Comyn by marriage. The Macdougalls harried Bruce mercilessly until the king-to-be finally routed them at the Battle of the Pass of Brander in 1309.

Even after Bruce had defeated the English at Bannockburn in 1314 and guaranteed Scottish independence, the wrangling for power between

The main source for the history of Orkney during the Viking period is the *Orkneyinga Saga*, compiled in Iceland sometime around 1200. A rip-roaring tale of battle, murder and political intrigue, it blends historical fact with oral tradition (and no small amount of poetic licence).

780	848	872	1263
Norsemen in longboats from Scandinavia begin to pillage the Scottish coast and islands, eventually taking control of Orkney, Shetland and the Western Isles.	Kenneth MacAlpin unites the Scottish and Pictish thrones, thus uniting Scotland north of the Firth of Forth into a single kingdom.	The King of Norway creates an earldom in Orkney, also governing Shetland; these island groups become a vital Viking base for raids and colonisation down the west of Scotland.	Norse power controls the entire western seaboard but is broken at the Battle of Largs, marking the retreat of Viking influence and eventual handing back of the western isles to Scotland.

THE LORDS OF THE ISLES

In medieval times, when overland travel through the Scottish Highlands was slow, difficult and dangerous, the sea lochs, kyles (narrow sea channels) and sounds of the west coast were the motorways of their time. Cut off from the rest of Scotland, but united by these sea roads, the west coast and islands were a world – and a kingdom – unto themselves. Dominated by Viking invaders for almost five centuries, the region later formed the heartland of the Lords of the Isles.

Descended from the legendary Somerled (a half-Gaelic, half-Norse warrior of the 12th century), the chiefs of Clan Donald claimed sovereignty over this watery kingdom. It was John Macdonald of Islay who first styled himself Dominus Insularum (Lord of the Isles) in 1353. He and his descendants ruled this vast territory from their headquarters at Finlaggan in Islay, backed up by fleets of swift *birlinns* and *nyvaigs* (Hebridean galleys), an intimate knowledge of the sea routes of the west, and a network of coastal castles that included Skipness, Dunstaffnage, Duart, Stalker, Dunvegan and Kisimul.

Clan Donald held sway over the isles, often in defiance of the Scottish king, from 1350 to 1493. At its greatest extent, in the second half of the 15th century, the Lordship of the Isles included all the islands on the west coast of Scotland, the west-coast mainland from Kintyre to Ross-shire, and the Antrim coast of northern Ireland. But in challenging the Scottish king for territory, and siding with the English king against him, Clan Donald finally pushed its luck too far.

Following a failed rebellion in 1493, the Lordship was forfeited to King James IV of Scotland, and the title has remained in possession of the Scottish, and later British, royal family ever since. 'Lord of the Isles' is one of the many titles held today by Prince Charles, heir to the British throne.

(and among) the Highland clans and the Scottish crown raged on for several centuries. Clan Campbell, supporters of Bruce, were rewarded for their continuing loyalty to the king with grants of land and titles, earning the bitter enmity of their rivals the Macdougalls and the Macdonalds. By the beginning of the 18th century, the chief of Clan Campbell had become the Duke of Argyll, owning most of the southwestern Highlands and capable of putting 5000 men into battle.

Much of the fighting that disrupted the Highlands during this period was between rival clans. The longest-running feud was between the Camerons and the Mackintoshs: following a battle over disputed land in 1337, the two clans remained sworn enemies for more than 300 years. The Battle of Mulroy (near Roy Bridge) in 1688, between Camerons and Macdonalds on one side and Mackintoshs on the other, turned out to be the last inter-clan battle before the Jacobite rebellions changed the Highlands forever.

1314	1320	1328	1468–69
Robert the Bruce wins a famous victory over the English at the Battle of Bannockburn, turning the tide in favour of the Scots for the next 400 years.	The Declaration of Arbroath asserts Scotland's status as an independent kingdom in submission to the pope.	Continuing raids on northern England force Edward II to sue for peace; the Treaty of Northampton gives Scotland its independence, with Robert I, the Bruce, as king.	Orkney and then Shetland are mortgaged to Scotland as part of a dowry from Danish King Christian I, whose daughter is to marry the future King James III of Scotland.

The Jacobite Rebellions

Jacobite, a term derived from the Latin for 'James', is used to describe the political movement committed to the return of the Stuart kings to the thrones of England and Scotland.

The 'Glorious Revolution' of 1688 saw the Catholic king James II (of England)/VII (of Scotland) deposed from the British throne, and replaced by his Protestant son-in-law William of Orange. From then until 1746 much of Highland history was dominated by the Jacobite rebellions that sought to restore a Catholic Stuart king to the British throne. Indeed, one of England's motivations for union with Scotland was fear of Jacobite sympathies in the Highlands being exploited by its enemy, the French.

A major manifestation of this fear was the building of government garrisons throughout the Highlands, notably Fort William, Fort Augustus and Fort George, and the driving of new military roads through the glens by General Wade and his successors. This wariness was well justified – there were Jacobite uprisings in 1689, 1708 and 1715.

By no means all of the Highland clans were Jacobite supporters, though. From his seat at Inveraray Castle, the Duke of Argyll, chief of Clan Campbell, served as the British government's political manager in Scotland for the first half of the 18th century. Many of the clans that joined in the rebellions did so more out of hatred towards the Campbells than support for the exiled Stuart king. Following the 1689 uprising, King William demanded that all Highland chieftains swear an oath of allegiance or suffer violent reprisals; Campbell soldiers were charged with making an example of the Macdonalds with the infamous Massacre of Glencoe.

In 1745 Charles Edward Stuart (better known as Bonnie Prince Charlie) landed in Scotland to claim the British crown for his father. Supported by an army of Highlanders, he marched southwards and captured Edinburgh in September 1745. He got as far south as Derby in England, but success was short-lived; a Hanoverian army led by the Duke of Cumberland pushed him back to the Highlands, where Jacobite dreams were finally extinguished at the Battle of Culloden in 1746. Many wounded Highlanders were executed by 'Butcher' Cumberland following the battle, but Charles escaped and fled to France via Skye, aided by Flora MacDonald; he later died in exile.

Bonnie Prince Charlie's flight after Culloden is legendary. He lived in hiding in the remote Highlands and islands for months before being rescued by a French frigate. His narrow escape from Uist to Skye, dressed as Flora MacDonald's maid, is the subject of the 'Skye Boat Song'.

The Highland Clearances

In the aftermath of the Jacobite rebellions, the government outlawed the wearing of Highland dress and the playing of the bagpipes. The Highlands were put under military control and private armies were banned. The ties of kinship and duty that once marked the relationship between Highland laird and clansman gradually transformed into the merely economic relationship of landlord and tenant. Lands that had been confiscated after 1745 were returned to their owners in the 1780s, but by then the chiefs had tasted the aristocratic high life and were tempted by the easy profits to be made from sheep farming.

1560	1603	1689	1692
As a result of the Reformation, the Scottish parliament creates a Protestant Church independent of Rome and the monarchy. The Latin Mass is abolished and the pope's authority denied.	James VI of Scotland inherits the English throne in the so-called Union of the Crowns, becoming James I of Great Britain.	First Jacobite uprising, led by John Graham of Claverhouse ('Bonnie Dundee'); a rebel victory at Killiecrankie is soon followed by defeat, but rebellion prompts building of a government garrison at Fort William.	The massacre of Glencoe causes further rifts between those clans loyal to the crown and those loyal to the old ways.

So began the Highland Clearances, one of the most shameful episodes in Scottish history. Not all of the people who left their homes in the late 18th and 19th centuries were forcibly evicted; in the Hebridean islands, for example, a combination of poverty, overcrowding and lack of suitable land led many to choose emigration. But some of the forced clearances, especially in Sutherland, were so brutal that newspaper reporting of the events caused a national scandal.

Under the pretext of agricultural 'improvement', the peasant farmers, no longer of any use as soldiers and uneconomical as tenants, were evicted from their homes and farms to make way for flocks of hardy Cheviot sheep – in the Highlands the year 1792 (when Cheviots were first introduced) was known for decades afterwards as *Bliadhna nan Caorach* (the Year of the Sheep). The most notorious events took place in Strathnaver, where Patrick Sellar – the factor (land agent) of the Duke of Sutherland – cleared people from their homes using dogs, and set fire to cottages while possessions were still inside. He was later charged with arson and culpable homicide, but was acquitted.

After the evictions a few cottars stayed behind to work the sheep farms, but most were relocated to desperate crofts on poor coastal land or fled to the cities in search of work. Many thousands emigrated – some willingly, some under duress – to the developing colonies of North America, Australia and New Zealand. All over the Highlands today, only a ruckle of stones among the bracken remains where once there were whole villages. The Mull of Oa on Islay, for example, once supported a population of 4000 – today there are barely 40 people there.

Although the Clearances took place two centuries ago, they remain an emotive subject in the Highlands today. They marked the final nail in the coffin of the old clan system, and the beginning of the depopulation of the Highlands, a process that is still going on. But it was rarely a straightforward story, and recent scholarship has challenged the popular image of poor tenants versus greedy landlords, claiming that in many cases the population pressure on marginal land had become unsustainable – something had to give. In bookshops from Oban to Inverness you'll find plenty of accounts of the Highland Clearances that offer food for thought.

Tartanry, Tourism & Deer Stalking

The pacification of the Highlands in the wake of the Jacobite rebellions led to a wave of adventurous travellers venturing north in search of the wild and the picturesque. The most famous of these were Samuel Johnson (compiler of the first *Dictionary of the English Language*) and his biographer James Boswell, who travelled to Inverness, Skye, Mull and Oban in 1773 and wrote separate accounts of their journey – both were bestsellers.

Top Historical Museums

Stromness Museum, Stromness

Shetland Museum, Lerwick

Strathnaver Museum, Strathnaver

Museum of Island Life, Skye

Arnol Blackhouse, Lewis

Highland Folk Museum, Newtonmore

Museum of the Isles, Skye

West Highland Museum, Fort William

Wick Heritage Centre, Wick

HISTORY TARTANRY, TOURISM & DEER STALKING

1707	1745–46	Late 1700s–early 1800s	1850–1900
Despite popular opposition, the Act of Union, which brings England and Scotland under one parliament, one sovereign and one flag, takes effect on 1 May.	The culmination of the Jacobite rebellions: Bonnie Prince Charlie lands in Scotland, gathers an army and marches south. He gains English territory but is defeated at the Battle of Culloden.	Lowland Scotland flourishes during the Industrial Revolution, but the Highlands suffer the misery of the Clearances and mass emigration.	The spread of the railways opens up the Highlands to tourism; wealthy southerners buy up huge tracts of land as sporting estates.

POWER FROM THE GLENS

The high rainfall and rushing rivers of the Scottish Highlands led to the region being a world pioneer in the development of hydroelectric power. In 1896 the Foyers generating station on Loch Ness was the first large-scale hydroelectric scheme in Britain, powering one of the world's first electric aluminium smelters. Its success led the British Aluminium Company to build a much larger scheme based on the Blackwater Dam north of Glen Coe – in fact, it built a whole town at Kinlochleven to house workers from the smelter and the power station. By 1911 the Highlands of Scotland were producing one-third of the world's aluminium.

A vision of bringing investment, employment and electricity to the economically depressed Highlands spurred the government into creating the North of Scotland Hydro-Electric Board (motto: 'Power from the Glens'). Over the next few decades the Hydro Board masterminded a series of vast civil engineering projects from Loch Awe to Glen Affric: by 1965, 78 dams had been built, with 54 power stations providing a total generating capacity of over 1000 megawatts.

Conscious of criticism that these developments would be detrimental to areas of great scenic beauty, the board decreed that the power stations be designed by architects in Modernist and International styles using local stone, and some were concealed underground. Many sites are now tourist attractions, including the Cruachan power station at Loch Awe, and the salmon ladder beside the dam at Pitlochry power station.

With today's emphasis on renewable energy sources, hydro power is back in fashion, and has the potential to supply up to one quarter of Scotland's homes. The country's biggest recent civil engineering project is the Glendoe Dam, hidden in the hills to the east of Fort Augustus, which came online in 2009.

Tales of this 'primitive' and 'unspoilt' region proved irresistible to the emerging Romantic movement in art and literature. Poets and artists toured the Highlands in search of the sublime, including William Wordsworth and Samuel Taylor Coleridge in 1803, and artist JMW Turner in 1831, the latter in the company of Sir Walter Scott. Scott himself penned a series of hugely popular historical novels – notably *Waverley*, *Rob Roy* and *The Pirate* – and the epic poems 'The Lady of the Lake' and 'The Lord of the Isles', all of which were set in the Highlands.

In fact, it was Scott who pretty much single-handedly invented the romantic, tartan-clad image of the Highlands. In 1822, Scott engineered a state visit to Edinburgh by King George IV – the first time a reigning British monarch had been to Scotland since 1650 – where the king was greeted by a stage-managed parade of Highlanders in traditional tartan costume. The king himself was persuaded to wear a kilt for the occasion, triggering a wave of tartan-mania amongst the fashionable classes of England.

George's successor, Queen Victoria, fell in love with the Highlands. Her consort Prince Albert purchased the Balmoral estate in 1852, and the royal

> Most clan tartans are in fact a 19th-century invention (long after the demise of the clan system), inspired partly by the writings of Sir Walter Scott.

1886	1914–32	1939–45	1970s
Rent strikes and land raids lead to the Crofters Holdings (Scotland) Act, which grants security of tenure to crofters for the first time.	Scottish industry slumps during WWI and collapses in its aftermath in the face of new Eastern production and the Great Depression. About 400,000 Scots emigrate between 1921 and 1931.	WWII sees the sea lochs of the Highlands used as marshalling areas for Arctic and Atlantic convoys. In Shetland, the Shetland Bus operation ferries agents and supplies to occupied Norway.	The discovery of oil and gas in the North Sea brings new prosperity to Aberdeen and the surrounding area, and also to the Orkney and Shetland Islands.

couple spent summer holidays there (a tradition still maintained by the royal family). After Albert's death in 1861, Victoria spent up to four months a year at Balmoral, often sneaking around the Highlands incognito in the company of her Scottish ghillie (attendant), John Brown. All this provoked enormous interest in the Highlands among the British upper and middle classes, sparking a wave of tourism assisted by the spread of the railways.

In the second half of the 19th century a decline in the profitability of sheep farming combined with the emergence of a wealthy nouveau-riche class in England led to a new phenomenon: the rise of the Highland sporting estate. Struggling Highland chiefs sold off their ancient lands to rich merchants from the south, who ran them as private fiefdoms of salmon fishing, grouse shooting and deer stalking. Today, more than 50% of the land area of the Highlands and islands is occupied by around 340 private sporting estates, two-thirds of them owned by absentee landlords.

John Prebble's classic *The High-land Clearances* (1963) is an emotive account of this controversial period of history. Eric Richards' book of the same name from 2007 takes a more balanced look at the events.

HISTORY CROFTING

Crofting

During the mass upheaval of the Highland Clearances, those who chose not to emigrate or move to the cities were forced to eke a living from narrow plots of marginal agricultural land, often close to the coast. This was a form of smallholding that became known as crofting. The small patch of land was not enough to produce a living on its own, and had to be supplemented by other work such as fishing and kelp gathering. Tenure was always precarious, as tenancies were granted on a year-by-year basis, and there was no guarantee of benefiting from any improvements made – on a whim of the landlord, a crofter could be evicted and lose not only the farm but also the house they'd built on it.

The economic depression of the late 19th century meant many crofters couldn't pay their rent. This time, the people resisted eviction, creating instead the Highland Land League and their own political movement, the Crofters' Party. Several of their demands were met by the government in the Crofters' Holdings Act of 1886, including security of tenure and fair rents.

But it failed to address the issue of the lack of land for new crofts. More rent strikes and land raids (occupations) followed, most famously in the Isle of Lewis, where a monument recalls the Pairc Deer Raid of 1887, when several hundred crofters killed a large number of deer in protest at their landlord's clearing of crofts to make way for deer stalking. Police and troops were sent to quell this 'riot', an over-reaction that only generated more public sympathy for the crofters.

Further legislation improved the situation, but it wasn't until 1976 that crofters won the right to purchase their own land and become owner-occupiers. Today in the Highlands and islands there are around 18,000 crofts (smallholdings) averaging 5 hectares in area, supporting a crofting population of around 33,000 people.

The effects of the Clearances were exacerbated by the potato famine of the 1840s. Between 1841 and 1861 the western Highlands and islands lost one-third of its population, mostly through emigration.

1999–2005	2003	2014	2014
Scottish parliament is convened for the first time on 12 May 1999. Among the first policies to be enacted are the reform of land laws, and the recognition of Gaelic as an official language.	Land Reform Act establishes the right of responsible access to private land, and the right of communities to buy the land they live on.	Around 340 sporting estates occupy more than 50% of the Scottish Highlands and islands, many owned by absentee landlords.	Scotland votes on and rejects becomiing a fully independent nation and so remains part of the United Kingdom.

Highland Culture

The native culture of Scotland's Highlands and islands – strongly influenced by clan history and the Gaelic language – is distinctive and colourful, ranging from evocative Gaelic poetry and foot-tapping fiddle music to graceful Highland dancing and the fast and furious sport of shinty.

An Leabhar Mor: The Great Book of Gaelic is a collection of 100 Gaelic poems (with English translations) dating from AD 600 to the present day, accompanied by specially commissioned artworks. Described as a '21st-century *Book of Kells*', it can be viewed online at www. leabharmor.net.

Literature

Gaelic Poetry

Little has survived of early Gaelic literature, although the monks of Iona and other Scottish monasteries are known to have written in their native language as well as in Latin. But as descendants of the Celts, the Gaels had a strong bardic tradition, with songs, poems, stories and stirring tales of historic events passed down from generation to generation by word of mouth.

Alexander Macdonald (Alasdair Mac Mhaighstir Alasdair; 1695–1770), a schoolmaster from Moidart, is widely regarded as one of the finest of Gaelic poets, and was a genuine bard of the Clanranald Macdonalds. An ardent Jacobite, he gathered with the clans at Glenfinnan in 1745, and fought at Culloden the following year. His poetry ranged from minute descriptions of nature and wildlife to satirical and political verse, as well as songs in praise of Bonnie Prince Charlie.

Another bard who fought in the Jacobite wars was Duncan Ban MacIntyre (Donnchadh Bàn Mac an t-Saoir; 1724–1812) of Glen Orchy. But 'Fair Duncan', as he was known, fought on the Hanoverian side under the Duke of Argyll. He was also illiterate, and his beautiful nature poems were composed and stored in his memory before being dictated for someone else to write down. A prominent monument to him stands on a hilltop above Dalmally.

The greatest Gaelic poet of modern times was Sorley MacLean (Somhairle MacGill-Eain; 1911–96) from the Isle of Raasay. He was a teacher who wrote powerfully about the Highland Clearances, the Spanish Civil War and WWII, but who also produced some of the 20th century's most moving and delicate love poetry.

MacLean's contemporary, Lewis-born Iain Crichton Smith (1928–98), was one of the most prolific writers of Gaelic poetry (though he also wrote widely in English). Notable collections include *Burn is Aran* (Water and Bread) and *Na Guthan* (Voices); his *Towards the Human* is a fine collection of essays and poems on Gaelic life.

No mention of Gaelic literature would be complete without a word about the poet and politican James Macpherson (1736–96), from Ruthven (near Kingussie), who caused a huge stir in 1761 with the publication of *Fingal, an Ancient Epic Poem in Six Books*. An avid collector of Gaelic poetry, Macpherson claimed to have discovered the works of Ossian, a 3rd-century Gaelic bard. *Fingal* and two subsequent volumes of Ossian's poetry were denounced as fake – Macpherson never produced the original Gaelic manuscripts – but nevertheless proved enormously popular. The epic poems were translated into several European languages, and strongly influenced the emerging Romantic movement. (The poems were also responsible for the naming of Fingal's Cave on the Isle of Staffa.)

20th-Century Highland Writers

The poet and storyteller George Mackay Brown (1921–96) was born in Stromness (in the Orkney Islands), and lived there almost all his life. Although his poems and novels are rooted in Orkney, his work transcends local and national boundaries. His novel *Greenvoe* (1972) is a warm, witty and poetic evocation of life in an Orkney community; his last novel, *Beside the Ocean of Time* (1994), is a wonderfully elegiac account of remote island life. His poetry has been published in collections such as *Travellers* (2001) and *Collected Poems: 1954–1992* (2005).

Another Orcadian worth looking out for is poet Edwin Muir (1887–1959), who wrote longingly about Orkney from his later life in Glasgow, and published the interesting travelogue *Highland Journey* in 1935.

Norman McCaig (1910–96) was born in Edinburgh but came from a Harris family and is widely regarded as the finest Scottish poet of his generation. He wrote eloquently about the Highlands and islands – his poem 'Climbing Suilven' is a superb description of what it feels like to climb a mountain, its images instantly recognisable to any hill walker. *Selected Poems* is probably the best collection of his work.

The hugely popular writer Neil Munro (1863–1930), born in Inveraray (in Argyll), is responsible for some of the best-loved books about the region, including the humorous *Tales of Para Handy,* featuring a rascally skipper and his boat the *Vital Spark,* which have been repeatedly dramatised on television, radio and the stage.

Caithness writer Neil M Gunn (1891–1973), born in Dunbeath, is celebrated as the best Scottish novelist of the 20th century, penning such evocative tales as *Morning Tide* and *The Silver Darlings,* a book about

Five Essential Highland Novels

Waverley (1814, Sir Walter Scott)

....

The Silver Darlings (1941, Neil M Gunn)

....

Whisky Galore (1947, Compton MacKenzie)

....

Consider the Lilies (1968, Iain Crichton Smith)

....

Greenvoe (1972, George Mackay Brown)

HIGHLAND CULTURE LITERATURE

THE GAELIC LANGUAGE

Scottish Gaelic (*Gàidhlig* – pronounced '*gah*-lic' in Scotland) is spoken by about 80,000 people in Scotland, mainly in the Highlands and islands. It is a member of the Celtic branch of the Indo-European family of languages, which has given us Gaelic, Irish, Manx, Welsh, Cornish and Breton.

Although Scottish Gaelic is the Celtic language most closely associated with Scotland, it was quite a latecomer to these shores. Other Celtic languages, namely Pictish and Brittonic, had existed prior to the arrival of Gaelic-speaking Celts from Ireland around the 5th century AD. These Irish settlers, known to the Romans as Scotti, were eventually to give their name to the entire country. As their territorial influence extended so did their language, and from the 9th to the 11th centuries Gaelic was spoken throughout the country. For many centuries the language was the same as the language of Ireland; there is little evidence of much divergence before the 13th century. Even up to the 18th century the bards adhered to the strict literary standards of Old Irish.

Gaelic culture flourished in the Highlands until the Jacobite rebellions of the 18th century. After the Battle of Culloden in 1746 many Gaelic speakers were forced from their ancestral lands, and the use of Gaelic was discouraged in favour of English. Although still studied at academic level, the spoken language declined, being regarded as little more than a mere 'peasant' language of no modern significance.

It was only in the 1970s that Gaelic began to make a comeback with a new generation of young enthusiasts who were determined that it should not be allowed to die. After two centuries of decline, the language is now being encouraged through financial help from government agencies and the EU. Gaelic education is flourishing from playgroups to tertiary levels, flowing on into the fields of music, literature, cultural events and broadcasting; now people from all over Scotland, and even worldwide, are beginning to appreciate their Gaelic heritage.

the herring industry. Sir Compton MacKenzie (1883–1972) spent much of his life on the island of Barra, where he is buried; his famous comedy *Whisky Galore* (made into a successful film in 1949) is based on the true story of islanders rescuing a cargo of whisky from the wreck of a ship off the island of Eriskay.

Scott & Stevenson

Sir Walter Scott (1771–1832) was Scotland's greatest and most prolific novelist. Although he was the son of an Edinburgh lawyer, and very much a Lowlander, Scott was a student of Highland history and legend, and many of his works are set north of the Highland line.

Scott's early works were rhyming ballads, such as 'The Lady of the Lake' (set in the Trossachs, about a medieval war between Highland clans and lowland nobles) and 'The Lord of the Isles' (about Robert the Bruce), both of which created a surge of tourism to their Highland settings.

His first historical novel – Scott effectively invented the genre – was *Waverley,* which recounted the adventures of Edward Waverley, a young English soldier who is sent north in 1745 to fight with the Hanoverian army against the Jacobites. It was published anonymously (in those days novels were considered a poor relation to poetry, and Scott wanted to be taken seriously as a poet), but was so successful that he could not refuse the demand for more. The so-called Waverley novels included more on a Highland theme, including *Rob Roy,* about the notorious MacGregor outlaw, and *The Pirate,* based on the life of John Gow, an Orkney adventurer.

Along with Scott, Robert Louis Stevenson (1850–94) ranks among Scotland's best-known novelists. Born in Edinburgh into a family of famous lighthouse engineers, Stevenson is known and loved around the world for classic tales that include *Kidnapped!,* set in the Highlands in the aftermath of Culloden, and *The Master of Ballantrae,* about a family torn in two by the Jacobite wars.

Music & Dance

Traditional Music

The Highlands and islands have always had a strong folk tradition, and in the 1960s the roots revival provided a forum for the Gaelic songs of Cathy-Ann MacPhee from Barra and Margaret Stewart from Lewis. Initially, most of the performers came from outside the region, but the arrival of the Boys of the Lough, headed by Shetland fiddler Aly Bain, introduced the world to authentic Highland folk music. Aly was probably the most influential folk musician Scotland has seen. He brought pipes, concertina, mandolins and other traditional instruments to a wide audience, recording with performers such as Tom Anderson and Phil Cunningham (see www.philandaly.com). Other much-admired fiddlers include Scott Skinner, Willie Hunter and Catriona MacDonald, who studied under the same master fiddler as Aly Bain.

The traditional melodies of the Highlands and islands reached a broader audience through the Gaelic compositions of Skye band Runrig, who transformed *ceilidh* music into stadium rock in the two decades following their formation in 1973. Other powerful ambassadors for Gaelic music included Capercaillie, Ossian and the Battlefield Band, which have all seen plenty of musicians from the Highlands and islands in their line-ups.

In recent years there has been a revival in traditional music, often adapted and updated for the modern age. Bands such as Shooglenifty blend Scottish folk music with anything from indie rock to electronica, producing a hybrid that has been called 'acid croft'.

The website www.scottish-folk-music.com is a useful source for listings of folk sessions, gigs, venues and bands, as well as providing the lyrics for popular Scottish folk songs.

The Scots folk songs that you will often hear sung in pubs and at *ceilidhs* draw on Scotland's rich history. A huge number of them relate to the Jacobite rebellions in the 18th century and, in particular, to Bonnie Prince Charlie – 'Hey Johnnie Cope', the 'Skye Boat Song' and 'Will Ye No Come Back Again', for example – while others relate to themes of working the land, emigration and the Highland Clearances.

Bagpipes

Although no piece of film footage about Scotland is complete without the drone of the pipes, this curious instrument actually originated in ancient Egypt and was brought to Scotland by the Romans.

The bagpipe consists of a leather bag held under the arm, kept inflated by blowing through the blowstick; the piper forces air through the pipes by squeezing the bag with the forearm. Three of the pipes, known as drones, play a constant note (one bass, two tenor) in the background. The fourth pipe, the chanter, plays the melody.

In 1747 the playing of the pipes was banned – under pain of death – by the British government as part of a scheme to suppress Highland culture after the Jacobite uprising of 1745, but the pipes were revived when Highland regiments were drafted into the British army towards the end of the 18th century. Highland soldiers were traditionally accompanied into battle by the skirl of the pipes, and the Scottish Highland bagpipe is unique in being the only musical instrument ever to be classified as a weapon.

Queen Victoria did much to repopularise the bagpipes with her patronage of all things Scottish. When staying at Balmoral she liked to be wakened by a piper playing outside her window. Competitive piping is still a popular pastime in the Highlands and islands – the sound of duelling bagpipes is quite an experience.

Scotland's most famous instrument has been reinvented by bands such as the Red Hot Chilli Pipers (www.redhotchillipipers.co.uk), who use pipes, drums, guitars and keyboards to create rock versions of traditional tunes that have been christened (tongue firmly in cheek) as 'Jock 'n' Roll'. They feature regularly at festivals throughout the country.

Highland Dancing

Another homespun art form that the Scots have made their own is dance. The most famous routines are the formal Highland Dances performed at Highland games, which date back to the foundation of Scotland. There are four official dance disciplines: the Sword Dance, Seann Triubhas, the Reel of Tulloch and the Highland fling.

The Sword Dance, or *gillie callum*, dates back to the legend that Malcolm Canmore celebrated his victory over a Macbeth chieftain by dancing over a crucifix made from his own claymore (sword) and the sword of his rival. The Seann Triubhas is attributed to the desire of Highlanders to shake off the hated *triubhas* (trousers) they were forced to wear instead of kilts after the 1745 rebellion.

A chilly congregation who danced to keep warm are credited with inventing the Reel of Tulloch, while the famous Highland fling was invented in the 1790s to mimic the movements of a stag; clansmen reputedly danced the steps on their targes (leather-covered shields).

Sport

Highland Games

According to oral tradition, Highland games date back to the kingdom of Dalriada and were essentially war games, allowing clan leaders to select their most skilled warriors for battle. In the 11th century King Malcolm

A *ceilidh* is an evening of traditional Scottish entertainment including music, song and dance. To find one, check the village noticeboard, or just ask at the local pub; visitors are always welcome.

Canmore is believed to have staged a royal contest to find the fastest runners in the kingdom to carry his messages across the Highlands.

Historical evidence for a tradition of annual clan games is patchy but the games certainly took off in the 19th century with the creation of the first Highland Societies. In 1848 Queen Victoria patronised the Braemar Highland Games and the tradition was incorporated into Highland legend.

Most of the activities in the games are based on equipment readily available to the average Highlander in ages past. The hammer throw was derived from the traditional mell used to drive fence-posts, while steelyard weights were thrown for distance and height. The caber (from the Gaelic for 'tree') was simply a tree trunk, and rounded river stones were used for putting the stone.

These days the traditional sporting events are accompanied by piping and dancing competitions, and attract locals and tourists alike. Games are held all over Scotland from May to September, with the biggest events staged at Dunoon, Oban and Braemar. You can find dates and details of Highland games at the Scottish Highland Games Association website (www.shga.co.uk).

The original Scottish Highland dress was not the kilt but the woollen plaid – a long length of tartan cloth wrapped around the body and over the shoulder. The modern kilt only appeared in the 18th century and was reputedly invented by Thomas Rawlinson, an Englishman!

Shinty

Shinty (*camanachd* in Gaelic) is a fast and physical ball-and-stick sport similar to Ireland's hurling, with more than a little resemblance to clan warfare. It's an indigenous Scottish game played mainly in the Highlands, and the most prized trophy is the Camanachd Cup. The cup final, held in September, is a great Gaelic get-together. The sport has long been dominated by a rivalry between the Kingussie and Newtonmore teams that stretches back more than a century, though Fort William and Kyles Athletic have come to the fore in recent years. The venue for the final is announced annually in February (see www.shinty.com).

THE TARTAN

This distinctive checked pattern, traditionally associated with the kilt, has become the definitive symbol of Scotland and the Highlands, inspiring skirts, scarves, blankets, ties, key-fobs and a thousand other saleable souvenirs. The pattern is thought to date back to at least the Roman period, though it has become romantically associated with the Gaels, who arrived from Ireland in the 6th century. What is certain is that a tartan plaid had become the standard uniform of Highlanders by the start of 18th century. Following the Battle of Culloden in 1746, the Disarming Act banned the wearing of Highland dress in an attempt to undermine the solidarity of the clans.

However, the ban was enforced only in the Highlands (it was repealed in 1782) and did not apply to the armed services, which in the second half of the 18th century included a large number of Highland regiments. The weaver William Wilson established a factory at Bannockburn to supply the army with tartan, experimenting with a wide range of new designs and colours. In 1778 the London Highland Society requested that clan chiefs submit a piece of their clan tartan to preserve the traditional designs, but most of the tartans recorded by the society were actually designed and woven by the Wilsons.

In the 19th century, tartan got caught up in the cult of so-called 'Balmorality' – Queen Victoria's patronage of Scottish culture – and many of the setts (tartan patterns) now associated with particular clans were created out of thin air by a pair of brothers known as the Sobieski Stuarts, who claimed descent from Bonnie Prince Charlie. The brothers' setts were based on a 'lost' document dating back to the 15th century and they published a hugely successful book of invented tartans, *The Costume of the Clans*, which became established as the genuine tartans of many Highland clans before their elaborate fraud was exposed. Today every clan, and indeed every football team, has one or more distinctive tartans, though few date back more than 150 years.

Each year in October there's an international match between Scotland and Ireland, played under composite shinty/hurling rules, and held alternately in Ireland and Scotland.

Curling

Curling, a winter sport which involves propelling a granite stone weighing 42lb (19kg) along the ice towards a target, was probably invented in Scotland in medieval times. Though traditionally Scottish, it was very much a minority sport until it got an enormous publicity boost when the British women's team (all Scots) won the gold medal in the 2002 Winter Olympics.

Scottish teams took gold in the men's world championship in 2006 and 2009, and silver in 2011 and 2012; and gold and silver in the women's world championship in 2013 and 2010 respectively. For more information, see royalcaledoniancurlingclub.org.

Landscape & Wildlife

Scotland's wildlife is one of its big attractions, and the best way to see it is to get out there: pull on the boots, sling on the binoculars, go quietly and see what you can spot. Many species that have disappeared from or are rare in the rest of Britain survive here.

Geography & Geology

The Scottish Ornithologists' Club website (www.the-soc.org.uk) has lots of interesting news and info for serious birders, including a useful section on where to birdwatch in Scotland.

Scotland covers 30,414 sq miles, about half the size of England. It can be divided into three areas: Southern Uplands, Central Lowlands, and the Highlands and islands.

South of a line joining Dunbar to Girvan lie the Southern Uplands, a range of rounded, heathery hills bordering England. The Central Lowlands comprise a broad slice from Edinburgh and Dundee in the east to Glasgow and Ayr in the west, home to the industrial belt and 80% of Scotland's population.

The Highland Boundary Fault, a geological feature, runs northeast from Helensburgh (west of Glasgow) to Stonehaven (south of Aberdeen) on the east coast. North of it lie the Highlands and islands, a mountainous area that makes up roughly two-thirds of the country. However, the low-lying, fertile agricultural belt that runs along the northeast coast from Aberdeen to Fraserburgh is usually lumped together, geographically and culturally, with the Lowlands.

The Highland hills – most of their summits reach the 900m to 1000m mark – were deeply dissected by glaciers during the last Ice Age, creating a series of deep, U-shaped valleys. The long, narrow sea lochs that today are such a feature of Highland scenery are, like Norway's fjords, glacial valleys that have been flooded by rising sea levels. Despite their pristine beauty, the wild, empty landscapes of the western and northern Highlands are artificial wildernesses. Before the Highland Clearances many of these empty corners of Scotland supported sizable rural populations.

Of Scotland's 790 islands, 94 are inhabited. To the west are the Inner Hebrides (from Islay to Skye) and the Outer Hebrides (Barra to Lewis). To the north are two other island groups, Orkney and Shetland, the northernmost outposts of the British Isles.

Moor & Mountain

Seventeen per cent of Scotland is forested, compared with England's 7%, Finland's 74% and a worldwide average of 30%.

Most of the Highland landscape consists of uncultivated heather moorland, peat bog and steep rocky mountains. Heather, whose tiny pink and purple flowers emerge on moor and mountain in August, is one of the symbols of Scotland, and also an excellent food source for the red grouse, an important game bird.

Peat bog – an endangered environment – covers large areas of the Highlands and islands, most notably in the Flow Country of Caithness and Sutherland, where it provides a haven for unusual plant species, such as the insect-eating sundew, and a nesting ground for birds that include golden plover, hen harrier, and red-throated diver.

Britain's largest land animal, the red deer, is present in large numbers, managed as a sporting asset for hunting estates. You're bound to see them if you spend any time in the Highlands; in winter especially, harsh weather will force them down into the glens to crop the roadside verges.

On the high mountain tops, and especially in the subarctic climate of the Cairngorm plateau, alpine plants thrive alongside bird species such as the snow bunting and the ptarmigan (a type of grouse). Seldom seen below 700m, the ptarmigan has feathered feet and is the only British bird that plays the Arctic trick of changing its plumage from mottled brown in summer to dazzling white in winter, the better to blend in with the snowfields. Another mountain resident that displays this feature is the blue mountain hare.

Perhaps the most majestic wildlife sight on moor and mountain is the golden eagle, which uses its 2m wingspan to soar on rising thermals. Almost all of the 400 or so pairs known to nest in the UK are to be found in the Scottish Highlands and islands, preferring remote glens and open moorland well away from human habitation.

The grassland habitat of the once-common corncrake (a summer visitor from Africa) was almost completely wiped out by modern farming methods, but it still breeds in pockets of sedge and iris in the Hebrides, including nature reserves in Islay, Coll and the Uists. Listen for their distinctive *krek-krek-krek* call – like a thumbnail drawn along the teeth of a comb.

Forest & Woodland

Although much of the Highlands was originally covered by the Caledonian forest – vast swathes of Scots pine in the inland glens, with coastal woods of oak, silver birch, alder and rowan – deforestation has reduced this to a few small pockets of native woodland; barely 1% remains. Important remnants of native Scots pine can be found at Rothiemurchus, Glen Affric and Beinn Eighe.

Managed regeneration forests are slowly covering more of the landscape, especially in the Highlands. Some 5000 sq miles (1.3 million hectares) of tree cover – 17% of the land area – now exists: not a huge figure, but an improvement on what it was (a mere 5% in 1900). About a third

Although the thistle is commonly used as a Scottish emblem, the national flower is the Scottish bluebell (*Campanula rotundifolia*; known in England as the harebell), which carpets the floor of native woodlands in spring. Loch Lomond is a good place to see them.

WINDING BACK THE CLOCK

Over the centuries many species have disappeared from Scotland, hunted into oblivion or left in the lurch after the destruction of their habitat or food supply. As a means of increasing biodiversity, there's a strong case for bringing some of them back. Though it has detractors, reintroduction of species has been implemented successfully in several instances. The red kite and the majestic white-tailed eagle, both absent from Britain since the 19th century, are now soaring in Scottish skies again. The latter, distinguishable by its yellow beak and talons, is found along the west coast and in the Hebrides, particularly on Mull and Skye – visitors can watch a nesting site via TV cameras at Aros Experience on Skye.

The European beaver was reintroduced to Knapdale, Argyllshire, in 2009 for a five-year trial period, a move opposed by some campaigners who felt beavers might negatively impact on forests or water quality. After a broadly successful trial, a mid-2015 decision will decide on the future of the Knapdale project. Meanwhile, several colonies of beavers have been living in the wild in the River Tay system for more than 20 years. No one knows for sure where they came from – whether escapees from a private collection, or deliberately introduced without permission – but they are thriving, and can be seen in several places, including the Loch of the Lowes nature reserve near Dunkeld.

But the mildly controversial beaver project pales beside events at the Alladale Wilderness Reserve in Sutherland, where the owner has already shipped in elk (moose), and plans to reintroduce wolves and bears.

of this is controlled by the government's Forestry Commission, which, as well as conducting managed logging, dedicates large areas to sustainable recreational use. The vast majority of this tree cover is coniferous, and there's a plan to increase it to 25% of land area by 2050.

Scotland's woods are home to 75% of Britain's red squirrel population; they've been pushed out in most of the rest of the country by the dominant greys, introduced from North America. The greys often carry a virus that's lethal to the reds, so measures are in place to try to prevent their further encroachment.

Other forest mammals that were slaughtered to the point of extermination in the 19th century include pine martens, polecats and wildcats. Populations of these are small and remote, but are slowly recovering thanks to their protected status and greater awareness.

The capercaillie, a black, turkeylike member of the grouse family, and the largest native British bird, was hunted to extinction in 1785 – then reintroduced from Sweden in 1837. Though still rare, it still inhabits forests of native Scots pine, notably in Rothiemurchus.

River & Lochs

One of the best-loved pieces of Scottish wildlife writing is *Ring of Bright Water* by Gavin Maxwell, in which the author describes life on the remote Glenelg peninsula with his pet otters in the 1960s.

It rains a lot in Scotland – some parts of the western Highlands get over 4500mm of rain a year, making it the wettest place in Europe – so it's not surprising there's plenty of water about. Around 90% by volume of Britain's fresh water is in Scotland; Loch Ness alone contains more than twice the volume of water in all of the lakes in England and Wales combined.

The most iconic of Scottish fish is the Atlantic salmon, which fights its way up Highland rivers to spawn. Salmon arrive in different rivers at different times of year between March and October, and are usually seen leaping waterfalls; good places to spot them include Pitlochry fish ladder and the Falls of Shin.

The majestic osprey (a fish-eating bird of prey absent from Scotland for most of the 20th century) nests in Scotland from mid-March through to September, after migrating from West Africa. There are around 200 breeding pairs and you can see nesting sites throughout the country, notably at Loch Garten in the Cairngorms and Loch of the Lowes near Dunkeld.

Coast & Islands

The waters off Scotland's north and west coasts are rich in marine mammals. Harbour porpoises are the most common sighting, though common and bottle-nosed dolphins are also seen. Minke whales are regular

JOURNEY OF THE SALMON

One of Scotland's most thrilling sights is the salmon's leap up a fast-flowing cascade, resolutely returning to the river of its birth several years before. The salmon's life begins in early spring, hatching in the gravel bed of a stream in some Scottish glen. Called 'fry' at this stage and barley an inch long, they stay for a couple of years, growing through the 'parr' stage to become 'smolt' when they turn silver, swim downstream and head out to sea.

Their destination could be anywhere in the North Atlantic, from the Faeroes to southern Greenland, but eventually, after one to three winters at sea, they return home to reproduce. Arriving all through the year, but most commonly in late spring and autumn, they enter the river of their birth (identified by its scent) and run up to the headwaters to spawn in November and December. Having spawned, most of the adult fish die and the cycle begins anew.

HIGHLAND GARDENS

As much as the untamed wildness of Scotland lifts the spirit, another of the country's delights is a more managed beauty – its numerous gardens, which emerge from harsh winter with a riotous explosion of colour in spring and summer. In the 19th century every castle and stately home worth its salt had a planned garden in the grounds; the milder parts of the country, particularly the Gulf Stream–warmed west coast, are absolutely studded with them.

From Benmore Botanic Garden in the south to Inverewe Garden in the north, there's a great deal more variety than anyone could reasonably expect at these latitudes. Among the most popular blooms with visitors are the colourful displays of rhododendrons and azaleas, introduced to Scotland from the Himalayas by 19th-century estate owners, which add a blaze of pink, purple, red and yellow to many a Highland hillside in May and June.

The National Trust for Scotland (p282) manages many of the finest gardens; its website is a good first stop to plan a route among the blooms.

summer visitors, and orcas (killer whales) are regularly sighted around Shetland and Orkney.

Seals are widespread. Both the Atlantic grey seal (identified by its Roman nose) and the common seal (with a face shaped more like a dog's) are easily spotted along the coasts, especially in the islands.

Otters are widespread in the Highlands and islands. They frequent both fresh and salt water, but are easiest to spot along the coast, where they time their foraging to coincide with an ebbing tide (river otters tend to be nocturnal). The best places to spot them are in the north and west, especially in Orkney, Shetland, Skye and the Outer Hebrides. The piers at Kyle of Lochalsh and Portree are otter 'hot spots', as the animals have learned to scavenge from fishing boats.

From May to August the sea cliffs of Orkney and Shetland and the north and west coasts of Scotland support some of the largest breeding colonies of seabirds in Europe, including 60% of the world's population of gannets and great skuas. Twenty-one of the British Isles' 24 breeding seabird species can be seen in Shetland, nesting in huge colonies: being entertained by the clownish antics of the puffins is a highlight for many visitors.

National Parks & Nature Reserves

Scotland has two national parks – Loch Lomond & the Trossachs National Park and the Cairngorms National Park. But national parks are only part of the story. There's a huge range of protected areas with a bewildering array of 25 distinct classifications. Fifty-one National Nature Reserves span the country, and there are also marine areas under various levels of protection.

News on endangered Scottish birds has generally been positive in the last couple of decades. The Royal Society for the Protection of Birds (www.rspb.org.uk) is active here, with 34 reserves in the Highlands and islands, and has overseen several success stories, including the reintroduction of the white-tailed eagle and the red kite.

Scotland accounts for one-third of the British mainland's surface area, but it has a massive 80% of Britain's coastline and only 10% of its population.

Environmental Issues

Scotland's abundance of wind and water means the government hasn't had to look far for sources of renewable energy. The grand plan is to generate half of the country's energy needs from renewable sources by 2020, and things look to be well on track. Scotland has been a European leader in the development of wind technology; wind farms now dot the hills and firths (estuaries), and the near-constant breeze in some areas means record-breaking output from some turbines.

The problem is that although everyone agrees that wind power is clean and economical, there's a powerful NIMBY (Not In My Back Yard) element who don't want the windmills spoiling their view. And it's not just the whirring blades, of course. A remote Highland wind farm is one thing, but the power lines trailing all the way down to the south have a significant visual and environmental impact.

Scottish Natural Heritage (www.snh.gov.uk) is the government agency responsible for the conservation of Scotland's wildlife, habitats and landscapes. A key initiative is to reverse biodiversity loss.

One of Scotland's major goals over the last decade or so has been to halt a worrying decline in biodiversity on land, in the air and in the sea. You can see progress reports on the Scottish Natural Heritage website, but a huge threat to existing species is, of course, climate change. A rise of a few degrees across the north would leave plenty of mountain plants and creatures with no place to go; it's already been speculated that the steady decline in Scotland's seabird population since the early '90s is partly caused by a temperature-induced decrease in certain plankton species.

The main cause of the worrying level of some fish stocks is clear: we've eaten them all. In 2010 the Marine (Scotland) Act was passed – it's a compromise solution that tries to both protect vulnerable marine areas and stocks and sustain the flagging fishing industry. But it may well be too little, too late.

Food & Drink

Traditional Scottish cookery is all about basic comfort food: solid, nourishing fare, often high in fat, that would keep you warm on a winter's day spent in the fields or out fishing. But a new culinary style known as Modern Scottish has emerged over the last two decades. Scotland's traditional drinks have also found a new lease of life in recent years, with single malts being marketed like fine wines, and a new breed of microbreweries springing up all over the country.

Scottish Specialities

Mince & Tatties

Haggis may be the national dish that Scotland is most famous for, but when it comes to what Scottish people actually cook and eat most often, the hands-down winner has to be mince and tatties (potatoes). Minced beef, browned in the pan and then stewed slowly with onion, carrot and gravy, is served with mashed potatoes (with a splash of milk and a knob of butter added during the mashing) – it's tasty, warming and you don't even have to chew it.

A Caledonian Feast by Annette Hope is a fascinating and readable history of Scottish cuisine, providing a wealth of historical and sociological background.

The Full Scottish

Surprisingly few Scots eat porridge for breakfast – these days a cappuccino and a croissant is just as likely – and even fewer eat it in the traditional way: with salt to taste, but no sugar. The breakfast offered in a B&B or hotel usually consists of fruit juice and cereal or muesli, followed by a choice of bacon, sausage, black pudding (a type of sausage made from dried blood), grilled tomato, mushrooms and a fried egg or two. If you're lucky, there'll be tattie scones (fried potato bread) as well.

Fish for breakfast may sound strange, but was not unusual in crofting (smallholding) and fishing communities, where seafood was a staple; many hotels still offer grilled kippers (smoked herrings) for breakfast, or smoked haddock poached in milk and served with a poached egg – delicious with lots of buttered toast.

Broth, Skink & Bree

Scotch broth, made with mutton stock, barley, lentils and peas, is nutritious and tasty, while cock-a-leekie is a hearty soup made with chicken

---

FOOD COSTS

The following price ranges refer to the cost of an average main course from the dinner menu:

£ less than £9

££ £9 to £18

£££ more than £18

Lunch mains are often cheaper than dinner mains, however, and many places offer an 'early bird' special with lower prices (usually available between 5pm and 7pm).

and leeks. Warming vegetable soups include leek and potato soup, and lentil soup (vegetarians beware: it's traditionally made using ham stock).

Seafood soups include the delicious Cullen skink, made with smoked haddock, potato, onion and milk, and *partan bree* (crab soup).

> It has been illegal to import haggis into the USA since 1971, as the US government declared that sheep lungs are unfit for human consumption.

Surf & Turf

Steak eaters will enjoy a thick fillet of world-famous Aberdeen Angus beef, and beef from Highland cattle is also much sought after. Venison from red deer is leaner and appears on many menus. Both may be served with a wine-based or creamy whisky sauce. And of course there's haggis, Scotland's much-maligned national dish.

Scottish salmon is famous worldwide, but there's a big difference between the now-ubiquitous farmed salmon (even the certified organic farmed salmon) and the leaner, tastier and considerably more expensive wild fish. Also, there are concerns over the environmental impact of salmon farms on the marine environment.

Smoked salmon is traditionally dressed with a squeeze of lemon juice and eaten with fresh brown bread and butter. Trout, the salmon's smaller cousin – whether wild, rod-caught brown trout or farmed rainbow trout – is delicious fried in oatmeal.

As an alternative to kippers you may be offered Arbroath smokies (lightly smoked fresh haddock), traditionally eaten cold. Herring fillets fried in oatmeal are good, if you don't mind picking out a few bones. Mackerel pâté and smoked or peppered mackerel (both served cold) are also popular.

Juicy langoustines (also known as Dublin Bay prawns), crabs, lobsters, oysters, mussels and scallops are also widely available.

OAT CUISINE

'Oats: a grain, which in England is generally given to horses, but in Scotland appears to support the people.' From *A Dictionary of the English Language* by Samuel Johnson (1709–84).

The most distinctive feature of traditional Scottish cookery is the abundant use of oatmeal. Oats grow well in the cool, wet climate of Scotland and have been cultivated here for at least 2000 years. Up to the 19th century, oatmeal was the main source of calories for the rural Scottish population. The crofter in his field, the cattle drover on the road to market, the soldier on the march – all would carry with them a bag of meal that could be mixed with water and baked on a girdle (a flat metal plate) or on hot stones beside a fire.

Long despised as an inferior foodstuff (see Johnson's sneering description above), oatmeal is enjoying a return to popularity as research has proved it to be highly nutritious (high in iron, calcium and B vitamins) and healthy (rich in soluble fibre, which helps to reduce cholesterol).

The best-known Scottish oatmeal dish is, of course, porridge, which is simply rolled oatmeal boiled with water. A lot of nonsense has been written about porridge and whether it should be eaten with salt or with sugar. It should be eaten however you like it – as a child in the 1850s, author Robert Louis Stevenson had his with golden syrup.

Oatcakes are another traditional dish that you'll certainly come across during a visit to Scotland, usually as an accompaniment to cheese at the end of a meal. A mealie pudding is a sausage-skin stuffed with oatmeal and onion and boiled for an hour or so. Add blood to the mixture and you have a black pudding.

Skirlie is chopped onions and oatmeal fried in beef dripping and seasoned with salt and pepper; it's usually served as a side dish. Trout and herring can be dipped in oatmeal before frying, and it can be added to soups and stews as a thickening agent. It's even used in desserts: toasted oatmeal is a vital flavouring in cranachan, a delicious mixture of whipped cream, whisky and raspberries.

HAGGIS: SCOTLAND'S NATIONAL DISH

Scotland's national dish is often ridiculed because of its ingredients, which admittedly don't sound promising – the finely chopped lungs, heart and liver of a sheep, mixed with oatmeal and onion and stuffed into a sheep's stomach bag. However, it actually tastes surprisingly good.

Haggis should be served with champit tatties and bashed neeps (mashed potatoes and turnips), with a generous dollop of butter and a good sprinkling of black pepper.

Although it's eaten year-round, haggis is central to the celebrations of 25 January, which honour Scotland's national poet, Robert Burns. Scots worldwide unite on Burns Night to revel in their Scottishness. A piper announces the arrival of the haggis and Burns' poem *Address to a Haggis* is recited to this 'Great chieftan o' the puddin-race'. The bulging haggis is then lanced with a dirk (dagger) to reveal the steaming offal within: 'warm, reekin, rich'.

Vegetarians (and quite a few carnivores, no doubt) will be relieved to know that veggie haggis is available in some restaurants.

Top 10 Seafood Restaurants

➡ Café Fish, Tobermory (p90)

➡ Waterfront Fishouse Restaurant, Oban (p84)

➡ Lochleven Seafood Cafe, Kinlochleven (p149)

➡ Badachro Inn, Badachro (p189)

➡ Summer Isles Hotel, Achiltibuie (p185)

➡ Captain's Galley, Scrabster (p179)

➡ Plockton Shores, Plockton (p192)

➡ Tigh an Eilean Hotel, Shieldaig (p190)

➡ Lochbay Seafood Restaurant, Stein (p204)

➡ Fish Market Restaurant, Mallaig (p159)

Vegetarians & Vegans

Scotland has the same proportion of vegetarians as the rest of the UK – around 8% to 10% of the population. Vegetarianism has moved away from the hippie-student image of a few decades ago and is now firmly in the mainstream. Even the most remote Highland pub usually has at least one vegetarian dish on the menu, and there are many dedicated vegetarian restaurants in towns and cities. If you get stuck, there's almost always an Italian or Indian restaurant where you can get meat-free pizza, pasta or curry. Vegans, though, may find their options a bit limited outside of Edinburgh and Glasgow.

Eating with Kids

Following the introduction of the ban on smoking in public places in 2006, many Scottish pubs and restaurants have had to broaden their appeal by becoming more family friendly. As a result, especially in the cities and more popular tourist towns, many restaurants and pubs now have family rooms and/or play areas. In this guide we have indicated restaurants that offer children's menus, high chairs and other child-friendly facilities with a family-friendly icon 👍.

You should be aware that children under the age of 14 are not allowed into the majority of Scottish pubs, even those that serve bar meals; and in family-friendly pubs (those in possession of a Children's Certificate), under-14s are only allowed in between 11am and 8pm, and must be accompanied by an adult aged 18 or older.

Clootie dumpling is a rich pudding made with currants, raisins and other dried fruits; it is wrapped in a linen cloth (or *cloot*, in old Scots) and steamed. It can be served freshly cooked with custard, or sliced cold the day after and fried in butter.

SSSSMOKIN!

Scotland is famous for its smoked salmon, but there are many other varieties of smoked fish – plus smoked meats and cheeses – to enjoy. Smoking food to preserve it is an ancient art that has recently undergone a revival, but this time it's more about flavour than preservation.

There are two parts to the process – first the cure, which involves covering the fish in a mixture of salt and molasses sugar, or soaking it in brine; and then the smoke, which can be either cold smoking (at less than 34°C), which results in a raw product, or hot smoking (at more than 60°C), which cooks it. Cold-smoked products include traditional smoked salmon and kippers. Hot-smoked products include *bradan rost* ('flaky' smoked salmon) and Arbroath smokies (haddock).

Kippers (smoked herring) were invented in Northumberland, in northern England, in the mid-19th century, but Scotland soon picked up the technique, and both Loch Fyne and Mallaig were famous for their kippers.

There are dozens of modern smokehouses scattered all over Scotland, many of which offer a mail-order service as well as an onsite shop. We recommend the following:

➔ **Inverawe Smokehouse** (☎0844 8475 49; www.smokedsalmon.co.uk; Inverawe, near Oban; ☻8.30am-5.30pm Mar-Oct) Delicate smoked salmon, plump juicy kippers.

➔ **Hebridean Smokehouse** (☎01876-580209; www.hebrideansmokehouse.com; Clachan, North Uist; ☻8am-5.30pm Mon-Fri year-round, 9am-5pm Sat Easter-Oct) Peat-smoked salmon and sea trout.

➔ **Salar Smokehouse** (☎01870-610324; www.lochduartsmokedsalmon.com; Lochcarnan, South Uist; ☻8.30am-4.30pm Mon-Fri) Famous for its flaky, hot-smoked salmon.

Cookery Courses

There are more than a dozen places that offer courses in Scottish cookery. Two of the most famous:

Kinloch Lodge Hotel (☎01471-833333; www.kinloch-lodge.co.uk; Kinloch, Isle of Skye) Courses in Scottish cookery and demonstrations using fresh, seasonal Scottish produce by Lady Claire Macdonald, author of *Scottish Highland Hospitality* and *Celebrations*. Fees include three nights accommodation at the hotel.

Nairns Cook School (☎01877-389900; www.nairnscookschool.com; 15 Back Wynd, Aberdeen) Two-day courses in modern Scottish cooking at the school owned by Scotland's top TV chef, Nick Nairn, author of *Wild Harvest* and *Island Harvest*.

What Are Ye Drinking'?

A Pint...

Scottish breweries produce a wide range of beers. The market is dominated by multinational brewers such as Scottish & Newcastle, but smaller local breweries generally create tastier brews, some of them very strong. The aptly named Skull Splitter from Orkney is a good example, at 8.5% alcohol by volume.

Many Scottish beers use old-fashioned shilling categories to indicate strength (the number of shillings was originally the price per barrel; the stronger the beer, the higher the price). The usual range is from 60 to 80 shillings (written 80/-). You'll also see IPA, which stands for India Pale Ale, a strong, hoppy beer first brewed in the early 19th century for export to India (the extra alcohol meant that it kept better on the long sea voyage).

Draught beer is served in pints (usually costing from £2.40 to £3.50) or half-pints; alcoholic content generally ranges from 3% to 6%. What the English call bitter, Scots call heavy, or export.

Modern Scottish is a style that should be familiar to fans of Californian Cuisine and Mod Oz (Australian). Chefs take top-quality Scottish produce – from Highland venison, Aberdeen Angus beef and freshly landed seafood to root vegetables, raspberries and Scottish cheeses – and prepare it simply, in a way that enhances the natural flavours, often adding a French, Italian or Asian twist.

Scottish Ales

The increasing popularity of real ales and a backlash against the bland conformity of globalised multinational brewing conglomerates has seen a huge rise in the number of specialist brewers and microbreweries springing up all over Scotland. They take pride in using only natural ingredients, and many try to revive ancient recipes, such as heather- and seaweed-flavoured ales.

These beers are sold in pubs, off-licences and delicatessens. Here are a few of our favourites to look out for:

➡ **Black Isle Brewery** (✑01463-811871; www.blackislebrewery.com; Old Allangrange; admission free) Has a range of organic beers.

➡ **Cairngorm Brewery** (✑01479 812222; www.cairngormbrewery.com; Dalfaber Industrial Estate) Creator of multi-award-winning Trade Winds ale.

➡ **Colonsay Brewery** (✑01951-200190; www.colonsaybrewery.co.uk; Scalasaig; ⊙ring for hours) Produces lager, 80/- and IPA.

➡ **Islay Ales** (www.islayales.com; Isle of Islay; ⊙10.30am-5pm Mon-Sat Apr-Sep, to 4pm Oct-Mar) Refreshing and citrusy Saligo Ale.

➡ **Isle of Skye Brewery** (✑01470-542477; skyeale.com; The Pier, Uig; ⊙9am-5pm Mon-Fri) Distinctive Hebridean Gold ale, brewed with porridge oats.

➡ **Orkney Brewery** (✑01856-841777; www.orkneybrewery.co.uk; Quoyloo) Famous for its rich, chocolatey Dark Island ale, and the dangerously strong Skull Splitter.

➡ **Valhalla Brewery** (✑01957-711658; www.valhallabrewery.co.uk; Haroldswick; tours £4.50) Brews the most northerly beer in Britain.

➡ **Isle of Arran Brewery** (✑01770-302353; www.arranbrewery.com) Produces light and hoppy Arran Blonde, and the highly addictive Arran Dark.

...Or a Wee Dram?

Scotch whisky (always spelt without an 'e' – 'whiskey' is Irish or American) is Scotland's best-known product and biggest export. The spirit has been distilled in Scotland at least since the 15th century.

As well as whiskies, there are whisky-based liqueurs, such as Drambuie. If you must mix your whisky with anything other than water, try a whisky-mac (whisky with ginger wine). After a long walk in the rain there's nothing better to put a warm glow in your belly.

At a bar, older Scots may order a 'half' or 'nip' of whisky as a chaser to a pint or half-pint of beer: a 'hauf and a hauf'. (Only tourists ask for 'Scotch' – what else would you be served in Scotland?) The standard measure in pubs is either 25mL or 35mL.

Top 10 Single Malt Whiskies – Our Choice

After a great deal of diligent research (and not a few sore heads), Lonely Planet's various Scotland authors have selected their 10 favourite single malts from across the country:

➡ **Ardbeg** (Islay) The 10-year-old from this noble Islay distillery is a byword for excellence. Peaty but well balanced. Hits the spot after a hill walk.

➡ **Bowmore** (Islay) Smoke, peat and salty sea air – a classic Islay malt. One of the few distilleries that still malts its own barley.

➡ **Bruichladdich** (Islay) A visitor-friendly distillery with a quirky, innovative approach – famous for very peaty special releases such as Moine Mhor.

➡ **Glendronach** (Speyside) Only sherry casks are used here, so the creamy, spicy result tastes like Grandma's Christmas trifle.

The website www.scottishbrewing.com has a comprehensive list of Scottish breweries, both large and small.

Scotland's most famous soft drink is Barr's Irn-Bru: a sweet fizzy drink, radioactive orange in colour, that smells like bubble gum and almost strips the enamel from your teeth. Many Scots swear by its restorative effects as a cure for a hangover.

FOOD & DRINK WHAT ARE YE DRINKING?

HOW TO BE A MALT WHISKY BUFF

'Love makes the world go round? Not at all! Whisky makes it go round twice as fast.' From *Whisky Galore* by Compton Mackenzie (1883–1972).

Whisky-tasting today is almost as popular as wine-tasting was in the yuppie heyday of the late 1980s. Being able to tell your Ardbeg from your Edradour is de rigueur among the whisky-nosing set, so here are some pointers to help you impress your friends.

What's the difference between malt and grain whiskies? Malts are distilled from malted barley – that is, barley that has been soaked in water, then allowed to germinate for around 10 days until the starch has turned into sugar – while grain whiskies are distilled from other cereals, usually wheat, corn or unmalted barley.

So what is a single malt? A single malt is a whisky that has been distilled from malted barley and is the product of a single distillery. A pure (vatted) malt is a mixture of single malts from several distilleries, and a blended whisky is a mixture of various grain whiskies (about 60%) and malt whiskies (about 40%) from many different distilleries.

Why are single malts more desirable than blends? A single malt, like a fine wine's terroir, somehow captures the essence of the place where it was made and matured – a combination of the water, the barley, the peat smoke, the oak barrels in which it was aged, and (in the case of certain coastal distilleries) the sea air and salt spray. Each distillation varies from the one before, like different vintages from the same vineyard.

How should a single malt be drunk? Either neat, or preferably with a little water added. To appreciate the aroma and flavour to the utmost, a measure of malt whisky should be cut (diluted) with one-third to two-thirds as much spring water (bottled, still spring water will do). Ice, tap water and – heaven forbid – mixers are for philistines. Would you add lemonade or ice to a glass of Chablis?

The most expensive bottle of whisky ever sold? A Lalique crystal decanter holding 6L of a unique blend of Macallan single malts sold for $628,205 at auction in Hong Kong in 2014.

➡ **Highland Park** (Island) Full and rounded, with heather, honey, malt and peat. Has an award-winning distillery tour.

➡ **Isle of Arran** (Island) One of the newest of Scotland's distilleries, offering a lightish, flavoursome malt with flowery, fruity notes.

➡ **Macallan** (Speyside) The king of Speyside malts, with sherry and bourbon finishes. The distillery is set amid waving fields of Golden Promise barley.

➡ **Springbank** (Campbeltown) Complex flavours – sherry, citrus, pear-drops, peat – with a salty tang. Entire production process from malting to bottling takes place on site.

➡ **Talisker** (Island) Brooding, heavily peaty nose balanced by a satisfying sweetness from this lord of the isles. Great postdinner dram.

➡ **The Balvenie** (Speyside) Rich and honeyed, this Speysider is liquid gold for those with a sweet tooth.

Survival
Guide

Directory A–Z

Accommodation

Scotland provides a comprehensive choice of accommodation to suit all visitors.

For budget travel, the options are campsites, hostels and cheap B&Bs. Above this price level is a plethora of comfortable B&Bs, pubs and guesthouses (£25 to £45 per person per night). Midrange hotels are present in most places, while in the higher price bracket (£65-plus per person per night) there are some superb hotels, the most interesting being converted castles and mansions, or chic designer options in cities.

If you're travelling solo, expect to pay a supplement in hotels and B&Bs, meaning you'll often be forking out over 75% of the price of a double for your single room.

Almost all B&Bs, guesthouses and hotels (and even some hostels) include breakfast – either full Scottish or a continental style – in the room price. If you don't want it, you may be able to negotiate a lower price, but not often.

Prices increase over the peak tourist season (June to September) and are at their highest in July and August. Outside of these months, and particularly in winter, special deals are often available at guesthouses and hotels.

If you're going to be in Edinburgh in August (festival month) or at Hogmanay (New Year), book as far in advance as you can – a year if possible – as the city will be packed.

For a few extra pounds, tourist offices have an accommodation booking service, which can be handy over summer. However, note that they can only book the ever-decreasing number of places that are registered with **VisitScotland** (☑0845 859 1006; www.visitscotland.com/accommodation). There are many other fine accommodation options that, mostly due to the hefty registration fee, choose not to register with the tourist board. Registered places tend to be a little pricier than nonregistered ones. VisitScotland's star system is based on a rather arbitrary set of criteria, so don't set too much store by it.

Most hotels and a rapidly increasing percentage of B&Bs can be found on general internet booking sites.

Bothies, Barns & Bunkhouses

Bothies are simple shelters, often in remote places; many are maintained by the Mountain Bothies Association (www.mountainbothies.org.uk). They're not locked, there's no charge – usually no toilet – and you can't book. Take your own cooking equipment, sleeping bag and mat. Users should stay one night only, and leave it as they find it.

Walkers can stay in camping barns – usually converted farm buildings – for around £5 to £10 per night. Take your own cooking equipment, sleeping bag and mat.

Bunkhouses, a grade or two up from camping barns, have stoves for heating and cooking and may supply utensils. They may have mattresses but you'll still need a sleeping bag. There will be toilets but probably no showers. Most charge from £10.

The **Shetland Amenity Trust** (☑01595-694688; www.camping-bods.com; ☉9am-5pm Mon-Thu, 9am-4pm Fri) has created a number of *bōds* – converted croft houses or fishing huts with bunks and washing and cooking facilities, but often no electricity or heating – many in remote and dramatic locations. Beds cost £8 to £10 but you will need to prebook through the trust in Lerwick, who will give you the keys.

B&Bs & Guesthouses

B&Bs – bed and breakfasts – are an institution in Scotland. At the bottom end you get a bedroom in a private house, a shared bathroom and the 'full Scottish' (juice, coffee or tea, cereal and cooked breakfast – bacon, eggs, sausage, baked beans and toast). Midrange B&Bs have en suite bathrooms, TVs in each room and more variety (and healthier options) for breakfast. Almost all B&Bs provide hospitality trays (tea- and coffee-making facilities) in bedrooms. Common B&B options range from urban houses to pubs and farms.

Guesthouses, often large converted private houses, are an extension of the B&B concept. They are normally larger and less personal than B&Bs.

Camping & Caravan Parks

Free 'wild' camping became a legal right under the Land Reform Bill. However, campers are obliged to camp on unenclosed land, in small numbers and away from buildings and roads.

Commercial camping grounds are often geared to caravans and vary widely in quality. There are numerous campsites across Scotland; **VisitScotland** (☑0845 859 1006; www.visitscotland.com/accommodation) lists a good selection of them on its website and on a free map, available at tourist offices.

Homestays & Hospitality Exchange

A convenient and increasingly popular holiday option is to join an international house-exchange organisation. You sign up for a year and place your home on a website giving details of what you're looking for, where and for how long. You organise the house swap yourself with

people in other countries and arrange to swap homes, rent free, for an agreed period. Shop around, as registration costs vary between organisations. Check out Home Link International (www.homelink.org.uk) and Home Base Holidays (www.homebase-hols.com) for starters.

Hostels

Numerous hostels offer cheap, sociable accommodation and in Scotland the standard of facilities is generally very good. The more upmarket hostels have en suite bathrooms in their dorms, and all manner of luxuries that give them the feel of hotels, if it weren't for the bunk beds.

Hostels nearly always have facilities for self-catering, and, apart from very remote ones, internet access of some kind. Many can arrange activities and tours.

In Highland areas you'll come across bothies – simple walkers' hostels and shelters – and in the Shetlands there are *böds* (characterful but basic shared accommodation).

INDEPENDENT & STUDENT HOSTELS

There are a large number of independent hostels, most with prices around £12 to £20 per person. Facilities vary considerably. Scottish Independent Hostels (www.hostel-scotland.co.uk/) is an affiliation of over 100 hostels in Scotland, mostly in the north. You can browse them online or pick up their free *Scottish Independent Hostels* map-guide from tourist offices.

SCOTTISH YOUTH HOSTEL ASSOCIATION

The **SYHA** (SYHA; ☑0845 293 7373; www.syha.org.uk) has a network of decent, reasonably priced hostels and produces a free booklet available from SYHA hostels and tourist offices. There are dozens to choose from around the country, ranging

from basic walkers' digs to mansions and castles. You've got to be a HI member to stay, but nonmembers can pay a £3 supplement per night that goes towards the £10 membership fee. Prices vary according to the month, but average around £16 to £20 per adult in high season.

Most SYHA hostels close from around mid-October to early March but can be rented out by groups.

Self-Catering Accommodation

The best place to start looking for this kind of accommodation is the website of **VisitScotland** (☑0845 859 1006; www.visitscotland.com), which lists numerous self-catering options all over Scotland. These options also appear in the regional accommodation guides available from tourist offices.

Other places to search:

Cottages & Castles (☑01738-451610; www.cottages-and-castles.co.uk) Offers a wide range of self-catering accommodation, as the name suggests.

Embrace Scotland (Association of Scotland's Self-Caterers; www.embrace-escotland.com) Association of self-catering properties with a searchable database of over 2500 across Scotland.

PRACTICALITIES

➡ **Newspapers** The Aberdeen-based daily newspaper *Press & Journal* covers the Highlands and islands, as does the weekly *Oban Times*. The *Daily Record* is a popular Labour-supporting tabloid, while the *Sunday Post* offers up rose-tinted nostalgia.

➡ **Radio** BBC Radio Scotland (AM 810kHz, FM 92.4-94.7MHz) provides a Scottish point of view.

➡ **Smoking** In Scotland you can't smoke in any public place with a roof that's at least half enclosed, which means pubs, bus shelters, restaurants and hotels (basically, anywhere you might want to).

➡ **TV** Watch BBC1 Scotland, BBC2 Scotland and STV for Scottish-specific programming. BBC Alba provides Gaelic-language TV.

➡ **Weights & Measures** Use the metric system for weights and measures, with the exception of road distances (in miles) and beer (in pints). The pint is 568mL, more than the US version.

Homeaway (www.homeaway.co.uk) A good choice for self-catering, with a wide portfolio and guest reviews.

NTS Holidays (☎0844 493 2108; www.nts.org.uk/holidays) The National Trust for Scotland has an excellent portfolio of up-market accommodation, including historic houses, lighthouse cottages and more.

Children

Scotland offers a range of child-friendly accommodation and activities suitable for families.

It's worth asking in tourist offices for local publications aimed at families. *The List* magazine (available at newsagents and bookshops) has a section on children's activities and events in and around Glasgow and Edinburgh.

The **National Trust for Scotland** (NTS; ☎0844-493 2100; www.nts.org.uk) and **Historic Scotland** (HS; ☎0131-668 8831; www.historic-scotland.gov.uk) organise family-friendly activities at their properties throughout the summer.

Children are generally well received around Scotland,

and every area has some child-friendly attractions and B&Bs. Even dryish local museums usually make an effort with an activity sheet or child-focused information panels.

A lot of pubs are family-friendly and some have great beer gardens where kids can run around and exhaust themselves while you have a quiet pint. However, be aware that many Scottish pubs, even those that serve bar meals, are forbidden by law to admit children under 14. In family-friendly pubs (ie those in possession of a Children's Certificate), accompanied under-14s are admitted between 11am and 8pm. There's no clear indication on which is which: just ask the barstaff.

Children under a certain age can often stay free with their parents in hotels, but be prepared for hotels and B&Bs (normally upmarket ones) that won't accept children; call ahead to get the low-down. More hotels and guesthouses these days provide child-friendly facilities, including cots. Many restaurants (especially the larger ones) have highchairs

and decent children's menus available.

Breastfeeding in public is accepted and is actively encouraged by government campaigns.

The larger car-hire companies can provide safety seats for children, but they're worth booking well ahead.

See also Lonely Planet's *Travel with Children*.

Customs Regulations

Travellers arriving in the UK from EU countries don't have to pay tax or duty on goods for personal use, and can bring in as much EU duty-paid alcohol and tobacco as they like. However, if you bring in more than the following, you'll probably be asked some questions:

➡ 800 cigarettes

➡ 1kg of tobacco

➡ 10L of spirits

➡ 90L of wine

➡ 110L of beer

Travellers from outside the EU can bring in, duty-free:

➡ 200 cigarettes *or* 100 cigarillos *or* 50 cigars *or* 250g of tobacco

➡ 16L of beer

➡ 4L of non-sparkling wine

➡ 1L of spirits *or* 2L of fortified wine or sparkling wine

➡ £390 worth of all other goods, including perfume, gifts and souvenirs

Anything over this limit must be declared to customs officers on arrival. Check www.hmrc.gov.uk/customs for further details, and for information on reclaiming VAT on items purchased in the UK by non-EU residents.

Discount Cards

Historic Sites

Membership of Historic Scotland (HS) and the National

Trust for Scotland (NTS) is worth considering, especially if you're going to be in Scotland for a while. Both are nonprofit organisations dedicated to the preservation of the environment, and both care for hundreds of spectacular sites. You can join up at any of their properties.

Historic Scotland (HS; ☑0131-668 8831; www.historic-scotland.gov.uk) A nonprofit organisation that cares for hundreds of sites of historical importance. A year's membership costs £48/89 per adult/family, and gives free entry to HS sites (half-price entry to sites in England and Wales). Also offers a short-term Explorer Pass – three days out of five for £29, seven days out of 14 for £38. Can be great value, particularly if you visit both Edinburgh and Stirling castles.

National Trust for Scotland (NTS; ☑0844-493 2100; www.nts.org.uk) NTS looks after hundreds of sites of historical, architectural or environmental importance. A year's membership, costing £50/87 for an adult/family, offers free access to all NTS and National Trust properties (in the rest of the UK). If you're 25 or under, it's a great deal at only £21.

Hostel Cards

If travelling on a budget, membership of the **Scottish Youth Hostel Association/Hostelling International** (SYHA; ☑0845 293 7373; www.syha.org.uk) is a must (annual membership over/under 16 years is £10/free, life membership is £100).

Senior Cards

Discount cards for those over 60 years are available for train travel.

Student Youth Cards

The most useful card is the International Student Identity Card (www.isic.org), which displays your photo. This gives you discounted entry to many attractions and on many forms of transport.

There's a global industry in fake student cards, and many places now stipulate a maximum age for student discounts or substitute a 'youth discount' for 'student discount'. If under 30 but not a student, you can apply for the European Youth Card (www.europeanyouthcard.org), which goes by various names in different countries, or an International Youth Travel Card (IYTC), also issued by ISIC. These cards are available through student unions, hostelling organisations or youth travel agencies.

Electricity

230V/50Hz

Food

For an overview of Scottish cuisine, see the Food & Drink chapter (p273).

Internet Access

➡ If you're travelling with a laptop, you'll find a wide range of places offering a wi-fi connection. These range from cafes to B&Bs and public spaces.

➡ Wi-fi is often free, but some places (typically, upmarket hotels) charge.

➡ There are increasingly good deals on pay-as-you-go mobile internet from mobile network providers.

➡ If you don't have a laptop or smartphone, the best places to check email and surf the internet are public libraries – nearly all of which have at least a couple of computer terminals, and they are free to use, though there's often a time limit.

➡ Internet cafes also exist in the cities and larger towns and are generally good value, charging approximately £2 to £3 per hour.

➡ Many of the larger tourist offices across the country also have internet access.

Legal Matters

➡ The 1707 Act of Union preserved the Scottish legal system as separate from the law in England and Wales.

➡ Police have the power to detain, for up to six hours, anyone suspected of having committed an offence punishable by imprisonment (including drugs offences).

➡ If you need legal assistance, contact the **Scottish Legal Aid Board** (☑0845 122 8686; www.slab.org.uk; 44 Drumsheugh Gardens, Edinburgh).

➡ Possession of cannabis is illegal, with a spoken warning for first offenders with small amounts. Fines and prison sentences apply for repeat offences and larger quantities. Possession of harder drugs is much more serious. Police have the right to search anyone they suspect of possessing drugs.

Maps

If you're about to tackle Munros, you'll require maps with far greater detail than the maps in this guide, or the ones supplied by tourist offices. The Ordnance Survey (OS) caters to walkers, with a wide variety of maps at 1:50,000 and 1:25,000 scales. Alternatively, look out for the excellent walkers' maps published by Harveys; they're at scales of 1:40,000 and 1:25,000.

Money

➜ The British currency is the pound sterling (£), with 100 pence (p) to a pound. 'Quid' is the slang term for pound.

➜ Three Scottish banks issue their own banknotes, meaning there's quite a variety of different notes in circulation. They are legal currency in England too, but you'll sometimes run into problems changing them. They are also harder to exchange once you get outside the UK.

➜ Euros are accepted in Scotland only at some major tourist attractions and a few upmarket hotels – it's always better to have sterling cash.

ATMs

ATMs (called cashpoints in Scotland) are widespread and you'll usually find at least one in small towns and villages. You can use Visa, MasterCard, Amex, Cirrus, Plus and Maestro to withdraw cash from ATMs belonging to most banks and building societies in Scotland.

Cash withdrawals from some ATMs may be subject to a small charge, but most are free. If you're not from the UK, your home bank will likely charge you for withdrawing money overseas; it pays to be aware of how much, as it may be much better to withdraw larger amounts less often.

Credit Cards

Visa and MasterCard cards are widely recognised, although many places will charge a small amount for accepting them. Charge

cards such as Amex and Diners Club may not be accepted in smaller establishments. Many smaller B&Bs do not take cards.

Moneychangers

Be careful using bureaux de change; they may offer good exchange rates but frequently levy outrageous commissions and fees. The best-value place to change money in the UK is at post offices, but only the ones in larger towns and cities offer this service. Larger tourist offices also have exchange facilities.

Tipping

➜ Tip 10% in sit-down restaurants, but not if there's already a service charge on the bill.

➜ In classy places, staff may expect closer to 15%.

➜ Service is at your discretion: even if the charge is added to the bill, you don't have to pay it.

➜ Don't tip in pubs: if the service has been exceptional over the course of an evening, you can say 'have one for yourself'.

➜ In taxis, round up to the nearest pound.

Opening Hours

In the Highlands and islands Sunday opening is restricted, and it's common for there to be little or no public transport.

Opening hours are as follows:

Banks 9.30am to 4pm or 5pm Monday to Friday; some are open 9.30am to 1pm Saturday.

Nightclubs 9pm or 10pm to 1am, 2am or later. Often only open Thursday to Saturday.

Post offices 9am to 6pm Monday to Friday, 9am to 12.30pm Saturday (main branches to 5pm Saturday).

Pubs & Bars 11am to 11pm Monday to Thursday, 11am to 1am Friday and Saturday, 12.30pm to 11pm Sunday; lunch is served

noon to 2.30pm, dinner 6pm to 9pm daily.

Shops 9am to 5.30pm (or 6pm in cities) Monday to Saturday, and often 11am to 5pm Sunday.

Restaurants Lunch noon to 2.30pm, dinner 6pm to 9pm or 10pm; in small towns and villages the chippy (fish-and-chip shop) is often the only place to buy cooked food after 8pm.

Public Holidays

Although bank holidays are general public holidays in the rest of the UK, in Scotland they only apply to banks and some other commercial offices.

Scottish towns normally have four days of public holiday, which they allocate themselves; dates vary from year to year and from town to town. Most places celebrate St Andrew's Day (30 November) as a public holiday.

General public holidays:

New Year 1 & 2 January

Good Friday March or April

Christmas Day 25 December

Boxing Day 26 December

Telephone
Mobile Phones

The UK uses the GSM 900/1800 network, which covers the rest of Europe, Australia and New Zealand, but isn't compatible with the North American GSM 1900. Most modern mobiles can function on both networks – but check before you leave home just in case.

Though roaming charges within the EU are due to be entirely eliminated in December 2015, other international roaming charges can be prohibitively high, and you'll probably find it cheaper to get a UK number. This is easily done by buying a SIM card (around £10 including calling credit) and sticking it in your phone. Your phone may be locked to your home network, however, so you'll have to either get it unlocked, or buy a pay-as-you-go phone along with your SIM card (around £50).

Pay-as-you-go phones can be recharged by buying vouchers from shops.

Phone Codes & Useful Numbers

Dialling the UK Dial your country's international access code then ☑44 (the UK country code), then the area code (dropping the first 0) followed by the telephone number.

Dialling out of the UK The international access code is ☑00; dial this, then add the code of the country you wish to dial.

Making a reverse-charge (collect) international call Dial ☑155 for the operator. It's an expensive option, but not for the caller.

Area codes in Scotland Begin with ☑01, eg Edinburgh ☑0131, Wick ☑01955.

Directory Assistance There are several numbers; ☑118500 is one.

Mobile phones Codes usually begin with ☑07.

Free calls Numbers starting with ☑0800 are free; calls to ☑0845 numbers are charged at local rates.

Time

Scotland is on GMT/UTC. The clocks go forward for 'summer time' one hour at the end of March, and go back at the end of October. The 24-hour clock is used

for transport timetables, but plenty of folk still struggle to get the hang of it.

Tourist Information

The Scottish Tourist Board, known as **VisitScotland** (☑0845 859 1006; www. visitscotland.com), deals with inquiries made by post, email and telephone. You can request, online and by phone, for regional brochures to be posted to you, or download them from the website.

Most larger towns have tourist offices (information centres) that open 9am or 10am to 5pm Monday to Friday, and on weekends in summer. In small places, particularly in the Highlands, tourist offices only open from Easter to September.

If you want to email a tourist office, it's townname@ visitscotland.com.

Travellers with Disabilities

Travellers with disabilities will find Scotland a strange mix of accessibility and inaccessibility. Most new buildings are accessible to wheelchair users, so modern hotels and tourist attractions are fine. However, most B&Bs and guesthouses are in hard-to-adapt older buildings, which means that travellers with mobility problems may pay more for accommodation.

Things are constantly improving, though.

It's a similar story with public transport. Newer buses have steps that lower for easier access, as do trains, but it's wise to check before setting out. Tourist attractions usually reserve parking spaces near the entrance for drivers with disabilities.

Many places such as ticket offices and banks are fitted with hearing loops to assist the hearing-impaired; look for a posted symbol of a large ear.

An increasing number of tourist attractions have audioguides. Some have Braille guides or scented gardens for the visually impaired.

VisitScotland produces the guide *Accessible Scotland* for wheelchair-bound travellers, its website (www. visitscotland.com/accom modation) details accessible accommodation and many tourist offices have leaflets with accessibility details for their area.

Many regions have organisations that hire wheelchairs; contact the local tourist office for details. Many nature trails have been adapted for wheelchair use.

Visas

➡ If you're a citizen of the EEA (European Economic Area) nations or Switzerland, you don't need a visa to enter or work in Britain – you can enter using your national identity card.

➡ Visa regulations are always subject to change, and immigration restriction is currently big news in Britain, so it's essential to check with your local British embassy, high commission or consulate before leaving home.

➡ Currently, if you're a citizen of Australia, Canada, New Zealand, Japan, Israel, the USA and several other countries, you can stay for up to six months (no visa

TIME DIFFERENCE BETWEEN SCOTLAND & WORLD CITIES

CITY	TIME DIFFERENCE
Los Angeles	8hr behind
Mumbai	5½hr ahead, 4½hr Mar-Oct
New York	5hr behind
Paris, Berlin, Rome	1hr ahead
Sydney	9hr ahead Apr-Sep, 10hr Oct, 11hr Nov-Mar
Tokyo	9hr ahead, 8hr Mar-Oct

required), but are not allowed to work.

➡ Nationals of many countries, including South Africa, will need to obtain a visa: for more info, see www. ukvisas.gov.uk.

➡ The Youth Mobility Scheme, for Australian, Canadian, Japanese, Hong Kong, Monegasque, New Zealand, South Korean and Taiwanese citizens aged 18 to 31, allows working visits of up to two years, but must be applied for in advance.

➡ Commonwealth citizens with a UK-born parent may be eligible for a Certificate of Entitlement to the Right of Abode, which entitles them to live and work in the UK.

➡ Commonwealth citizens with a UK-born grandparent could qualify for a UK Ancestry Employment Certificate, allowing them to work full time for up to five years in the UK.

➡ British immigration authorities have always been tough; dress neatly and carry proof that you have sufficient funds with which to support yourself. A credit card and/ or an onward ticket will help.

Women Travellers

Solo women travellers are likely to feel safe in Scotland.

The contraceptive pill is available only on prescription; however, the 'morning-after' pill (effective against conception for up to 72 hours after unprotected sexual intercourse) is available over the counter at chemists.

Transport

GETTING THERE & AWAY

Flights, tours and rail tickets can be booked online at lonelyplanet.com/bookings.

Air

There are direct flights to Scottish airports from England, Wales, Ireland, the USA, Canada, Scandinavia and several countries in Western, Central and Eastern Europe. From elsewhere, you'll probably have to fly into a European hub and catch a connecting flight to a Scottish airport – London, Amsterdam, Frankfurt and Paris have the best connections. This will often be a cheaper option anyway if flying in from North America.

Airports

Scotland has four main international airports: Aberdeen, Edinburgh, Glasgow and Glasgow Prestwick, with a few short-haul international flights landing at Inverness. London is the main UK gateway for long-haul flights. Sumburgh on Shetland has summer service from Norway.

Aberdeen Airport (ABZ; ☑0844 481 6666; www.aberdeenairport.com)

Edinburgh Airport (EDI; ☑0844 448 8833; www.edinburghairport.com)

Glasgow Airport (GLA; ☑0844 481 5555; www.glasgowairport.com)

Glasgow Prestwick (PIK; ☑0871 223 0700; www.glasgowprestwick.com)

Inverness Airport (INV; ☑01667-464000; www.hial.co.uk)

Land

Bus

Buses are usually the cheapest way to get to Scotland from other parts of the UK. The main operators:

Megabus (☑0900 1600 900; www.megabus.com) One-way fares from London to Glasgow from as little as £8 if you book well in advance (up to 45 days). Has some fully reclinable sleeper services.

National Express (☑08717 818178; www.nationalexpress.com) Regular services from London and other cities in England and Wales to Glasgow and Edinburgh.

Scottish Citylink (☑0871 266 3333; www.citylink.co.uk) Daily service between Belfast and Glasgow and Edinburgh via Cairnryan ferry.

Car & Motorcycle

Drivers of EU-registered vehicles will find bringing a car or motorcycle into Scotland fairly easy.

The vehicle must have registration papers and a nationality plate, and you must have insurance. The International Insurance Certificate

---

CLIMATE CHANGE & TRAVEL

Every form of transport that relies on carbon-based fuel generates CO_2, the main cause of human-induced climate change. Modern travel is dependent on aeroplanes, which might use less fuel per kilometre per person than most cars but travel much greater distances. The altitude at which aircraft emit gases (including CO_2) and particles also contributes to their climate change impact. Many websites offer 'carbon calculators' that allow people to estimate the carbon emissions generated by their journey and, for those who wish to do so, to offset the impact of the greenhouse gases emitted with contributions to portfolios of climate-friendly initiatives throughout the world. Lonely Planet offsets the carbon footprint of all staff and author travel.

(Green Card) isn't compulsory, but it is excellent proof that you're covered.

If driving from mainland Europe via the Channel Tunnel or ferry ports, head for London and follow the M25 orbital road to the M1 motorway, then follow the M1 and M6 north.

Train

Travelling to Scotland by train is faster and usually more comfortable than the bus, but more expensive. Taking into account check-in and travel time between city centre and airport, the train is a competitive alternative to air travel from London.

East Coast (☑03457 225 225; www.eastcoast.co.uk) Trains between London Kings Cross and Edinburgh (4½ hours, every half hour).

Eurostar (www.eurostar. com) You can travel from Paris or Brussels to London in around two hours on the Eurostar service. From St Pancras, it's a quick and easy change to Kings Cross or Euston for trains to Edinburgh or Glasgow. Total journey time from Paris to Edinburgh is about eight hours.

ScotRail (☑08457 55 00 33; www.scotrail.co.uk) Runs the *Caledonian Sleeper,* an overnight service connecting London Euston with Edinburgh, Glasgow, Stirling, Perth, Dundee, Aberdeen, Fort William and Inverness.

National Rail Enquiry Service (☑08457 48 49 50; www.nationalrail.co.uk) Time-

table and fares info for all trains in Britain.

Virgin Trains (☑08719 774 222; www.virgintrains.co.uk) Trains between London Euston and Glasgow (4½ hours, hourly).

Sea

Car Ferry

Car-ferry links between Northern Ireland and Scotland are operated by **Stena Line** (☑08447 70 70 70; www. stenaline.co.uk; passenger £20-29, driver plus car £99-150) and **P&O** (☑08716 64 20 20; www. poferries.com). Stena Line travels the Belfast–Cairnryan route and P&O Irish Sea the Larne–Troon and Larne–Cairnryan routes.

The prices in the table are a guide only; fares are often less than quoted here.

GETTING AROUND

Public transport in Scotland is generally good, but it can be costly compared with other European countries. Buses are usually the cheapest way to get around, but also the slowest. With a discount pass, trains can be competitive; they're also quicker and often take you through beautiful scenery.

Traveline (☑0871 200 22 33; www.travelinescotland.com) provides timetable info for all public-transport services in Scotland, but can't provide

fare information or book tickets.

Air

Most domestic air services are geared to business needs, or are lifelines for remote island communities. Flying is a pricey way to cover relatively short distances, but certainly worth considering if you're short of time and want to visit the Hebrides, Orkney or Shetland.

Airlines in Scotland

Eastern Airways (☑0870 366 9100; www.easternairways. com) Flies from Aberdeen to Stornoway and Wick.

Flybe/Loganair (☑01857-873457; www.loganair.co.uk) The main domestic airline in Scotland, with flights from Glasgow to Barra, Benbecula, Campbeltown, Islay, Kirkwall, Sumburgh, Stornoway and Tiree; from Edinburgh to Inverness, Kirkwall, Sumburgh, Stornoway and Wick; from Aberdeen to Kirkwall and Sumburgh; and from Inverness to Kirkwall, Stornoway and Sumburgh. It also operates interisland flights in Orkney and Shetland, and from Barra to Benbecula.

Hebridean Air (☑0845 805-7465; www.hebrideanair. co.uk) Flies from Connel airfield near Oban to the islands of Coll, Tiree, Colonsay and Islay.

Bicycle

Scotland is a compact country, and travelling around by bicycle is a perfectly feasible proposition if you have the time. Indeed, for touring the islands a bicycle is both cheaper (for ferry fares) and more suited to their small sizes and leisurely pace of life. For more information see http://active.visitscotland. com and the **Sustrans** (www. sustrans.org.uk/scotland/national-cycle-network) pages on the National Cycle Network.

FERRIES TO/FROM NORTHERN IRELAND

CROSSING	DURATION	FREQUENCY	FARE PASSENGER/ CAR (£)
Belfast–Cairnryan	2¼hr	5-6 daily	29/90
Larne–Cairnryan	2hr	6-8 daily	28/96
Larne–Troon	2hr	2 daily (late Mar–early Sep)	28/96

Boat

The main car-ferry operators to Scotland's larger islands are CalMac (west coast) and Northlink (Orkney and Shetland), but there are many other car and passenger-only ferries, often run by the local council, serving smaller islands and making short sea crossings.

Taking your car on a ferry – particularly to the farther-flung islands – can be expensive; you might save some money by hiring a car once you arrive there. Bicycles, on the other hand, travel free on most car ferries (there may be a small charge for bikes on passenger ferries).

It's recommended that you make reservations for ferry crossings if you're travelling by car, especially in summer; the Mallaig to Armadale (Skye) ferry in particular can get very busy, with long waits for those without bookings. Reservations are not needed for foot passengers and bicycles.

Caledonian MacBrayne (CalMac; ☎0800 066 5000; www.calmac.co.uk) Serves the west coast and islands. Comprehensive timetable booklet available from tourist offices.

CalMac Island Hopscotch offers more than 20 tickets, giving reduced fares for various combinations of crossings; these are listed on the website and in the CalMac timetable booklet. **Island Rover** tickets allow unlimited ferry travel for £59/85 for a foot passenger for eight/15 days, plus £275/410 for a car or £138/207 for a motorbike. Bicycles travel free with foot passengers' tickets.

Northlink Ferries (☎0845 600 0449; www.northlink ferries.co.uk) Ferries from Aberdeen and Scrabster (near Thurso) to Orkney, from Orkney to Shetland and from Aberdeen to Shetland.

ROAD EQUIVALENT TARIFF

The Scottish Government has introduced a scheme called the Road Equivalent Tariff (RET) on certain ferry crossings. This reduces the price of ferry transport to what it would cost to drive the same distance by road, in the hope of attracting more tourists and reducing business costs in the islands. This has been permanently adopted on routes to the Western Isles, Coll and Tiree and is being trialled for Islay, Gigha, Colonsay and Arran. Fares on these crossings have been cut by around 40%, and initial signs are that the scheme has been successful, with tourist numbers up by 25% to 40%. Expect it to be adopted for other west-coast islands during the lifespan of this book.

Bus

Scotland is served by an extensive bus network that covers most of the country. In remote rural areas, however, services are more geared to the needs of locals (getting to school or the shops in the nearest large town) and may not be conveniently timed for visitors.

First (www.firstgroup.com) Operates local bus routes in several parts of Scotland.

Scottish Citylink (☎0871 266 3333; www.citylink.co.uk) National network of comfy, reliable buses serving all main towns. Away from main roads, you'll need to switch to local services.

Stagecoach (www.stage coachbus.com) Operates local bus routes in many parts of Scotland.

Bus Passes

Holders of a National Entitlement Card (www.entitle mentcard.org.uk), available to seniors and disabled people who are Scottish citizens, get free bus travel throughout the country. The youth version, for 11- to 26-year-olds, gives discounted travel, and SYHA members receive a 20% discount on Scottish Citylink services. Students do, too, by registering online.

The Scottish Citylink Explorer Pass offers unlimited travel on Scottish Citylink (and selected other bus routes) services within Scotland for any three days out of five (£41), any five days out of 10 (£62) or any eight days out of 16 (£93). Also gives discounts on various regional bus services, on Northlink and CalMac ferries, and in SYHA hostels. Can be bought in the UK by both UK and overseas citizens.

Car & Motorcycle

Scotland's roads are generally good and far less busy than in England, so driving's more enjoyable.

Motorways (designated 'M') are toll-free dual carriageways, limited mainly to central Scotland. Main roads ('A') are dual or single carriageways and are sometimes clogged with slow-moving trucks or caravans; the A9 from Perth to Inverness is notoriously busy.

Life on the road is more relaxed and interesting on the secondary roads (designated 'B') and minor roads (undesignated), although in the Highlands and islands there's the added hazard of suicidal sheep wandering onto the road (be particularly wary of lambs in spring).

At around £1.30 per litre (equivalent to around US$8 per US gallon), petrol's expensive by American or Australian standards; diesel is about 8p per litre more expensive. Prices tend to rise as you get further from the main centres and are more than 10% higher in the Outer Hebrides. In remote areas petrol stations are widely spaced and sometimes closed on Sunday.

Hire

Car hire in the UK is competitively priced by European standards, and shopping around online can unearth some great deals, which can drop to as low as £12 per day for an extended hire period. Hit comparison sites like Kayak (www.kayak.com) to find some of the best prices.

The minimum legal age for driving is 17 but to rent a car, drivers must usually be aged 23 to 65 – outside these limits special conditions or insurance requirements may apply.

If planning to visit the Outer Hebrides or Shetland, it'll often prove cheaper to hire a car on the islands, rather than pay to take a hire car across on the ferry.

The main international hire companies:

Avis (www.avis.co.uk)

Budget (www.budget.co.uk)

Europcar (www.europcar.co.uk)

Hertz (www.hertz.co.uk)

Sixt (www.sixt.co.uk)

Tours

There are numerous companies in Scotland offering all kinds of tours, including historical, activity-based and backpacker tours. It's a question of picking the tour that suits your requirements and budget.

Discreet Scotland (☑07989-416990; www.discreetscotland.com) Luxurious private tours in an upmarket 4x4 that range from day trips from Edinburgh to full weeks staying in some of Scotland's finest hotels.

Haggis Adventures (☑0131-557 9393; www.haggisadventures.com) Offers fun backpacker-oriented tours, with longer options taking in the Outer Hebrides or Orkney.

Hebridean Island Cruises (☑01756-704700; www.hebridean.co.uk) Luxury small-boat cruises around the west coast, Outer Hebrides and northern islands.

Mountain Innovations (☑01479-831331; www.scotmountainholidays.com.co.uk) Guided activity holidays and courses in the Highlands: walking, mountain biking and winter mountaineering.

Rabbie's (☑0131-226 3133; www.rabbies.com) One- to five-day tours of the Highlands in 16-seat minibuses with professional driver/guide.

Scot-Trek (☑0141-334 9232; www.scot-trek.co.uk) Guided walks for all levels; ideal for solo travellers wanting to link up with others.

Timberbush Tours (☑0131-226 6066; www.timberbush-tours.co.uk) Comfortable small-group minibus tours around Scotland, with Glasgow and Edinburgh departures.

Train

Scotland's train network extends to all major cities and towns, but the railway map has a lot of large, blank areas in the Highlands and the Southern Uplands where you'll need to switch to road transport. The West Highland line from Glasgow to Fort William and Mallaig, and the Inverness to Kyle of Lochalsh line, offer two of the world's most scenic rail journeys.

The **National Rail Enquiry Service** (☑08457 48 49 50; www.nationalrail.co.uk) lists timetables and fares for all trains in Britain.

ScotRail (☑08457 55 00 33; www.scotrail.co.uk) Operates most train services in Scotland; website has downloadable timetables.

Costs & Reservations

Train travel is more expensive than bus, but usually more comfortable: a standard return from Edinburgh to Inverness is around £50 to £75 compared with £30 to £50 on the bus.

Reservations are recommended for intercity trips, especially on Fridays and public holidays. For shorter journeys, just buy a ticket at the station before you go. On certain routes, including the Glasgow–Edinburgh express, and in places where there's no ticket office at the station, you can buy tickets on the train.

Children under five travel free; those five to 15 years usually pay half-fare.

Bikes are carried free on all ScotRail trains but space is sometimes limited. Bike reservations are compulsory on certain train routes, including the Glasgow–Oban–Fort William–Mallaig line and the Inverness–Kyle of Lochalsh line; they are recommended on many others. You can make reservations for your bicycle from eight weeks to two hours in advance at main train stations, or when booking tickets by

---

SINGLE-TRACK ROADS

In many country areas, especially in the Highlands and islands, you will find single-track roads that are only wide enough for one vehicle. Passing places (usually marked with a white diamond sign, or a black-and-white striped pole) are used to allow oncoming traffic to get by. Remember that passing places are also for overtaking – pull over to let faster vehicles pass if necessary. It's illegal to park in passing places.

THE WEST HIGHLAND LINE

The West Highland Railway runs between Mallaig and Fort William through some of Scotland's wildest and most spectacular mountain scenery, and some of Britain's finest hiking terrain.

Stations such as Arrochar & Tarbet, Crianlarich, Bridge of Orchy and Spean Bridge allow you to set off on an endless array of wonderful mountain walks, direct from the platform. There are several opportunities for circular walks, or you can get off at one station, have yourself a jolly tramp, then jump on another train from another station. From Fort William Station it's only a few miles' walk to Britain's highest peak, Ben Nevis.

Possibly the most intriguing place to get off the train is at Corrour, which, at 408m, is Britain's highest and most remote station (there's no road access). It lies in the middle of Rannoch Moor, which was so soft and boggy that the line here had to be laid on a platform of earth, ashes and brushwood. It's a tribute to the railway's Victorian engineers that it has remained in place for over a century and nobody has ever managed (or wanted) to build a road up here. Film buffs will already know that Corrour is where Renton, Sick Boy, Spud and Tommy got back to nature in the film Trainspotting; unlike them, however, you won't be disappointed: from Corrour you can reach lonely peaks or wind your way through remote valleys that are out of reach to mere motorists.

Beyond Fort William the train runs through more glorious scenery and across the Glenfinnan Viaduct (of Harry Potter film fame) to Mallaig – the **Jacobite Steam Train** (☎0844 850 4685; www.westcoastrailways.co.uk; day return adult/child £34/19; ☺ daily Jul & Aug, Mon-Fri mid-May–Jun & Sep-Oct) also plies this section of the line – from where it's a short ferry ride to the Isle of Skye.

---

phone (☎0845 755 0033) or online.

There's a bewilderingly complex labyrinth of ticket types. In general, the further ahead you can book, the cheaper your ticket will be.

Advance Purchase Book by 6pm on the day before travel; cheaper than Anytime.

Anytime Buy any time and travel any time, with no restrictions.

Off Peak There are time restrictions (you're not usually allowed to travel on a train that leaves before 9.15am); relatively cheap.

It's always worth checking the ScotRail website for current family or senior offers.

Discount Cards

Discount railcards are available for people aged 60 and over, for people aged 16 to 25 (or mature full-time students), two over-16s travelling together, and for those with a disability. The **Senior Railcard** (www.senior-railcard. co.uk; per year £30), **16-25 Railcard** (Young Persons Railcard; www.16-25railcard. co.uk; per year £30), **Two Together Railcard** (www.

twotogether-railcard.co.uk; per year £30) and **Disabled Persons Railcard** (www. disabledpersons-railcard. co.uk; per year £20) are each valid for one year and give one-third off most train fares in Scotland, England and Wales. You'll find they pay for themselves pretty quickly if you plan to take a couple of long-distance journeys or a handful of short-distance ones. Fill in an application at any major train station. You'll need proof of age (birth certificate, passport or driving licence) for the Young Persons and Senior Railcards (proof of enrolment for mature-age students) and proof of entitlement for the Disabled Persons Railcard. You'll need a passport photo for all of them. You can also buy railcards online, but you'll need a UK address to have them sent to.

Train Passes

ScotRail has a range of good-value passes for train travel. You can buy them online or by phone or at train stations throughout

Britain. Note that Travelpass and Rover tickets are not valid for travel on certain (eg commuter) services before 9.15am weekdays.

Central Scotland Rover Covers train travel between Glasgow, Edinburgh, North Berwick, Stirling and Fife; costs £36.30 for three days' travel out of seven.

Freedom of Scotland Travelpass Gives unlimited travel on all Scottish train services (some restrictions), all CalMac ferry services and on certain Scottish Citylink coach services (on routes not covered by rail). It's available for four days' travel out of eight (£134) or eight days out of 15 (£180).

Highland Rover Allows unlimited train travel from Glasgow to Oban, Fort William and Mallaig, and from Inverness to Kyle of Lochalsh, Aviemore, Aberdeen and Thurso. It also gives free travel on the Oban/Fort William–Inverness bus, on the Oban–Mull and Mallaig–Skye ferries, and on buses on Mull and Skye. It's valid for four days' travel out of eight (£81.50).

Glossary

For a glossary of Scottish place names, see p56.

bag – reach the top of (as in to 'bag a couple of peaks' or '*Munro* bagging')

bailey – the space enclosed by castle walls

birlinn – Hebridean galley

blackhouse – low-walled stone cottage with thatch or turf roof and earth floors; shared by both humans and cattle and typical of the Outer Hebrides until the early 20th century

böd – once a simple trading booth used by fishing communities, today it refers to basic accommodation for walkers etc

bothy – hut or mountain shelter

brae – hill

broch – defensive tower

burgh – town

burn – stream

cairn – pile of stones to mark path or junction; also peak

camanachd – Gaelic for *shinty*

ceilidh (*kay*-li) – evening of traditional Scottish entertainment including music, song and dance

Celtic high cross – a large, elaborately carved stone cross decorated with biblical scenes and Celtic interlace designs dating from the 8th to 10th centuries

chippy – fish-and-chip shop

Clearances – eviction of Highland farmers from their land by *lairds* wanting to use it for grazing sheep

Clootie dumpling – rich steamed pudding filled with currants and raisins

close – entrance to an alley

corrie – circular hollow on a hillside

craic – lively conversation

craig – exposed rock

crannog – an artificial island in a *loch* built for defensive purposes

crofting – smallholding in marginal agricultural areas following the Clearances

Cullen skink – soup made with smoked haddock, potato, onion and milk

dene – valley

dirk – dagger

dram – a measure of whisky

firth – estuary

gloup – natural arch

Hogmanay – Scottish celebration of New Year's Eve

howff – pub or shelter

HS – Historic Scotland

kyle – narrow sea channel

laird – estate owner

linn – waterfall

loch – lake

lochan – small *loch*

machair – grass- and wildflower-covered dunes

makar – maker of verses

Mercat Cross – a symbol of the trading rights of a market town or village, usually found in the centre of town and usually a focal point for the community

motte – early Norman fortification consisting of a raised, flattened mound with a keep on top; when attached to a *bailey* it is known as a motte-and-bailey

Munro – mountain of 3000ft (914m) or higher

Munro bagger – a hill walker who tries to climb all the *Munros* in Scotland

NNR – National Nature Reserve, managed by the *SNH*

NTS – National Trust for Scotland

nyvaig – Hebridean galley

OS – Ordnance Survey

Picts – early inhabitants of north and east Scotland (from Latin *pictus*, or 'painted', after their body paint decorations)

provost – mayor

RIB – rigid inflatable boat

rood – an old Scots word for a cross

RSPB – Royal Society for the Protection of Birds

Sassenach – from Gaelic 'Sasannach': anyone who is not a Highlander (including Lowland Scots)

shinty – fast and physical ball-and-stick sport similar to Ireland's hurling

SMC – Scottish Mountaineering Club

SNH – Scottish Natural Heritage, a government organisation directly responsible for safeguarding and improving Scotland's natural heritage

sporran – purse worn around waist with the kilt

SSSI – Site of Special Scientific Interest

SYHA – Scottish Youth Hostel Association

wynd – lane

Behind the Scenes

SEND US YOUR FEEDBACK

We love to hear from travellers – your comments keep us on our toes and help make our books better. Our well-travelled team reads every word on what you loved or loathed about this book. Although we cannot reply individually to your submissions, we always guarantee that your feedback goes straight to the appropriate authors, in time for the next edition. Each person who sends us information is thanked in the next edition – the most useful submissions are rewarded with a selection of digital PDF chapters.

Visit **lonelyplanet.com/contact** to submit your updates and suggestions or to ask for help. Our award-winning website also features inspirational travel stories, news and discussions.

Note: We may edit, reproduce and incorporate your comments in Lonely Planet products such as guidebooks, websites and digital products, so let us know if you don't want your comments reproduced or your name acknowledged. For our privacy policy visit lonelyplanet.com/privacy.

AUTHOR THANKS

Neil Wilson

Many thanks to all the helpful and enthusiastic staff at TICs throughout the country, and to the many travellers I met on the road who chipped in with advice and recommendations. Thanks also to Carol Downie, and to Steven Fallon and Keith Jeffrey, Steve Hall, Russell Leaper, Brendan Bolland, Jenny Neil, and Tom and Christine Duffin. Finally, many thanks to co-author Andy and to the ever-helpful and patient editors and cartographers at Lonely Planet.

Andy Symington

Many thanks are due in many places, but firstly to Jenny Neil and Brendan Bolland for a big welcome and cracking cemetery stay and to Juliette and David Paton for guaranteed warm and generous hospitality. Old mate Hugh O'Keefe was grand company on the Highlands' winding roads, while John Campbell brightened an Unst evening. Gratitude goes also to Eleanor Hamilton, Cindy-Lou Ramsay, Riika Åkerlind, the Jackson-Hevia family and numerous helpful folk met along the way. Big thanks to Neil for coordinating and Taybank pints, and cheers to James, Cliff and the LP team for a top organising job.

ACKNOWLEDGMENTS

Climate map data adapted from Peel MC, Finlayson BL & McMahon TA (2007) 'Updated World Map of the Köppen-Geiger Climate Classification', *Hydrology and Earth System Sciences,* 11, 163344.

Cover photograph: Red deer stag, Glen Strathfarrar, Inverness-shire; Ann & Steve Toon/Alamy

THIS BOOK

This 3rd edition of Lonely Planet's *Scotland's Highlands & Islands* guidebook was researched and written by Neil Wilson and Andy Symington. The previous edition was also written by Neil Wilson and Andy Symington and Joe Bindloss and Clay Lucas wrote the 1st edition. This guidebook was commissioned in Lonely Planet's London office, and produced by the following:

Destination Editor James Smart

Coordinating Editor Andrea Dobbin

Product Editor Tracy Whitmey

Book Designer Wibowo Rusli

Senior Cartographer Mark Griffiths

Assisting Editor Melanie Dankel

Cover Researcher Naomi Parker

Thanks to Sasha Baskett, Penny Cordner, Ryan Evans, Larissa Frost, Jouve India, Alice MacDonald Long, Kate Mathews, Claire Naylor, Karyn Noble, Katie O'Connell, Pascal Theze, Diana Wilson, Tony Wheeler

Index

Map Legend

Sights

- Beach
- Bird Sanctuary
- Buddhist
- Castle/Palace
- Christian
- Confucian
- Hindu
- Islamic
- Jain
- Jewish
- Monument
- Museum/Gallery/Historic Building
- Ruin
- Shinto
- Sikh
- Taoist
- Winery/Vineyard
- Zoo/Wildlife Sanctuary
- Other Sight

Activities, Courses & Tours

- Bodysurfing
- Diving
- Canoeing/Kayaking
- Course/Tour
- Sento Hot Baths/Onsen
- Skiing
- Snorkelling
- Surfing
- Swimming/Pool
- Walking
- Windsurfing
- Other Activity

Sleeping

- Sleeping
- Camping

Eating

- Eating

Drinking & Nightlife

- Drinking & Nightlife
- Cafe

Entertainment

- Entertainment

Shopping

- Shopping

Information

- Bank
- Embassy/Consulate
- Hospital/Medical
- Internet
- Police
- Post Office
- Telephone
- Toilet
- Tourist Information
- Other Information

Geographic

- Beach
- Hut/Shelter
- Lighthouse
- Lookout
- Mountain/Volcano
- Oasis
- Park
- Pass
- Picnic Area
- Waterfall

Population

- Capital (National)
- Capital (State/Province)
- City/Large Town
- Town/Village

Transport

- Airport
- Border crossing
- Bus
- Cable car/Funicular
- Cycling
- Ferry
- Metro station
- Monorail
- Parking
- Petrol station
- S-Bahn/Subway station
- Taxi
- T-bane/Tunnelbana station
- Train station/Railway
- Tram
- Tube station
- U-Bahn/Underground station
- Other Transport

Note: Not all symbols displayed above appear on the maps in this book

Routes

- Tollway
- Freeway
- Primary
- Secondary
- Tertiary
- Lane
- Unsealed road
- Road under construction
- Plaza/Mall
- Steps
- Tunnel
- Pedestrian overpass
- Walking Tour
- Walking Tour detour
- Path/Walking Trail

Boundaries

- International
- State/Province
- Disputed
- Regional/Suburb
- Marine Park
- Cliff
- Wall

Hydrography

- River, Creek
- Intermittent River
- Canal
- Water
- Dry/Salt/Intermittent Lake
- Reef

Areas

- Airport/Runway
- Beach/Desert
- Cemetery (Christian)
- Cemetery (Other)
- Glacier
- Mudflat
- Park/Forest
- Sight (Building)
- Sportsground
- Swamp/Mangrove

OUR STORY

A beat-up old car, a few dollars in the pocket and a sense of adventure. In 1972 that's all Tony and Maureen Wheeler needed for the trip of a lifetime – across Europe and Asia overland to Australia. It took several months, and at the end – broke but inspired – they sat at their kitchen table writing and stapling together their first travel guide, *Across Asia on the Cheap*. Within a week they'd sold 1500 copies. Lonely Planet was born.

Today, Lonely Planet has offices in Franklin, London, Melbourne, Oakland, Beijing and Delhi, with more than 600 staff and writers. We share Tony's belief that 'a great guidebook should do three things: inform, educate and amuse'.

OUR WRITERS

Neil Wilson
Coordinating Author, Walking the West Highland Way, Inverness & the Central Highlands, Northern Highlands & Islands Neil was born in Scotland and, save for a few years spent abroad, has lived here most of his life. A lifelong enthusiasm for the great outdoors has inspired hiking, biking and sailing expeditions to every corner of the country. Researching this edition took him from the country's most westerly point at Ardnamurchan Lighthouse to its most easterly at Fraserburgh, and to every corner of beautiful Perthshire where he now lives. Neil has been a full-time author since 1988 and has written around 65 guidebooks for various publishers, including the Lonely Planet guides to Edinburgh and Scotland.

Andy Symington
Southern Highlands & Islands, Northern Highlands & Islands, Orkney & Shetland Andy's Scottish forebears make their presence felt in a love of malt, a debatable ginger colour to his facial hair and a love of wild places. From childhood treks up the M1 he graduated to making dubious road-trips around the firths in a disintegrating Mini Metro and thence to peddling whisky in darkest Leith. Whilst living there, he travelled widely around the country in search of the perfect dram, and, now resident in Spain, continues to visit very regularly.

Published by Lonely Planet Publications Pty Ltd
ABN 36 005 607 983
3rd edition – Feb 2015
ISBN 978 1 74220 992 0
© Lonely Planet 2015   Photographs © as indicated 2015
10 9 8 7 6
Printed in Singapore